S0-BSZ-130

THE UNITED STATES CONGRESS
People, Place, and Policy

The Dorsey Series in Political Science
Consulting Editor Samuel C. Patterson *The University of Iowa*

The
UNITED STATES CONGRESS
People, Place, and Policy

Charles O. Jones
University of Virginia

1982

THE DORSEY PRESS   Homewood, Illinois   60430
IRWIN-DORSEY LIMITED   Georgetown, Ontario   L7G 4B3

© THE DORSEY PRESS, 1982

All rights reserved. No part of this publication may be reproduced, stored in a retrieval system, or transmitted, in any form or by any means, electronic, mechanical, photocopying, recording, or otherwise, without the prior written permission of the publisher.

ISBN 0-256-02663-7
Library of Congress Catalog Card No. 81– 68064

Printed in the United States of America

1 2 3 4 5 6 7 8 9 0 MP 9 8 7 6 5 4 3 2

For Vera

Preface

In this book, I have tried to provide readable text to acquaint students with the every day workings of the United States Congress. This remarkable institution is incredibly complex but captivating nonetheless. For me, and for many of my colleagues, studying Congress has become habit-forming. To paraphrase a famous commercial: "Betcha can't study it just once." In these pages I want to project to the students my own interest and excitement about the institution.

The book has several features. After an introductory chapter I quite unabashedly seek to attract the reader with a sort of "you are there" report on a week on Capitol Hill. Alexis de Toqueville spoke of "this ceaseless agitation" as characterizing so much of what he admired in American politics. For him this activity was "the greatest advantage of democracy." I have tried to capture that spirit of action in my description of what went on in Congress during the week of April 18 to 22, 1977. Other features of the book include:

An emphasis on historical background where appropriate.

Special attention to the many important differences between the House of Representatives and the Senate.

Provision of up-to-date data on elections and congressional organization.

Illustrations of rules and procedures drawn from congressional documents.

Treatment of the increasingly important role for congressional staff.

Detailed analysis of the formalities associated with making law.

Analysis of the role of Congress in the broader policy process.

A review of major congressional reforms in the 20th century.

After the introductory chapters (1 and 2), the book is organized in accordance with the subtitle: people, place, and policy. Chapters 3 through 7 identify the people who populate Capitol Hill—describing the growth in numbers, who these people are and how they got there, and how their functions have changed over time. Also included is a chapter on the people who come to Congress in order to get something.

Chapters 8 through 12 focus on the place. They provide detailed treatments of committees, political parties, and floor procedures for each house. The significant differences between the chambers are particularly noted. And the fascinating procedures by which the two houses get together are described.

Chapters 13 through 15 turn to policy—first examining the crucial role Congress plays in program development, then turning to the recent activities of Congress in program execution. Particularly emphasized is congressional participation in the policy networks that are so significant in the policy process. Chapter 15 treats congressional policy toward itself—that is, the matter of organizational, political, and procedural reform through the decades of this century. A final chapter reviews issues raised throughout the book and develops conclusions about where Congress stands today in the American political system.

One of the many captivating features of Congress is its ever-changing nature. Even as these words are written we observe new patterns in relationships between a confident president and a divided Congress. Still there are certain basic characteristics of the institution that persist. I hope I have captured enough of these to allow students to understand what is new about Congress and what is not.

Charles O. Jones

Acknowledgments

The idea for this book grew out of discussions between Samuel C. Patterson and me as we vacationed with our families on Georgian Bay, Ontario, Canada, in August 1976. He had recently become consulting editor for The Dorsey Press. I had been thinking about a book on Congress for some time. Not surprisingly, our visit resulted in a plan for me to write a book under his editorship.

First a word about this Pat Patterson. We have been close friends since we met in an introductory American government course at the University of South Dakota in 1949. William O. Farber was our teacher. He guided us into the study of government and politics. We followed Bill Farber's advice and pursued graduate study at the University of Wisconsin, primarily working with Ralph K. Huitt and Leon D. Epstein. We have never taught at the same institution, but we have remained the closest of colleagues. Our conversations over a period of nearly 35 years of companionship have covered practically every aspect of the study of politics. Since he was an editor first (of the *American Journal of Political Science*), he was of tremendous help to me when I became editor of the *American Political Science Review*. But that orderly mind of his has set me straight on most of my professional endeavors. Pat Patterson has had an enormous impact on my career in political science, and this seemed a good place to acknowledge my debt to him.

The enterprise we discussed in August 1976 was a small, readable text on the United States Congress. You see the result. At this point I am less struck by the length of the eventual product than by the fact that I slighted many topics I had planned to cover. I have touched lightly on the presidential role in congressional work; the complex associations among bureaucrats, political executives, and Congress; various intergovernmental policy and political connections that are made on Capitol Hill; and the change in the congressional agenda through time. I also intended to offer detailed illustrations of legislation—from the problem to the law. Perhaps the lesson is that a short book about Congress cannot be written until one has written a long book. Beyond that lesson, however, is the humility one experiences in trying to comprehend, then communicate, the incredibly intricate contacts and activities among people, place, and policy on Capitol Hill.

I want to acknowledge the assistance of many other persons in addition to Pat Patterson. First are the many outstanding scholars in my cohort of congressional scholars. Imagine being associated with Joseph Cooper (1961), Roger H. Davidson (1963), Richard F. Fenno, Jr. (1956), Robert L. Peabody (1960), Nelson W. Polsby (1961), and Randall B. Ripley (1963) (year of Ph.D. in parentheses). These people changed the face of congressional research, and I was fortunate enough to have been able to consult and work with them. Readers will note my frequent reference to their work in these pages, but beyond that I have profited from frequent conversations with them about our mutual interest in what goes on under that dome on the Hill. It should also be recorded that Neil MacNeil, chief congressional correspondent for *Time* magazine, made it his business to promote the work of this generation of scholars. My close personal friendship with MacNeil permitted me to tap his own impressive storehouse of wisdom and knowledge of Congress.

Second I must mark by debt to four colleagues at the University of Pittsburgh. For 12 years I enjoyed the double advantage of membership in the cohort plus association with major legislative scholars at Pitt. William J. Keefe and Morris S. Ogul have written the leading text on American legislatures (now in its fifth edition). Holbert N. Carroll wrote a superb book on the House Committee on Foreign Affairs. And Bert A. Rockman has studied the connections between legislators and bureaucrats. All four have contributed immeasurably to my understanding and teaching of Congress. Keefe also read several chapters of this book, offering sensible improvements. Bert Carroll served as book review editor of the *American Political Science Review*, and thus we frequently lunched together. He listened patiently as I talked out the structure of this book, always reacting diplomatically in getting me on the right track.

Third I owe a tremendous debt of gratitude to Janet Altenbaugh, my personal secretary at the University of Pittsburgh. She transcribed tapes, typed and retyped hundreds of pages of manuscript, made tables and figures out of hand-formed scratchings, and kept account of what went where. Having all of this done efficiently and effectively is impressive, having it done cheerfully as well is astounding. This recognition is essential but pitifully small.

Several graduate students also assisted me in the development of this book. In particular I should mention Christopher J. Bosso, David Kozak, Sharon Fitzgerald Lukish, Dieter Matthes, Margaret Eaholtz Scranton. I must say that I have been favored with the opportunity of working with excellent and enthusiastic students over the years.

I also want to thank three qualified and constructive reviewers — Charles S. Bullock, III, University of Georgia; Samuel H. Kernell, University of California, San Diego; and Norman J. Ornstein, Catholic University. Each was helpful in providing comments and criticisms. Since they are of a newer cohort of congressional scholars, I was particularly pleased that they found some things to like in this book.

The dedication reads: For Vera. That is small acknowledgment in print for a person who contributes so much to my life. But the recognition in thought is vast, as we both are aware. Joe and Dan know it too.

C. O. J.

Contents

List of tables xix

1. The United States Congress 1

   Historical perspectives on Congress, 3
   Studying the modern Congress, 9

2. "This ceaseless agitation" 13

   The billion dollar Congress, 14
   "When are the Girl Scouts coming in?" 16

3. Who is Congress? 53

   The growing Congress, 54
   Characteristics of the congressional population, 62
   Summary, 69

4. How representatives are chosen 71

   Creating the district, 71
   Types of House elections, 76
   Once in, 78
   Recruitment, 84

Campaigning, 94
Spending money to win, 98
Regulating campaign finance, 101
Summary, 105

5. How senators are chosen 106

What they represent, 107
Types of elections, 109
Changing tenure, 114
Why do senators lose? 117
Recruitment, 119
Campaigning, 127
Summary, 132

6. Staff recruitment and turnover 133

Personal offices, 135
Committees, 139
Research support agencies, 144
Summary, 145
How they came to be there: Concluding remarks, 146

7. Who comes to Congress, what do they want, and how do they get it? 149

What determines who comes? 150
Who in fact comes? 153
What do they want? 162
How do they get it? 166
The special case of constituents, 169
The special case of foreign groups, 175
Conclusion, 177

8. How the House organizes to do its work: Offices and committees 179

The problem of representation, 179
House and Senate—general differences, 184
Organizing the House of Representatives, 185

9. How the House organizes to do its work: Parties and floor action 222

The political party system, 222
Unofficial groups, 238
Organizing the work on the floor, 245
Conclusion, 264

10. Organizing the Senate 265

Organizing to represent and serve the state, 267
Organizing to make law, 272

11. **Beyond the committees in the Senate: Political parties and floor action** **294**

Party leadership, 295
Party organization, 302
Party at work, 305
Organizing the work on the floor, 308
Summary, 325

12. **Getting together in the legislative process** **326**

Getting the House and Senate together, 326
Getting together with the president, 343
Summary, 351

13. **Congress and the policy process: Program development** .. **352**

The policy process, 354
Policy networks, 358
Congress and program development activities, 365
Comparing action on specific bills, 374
Conclusion, 377

14. **Congress and the policy process: Program execution** **379**

Traditional involvements, 381
The new involvements—Congress reaches out, 398
Congress as a total policy process, 404
Program execution activities and policy networks, 406
Conclusion, 408

15. **Reforming the Congress: When and how** **409**

The reform psychology, 411
Analyzing congressional reform, 413
Reform eras, 417
Conclusion, 435

16. **People, place, and policy** **437**

People, 438
Place, 439
Policy, 441
Where does Congress stand today? 442

Appendix: Writing a term paper on Congress **444**

References **452**

Additional sources **463**

Index **469**

List of tables

2 — 1. Appropriations for Congress—selected fiscal years 15

2 — 2. Senate committee and subcommittee meetings, April 18 — 22, 1977 19

2 — 3. House committee and subcommittee meetings, April 18 — 22, 1977 20

2 — 4. Schedule of the Speaker of the House, April 19 — 20 28

2 — 5. Schedule of the minority leader, April 19 — 20 29

2 — 6. Schedule of Morris K. Udall, chairman, Committee on Interior and Insular Affairs, April 19 — 20 31

2 — 7. Schedule of William S. Cohen (R — Maine), April 19 — 20 32

2 — 8. Schedule of Senator Edmund S. Muskie, April 19 — 20 32

2 — 9. Schedule of Senator George McGovern, April 19 — 20 33

2 — 10. Schedule of Senator H. J. Heinz, III, April 19 — 20 34

2 — 11. Action in the House Chamber, April 18 — 22 36

2 — 12. Action in the Senate Chamber, April 18 — 22 37

2 — 13. Coverage of Energy Week in Washington by seven newspapers 45

2 — 14. Congressional coverage by seven newspapers, April 18 — 24 45

2 — 15. Coverage of president's energy message and reaction, April 21, 1977 ... 48

3 — 1. The Headquarters Establishment at Washington in 1802 and 1829...... 55

3 — 2. Percentage growth in personal and committee staff since 1947 58

3 — 3. Personnel employed by Congress, 1979 59

3 — 4. Occupational background of House members, 91st — 97th Congresses .. 64

3 — 5. Occupational background of senators, 91st — 97th Congresses 64

3 — 6. Average age of members of Congress, 91st — 97th Congresses.......... 65

3 — 7. Religious affiliation of members of Congress, 91st — 97th Congresses ...   66

4 — 1. Size of the House of Representatives, 1789 — present   74

4 — 2. Number and percentage of House incumbents winning reelection,
        1956 — 1980   79

4 — 3. Party turnover for House seats for selected time periods   80

4 — 4. Marginal seats, retirements, and membership turnover, 1956 — 1976   82

4 — 5. High opportunity districts for prospective Democratic candidates   86

4 — 6. Life cycle of replacements 40 and under   87

4 — 7. Primary opposition for Democratic candidates in 74 selected
        districts, 1974   90

4 — 8. Advantages of the "worst case" Democrats in 1974   93

4 — 9. Number of districts with limited campaign expenditures in 1976   98

4 — 10. House campaign expenditures, 1974 — 1978   104

5 — 1. Senatorial classes, First Congress (1789 — 1791)   110

5 — 2. The Class 1 Senate seat in Pennsylvania, 1789 — present   111

5 — 3. Number and percentage of senatorial incumbents winning reelection,
        1956 — 1980   115

5 — 4. Voter recognition, rating, and contact with House and Senate
        candidates, 1978   118

5 — 5. First and last public office of senators, Matthews sample of 180   121

5 — 6. First and last public office of senators, 95th Congress   122

5 — 7. High opportunity states for opposition party, 1974, 1976
        Senate elections 124

5 — 8. Primary opposition for senatorial candidates, high-opportunity
        seats, 1974, 1976   126

5 — 9. Senate campaign expenditures, 1974 — 1978   129

6 — 1. Home-based personal staff for representatives and senators   137

6 — 2. Assembling two subcommittee staffs — House Committee on Interstate
        and Foreign Commerce   143

7 — 1. Organizations represented before the House Subcommittee on Health
        and the Environment in regard to clean air legislation, March
        13 — 26, 1975 . . . .   154 — 55

7 — 2. Ratings of lobbying techniques by lobbyists and congressional
        respondents   167

7 — 3. Who comes to Congress representing foreign governments?   176

8 — 1. Variations in representative relationships   180

8 — 2. Organizing to represent in the House — the perquisites   186

8 — 3. Typical staff positions in a House Washington office   190

8 — 4. From a bill to a law . . . .   194 — 195

8 — 5. Committees and subcommittees, House of Representatives,
        96th Congress . . . .   198 — 202

8 — 6. Committee and subcommittee positions, 96th Congress   203

8 — 7. Committees and subcommittees ranked by ratios of Democrats
        to Republicans   204

8 — 8. Assigning members to committees — the workload   208

8 — 9. Staff assignments for Committee on Interstate and Foreign
        Commerce and its subcommittees . . . .   217 — 18

9 — 1. Party committees, House of Representatives, 97th Congress   227

9 – 2. Major party leaders, House of Representatives, 97th Congress
(1981 – 1982) 232
9 – 3. Party unity scores, U.S. House of Representatives, 1961 – 1980 235
9 – 4. Designated days in House legislative month 248
9 – 5. The flow of work on the House floor—major legislation 258
10 – 1. Organizing to represent in the Senate—the perquisites 268
10 – 2. State offices for senators, number and staff, 95th Congress 271
10 – 3. Committees and subcommittees, Senate, 96th Congress .... 273 – 76
10 – 4. House and Senate standing committee counterparts 277
10 – 5. Senate committee and subcommittee positions, 96th Congress 278
10 – 6. Senate committee and subcommittee ratios, Democrats to Republicans,
96th Congress 281
10 – 7. Assigning senators to standing committees—the workload 284
10 – 8. Examples of Senate committee assignments, 1979 284
10 – 9. Subcommittee membership change, 95th to 96th Congress; Senate
Committee on Agriculture, Nutrition, and Forestry 287
10 – 10. Staff assignments for Senate Committee on Governmental Affairs
and its subcommittees .... 289 – 91
11 – 1. Senate floor leaders, 1911 – 1983 .... 300 – 301
11 – 2. Major party leaders, Senate, 97th Congress (1981 – 1982) 303
11 – 3. Party unity scores, U.S. Senate, 1961 – 1980 307
11 – 4. Average party support for president's program, 1961 – 1980, House
and Senate 308
11 – 5. The Senate at work—September 28, 1979 318
11 – 6. The flow of work on the Senate floor—major legislation under
unanimous consent agreements 319
11 – 7. Senate cloture votes, 1917 – 1977 323
12 – 1. Sequence of House and Senate floor action on Conferences Report
on 1979 Supplemental Appropriations .... 338 – 39
12 – 2. Joint committees, 89th – 96th Congresses 343
12 – 3. Presidential vetoes, 1965 – 1977 348
13 – 1. The policy process 355
13 – 2. The distribution of policy activities in the U.S. Constitution 356
13 – 3. Characteristics of policy networks 362
13 – 4. Variation in participation in program development activities
(14 bills, 89th Congress) 375
14 – 1. Expected participation in traditional cozy little triangles:
Problem definition to program evaluation 407
15 – 1. The Reed and Cannon Reforms analyzed 422
15 – 2. Consolidation of standing committees, Legislative Reorganization
Act of 1946 425
15 – 3. The major post-World War II reforms analyzed 426
15 – 4. The decade of congressional reform, 1970 – 1979 429
15 – 5. The reforms of the 1970s analyzed 433
A – 1. Studying how a bill becomes a law 445
A – 2. Studying the members of Congress 450

1 The United States Congress

The Continental Congress met in York, Pennsylvania, in the fall of 1777 to establish a confederation. It began work in Lancaster but only held one session there. "It was deemed the part of wisdom to put a good-sized river [the Susquehanna], in addition to the many miles, between them and the British army" (Burnett, 1964: 248). And so the delegates moved across the river to York. The issue of voting in the new Congress came up immediately and was resolved in favor of one vote for each state. On October 14 the issues of the size of state delegations and length of terms for delegates were resolved. The results are contained in Article V of the Articles of Confederation—our first national constitution.

> Article V. For the more convenient management of the general interests of the united states, delegates shall be annually appointed in such manner as the legislature of each state shall direct. . . .
>
> No state shall be represented in Congress by less than two, nor by more than seven Members; and no person shall be capable of being a delegate for more than three years in any term of six years. . . .
>
> In determining questions in the united states in Congress assembled, each state shall have one vote.

In commenting on these provisions, Edmund Cody Burnett declared that "Congress effectively inoculated itself with the germ of pernicious anemia" (1964: 250). A British observer, James Bryce, wrote that: "This Confederation, which was not ratified by all the States till 1781, was rather a league than a national government" (Bryce, 1915: 20). The Articles themselves declared as much in Article III: "The said states hereby severally enter into a firm league of friendship with each other." The league was not to last. In a sequence of actions familiar to all, a group met in Annapolis, Maryland, to discuss trade problems; this group recommended that Congress authorize "a future Convention, with more enlarged powers;" and the Congress did, on February 21, 1787, pass a resolution authorizing the Constitutional Convention (Tansill, 1927: 46).

> Resolved that in the opinion of Congress it is expedient that on the second Monday in May next a Convention of delegates who shall have been appointed by the several states be held at Philadelphia for the sole and express purpose of revising the Articles of Confederation and reporting to Congress and the several legislatures such alterations and provisions therein as shall when agreed to in Congress and confirmed by the states render the federal constitution adequate to the exigencies of Government and the preservation of the Union.

Shortly after the delegates finally assembled in late May 1787, Edmund Randolph of Virginia introduced a bold plan for a new government. On the very next day, Randolph went even further by introducing a resolution "that a Union of the States merely federal will not accomplish the objects proposed by the articles of Confederation" and "that a *national* Government ought to be established consisting of a *supreme* Legislative, Executive and Judiciary."[1] The resolution was adopted and, according to Alfred H. Kelly and Winfred A. Harbison (1948: 124)

> The Convention had thus committed itself to a serious breach of its authority. Called to amend the Articles, a majority of the delegates had boldly decided to disregard their instructions and instead to create an entirely new frame of government.

Had the Convention decided to stay within its charge, it probably would have adopted the features of the so-called New Jersey plan, introduced by William Paterson on June 15. Significantly this plan did not change the unicameral legislature of the Articles, but it did give it more authority. Had it been accepted we may well have developed a parliamentary system since Congress was "authorized to elect a fed-

---

[1] Taken from James Madison's notes at the Constitutional Convention as recorded in Tansill, 1927: 120. Emphasis was Madison's.

eral Executive" (Tansill, 1927: 205). But the New Jersey plan was not adopted.

The Randolph or Virginia plan provided for a two-house legislature. The pertinent provisions were as follows (Tansill, 1927: 116 – 17):

    3. Resolved that the National Legislature ought to consist of two branches.

    4. Resolved that the members of the first branch of the National Legislature ought to be elected by the people of the several States. . . .

    5. Resolved that the members of the second branch of the National Legislature ought to be elected by those of the first, out of a proper number of persons nominated by the individual Legislatures.

Having agreed on two houses, the Convention then determined the basis of representation for each. The conflicts between the large and small states need not be reviewed here. Suffice it to say that they occupied a great deal of time and debate in Philadelphia. The final results are contained in Article 1 of the Constitution—a House of Representatives "composed of Members chosen every second year by the People of the several States" and a Senate "composed of two Senators from each State, chosen by the Legislature thereof, for six years."

So the United States Congress was born. There had never been any institution quite like it for governing a nation. It remains an extraordinary legislature in the world today. And it is constantly undergoing change. As William J. Keefe rightly observes (1980: 143): "No new Congress is the same as the previous one. Congresses differ from one session to the next and in some respects even from one month to the next." What an exciting if complex institution to explain.

HISTORICAL PERSPECTIVES ON CONGRESS

What did the founding fathers think they had created in Article I? And what functions have been attributed to Congress through time? Sampling various perspectives on the role of Congress serves the useful purpose of illustrating the adaptability of this institution to the dynamics of national politics. Not only does its role shift with the political context, but it may even appear to serve different functions for different people at any one time. This adaptability should not surprise us. It is well suited to the interdependency of institutions so carefully devised by the framers. So let's turn first to the creation.

In their analysis of political bargaining in the United States, Robert A. Dahl and Charles E. Lindblom observe that "no unified, cohesive, acknowledged, and legitimate representative-leaders of the 'national majority' exist in the United States" (1953: 336). Other political systems are designed to facilitate the development and expression of national majorities. In our case, however (Dahl and Lindblom, 1953: 336):

> The convention did its work so well that even when a Congressional majority is nominally of the same party as the president, ordinarily they do not speak with the same voice.
>
> On a great many questions the "preferences of the greater number" or "the majority" is a fiction. But even if there were a national majority in the United States, it could not rule unless it were so overwhelmingly large as to include within its massive range the diverse "majorities" for which different elements in the bureaucracy, the president, and congressmen all claim to speak.

What Dahl and Lindblom have described sounds like a football team unable to score even when the opposing players leave the field! What possible rationale could there be for devising a system with so many internal checks? The answer to this question is found in *The Federalist*, that remarkable set of essays by Alexander Hamilton, John Jay, and James Madison, written in support of ratification of the Constitution. The argument, greatly simplified, goes something like this.[2]

Republicanism

It is essential to such a government that it be derived from the great body of the society, not from an inconsiderable proportion, or a favored class of it; otherwise a handful of tyrannical nobles . . . might aspire to the rank of republicans (Number 39).

Separation of powers

The accumulation of all powers, legislative, executive, and judiciary, in the same hands, whether of one, a few, or many, and whether hereditary, self-appointed, or elective, may justly be pronounced the very definition of tyranny (Number 47).

Legislative primacy

In republican government, the legislative authority necessarily predominates (Number 51). Its constitutional powers being at once more extensive, and less susceptible of precise limits, it can, with the greater facility, mask, under complicated and indirect measures, the encroachments which it makes on the coordinate departments (Number 48).

Legislative expansion

We have seen that the tendency of republican governments is to an aggrandizement of the legislative at the expense of the other departments (Number 49).

---

[2] The quotations are taken from the Modern Library edition of *The Federalist*, in the following sequence: pp. 244, 313, 338, 323, 330, 338, 338, 337.

Bicameralism

The remedy for this inconveniency [natural legislative primacy and expansion] is to divide the legislature into different branches; and to render them, by different modes of election and different principles of action, as little connected with each other as the nature of their common functions and their common dependence on the society will admit (Number 51).

Checks and balances

It may even be necessary to guard against dangerous encroachments by still further precautions (Number 51). Ambition must be made to counteract ambition (Number 51).

As collected these pronouncements add up to an extraordinarily cautious approach to government making. The people must be represented in government, but not all in one place. Given the power of the idea of popular representation, the legislature is bound to dominate and one simply cannot permit that to happen. Therefore it is necessary to divide the legislature and, as well, give the other branches some authority to override its judgments. This remarkable balancing act between institutional independence and dependence produced an ambiguity in the political and policy functions to be performed by each branch. This ambiguity, in turn, has led to widely varying interpretations regarding the proper role of Congress in the national policy process. Among the more prominent interpretations are those promoting legislative primacy, presidential primacy, and mixed government (either cooperative or adversarial).[3]

Legislative primacy

The inevitability of legislative primacy led James Madison and his coessayists in *The Federalist* to justify the need for checks and balances. Their statement on the subject (see above) provides the rationale of those supporting legislative superiority—legislators come from the people. But it was left to John C. Calhoun in 1817 to provide the most eloquent statement on the subject. Then serving in the House of Representatives from South Carolina, Calhoun articulated the view that the separation of powers by no means implied equality of power among the branches. Congress was unquestionably supreme because of its close connections to the people.

---

[3] These categories benefit from the discussion in Davidson et al., 1966, Chapter 1. They propose three theories—literary ("a restatement of the constitutional formulation of blended and coordinate powers"), executive-force ("the executive initiates and implements; the legislature modifies and ratifies"), and party-government ("not a theory about Congress . . . but rather a proposal to reconstruct the American party system").

The prevailing principle [for our structure of government] is not so much a balance of power as a *well-connected chain of responsibility*. That responsibility commenced here, and this House is the centre of its operation. The members are elected for two years only; and at the end of that period are responsible to their constituents for the faithful discharge of their public duties. . . .

If we turn our attention to what are called the co-ordinate branches of our Government, we find them very differently constructed. The Judiciary is in no degree responsible to the people immediately. To Congress, to this body, is the whole of their responsibility. Such, too, in a great measure is the theory of our Government as applied to the Executive branch. It is true the President is elected for a term of years, but that term is twice the length of ours [in the House]; and, besides, his election is in point of fact removed in all of the States three degrees from the people; the Electors in many of the States are chosen by the State Legislatures. . . .

This, then, is the essence of our liberty; Congress is responsible to the people immediately, and the other branches of Government are responsible to it (Hyneman and Carey, 1967: 150 − 51; emphasis added).

The chain of responsibility theory was certainly forceful before the popular election of presidential electors. By 1836, however, in only one state, Calhoun's own South Carolina, were electors still chosen by the state legislature. All other states held popular elections, thus permitting the president to claim legitimacy by reason of direct public approval. Still many members of Congress and others continue to rationalize legislative superiority within the national political system.

Presidential primacy

On March 15, 1789, Thomas Jefferson wrote to James Madison expressing concerns about the new government:

The tyranny of the legislature is really the danger most to be feared, and will continue to be so for many years to come. The tyranny of the executive power will come in its turn, but at a more distant period.[4]

The dominance of the executive over Congress may be said to have developed as a consequence of the growing complexity of issues facing the national government. Though these forces were understood by Woodrow Wilson, it was not until the Franklin D. Roosevelt administrations that developments shaped the modern presidency and encouraged its imperial quality. Certainly by the end of the 19th century, Congress was the premier institution in Washington. In his classic work, *Congressional Government*, Woodrow Wilson confirmed Madison's fears about the legislature. (1913: 43, 45, 57).

---

[4] Quoted in de Toqueville, 1945: 270. This incredibly prescient statement was first brought to my attention in Schlesinger, 1973: 377.

> . . . the power of Congress has become predominant . . . Accordingly it has entered more and more into the details of administration, until it has virtually taken into its own hands all the substantial powers of government. . . . Any one who is unfamiliar with what Congress actually does and how it does it . . . is very far from a knowledge of the constitutional system under which we live.[5]

Two world wars and a great depression contributed a vastly strengthened presidency to national politics. Dubbed the imperial presidency by Arthur Schlesinger, Jr., the White House came to be the center of decisionmaking. Fred I. Greenstein concludes that with the Franklin Roosevelt administrations "the presidency began to undergo not a shift but rather a metamorphosis" (in King, 1978: 45). The justification for expansion of executive authority was manifold. Among the more important reasons cited were the priority of international politics, the growing complexity of domestic issues, and the national constitutuency represented by the president. Schlesinger believes that the Nixon presidency brought matters to a head by forcing public realization of the extraordinary growth of power in the executive branch (1973: 377):

> The imperial presidency, created by wars abroad, was making a bold bid for power at home. The belief of the Nixon administration in its own mandate and in its own virtue, compounded by its conviction that the republic was in mortal danger from internal enemies, had produced an unprecedented attempt to transform the presidency of the Constitution into a plebiscitary presidency. If this transformation were carried through, the president, instead of being accountable every day to Congress and public opinion, would be accountable every four years to the electorate. Between elections, the president would be accountable only through impeachment and would govern, as much as he could, by decree.

Those promoting presidential primacy are not typically endorsing executive imperialism. They believe that the president alone can initiate large-scale integrated policy proposals to treat the complex issues of the modern era. Congress has a role in modifying these proposals and has a responsibility to check excesses of presidential power. This group remains steadfast, however, in the belief that the presidency has become the primary institution in the national policy process.

Mixed government—cooperative mode

Another view is that neither branch works for the other. Both are viewed as contributing within their spheres of authority, knowledge,

---

[5] By 1900 Wilson had already expressed doubts that Congress was predominant. See the preface to the 15th edition of *Congressional Government*.

and expertise. It may be that this cooperation is what the framers intended. Unfortunately, however, they created many impediments to its realization. The separation of the election bases for the two institutions, as well as for the two houses of Congress, plus the checks each can impose on the actions of the other virtually make cooperation an unnatural act. Theoretically, political parties provide a means for joining the two institutions in a common cause and many persons have recommended as much. The Committee on Political Parties of the American Political Science Association described the potential role for parties as follows (1950:   89):

> The president could gain much when party leaders in and out of Congress are working together with him closely in matters concerning the party program. As party head, the president could then expect more widespread and more consistent support from the congressional leaders of his party. These, in turn, would present a more united front. As a result, on issues where the party as a party could be expected to have a program, the program of the party, of the party leaders in each house of Congress, and of the president would be the same program, not four different programs.

The committee also envisaged a rational division of responsibility emerging from a strengthened party system. The president would initiate proposals for congressional consideration, depending on political parties to provide support. Congress benefits from "prior effort and concrete recommendations." The president gains "dependable political support" (1950:   94).

This solution may sound attractive, but the separation of election base can result in insuperable obstacles to cooperation. Thus, for example, the cooperative mode as worked through the party system breaks down when a president of one party faces congressional majority leaders of the other party.[6] Even when the same party controls both, however, major differences may develop with few effective means for their resolution.

Mixed government—adversarial mode

By this view, Congress and the presidency are coequal and competitive. The separation is accepted as is the improbability of strengthened political parties acting to promote cooperation. Each branch may be expected to encroach on the other with the court enforcing the separation where constitutional bounds are violated. I know of no one who publicly advocates this particular pattern of

---

[6] The voters have shown a propensity in recent years to split their tickets. Between 1947 and 1981, the Congress and the White House were controlled by different parties nearly half of the time (16 of 34 years). In the 1980 elections another variation was introduced: a Republican president and Senate, a Democratic House of Representatives.

institutional behavior. But it has been characteristic of interbranch relations during periods in which different parties control the White House and Congress (e.g., Truman and the 80th Congress, Nixon and the 93d Congress). Thus it results from each branch accepting its *own* primacy and refusing to yield to the other.

STUDYING THE MODERN CONGRESS

Note that the interpretations above are more than mental images of what should be. They also are useful descriptions of particular presidential-congressional relations, even in the 20th century. For example:

Congressional primacy: The Cannon era (1902 − 10, when Joseph G. Cannon was Speaker of the House), the weak president era (1920s—Harding, Coolidge, Hoover).

Presidential primacy: The Roosevelt era (1933 − 45), variable in the post-World War II era.

Cooperative mode: The early Wilson and Johnson administrations (1913 − 17, 1964 − 66).

Adversarial mode: The several administrations with split-party control (Wilson, 1919 − 20; Truman, 1947 − 48; Eisenhower, particularly 1959 − 60; Nixon-Ford, 1973 − 76), but also characterizing some relationships in Kennedy, 1961 − 63; Johnson 1966 − 68; and Carter, 1977 − 81 despite Democratic control of both branches.

This review of historical perspectives as descriptions of reality tells us something else of profound importance about the Congress. Given the emergence of complex foreign and domestic issues in the 20th century, one might have expected Congress to suffer steady decline in influence. After all, how can a two-house legislature hope to grapple with the social, economic, and political issues of a technocratic society? It is true that Congress has had to accept a lesser role at various times since the 1930s, but the graph of legislative power is one of peaks and valleys not one of straight linear decline. And as of this writing Congress is definitely on one of the peaks.

Remarkable as it may seem, then, this awkwardly structured policy institution continues to position itself at the very center of national decision-making. In an era that invites the creation of efficient hierarchies, one is faced with having to explain the important political and policy functions performed by an inefficient and nonhierarchical Congress. How can this body even presume to participate actively in the development of programs to resolve such issues as energy supply and use, deterioration of the environment, redistribution of resources, complex questions associated with human relations? And how do the members justify getting involved in foreign policy issues—including going to war?

In large part Congress can justify its influential participation in the national policy process because of the persistent devotion in the country at large to the idea of political representation. The republican principles espoused by Madison remain strong today as does the practical expression of these principles by a legislature. In fact, Congress comes under particularly heavy criticism if it appears not to represent dominant opinions in the society. The point is that Congress continues to have power in the political system because most people want it that way. At the same time, however, it is as predictable as night following day that a representative body will be subject to constant criticism. Why? Simply because support for representation as an abstract principle by no means guarantees support for specific representative acts in regard to resolving public problems. In fact, almost any decision by a representative produces some winners and some losers. The losers may criticize the act, however, without abandoning their faith in representation as a way of doing business. The trick for Congress is to prevent the losers from drawing this second conclusion—that the whole system has gone wrong. The importance of events in the 1960s and 1970s (Vietnam, civil rights, the women's rights movement, environmental concerns) was precisely because they resulted in challenges to the current structure for realizing republican principles. It was not altogether surprising, therefore, that Congress sought to alter that structure—enacting more reforms in the 1970s than in any other period in its history.

Studying the modern Congress is an uncommonly challenging endeavor. I have always believed that but I am even more persuaded after having written this book. The task would be greatly simplified if there were just one commonly accepted perspective on its role, or if it had less authority to get involved in all phases of all public issues, or if it would just stay in one place. But there are many perspectives on its role, it does have great power, and it is a moving target. This variability itself tells us something important about the institution—that it adapts to the changing national political environment, suggesting again how important it is since lesser structures resist change and suffer accordingly.

The plan of the book changed in an important way as it was written. I began with an organization designed to respond to the question posed earlier: Why does Congress continue to be such an important policymaking institution? My answer drew directly from Madison and his coessayists of *The Federalist*. Congress has impressive constitutional power of approval in virtually all important issue areas and can justify exercising this power as long as it remains a representative institution. Further, the power of approval naturally leads legislators to participate in other policy activities as well (something Madison worried about—"aggrandizement of the legislative at the expense of the other departments"). The organization of the book flowed naturally from these ideas. I had to explain the who, what, and how of Congress.

> The people: Who are these representatives? How do they get there? Who else works on Capitol Hill? Who comes to Congress to get approval?
>
> The institution: How is it organized to give approval? How do the House and Senate differ? How do the bodies get together?
>
> The policy process: How does Congress participate in other policy activities besides program approval? How does this participation vary over time and across issues?
>
> Reform: Why and when does Congress reform itself? What are the effects of these reforms?

The reader will note that this organization essentially remains. After an initial chapter (Chapter 2) in which I portray the astonishing amount of human activity so characteristic of life on Capitol Hill, I turn to an analysis of people (Chapters 3 – 7), institution (Chapters 8 – 12), policy process (Chapters 13, 14), and congressional reform (Chapter 15), concluding with a few observations about this remarkable institution (Chapter 16). What changed rather dramatically was the proportion of attention devoted to each topic. I intended to write two relatively brief chapters on the institution—one on each house. When it came to the writing, however, those two short chapters became five rather lengthy chapters. I came to believe that the formal organization of Congress to exercise its power of approval required more explication than I had originally intended. Why? This extraordinary authority to legitimize government programs brings people to Congress and justifies members getting involved in other ways in the policy process (defining problems, initiating proposals, overseeing administration).

In my earlier version of this chapter I asked the reader to picture Congress as *a population for prospective and ongoing policy networks.* My idea simply was that legislators and their aides are drawn into policy or issue-centered networks or systems to participate in many ways toward the goals of developing and administering government programs. I still believe that is a useful way to look at Congress. What it lacks, however, is *sufficient emphasis on the reasons why other policy actors should care to involve legislators.* The principal justification is that Congress has the formal authority to pass laws, to say yes or no. Therefore, the means by which the two houses organize to accomplish this vital function require the careful attention of all students— including those who are primarily interested in the broader policy process. Also significant, of course, is the impact of this formal approval function on the behavior of legislators as actors in other policy activities.

My discovery and subsequent shift in emphasis led me to try and fold two books into one. The first book seeks to describe and analyze the role of Congress in the national policy process. The second intends to provide a detailed guide to the important formal workings of the institution. I have tried to knit the two together rather than writing separate texts. The work begins in the next chapter by sampling how it all comes together during one week in April 1977.

2 "This ceaseless agitation"

Sometimes it takes an outsider to tell us about ourselves. Alexis de Tocqueville accomplished this goal for generations of Americans. His pen recorded what his eyes saw and his mind absorbed. Thus, for example, the political busyness we take for granted, he marked as extraordinary (1945 ed.:   249):

> It is not impossible to conceive the surprising liberty that the Americans enjoy; some idea may likewise be formed of their extreme equality; but the political activity that pervades the United States must be seen in order to be understood. No sooner do you set foot upon American ground than you are stunned by a kind of tumult; a confused clamor is heard on every side, and a thousand simultaneous voices demand the satisfaction of their social wants. Everything is in motion around you.

"This ceaseless agitation," de Tocqueville observed, is probably "the greatest advantage of democracy" (1945 ed.:   251). Much of this activity can be viewed in legislatures, but it is by no means limited to those institutions.

> The great political agitation of American legislative bodies . . . is a mere episode, or a sort of continuation, of that universal movement

13

which originates in the lowest classes of the people and extends succes-
sively to all the ranks of society. It is impossible to spend more effort in
the pursuit of happiness (1945 ed.:   250).

America is as politically busy today as when de Tocqueville visited.
It remains one of the most striking features for foreign visitors or when
we return from travel abroad. While the scurrying about may be
watched in any number of settings, perhaps the most comprehensive
view is in the institution that is the subject of this book—that is, the
United States Congress. Most of the world's legislative chambers are
relatively quiet and confined places. Congress is noisy, bustling, and
sprawling. Nelson W. Polsby has captured these differences (in Polsby
and Greenstein, eds. 1975:   275 — 76):

> It is instructive . . . for the student of the United States Congress to
> visit the mother of parliaments at Westminster, or the Italian Chamber
> of Deputies, or the Knesset in Jerusalem. In Washington, the Capitol
> building teems with life, and the business of Congress overflows into five
> giant office buildings nearby [and, it should be added, new buildings
> either being acquired or built]. Senators and representatives each have a
> suite of offices and a staff to help in their very individual relationships
> with the people back home who nominated and elected them. Xerox
> and mimeograph machines hum. Committees and subcommittees
> abound, all with projects, personnel, budgets, press releases, hearings.
> Political careers are in such a system plainly a product of much entre-
> preneurial activity—as well as good fortune.
>   The contrast with life in Westminster or at the Montecitorio is strik-
> ing: to someone accustomed to the hurly-burly of Capitol Hill, the lei-
> surely pace, the absence of activity, the paucity of actual working
> facilities in and around a parliament is memorable. The visitor who takes
> the guided tours is reminded of the apocryphal query voiced by the
> American who is taken around the beautiful Moscow subway: Where are
> the trains?

The purpose of this chapter is to portray this congressional busyness. Following a few observations about the astonishing growth of
Congress in the past few years, I will illustrate what goes on by reporting on a single week's activities on Capitol Hill. Quite by chance I
selected the week in which President Carter introduced his energy
program. Of course, no week is typical, but every week is interesting. I
selected one that happened to be more interesting than most.

THE BILLION DOLLAR CONGRESS

In his last State of the Union Message, President Gerald R. Ford
made some observations about the budget of Congress.

> I cannot help but observe that while the White House staff and the
> Executive Office of the president have been reduced and the total num-
> ber of civilians in the executive branch contained during the 1970s, the

legislative branch has increased substantially, although the membership of the Congress remains at 535. Congress now costs the taxpayers more than a million dollars a year per member; *the whole legislative budget has passed the $1 billion mark.*[1]

Congressional leaders were not pleased with this reference to a billion-dollar Congress. But they could hardly deny the dramatic growth taking place on Capitol Hill. Table 2 – 1 shows the growth in

TABLE 2– 1
Appropriations for Congress—selected fiscal years ($ millions)

	1967	1970	1973	1976	1977	1980	*Percent increase* 1967 – 80*
Senate	39.7	54.8	79.1	118.8	137.3	206.9	421
House	77.7	104.8	141.6	206.4	241.8	312.9	303
Joint items	9.7	13.2	26.0	54.8	55.5	60.2	521
Office of Technology Assessment	—	—	—	6.5	6.6	11.0	69
Congressional Budget Office	—	—	—	—	9.3	12.1	30
Architect of Capitol	14.3	24.0	26.4	40.8	60.5	62.8	339
Library of Congress	30.0	43.9	78.3	116.2	137.9	177.5	492
Government Printing Office	42.7	40.0	63.7	145.3	140.8	111.1†	160
General Accounting Office‡	48.5	63.0	96.2	135.9	150.6	200.3	313
Cost-Accounting Standards Board	—	—	1.7	1.6	1.7	1.3	– 24
Botanic Gardens	0.5	0.6	0.8	1.2	1.2	1.5	200
Copyright Royalty Commission	—	—	—	—	0.3	0.5	67
Totals§	263.1	344.3	513.8	827.5	943.5	1,158.1	340
Average per member (in millions)	0.5	0.6	1.0	1.5	1.8	2.2	
Average per member (items 1– 8)	0.4	0.5	0.8	1.3	1.5	1.8	

* Percent increase from first entry for recent items.
† In 1977 Congress reallocated the GPO budget requiring agencies to pay for their entries into the *Federal Register*. The effect was to reduce the amount included in the legislative budget.
‡ Included in independent offices appropriations in 1967.
§ May vary slightly from official totals due to rounding.
SOURCE: Various issues of *Congressional Quarterly Weekly Report.*

appropriations for the legislative branch, 1967 – 80. Even discounting the inclusion of such a curious item as the Botanic Gardens (incorporated into the legislative budget for historical reasons), the increase is rather phenomenal—indeed, more than twice that of the budget overall. Further, the growth is considerably greater than in the recent past

---

[1] *Congressional Quarterly Weekly Report,* January 15, 1977, p. 91.

(340 percent increase, 1967 – 80, as compared to a 74 percent increase in legislative branch appropriations, 1957 – 67).

An immediate response on Capitol Hill to charges of excessive growth was to adjust the budget. The members pointed out that many items which were traditionally included in the legislative branch appropriations belonged elsewhere. Thus, for example, the Government Printing Office budget was reallocated. And the appropriations were divided into those associated with congressional operations and those associated with related agencies. With this arrangement, the Library of Congress appropriations were divided between general support (allocated to related agencies) and the Congressional Research Service (included in congressional operations). By these methods, Congress was able to argue that its operational budget remained below $1 billion. On the other hand, this division does not reduce the rate of growth in the congressional budget—just the opposite. Whereas the overall growth, 1967 – 80, is 340 percent, the growth in those items that are unarguably congressional (1 – 5 in Table 2 – 1) is 375 percent!

But we do not want to be distracted by arguments about what should or should not be included in the congressional budget. The purpose of Table 2 – 1 is to provide an indicator of congressional activity. Dollars translate into people doing things. And by this measure more people on Capitol Hill are doing more things—more than has been the case in the past and more than is the case for any other legislature in the world.

By almost any measure—expenditures, staff growth, bills and resolutions introduced, committee and subcommittee meetings, groups testifying—our national legislature is a veritable beehive of activity. De Tocqueville would probably react to all of this with awe. For whatever he observed in the 1830s pales when compared to what goes on in Washington today. But let's go to Washington and observe a particular week on Capitol Hill—April 18 – 22, 1977.

"WHEN ARE THE GIRL SCOUTS COMING IN?"

It was April 20, 1977, and President Jimmy Carter was to deliver his first address before the Congress. The subject was of vital interest to all Americans—that is, future energy supply and use. This event was the highlight of the week I had chosen to concentrate on for this book. As I walked toward the Capitol on the way to my first appointment of the day, a CBS news truck had already arrived, and the police were putting ropes in place for crowd control. My 9:30 A.M. appointment was with an aide to the Speaker of the House of Representatives. The aide was late, and so I sat and read the newspaper in the large room outside the Speaker's ceremonial office—a room housing several staff aides and secretaries. At approximately 9:35 A.M. Speaker Thomas P. "Tip" O'Neill entered. I wondered to myself what would be on the Speaker's mind on this important day. He answered my question as he turned to a secretary and asked two questions:

1.   "What about Fowler? Is that all set?" (Wyche Fowler had just been elected to fill the Georgia House seat previously held by United Nations' Ambassador Andrew Young. The Speaker was asking about Fowler's committee assignments.)
2.   "When are the Girl Scouts coming in?" (A group of Girl Scouts from O'Neill's Boston district was scheduled to come in and take pictures of the Speaker.)

This brief episode illustrates a fundamental congressional characteristic. Whatever else may be going on, all members of Congress must remain attentive to their states and districts. I do not mean to suggest by this episode that Speaker O'Neill judges the Girl Scouts as important as the president's energy message—only that he rightly must give them attention too.

But there is another sense in which it is useful to begin this section with such a story. The week of April 18 — 22 will be recorded as Energy Week. As will be amply demonstrated below, however, Congress had a full agenda even without the president's proposals. So, despite the press and media attention which marked this as the president's week, Congress was busy with mayors, industrialists, union representatives, generals, Indians, departmental secretaries, scientists, farm groups, and Girl Scouts.

The week

President Carter began the week by speaking to the American people. In a televised address, the President said:

> Tonight I want to have an unpleasant talk with you about a problem unprecedented in our history. With the exception of preventing war, this is the greatest challenge our country will face during our lifetimes. The energy crisis has not yet overwhelmed us, but it will if we do not act quickly.[2]

The effort would be the "moral equivalent of war," and therefore the president felt compelled to blitz Congress and the media with his analysis of the problem and the proposals he judged would be effective solutions.

On Wednesday evening at nine o'clock eastern time, the president presented his proposals to Congress. This speech too was televised nationally. The president appeared nervous, and the speech was not

---

[2] *Congressional Quarterly Weekly Report,* April 23, 1977, p. 753.

well delivered. There was little applause, even from the galleries. But it was an important event, and it dominated the week for the media.

Still President Carter was not satisfied that the program had been sufficiently launched. He held a press conference on Friday, April 22. It was also televised, and as intended, the energy program dominated the questioning. At one point a reporter asked whether the president may not be engaged in "overkill . . . with the American people and especially with Congress in terms of getting your program on energy through." The president agreed but thought it justified.

> I cannot disagree with you. There is a danger of overexposure, of me in my presentation to the news media and to the American people. But I think this is an extraordinary week, and I doubt that it will be repeated in the future.[3]

This major national event serves our purposes well. Not only does it fix the time for the reader, but it illustrates how the president can dominate the news. The fact is that April 18 — 22 would have been an important week on Capitol Hill without the president's message. Congress was returning from what is referred to in the House as a district work period and in the Senate as a nonlegislative period (formerly called the Easter recess in both houses). Thus, a full agenda was awaiting action. So let's look at what was going on whether or not the president made an appearance on April 20. Later we can return to evaluate the significance of the main event from the public's perspective. We will start with the committees, then consider the schedules of individual members, the action in each chamber, and the work of other associated persons.

The week in committees

One hardly has to look beyond the totals in Tables 2 — 2 and 2 — 3 to establish the point that Congress was quite heavily engaged during the week, April 18 — 22. House committees and subcommittees held 143 meetings; Senate committees and subcommittees held 107 meetings—an overall total of 250 meetings! It does not take much imagination to realize the amount of activity associated with 250 meetings in such a concentrated period of time. While several of these meetings touched on energy problems and policies, none was specifically directed to the president's energy program. Those meetings would come later after the program had been introduced as legislation.

But Tables 2 — 2 and 2 — 3 tell us much more that is helpful in understanding how Congress does its work. First note that both hear-

---

[3] *Congressional Quarterly Weekly Report*, April 30, 1977, pp. 813 — 14.

TABLE 2-2
Senate committee and subcommittee meetings, April 18-22, 1977

Committee	Number of meetings on each day					Totals	Number of markup	Number closed
	18	19	20	21	22			
Agriculture/Nutrition/ Forestry	—	1	1	1	1	4	4	0
Appropriations*	3	6	4	5	5	23	0	0
Armed Services*	2	3	3	2	1	11	8	9
Banking/Housing/Urban Affairs	1	1	1	1	1	5	0	0
Budget	—	—	—	—	1	1	0	0
Commerce/Science/ Transportation*	—	2	2	2	1	7	0	0
Energy/Natural Resources*	2	3	1	1	—	7	2	0
Environment/Public Works* ...	1	1	1	1	—	4	0	0
Finance	—	1	—	1	—	2	0	0
Foreign Relations*	—	1	3	3	2	9	1	0
Governmental Affairs	—	2	1	3	2	8	1	0
Human Resources	—	1	2	2	2	7	3	0
Judiciary	1	2	1	1	—	5	0	0
Select/Aging	—	1	—	1	—	2	0	0
Select/Intelligence	—	—	2	1	1	4	1	2
Select/Small Business	—	—	1	1	—	2	0	0
Joint Economic	—	—	1	1	1	3	0	0
Conference	—	—	—	1	1	2	0	0
Republican Policy	—	—	—	1	—	1	0	1
Grand totals	10	25	24	29	19	107	20	12

* Most meetings were in subcommittees.
SOURCE: Taken from "Activities Today in Congress," the *Washington Post*, April 18-22, 1977.

ings or other regular meetings *and* markup sessions are recorded. The latter are meetings in which the committee and its staff review and amend the bill for the last time before the vote. Until 1973, the markup sessions were normally closed to the public.[4] In that year, however, provisions were made in both houses to conduct this business in the open. Thus, the public can attend most markup sessions of committees and subcommittees, and they are now regularly listed each day in the Washington newspapers. During the week of April 18 — 22, the Senate held a total of 20 markup sessions; the House 38. This is a smaller proportion of the total committee sessions than would be characteristic of a week later in the year since relatively little legislation is ready for markup in April.

Second, while we are on the subject, also note that the number of closed meetings is very low. No House meetings were closed during

---

[4] See *Congressional Quarterly Weekly Report*, February 16, 1974, p. 369, for comparative figures on open and closed meetings in the post-World War II period.

TABLE 2–3

House committee and subcommittee meetings, April 18– 22, 1977

Committee*	Number of meetings on each day						Number
	18	19	20	21	22	Totals	of markup
Agriculture	—	3	4	2	1	10	8
Appropriations	2	6	5	5	2	20	0
Armed Services	—	1	1	1	—	3	0
Banking/Finance/Urban Affairs	—	2	2	2	1	7	2
District of Columbia	—	—	1	1	—	2	0
Education/Labor	—	2	2	3	1	8	0
Government Operations	1	2	1	1	—	5	0
House Administration	—	3	2	1	—	6	0
Interior/Insular Affairs	1	3	2	3	2	11	4
International Relations	1	5	3	3	—	12	7
Interstate/Foreign Commerce	2	3	3	5	2	15	7
Judiciary	1	1	1	4	2	9	5
Merchant Marine/Fisheries	—	1	1	1	—	3	0
Post Office/Civil Service	—	2	2	1	—	5	1
Public Works/Transportation	1	2	2	2	—	7	0
Rules	—	1	—	—	—	1	0
Science/Technology	—	—	2	—	—	2	1
Small Business	2	1	1	1	—	5	0
Standards/Official Conduct	—	—	—	1	—	1	0
Veterans' Affairs	—	2	2	1	—	5	0
Ways/Means	1	1	1	—	—	3	3
Select/Aging	—	—	1	—	1	2	0
Select/Assassinations	1	—	—	—	—	1	0
Grand totals	13	41	39	38	12	143	38

* Most meetings were in subcommittees.
SOURCE: Taken from "Activities Today in Congress," the *Washington Post*, April 18–22, 1977.

this week. And only 12 Senate meetings were closed. Of these, nine were markup sessions (eight in the sensitive areas dealt with by the Committee on Armed Services) and one was a meeting of the Republican Policy Committee, which is not subject to the Senate rules. In total this represents less than one half of one percent of all meetings.

Third, much of the work in the early part of the session is done in subcommittees. In the Senate 70 of the 107 meetings (65 percent) were in subcommittees. Even more House business was conducted in subcommittees—115 of the 143 meetings (over 80 percent).

Two other observations are worth making. While the House holds more meetings in absolute numbers (143 compared to 107 in the Senate), the number in proportion to members is greater in the Senate. And the workload varies considerably through the week. Note that Congress continues to be essentially a Tuesday to Thursday institution. The Senate held 74 percent, the House 82 percent, of its meetings during this period. This is not unusual—studies of legislative workload show virtually the same breakdown through a legislative session.[5]

Now let's try to make this all a little more meaningful by making reference to specific committees and subcommittees. It would, of course, be impossible for one person to visit even a small percentage of these meetings. In addition to the problem of sheer numbers, most of the meetings occur in the morning (normally around 80 percent occurring between nine and noon). So there is a heavy concentration of activity in the committee rooms before the House and Senate convene. Still one can sample various types of committee meetings in a week's time, and that is what I did.

Perhaps the best way to convey impressions is simply to chronicle two days—one spent on the House side, the other on the Senate side. What follows then are my notes taken for the days indicated.

April 20, 1977. I had the appointment with one of the Speaker's staff assistants that I referred to earlier. I wanted to talk with him about the Speaker's schedule for the week—what was important, how the schedule was developed, and what were the driving forces for the Speaker's daily commitments. It soon became clear that I had caught the aide on a bad day. In a series of brief and unhelpful responses, he was telling me mostly to get out of his hair. I soon obliged (actually much of our time together was taken up with the aide reviewing a press release on the soon-to-be announced Ad Hoc Committee on Energy). On my way out, I glanced into the Speaker's office to see the Girl Scouts snapping pictures. I paused outside to record some thoughts, the most memorable of which was: Staff of important people often perceive themselves as even more important. Not a bad lesson, I thought, well worth conveying to students who might some day either become staff or be forced to deal with them.

I then walked over to the Rayburn House Office Building to attend a markup session of the Committee on Interstate and Foreign Commerce. They were working on the Clean Air Act of 1977. On the way I stopped briefly to visit with friends who were working for the newly established House Commission on Administrative Review—the so-called Obey Commission, after its chairman, David R. Obey (D—Wisconsin). Here was yet another miniworld of activity on Capitol Hill—a highly qualified staff engaged in the study of how the House is organized and administered. Their work was intended to result in important rules changes but little came of their efforts.

The markup session was already in progress when I entered 2123

---

[5] See U.S. Congress, House, Commission on Administrative Review, *Scheduling the Work of the House,* 94th Congress, second session, 1976, pp. 6 — 8, and U.S. Congress, Senate, Commission on the Operation of the Senate, *Legislative Activity Sourcebook: United States Senate,* 94th Congress, second session, pp. 6 — 11.

Rayburn. Approximately 20 of the 43 committee members were in attendance. Harley O. Staggers (D—West Virginia), chairman of the full committee, formally chaired the meeting but Paul G. Rogers (D—Florida) was the substantive leader on this particular bill. Rogers chaired the Subcommittee on Health and Environment which had produced the Clean Air bill, and thus he managed it before the full committee. The clerk droned on, reading the bill in its entirety. Efforts to dispense with the reading were objected to by James M. Collins (R—Texas) who was seeking to delay the bill. Younger Democrats on the Committee were clearly perturbed by this behavior. Rogers consulted with staff aides, seemingly confident that he had the votes to pass the bill after all the delays. At least he projected that confidence to this observer, and I left to attend another committee meeting.

The Committee on Science and Technology was holding a markup session on the legislative authorization for nonnuclear programs of the Energy Research and Development Administration (ERDA). The chairman of the committee was not in attendance, so the second-ranking Democrat, Don Fuqua of Florida, was in the chair. Walter Flowers (D—Alabama) performed the role of substantive leader on the bill since his subcommittee had done the work. Approximately the same number of members was in attendance as with the Commerce Committee session I had just left. While I was there a technical point was raised by one of the members, and the legal counsel for ERDA was asked to step forward and respond. Relatively few staff were in attendance, but those who were there performed the critical function of interpreting the language of the bill for the members. I noted that one member, Louis Frey (R—Florida), was obviously running between this committee and the one I had just left. I then counted seven other members of the Science and Technology Committee who also served on the Commerce Committee. Small wonder that not all members were in attendance. It is hard to be in two places at once. After listening to more clarification of technical points in the bill, it occurred to me how useful these sessions were for familiarizing the full committee with the legislation. After all, not all of them would have served on the subcommittee which had held hearings on the bill.

On my way to lunch at the Capitol, I stopped briefly to watch the West Springfield, Massachusetts, high school band form on the Capitol steps. Once in formation, a picture would be taken with their congressman, in this case the powerful Edward P. Boland (D—Massachusetts), a close friend of the Speaker.

My luncheon appointment was with William S. Cohen (R—Maine). Cohen received considerable favorable publicity as an earnest and able member of the Committee on Judiciary during the impeachment hearings. He is characteristic of a new type of member who shows independence, initiative, and a wide range of interests. We discussed his recently published book of poetry and his plans for a book on Congress as well as the progress of the new administration and his plans to run for the Senate in Maine in 1978 (P.S.—he ran and won). While we were there, Cohen's Republican colleague from Maine's first district, David Emery, came in with a group of constituents. The House dining room is frequently used for both social and political purposes: that is, treating constituents, meeting with lobbyists, discussing business with other members, even exchanging views with a professor.

After lunch I walked back to the House office buildings, this time to the Longworth Building in order to attend a hearing of the Subcommittee on Livestock and Grains, Committee on Agriculture. Very nearly the whole subcommittee was in attendance (13 of the 17 members), and the discussion was quite intense. Department of Agriculture witnesses were testifying on the feed grains and wheat sections of the general farm bill. The atmosphere contrasted rather sharply with the earlier meetings. Here was very much a clientele-oriented committee. There was talk about "our farmers." Ruddy complexions and a mix of southern and flat midwestern accents were evident. Very few staff were present. House members on the Committee on Agriculture know their subject well. The press was in attendance, no doubt representing the several weekly farm papers as well as daily newspapers from rural areas. Mostly I got the impression that when I entered 1301 Longworth, I had penetrated a true community in which there was common understanding, if not always agreement. It was impressive and quite different from what I had observed in the other two meetings on that day.

It was 2:30 P.M., and the Speaker was holding a press conference in 15 minutes. So I left the world of the farm and walked back over to the Capitol. The Speaker holds daily press conferences in his ceremonial office, H—210. This particular day was significant because of the president's energy message that evening. The press gathered in H—209, and at 2:45 P.M. the doors to H—210 opened. The Speaker sat behind his desk with Majority Leader James C. Wright, Jr., of Texas seated on his right and Caucus Chairman Thomas S. Foley of Washington seated on his left. The press representatives crowded around the desk. The Speaker's staff aides were sprinkled throughout the room. It is sufficient at this point simply to observe that the whole scene was awkward. In striking contrast to presidential news conferences, the Speaker remained seated and had to look up to the standing journalists. Many people could not see the Speaker, and some could not hear—either the questions or the answers. There were occasional pauses in the questioning. The conference was mercifully ended when a staff aide said: "Mr. Speaker, the House is about to go into session."

I quickly exited in order to get to a typewriter and record the few notes I had taken. On the way over to the Cannon House Office Building, I observed John J. Rhodes (R—Arizona) walking briskly to the Capitol. Rhodes is the minority leader and was headed into the House chamber. He was, no doubt, coming from having dealt with some congressional district matters in his office in the Rayburn House Office Building. As minority leader he also has an office in the Capitol itself. Though members can get to the Capitol through underground walkways or subway cars from the Rayburn Building, on a nice day they often prefer to walk outside.

The House then convened at 3:00 P.M.—an unusually late hour dictated by the evening session at which the president would speak. Recess came at 6:38 P.M., with provision for reconvening at approximately 8:40 P.M. The details of House floor action will be discussed later.

April 21, 1977. I decided to spend this day on the Senate side. I first went to Room 357 in the Russell Office Building to observe a hearing on the Youth Employment Act before the Subcommittee on Employment, Poverty, and Migratory Labor of the Committee on Human Resources. When I arrived the hearing room was packed—hardly a seat available. Many staff persons from the National League of Cities were in attendance along with other interested group representatives. The witnesses and their supporters exchanged views while waiting for the subcommittee to come to order. Behind the dais at least a dozen staff aides were busily engaged in preparations for the hearings. Finally, at 10:45 A.M., just 15 minutes late, Senator Gaylord Nelson (D—Wisconsin), chairman of the subcommittee, entered. After a bit of "staff hovering" around him, Senator Nelson called the subcommittee to order. Mayor Kenneth Gibson of Newark, representing the U.S. Conference of Mayors, testified first, followed by Phylis Lamphere of the National League of Cities. Senator Harrison Williams (D—New Jersey) arrived at 10:50 A.M. for Mayor Gibson's testimony (strictly a courtesy for the Newark mayor—Williams was then chairman of the full committee but not a member of the subcommittee). No other Senators attended the hearing while I was there, though several staff aides stopped by to pick up statements.

Upon leaving 357 Russell, I noted a crowd of reporters around 335 Russell—the location of the Senate Republican Policy Committee. The committee was in session to evaluate the president's energy proposals as offered the night before. Senators Howard Baker (R—Tennessee), the Senate minority leader, and John Tower (R—Texas), chairman of the Senate Republican Policy Committee, later held a press conference criticizing the Carter program. It occurred to me as I passed by the awaiting group of reporters how the major event of the week was tracked by the press passing by all of the other multifaceted activities which were occurring in the same buildings.

Anxious to witness a Senate committee markup session, I then went to the Dirksen Office Building to watch the full Committee on Human Resources work on the Education of the Handicapped Act. Unfortunately, either they had already adjourned, or the meeting was postponed. An appropriations subcommittee was the next type of meeting on my list, and one was in session in 1114 Dirksen (the newest of the two Senate office buildings). The Subcommittee on Interior of the Committee on Appropriations was meeting to consider appropriations for the Bureau of Indian Affairs, Department of the Interior. Testimony was being received on health-care problems for Indians as I entered. Here again was a strikingly different scene. Most of those in attendance were Indians. The young people were dressed in jeans and bright shirts; the older men were dressed in suits but no ties. Various stories of inadequate health care facilities were told and duly entered into the record. The only senatorial ears present belonged to Henry Bellmon of Oklahoma, the lowest ranking *Republican* on the subcommittee. Three or four staff persons were also present. One other note: placed behind the dais was an enormous chart with details of the schedule for the Senate Committee on Appropriations. With the passage of the Budget and Impoundment Control Act of 1974, the congressional budget process requires a much more precise timetable than in the past. More about that in later chapters.

Checking my schedule of committee meetings, I noted that the Subcommittee on State, Justice, Commerce, and the Judiciary; Committee on Appropriations was in session in S—146, a very small room on the Senate side of the Capitol. As I entered, Paul Warncke, newly appointed director of the Arms Control and Disarmament Agency, was leaving. Senator Edward W. Brooke (R—Massachusetts) was also making his exit. Representatives of the United States Information Agency were the next witnesses in the sequence of foreign policy agencies testifying for their budget requests. Senators Ernest F. Hollings (D—South Carolina), Patrick J. Leahy (D—Vermont), and Ted Stevens (R—Alaska) remained to hear the justification, along with three or four staff aides. Throughout the week I observed that the number of senators in attendance was directly proportional to the relative national importance of the witnesses.

My luncheon companion on this day was a former Senate staff aide now serving as a lobbyist for El Paso Alaska Company. He was on Capitol Hill on April 21 to "educate" legislators and their aides on the benefits of the Trans-Alaska Gas Project. I mention this only because it illustrates a rather common pattern in which former senators, representatives, and legislative staff capitalize on their contacts and Capitol Hill familiarity to benefit various groups. Since it happens on both sides of many issues and since it is difficult to control how free citizens earn their keep, it is highly likely that the practice will continue.

I returned to the Dirksen Office Building in the afternoon. First I peeked into Room 1220, one of the largest hearing rooms in the building. A Food Day Conference on World Hunger was underway sponsored by Senator Mark Hatfield (R—Oregon) and the Center for Science in the Public Interest. Here was an event not listed on the regular schedule of Senate activities for April 22.

But my mission this afternoon was to attend a confirmation hearing, still another type of committee meeting. The Senate Committee on Foreign Relations was in session to consider several ambassadorial nominations. I had predicted in advance that senatorial attendance would be high since former Senate Majority Leader Mike Mansfield of Montana was one of the nominees—to be ambassador to Japan. I was not disappointed. I counted 10 senators and between 15 and 20 staff persons. Several reporters were also in attendance, including representatives of the foreign press. The audience included many foreign nationals from the embassies of countries to which the ambassadors were being assigned. I could not help but reflect on the variety of settings I had observed on this day—from the mayors, Indians, and administration officials in the morning to the international milieu in the afternoon. The hearing itself was mostly a love-in. The members of the committee tried to outdo one another in their praise for the Mansfield appointment. This too was expected. For in Mike Mansfield, the Senate had an opportunity to confirm one of its own to an important post.

I left as Senator Daniel P. Moynihan (D—New York), and one of our own in political science, was introducing the nominee to be our permanent representative to NATO. I spent the remainder of the afternoon talking to Senate staff persons.

Summary.   Though I have spent a great deal of time on Capitol Hill in the last 20 years, I must say that these committee visits were impressive for several reasons. It is one thing to read about the number and variety of interests served by the committee system. It is quite another to witness it and realize that even in a full day one can only sample the activity. Thus, for example, I attended parts of three House committee meetings on April 20, yet 36 other meetings were taking place that day just in the House (an additional 24 in the Senate).

I was also reminded again of the differences between the House and the Senate. Attendance at meetings among House members was uniformly higher than among senators. I attended several meetings during the week on the Senate side in which only one or two senators were present. On the other hand, the staff is much more in evidence in Senate committee meetings. It was not an uncommon sight to have a single senator conducting a hearing with a dozen staff hovering about.

Finally, the variety and complexity of issues being dealt with generate a respect for the knowledge and skill required by modern legislators. While it is true they can't know everything as individuals, it is the case that they have established an impressive network for receiving and processing demands, information, proposals, and complaints. A week's visit does not capture the intricacies of this network. What it does is to permit the observer to experience an initial sense of absolute chaos and gradually to identify the underlying structure and rationale. Having reached this second stage—that is, sensing that all of this activity may in fact have a purpose—one is then prepared to explore the institution in a more orderly fashion. And that is one of the reasons why I thought I would begin with this montage rather than the more traditional description of constitutional authority and legislative purposes. Hopefully I will be successful here in projecting my experience into your cognitive map.

The week for the members

The committee meetings give us an indication of how individual members spent the week of April 18 – 22. But there is much more. I asked the staff of certain representatives and senators to keep their weekly schedules so that I might show the nature and variety of appointments. Before introducing those, however, I think the problems I had in getting them provide some important lessons about the lives of senators and representatives.

Most, but not all, members are provided with a daily schedule of meetings and appointments—often on a 3 × 5 card. What I found was that senators are more likely to have these schedules typed up and available. I also found that the schedule is not always preserved nor is it corrected if it is retained in the records. The staff of House Majority Leader James C. Wright, Jr., informed me that they provided Wright with a daily schedule, he personally made many changes as the day progressed, but they never asked for it back. I was not successful in getting them to provide me with even the original version of the schedule. An aide to Speaker O'Neill informed me that they do not take the time to revise his daily schedule at the end of the day. "We have no sense of history, I guess." I was able to get different versions of the Speaker's schedule for the week, however.

I also observed that unless you are persistent, actually going to the office in question to pick up the schedule, you may not get it at all. Where the staff was not able at the moment to give me the schedule, I left my name and address for it to be sent. I was successful in getting only one of six members' schedules and one of five staff persons' schedules in this way. The lesson here is not that either the members or the staff are uncooperative. Rather they simply are too busy with today to think about yesterday. They all live by frantic schedules and they seldom have, nor want, the luxury in time to look back. In fact, I concluded that many on Capitol Hill are hooked on busy schedules. They can no more easily cope with a free day than can the junkie cope with going cold turkey. By its very nature, however, the need for a schedule fix is unlikely to be accompanied by a time perspective. Most members of Congress and their immediate staff live in the short run, and I do mean *run*. They exist in a rather fast-paced time capsule, and despite the complaining, they like it that way.

On the House side, my small sample of schedules includes those of the Speaker, the then Minority Leader, John J. Rhodes, Interior Committee Chairman Morris K. Udall, and a rank-and-file member, William S. Cohen. I offer these as examples only, making it clear in advance that they are not necessarily representative, nor are they likely to reflect all of the activities of these members during the days indicated.

Rather than repeat the rather lengthy and sometimes repetitive schedules for each day, I have selected two days only for illustrative purposes—April 19 and 20. I will provide supplementary information in discussing each person. The Speaker's schedule is summarized in Table 2 − 4. Note how his various appointments and meetings reflect

TABLE 2− 4
Schedule of the Speaker of the House, April 19– 20

Day	Hour	Appointment
April 19	8:00	White House breakfast—budget and defense matters discussed with Secretary of Defense Brown. Briefing on energy plan by Dr. Schlesinger in State Dining Room after breakfast.
	10:30	Meet with representatives of Outdoor Advertising.
	10:45	Meet with Colonel Jack Sanderson about Marine Corps Reserve.
	11:00	Meet with Representative Eckhardt (D −Texas).
	11:30	Courtesy call from German ambassador and mayor of Hamburg.
	11:30	Leadership meeting.
	11:45	Press conference.
	12:00	The House convenes.
	1:30	Meeting of Steering and Policy Committee about committee assignments for Representative Wyche Fowler (D– Georgia).
	3:30	Meet with Representatives Lee Hamilton (D– Indiana), Clement Zablocki (D– Wisconsin) and Roy Jenkins, president, European Community Commission.
	5:30	Reception—National Alliance of Postal and Federal Employees.
	6:00	Reception—Massachusetts Building and Construction Trades.
	7:30	Dinner for Liberian ambassador.
April 20	8:15	Breakfast with representatives of Armco Steel Corporation—brief speech.
	9:00	Meeting of Democratic Caucus on energy.
	9:40	Girl Scouts take pictures.
	10:30	Meet the Harvard Democratic Club—brief speech.
	11:45	Meet with Boston Building Trades.
	2:30	Leadership meeting.
	2:45	Press conference.
	3:00	The House convenes.
	3:30	Meeting of Steering and Policy Committee on budget.
	9:00	Joint Session of Congress to hear president's energy message.

the principal responsibilities of the Speaker. He begins April 19 with a breakfast at the White House. Surely one of his major duties is to maintain close contact with the president and his program. Then throughout the two days he is seen meeting with constituents, interest group representatives, and members of his party in the House. He also performs his more formal leadership responsibilities in presiding over the Steering and Policy Committee and, of course, the House itself, as well as engaging in certain ceremonial or courtesy functions.

The minority leader's schedule is almost as diverse as the Speaker's (see Table 2 – 5). He too must be available for various interests and

TABLE 2– 5
Schedule of the minority leader, April 19– 20

Day	Hour	Appointment
April 19	7:30	Breakfast at American Enterprise Institute about election reform legislation.
	9:30	Meet with representatives of Armco Steel—with Senator Henry Jackson (D– Washington), give 12– 15 minute summary of Carter's first 90 days.
	11:00	Meet with representatives of Youngstown, Ohio, Chamber of Commerce—brief speech.
	12:00	The House convenes.
	1:00	Meeting of the Policy Committee on Renegotiation Act and Universal Voter Registration.
	2:15	Appointment to discuss missile program.
	3:30	Meet with representatives of Associated Builders of Phoenix.
	4:00	Meet with representatives of Arizona Corporation Commission.
	5:00	Meet with SOS group.
	5:00	Reception—American Library Association.
	5:00	Reception—National Alliance of Postal and Federal Employees.
	6:00	Reception for William Brock, Chairman of National Republican Committee.
April 20	8:00	Breakfast with SOS and Chowder and Marching Society.
	9:30	Meet with Arizonan just appointed special assistant to surgeon general.
	10:00	Meet with members of White Mountain Apache Tribe.
	10:30	Meet with banking representative.
	11:00	Meet with candidate for office in California.
	2:00	Attend lecture by Herman Kahn.
	3:00	The House convenes.
	3:15	Meet with Ways and Means Republicans about taxes.
	5:00	Meet with Phoenix postal representatives.
	7:30	Leadership meeting.
	9:00	Joint Session of Congress to hear president's energy message.

members of his party. Note, however, that just as with Speaker O'Neill's busy schedule, John J. Rhodes finds time for constituents to express their special, even parochial interests. Not even leaders can afford to ignore their roles as elected representatives of relatively small geographical areas. And of course with a Democrat in the White House, the minority leader no longer made frequent trips to the other end of Pennsylvania Avenue. It is interesting to note that while Speaker O'Neill was breakfasting at the White House, Rhodes was taking his eggs at the American Enterprise Institute—generally acknowledged to be a conservative-oriented policy research institute.

I was once a constituent of Representative Morris K. Udall (D—Arizona). My respect for him has grown through the years. He is now an important substantive policy leader in the House of Representatives. He is chairman of the Committee on Interior and Insular Affairs—a most important committee for the western United States— and its Subcommittee on Energy and the Environment. In addition he is the second-ranking Democrat on the Committee on Post Office and Civil Service and the Ad Hoc Select Committee on the Outer Continental Shelf. Further, he was included on the Speaker's new Ad Hoc Select Committee on Energy. Thus Udall's life is dictated by committee meetings, as is clearly reflected in his schedule (see Table 2 − 6). Note that he often has more than one meeting scheduled for the same time. With his colleagues, however, he finds time to meet constituents and group representatives. In addition he must satisfy the demands of his status as a national personality. Thus, frequent appearances on television and radio are often a part of his daily schedule.

Finally, note that Representative Cohen—a relatively junior member in his third term—spent most of his scheduled time in committee work and meeting with constituents. While obviously a less glamourous schedule, it must be emphasized that this daily contact with the people and problems of a congressional district just happens to be vital to the representative process. Thus we witness in this small sample of schedules how it is that leaders are pulled toward the important majority-building function that is essential for lawmaking, while the rank-and-file members are pulled toward the representational function so essential for societal stability.

One other relevant observation about these schedules is that the leadership is directly touched by the national event of the week—that is, the president's energy proposals. O'Neill is briefed in advance, and by late Friday afternoon he is found meeting with the Democrats of the newly appointed Ad Hoc Committee on Energy to develop a strategy. Rhodes is interviewed on CBS news on the day after the energy message and on the following Monday is in a Republican leadership meeting on the energy proposals. While other members obviously follow what is going on, still 'their principal activities are driven more by what happened yesterday or the day before than what is happening today. I emphasize this point as yet another reminder of the principal lesson of this chapter—that is, that Congress is an on-going institution with an incredible number of daily commitments and involvements. For most members the president's energy proposals would come to influ-

TABLE 2– 6
Schedule of Morris K. Udall, chairman, Committee on Interior and Insular Affairs,
April 19– 20

Day	Hour	Appointment
April 19	9:00	Briefing of Interior Committee by building trades representatives.
	9:15	Briefing on energy program by Dr. Schlesinger in White House State Dining Room.
	9:45	Vote in Interior Committee to report on H.R. 2 (strip-mining bill).
	10:00	Subcommittee on Civil Service, Post Office and Civil Service Committee, Democrats caucus on Hatch Act reform.
	10:15	Joint meeting of Subcommittees on Mines and Mining, and Indian Affairs and Public Lands (hearing).
	11:30	Meet with representatives of the Arizona Corporation Commission.
	11:45	Meet with representative of the National Education Association.
	12:00	Office appointments.
	2:00	Meeting of the Board of the Office of Technology Assessment.
	4:00	Meet with representative of Tenneco about Alaska pipeline.
	4:30	"Congress Watch" (television program).
	5:00	Address Harvard/Radcliffe Democratic Club.
	5:30	Meet with representatives of the Arizona building trades.
	5:00– 7:00	Reception—Egg and Poultry Dealers.
	5:30– 7:30	Reception—Water Systems Council.
	6:30– 8:30	Reception—House of Commons Expenditure Committee, British Embassy.
April 20	8:00	Breakfast with John Gilligan.
	9:00	Meeting of Democratic caucus.
	9:45	Meeting of Interior Committee (business).
	10:00	Meeting of Subcommittee on Water and Power (hearing).
	12:20	Phone interview, CBS radio, Boston.
	12:30	Meet with Arizonan just appointed special assistant to surgeon general.
	2:30	Reception for House of Commons Expenditure Committee.
	4:30	Meeting with Herman Kahn.
	5:00– 6:30	Attend discussion of American Association for Advancement of Science.
	5:30	Attend dinner for Herman Kahn.
	7:00	Television taping, WTTG.
	9:00	Joint Session of Congress to hear president's energy message.

ence their activities when the new program as legislation was itself fitted into the daily routine of committee hearings, markups, office visits by lobbyists, and so on.

Senators' schedules are equally interesting and revealing. I offer three examples, again limiting the sample to just two days—April 19 and 20. Included is a senior Democrat, committee chairman, and former vice presidential nominee, Edmund S. Muskie (Maine); a former Democratic presidential nominee, George McGovern (South Dakota);

TABLE 2–7
Schedule of William S. Cohen (R– Maine), April 19– 20

Day	Hour	Appointment
April 19	9:30	Meeting of Judiciary Committee.
	10:00	Meeting of Subcommittee of Small Business Committee.
	12:00	Luncheon appointment.
	1:45	Meet with constituents (photo).
	2:00	Meet with representatives of hatcheries.
	2:45	Meet with constituents.
	3:30	Reception —General Mills Family Leaders of Tomorrow (constituent was winner of Maine fellowship).
	5:00	Reception —American Library Association.
April 20	10:00	Meeting of Judiciary Committee.
	1:00	Meet with representatives of St. Regis Paper Company.
	1:30	Meet with constituents (photo).
	1:45	Meet with constituents (photo).
	2:00	Meet with constituents (photo) —also discuss Greenville Sewer Project.
	5:00	Meeting of Wednesday group (Republican members of the House).
	9:00	Joint Session of Congress to hear president's energy message.

and a very junior but nationally prominent Republican, H. J. Heinz, III (Pennsylvania). The first two are no longer in the Senate—Muskie resigned to accept the position of secretary of state; McGovern was defeated in 1980. No schedule is necessarily typical, but these three reflect some of the major appointments and contacts of senators.

First note that in every case the senator had committee meetings which overlapped. Given the multiple committee assignments, this is, of course, a frequent occurrence for senators. It helps to explain why

TABLE 2–8
Schedule of Senator Edmund S. Muskie, April 19– 20

Day	Hour	Appointment
April 19	9:30	Meeting of Subcommittee on Water Resources (hearing).
	10:00	Meeting of Committee on Governmental Affairs (hearing).
	11:00	Meet with Hank Simpson, Jr., Simpson Egg Farms, Winthrop, Maine.
	12:15	The Senate convenes.
	1:00	Meeting of Special Committee on the Aging.
	4:30	Depart for U.S. Naval Academy.
	Evening	Speech, U.S. Naval Academy.
April 20	9:15	Meeting of Committee on Governmental Affairs (hearing).
	9:30	Meeting of Subcommittee on Water Resources (hearing).
	12:30	The Senate convenes.
	12:30	Luncheon appointment.
	4:00	Meet with representative of St. Regis Paper Company.
	6:00	Reception in honor of Senator Eastland.
	9:00	Joint Session of Congress to hear president's energy message.

TABLE 2–9
Schedule of Senator George McGovern, April 19– 20

Day	Hour	Appointment
April 19	8:30	Meeting of Committee on Agriculture, Nutrition, and Forestry (markup).
	10:00	Meet with representatives of United Brands (with meat-packing affiliate company in Sioux Falls, South Dakota).
	10:00	Meeting of Committee on Foreign Relations (markup).
	12:15	The Senate convenes.
	12:15	Luncheon appointment.
	1:30	Testify before Special Committee on the Aging.
	2:00	Meet with the president, White House.
	2:30	Office appointment.
	2:45	Office appointment.
	3:30	Reception – General Mills Family Leaders of Tomorrow (South Dakotan involved).
	4:00	Coffee for Mr. Roy Jenkins, president of European Economic Community.
	8:00	Dinner for Secretary of State Cyrus Vance.
April 20	8:00	Stop by breakfast of Upper Midwest Council.
	8:00	Meeting of Committee on Agriculture, Nutrition, and Forestry (markup).
	10:30	Meeting of Subcommittee of International Operations.
	12:00	Lunch with Agriculture Committee staff.
	12:30	The Senate convenes.
	2:00	Press interview.
	2:30	Meeting of Subcommittee on Arms Control.
	3:00	Meet with delegation from Huron College, Huron, South Dakota.
	6:00	Reception in honor of Senator Eastland.
	9:00	Joint Session of Congress to hear president's energy message.

attendance at these meetings is very low. Second, I would direct your attention to Senator Muskie's April 19 speech at the U.S. Naval Academy. That was but one of four speeches delivered outside Washington during the week (the other three were in Lexington, Kentucky, on April 21; Harrisburg, Pennsylvania, on April 23; and New York City on April 24). Senators are major public figures and are often responsive to a national as well as statewide constituency. Small wonder that Senator Muskie's committee hearings were not even listed on the daily schedule as handed to me. (I simply entered them based on his committee assignments). Third, observe the rather heady appointments and receptions on Senator McGovern's schedule—a meeting with the president, a coffee with the president of the European Economic Community, a dinner with the secretary of state—all in one day. On other days during the week (not included in Table 2 – 9), McGovern had lunch with a group from the Department of State, a coffee with the prime minister of Portugal, and a luncheon with a minister of Foreign Affairs. While a select few House members may have such appointments, whey are experienced by many senators. It cannot be em-

TABLE 2– 10
Schedule of Senator H. J. Heinz, III, April 19– 20

Day	Hour	Appointment
April 19	8:30	Stop by breakfast of representatives of National Alliance of Postal and Federal Employees.
	9:30	Committee on Banking, Housing, and Urban Affairs to meet with representatives of Building and Construction Trades Department, AFL– CIO.
	10:00	Meeting of Committee on Banking, Housing, and Urban Affairs (hearing).
	10:30	Meeting of Committee on Governmental Affairs (hearing).
	12:00	Photo with high school students on Capitol steps.
	12:15	The Senate convenes.
	12:30	Luncheon, Senate Republican Policy Committee.
	12:45	Meeting of Pennsylvania congressional delegation.
	2:00	Meeting of legislative staff.
	3:00	Meet with representatives of Armco Steel.
	4:30	Meet with Montgomery county chapter of National Association of Retired Federal Employees.
April 20	7:50	Office appointment.
	9:15	Meeting of Committee on Governmental Affairs (hearing).
	9:30	Meeting of Committee on Banking, Housing, and Urban Affairs (hearing).
	12:30	The Senate convenes.
	12:30	Meeting of the Wednesday Club (Republican Senators).
	12:30	Luncheon of Pennsylvania delegation (hosted by Pennsylvania State University).
	2:00	Meet with president of Pennsylvania State University.
	3:00	Meet with president of Boeing Vertol.
	5:30	Reception —WCAU– TV (Philadelphia).
	9:00	Joint Session of Congress to hear president's energy message.

phasized too often that these really are two quite different legislative chambers.

And finally, all three schedules show that however cosmopolitan the senator, he must pay heed to state interests. It is no coincidence that the most junior of the senators, Heinz of Pennsylvania, has the most such appointments, but even national figures like Muskie and McGovern also find time in their busy schedules to see egg farmers, local industrialists, meat-packers, and college students.

Unfortunately it is not possible to do more than provide these few illustrative schedules. They are sufficient to emphasize the many worlds of individual legislators, however. The reader can well imagine the incredible network of communication and contact associated with the weekly schedules of 535 members of Congress. Having set that clearly in mind, consider the activities of thousands upon thousands of congressional staff, various legislative support personnel (e.g., in the Congressional Research Service, Congressional Budget Office, etc.), bureaucrats serving legislative purposes, political executives spending time on legislative matters, and lobbyists—all actors in lawmaking.

Reviewing the schedule of any one of these persons will give us a slightly different perspective on the week, the day, the hour which we may choose for comprehending the scope of activity on Capitol Hill.[6]

The week in the chambers

Still another sighting can be taken for the week of April 18 — 22 by observing what went on in the House and Senate chambers. This activity is not separable from either the members or the committees. Rather we simply catch a glimpse of their work in another arena.

Tables 2 — 11 and 2 — 12 summarize the activities in the two chambers for the week in question. Before treating each house separately, certain general characteristics should be noted. Observe that the tables show the extent to which the chambers are the points of initiation and termination of legislative action. Bills are introduced, presidential messages received, and major legislation is debated and passed. What happens in between, of course, is the extensive work of the committees. Also illustrated once again is the filtering action which reduces the number of bills which actually reach the floor (though this particular week was untypically low in the number of bills passed).

The House spent most of its floor time, April 18 — 22, on three pieces of legislation. On Tuesday attention was directed to the authorization of appropriations for research and development programs in the Environmental Protection Agency. Basically noncontroversial, the bill (H.R. 5101) was allotted only one hour of debate, and not even that much time was consumed. Following the adoption of relatively minor amendments, the bill passed overwhelmingly, 358 — 31.

The Export Administration Amendments were the subject of debate on Wednesday, April 20. Of particular interest were provisions which would ban American participation in the Arab boycott of Israel. Again one hour of debate was provided, but this time it was all used. The legislation (H.R. 5840) came from the Committee on International Relations (now the Committee on Foreign Affairs), which had devoted 13 days of hearings to its consideration. It was unanimously reported out of the committee. Though unquestionably a controversial issue, the bill was "the product of much give-and-take" between the executive branch, the Congress, and affected interest groups.[7] Here was an example of a congressional committee serving effectively to strike the

---

[6] For example, I asked David Cohen, then the president of the citizens lobby, Common Cause, for his telephone log during the week. Among other things, the log reminds one about how much work is done over the phone. In addition, however, it is fascinating to see the types of people Cohen communicates with—journalists, members of Congress, congressional staff, administration officials and staff, scholars, other lobbyists— and the variety of topics discussed. The sheer volume of communication stimulated by the existence and form of the United States Congress is staggering.

[7] See account in *Congressional Quarterly Weekly Report,* April 23, 1977, p. 734.

TABLE 2 – 11

Action in the House Chamber, April 18 – 22

	18	19	20	21	22	Totals
Bills introduced	29 – 1 – 4*	82 – 2 – 14	91 – 3 – 12	84 – 1 – 14	21 – 0 – 2	307 – 7 – 46
Bills reported	7	3	2	2	1	15
Legislation debated	—	1†	1‡	1§	→	3
Legislation passed	2	4	3	2	—	11
Roll-call votes	1	3	2	3	2	11
Presidential messages	3	—	2	—	2	7
Time in session	46 minutes	2 hours 30 minutes	(1) 3 hours 38 minutes; (2) 56 minutes	7 hours 32 minutes	4 hours 8 minutes	19 hours 30 minutes

* The sequence for the numbers is as follows: public bills, private bills, resolutions.
† Authorizing appropriations to the Office of Research and Development, Environmental Protection Agency, fiscal year, 1978.
‡ Export Administration Amendments of 1977.
§ Department of Defense authorization, fiscal year, 1978.
SOURCE: Compiled from information in the "Daily Digest" of the *Congressional Record*, April 18 – 22, 1977.

TABLE 2–12
Action in the Senate Chamber, April 18–22

	18	19	20	21	22	Totals
Bills introduced	4 – 0*	24 – 2	18 – 0	24 – 4	9 – 5	79 – 11
Bills reported	5	1	22	5	3	16
Nominations	7†	—	2	5	—	14
Treaties	2	—	—	—	—	2
Legislation debated	1‡					1
Legislation passed	1	2	—	—	1	4
Conference agreed to	—	1	1	—	—	2
Roll-call votes	—	—	1	4	—	5
Confirmations	—	—	3	1	—	4
Presidential messages	2	—	2	—	2	6
Time in session	1 hour 45 minutes	6 hours 29 minutes	5 hours 19 minutes	5 hours 50 minutes	3 hours 55 minutes	24 hours 29 minutes

* The sequence for the numbers is as follows: bills, resolutions.
† Excludes lesser military appointments.
‡ Tax Reduction and Simplification Act of 1977.
SOURCE: Compiled from information in the "Daily Digest" of the *Congressional Record*, April 18 – 22, 1977.

bargain on a difficult issue. As Representative Clement J. Zablocki (D—Wisconsin), chairman of the Committee on International Relations indicated in the debate:

> True, there are sections that are controversial; but we have tried to make it as noncontroversial as possible. . . . Mr. Chairman, this bill represents nearly a year's work by the Committee on International Relations.[8]

After two relatively minor amendments, the bill passed overwhelmingly—364 — 43.

The first important piece of business on Thursday was the resolution to establish an ad hoc committee on energy. This was the initial response by the House to the president's energy message of the evening before. The Committee was directed

> to consider and report to the House on the message of the president . . . , on other messages or communications related thereto, and on any bill or resolution which the Speaker may sequentially refer thereto which the Speaker determines relates to the substance of the president's message.[9]

With broad bipartisan support, the creation of the committee was agreed to without a roll call vote.

The House then moved to consider the largest supplemental appropriations bill to be passed by the Congress since the World War II period.[10] The $29 billion measure was in the form of a conference report, that is, the compromise version between different House and Senate bills enacted earlier. Following some partisan needling by the Republicans, the conference report was adopted on a roll-call vote, 264 — 142.

Most of the debating time on Thursday and Friday was devoted to the important authorization legislation for the Department of Defense. Two hours of debate were allotted to the legislation. Described as sluggish, the debate was poorly attended. Representative Robert Bauman (R—Maryland) observed that: "during the entire time of this debate there were no more than 30 members on the floor, and most of those present were members of the Committee on Armed Services."[11] Amendments were considered on Friday, thus providing a further opportunity for discussion of the bill, but action was not completed. At the close of business on Friday, Majority Leader James C. Wright announced that consideration of the Defense Department authorization bill would be concluded on Monday, April 25.

---

[8] *Congressional Record* (daily edition), April 20, 1977, p. H3267.

[9] *Congressional Record* (daily edition), April 21, 1977, p. H3349.

[10] *Congressional Record* (daily edition), April 21, 1977, p. H3355.

[11] *Congressional Record* (daily edition), April 21, 1977, p. H3403.

In summary, in its first week back after the Easter district work period, the House floor was not as active as normal. Important but basically noncontroversial legislation was debated and passed. Relatively few roll-call votes were taken (22 were recorded the following week), and less than 20 hours were spent in session (only 46 minutes on the first day back—see Table 2 − 11).

On the Senate side, the bulk of the debating time was devoted to a single piece of legislation—the Tax Reduction and Simplication Act of 1977. This week-long debate provides yet another example of House-Senate differences. Seldom does the House devote so much time to debating one bill. And indeed, the Senate did not complete its action on the bill until the following Friday—April 29. The debate began on Tuesday since few senators had returned on Monday. The first order of business was for Senator Russell Long (D − Louisiana), chairman of the Committee on Finance, to ask the Senate to delete the famous $50 tax rebate from the bill. At one point this rebate was an important part of President Carter's economic stimulus package. The president had changed his mind about the proposal, however, and asked that the rebate provision be withdrawn. Chairman Long was not so cooperative in regard to certain business tax credits which the president had also asked be stricken. Senators Dale Bumpers (D − Arkansas) and Edward M. Kennedy (D − Massachusetts) moved to recommit the tax bill to the Committee on Finance with instructions to delete the special tax credits. That motion led to a rather heated debate that took up the better part of two days. On Thursday, Chairman Long prevailed and the Bumpers − Kennedy motion (supported by President Carter) was defeated on a roll-call vote, 20 − 74.

In other actions on Friday the Senate agreed to the conference report on supplemental appropriations (the $29 billion approved by the House on Thursday). And in another role which distinguishes the Senate from the House, four nominations were confirmed during the week, including former Senator Mike Mansfield to be ambassador to Japan. Mansfield was approved on the same day that he appeared before the Committee on Foreign Relations.

At 9 o'clock and 1 minute P.M., the doorkeeper announced the president of the United States.

The president of the United States, escorted by a committee of senators and representatives, entered the Hall of the House of Representatives, and stood at the clerk's desk.

[Applause, the members rising].

The Speaker: Members of the Congress, I have the high privilege and the distinct honor of presenting to you the President of the United States.

[Applause, the members rising].[12]

---

[12] *Congressional Record* (daily edition), April 20, 1977, p. H3328.

The national event that dominated the week's news also occurred within Congressional chambers—in the hall of the House of Representatives. Aside from the event itself, however (i.e., the speech by the president), one witnessed little by way of direct action related to the energy program. The House established its Ad Hoc Committee on Energy. Several members in both houses reacted to the president's message by entering remarks in the *Congressional Record*. But for the most part, the House and Senate in chambers continued to work on legislation which had been developed by their respective committees. Even though it was a relatively light week on the floor, the diversity and importance of the measures debated—tax reform, Defense Department authorization, environmental research, international trade and boycotts, a $29 billion appropriation—illustrate the diverse demands to be met by the modern Congress.

The week for others

If it is difficult to imagine the activity of 535 members of Congress during a busy week, consider the task of comprehending the work of some 20,000 others who are in some fashion associated with the work of Capitol Hill. In general, one could predict that the important staff personnel in offices and committees would be spending their time on the principal responsibilities of the members themselves—that is, serving the state or district and legislating. My visits with a number of staff persons during my wanderings on Capitol Hill, April 18 – 22, confirmed these expectations.

On the Senate side, I walked in on the tail end of a staff meeting in Senator Heinz's office. Since the room was very crowded, the first question I asked Geoffrey Garin, the legislative assistant, after the meeting was: "What is the size of the staff?" The answer was 33 people in the Washington office and 22 in Pennsylvania (11 in Pittsburgh, 9 in Philadelphia, and 2 in Harrisburg). I remember thinking at the time that this was probably at least as much patronage as was available to some cabinet officers. But more about that later when we discuss congressional offices in a more systematic manner. Garin himself was busy on legislation. He pointed out that all of the case work—that is, the individual servicing of constituents' requests—is handled in the state offices, a procedure adopted by more and more Senate staffs.

Dr. Karl Braithwaite (Ph.D. in political science) works for the Subcommittee on Environmental Pollution of the Committee on Environment and Public Works. Senator Muskie is the subcommittee chairman, and so Braithwaite works for Muskie—more patronage. The clean air bill was in its final stages in the committee, and Braithwaite was totally involved in that legislation. On the particular day that I had lunch with him, he was (1) enlisting the assistance of Dr. John Middleton (former national air-pollution control director) in regard to certain aspects of the bill, (2) trying to find rooms to hold a markup session for the bill, and (3) drafting language that would undo an amendment passed earlier in the committee which he judged unfriendly. He left no doubt about how he spent his week. Whereas the president's energy message might well have an impact on environmental pollution, Braithwaite's immediate concern was this year's clean air legislation.

I have known George V. Cunningham for over 30 years, and so it was a pleasure as usual to stop by Senator McGovern's office to visit with him. Cunningham is the administrative assistant for McGovern and thus manages the office and deals with problems in the state. Primarily his legislative work is that which is state-related. In fact when McGovern was running for president, it was not gross exaggeration to say that Cunningham was South Dakota's senior senator when it came to state service. He estimated that he spent the week of April 18 – 22 as follows:

Answering mail	11 hours
Meeting with groups on pending legislation	20 hours
Legislative work	15 hours
Telephone contacts	4 hours
Office administration	5 hours
Miscellaneous	5 hours
Total	60 hours

He pointed out that while the state offices will do the leg work on constituency matters, all the correspondence is done in Washington. "We don't like to have the boss's name signed by others."

Another friend was just completing his work as a staff member of the Senate Temporary Select Committee to Study the Committee System. Dr. Norman J. Ornstein is a political scientist normally located at Catholic University. During the week of April 18 – 22 he was engaged in writing a report on the effects of the changes which had been instituted in the Senate committee system as a result of the work of the select committee. We talked about all of the different worlds that some people lump together as one in describing "the" Congress. He observed that still another set of relationships was that on the floor, between the senators themselves — "above and beyond the staff, where the fellows get together."

My experience on the House side confirmed what I had found in the Senate. The office staff personnel were principally working on constituency-related matters (which might, of course, later require legislation or might be the result of pending or existing legislation). Maureen Drummy then worked for Representative William A. Steiger

(R—Wisconsin).[13] I have visited with her many times. She is always seated behind a mound of letters to be answered. On this particular day three huge stacks of mail from right to lifers were awaiting some disposition. Their concern about an amendment to the legal services bill was going to take up much of her week.

Dr. Joseph Cooper is another political scientist who was then working on Capitol Hill. He served as staff director for the Commission on Administrative Review, a group of House members and citizens directed to study administrative operations and services of the House of Representatives. When I saw Cooper he was sitting with Allan Katz, general counsel for the commission, on a bench near the subway in the Rayburn Building. They explained to me that their offices were simply too congested to conduct a meeting—a not uncommon problem on the Hill. Their concerns during this week were no different than for the past several weeks—that is, how to conduct several large studies of the administrative, financial, and work management problems of the House in a very short time period. Most congressional committees want immediate responses to unanswerable questions.

I have already alluded to the activities of one of the Speaker's assistants as he sought to keep one step ahead of his boss's frantic schedule. Because of his position, his week was influenced more by national events than was true for the other staff referred to here. I wanted to mention one other person whom I visited, however, because his problems so closely paralleled those of Karl Braithwaite on the Senate side. John Gabusi was then the chief administrative officer for the House Committee on Interior and Insular Affairs (later he served as assistant secretary for management in the Community Services Administration). A former Udall aide, (Udall is chairman of the Interior Committee), Gabusi was frantically trying to find space for a committee hearing at the time I stopped by. He noted that they might have to rent hotel space since meeting rooms were most difficult to get at the last minute. Braithwaite, you will recall, was having similar problems on the other side. In addition to his administrative work for the committee, Gabusi continued to handle political work for Udall and tried to keep up with some of the substantive problems before the Interior Committee. It is a point worth making that seldom are congressional staff personnel able to limit their responsibilities to one clearly defined area. More than most professional people, they must learn to live with unfinished assignments, fresh demands every day, constant interruption, impossibly short deadlines, and lots of noise.

I hesitate to provide a summary from such a small sample of staff

---

[13] Representative Steiger has since died. A promising young Republican politician, he died of a heart attack on December 4, 1978, at the age of 40.

persons. I only mean to suggest that you permit the activities described here to direct your attention to the many individualized, even autonomous operations which take place on Capitol Hill. To paraphrase de Toqueville, the political and policy activity that pervades the Congress must be seen in order to be understood. I would add that when one begins to include the staff perspective, seeing is not as easy as one might think. For the more constituency-oriented staff, one can only estimate the total amount of activity which might result from a staff contact. The more legislative-oriented staff too are in continual communication with the bureaucracy, the state or district, and interest groups. Thus the part of their work that one actually witnesses may in fact be quite small compared to the total amount of activity associated with the issue at hand.

With the above statements I begin to set the outer limits of my own capacity to describe this week on Capitol Hill. It becomes physically impossible to trace the many lines of activity just for those persons with whom I came into contact. But I can advise you of various other groups of actors on Capitol Hill during this week. First would be the legions of administration officials who march up to the Hill every day—to testify before committees, consult with members and staff, provide information vital to lawmaking, participate in the writing of reports and the laws themselves. Second are the equally large masses of lobbyists performing many of the same functions for the special interests they represent. Then there are the publicists who selectively cover all of this marching to and fro—that is, the reporters, columnists, photographers, television crews. The astute observer can see many of these operators at work by simply wandering into hearing rooms, the members' offices (they are the persons sitting in the cramped space near the receptionist's desk), the cafeterias, and the halls of the Capitol and office buildings. Count it a poor day if you don't recognize at least one cabinet secretary, columnist, or television reporter.

Coverage—what the nation learned about the week

If congressional activity must be seen to be understood, then it is perfectly in order in this chapter to ask what the nation saw or read about the week of April 18 — 22. Perhaps one of the problems in citizen understanding of and appreciation for Congress is that the public does not learn a sufficient amount about this most basic of democratic institutions. To find out, I monitored CBS news coverage of the week and collected a small sample of newspapers; the *Washington Post*, the *New York Times*, the *Chicago Tribune*, the *Pittsburgh Press*, the *Des Moines Register*, the *Houston Chronicle*, and the *Iowa City Press-Citizen*.

As expected, the CBS news coverage focused on President Carter and his proposed energy program. The news on Congress was as follows:

Monday: Congress mentioned only as being requested by Carter to delay automobile emission controls and as unlikely to favor the cut back of water projects (referred to by Cronkite as their pet projects.)

Tuesday: Testimony before the Senate Special Committee on the Aging was viewed. Senior citizens were shown favoring food stamps. And in his comments, Eric Sevareid mentioned probable congressional reaction to the president's energy proposals.

Wednesday: Mention was made of the fact that the House passed legislation severely limiting U.S. participation in Arab boycotts of Israel.

Thursday: Initial congressional reaction to the Carter energy program was aired.

Friday: Mention was made of Carter's meeting with Senator Long (D—Louisiana) in regard to the tax bill. A CBS special program to be aired later in the evening was previewed, with appearances by some congressmen.

What this summary suggests is obvious—those who get their news from CBS would have hardly known Congress was in session during the week of April 18 — 22 except to hear President Carter present his energy program. This lack of coverage is a frequent complaint on Capitol Hill. This small sample suggests there is some basis for dissatisfaction.

Selected newspaper coverage for the week is analyzed in Tables 2 — 13, 2 — 14, and 2 — 15. In general the tables demonstrate what one would expect—that is, coverage of the White House far exceeds that of Congress. The specific extent of this imbalance is worth emphasizing, however. Table 2 — 13 shows the number of articles devoted to subjects involving the president, Congress, and the energy program. As can be seen, 61 percent of the stories were devoted to the energy problem, the president's program, and various reactions to that program. Another 9 percent of the stories were directed to other presidential actions and 3 percent to congressional reactions to these initiatives. Stories focused solely on the week in Congress, that is, the actions on Capitol Hill, constituted 23 percent of the total (items 7 and 8 among the subjects).

Of course, the number of stories does not tell us very much about the amount of coverage. Table 2 — 14 shows the column inches devoted to congressional action for the week. Several important observa-

TABLE 2 – 13
Coverage of Energy Week in Washington by seven newspapers

Subject	Number of articles	Percent of total articles
1. President's energy program	148	32
2. Congressional reaction to energy program	31	7
3. Reaction by others	63	14
4. Energy problem (general)	37	8
5. Other Carter actions during the week	42	9
6. Congressional reaction to other Carter actions	14	3
7. Congressional actions (other than energy)	99	21.5
8. Congress (general)	7	1.5
9. Carter (general)	19	4
Totals	460	100

SOURCE: Compiled from stories in the *Washington Post*, the *New York Times*, the *Pittsburgh Press*, the *Chicago Tribune*, the *Des Moines Register*, the *Houston Chronicle*, and the *Iowa City Press-Citizen*.

TABLE 2 – 14
Congressional coverage by seven newspapers, April 18 – 24

	Column inches devoted to				
Newspaper	House	Senate	Conferences	Other	Total
Washington Post	121^{1}/2	77^{1}/2	0	72^{1}/2	281^{1}/2
New York Times	27^{1}/4	108^{3}/4	13	26^{3}/4	175^{3}/4
Pittsburgh Press	10^{3}/4	37^{3}/4	4^{1}/2	14^{1}/2	67^{1}/2
Chicago Tribune	8^{1}/2	24	0	3^{1}/2	36
Des Moines Register	6	78^{1}/4	0	105^{3}/4	190
Houston Chronicle	91^{1}/4	24^{1}/4	0	62^{1}/4	177^{3}/4
Iowa City Press-Citizen	0	38^{1}/2	0	0	38^{1}/2
Totals	265^{1}/4	389	17^{1}/2	285^{1}/4	967

SOURCE: Compiled from stories in the seven newspapers.

tions can be made about this display of newspaper coverage. Not unexpectedly the *Washington Post* provided the most comprehensive overview of congressional activities. It devoted more space to Congress than the other newspapers, and its coverage was the most balanced between the House and Senate. The *Houston Chronicle* concentrated more attention on the House—most unusual for newspapers. By comparison, the other newspapers, including the *New York Times*, concentrated primarily on the Senate. These five other newspapers devoted only 52^{1}/2 column inches to House action (floor and committees) compared with 287$^{1/4}$ column inches for the Senate.[14] The congressional action receiving the most attention was, of course, the tax bill being debated in the Senate. In particular the $50 rebate and the business tax credits received rather widespread reporting (a total of 176$^{1/4}$ column inches devoted to floor and committee action—18 percent of the total space for congressional action during the week). By contrast, the passage of the largest supplemental appropriations bill in history received *a total of 7 $^{1/2}$ column inches in total* (all newspapers). In fact, the latter piece of legislation meant more to the taxpayer than the $50 rebate since at $29 billion it represented $135 for every man, woman, and child in the nation. Why this difference in coverage? The $50 rebate was a part of the president's program. The $29 billion appropriations bill was a part of routine business between Congress and the executive.

Turning specifically to the committees, one does not have to wonder why the public knows so little of this ceaseless activity on Capitol Hill. The answer is that very little attention is paid to it in the press. Of the 250 committee meetings referred to earlier (see Tables 2 − 2 and 2 − 3), only a very few were covered in this sample of seven newspapers. Only one House committee action was picked up by more than three newspapers. The approval of the strip-mining bill by the House Committee on Interior and Insular Affairs was noted by five papers— two of which devoted 1$^{1/2}$ column inches each to the development. Although Senate committees received considerably more coverage than House committees, still the totals are not impressive in light of the amount of activity. Those covered by more than two papers included:

	Stories	Column inches
Agriculture. Nutrition, and Forestry	5	46$^{1/4}$
Commerce, Science, and Transportation	3	14$^{3/4}$
Finance	6	52$^{3/4}$
Foreign Relations	7	52
Judiciary	5	19

Of course, it must be noted that the number of stories does not represent the number of committee meetings covered. In most cases, only one committee action was reported, as with the $50 rebate in the

---

[14] Only the stories themselves were measured. Headlines, by-lines, pictures, and charts were not included. It should be noted that spacing did vary among the papers, with *The New York Times* the most tightly spaced and thus probably containing more words per column inch than the others.

Finance Committee, or the increase in federal judges being considered by the Judiciary Committee.

Next consider the number of stories about Congress which were not directly related to formal action in the committees or the chambers (the column marked "other" in Table 2 – 14). A total of 285 1/4 column inches (29 percent of the precious space devoted to Congress) went to this type of story—20 column inches more than was allocated to the 143 committee meetings and the three or four major floor actions in the House of Representatives during the week. And what were the subjects of these miscellaneous stories? Of the 18 stories in this category, 9 dealt with ethical problems, deals, or were otherwise unflattering to Congress.

Three final observations. Aside from the *Washington Post* and the *New York Times*, most of the news stories on Congress come from sources other than the staff of the newspaper in question. Over half of the stories came from the wire services (Associated Press, United Press International). Of the 60 stories in the papers other than the *Post* and the *Times*, only 10 were written by local staff (6 for the *Des Moines Register* and 4 for the *Houston Chronicle*). Second, it is interesting to note that congressional action during this week was not the subject of columnist or editorial attention. Only one editorial dealt with matters before Congress and this week's congressional action did not stimulate comment from any national columnists carried by these six newspapers. Third, all seven newspapers also ran stories on local congressmen most of which were the result of news dispatches from the members' offices. These were not included in the totals.

Turn now to Table 2 – 15 which summarizes the coverage devoted to *just one day*, April 21, the day following the president's energy message to Congress. More space was allocated to the energy program (983 1/2 column inches) on this one day than was given to congressional action for the full seven-day week (967 column inches). When one adds the reactions of Congress, the columnists, and others (principally industry), the total for this one day far exceeds that for Congress for the week. Observe, however, that relatively little space was allocated to congressional reaction—114 1/4 column inches for all seven newspapers; approximately one fourth of that given to reaction by others. The figures speak for themselves. And what they say mostly is that what I saw on Capitol Hill the week of April 18 – 22 is not what citizens in these seven cities read about in their daily newspapers.

Are the national news magazines any more comprehensive in their coverage? *Time* and *Newsweek* were examined for the weeks of April 25 and May 2.[15] *Time* devoted one story and 24 1/2 column inches to congressional reactions to Carter programs. This total represented 4 percent of total space for all the national political subjects treated in these two issues and, it might be pointed out, hardly a chemical trace

TABLE 2 – 15
Coverage of president's energy message and reaction, April 21, 1977

| | | Column inches devoted to | | | |
	Program	Congressional reaction	Columnist reaction	Other reaction	Totals
Washington Post	180*	$18^{1}/_{2}$	$52^{1}/_{4}$	$63^{1}/_{2}$	$314^{1}/_{4}$
New York Times	$319^{1}/_{2}$†	$16^{1}/_{2}$	$30^{1}/_{2}$	$10^{1}/_{4}$	$376^{3}/_{4}$
Pittsburgh Press	84	0	30	$47^{3}/_{4}$	$161^{3}/_{4}$
Chicago Tribune	$77^{1}/_{4}$	18	0	0	$95^{1}/_{4}$
Des Moines Register	$172^{1}/_{2}$*	$24^{3}/_{4}$	14	$20^{1}/_{2}$	$231^{3}/_{4}$
Houston Chronicle	117	28	34	62	241
Iowa City Press-Citizen	$33^{1}/_{4}$	$8^{1}/_{2}$	0	$45^{1}/_{4}$	87
Totals	$983^{1}/_{2}$	$114^{1}/_{4}$	$160^{3}/_{4}$	$249^{1}/_{4}$	$1,507^{3}/_{4}$

* Includes text of president's message.
† Includes text of message and fact sheet issued by the White House.
SOURCE: Compiled from stories in the seven newspapers.

of the space in the full magazine. No column inches at all were devoted to the many other activities on Capitol Hill described earlier in this chapter.

Newsweek offered even less coverage than *Time*. No individual stories were devoted to congressional action or reaction during the week. A mere $7^{1}/_{2}$ column inches in another story were allocated to congressional reaction to the energy program. Compare this total with the $105^{1}/_{4}$ column inches on reactions by others. This despite the fact that Congress, not "others" had to approve the program.[16]

Unquestionably it would be too much to expect that the media would cover all of the activities on Capitol Hill during a week. One might logically argue that congressional coverage would and should be even less during a week in which the president is proposing a national energy program. It is not necessary for us to debate either of these points. The purpose of this exercise has been merely to discover the extent of coverage during the week in question. It is sufficient to note that (1) Capitol Hill was a busy part of our government during the week of April 18 – 22, and (2) the American people learned hardly a smidgen about congressional action that directly affected them. The

[15] The two issues were examined since reaction to the energy program could not be included in the April 25 issue due to printing deadlines.

[16] An additional story on members in their districts during the Easter break was included in the April 25 *Newsweek* (15 column inches — twice as much as was devoted to congressional reaction to the energy proposals).

results of this limited analysis of the media alone justified including this chapter in the book.[17]

Concluding observations

At the end of my week on Capitol Hill, I recorded a number of observations. I offer them here more as personal reflections than as a systematic summary of the chapter. The individual tabular and narrative descriptions should speak for themselves. These final thoughts are in the form of thematic impressions about the functioning of Congress in the political system.

First I stress the theme of diversity. Although it is a commonplace observation that Congress copes with an enormous number and variety of issues, I doubt that any of us comprehend either the scope of the problems treated or the staccato-like trumpeting of diverse demands throughout the congressional day and week. At least I can faithfully report that I felt re-educated on this matter from my week of concentrated observation. A corollary theme is that of the incredible number of contact points on Capitol Hill for those with wants and needs. At any point in time, one can assume that hundreds of contacts are being made between lobbyists, agency personnel, representatives of the current administration, and the press, on the one hand, and the members and staff of Congress on the other. The settings in which these formal and informal contacts are made include member and staff offices, hallways, committee rooms and offices, cafeterias and dining rooms, and caucus rooms.

A related theme of extraordinary importance and subtlety is that of redundancy. At first one might understandably deplore the extent to which the same issue is reviewed, explored, outlined, presumably resolved, and raised again. Yet to watch it all happening reveals definite purposes associated with such repetition. For what one sees is a continuous reassessment of issues, processes, and policies. New actors and perspectives are easily integrated into a repetitive round of discourse because their contributions can be evaluated against the core formulas which form the basis of the conversation. Seldom is any one actor successful in challenging the base itself, although that is not unheard of, and President Ronald Reagan appears determined to try.

---

[17] It should be noted that various specialized publications would have carried stories on this week on Congress. Farm journals, trade journals, association and citizen group newsletters, and so on, normally cover hearings and other significant congressional actions of interest to their readers. Such forms of communication confirm the suspicions of those who see government as a triumvirate of bureaucrats, legislators, and lobbyists.

The redundancy also performs an important memory function. Given the daily assaults on a member's capacity to maintain continuity, recapitulation becomes absolutely essential. Briefings go on several times a day as the member moves from office to committee hearing or markup to office to chamber floor and back to office, and so on. Even without briefings, however, members normally know what is happening when they enter each of these settings because of the continuous recapitulation. It is all rather like a soap opera. One can miss several days, even weeks, without loss of familiarity.

At the end of this week in particular, I marked the manner in which a major issue or event overlaid the more routine business of the Hill. The president's energy message was the national event of the week. Yet it had little effect on the daily operation of Congress. The leadership was pulled toward the event, but most members and staff went about their business, pausing only to attend the joint session or watch the president on television. The national press, of course, is the carrier of the event. They sustain it through the day, the week, or however long the president wishes to extend it, within reason. In my wanderings during the week, I frequently crossed paths with the national press when I would pass a leadership office. But what really impressed me upon reflection was that I could enter a bit of Wisconsin, South Dakota, Maine, or Texas in the offices of members, then observe the playing out of a vitally important regional or national issue in a committee room, yet occasionally encounter the world of large issues and grand designs—the "moral equivalents of war," if you will. I also came to understand as never before that these three worlds are highly interrelated. Grand designs (e.g., a national energy policy) eventually are influenced by the parochialism of a member's office and the continuity, even redundancy, of issue review in the committees. In fact, before long the president's program was subjected to those congressional processes referred to earlier with unsatisfactory results for the White House.

My notes at the end of the week reminded me that what I observed was more dedicatedly issue or policy oriented than I had remembered from the past. In an influential book, David R. Mayhew states, "I shall conjure up a vision of United States congressmen as single-minded seekers of reelection" (1974: 5). In light of this electoral goal, Mayhew makes quite rational much of the organization and operation of Congress. What I observed does not deny this proposition but it does modify it. I concluded that a great many people on Capitol Hill are involved in problem solving without knowing all that much about what will get a member reelected. No doubt this feature is a result of the expansion of staff over the past few years. And unquestionably much of this work by specialized staffs is still filtered through a district-and-state oriented process. I am simply recording my impressions and speculating that it may be more difficult in the future to maintain a national legislature with a single-minded electoral preoccupation. The more Congress is involved in complex issue analysis and policy formulation (possibly as a result of increased staff capabilities), the less will members be able to determine constituency effects. This theme deserves treatment later when we discuss congressional staff in more detail.

A related theme is that of the changing role of legislative staff. One is tempted to inquire as to their effect on the legislative process when attending Senate committee hearings in which one senator and a dozen or more staff aides are present or in which committee members rely primarily on the staff during the vital markup stage of legislation. Who leads whom is a relevant question to ask of the present Congress.

Finally I came away with even greater respect for the committee hearings process—both for what happens there and certainly for what a student can learn in that setting. It is interesting to think about the hearings as theater, particularly when involving administration witnesses. The staffs on each side—executive and legislative—set the stage, write the scripts, manage the cue cards, whisper new lines, sweep up afterwards. The principals enter—a cabinet secretary and supporting staff on one side, a few senators with their aides on the other. The preparations on each side are played out in the form of initial statements, questions, and answers. When the unexpected arises, staff lips whisper into one attentive ear of each principal actor, the other ear receiving a response or question from the other side. Occasionally there is a pause during which consultations occur on both sides.

One cannot help but wonder why everyone is so cautious—sticking to the script, consulting so frequently, promising a full response later. The reason is simple. Contrary to what many say about congressional hearings, they are important public policy events. The key word is *public*. The administration witnesses are being put on record. The work of their agency is being examined and justified. The legislators are providing cues as to what is or is not acceptable policy interpretation. Lobbyists are recording their group's interests in a particular policy and possibly indicating areas of compromise. These words restate the ground rules or boundaries of policy discourse; they constitute important formal talk to be relied on later. Cooperation, interpretation, and accommodation may occur informally, but the formal record must reflect the on-going institutional relationships. One comes to realize what the term *institution* really means in such settings. It is particularly fascinating for students of government to observe these points in the process during which individuals perform institutional roles. This phenomenon can be witnessed in committee hearings where an industrialist, lawyer, or professor understands and assumes the role of a senator or cabinet secretary—speaking and acting not only as a person but as a member of an established group with historical ties and future intentions.

3 Who is Congress?

In the month of October, 1800, a small "packet sloop," laden with all the records, archives and furniture which the infant Republic possessed, sailed from Philadelphia, where Congress then sat, up the Potomac to the new seat of government (Hazelton, 1897: 25).

It is extraordinarily difficult for me to look at the grandeur of Capitol Hill and imagine what it must have been like when the government was first getting established in Washington, D.C. In James Sterling Young's description of these early days, he observes that both the city and its government buildings were unattractive. No one much liked Washington—neither those who had to come there on business nor those who had to live there.

Hardly an aspect of the outpost on the Potomac was spared their scorn. The climate was intolerable. The place was a menace to health, pervaded with "contaminated vapour" which brought on all manner of "agues and other complaints." Washington was a "desert city," an

53

"abomination of desolation." The public buildings were either pretentious to the point of bad taste or "large naked ugly buildings" sur-
rounded with fences "unfit for a decent barnyard" (Young, 1966:   49).

The Capitol Building, which has come to symbolize Washington was,
in 1814, two wings connected only by a wooden walkway. It was not
until 1807 that the House had its own chamber. And the whole building was none too sound. Young describes it this way (1966:   44 — 45).

> Commanding the terrain from the tallest hill, the Capitol was built
> to be seen. But failure to erect the central portion, connecting the Sen-
> ate and House wings, made it an architectural monstrosity—twin boxes
> of white stone on a shrubless heath of hard-packed stone dust, the
> void between them bridged by a covered boardwalk resembling the
> construction sheds that dotted the grounds. . . . Behind the showy
> facade shoddy workmanship and poor design soon became apparent.
> Part of the ceiling fell in 1803, narrowly missing the vice president's
> chair. Columns supporting the gallery split open. . . . Printed notices
> warned spectators in the balcony "not to place their feet on the board
> in the front of the gallery, as the dirt from them falls upon senators'
> heads."

The two-winged monstrosity was set ablaze by Sir George
Cockburn and his men on August 24, 1814, as the British occupied
Washington in the unfortunate War of 1812. Rather roundly con-
demned at the time even by the English, this act of arson turned out
to be merciful. The building was rebuilt by 1817 to include the original two wings and a domed center portion (though not the dome we
know today) (Hazelton, 1897:   33 — 37).

THE GROWING CONGRESS

It was not at all difficult to comprehend who was Congress during
these early days. In 1802 the legislative branch was comprised of 152
persons most of whom (91 percent) were the members themselves. As
noted in Table 3 — 1, the legislative branch was larger than the executive branch by some 20 persons. By 1829 the congressional population had nearly doubled. But the expansion was the result of adding
more members to the House and Senate.

The members also lived on or very near Capitol Hill—many in
boarding houses. They could easily walk to the Capitol. "A complete
and self-contained village community" grew up over the first three
decades (Young, 1966:   71). And though the White House was only a
mile and a half away, one had to cross the Tiber River and fight the
morass and thicket of a virtual swamp to make the trip. Thus, two
communities developed—one executive, one legislative—and the
separation of powers become something more than a theory.

By the end of the 19th century one gets a quite different report on

TABLE 3 — 1
The Headquarters Establishment at Washington in 1802 and 1829*

	1802	1829
Executive branch:		
Presidency	2	2
Treasury Department and Post Office	89	226
War Department	19	34
Navy Department	11	23
State Department (including Patent Office)	10	32
Attorney General's Office	1	1
Total	132	318
Legislative branch:		
Vice president	1	1
Senators	32	48
Representatives	106	225
Ancillary personnel (clerks, officers, librarian)	13	25
Total	152	299
Judicial branch:		
Supreme Court justices	6	7
Clerk	1	1
Total	7	8
Grand total	291	625

* Does not include personnel at the Washington Navy Yard, the federal employees
serving the District of Columbia, or the federal employees serving outside Washington or in the military service.
SOURCE: Young, 1966: 31.

the city of Washington. Instead of leaving (Young reported that "from
1797 to 1829 . . . more senators resigned than failed to be reelected
by their state legislatures" 1966: 57), many members stayed in Washington after being defeated.

> There is something about the place that fascinates them. It is a
> clean, beautiful city with many charms. The town they come from is
> dirty and ugly with nothing pleasing to the eye. The contrast is so great
> that they cannot face the change (Stealey, 1906: 18).

In a book about his own career, *Twenty Years in the Press Gallery*, O.
O. Stealey, correspondent of the *Louisville Courier-Journal*, believed
that (1906: 38):

> Washington is destined to be the most beautiful and most magnifi-
> cent city in the world. . . . With the finest group of public buildings in
> the world, a wealth of broad avenues and circles and ornamental
> grounds that tells us of a spaciousness that is unrivalled, the noble
> river and the beauties and historic interest of the surrounding country,
> there are certainly attractions enough in Washington, not only to allure
> visitors but to make them wish that they might live here.

But while the description of the city had changed by 1900, the response to the question, who is Congress, remained more or less the

same as in that earlier age. The answer was the elected representatives and senators. Stealey concludes that: "By all odds the hardest work a congressman has to do is the writing of reports on bills before his committee" (1906: 16). Staff assistance was still a new development. It was not until 1856 that the House Committee on Ways and Means and the Senate Committee on Finance hired full-time clerks (Kofmehl, 1977: 3). And personal staff assistance was provided for in the Senate in 1885 ($6 a day) and in the House in 1893 ($100 a month). Stealey noted the importance of these clerks, in part because they could make contact with their counterparts downtown (the beginnings of cozy little triangles?) (1906: 33).

> The value of an efficient secretary or clerk to a congressman can hardly be overestimated. One wonders now how they once did without them, they release the members from so many burdens and so much tedious work, exhausting of mind and time. Since the government allowed each member a clerk at a salary of $100 per month all the calls upon congressmen from their constituents have generally received prompt attention. Then these clerks to members, can, as a rule, if they are bright and capable, get more things done than the members can themselves. This is because they cultivate the acquaintance and friendship of the private secretaries of the cabinet officers, and these officials can do lots of things that the cabinet officer himself would not think or inconvenience himself to do.

Between the period of Stealey's observations and the 1940s, Congress was slowly emerging as something more than its elected members. The Legislative Reference Service of the Library of Congress and the Office of Legislative Counsel were established in 1914 and 1918 respectively, committee staffs began to grow after 1900, as did the number of positions associated with administering House and Senate business. Still for the most part, those describing Congress concentrated heavily on the membership. In his book, *This is Congress* (1943), Roland Young talked about the need for additional staff assistance, particularly for performing legislative as distinct from political functions. He judged that both the members and the committees needed more staff. But he warned that:

> Such a staff need not be large, and indeed, there are distinct disadvantages in having a large staff working for Congress. If Congress had a large staff of its own, effective congressional control would be transferred from Congress to a congressional bureaucracy; one set of bureaucrats would give orders to another set, and the lines of power would be immensely confused. A large staff of congressional experts would become rivals of administrative experts, and the result might be confusion rather than cooperation (Young, 1943: 102).

The Legislative Reorganization Act of 1946 specifically provided for additional staff assistance for committees and increased clerk-hire allowance for members. In 1955 the standard work on Congress, *The Legislative Process in Congress*, by George B. Galloway, included a chapter on congressional staff aides. For the first time, the answer to the question who is Congress elicited a somewhat more inclusive response. Galloway included the Legislative Reference Service, the Office of Legislative Counsel, the Coordinator of Information, and the staffs of committees, members, and the two houses, among the participants in the legislative process (1955: Ch. 17).

Figures 3−1 and 3−2 show the sizeable increases immediately following the passage of the Legislative Reorganization Act of 1946.

FIGURE 3−1
Growth of House and Senate committee staff, 1930 − 1979 (selected years)

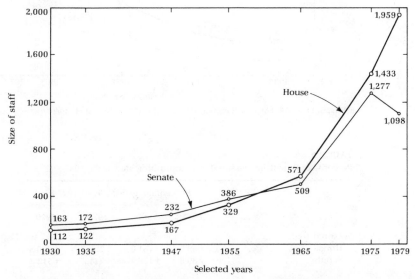

SOURCE: 1930, 1935: Fox and Hammond, 1977: 171; 1947 − 79: Schneider, 1980: 539; Bibby, et al., 1980: 70; Malbin, 1980: 253. Does not include select and special committee staffs.

But they show even greater growth after that period. The percentage growth is really quite phenomenal, as is shown in Table 3 − 2. Note that the Senate personal staff growth is greater than that in the House, but the reverse is true for committee staff growth (i.e., House committee staff growth is far greater than that for the Senate). Senate committee staff has declined in the most recent count. The total growth for all staff—personal and committee—for the period 1947 to 1979 is 465 percent. Unquestionably Capitol Hill has the fastest growing bureaucracy in town.

Personal and committee staffs do not constitute the whole of congressional bureaucrats. Table 3 − 3 shows the additional personnel

FIGURE 3 – 2
Growth of House and Senate personal staff, 1930 – 1979 (selected years)

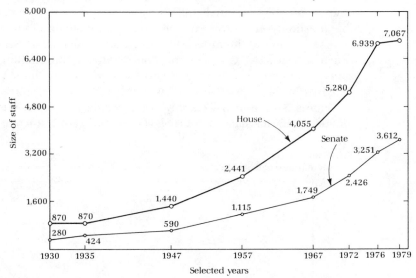

SOURCE: 1930 – 76: Fox and Hammond, 1977:   171; 1979: Bibby, et al., 1980:   67.

TABLE 3 – 2
Percentage growth in personal and committee staff since 1947

	Percentage growth from 1947 to:			
	1957	1967	1972	1979
Personal staff:				
House	+69.5	+181.6	+266.7	+390.8
Senate	+89.0	+196.4	+311.2	+512.2
	1955	1965	1975	1979
Committee staff:				
House	+97.0	+241.9	+758.1	+1073.1
Senate	+66.4	+119.4	+450.4	+ 373.3

SOURCE: Calculated from data in Figures 3 – 1 and 3 – 2.

who populate the Hill or work for Congress. Over 17,000 persons work directly for the two houses to assist in the daily operations. The General Accounting Office (GAO) and Library of Congress serve many purposes. Even if we count just 30 percent of GAO personnel and those library employees who work for the Congressional Research Service, the total figure is still nearly 25,000. For most legislatures of the world, the population you see in the debating chambers is the population you get for the institution. Clearly this is not the case for Congress or for an increasing number of state legislatures. The 538 senators, rep-

TABLE 3 – 3
Personnel employed by Congress, 1979

	Number	Totals
House:		
Committee staff*	2,073	
Personal staff	7,067	
Leadership staff	162	
Others	1,487	10,787
Senate:		
Committee staff*	1,217	
Personal staff	3,612	
Leadership staff	170	
Others	1,351	6,350
Joint Committee staff	138	138
Support agencies:		
General Accounting Office	5,303	
Library of Congress	5,390	
(Congressional Research Service)	(847)	
Congressional Budget Office	207	
Office of Technology Assessment	145	11,045
Miscellaneous:		
Architect	2,296	
Capitol Police	1,167	3,463
Total		31,783†

* Includes select and special committee staff—thus explaining the difference from figures in Fig. 3 – 1.
† The total is 23,528 if one includes just the Congressional Research Service from the Library of Congress and 30 percent of the General Accounting Office.
SOURCE: Bibby, et al., 1980:   68.

resentatives, delegates (three — one each from the District of Columbia, Guam, and the Virgin Islands), and one resident commissioner (from Puerto Rico) have a great deal of staff and organizational support.

By contrast, the Canadian parliament, which is the second most heavily staffed legislature in the world, has a staff of 3,300 (Malbin, 1980:   10). Consider the situation for the House of Commons in Great Britain.

> Nor do the committees or their members have much in the way of staffing. Ordinarily, each committee will have only one clerk of the House available to it. Further individual members have no research staffs of their own. Several together have an office room and may employ a secretary (each member is given a very limited amount of funds to do this). Members are also entitled to use the research staff of the House of Commons Library, but the staff at the library comprises so few professional persons that there is a ratio of MPs (excluding ministers) to staff of over 40 to 1 (Schwarz and Shaw, 1976:   75).

Interestingly enough, the ratio is the reverse for Congress—that is, 40 to one, staff to members.

Housing all of these people continues to pose a serious problem. Until the turn of the century, the members had to work from their desks or seats in the House and Senate. Congress was then the U.S. Capitol. The committees began to press for space first and by the end of the century space was being rented in nearby buildings. The first office buildings were completed in 1908 for the House and 1909 for the Senate. Today, the House has three buildings (named for three of its most notable Speakers—Cannon, Longworth, and Rayburn), the Senate has two (named for two recent senators—Russell and Dirksen) and is expanding one of the buildings. Both institutions have purchased other nearby buildings in addition to renting space in other buildings.[1] Still the space problem is severe for this large congressional population.

Also very much a part of the congressional complex is the Library of Congress. Originally housed in the Capitol, the library got its own building in 1897. A second building was added in 1939, and a third has just been completed. The newest building—named for James Madison—has more floor space than the Pentagon. The new building raised considerable controversy because of its cost and because many House members saw it as additional office space for them.

The accompanying map shows the location of the various buildings in the congressional complex. Picture it with a population of approximately 20,000 regulars plus many thousands of tourists, lobbyists, advisors, and administration personnel, and your mind's eye will begin to capture the nature of this ceaseless agitation.

The purpose of this all too brief historical review has been to point out that a great deal has happened in the last two or three decades to expand our image of what and who constitutes Congress. No longer can we concentrate only on the elected senators and representatives (see Figure 3 – 3). At minimum, we must include as well the following sets of personnel:

Individual member staffs.

Committee staffs.

Administrative staff (House and Senate).

Research and support services:
    Congressional Research Service.
    Congressional Budget Office.
    Office of Technology Assessment.
    General Accounting Office.
    House Information Systems.
    Office of the Legislative Counsel.
    Office of the Law Revision Counsel.

---

[1] See Congressional Quarterly, *Guide to the Congress of the United States*, (Washington: Congressional Quarterly, 1972), pp. 382 – 89.

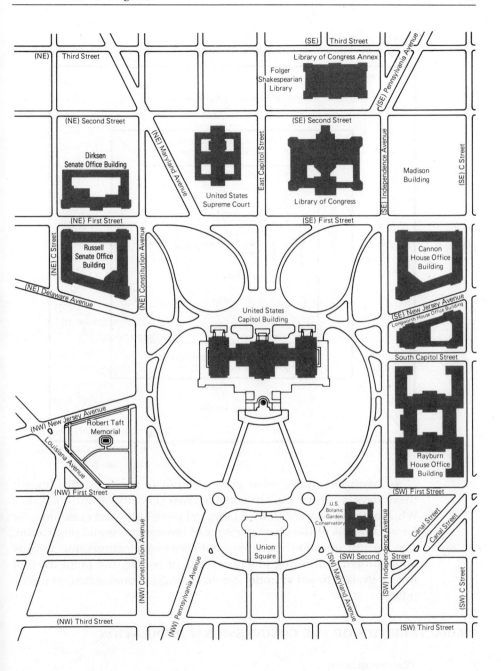

(SE) Third Street

(NE) Third Street

Library of Congress Annex

Folger
Shakespearian
Library

(SE) Pennsylvania Avenue

(NE) Second Street

(SE) Second Street

(NE) Maryland Avenue

(SE) Independence Avenue

(SE) C Street

Dirksen
Senate Office Building

United States
Supreme Court

East Capitol Street

Library of Congress

Madison
Building

(NE) First Street

(SE) First Street

(NE) C Street

Russell
Senate Office
Building

(NE) Constitution Avenue

Cannon
House Office
Building

(NE) Delaware Avenue

(SE) New Jersey Avenue

Longworth House Office Building

United States
Capitol Building

South Capitol Street

(NW) New Jersey Avenue

Robert Taft
Memorial

Louisiana Avenue

Rayburn
House Office
Building

(NW) First Street

(SW) First Street

Canal Street

Canal Street

U.S.
Botanic
Garden
Conservatory

(NW) Constitution Avenue

(SW) Independence Avenue

Union
Square

(SW) Second Street

(SW) Maryland Avenue

(SW) C Street

(NW) Pennsylvania Avenue

(NW) Third Street

(SW) Third Street

FIGURE 3 – 3
The growth of the congressional population

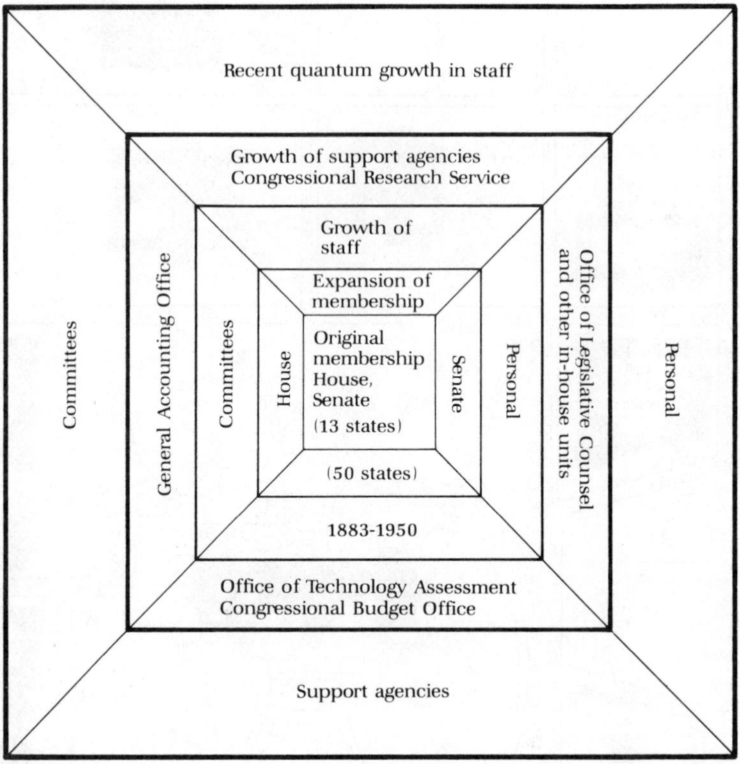

So having identified what groups populate the legislative branch these days, we turn now to consider two very important questions: Who are these people? How did they get there? The first question calls for an analysis of the characteristics of the congressional population. The second question requires us to consider elections and various appointment and hiring practices. And, of course, the point of all of this analysis is to aid in understanding congressional action on public policy.

CHARACTERISTICS OF THE CONGRESSIONAL POPULATION

The members

One of the more obvious characteristics of the congressional population in recent decades is, of course, its predominantly Democratic cast. The Republicans lost their majority status in Congress during the early years of the depression (losing the House in 1930 and both houses in 1932) and have regained it only twice since (1946 and 1952). The party split in the House and Senate since 1952 is shown in Figure 3 — 4. As indicated, the Republicans were able to stay reasonably close to the Democrats after losing their majority status in the 1954 and 1956

FIGURE 3 — 4
Party split in the House and Senate, 1952 — 1980

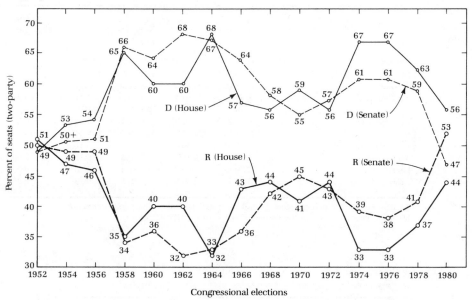

Congressional elections

elections. The 1958 election was a disaster, however, with the Republicans reduced by 47 in the House and 13 in the Senate (the highest number of Senate losses in the history of the party). Just as they were beginning to recover, they suffered setbacks in 1962 and 1964 in the Senate and House respectively. Recovery again seemed possible during the period 1966 — 72, but the 1974 elections once again pushed the Democratic majorities over 60 percent. The Republicans began to improve in the 1978 elections and stunned everyone by winning control of the Senate in 1980. The gain of 12 seats by Republicans was their second largest since 1868. During the full period of the 14 elections, the Democrats won 3,605 of the 6,094 House seats (59.2 percent) and 812 of the 1,388 Senate seats (58.5 percent). Interestingly enough, Republicans were elected to the White House in five of the eight elections during this period. But more about that later when we discuss presidential-congressional relations.

We begin then by noting that the smallest, but presumably most important, group of persons in the congressional population—the members themselves—are mostly Democrats. The occupational background of the members is displayed in Tables 3 — 4 and 3 — 5. Several observations can be made about the information provided there. Most striking is the dominance of lawyers in Congress. Two thirds of the

TABLE 3 — 4
Occupational background of House members, 91st — 97th Congresses

Occupation	Congress				Percent change 91st — 97th
	91st*	93d	95th	97th	
Agriculture	34 (8%)	38 (9%)	16 (4%)	28 (6%)	−2
Business/banking	159 (37)	155 (36)	118 (27)	134 (31)	−6
Educator	59 (14)	59 (14)	72 (17)	59 (14)	—
Engineering	6 (1.4)	2 (0.5)	2 (0.5)	5 (1)	−0.4
Journalism	39 (9)	23 (5)	14 (3)	21 (5)	−4
Labor leader	3 (0.7)	3 (0.7)	6 (1.4)	5 (1)	+0.3
Law	242 (56)	221 (51)	223 (51)	194 (45)	−11
Law enforcement	2 (0.5)	2 (0.5)	7 (2)	5 (1)	+0.5
Medicine	5 (1)	5 (1)	2 (0.5)	6 (1.4)	+0.4
Clergy	2 (0.5)	4 (0.9)	6 (1.4)	3 (.7)	+0.2
Scientist	1 (0.2)	2 (0.5)	2 (0.5)	0 (0)	−0.2

*Totals exceed 100 percent since several members have more than one occupation.
SOURCE: Various issues of the *Congressional Quarterly Weekly Report.*

TABLE 3 — 5
Occupational background of senators, 91st — 97th Congresses

Occupation	Congress				Percent change 91st — 97th
	91st	93d	95th	97th	
Agriculture	16*	11	9	9	−7
Business/banking	25	22	24	28	+3
Educator	14	10	12	10	−4
Engineering	2	2	0	2	—
Journalism	8	5	4	7	−1
Labor leader	0	0	0	0	—
Law	68	68	68	59	−9
Law enforcement	0	0	0	0	—
Medicine	0	1	1	1	+1
Clergy	0	0	1	1	+1
Scientist	1	0	1	1	—

*With 100 senators, the number in each category represents the percentage.
SOURCE: Various issues of the *Congressional Quarterly Weekly Report.*

senators and normally over half of the representatives have been lawyers.[2] They are declining in numbers, however—down 11 percent in

---

[2] Lawyers constitute less than one half of one percent of the civilian work force. U.S. Department of Commerce Bureau of Census, *Statistical Abstract of the United States* (Washington, D.C.: U.S. Government Printing Office, 1976), p. 373.

the House, 9 percent in the Senate. The next largest category is that of business and banking, with a fourth to a third of the representatives and a fourth of the senators so identified. Of the other occupations, education is well represented and appears to be growing, at least in the House. Teachers at all levels, kindergarten through graduate school, represent less than 5 percent of the labor force. The decline in agriculture as a source of employment among the general public is reflected in both houses, though the Senate continues to get a sizeable number of members with agricultural experience.

Overall, then, the members of Congress have predominantly white-collar working experience. Who speaks for the nearly one third of the labor force engaged in blue-collar work? Most governments in the world have strong, direct representation through the unions or labor parties. In the United States Congress, however, only a handful of members have direct occupational experience with labor unions — less than 1 percent in the House and none at all in the Senate. This is not to suggest that working people are not represented in Congress. It is only to point out that organized labor has not been successful in electing its own leadership to Congress. It is interesting to speculate about the policy implications of this fact — a matter we will reserve for a later chapter.

Table 3 — 6 displays the trends in the average age of the members as well as the range of ages in each house. The decline in average age is

TABLE 3 — 6
Average age of members of Congress, 91st — 97th Congresses

	91st	92d	93d	94th	95th	96th	97th	Change 91st — 97th
Senators:								
Average	56.6	56.4	55.3	55.5	54.7	52.7	52.5	−4.1
Range	36 − 79	36 − 80	30 − 80	31 − 78	34 − 78	35 − 81	32 − 79	
Representatives:								
Average	52.2	51.9	51.1	49.8	49.3	48.8	48.4	−3.8
Range	30 − 82	30 − 82	28 − 80	26 − 82	27 − 77	26 − 78	27 − 80	
Congress	53.0	52.7	52.0	50.9	50.3	49.5	49.2	−3.8

SOURCE: Congressional Quarterly, Inc., *Congressional Quarterly Almanac,* 1979, p. 3.

one of the more interesting developments in congressional characteristics. Once criticized for harboring old men, the Congress has become a more youthful institution. Note that there is a steady decline in the average age of both houses for each succeeding Congress. The average for the Congress overall drops below 50 for the first time in the 96th Congress. When the 95th Congress convened, a total of 91 House members (21 percent) were less than 40 years old; 40 (9 percent) were less than 35; and 5 were less than 30. Those under 40 were either educated or were just beginning their occupational careers during the turbulent and exciting 1960s. Thus in a sense this important decade in recent American history is finally beginning to have its impact on Congress. I refer to this process as the greening of Congress—that is, the gradual process by which the mood of the 1960s and early 1970s was finally transmitted to Capitol Hill through successive elections. This process has occurred to a greater extent in the House than in the Senate, where only six senators were under 40 in the 95th Congress (a mere 6 percent). Further greening occurred in the Senate in 1978, however, when eight new senators under 40 were elected and to a lesser extent in 1980 when four were elected. One other point worth making about the age of the members of Congress is that they are now all of the 20th century. After the 1978 elections only one senator, Milton Young (R—North Dakota) was born before 1900 and he retired in 1980. At the opening of the 90th Congress in 1967, 21 senators (over one fifth of the chamber) and 30 representatives (7 percent) were born in the last century. If for no other reason this change would seem to be important for symbolic purposes.

Table 3—7 on religious affiliation of members requires little comment. The distribution has remained relatively stable, with a slight dip in Protestant representation being the most notable change. Compared to the general population, Protestants still tend to be overrepresented in both chambers, Catholics underrepresented, and Jews represented almost exactly in proportion to their numbers.

TABLE 3—7
Religious affiliation of members of Congress, 91st—97th Congresses

Affiliation	91st	93d	95th	97th	Percent change 91st—97th
Senators:					
Protestant	81*	79	76	71	−10
Catholic	13	14	13	17	+ 4
Greek Orthodox	0	1	2	2	+ 2
Mormon	4	4	4	4	—
Jewish	2	2	5	6	+ 4
None (or unavailable)	0	0	0	0	—
Representatives:					
Protestant	305 (70%)	305 (71%)	273 (63%)	275 (63%)	− 7
Catholic	96 (22)	100 (23)	121 (28)	119 (27)	+ 5
Greek Orthodox	3 (0.7)	3 (0.7)	3 (0.7)	3 (0.7)	—
Mormon	6 (1.4)	7 (1.6)	7 (1.6)	7 (1.6)	+0.2
Jewish	17 (4)	12 (2.7)	23 (5.3)	27 (6.2)	+2.2
None (or unavailable)	7 (1.6)	5 (1.2)	8 (1.8)	4 (0.9)	−0.7
Totals	434	432	435	435	

* Figures also represent percentages since there are 100 senators.
SOURCE: Various issues of the *Congressional Quarterly Weekly Reports.*

Other important groups in the society remain poorly represented in the congressional membership. The House of Representatives in the 97th Congress had only 19 women members (just over four percent) and 18 black members (including one nonvoting delegate from the District of Columbia). In 1978 the one black senator, Edward W. Brooke (R—Massachusetts) was defeated and one woman senator was elected—Nancy L. Kassebaum (R—Kansas). A second woman senator, Paula Hawkins (R—Florida), was elected in 1980.

The staff

Not untypically the study of congressional staff lags behind its growing importance in the policy process. As a consequence, it is difficult to present comparable data for the many different types of staffs on Capitol Hill. It is possible that we will never have reliable data for comparative purposes. Turnover of staff is higher than for the membership, and there is less general interest in staff characteristics. These problems do not diminish the significance of such data, however, and it seems apparent that interest in congressional staff is increasing with its growing importance in the policy process.

What limited data are available show that all types of staff (personal, committee, administrative, support agency) reflect, in the aggregate, the Democratic Party dominance of Congress. That is to be expected. Congress is an institution of representatives elected within the political party structure. Staff is hired within this political context. This is not to say that such persons are not professional or expert in their respective fields. It is to suggest that professionalism in Congress is practiced within a political even partisan context. The election of a Republican majority in the Senate in 1980 was therefore accompanied by a massive turnover in staff. It was estimated that Republicans would gain 500 committee staff positions and would have gained more except for the fact that a two to one split between the majority and minority had just gone into effect.[3]

Other characteristics of staff demonstrate the changes which Congress is undergoing. The expanded staff in recent years is a relatively young staff. Studies of congressional staff by Harrison W. Fox, Jr., and Susan W. Hammond show that nearly half of the personal staff professionals in the Senate are under 35 and a sizeable majority of them in the House are under 30. Typically committee professional staff are older—16 percent under 30, 40 percent under 40 (Fox and Hammond, 1977: 146).

Fox and Hammond report that liberal arts and law are the most prevalent educational background among staff members, but increas-

---

[3] *National Journal,* November 29, 1980, p. 2025.

ingly staff are hired with expertise from more specialized areas. "The trend is for younger staff to have higher levels of education than older staff."[4] This difference in age and education between personal and committee staffs could conceivably create tension in the future if it does not already exist in some cases. Actually there is evidence to suggest that committee staff is viewed as the congressional bureaucracy by the personal aides to the members.

Another important characteristic of staff to examine is that of occupational background. What previous experience do they bring to the job? Obviously in the case of very young staff, the answer is none at all. Many staff go to work for congressmen and senators right out of college, graduate school, or law school. Fox and Hammond report also that relatively few staff have worked elsewhere in the federal government.

> In nearly a third of House offices, no professional staff member had worked in any other branch of the Federal Government. Even on committee staff, 57.2 percent had not worked in a federal department.[5]

Significantly, therefore, an expanding and increasingly important policymaking staff is drawn from a population *with little direct experience in the private world of work*. In his interesting study of congressional staff, Michael J. Malbin points out that many staff are young lawyers from the best schools (1980: 20):

> They are paid well (salaries of $40,000 and above are common for committee professionals), and they are allowed to exercise a great deal of power at a relatively young age. The experience is exhilarating for a while. . . . But for most of the professionals the exhilaration does not last forever.

These energetic young professionals have a lot to give, but a lot is also demanded. As Malbin reports, the members "hire them young, burn them out, and send them on" (1980: 20).

Other characteristics of interest are those of the legal residence of staff and tenure in any one job. As expected, most personal staff continue to maintain residence in the state or district but less so than in the past. As members expand their Washington staffs to include subject matter experts, there is less need or pressure to insure that these professionals are from the home area. Whether or not they live in the district or state, however, personal staff remain attentive to the impact of a particular piece of legislation on the constituency. Committee staff

---

[4] Harrison W. Fox, Jr., and Susan Webb Hammond, "Recent Trends in Congressional Staff," unpublished paper delivered at Southern Political Science Association, Atlanta, Georgia, November 4 – 6, 1976, p. 10.

[5] Fox and Hammond, "Recent Trends," p. 13.

typically take up residence in the Washington area, though many continue to be from the state or district of the member who appoints them.

Fox and Hammond report that tenure among Hill staff tends to be relatively brief—at least in any one position. The average tenure of legislative assistants in the House was 2.3 years. Even committee staff have limited time in one job—nearly 50 percent with less than four years in one study.[6] Robert H. Salisbury and Kenneth A. Shepsle found evidence to support the view that the high turnover of staff "results in part from the fact that many staffers look upon their Hill service as a credentialing experience and hope to fulfill their main life ambitions elsewhere" (1981: 393). Committee staffers were more likely to stay longer but not as long as executive branch bureaucrats. Salisbury and Shepsle also found that staff tended to follow the member. Many move in tandem with their member-patron as he or she shifts committee or subcommittee assignments or changes houses (typically moving to the Senate) (1981: 387—90).

It is possible that the remarkable growth in Hill staff will in time contribute to greater careerism among congressional staff of all types. Tenure in any one position may remain relatively brief (though that may change as well), but some of the tendencies characteristic of other bureaucracies may be realized with congressional staff too— particularly committee staff and the personnel of the various support agencies (Office of Technology Assessment, Congressional Budget Office, and the Congressional Research Service).

SUMMARY

In summary, the available evidence on the characteristics of the congressional population suggest important changes that warrant careful study. What are the policy implications of a younger Congress? Of a rapidly growing, young staff with limited occupational background? Of higher turnover among both members and staff? Of the development of three competitive staff worlds—personal, committee, and support agencies (i.e., OTA, CRS, CBO)? These are but some of the questions which make these characteristics of greater interest than ever before.

Who is Congress has come to be a most interesting and difficult question to answer. Thirty years is not a long time in history, yet it is clearly a very long time ago for Congress. In 1948—49, the House and Senate were trying to adapt to a post-World War II society. Congress had played a relatively minor role in the conduct of the war, and

---

[6] Fox and Hammond, "Recent Trends," p. 9.

members were sensitive to the need to modernize. Even at that time the institution was the most powerful and complex legislative body in the world. But those who described and analyzed it then would hardly recognize it today. By the 1950s, and certainly by the 1960s, we Americans had gotten used to a strong and intricately differentiated executive branch. Now we observe the same developments in the legislative branch.

4 How representatives are chosen

We turn now to the important question of how this congressional population came to be in Washington, directing attention first to the representatives and how they are elected. It is appropriate to treat House and Senate elections separately. The voters go to the polls on the same day for both, but often this is the only characteristic the two elections have in common. The constituencies are different (except in those few states with only one representative), senators' terms are three times longer than those for representatives, only a third of the Senate is up for election every second year, Senate campaigns have come to be multimillion dollar operations in many states, candidates for the Senate normally have greater name familiarity among the voters, and national media attention is not untypical for many Senate races while it is rare for House races. Thus, while many journalists and scholars continue to group these unlike events as *congressional elections,* we will discuss them in separate chapters and then examine the largest population on Capitol Hill—the staff—in Chapter 6.

CREATING THE DISTRICT

The first matter to consider is the creation of congressional districts. The whole state is a two-member district for the U.S. Senate. For

House representation, however, each state must first be instructed on the number of representatives it may elect (apportionment), and then district lines are drawn, that is, constituencies are created (districting). The constitutional provisions relating to this process are rather unspecific:

Article I, Section 2

The House of Representatives shall be composed of Members chosen every second Year by the People of the several States, and the Electors in each State shall have the Qualifications requisite for Electors of the most numerous Branch of the State Legislature.

* * * * *

Representatives and direct Taxes shall be apportioned among the several States which may be included within this Union, according to their respective Numbers. . . . The actual Enumeration shall be made within three Years after the first Meeting of the Congress of the United States, and within every subsequent Term of ten Years, in such Manner as they shall by Law direct. . . .

Article I, Section 4

The Times, Places and Manner of holding Elections for Senators and Representatives, shall be prescribed in each State by the Legislature thereof; but the Congress may at any time by Law make or alter such Regulations, except as to the Places of chusing Senators. . . .

Article I, Section 5

Each House shall be the Judge of the Elections, Returns and Qualifications of its own Members.

These provisions set the two-year term for representatives and a 10-year term for their districts. But several questions remained to be answered along the way by political bodies. Who may vote in a House election? The state legislature makes that determination when it sets qualifications for its own lower house. Who does the apportioning every 10 years? Congress "shall by Law direct" the manner in which apportioning will occur. Who draws the district lines? The state legislature shall prescribe "the Times, Places and Manner of holding Elections for . . . Representatives . . .", subject to any alterations Congress wishes to make at any time.

The early history of House elections—the only national elections originally determined by popular vote—was somewhat chaotic.[1] States had provisions for majority election (sometimes resulting in many runoff elections), multimember districts (two, three, even four mem-

---

[1] I have found the historical discussion of apportionment and districting in Congressional Quarterly, *Guide to U.S. Elections* (Washington, D.C., 1975), pp. 523–39, to be very useful in preparing this section.

bers from a single district), House elections in odd-numbered years, and electing all members at-large. Further, the practice of gerrymandering—shaping district lines so as to favor one political party—was widespread. Of course, the problem of constituting a national lower House on the basis of population is more complex in an expanding federal system than one might suppose. Consider the following questions:

1. How does one handle the problem of population growth? Increase the size of the legislature? Or set the number of representatives and shift seats among the states?
2. What about the admission of new states? Is their representation to be taken from the other states?
3. How does one handle the problem of fractions beyond the first 50 seats (all states are guaranteed at least one seat)?
4. How much discretion should state legislatures be permitted in drawing district lines?
5. Does election of representatives "by the People of the several States" also require equality in the size of congressional districts?

These difficult questions have been answered in various ways through the years. Table 4 — 1 shows that until 1912 increased population was regularly accommodated by increasing the size of the House. Only in 1842 was the House actually reduced in size. Any admission of new states was treated in the same way with the result that House membership at the end of the decade was normally slightly higher than at the beginning. In 1911 this politically attractive method of handling the problem was replaced by the more difficult process of having to make adjustments within the same universe. Thus between 1789 and 1911 all but the original 13 states typically experienced increased representation (the original 13 were particularly reduced in number of representatives with the 1842 reapportionment act—a loss of 31 seats). After 1911, however, Congress had to make many adjustments. When the 1920 census was taken, the beginnings of the rural-to-urban and east-to-west population movements presented such difficulties for the membership that no reapportionment act was passed, in direct violation of the Constitution. Not until 1929 was Congress able to enact legislation to direct the apportionment following the 1920 census. The 1929 act essentially established an automatic reapportioning process based on 435 seats and by which the Bureau of the Census would report to Congress on how the seats should be allocated among the states. Thus this sensitive political matter was transferred to a bureaucratic agency, a practice Congress has relied on from time to time for difficult issues.

The problem of how to handle fractions has been treated in various ways. The initial methods resulted in great inequalities and thus many

TABLE 4 – 1
Size of the House of Representatives, 1789 – present

Year	Membership after apportionment	Number of new states admitted	Membership at end of decade
1789	65		
1792	105	3[a]	106
1802	141	1	142
1812	181	6[b]	186
1822	213	1[c]	213
1832	240	2	242
1842	223	5	232
1852	233	2	237
1862[d]	241	4[e]	246
1872	292[f]	1	293
1882	325	6	332
1892	356	1	357
1902	386	1	391
1912	433[g]	2	435
1952	435	2	437
1962	435[h]	0	435

[a] Vermont (1791) and Kentucky (1792) admitted in time to be included in the 1790 reapportionment.
[b] Massachusetts originally allocated 20 representatives in 1811 with the understanding that 7 would be allotted to Maine when it became a state.
[c] Missouri (1821) admitted in time to be included in the 1820 reapportionment.
[d] The working House of Representatives was considerably smaller during this period due to the secession of southern states.
[e] Kansas (1861) was admitted in time to be included in the 1860 reapportionment.
[f] Originally the 1872 reapportionment act fixed the House size at 283, but a supplemental act increased the size to 292.
[g] The 1911 reapportionment act set the House size at 433, with two additional representatives to be added when Arizona and New Mexico were admitted—for a permanent limit of 435.
[h] Efforts in 1961 permanently to expand the House size to accommodate the admission of Alaska and Hawaii were defeated.
SOURCE: Compiled from data in Congressional Quarterly *Guide to U.S. Elections,* 1975, p. 531; and *The World Almanac,* 1977 edition.

efforts were made to develop another system. Congress finally settled on the so-called method of equal proportions in 1941, and that is what is used today.

Congress has also instructed state legislatures from time to time on drawing district lines. Must there be district boundaries at all? Should districts be contiguous? What about multimember districts? Should gerrymandering be controlled? Congress sought to deal with some of these matters in the 1842 apportionment act—requiring contiguity and single-member districts. The 1872 act added a provision that the districts should have "as nearly as practicable an equal number of inhabitants." And the 1911 act required that the districts be as compact as possible. Enforcing these provisions was difficult, however, and for the most part, state legislatures continued to draw district lines in a manner that accommodated partisan alignments within the state.

The redistricting situation by the 1960s was somewhat of a national scandal. There were absolutely wild differences in the population of congressional districts.[2] The 20 largest districts in 1960 ranged from 621,935 to 951,527; the 20 smallest from 177,431 to 252,208 (Baker, 1966: 79). The population difference between the largest and smallest districts was a staggering 774,096—three quarters of a million people! Further, district lines were drawn in strange and wondrous ways in some states—and not at all in other states. The Oklahoma first district was not even contiguous. The South Dakota first and second were divided by the Missouri River—a natural boundary—despite the fact that one district was almost three times larger in population than the other. New Mexico and North Dakota each elected their two represen- tatives at large. Connecticut elected five representatives by district and one at large (as did other states when they could not agree on a redistricting plan).

It seemed that the situation was ripe for intervention by the Su- preme Court. As it turned out, the Court warmed up to the con- gressional districting situation by first declaring that the federal courts could decide state legislative district cases (*Baker* v. *Carr,* 1962). The Court then proceeded in a series of cases to establish a one-person, one-vote principle. In *Wesberry* v. *Sanders* (1964) the Court declared that "as nearly as practicable one man's vote in a congressional elec- tion is to be worth as much as another's." The decision was based on Article I, Section 2 of the Constitution—that is, "The House of Rep- resentatives shall be composed of Members chosen every second Year *by the People of the Several States"* (McKay, 1965: 92, emphasis added). Thus it was that the question of equality of representation (number 5 above) was answered. As a result of the redistricting follow- ing the Wesberry decision Congress is as equally districted as could be expected given the continuing problems of apportioning within a fed- eral system (e.g., the requirement that all states have at least one rep- resentative). As Samuel C. Patterson observes: "Without a change in the Constitution, it is impossible to make congressional districts perfectly equal in population" (in King, 1978: 136).

To summarize, congressional districts are now created by a process beginning with the decennial census. The Bureau of the Census calcu- lates the number of representatives a state may elect based on popula- tion changes since the last census, an absolute limit of 435 members, and utilizing the method of equal proportions. The clerk of the House passes this information on to the governors of the 50 states, and the legislatures in those states with changes are then bound to redistrict by a one-person, one-vote criterion. Should the legislature fail to meet these responsibilities, the federal courts may intervene. But states with

---

[2] Though as Samuel C. Patterson notes, the actual number of extreme cases has never been great in this century (in King, 1978: 136 – 37).

internal population shifts (e.g., rural to urban) also must redistrict if the shifts seriously jeopardize the equality principle.

TYPES OF HOUSE ELECTIONS

Next we turn to the many different types of elections involving candidates for the House of Representatives. Many have to run twice in an election year—once to get the nomination and again to win the seat. The primary election is an American phenomenon in which one has the right to be the party's nominee. Since the election is open to all candidates who qualify, one can in essence win the party's label whether or not the leadership approves. Americans have come to accept this practice of electing the nominees, but the rest of the world tends to look upon this procedure as very curious since it typically undermines party responsibility.

Further confusion is introduced by the failure to hold primary elections on a single day. In fact, they are typically spread over an eight-month period. In 1978 the first congressional primary was held in Illinois on March 21 (with a filing deadline of December 19, 1977), the last in Hawaii on October 7. How can one generalize about our nominating politics when the process is spread over two thirds of the year? Further complications are introduced in nine southern states which provide for runoff primaries if no candidate receives a majority of the vote the first time around. Potentially then some candidates may have to run in *three elections.* The 50 states scheduled primaries or runoffs on 25 different dates in 1978! This statistic alone demonstrates the extent to which elections for the House of Representatives can become individualized events. Additionally, however, the primaries may vary by the nature and extent of opposition:

1. No opposition for either (or any) party's candidate.
2. Opposition for both (or all) party candidates.
3. Opposition for only one party's candidate.
4. Variation in the number of candidates in 2 and 3 above.

House elections may also vary depending on who else is running at the time. Typically the most significant running mate for a House member is a presidential candidate. In particular, the presidential race has the effect of increasing turnout over the so-called midterm elections. The average decline in turnout, presidential to midterm election, is 13.6 percent, or approximately 14 million voters (an average of over 32,000 for each congressional district). No doubt House incumbents get used to this roller coaster (see the dotted line in Figure 4—1 between the presidential and midterm elections), but it can't help but influence their political lives. Note that the subsequent increase in turnout has been on the average somewhat smaller than the decline

FIGURE 4–1

Voter turnout, House elections, 1952–1978

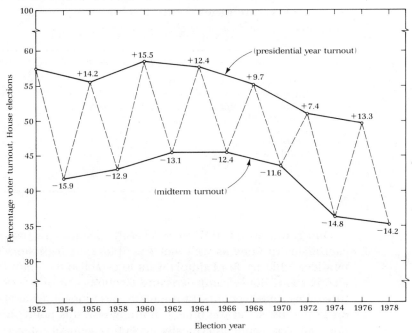

SOURCE: *Statistical Abstract of the United States*, 1979, p. 513.

(12.1 percent average increase). The reason for this difference is evident from the steady decline in turnout for House elections in presidential years. In fact, the two trend lines were beginning to merge, 1960–72, but they spread again with the shockingly low turnout in the 1974 House elections, when only 36.2 percent of the eligible voters bothered to go to the polls and again in 1978 when turnout fell to the lowest point since 1942 (when many eligible voters were overseas). This trend from low to lower turnout happens to coincide with a reduction in the number of marginal districts, but more about that later.

House elections may also vary in the extent to which candidates for other offices are seeking election. Every third election, House candidates will run without a senatorial candidate on the ticket. Occasionally this will occur in a midterm election so that no other national-level candidates will be running in the state. Thus in 1974 candidates for House seats in 16 states did not have to contend with Senate contests either for gaining the voter's attention or competing for the campaign dollar. In 9 of these 16 states, however, governors were being elected—presenting yet another variation in the context within which a House election occurs. Finally it occasionally happens that two Sen-

.   ate seats will be contested. This situation occurs when an incumbent resigns or dies during a term and a special election is held. To summarize, House candidates may be involved in any one of eight types of elections classified by who else is running:

	Presidential year	Midterm year
Senate and gubernatorial candidates running	1	2
Senate candidates running	3	4
Gubernatorial candidates running	5	6
No statewide candidates running	7	8

One could go on and on to classify elections in terms of other candidates running as well—for example, state legislators or important local officials. But I simply want to establish the point that generalizing about House campaigns and elections can be a very risky venture unless one accounts for the many variations in what else is going on in the district at the time. If nothing else this point should make one cautious about uncritically accepting general interpretations of congressional elections—including those offered here.

ONCE IN

Before discussing the recruitment of candidates and campaigning, it bears emphasis that once in representatives tend to stay in office if they want to. Table 4 − 2 shows the rate of return of incumbent members of the House of Representatives seeking reelection. In general the data show that normally a large number of incumbents seek reelection, very few get defeated in primaries (reaching 3 percent only twice in the period measured), and a large majority win in the general election as well (high turnover being 10 percent). For the most part, a new House of Representatives is made up of faces from the old House. Note that normally over 80 percent of the total House has returned (last column in Table 4 − 2), and in 1968 over 90 percent of the members carried over.

It is also the case that when an incumbent retires, seeks other office, or dies, chances are good that the party will hold on to the seat. Thus, for example, in 1976, 41 of the 51 seats in districts where the incumbent was not running were won by the same party which had held the seat previously. Even in 1974, a year of relatively high turnover (see Table 4 − 2), 30 of the 44 nonincumbent districts were won by the same

TABLE 4 — 2
Number and percentage of House incumbents winning reelection, 1956 — 1980

Year	Incumbents seeking reelection	Lost in primary	Lost in general election	Returned to House	As percent of whole House
1956	411 (94.5%)	6 (1.5%)	16 (3.9%)	389 (94.6%)	89.4%
1958	396 (91.0%)	3 (0.8%)	37 (9.3%)	356 (89.9%)	81.8
1960	405 (93.1%)	5 (1.2%)	25 (6.2%)	375 (92.6%)	86.2
1962	402 (92.4%)	12 (3.0%)	22 (5.5%)	368 (91.5%)	84.6
1964	397 (91.3%)	8 (2.0%)	45 (11.3%)	344 (86.6%)	79.1
1966	411 (94.5%)	8 (1.9%)	41 (10.0%)	362 (88.1%)	83.2
1968	409 (94.0%)	4 (1.0%)	9 (2.2%)	396 (96.8%)	91.0
1970	401 (92.2%)	10 (2.5%)	12 (3.0%)	379 (94.5%)	87.1
1972	390 (89.7%)	12 (3.1%)	13 (3.3%)	365 (93.6%)	83.9
1974	391 (89.9%)	8 (2.0%)	40 (10.2%)	343 (87.7%)	78.9
1976	384 (88.3%)	3 (0.8%)	13 (3.4%)	368 (95.8%)	84.6
1978	382 (87.8%)	5 (1.3%)	19 (5.0%)	358 (93.7%)	82.3
1980	398 (91.5%)	6 (1.5%)	31 (7.8%)	361 (90.7%)	83.0
Average (1956 — 80)	398 (91.5%)	7 (1.8%)	25 (6.3%)	367 (92.2%)	84.2%

SOURCE: *Congressional Quarterly Weekly Report*, April 5, 1980, p. 908 and Bibby, et al., 1980: 14.

party. Of course as expected, the minority party often suffers in these exchanges. All but one of the 14 districts in 1974 and 3 of the 10 districts in 1976 that were won by the other party were taken from the Republicans by the Democrats. Put another way, under normal circumstances the Democratic Party has a better chance of holding a district when an incumbent retires than the Republican Party.[3]

Another interesting development is the reduced competition for House seats. It seems that (1) there is less party turnover in congressional districts than in the past, and (2) there are fewer marginal districts (i.e., those won by less than 55 percent of the vote). Table 4 — 3 presents evidence on the first point. The number of congressional districts won by the same party in every election during the period measured increased to nearly 80 percent of the total districts by 1952 — 60. During the most recent period, the number declined, but it must be remembered that this was a time of much redistricting as a result of court cases. The actual number of changes as a percent of potential change (a measure of turnover) increased only slightly over the previous period (and declined slightly—to 7.2 percent—if changes strictly accountable to districting are excluded from the calculations) (Bullock, 1975: 574).

David R. Mayhew offers evidence in support of the second point above. He studied the percentages of victory for incumbent con-

---

[3] The 1980 election was by no means normal in any respect. Nine districts switched parties of the 34 in which the incumbent retired or ran for another office. Of these nine, eight were won by the Republicans.

TABLE 4 – 3
Party turnover for House seats for selected time periods

Time period	Districts held by same party	Total number of party changes in other districts	Percent turnover*
1914 – 26	270 (62.1%)	308	11.8
1932 – 40	304 (69.9%)	184	10.6
1942 – 50	322 (74.0%)	119	11.9
1952 – 60	340 (78.2%)	135	7.8
1962 – 70	315 (76.5%)†	136	8.2

* Calculated by dividing the actual number of changes by the potential number of changes in a particular election period.
† Bullock included only districts which existed for at least four of the five elections in the period.
SOURCE: Data for 1914 – 26 taken from Hasbrouck, 1927: Ch. ix; for 1932 – 40, 1942 – 50, and 1952 – 60, from Jones, 1964: 465; and for 1962 – 70 from Bullock, 1975:   575.

gressmen and found that "the number . . . running in the marginal zone has roughly halved over the 16-year period [1956 – 72]" (Mayhew, 1974b: 304). The number of incumbents winning by less than 55 percent had declined from approximately 20 percent in the late 1950s to just over 8 percent in 1970 and 1972. Robert S. Erikson estimates that during the 1950s the incumbency advantage was worth about 2 percent—not a spectacular amount, and Erikson doubted that it explained the low turnover of membership. He found a marked increase in advantage during the 1960s, however—to 5 percent (1971 and 1972). The shift was particularly strong in the 1966 to 1970 period, which coincides with the decline in marginal seats shown by Mayhew. Thus it would seem that at least for the 1960s and early 1970s individual House members were less threatened by electoral competition than in the past.

Mayhew suggests five possible explanations for the decline in incumbent marginality: drawing district lines to protect incumbents, better advertisement by members, "getting more political mileage out of federal programs," greater skill at position taking, more reliance by voters on an "incumbency cue" in voting (1974b: 304 – 13). Morris P. Fiorina sought to determine which of these factors was influential. He rejected the district line, personal advertising, and incumbency cue hypotheses. In his judgment incumbents have created constituency dependence on them by increasing the number of domestic programs and bureaucratic agencies to administer these programs (Fiorina, 1977:   52 – 53).

> To explain the vanishing marginals we need only argue that over the past quarter of a century expanded constituency service and pork-barrel opportunities have given the marginal congressman the opportunity to

> switch 3 to 5 percent of those who would otherwise oppose him on
> policy grounds to his supporting coalition. Considering the magnitude
> of the growth in the federal role . . . such a shift seems eminently
> plausible.

These various explanations for greater incumbency safety are based
on the assumption that the trend itself will either continue or smooth
out at the low levels of marginal seat distribution realized in 1970 and
1972. In 1974, however, the marginals reappeared. Over 70 seats were
won in the 50 to 54.9 percent range, the most since 1965 and more
than in 1970 and 1972 combined. Cover and Mayhew judged that this
result was "probably ephemeral" (Dodd and Oppenheimer, 1977: 59).

> With biennial vote swings smaller in size, the trough in the bimodal
> distribution is likely to shift back to the middle of the marginal range,
> yielding what have come to be normal election patterns like the one in
> . . . 1972.

The results in 1976 and 1978 appear to sustain this judgment. Once
again the number of representatives winning by 60 percent or more
exceeded 70 percent.

This matter of incumbency advantage has held a special fascination
for students of Congress, perhaps because of a belief that elections
should produce high turnover—throw the rascals out and all that.
Whatever the reason the subject has been studied with great intensity
in recent years. Much attention has been focused on what incumbents
do to stay in office—trips home, constituency service, mail, more staff
presence in the district, and so on. But as Barbara Hinckley points out:
"The advantage may be less a matter of what incumbents do right than
of what challengers do wrong—or do not do at all" (1980: 442). The
1978 National Election Study included a number of questions designed to find out how much voters knew about incumbents and
challengers and where they got their information. The results are interesting (Hinckley, 1980; Mann and Wolfinger, 1980):

1. More than twice as many voters recognize and can evaluate or rate
    the incumbent as compared to the challenger (93 percent to 44
    percent—see Table 5 — 4).[4]
2. A large majority of voters have a positive feeling about the incum-
    bent as compared to the challenger (73 percent to 17 percent—56
    percent don't know or can't rate the challenger).
3. Very few voters give the incumbent a poor or very poor rating
    when evaluating job performance (only 4 percent).

---

[4] In earlier surveys voters were asked to name a candidate. Very few could. Now
voters are asked for name recognition, which is what they experience in the voting
booth. Thomas E. Mann found major differences between name recall and recognition
for Representative Alan Howe (19 and 89 in November 1975, 41 and 99 in August 1976).
(1978: 31).

4. Voter contact with the incumbent is much greater than with the challenger—whether in direct meeting, attendance at a meeting, talk with a staff person, receipt of mail, through family or a friend, or through the media (any type of contact: 90 percent for incumbent, 44 percent for the challenger).

5. Contact with a candidate reduces defections from the candidate's party (for example, where voters from the challenger's party have had contact *only* with the incumbent, 72 percent of them defected to vote for the incumbent; 46 percent of these voters defected if they had contact with both candidates).

These results demonstrate the overwhelming advantage of the House incumbent among the voters. Whether this advantage is the consequence of incumbent effort or challenger incompetence is not altogether clear. Thomas E. Mann and Raymond E. Wolfinger are undoubtedly correct in observing that victory for incumbents "is enhanced by the absence of a serious challenge and the greater likelihood of a lopsided partisan balance in the . . . House constituency" (1980:   631). Once in an incumbent may *be* the district—that is, since most House districts are artificially drawn, often cutting across several jurisdictions, the member comes to define, perhaps even to create, the interests within those lines on a map. The situation in the Senate is dramatically different (see Chapter 5).

The immediate policy implications of these developments are not altogether clear. Once in the members have a very good chance of staying if they choose to do so. And further, most of them have supported a broad domestic program in recent years that commands greater attentiveness on their part to the district. Fiorina among others is quite correct in observing that many social programs enacted in the last two decades result in more constituent demands on their Washington-based representatives. It just so happens that good constituency service of this kind may result in good electoral politics and incumbents may therefore be favored to an even greater extent than in the past. It is interesting, however, that the greatest electoral advantage appears to come not from specific contact between voters and the member's office but rather in the greater recognition afforded by the member's district presence (Mann and Wolfinger, 1980:   628).

It should be emphasized that a higher return of incumbents does not necessarily mean less turnover in the membership. First, the number of voluntary retirements has increased in recent years, due in part to the more generous pension benefits for members and possibly to the greater demands mentioned earlier. In 1974 a post-World War II record of 44 House members voluntarily withdrew (either retiring or running for another office). This record fell in 1976 when 47 House members decided not to run again and again in 1978 when 49 members declined to run.[5] Thus, the greater incumbency advantage is offset by inducements to retire or run for other offices. Table 4 – 4 offers evidence in support of this conclusion. The 11 elections, 1956 –

TABLE 4 – 4
Marginal seats, retirements, and membership turnover, 1956 – 1976

Elections	Average percentage of marginal seats*	Average number of retirements	Average percentage of total membership returned
Group I (1956 – 66)	18.4%	26	84.1%
Group II (1968 – 76)	11.7	36	85.1

* 50 to 54.9 percent.
SOURCE: Calculated from data in Mayhew, 1974; election returns for 1974 and 1976 in *Congressional Quarterly Weekly Reports;* and *Congressional Quarterly Weekly Report,* April 24, 1976, p. 100.

76, are divided into two groups. The first group of six has the higher average percentage of marginal seats (won in the 50 to 54.9 percent range) and the lower average number of retirements. The second group of five has a lower average percentage of marginal seats but a higher average number of retirements. As shown in the final column, the difference in the average percentage of members returning for each set is negligible. The conclusion is therefore that membership turnover has not changed a great deal; that the stability of the institution from this perspective remains very much what it has been in the recent past.

A second consideration of policy importance is that whereas greater constituency service is required by the many social and regulatory programs of the 1960s and 1970s, it also follows that the legislative program itself is heavier than in the past. Thus members are not free to devote all of their time and effort to constituency service. The domestic legislative agenda is more demanding of their time than ever before. This condition, of course, presumably contributes to the greater number of retirements. "In their retirement announcements, many of the members cited the increased workload that House service demanded of them."[6]

---

[5] *Congressional Quarterly Weekly Report,* April 24, 1976, p. 1003 and July 1, 1978, p. 1670. Joseph Cooper and William West analyze the reasons for retirements in Dodd and Oppenheimer, 1981: chapter 4.

[6] *Congressional Quarterly Weekly Report,* April 24, 1976, p. 1003.

RECRUITMENT

It might appear obvious that the policy-related behavior of the members of Congress would be influenced by how and why they got into politics. Despite this fact, there are few systematic studies of how members of Congress are recruited. Of course given the high rate of return for incumbents, the principal recruiting to be done is for challenging candidates. Having just read the previous section on incumbency advantage, can you imagine trying to convince a friend to run for a House seat against the incumbent? Yet the political party leaders often have to do that—find congressional candidates who are bound to lose, primarily as "ticket fillers."[7] The party also may even select winning candidates in the few remaining areas where it is strong enough to determine such matters (as in inner-city Chicago). Where the local party has been instrumental in their selection, House members naturally tend to be oriented to the interests and needs of the city and district. In his study of Chicago, Leo Snowiss found that congressional Democrats were not "knowledgeable about and capable of significantly contributing to the formulation of important national policies." Rather they were anxious to get the city what it needed (Snowiss, 1966: 637):

> Their practical, instrumental outlook and their preoccupations with tangible, highly specific goals have helped them to acquire much of value for the city. . . . Pursuing limited, specific, tangible goals, they have been able to exercise considerable influence over the disposition of federal public works. . . . Rivers and harbors, highways, and housing have been their forte.

Snowiss found that the suburban Republican members were not recruited by the party and tended to be issue-oriented conservatives (1966: 632).[8]

From these fragments of evidence we begin to understand the need to study this matter of recruitment, to analyze the where, who, how, and why of candidate selection. We can do no more than begin this

---

[7] In their study of defeated congressional candidates, Robert J. Huckshorn and Robert C. Spencer found that party leaders were mentioned more often than others as influential in the decision to run (1971: 49). Many candidates are, in fact, self-starters, however (no doubt ignorant of their chances of success). Jeff Fishel found that more Democratic congressional challengers were consistently self-starting than party or group sponsored. Republicans were slightly more often party sponsored. (Fishel, 1973: 58). Thomas A. Kazee shows that for many House candidates the campaign is a rewarding experience despite the odds. And for some it appears to be a no lose situation—"defeat . . . does not end one's career . . ." and "political candidacy seems to enhance . . . self-esteem and community commitment" (1980: 96).

[8] David M. Olson has classified political parties in the congressional district into four types—organizational, bifactional, multiple component, and atomistic. Each type provides a special political setting for the member back in the district, but the impact of each in Washington is slight (1978: 239 —63).

analysis, but the effort will illustrate the policy relevance of recruitment. Consider the 1974 election. The combination of Watergate and economic issues favored the Democrats. Let's review the where, who, how, and why of Democratic candidates with a potential for winning in 1974.

Where

The *where*, of course, refers to the districts that offer the greatest opportunities for the prospective candidate. First in this category are the open districts—that is, those where the incumbent is not running because of retirement, decision to run for another office, or primary defeat. Typically such districts show a reduced margin for the incumbent party—referred to as the retirement slump. In recent years the advantage to the challenger has been on the average over 5 percent and as much as 11 percent in 1972 (in Dodd and Oppenheimer, 1981: 70). Redistricting may also alter the incumbent's advantage. After all it is disorienting to anyone to return home and find that a new family has moved in.

Second are the marginal districts. In 1974 one naturally expected the Democrats to have the advantage in winning 1972 marginal seats because of the issues. In fact, it was not unreasonable in 1974 for Democrats to look beyond those Republican seats won in 1972 by 50 to 54.9 percent. Democratic landslide elections in 1968 and 1964 resulted in capturing many Republican seats that had been won by the 55 to 59.4 percent and beyond in 1956 and 1962, respectively.

For present purposes, we will examine these high opportunity cases to determine what can be learned about recruitment. Specifically we will concentrate first on those districts where Democratic candidates might reasonably judge that they had a good chance to win. Then we will look even more closely at those who did in fact win to see whether any conclusions might be drawn about the policy impact of how and why they ran.

Table 4−5 displays the high opportunity districts for 1974. As expected, the new Democratic candidates did extremely well in those districts previously held by Democrats, winning 25 of 27 (categories 1 and 2 in Table 4−5). By definition they did well where they had a redistricting advantage over an incumbent Republican (category 7 in Table 4−5). Democrats also won 47 additional Republican seats in 1974−13 of the 24 open districts (categories 3 and 4), 13 of 25 in the 50 to 54.9 percent marginal range, and 9 of the 31 in the 55 to 59.9 percent marginal range. Categories 3 to 7 account for 37 of the 49 Republican districts lost to Democrats. The remaining 12 may properly be termed *upsets*. The range of 1972 Democratic percentages for these districts was from 24.1 to 39.8. All but two of these districts were rated as

TABLE 4-5
High opportunity districts for prospective Democratic candidates

District type	Total in 1974	Won by Democrat
1. Incumbent Democrat retiring or running for other office	22	21 (95.5%)
2. Incumbent Democrat vulnerable to primary loss	5*	4 (80.0%)
3. Incumbent Republican retiring or running for other office	21	12 (57.1%)
4. Incumbent Republican loses primary	3	1 (33.3%)
5. Incumbent Republican candidate won by 50-54.9 percent in 1972	25	13 (52.0%)
6. Incumbent Republican candidate won by 55-59.9 percent in 1972	31	9 (29.0%)
7. Redistricting advantage	2	2 (100.0%)

* Includes only those districts in which a Democratic incumbent was defeated by a primary opponent.
SOURCE: Compiled from data in Richard Scammon, ed., *America Votes 11* (Washington, D.C.: Congressional Quarterly, 1975).

favoring the Republicans by the *Congressional Quarterly* (four were rated safe Republican).[9] In two instances, however, the Republican incumbent was a member of the House Committee on the Judiciary and had supported President Nixon during the impeachment proceedings.

Who

Who were these new Democratic recruits? How do they compare with the members they replaced? Do they have characteristics in common? The age differences between the new and the old representatives are very striking—an average age of 40.2 for those coming in, 55.5 for those going out. Only eight replacements were 50 years or older as compared to 53 of the incumbents. Over one half (42) of the replacements were 40 or under. None of these results is very surprising since many new members replaced retirees. The replacement process in 1974 deserves special attention, however, since it was the first infusion of the 1960s awareness into the House of Representatives. Consider the life cycles for those members 40 and under. As indicated in Table 4-6 the 1974 class included several members educated or

[9] See *Congressional Quarterly Weekly Report,* October 12, 1974.

TABLE 4 – 6
Life cycle of replacements 40 and under

Event	Age		
	30	*35*	*40*
Born	1944	1939	1934
High School graduation	1962	1957	1952
Military service	*	1959	1954
College graduation	1966	1963	1958
Law School graduation	1968 – 69†	1965 – 66	1960 – 61

* Only two members under 35 had military service.
† Some law schools admit students with three years of college.

moving into the work force in the 1960s. Generational changes of this type in the past were not so significant. It is generally agreed, however, that the civil rights movement and the Vietnam War produced a new consciousness that was not immediately represented in the House (turnover in 1968 was extremely low—see Table 4 – 2). The large Democratic freshman class of 1974, therefore, was of particular importance in shaping a new Congress.

The occupational differences between the two groups were not enormous, but they may be suggestive of what is to come. The replacements were drawn less from agriculture (the most striking difference), business and banking, and law, and had less public service/political experience. There were also fewer veterans among the replacements. In fact, only two members under 35 were veterans. An all-voluntary military may well cause problems for Department of Defense appropriations in the future as fewer members of Congress have military experience. Educators and journalists show slight increases. If anything, one would conclude that the 1974 Democrats were less oriented toward business than their predecessors.

I also examined roll-call voting scores for the replacements and those whom they replaced. The *Congressional Quarterly* compiles scores for presidential support (the percent of roll-call votes that a member supported a presidential position), conservative coalition support (the percent of votes where a member supported a bipartisan conservative majority on legislation), and party unity (the percent of votes on which members were on the same side as their party's majority). These scores are very useful in getting a general impression of how members compare with one another on a whole series of votes. I compared the 1975 scores of the replacements with the 1974 scores of the replaced. There were only minor differences between outgoing and incoming Democrats as regards presidential or conservative coalition support. The new Democrats, however, were significantly more supportive of their party than the outgoing Democrats.

The pattern for Democrats replacing Republicans was quite different, as one would expect. These new members provided less support for the Republican president than their Republican predecessors (32.5 percent on the average compared to 50.4 percent) and considerably less support of the conservative coalition (26.2 percent compared to 67.5 percent). These Democrats too showed more support for their party than the Republicans showed for theirs. All in all, the Democratic replacements demonstrated a more liberal performance on these scores than their predecessors.

Finally it is interesting to look at how the new Democrats scored as compared to all Democrats in 1975. They supported the president slightly less (35 percent compared to 38 percent for all Democrats), contributed fewer votes to the conservative coalition (59 percent compared to 63 percent among southern Democrats; 16 percent compared to 20 percent among northern Democrats), and provided impressively greater party support than the rest of their colleagues (79 percent compared to 69 percent for all Democrats).

In summary, the who of the successful 1974 Democratic recruits was a new generation of legislators considerably younger than those they replaced and presumably very aware of the important social changes experienced in the 1960s. For present purposes it is enough to record these differences as essential for understanding the policy changes in Congress in 1974 and beyond. Richard F. Fenno, Jr., once observed that: "We shall get a different kind of Congress when we elect different kinds of congressmen or when we start applying different standards of judgment to old congressmen" (in Ornstein, 1975: 287). Both appear to have happened beginning in 1974. It is important to observe then that some policy change is traceable to certain landmark elections.

How and why

In his interesting study of Connecticut legislators, James David Barber poses three questions a potential candidate might ask (1965: 11):

1. Do I want it? (motivation)
2. Can I do it? (resources)
3. Do they want me? (opportunity)

Some form of positive response is required for all three questions. As Barber points out, however, the reasoning behind the response may vary considerably. In fact, later in the book Barber identifies four types of legislators based on self estimates of, among other things, motivation, resources, and opportunities: the spectator, advertiser, reluctant, and lawmaker (1965: 214).

> For three types—the Spectators, Advertisers, and Reluctants—much of [the legislator's] behavior represents compensation. For three quite different reasons these individuals seek in politics opportunities for enhancing and protecting a sense of self-approval, employing strategies symptomatic of relatively low self-esteem. The Lawmakers, on the other hand, tend to evaluate themselves rather more highly and thus to be much less concerned with bolstering their egos.

Unfortunately I lack sufficient evidence with the 74 Democratic members examined here to do an in-depth analysis of how they rationalize their entry into congressional politics. It is sufficient for present purposes to note that motivations, resources, and opportunities vary considerably and to suggest that this variation itself may help to explain the behavior of representatives as participants in the policy process. We will consider each of the factors in turn—motivation, resources, and opportunity—and then make a judgment about the impact of each on the representatives as they assume their responsibilities in Washington.

Almost by definition one would expect motivation to be high for these candidates. These were high opportunity districts for Democrats and therefore candidates might be expected to be highly motivated. In fact, such districts should attract a number of candidates, probably in relation to the certainty of victory in the general election. Table 4−7 shows that this is more or less the case. Note that the average number of opponents is greatest for the redistricted seats and those in which a Democratic incumbent retired or ran for another office. The districts in which Republicans were, by choice, not returning also attracted a number of candidates. The only puzzle is why so few candidates sought the nomination in the Republican districts won by 50 to 54.9 percent in 1972.

So the first conclusion is simply that a candidate in this group must have wanted it to engage in such intense primary competition. Another indicator of motivation is whether a candidate had run for the House in the past. A total of 13 in this group of 74 ran in 1972; 6 ran in 1970. Four candidates were former members of the House and were back to try again. Finally, all but one of these members sought reelection in 1976. Bear in mind, however, that for the most part these candidates were running in high-opportunity districts. The motivation for challenging candidates in hopeless races would naturally be considerably less.

Can I do it is, as Barber indicates, a question of resources and personal situation. It is no coincidence that many legislators are law-

TABLE 4−7
Primary opposition for Democratic candidates in 74 selected districts, 1974

Type of district	Total in category	Number with primary	Average number of candi- dates	Average percent of nominee
1. Democratic incumbent does not run	21	19	5.1	43.3* 47.1
2. Democratic incumbent suc- cessfully challenged	4	4	1.3	49.8
3. Republican incumbent does not run	12	11	3.1	55.5
4. Republican incumbent suc- cessfully challenged	1	1	1.0	62.0
5. Republican won by 50− 54.9 percent in 1972	13	9	2.0	60.9
6. Republican won by 55− 59.9 percent in 1972	9	7	3.4	53.1
7. Democratic redistricting advantage	2	2	5.5	44.0
8. Republican won by over 60 percent in 1972	12	8	3.1	53.1* 55.4
Total	74	61		

* The first figure represents the average percentage before the runoff election. There were four runoff elections—three in category 1; one in category 8.
SOURCE: Compiled from data in Richard M. Scammon, ed., *America Votes 11* (Washington, D.C.: Congressional Quarterly, 1975).

yers, businessmen, or teachers. These occupations permit flexible work scheduling, an essential requirement for campaigning and taking on the responsibilities of the job should the candidate win. Here is what Barber says (1965: 233):

> The *availability* of candidates depends to a large extent on their ability to arrange their affairs to accommodate an extended sojourn in a distant place. This tends to limit candidates to (1) those who can give up what they are doing without financial sacrifice, (2) those in flexible occupations who can postpone or temporarily pass on to others their current duties, and (3) those whose superiors are willing to release them for candidacy and office holding.

I have already noted the occupational characteristics of the 74 Democrats selected for study here. There were no plumbers or carpenters or auto mechanics (though, interestingly enough, there was one housepainter—Beard of Rhode Island).

Another dimension to the resources question is the previous legislative or political experience of the candidate. Can I do it may also refer to capability and style as well as convenience. Almost three fourths of the 74 Democratic candidates were judged by the *Congressional Quarterly* to have had significant public service or political occupational experience. Of these, 4 were former members of the House, 16 served as state representatives, 2 as state senators, 5 as both, and 6 were at one time aides to U.S. senators or representatives. In addition, seven candidates had local legislative experience on city councils or county boards of supervisors and four served as mayors. A number of candidates also had other political experience — in Washington with federal agencies, in law enforcement (primarily as public attorneys), as county officials, as party officials, and in running for other offices.

But what of the 20 candidates who were not rated by the *Congressional Quarterly* as having had public service or political occupational experience? Nine of these 20 ran for the House in 1970, 1972, or both. Five others had had varying types of political experience, leaving just six candidates with virtually none. Interestingly the less marginal districts had the larger number of political neophytes. This is as one would expect. It just so happens that every so often newcomers do win seats which normally would be safe for the incumbent party. For the rest, however, Robert J. Huckshorn and Robert C. Spencer, in their study of defeated congressional candidates, raise some doubts as to whether the exercise is worth the effort—for anyone involved (1971: 87).

> . . . congressional elections are often waged by neophytes who have started themselves on the road to high public office. More often than not the entire party is damaged by the ensuing confusion and by a directionless campaign at this important middle level.

Still lightening does strike, more often for majority-party candidates than for minority-party candidates, however. Thus, at this important middle level many, if not most, challenging candidates think they have the resources to win.

The third consideration is what Barber refers to as the opportunity. "However strong his motives, however ready he stands to serve, the potential candidate remains on the sidelines until and unless some practical opportunity presents itself" (1965: 237). Stimson Bullitt likens the situation to that of a surf rider. "The decision as to when to run for office . . . is taken partly in the manner of a surf rider who bides his time until the right wave looms up then rides his board upon it to the beach" (1961: 81). We have already stressed that most of these districts provided practical opportunities for Democratic candidates, that is, either Democrats or Republicans were not running again or Republican incumbents were vulnerable for one reason or another. Something more is implied by Barber's question, Do they want me, however. The opportunity should be complemented with indications of support for the candidacy. This support might be directly interpreted from the candidate's previous political experience or indirectly assumed from events within the district. Direct encouragement might legitimately be interpreted from:

Previous electoral victories (e.g., at the state and local levels).

Narrow electoral losses in a previous challenge to incumbent.

Large increase in electoral percentage over a previous election.

Previously a Democratic district.

Active political party support.

Active support from interest groups or volunteers.

Support may also be legitimately expected to flow from other events:

Redistricting to favor your party.

Population change within the district.

Ticket advantage (i.e., strong candidates for other offices).

Issue disadvantage for the incumbent (e.g., Watergate or the economy in 1974).

Personal disadvantage for the incumbent (e.g., age, indictment, personal/family problem of some kind).

The record shows that many of the 74 Democrats studied here had one or more of these advantages. That is, they had ample encouragement to run for Congress. Even if we take the worst cases—that is, districts in which Republican incumbents won by more than 60 percent in 1972—we see that several candidates had reason to estimate that they were wanted. Of course one might argue that all Democratic candidates were more optimistic than usual as a result of Watergate, but this issue affected districts and Republican candidates differently. For example in North Carolina two presumably safe Republican seats fell to the Democrats in part it seems because of Senator Sam Ervin's prominent role as chairman of the Senate Watergate hearings. In other districts, the combination of issues, population shifts, previous campaigns, and the age or overconfidence of incumbents provided the Democratic challengers with reasons to be encouraged.

The 1974 Democratic freshman class has been marked as having had a profound influence on Congress. Elected at a virtual fever pitch of emotion concerning political ethics, these representatives received considerably more attention than is normal for newcomers to Congress. We do not have the full complement of evidence required by Barber's categories, but from what has been presented it would seem that an unusually high number of *lawmakers* went to the House of Representatives in 1975. Pressed by their own conceptions of the job to

TABLE 4 – 8
Advantages of the "worst case" Democrats in 1974

Candidate	District	Democratic percentage 1972	Democratic percentage 1974	Advantage
Timothy Wirth	Colo., 2	33.5	51.9	Population change, issue advantage, ticket advantage
Elliot Levitas	Ga., 4	24.1	55.1	Previous victories, issue advantage
Martin A. Russo	Ill., 3	37.7	52.6	Party support, incumbent disadvantage
David W. Evans	Ind., 6	35.2	52.4	Previous electoral experience, issue advantage, incumbent disadvantage
Philip H. Hayes	Ind., 8	36.6	53.4	Previous electoral experience, potential Democratic district, group support, issue advantage
William J. Hughes	N.J., 2	34.3	58.1	Previous electoral experience, population change, issue advantage, incumbent disadvantage
Thomas J. Downey ...	N.Y., 2	33.2	52.2	Population change, incumbent disadvantage
Edward W. Pattison ...	N.Y., 29	30.1	54.5	Previous electoral experience, population change, incumbent disadvantage
Stephen L. Neal	N.C., 5	35.2	52.2	Potential Democratic district, issue advantage
W. G. Hefner	N.C., 8	39.8	57.0	Potential Democratic district, issue advantage
Glenn English	Okla., 6	27.3	54.5	Previous political experience, incumbent disadvantage
James Weaver	Ore., 4	37.4	52.9	Previous political experience, potential Democratic district, population change

SOURCE: Compiled primarily from data in Michael Barone, et al., *The Almanac of American Politics* (New York: E. P. Dutton, 1975).

be done and an unusual amount of media attention, these new members exhibited many of the lawmaker characteristics (1965: 216).

Defining characteristics: High in activity, high in willingness to return.

General legislative style: Attention to substantive tasks.

Background and expectations: Like Advertisers, young and mobile, but with deeper and more varied political roots and much more interest in full-time elective office.

Nominations: Seeks nomination in larger, moderately competitive, highly educated constituency. Offers interest and competence in issues.

Reactions: Concentrates on bills, decisions. Pleased at opportunity to produce desired legislation, participate in rational process, work cooperatively with others.

Self: Strong sense of individuality, personal standards. Stresses rationality; sense of the self as developing maintains and enhances self-approval.

Strategies: Conscious definition of central political roles.

Pattern persistence and change: Pattern meets strong needs for rational mastery, but environmental support varies. May turn to other arenas.

Legislative work: Makes most significant contributions, aided by congruence between personal strategies and legislative task organization. But may neglect need for inspiration, get impatient with formal properties.

Political future: Long, depending on competing demands for his talents and availability of productive political institutions.

The 1974 Democratic freshmen were highly motivated, generally confident of their resources, and nearly overcome with opportunities. Their positive affectation fits the lawmaker role as described by Barber. It also helps to explain a lot of what has happened in Congress since their election. To summarize: elections, political conditions in the district, personal motivations and experience, resources and opportunities all are important in the recruitment and election of legislators and provide important clues for understanding the policy behavior of representatives.

CAMPAIGNING

Once recruited and nominated, most candidates for the House of Representatives must campaign for the office by running against someone else. I have already noted that incumbents have a tremendous advantage in these contests. Their edge begins with their knowing long in advance that they are likely to be a candidate and can, therefore, perform accordingly in the exercise of their duties as a congressman. Thus it is that many members often describe their job as one of constant campaigning. "I campaign all the time. It's just that as the election approaches, decisions have got to be made—like brochures and schedules" (in Jennings and Zeigler, 1966: 33).

While it may be true that the successful House member engages in a kind of perpetual campaign, still, as suggested above, every second year there are periods of intense activity back home. It is this prescribed period of campaigning between the primary and the general election that we turn to now.

The first point to make is, of course, that objectively the campaign represents a different challenge in different congressional districts. Consider some extreme cases on selected census characteristics.

Population per square mile:
  Alaska at large, 0.5
  New York, 18th district, 77,922

Population change, 1960 − 70:
  California, 39th district, +130.3%
  South Dakota, 2d district, −4.2%

Percent black:
  Illinois, 1st district, 88.9%
  Minnesota, 7th district, 0.07%

Median family income:
  Illinois, 10th district, $16,576
  Mississippi, 3d district, $5,320[10]

The point is obvious. Planning a campaign to reach just over 300,000 people in the 566,432 square miles of Alaska is necessarily an enterprise of a quite different order than that to reach the 470,000 people crammed into the six square miles of New York's 18th district on Manhattan Island. But districts differ in other ways too that are relevant for understanding the nature of congressional campaigning. Several of these factors have been discussed in other settings, but are worth emphasis here:

Percentage of victory for the incumbent in the previous election

Reapportionment and redistricting

Voting turnout[11]

Issues and their effect

Type of election (presidential, mid-term, senator running, etc.)

Strength of opponent (including financing)

Timing of primary[12]

Any one of these factors may be influential in shaping the talk, expense, travel, and organization of the campaign. Thus look for consid-

---

[10] Data taken from U.S. Department of Commerce, Bureau of the Census, *Congressional District Data Book 93d Congress* (Washington, D.C.: U.S. Government Printing Office, 1973).

[11] For example in 1976 in two hotly contested districts, turnout differed widely. In the South Carolina fifth, 29 percent of the total population voted; in the Iowa first, 45 percent of the total population voted. Kenneth L. Holland (D) won the South Carolina fifth with 51.6 percent; James Leach (R) won the Iowa first with 52.1 percent.

[12] In 1978, congressional candidates in Illinois knew who their opponents were on March 21, over seven months in advance of the general election. Candidates in Hawaii, on the other hand, have only a month of campaigning after winning the primary.

erable variation among congressional districts when observing electoral politics.

All of the above factors are objective in the sense that they are measurable and we can agree in advance about the differences. There are also subjective considerations to mention in passing. Whatever objective differences exist, campaign behavior may also vary because of how the candidates view the challenge. Thus, for example, Huckshorn and Spencer report that many candidates challenging incumbents were optimistic beyond realism (1971:   87):

> [An] overwhelming number of [challenging] candidates . . . ran for unselfish reasons. Most of these candidates ran hopeless, badly financed campaigns at great personal sacrifice and with little prospect of reward. Relatively few indicated that their personal interests were of prime importance; indeed, there are far easier, cheaper, and more effective ways to accomplish personal advancement.

On the other side of the coin are the objectively safe incumbents who feel threatened by having any opposition at all. For many decades southern Democrats who won the primary were assured reelection, often because no Republican challenged them in the general election. Beginning in the 1960s, however, Republicans began to contest these districts, and Democratic incumbents typically reacted by waging a much more active campaign than was warranted by the challenge.

Then, of course, whatever the facts seem to be, candidates are convinced to campaign with a particular intensity and style because they are uncertain as to what makes a difference. Elsewhere I have observed that in campaigns "the candidate relies on the shotgun rather than the rifle" (in Jennings and Zeigler, 1966:   29). William Gore and Robert Peabody speak of a "spray of stimuli" in characterizing the various appeals during a campaign (1958:   65). And Richard F. Fenno, Jr., reports that (1978:   17):

> The fact is . . . that although representatives campaign furiously— and sometimes quite systematically—against their challengers, there remains a sizeable residue of uncertainty as to which campaign activity is related to which element of their support. . . . They worry about reelection support because they don't know for sure how to go about getting reelected. . . . They often decide . . . to campaign "just the way we did last time."

Whereas we know objectively that campaigns vary district-to-district, what we don't know, either as candidates or students of elections, is what technique works when and with whom. Campaigning remains more of an art than a science and thus continues to depend heavily on the subjective—on how candidates and their aides perceive the objective elements listed earlier. Alan L. Clem collected descriptions of seven 1974 congressional campaigns. He identified 14 variables that might help to explain what happens in a campaign (1976:   6 −13). The number of variables alone tells us something—that campaigns differ a lot. What is most common among the many districts is an uncertainty that leads to a frantic effort to touch as much of the district as possible, responding along the way to each and every effort to contact the candidate. Several years ago I sought to satisfy my curiosity about this campaign life of the members, and so I selected two very different districts (one in the most rural district of Maine, the other in midtown Manhattan) and followed the incumbent as he campaigned. Here is what I concluded (in Jennings and Zeigler, 1966: 29, 31):

> Both Mr. Rural and Mr. Urban . . . sensed, if they did not know for certain, that victory would come if they worked hard until election day. Their efforts were tireless. Despite the differences in techniques, organization, and financial resources, both candidates were trying to establish (or, rather to reestablish) themselves in the minds of party workers and voters as energetic, knowledgeable, educated, capable, aware representatives of the people. They stressed their expertise. They talked about their record. They enjoyed being asked to unravel complicated issues. If anything, they—not the constituents—were the instructors . . . both saw the campaign as a period in which they would meet as many people as possible in order to impress voters that they were well represented in Washington.

Of course, finding those voters represented quite a different challenge for each candidate.

> On one typical day, Mr. Rural traveled 215 miles, spent 17 hours, and met or talked to approximately 300 people. In the same time, Mr. Urban met or talked to from three to five times that many people, and his travel distance was measured in city blocks (in Jennings and Zeigler, 1966: 31).

It must be acknowledged that many people are in politics precisely because they like to be in demand in this way. The fast pace and scheduling problems make life interesting for them. Former Representative Clem Miller (D — California) described his life during a congressional recess (when the pace is very much like that during a campaign) as follows (1962: 75):

> When we first begin a tour, the commitments are well spaced out. But as time goes on, the schedule becomes choked with a succession of extra events that make each day tighter and tighter. Telephone calls begin to follow us around from place to place. Can I spare a few minutes of this? Can I see that person for five minutes? Can I talk to the annual meeting of the Soil Conservation District directors? It may mean skimping on lunch, shaving travel time, and postponing bedtime, but we generally work them in.

Miller conceded that "it's an exhilerating experience but an exhausting one" (1962: 77). Tragically Clem Miller was killed in an airplane accident, October 7, 1962, campaigning for reelection.

SPENDING MONEY TO WIN

One reasonable indicator of whether or not an active campaign is under way in a congressional district is the amount of money a candidate spends (or at least reports spending). Table 4 −9 shows a surpris-

TABLE 4 − 9
Number of districts with limited campaign expenditures in 1976

	Democratic candidate	Republican candidate	Total districts
Districts with no major party opponent	45	4	49
Districts in which one candidate reported expenditures of less than $10,000	32*	79	111
(less than $5,000)	(16)	(55)	
(less than $1,000)	(3)	(23)	
(no expenses reported)	(0)	(12)	
Districts in which both candidates reported expenditures of less than $10,000			4†
Total districts			164

* Includes two incumbents.
† Includes four Democratic incumbents.
SOURCE: Compiled from data in *Congressional Quarterly Weekly Report*, October 29, 1977. Includes both primary and general election expenditures.

ingly high number of districts which, by this measure, had little or no general election campaigning. The expenditures reported are for both the primary and general elections. Thus we can assume that in most instances where a challenger spent less than $10,000 the incumbent's expenditures were primarily directed to the primary or were designed to maintain contact with the district and were not campaign-oriented in the normal sense. The 164 districts identified in Table 4 −9 constitute nearly 40 percent of the total number. The average percentage of those spending less than $10,000 suggests they were wise—the Democrats averaged 30.6 percent, the Republicans 22.4 percent.

At the other end of the scale are the few districts in which at least one candidate reported expenditures in excess of $200,000. In 1976 there were 21 districts in which one candidate spent over $200,000 and five more in which both candidates spent over $200,000. In some of the former districts, most of the money was spent in the primary. For example in the Texas first district, Sam B. Hall, Jr., won the Democratic nomination in a runoff primary, then won the seat by 83.7 percent of the vote.

Not surprisingly the most money is typically spent in those districts that are hotly contested often because there is no incumbent. In 23 particularly close races in 1976 candidates reported expenditures of nearly $11 million, with both Democrats and Republicans averaging over $200,000 a piece (compared to an average expenditure of just over $70,000 for all House candidates in 1976).[13] In 11 of the 23 districts there was no incumbent running. In nine other of these districts the incumbent had won in 1974 by an average of 52 percent of the two-party vote, thus making them high opportunity districts for challengers. The California 27th takes honors for total expenditures in 1976. A Republican incumbent retired in 1976, and both parties had primary battles. Democrat Gary Familian won over seven other candidates with 35 percent of the vote; Republican Robert K. Dornan won over five other candidates with 31.6 percent of the vote. Familian reported expenditures of $637,080; Dornan reported $403,675. The general election campaign expenditures just escalated according to both candidates. "We were playing catch up," according to Dornan. "If he didn't go to television, we wouldn't have. If he didn't go to radio, we wouldn't have." Familian agreed that "It was a vicious circle."[14]

What these examples tell us once again is to be cautious about glib generalities in discussing House elections. One lesson above all comes through loud and clear—the membership of the House of Representatives in any one Congress has had varied recruitment and campaign experience. Thus to the extent that such experience influences how members participate in the policy process, it follows that this participation too will vary markedly from one member to the next.

In their study of House campaigns, Hart Research Associates concluded that most were "mom and pop operations, low on both money and professionalism."[15] Anyone ever associated with a congressional campaign would agree. The initiative and drive in these races, as compared to Senate campaigns, comes from the candidate and immediate staff, advisers, and friends. Again the incumbents have the advantage of existing organizations—one in Washington and one or more back in the district. Challengers have to create something new and go begging for money. The party is of only limited assistance in this effort in part because no political party unit quite fits the congressional district. Remember that the districts are subject to change. They cut across permanent governmental jurisdictional boundaries within a state— that is, those of cities, counties, and townships. As Huckshorn and Spencer put it: "the average candidate for Congress must build his organization across municipal and county party lines and must seek to weld together a highly personal campaign team (1971: 90−91).

---

[13] Calculated from data in *Congressional Quarterly Weekly Report*, October 29, 1977, pp. 2305−11, and Bibby et al., 1980: 31.

[14] *Congressional Quarterly Weekly Report*, October 29, 1977, p. 2300.

[15] As reported in *Congressional Quarterly Weekly Report*, October 29, 1977, p. 2300.

This is well worth remembering for its possible policy implications. That is, most members who get to Washington can legitimately claim that they got there on their own!

Does the national, state, or local party assist candidates once they form their own organization? The answer is some but not very much. In his study of congressional challengers in the 1964 election, Jeff Fishel found that a large majority of his respondents judged that the national and local party provided some, not much, or no campaign assistance. Huckshorn and Spencer too found that losing candidates believed lack of party support, particularly at local and state levels, was important in their defeat (inadequate organization and lack of money were cited as the most important factors). Incumbents and challengers in marginal districts have the advantage of financial aid from the Democratic and Republican congressional campaign committees. But this aid does not normally constitute a major part of campaign finances. Party committees of all types contributed 8 percent of the total reported receipts for House campaigns in 1976; 7 percent in 1978. The largest percentage in both years came from individual contributions of $100 or less (36 and 34 percent, respectively), again emphasizing the personal nature of these campaigns. Contributions to House candidates from nonparty political action committees (the PACs) increased from 22 percent to 26 percent of the total from 1976 to 1978 (causing concern by many who fear the influence of the PACs) (Malbin, 1978: 26).

It is important to emphasize the out of the hat organizational characteristics of House campaigns for at least two reasons. First it puts in perspective the more systematic descriptions of how campaigns are conducted—for example, the planning or strategy phase, the organizational and funding phase, the implementation phase, and so on. It is not that these activities are ignored. It is rather that typically they are both less systematic and grandiose than one might think. Second, as Richard F. Fenno, Jr., has suggested in his book *Home Style*, much of what goes on in the district is revealing of what one might expect to be represented in Washington.

Do incumbents win because they spend more money? Well they do typically spend more money (Jacobson, 1980: 54–55; 58–59). In 1978 on an average, incumbents reported spending over 50 percent more than challengers (Mann and Wolfinger, 1980: 627). But as suggested earlier, where incumbents were the safest, both they and their challengers spent less. The big money was spent in those districts where the incumbent won by less than 60 percent or lost. In fact in 1978, 19 victorious challengers spent an average of $217,083 compared to $200,607 spent by the incumbents they defeated. Results like this support the conclusion of Gary C. Jacobson that (1980: xv):

Campaign spending matters, and it matters most to candidates who are not incumbents. Indeed . . . what incumbents spend makes relatively little difference. Whether or not campaigns are seriously contested depends on the resources mobilized by nonincumbents.

This analysis complements that associated with the view stated earlier that incumbents stay in office in part—perhaps in large part—because they lack significant opposition. Presumably if all challengers could raise a million dollars they would stand a good (certainly better) chance of winning regardless of what the incumbent does. And Jacobson's logical conclusion is that public financing of congressional campaigns (a frequently proposed reform in recent years) is likely to assist challengers and thus lead to more competitive elections. "The more spending by all candidates, the better challengers are likely to do" (1980: 219).

REGULATING CAMPAIGN FINANCE

The matter of regulating the funding of campaigns deserves special attention because of the changes in recent years. The Federal Corrupt Practices Act of 1925 set limits on general election campaign expenditures for both House and Senate races, prohibited contributions from certain groups, controlled a few corrupt practices, and required reports to be filed. The act had so many loopholes, however, that it was virtually unenforceable. The excesses in campaign financing during the 1972 presidential election led directly to demands for reform. As John Gardner, then president of Common Cause put it:

The Watergate is not primarily a story of political espionage, nor even of White House intrigue. It is a particularly malodorous chapter in the annals of campaign financing. The money paid to the Watergate conspirators before the break-in—and money passed to them later—was money from campaign gifts.[16]

The Federal Elections Campaign Amendments of 1974 provided the most extensive controls ever enacted. It dealt with both presidential and congressional campaigns and, for the first time, included primary elections as well. The law had the following major provisions as far as congressional elections were concerned:[17]

1. Contributions were limited ($1,000 per individual for each primary, runoff, and general election, up to $25,000 total; $5,000 per

---

[16] Quoted in Congressional Quarterly, *Congress and the Nation Vol. IV, 1973–1976*, (Washington, D.C.: Congressional Quarterly, Inc., 1977), p. 988.

[17] For a fuller summary of the provisions and legislative action see *Congress and the Nation Vol. IV, 1973–1976*, pp. 988–1000. This discussion relies heavily on the material presented in this volume.

organization, political committee, or political party organization for each election, no aggregate limit) (altered by the 1976 act).

2. Candidates and their families were limited on how much they could contribute to their own campaigns ($35,000 for Senate races; $25,000 for House races) (later voided by the Supreme Court).

3. Spending was limited as follows (all later voided by the Supreme Court):

    a. Senate primaries: $100,000 or eight cents per eligible voter, whichever greater; Senate general elections: $150,000 or 12 cents per eligible voter, whichever greater.

    b. House primaries and general elections: $70,000 for each.

    c. National parties were limited to $10,000 per House candidate; $20,000 or two cents per voter (whichever greater) per Senate candidate.

4. Created an eight-member, bipartisan Federal Election Commission for administering the new law (later voided in this form by the Supreme Court).

5. Required each candidate to establish one central campaign committee and file regular reports with the Federal Election Commission (before and after each election) (altered by the 1976 Act).

6. Increased fines for violations (altered by the 1976 Act).

The attentive constitutional scholar would note possibilities for freedom of speech violations in this law—that is, to curb either contributions or spending is to limit one form of expression. A court case ensued and in *Buckley* v. *Valeo* (424 U.S. 1, 1976), the Supreme Court did hold certain sections of the law invalid. Campaign spending limits, but not individual or committee contributions, were held unconstitutional First Amendment violations. The Court also voided the limits on how much candidates themselves and their families could contribute to their own campaigns. Finally, the Federal Elections Commission was held to be unconstitutionally composed since some members were appointed by the Speaker of the House and the president pro tem of the Senate to perform executive-type functions (a violation of the separation of powers).

Congress quickly reconstituted the Federal Elections Commission as a presidentially appointed body with congressional approval and it established new limits on contributions. The 1974 Act only set limits on how much individuals and committees could contribute to candidates. The 1976 act also limited contributions to national party committees ($20,000 for individuals; $15,000 for a multicandidate committee) and to other political action committees ($5,000 for individuals; $5,000 for a committee). The Republican and Democratic national party and campaign committees were also made an exception to the senatorial candidate contribution limits imposed on other committees. They were permitted to contribute up to $17,500 per senatorial candidate. Finally, the penalties for violation were made even more stringent than in the 1974 act.

It is interesting to speculate about the motivations and policy effects of these changes in the law. Presumably the reforms themselves were driven by policy considerations. That is, one assumed that with no control over contributions or spending, special interests could buy access to a representative so as to influence his or her legislative behavior. Unfortunately, it is not altogether clear how the new law will prevent this access. But in any event, neither the reformers themselves nor students of legislative behavior have provided systematic analyses of what precisely happened before or what is likely to happen now. What is possible right now is to examine the increases in expenditures (the reporting has improved dramatically) and the sources of contributions (with special attention to the political action committees—the PACs).

Table 4 −10 shows the increases in expenditures, 1974 −1976 and

TABLE 4 −10
House campaign expenditures, 1974 −1978

	1974	1976	Percent change	1978	Percent change
All candidates	44.1*	60.0	(+36.1)	86.7	(+44.5)
All Democrats	23.4	32.0	(+36.8)	45.8	(+43.1)
All Republicans	20.6	28.1	(+36.4)	40.9	(+45.7)
Number spending less than $50,000	444	365	(−17.8)	293	(−19.7)
Number spending more than $200,000	10	31	(+210)	128	(+313)

* In millions.
SOURCE: Calculated from Bibby et al., 1980: 26−37.

they are impressive. Even accounting for the fact that improved reporting naturally tends to produce larger figures, the totals show that a lot of money is being spent on House races. Is it too much? That is a hard question to answer in the abstract but it is an interesting question for campaign finance reformers to ponder. Given what has been said about incumbency advantage in elections, it is hard to be for limiting spending *and* high turnover in House seats. If Jacobson is correct, more spending by all candidates threatens incumbents. And as Michael J. Malbin points out (1979: 28):

> What poses a greater threat to our representatives, the high cost of campaigning or the entrenched power of incumbency? As the situation stands now, the staff and perquisites available to incumbents make them almost unbeatable except by someone who can spend a lot of money on

the effort. Is the amount spend by challengers too much? The cost of campaigns now comes to less than the nation's advertising budget for soap, while the cost of running the federal government exceeds one fifth of the gross national product. In light of this, how can anyone seriously claim that the cost of keeping the incumbents on their toes is too high?

Having only recognized, not solved, the dilemma posed by escalating costs and incumbency advantage, we move on to consider the problem of where the money comes from. Earlier I indicated that many House campaigns are run as relatively small enterprises, with the largest percentage of contributions coming from those giving $100 or less. Individual contributions of all sizes amounted to 59 percent of funds raised for House races in 1976, 57 percent in 1978 (Malbin, 1979:   26). The next largest source of contributions is the PACs, and this has caused concern among many observers of congressional elections. On the average, the nonparty PACs (representing business, labor, or some ideological inclination—conservative or liberal) provided about one fourth of the funds to House candidates. Total PAC contributions to congressional campaigns have unquestionably increased, in part because of the increase in the number of PACs. In 1978 there were 303 labor and 450 business PACs; in 1980 labor PACs had increased to 318, but business PACs had mushroomed in number to 1,226.[18] Contributions to the parties also shifted. Democrats had traditionally received most of the PAC funds, but in 1980 Republican candidates were the principal beneficiaries. And the total PAC contributions predictably went up in 1980—as they had in previous years.

Labor has had political action committees for a long time (thus the traditional advantage for Democratic candidates from PAC contributions). Until 1974, however, corporations were banned from organizing PACs if they had federal contracts. Most large corporations either were doing business with the government or wanted to do so. This ban was lifted in 1974, hence inviting an increase in PAC organization and involvement in campaigns. Serious thought is being given to this increase in PAC contributions by Common Cause and others, and further campaign finance reform may be enacted in the future.

Regulating campaign contributions and spending has proved to be difficult. First there are the constitutional considerations associated with the First Amendment freedoms. The courts have said that money has a right to talk too. Second the whole issue is naturally teeming with partisan manuevering. Every proposal for change is understandably examined carefully for any advantage that might be gained by each party. Third the motivations for reform often grow out of desires for other kinds of changes—reducing the incumbency advantage, preventing access to representatives through the use of money,

---

[18] *Congressional Quarterly Weekly Report,* November 22, 1980; p. 3405.

getting the fat cats out of politics, improving policy results, and so on. Unfortunately, however, the science of reform is so undeveloped that the changes often lead to unforeseen often undesirable consequences not the least of which is a cycle of reforming the reforms even before the full effects are known.

SUMMARY

Looking back at this House membership component of the congressional population several lessons stand out as useful for understanding how, when, and why they might become involved in various networks.

1. The method by which a modern district is created induces an attentiveness back home. Aside from the few at-large districts, no representative can assume that the district will remain unchanged over a long period of time.
2. Representatives face very different types of electoral situations, both through time and across districts.
3. Incumbents have a definite edge in elections which may be reduced by redistricting or by the emergence of a dominant issue.
4. Recruitment is basically an unsystematic process which appears to play an idiosyncratic role in legislative behavior.
5. Campaigns are mostly individualized efforts by candidates who have learned to fend for themselves.
6. Campaign spending in House races has increased in recent years but not enough to improve the chances of challengers by very much. The new regulations have encouraged more contributions and spending.

David R. Mayhew, in *Congress: The Electoral Connection,* assumes "that United States congressmen are interested in getting reelected — indeed, in their role here as abstractions, interested in nothing else" (1974a: 13). Mayhew found that assumption useful in rationalizing how congressmen act. However useful to him, the statement oversimplifies the process and thus hides about as much as it reveals. What has been described here does not suggest that Mayhew is wrong, only that many forces are at work to complicate the reelection effort. He "conjure[s] up a vision of United States congressmen as single-minded seekers of reelection" (1974a: 5). Based on the preceding review we conjure up an image of representatives who are attentive to their constituencies; adaptive to changing conditions in the district, possibly even new boundary lines; and forced by several circumstances to arrange their own set of dependencies and collect their own resources. I think that this image will help us later to understand the participation of members in policy development.

5 How senators are chosen

Former Speaker Thomas B. Reed 1889 – 91, 1895 – 99 (R – Maine) once fictionalized a situation in which the president had come to be elected by the Senate. At the first election, the chief justice of the Supreme Court announced the result:

> Seventy six Senators [then the total number of senators] had each received one vote. For a moment a stillness as of death settled on the multitude. Never until that moment had the people realized that, like the Deacon's One Hoss Shay, the Senate of the United States was one level mass of wisdom and virtue, perfect in all its parts, and radiant from North to South with that light of intelligence which never shone on sea or shore. (McCall, 1914: 252).

Though engaging in his special brand of sarcasm, Speaker Reed was certainly correct in the implication that the United States Senate is a thing unto itself. Nelson W. Polsby calls it "a great forum, an echo chamber, a publicity machine" (1970: 487). Elsewhere I have described it as "an institution of 'functional self-indulgence'—a sort of adult 'Summerhill' . . . based on a remarkably human proposition: that social gain will be realized by permitting . . . self-promotion among the membership" (in Dodd and Oppenheimer, 1977:   249). I think the following discussion will support this image of a very special and distinctive institution.

WHAT THEY REPRESENT

In our first government under the Articles of Confederation, the one-house legislature was based on a concept of equal representation. States could send between two and seven representatives, but each state had only one vote. No one doubted that a central issue in forming a new government would be the maintenance of state sovereignty in devising the basis for representation in the legislature. It was, after all, the states that had been made independent by the revolution. A central government scarcely existed.

Likewise, when the Constitution was written, equality of representation for the states was fought for by those who estimated that a proportional representation system would be a great disadvantage for the small states. "The Senate, the principal compromise of the Constitution, brought to an end the great controversy over the method of representation—by states or by population" (Rogers, 1926:   10). Writing in *The Federalist* (Number 62), either Alexander Hamilton or James Madison observed that one could justify in theory a government "founded on a mixture of the principles of proportional and equal representation" (1937:   401 − 2).

> But it is superfluous to try, by the standard of theory, a part of the Constitution which is allowed on all hands to be the result, not of theory, but "of a spirit of amity, and that mutual deference and concession which the peculiarity of our political situation rendered indispensable."

> * * * * *

> In this spirit it may be remarked, that the equal vote allowed to each State is at once a constitutional recognition of the portion of sovereignty remaining in the individual States, and an instrument for preserving that residuary sovereignty.

This equal representation for jurisdictions was set forth in the following language in Article I, Section 3:

> The Senate of the United States shall be composed of two Senators from each State, chosen by the Legislature thereof, for six Years; and each Senator shall have one Vote.

Not content with this provision, the proponents of equal representation also included a guarantee in the amending provisions of Article V: "no State, without its Consent, shall be deprived of its equal Suffrage in the Senate."

Several important changes were made which made the Senate quite different from the unicameral Congress under the Articles.

1. The number of members (referred to as delegates in the Articles; senators in the Constitution) is uniform for all states (two each) rather than variable.
2. Senators' terms are for six years rather than three (actually under the Articles no delegate could serve "for more than three years in any term of six years").
3. Each senator has one vote rather than one vote for each state.
4. One third of the Senate is elected every second year rather than the annual appointment of all delegates under the Articles.

Despite these differences, one must acknowledge that the historical concept of representing jurisdictional sovereignty did carry over from our earliest Congress to the legislature formed by the Constitution. It is interesting to note that whereas many states sought to emulate this arrangement in forming their legislatures the Supreme Court, in *Reynolds* v. *Sims,* 1964, declared that both houses of a state legislature must be apportioned on a population basis. State senates are no longer permitted to follow the United States Senate precedent.

This representational base is only one of the features that make the Senate a unique institution. We have grown so accustomed to the idea of representing area that we seldom reflect on the practical consequences. In fact it was not such a serious problem in the early days of the republic. The disparity between the largest and smallest state, while sizeable, was not outrageous. In 1790, the largest state, Virginia, was approximately 12 times larger than the smallest, Delaware. In 1970, however, California with a population of 20 million was nearly 67 times larger than Alaska with 300,000. Further, Virginia's population was much closer to that of the majority of the states in 1790 than was California's in 1970. Besides Delaware, Virginia was over five times larger than just two other states (Georgia and Rhode Island). In 1970, California's population was over five times larger than 34 states (nearly 70 percent of the states); ten times larger than 19 states (nearly 40 percent of the states).

While there are many ways to make the point, it all comes down to the same conclusion. The United States Senate is a collection of representatives with remarkably different constituencies given the democratic, one-person, one-vote basis of much of the rest of the political system. Senators S. I. Hayakawa and Alan Cranston of California (at this writing) have more people to represent just in the Riverside-San Bernadino-Ontario metropolitan area outside Los Angeles than do the *six* senators from Alaska, Vermont, and Wyoming. California senators face an enormous challenge in campaigning, reflecting the interests and demands of constituents, and creating a staff organization that is responsive to problems within the state.

One of the more obvious consequences of the one-state, two-senators rule is the inevitable inequity in staff allowances. A formula has been devised to provide more staff for the more populous states, but the very largest states don't have the votes to force full equality. Thus, California has approximately twice the staff allowances of Alaska, not the 67 times suggested by the difference in population. As a result, the citizens of Alaska and Wyoming have about $1.20 worth of staff assistance on a per capita basis for each senator; the citizens of California and New York have less than five cents worth![1] Of course, the Supreme Court has never been able to apply the one-person, one-vote rule to the Senate and so one person, one equal share of staff has never even arisen. It is an issue worth examining, however, given the wide disparity in staff assistance among senators.

Small-state senators would argue that their job in Washington is every bit the equal of large-state senators. That is, they have an equal number of committees and must act on legislation of national concern and interest. I have never heard one argue that the constituency service challenge is in any sense equal, however, suggesting that the home-based staff might be reduced for these senators rather than dramatically enlarged for large-state senators. As will be discussed later, the problem in any such change is in defining what is *home-based* staff since each office organizes the work differently. Some handle constituency problems in the state, others in Washington, many in both.

But we are beginning to get ahead of the story line. For present purposes it is enough to recall the fact that senators represent something called states. Having just two from each accepts and reinforces the concept of sovereignty (i.e., equality in the independence of authority) and contributes to the special nature of the Senate as a legislative body. Senators are not just representatives; they are also ambassadors of sovereign states.

TYPES OF ELECTIONS

Much of the discussion of House elections applies to the Senate as well. That is, senators, too, often face primaries, sometimes runoffs. They also must occasionally compete with other major candidates running at the same time. House elections always coincide with a senator's election but are not normally as distracting for senators as a

---

[1] Susan Webb Hammond, "The Operation of Senators' Offices," in U.S. Senate, Commission on the Operation of the Senate, *Senators: Offices, Ethics, and Pressures*, 94th Cong., 2d Sess., 1977, p. 4.

senatorial race is to House members (either in drawing funds or in diverting public attention). Senators run with the president every other election, just as do House members. The difference is, of course, that senators normally run only once every six years. Thus, for example, Senator H. John Heinz, III (R — Pennsylvania) was first elected in 1976 (a presidential year), his term expires in 1982 (a midterm year), and again in 1988 (a presidential year). And senators also will occasionally run with gubernatorial candidates except in those few states where governors are elected in odd-numbered years.

But the more interesting feature of Senate elections is historical in nature. Recall that Article I, Section 3 calls for state legislatures to choose senators. And three classes were established so as to provide continuity in the Senate. The first class was up for reappointment after two years, the second class after four years, and the third class after six years. Therefore all senators terms would be six years. The initial classes were determined by lot, though no state had two senators in the same class so as to avoid having both elected at the same time. The original distribution is listed in Table 5 — 1. When states were admit-

TABLE 5 — 1
Senatorial classes, First Congress (1789 — 1791)

Class 1 (two-year terms)	Class 2 (four-year terms)	Class 3 (six-year terms)
Ellsworth, Conn.	Bassett, Del.	Johnson, Conn.
Read, Del.	Few, Ga.	Gunn, Ga.
Carroll, Md.	Strong, Mass.	Henry, Md.
Dalton, Mass.	Wingate, N.H.	Langdon, N.H.
Elmer, N.J.	Paterson, N.J.	King, N.Y.
Schuyler, N.Y.	Johnston, N.C.	Hawkins, N.C.
Maclay, Pa.	Stanton, R.I.	Morris, Pa.
Foster, R. I.	Butler, S.C.	Izard, S.C.
Grayson, Va.	Lee, Va.	

SOURCE: *Biographical Directory of the American Congress, 1774 — 1971* (Washington, D.C.: U.S. Government Printing Office, 1971), pp. 51 — 52.

ted, the new senators drew their class by lot. Thus, the integrity of the classes has been maintained with the expansion of the Senate.

It is edifying to trace the history of a particular Senate seat through time. Table 5 — 2 shows the men who have held one of the Pennsylvania Senate seats from 1789 to the present. This particular seat was in Class 1. That is, William Maclay, by lot, drew an initial two-year term. The six-year term sequence then began in 1790, with the most recent election at this writing being 1976 (186 years, 31 six-year terms). Several points are worth noting in Table 5 — 2. This particular seat was vacant

TABLE 5–2
The Class 1 Senate seat in Pennsylvania, 1789– present

Senator	Party*	Service	Reason for leaving
William Maclay	D– R	1789– 91	Retired
Vacancy		1791– 93	
Albert Gallatin	D– R	1793– 94	Election declared void†
James Ross	F	1794– 1803	Not reelected
Samuel Maclay	D– R	1803– 09	Retired
Michael Leib	D– R	1809– 14	Appointed postmaster in Philadelphia
Jonathan Roberts	D– R	1814– 21	Not reelected
Vacancy		1821	
William Findlay	D– R	1821– 27	Appointed director of the U.S. Mint
Isaac D. Barnard	F	1827– 31	Resigned
George M. Dallas	D	1831– 33	Declined reelection
Samuel McKean	D	1833– 39	Not reelected
Vacancy		1839– 40	
Daniel Sturgeon	D	1840– 51	Retired (later treasurer)
Richard Brodhead	D	1851– 57	Not reelected
Simon Cameron	R	1857– 61	Appointed secretary of war
David Wilmot	R	1861– 63	Retired
Charles R. Buckalew	D	1863– 69	Not reelected
John Scott	R	1869– 75	Retired
William A. Wallace	D	1875– 81	Not reelected
John I. Mitchell	R	1881– 87	Accepted judgeship
Matthew S. Quay	D	1887– 99	Deadlock in legislature
Vacancy		1899– 1901	
Matthew S. Quay	R	1901– 04	Death
Philander C. Knox	R	1904– 09	Appointed secretary of state
George T. Oliver	R	1909– 17	Retired
Philander C. Knox	R	1917– 21	Death
William E. Crow	R	1921– 22	Death
David A. Reed	R	1922– 35	Defeated
Joseph F. Guffey	D	1935– 47	Defeated
Edward Martin	R	1947– 59	Retired
Hugh Scott	R	1959– 77	Retired
H. John Heinz, III	R	1977–	

* Key to parties: D– R = Democratic– Republican; F = Federalist; D = Democratic, R = Republican.
† Albert Gallatin was declared ineligible for not having been a citizen of the United States for nine years.
SOURCE: Congressional Quarterly, *Guide to U.S. Elections* (Washington, D.C.: Congressional Quarterly; 1975) p. 475; and *Biographical Directory of the American Congress, 1774– 1961* (Washington D.C.: U.S. Government Printing Office, 1961).

on four occasions (1791 – 93, 1821, 1839 – 40, 1899 – 1901). Vacancies were not uncommon since state legislatures failed to reach agreement on who should represent the state in the Senate. The Constitution was not of much assistance in determining how state legislatures were to select senators. Some states required a majority of each house sitting separately; others elected senators in joint session. In 1866 Congress sought to make the process more uniform and enacted the following procedures:

1. The first ballot by each house separately.
2. If no candidate received a majority, subsequent ballots by joint sessions.
3. The first ballot taken on the second Tuesday after the new legislature organized.
4. Subsequent ballots taken on every legislative day thereafter until a candidate is elected.[2]

In the Pennsylvania Class 1 seat, the legislature adjourned in 1899 without electing a senator. The governor then appointed the incumbent, Matthew S. Quay, to the seat but the Senate refused to seat him since the vacancy had occurred during the time the legislature was in session and the Constitution clearly specifies that governors may make temporary appointments only when a vacancy occurs during a legislative recess. Delaware actually went without any representation in the Senate between 1901 and 1903. The legislature was deadlocked by a factional dispute in the Republican Party. The Class 1 seat was left unfilled in 1899; the Class 2 seat was open in 1901 and it too was left unfilled until 1903.

Note also the difference in average length of term before and after the direct election of senators. The average length of service for the 20 senators (excluding Gallatin) before direct election was slightly over 6 years; the average length of the 5 senators (excluding Crow, who was a gubernatorial appointee and never elected) after direct election was slightly under 12 years. Only Daniel Sturgeon and Matthew S. Quay were elected to two full terms in the earlier period.

Finally, many senators in the early period voluntarily left the Senate after one term or before. The high turnover was not entirely due to party shifts in the legislature. Some were appointed to other positions; others simply retired. This high turnover was not peculiar to Pennsylvania. Georgia had 24 Class 2 and 16 Class 3 senators (excluding appointees not later elected) before direct election (a 116-year period— actually 126 years, but Georgia was not represented for 10 years in the Civil War period). Since direct election—a 64-year period—they have had but four each of Class 2 and Class 3 senators. We will have more to say about this greater longevity of senators at a later time.

Pressure for the direct election of senators developed over a period of years. The House passed constitutional amendments on five occasions toward the end of the old and beginning of the new century, but the Senate did not act. Of course, selection of senators was frequently an issue in state legislative elections, but this was hardly a substitute for direct election. The states themselves started to act after the turn of the century. Oregon was the first state to enact a law providing for a

---

[2] A portion of this discussion relies on that in Congressional Quarterly, *Guide to U.S. Elections* (Washington, D.C.: Congressional Quarterly, 1975), p. 448.

sort of advisory popular election of senators. Legislatures were not bound by the results, but in 1908 a Republican legislature selected a Democrat who had won the popular poll and thus set an important precedent. Several other western and midwestern states adopted the Oregon method.[3] George W. Norris (R — Nebraska, 1913 — 43) describes how the process worked in his case (1961: 162):

> Under the Oregon plan the political parties were able to nominate candidates at the primaries for the United States Senate. I won the Republican nomination, and A. C. Shallenberger . . . was the Democratic choice. . . .
>
> Mr. Shallenberger and I fought out the campaign in 1912 in precisely the same fashion that we would have campaigned had there been a direct vote. . . . We had accepted the pledge made by candidates to the state legislature as binding, although this action was merely a matter of honor.
>
> In the November election a strange development took place. I defeated Mr. Shallenberger, to discover that the majority of the members of the legislature were Democrats. Among some of the more reactionary Democrats a feeling quickly developed they should endeavor to induce members of the legislature to disregard the pledge given under the Oregon plan and elect a United States senator who was a Democrat. It was nipped in the bud before it got very far. Statements from a few of the most prominent Democrats . . . that they considered themselves honor-bound to fulfill their pledge . . . quickly settled the move of these reactionaries.

It was in large part because of the policy implications of party and state legislative control of United States senators that pressure developed to change the procedure. James Bryce describes the process typically employed (1915: 100):

> Choice by a legislature had come to mean choice by party majority in a legislative caucus, and the determination of that caucus had often been prearranged by a small group of party managers; or if that did not happen secretly, it had been settled in a party convention which directed the members of the party in the legislature how to cast their votes. There was anyhow little room left for free selection by the legislature.

The direct election of senators was consonant with several reforms undertaken during this period to break the hold of political parties over elections and the legislative process (others included the direct primary, presidential primaries, and reduction of the Speaker's power).

The 17th Amendment was ratified May 31, 1913. It changed two important words: "*chosen* by the *Legislature* thereof" to "*elected* by the

---

[3] See *Guide to U.S. Elections*, pp. 450 — 51; Bryce, 1915: 100 — 102.

people thereof." The amendment also provides that a state legislature can empower the governor to make temporary appointments in the case of vacancies "until the people fill the vacancies by election as the legislature may direct." Blair Lee (D — Maryland) was the first popularly elected senator, in a special election, November 1913. The 1914 midterm election was the first test of the new method, however. Fears that incumbents would be defeated were allayed when 23 of 25 senators elected previously by state legislatures and seeking reelection were returned. None was defeated in the general election; the two not returned failed to get renominated.[4]

One is taken by the justification for the original plan of having state legislatures select senators. Hamilton or Madison argued that (1937: 401, my emphasis):

> It is recommended by the double advantage of favoring a select appointment, and of giving to the state governments such an agency in the formation of the federal government as must secure the authority of the former, and *may form a convenient link between the two systems.*

This summary well characterizes the Senate as a council of ambassadors who presumably are there to reflect the interests and problems of the state and its government. This important connection was eliminated with the direct election of senators. Also reduced was the role and influence of the state political party, with important consequences in Congress. Thus the historical shift in type of election to the Senate appears to have had significant consequences, few of which have ever been studied systematically but all of which certainly deserve full discussion by students of politics.

CHANGING TENURE

The point was made in Chapter 4 that once in, House members have a very good chance of staying in office. In a study of incumbency return in the post-World War II period, Warren L. Kostroski concluded that the figures for the Senate were very much like those of the House. "Both rates are highly and unexpectedly close" (1973: 1217). Kostroski looked only at those elections in which an incumbent was running, however. He did not include incumbents who retired, ran for other office, or lost in primaries. When these senators are included one notes quite striking differences in the rate of return compared to the House. On an average the following percentage differences from House races are noted in comparing the data in Tables 4 — 2 and 5 — 3:

1. A lower percentage of incumbent senators seek reelection.
2. A higher percentage of senators lose in both the primaries and general election.

---

[4] *Guide to U.S. Elections,* p. 451.

3. A significantly lower percentage of incumbents are returned to the Senate.

Two other important observations can be made in comparing the House and Senate figures. First, the Senate results vary much more dramatically from one election to the next than do the House results. The range of incumbent return is from 55.2 percent in 1980 to 96.6 percent in 1960 (a 41.4 percent difference) of the senators seeking reelection and from 42.9 percent in 1978 to 82.4 percent in 1960 (a 39.5 percent difference) of all seats up for reelection in any one year. The comparable ranges for the House are 86.6 to 96.8 percent in the return of incumbents (a 10.2 percent difference) and 78.9 to 91.0 percent in the return of all representatives (a 12.1 percent difference). Predicting Senate elections appears to be a risky enterprise given these large variations.

Second, there are striking differences between the first six elections (1956 – 66) and the next seven (1968 – 80). Observe the averages for these two periods at the bottom of Table 5 – 3. Here is impressive evidence that the United States Senate has undergone important changes in recent years. On an average nearly 45 percent of a particular class failed to return in this second period (1968 – 80) for one reason or another; just over 30 percent suffered primary or general election defeats. Of course in the Senate the turnover in any one year is

TABLE 5– 3
Number and percentage of senatorial incumbents winning reelection, 1956– 1980

Year	Number of elections	Incumbents seeking reelection	Lost in primary	Lost in general election	Returned to Senate	As percent of whole group	As percent of whole Senate*
1956	35	29 (82.9%)	0 (0.0%)	4 (13.8%)	25 (86.2%)	71.4%	90%
1958	34	28 (82.4%)	0 (0.0%)	10 (35.7%)†	18 (64.3%)	52.9	84
1960	34	29 (85.3%)	0 (0.0%)	1 (3.4%)	28 (96.6%)	82.4	94
1962	39	35 (89.7%)	1 (2.9%)†	5 (14.3%)‡	29 (82.9%)	74.4	90
1964	35	33 (94.3%)	1 (3.0%)	4 (12.1%)†	28 (84.8%)	80.0	93
1966	35	32 (91.4%)	3 (9.4%)†	1 (3.1%)	28 (87.5%)	80.0	93
1968	34	28 (82.4%)	4 (14.3%)	4 (14.3%)	20 (71.4%)	58.8	86
1970	35	31 (88.6%)	1 (3.2%)	6 (19.4%)‡	22 (71.0%)	62.9	87
1972	33	27 (81.8%)	2 (7.4%)†	5 (18.5%)	20 (74.1%)	60.6	87
1974	34	27 (79.4%)	2 (7.4%)†	2 (7.4%)	23 (85.2%)	67.6	89
1976	33	25 (75.7%)	0 (0.0%)	9 (36.0%)	16 (64.0%)	48.5	83
1978	35	25 (71.4%)	3 (12.0%)‡	7 (28.0%)†	15 (60.0%)	42.9	80
1980	34	29 (85.3%)	4 (13.8%)	9 (31.0%)	16 (55.2%)	47.1	82
Averages:							
1956– 80	34.6	28.3 (81.8%)	1.6 (5.7%)	5.2 (18.4%)	22.2 (78.4%)	64.2	86.8
1956– 66	35.3	31.0 (87.8%)	0.8 (2.6%)	4.2 (13.5%)	26.0 (83.9%)	73.7	90.7
1968– 80	34	27.4 (80.6%)	2.3 (8.4%)	6.0 (21.9%)	18.9 (69.0%)	55.6	84.9

* Those incumbents elected added to those not up for reelection.
† Includes one appointee seeking election to a full term.
‡ Includes two appointees seeking election to a full term.
SOURCE: *Congressional Quarterly Weekly Report,* April 5, 1980, p. 908, and Bibby et al., 1980: 15.

limited due to the fact that only one third of the full membership is normally up for reelection (with any additions due to special elections for deaths or midterm resignations). If, however, we look at the last three elections (1976, 1978, 1980), the turnover is quite astonishing. Of the 99 senators up for reelection in this period, 23 retired or did not seek reelection for other reasons and 32 were defeated in either the primary or general election. Here then is a turnover of 55 senators for the three-election periods, which means that when the 97th Congress met over half of the members of the Senate were serving their first term! Note also the final column in Table 5 — 3. With two thirds of the Senate not up for reelection one naturally expects the Senate to have a higher return on total membership in any one election than the House. Such is the case, 1956 — 66 (an average 90.7 percent return for the whole Senate compared to an average return rate of 84.1 percent for the House). In the 1968 — 80 period, however, the figures are nearly the same, 84.9 percent for the Senate, 84.8 percent for the House. And in the last three elections in Table 5 — 3, an average of 81.6 percent of the Senate has returned compared to 83.3 percent of the House. This is truly a stunning figure given the fact that the Senate begins an election with 67 percent of its members already in place and the House begins with none (or those few who have no opposition). Staggered Senate terms actually have provided *less* continuity in membership in recent elections than coincident House terms. As the chairman of the National Republican Senatorial Committee in 1980, Senator H. J. Heinz, III (Pennsylvania), observed: "Being an incumbent Senator is increasingly hazardous to one's political health."[5]

This increased turnover has reduced the average length of service of senators over the past decade. In 1967, the senators had nearly 11 years service on the average (11.4 for Democrats, 9.5 for Republicans); in 1977 this average dropped to just over 9.5 years service (10.3 for Democrats, 8.2 for Republicans), and in 1981 it was down to 7.5 years service (10 for the Democrats and 5.3 years—less than one term—for the Republicans). But these averages do not tell the full story. In 1971, just over a quarter of the senators (27) were serving their first term (i.e., had been elected in the last three elections). In 1981 over half (55) were freshmen! What an astounding change. The cartoon image of white-haired and heavy-jowled senators with string ties is simply no longer appropriate.

Who is the Senate requires a quite different response in the late 1970s than for the recent past. After many years of relative stability in membership, the world's most extraordinary legislative body is clearly undergoing important changes. The full implications are not clear as

[5] National Republican Senatorial Committee, *1980 Senate Races,* July 11, 1980, p. 2.

yet but we will later seek to identify the more important policy developments that appear traceable to these changes.

WHY DO SENATORS LOSE?

I observed in Chapter 4 that scholars have been intrigued with the matter of a high return of incumbents in the House. Every bit as interesting is the question of why Senate incumbents have been treated so badly at the polls. Lacking data on the subject one might make a very good case for just the opposite result. After all, House members must run frequently and thus are continually exposed to their electorates. Relatively few House members serve in leadership positions and therefore most do not get national attention.

Senators, on the other hand, have long terms in which to ingratiate themselves with their publics. They also have large staffs and more access to the media. Television reporters are more likely to focus on senators than representatives when seeking congressional opinion on major issues. Thus many senators have the opportunity to become national figures. In fact many senators are touted as presidential candidates. Also, given the smaller number of senators most either chair or serve as ranking minority members on a committee or subcommittee and thus are in a position to (1) get additional staff and (2) aid their states directly from this leadership position. The case seems quite strong that incumbent senators should be invulnerable—or at least as safe as House members. But they are not. In the 1980 elections 18 senators with combined Senate service of nearly 300 years either retired or were defeated in primaries or the general election. The chairmen of the Committees on Agriculture, Nutrition, and Forestry; Appropriations; Foreign Relations, Select Intelligence; and Select Small Business were all defeated. Why?

The analysis of this question begins by reminding ourselves why it is that incumbent representatives win. Recall their advantage in voter recognition over their challengers. Theirs is an electoral environment that they can control. The state legislature gives the district life, but the representative gives it meaning. All House members have a concept of what this geographical area is—as a population and a place to get reelected (Fenno, 1978: chapter 1).

Senators represent sovereign states and are much less in control of their electoral environment. "Other elections occur within the state that may affect them; they have little contact with the state government and little or no control over it (in Sandoz and Van Crabb, 1981:   99). Senators are therefore directly affected by events within their constituencies. They are politically exposed to a much greater extent than representatives.

Still, until recently, incumbent senators had respectable return rates—falling below 70 percent just once between 1956 and 1974 (see Table 5– 3).[6] What appears to be happening recently is that challengers to incumbent senators are more successful than their House counterparts in achieving recognition among the voters. Table 5 – 4 shows

TABLE 5– 4
Voter recognition, rating, and contact with House and Senate candidates, 1978

	House			Senate		
Percent of voters who:	In-cumbent	Chal-lenger	Difference	In-cumbent	Chal-lenger	Difference
1. Recognized and rated	93%	44%	−49%	96%	86%	−10%
2. Rated positively	73	17	−56	61	48	−13
3. Had some contact	90	44	−46	94	82	−12
4. Received mail from	71	16	−55	53	32	−20
5. Read about	71	32	−39	73	63	−10
6. Heard on radio	34	15	−19	45	37	− 8
7. Saw on TV	50	24	−26	80	70	−10

SOURCE: Mann and Wolfinger, 1980: 623– 27.

huge differences in voter recognition, rating, and contact with House and Senate challengers in the 1978 congressional elections. "In Senate elections, voters choose between two candidates they tend to recognize and remember contact with" (Hinckley, 1980:   459). In fact the high percentage of voter recognition and contact with challengers nearly equals that of House incumbents. And a higher percentage of voters see Senate challengers on television or hear them on radio than see or hear House incumbents (a result of the fact that many House candidates rely more on mail than broadcast media).

Do these results support the view that the incumbency advantage melts away if the challenging candidate is successful in becoming known to the voters? Not quite. After all we don't have trend data showing the change in recognition over time for each set of elections. And we must be very cautious about generalizing from Senate to House elections. But we certainly do pick up important clues from Table 5 – 4 about why it is incumbent senators are losing in such great numbers. What were identified as advantages may be just the opposite in a period of voter dissatisfaction with the performance of the national government. As Alan I. Abramowitz concludes (1980:   633):

> Several factors may help to explain the difference between House and Senate elections. A House district is more likely to be dominated by one

---

[6] Though the immediate post—World War II period witnessed high turnover in the Senate—averaging 62.5 percent, 1946 – 52 (Bibby, et al., 1980:   15).

party than a state. In addition, Senate challengers generally appear to wage more visible and effective campaigns than House challengers. . . . Finally, voters may use different criteria to evaluate the performance of senators and representatives. Senators appear to be associated more often with controversial national issues than representatives, whose positions on such issues do not generally receive as much publicity. Their greater prominance in the media may result in senators having less control than representatives over the information which voters receive about their performance.

There is bitter irony in this analysis for senators. The Senate has long been viewed as the epitome of legislative service—a goal to strive for by state legislators and members of the House of Representatives. But when times are bad, the greater prominence, sustained in part by the impressive resources available to senators, insures (1) more serious challenges and (2) increased likelihood that the senator will be identified with the national politics that is blamed for the bad times. A natural response on the part of incumbents to these developments is to spend more—thus contributing to cost spirals in campaigning.

RECRUITMENT

The House and Senate are, of course, coequal legislative bodies. While their specific powers and duties differ somewhat, the very nature of the compromise that led to the establishment of the two bodies suggested institutional equality. In their day-to-day relationships, the House and Senate treat each other as coequal bodies. The president, too, cannot afford to favor one chamber over the other where each has authority to act. Still, primarily due to their smaller numbers and longer terms, senators are judged to be more important than House members. The House as a body may be equal to the Senate; individual members are not. Whereas many House members resign to run for the Senate, the reverse simply does not happen. The one former senator in the House at this writing (Claude Pepper, D — Flordia) was defeated in a senatorial primary and subsequently ran for a House seat. When Representative William S. Cohen (R — Maine) ran for the Senate in 1978, his friend, Thomas Railsback (R — Illinois) said: "Just remember when you get to the Senate, don't become like the rest of those bastards" (Cohen, 1981: 25). When he won a Senate seat, the new Senator Cohen reported that (1981: 27):

> During the first six weeks of 1978, I received more invitations to speak than I had had during the entire two preceding years. I do not recall a commensurate increase in wisdom during that six-week period which justified new confidence in my judgment. In fact, I had even less confidence in my judgment.

> The morning after President Carter recognized China, I received a
> call from a reporter from a major newspaper. She had eight questions
> concerning the decision. . . .
>
> As a member of the House, I would not have been called for my
> opinion. But it is implicitly assumed by the press, local as well as na-
> tional, that a senator does have an opinion.

I make this point about the greater prestige of senators because
recruitment is not normally a major problem, particularly in recent
years when Senate seats are increasingly competitive. As with House
seats, there are differences among the states, to be sure. Thus Republicans in particular will still concede senatorial races for lack of a willing
candidate. But this too has changed through the years. Between 1948
and 1962, Republicans conceded an average of four Senate seats to the
Democrats each election, mostly in the South. Between 1964 and 1980
an average of just one seat was conceded by Republicans.

Several factors make it easier to generalize about Senate recruitment
as compared to that in the House. First, appointments by governors
are frequent when a senator dies or resigns in midterm. The constitutional provision reads as follows (17th Amendment): "the legislature of
any State may empower the executive thereof to make temporary appointments until the people fill the vacancies by election as the legislature may direct." One might expect that such an appointment would
be a sizeable advantage in winning election. The record does not support this conclusion, however. In the first place, appointments are
frequently made with the understanding (explicit or implicit) that the
appointee will not run. Wives of senators are occasionally appointed
(as with Muriel Humphrey upon the death of her husband in 1978), or
distinguished members of community and state are chosen for whom
the short term is an honor, a full term would be a burden. Occasionally
governors appoint themselves, a practice that is apparently not looked
upon with favor by the electorate since such persons frequently lose in
the subsequent election (only Albert B. Chandler, D—Kentucky, was
successful of the eight governors who have tried this ploy).[7] During the
period 1968—78, 11 senatorial appointments were made by governors.
Of these, three didn't seek election, one was ineligible to succeed
himself (Arkansas law does not permit an appointee to run for the
office), four lost in the primary, two lost the general election, and one
was subsequently elected.

Second, the career lines of senators are somewhat more fixed than
in the House. For Woodrow Wilson, writing in 1885, the obvious place
to recruit senators was in the House of Representatives (1885:   195).

> There cannot be a separate breed of public men reared specially for
> the Senate. It must be recruited from the lower branches of the rep-

---

[7]*Congressional Quarterly Weekly Report*, March 25, 1978, p. 460.

resentative system, of which it is only the topmost part. No stream can be purer than its sources. The Senate can have in it no better men than the best men of the House of Representatives; and if the House of Representatives attract (sic) to itself only inferior talent, the Senate must put up with the same sort. I think it is safe to say, therefore, that though it may not be as good as could be wished, the Senate is as good as it can be under the circumstances. It contains the most perfect product of our politics, whatever that product may be.

It is not difficult to determine whether Wilson is right about this career line. James Bryce found that 36 of the 92 senators in the 61st Congress (39.1 percent) and 28 of the 96 senators in the 62nd Congress (29.2 percent) had served in the House. An even higher percentage had served in state legislatures (42.4 and 40.6 percent respectively). He also noted that "many [senators] had been judges or state governors" (1915: 118 — 19).

Donald R. Matthews produced a more systematic study of the channels to the Senate in 1960. Based on an examination of the biographical data of 180 senators from the 1950s, Matthews showed that nearly 50 percent of his sample began public service careers in law enforcement or the state legislature (see Table 5 — 5). On the other

TABLE 5 — 5
First and last public office of senators, Matthews sample of 180

	Percent first	Percent last
U.S. Senator/none	9%	9%
Governor	2	20
Representative	4	25
State legislator	21	9
State official	4	2
Local official	14	6
Law enforcement	28	13
Administrative official	14	16
Congressional staff	3	1
	100%	101%

SOURCE: Matthews, 1960: 51, 55. The figures for the last public office were recomputed. Matthews did not include those with *no* last public office.

hand, 45 percent moved from governorships or the House of Representatives into the Senate (i.e., as the last public office held before winning a Senate seat). Matthews was led to conclude (1960: 66):

the "typical" senator started a political career shortly after graduating from college by being elected state legislator or becoming a prosecuting attorney or some other kind of law-enforcement officer. . . . The chances are that he was elected to the Senate while, or shortly after serving as a state governor or member of the House of Representatives.

Table 5 – 6 shows some changes in this distribution for the 95th Congress (1977 – 79). Law enforcement and the state legislature still

TABLE 5 – 6
First and last public office of senators, 95th Congress

	First					Last				
	D	(Per- cent)	R	(Per- cent)	Total	D	(Per- cent)	R	(Per- cent)	Total
U.S. senator/none	4	6.5%	6	15.8%	10	4	6.5%	6	15.8%	10
Governor	1	1.6	0	0.0	1	7	11.3	6	15.8	13
Representative	7	11.3	4	10.5	11	18	29.0	12	31.6	30
State legislator	26	41.9	10	26.3	36	11	17.7	5	13.2	16
State official	2	3.2	1	2.6	3	7	11.3	3	7.9	10
Local official	6	9.7	8	21.1	14	4	6.5	5	13.2	9
Law enforcement	7	11.3	6	15.8	13	5	8.1	0	0.0	5
Administrative official	6	9.7	1	2.6	7	5	8.1	1	2.6	6
Congressional staff	3	4.8	2	5.3	5	1	1.6	0	0.0	1
Total	62		39		100	62		38		100

SOURCE: Compiled from biographical data in Michael Barone, et al., *The Almanac of American Politics*, 1978 (New York: Dutton, 1977).

spawned about half the political careers but the distribution between the two is quite different. State legislative experience was the entry point for 36 percent of the senators (15 percent greater than for Matthews' sample); law enforcement 13 percent (15 percent less than for Matthews' sample). The only other major changes in the left column in Tables 5 – 5 and 5 – 6 are those for the House of Representatives (7 percent greater in the 95th Congress) and administrative officials (7 percent less).

Turning to the last positions held before election to the Senate, note that again the combined figure for governor and the House of Representatives is close to that in the earlier period (43 percent as compared to 45 percent for Matthews' sample). But the distribution is different in this case as well. The number coming from the House has increased, the number from governorships has decreased. Other changes too are notable—more state legislators and state officials (other than governor); fewer law enforcement and federal administrative officials.

What explains these differences? It is difficult to say with any confidence. It is true that the job of governor became less attractive during the 1960s. The financial problems of many states resulted in high turnover among governors, with the effect that this position was not as attractive as a launching pad for either the Senate or the presidency. Perhaps this development also explains the increase in state legislators and other elected officials as the last step before Senate election. These persons no longer view the governorship as the logical next step on the way to the Senate. Rather they make their move from less politically sensitive positions.

To return now to Wilson's observation, we can see from at least three different periods that a consistently high percentage of senators do indeed come from the House of Representatives (normally close to 30 percent). Bryce also found that a large number of senators had state legislative experience. In the 95th Congress over 40 percent of the senators served in a state legislature at some point (very much the same proportions that Bryce found), and the combined percentages of members with major legislative experience (in the House or state legislature) as a last position before election to the Senate is a healthy 46 percent (see Table 5 − 6, last column). All of this evidence tends to support the thrust of Wilson's observation. It does not necessarily permit the conclusion that the Senate "contains the most perfect product of our politics," but the movement from the House, the state legislatures, governorships, and major state and federal elective and administrative posts, does indicate that the Senate is judged by many to be a very special place. Further support for this view is found in the number of presidential and vice presidential candidates spawned from the Senate. As the 95th Congress opened, four presidential candidates (Goldwater, 1964; Humphrey, 1968; McGovern, 1972; and Thurmond, 1948); four vice presidential candidates (Dole, 1976; Eagleton, a candidate for the first few weeks of 1972; Muskie, 1968; and Sparkman, 1952); one former vice president (Humphrey, 1965 − 69); and innumerable presidential aspirants (e.g., Bayh, Bentsen, Byrd, Church, Jackson, Kennedy, Muskie) were in the chamber.[8]

Where do the new senators come from? What are they like? How and why did they run? Just as in the House, there are certain high opportunity situations for senatorial candidates. Table 5 − 7 shows these for two election years, 1974 and 1976. No seats switched parties outside these high opportunity states. In 1974 the Democrats were successful in winning five of the vulnerable Republican seats; Republicans won only one of the Democratic seats. In 1976 the Republicans had more luck in winning Democratic seats (winning seven) but they were not able to hold their own vulnerable seats, and thus their gains were cancelled by seven Democratic wins.

Like their counterparts in the House, the new senators in 1974 and 1976 were significantly younger than those they replaced. The 1974

[8] The 95th Congress may have been a high-water mark for such persons. The 97th Congress (1981 − 83) had just two presidential candidates and two vice presidential candidates (though still many senators with presidential ambitions).

TABLE 5–7
High opportunity states for opposition party, 1974, 1976 Senate elections

Situation	Total in 1974	Won by Democrat	Total in 1976	Won by Democrat
1. Incumbent Democrat retiring	3	2	4	2
2. Incumbent Democrat loses primary	2	2	0	0
3. Incumbent Republican retiring	4	3*	4	3
4. Incumbent Democrat previous margin 50–54.9 percent	5	5	5	2
5. Incumbent Democrat previous margin 55–59.9 percent	2†	2	5	3
6. Incumbent Republican previous margin 50–54.9 percent	4	1	4	4
7. Incumbent Republican previous margin 55–59.9 percent	3	1	3	0
Totals	23	16 (69.6%)	25	14 (56.0%)

* Includes John Durkin who won a second election in 1975 against Louis Wyman in New Hampshire. The first election ended in a virtual tie.
† Includes Adlai Stevenson who won a special election in 1970.
SOURCE: Compiled from data in various issues of the *Congressional Quarterly Weekly Reports* and Richard Scammon, ed., *America Votes 11* (Washington, D.C.: Congressional Quarterly, 1975).

group was 19 years younger on the average (47 as compared to 66), the 1976 group 15 years younger (48 as compared to 63). The younger for older rule was rather dramatically broken in 1976 with the election of S. I. Hayakawa (R–California). At 70 he replaced a 42-year-old (John Tunney). If these two are dropped from the averages, the spread in ages is nearly 20 years for 1976. The age ranges for the two new groups are: 1974, 34 to 53 for the new, 48 to 82 for the old; 1976, 38 to 70 for the new, 42 to 76 for the old.

In occupation and religion, the new groups look remarkably like the old for both years. Certainly there are not significant enough changes to merit comment. The voting scores do hold some surprises, however. The nine Democratic and two Republican replacements in 1975 actually provided President Ford with more support on the average than did the five Democratic and six Republican incumbents in 1974. And a quite evenly split group of replacements provided more support for President Carter in 1977 than was supplied in 1976 to President Ford by those replaced. The new Democrats were significantly more supportive of Carter than the old Democrats were of Ford (73.4 percent compared to 28.2 percent). On the other hand, the new Republicans were relatively kind to the new president—offering only slightly less support than they did for their own president in 1976 (48.9 percent for Carter in 1977; 59.9 percent for Ford in 1976). Perhaps this result is attributable to the fabled honeymoon year for new presidents.

Two other observations are worth making. The support for the conservative coalition was reduced by the heavily Democratic replacement group in 1975 but increased by the more partisanly balanced group in 1977. And party unity was increased in both years (in part a consequence of low attendance records of certain campaigning or retiring senators).

Relatively few important differences are noted when comparing the voting scores of the 1974 and 1976 replacements with the rest of their colleagues. The only consistent difference is that, as with the new House members, the new senators tend to score higher on party unity. The other notable differences are that both northern and southern Democratic replacements provided less support for the conservative coalition in 1975; whereas northern Democratic and Republican replacements provided more support for the coalition in 1977. Since conservative coalition support rose throughout the Senate in 1977, perhaps the new members, fresh from the hustings, reflected the trend more than their colleagues.

We cannot let this topic of new senators for old pass without commenting on the remarkable 1980 Senate elections. Most prognosticators judged that the Republicans would make gains based on the fact that Democrats held 24 of the 34 seats up for election. But these predictions did not exceed a five- or six-seat Republican gain. Even the National Republican Senatorial Committee estimated that "Republicans will be the Senate majority no later than 1982."[9] The results, however, challenged Ronald Reagan's landslide for election eve surprises. The Republicans retained all 10 seats held before and won 12 seats previously held by Democrats. Republicans organized the Senate in 1981 for the first time since 1953. For the third time in this century a Republican president was faced with split-party control in Congress (a Democratic House, Republican Senate).[10] As before the new senators were younger than those they replaced (47 as compared to 58). But the ideological shift was conservative (Sandoz and Van Crabb, 1981: 104).

How and why do people run for the United States Senate? Barber's three questions are again useful as a means for developing a response: Do I want it? Can I do it? Do they want me? Conclusions differ very little, if at all, from those for House candidates in the high opportunity districts. That is, with few exceptions, motivation is high if the opportunity presents itself to run for the Senate. Given the importance of the office, the personal resources of candidates are normally high. More often than not, important people seek Senate seats, people

---

[9] National Republican Senatorial Committee, *1980 Senate Races,* July 11, 1980, p. 2.

[10] The other occasions — 1911 – 12 for William Howard Taft and 1931 – 32 for Herbert Hoover.

with electoral experience who have had earlier occasions to judge whether or not they are wanted in politics.[11] Table 5−8 shows the primary opposition for senatorial candidates running for high opportunity seats in 1974 and 1976. Note first of all that primary opposition

TABLE 5−8
Primary opposition for senatorial candidates, high-opportunity seats, 1974, 1976

Type of seat	Year	Total in cate-gory	Number with primary R	Number with primary D	Average number of candidates R	Average number of candidates D	Average percent of nominees R	Average percent of nominees D
1. Democratic incumbent does not run	1974	3	3	2	3	6.5	71.1	54.5
	1976	4	3	4	3.3	6	59.4	54.0
2. Democratic incumbent successfully challenged	1974	2	1	2	2	2	64.8	59.7
	1976	0	−	−	−	−	−	−
3. Republican incumbent does not run	1974	4	3	3	2.3	5.7	69.9	$\left(\begin{smallmatrix}51.4\\61.7\end{smallmatrix}\right)$*
	1976	4	4	4	3	3.3	65.6	55.5
4. Republican won by 50−54.9 percent last time	1974	4	2	4	2.5	4.3	87.4	$\left(\begin{smallmatrix}57.4\\59.9\end{smallmatrix}\right)$*
	1976	4	1	4	2	6	70.5	47.4
5. Republican won by 55−59.9 percent last time	1974	3	1	3	2	5.7	75.8	44.8
	1976	3	0	0	−	−	−	−
6. Democrat won by 50−54.9 percent last time	1974	4	2	2	5	3.5	58.8	68.9
	1976	5	4	4	4.8	4.3	61.4	59.2
7. Democrat won by 55−59.9 percent last time	1974	2	2	1	2.5	2	68.6	82.9
	1976	5	5	3	3.4	2.3	68.3	89.4

* The first figure represents the average percentage before the runoff election; the second with a runoff—one in each category.
SOURCE: Compiled from data in Richard M. Scammon, ed., *America Votes 11, 12* (Washington D.C.: Congressional Quarterly, 1975, 1977).

is rather intense in the open seats and where the incumbent won last time by less than 55 percent of the vote. Note also that there are important differences between the Republicans and Democrats. Democrats have more candidates running and the races are closer on an average. They also have more primaries. By this measure alone, one would be led to conclude that Democrats want it more than Republicans, but of course, they are in the majority party and thus have more good opportunities to win than Republicans.

[11] The 1978 election was somewhat of an exception in this regard. Of the 20 newly elected senators, seven had not held any major elective public office and five of these had not held a major public position of any kind. Gordon Humphrey, R−New Hampshire, was a pilot for Allegheny Airlines before being elected to the Senate.

Recruiting for the United States Senate is not a major problem. The institution itself continues to attract high quality candidates—at least as measured by socioeconomic status and previous political experience. There is evidence, therefore, for senators to consider themselves, in Wilson's words as "the most perfect product of our politics." Attitude is important for sustaining any institution. It just may be that through the decades attitude and structure have complemented one another in the case of the Senate to produce the unique legislative body we know today.

CAMPAIGNING

Senatorial campaigns vary so much from one state to the next and have changed so much through time that it is presumptuous to even open the subject in so short a space. Still these variations and changes are significant to a full understanding of the Senate as a major institution of public policy and so some effort must be made to treat that topic. As has already been discussed, before the passage of the 17th Amendment senators first campaigned for votes in the state legislature. Typically candidates had to gain the support of state legislative party leaders, making it difficult for self-starters to succeed. With the acceptance of senatorial primaries in some midwestern and western states, candidates were somewhat freed from prior commitments to party ties and new faces began to appear.

In certain states the reform mood that led to senatorial primaries, and later the 17th Amendment, also resulted in successful third parties. Thus for example, in Wisconsin the Progressive Party won control of the state legislature with the reelection of Robert M. LaFollette as governor. The Wisconsin Class 2 seat was to be selected in 1905 by this new legislature. Many candidates were interested, but LaFollette was concerned that conflict over the election might interfere with the enactment of his program. The solution?

> It became evident that a senator must be elected before the legislative program could be achieved. Throughout the state and in the legislature a strong sentiment existed to elect Bob. He was the only man who could be elected without a prolonged, bitter conflict which might engender animosities that would defeat the legislation pledged in the platform.
>
> At a joint session of the legislature on January 25 [1905] Bob was elected United States senator, receiving 100 out of 123 votes cast (LaFollette and LaFollette, 1953: 189).

So the governor was elected to the Senate. LaFollette proceeded to serve out the year as governor so as to shepherd his program through the legislature. He then took the oath of office as a senator nearly one year later on January 4, 1906, beginning a 20-year career in the Senate.

While campaigning for state legislative votes also varied from state to state, the popular election of senators introduced a whole new set of variations. First consider the fundamentals about senatorial elections which make them so different from House elections. All but the at-large districts in the House are changed to reflect population shifts so as to keep them as equal as possible. Senators represent whole states, however, and no effort is made to adjust for enormous population shifts. In 1910 a California senator represented 2.6 percent of the total U.S. population; in 1970 that figure was nearly 10 percent. Conversely a Pennsylvania senator represented 8.3 percent of the total population in 1910 and 5.8 percent in 1970. The populations of both states had grown in this period, but the total for California had gone from 2.4 million in 1910 to 20 million in 1970. The number of Californians increased by more than 4.2 million just in the decade between 1960 and 1970 alone—500,000 more than the combined populations of Montana, Nebraska, Wyoming, and the two Dakotas. These five plains states realized a net gain of 64,000 between 1960 and 1970—the two Dakotas actually lost population.

The other fundamental feature of Senate elections is of course the six-year term. Three-, four-, five-, six-, seven-, nine-year terms and "during good behaviour," were all proposed at the constitutional convention. The majority sentiment favored a longer term than for House members so as to check the popular tendencies of the lower chamber. The six-year term provides the longest period between elections for any elected official in the national government. Effectively it gives senators five years or more before they have to file for renomination. House members may have had to conduct four campaigns in that period—two primary, two general election. Small wonder that they think about moving to the Senate.

Most senatorial campaigns are managed by professionals and include television and radio spots, extensive polling, and policy research. The costs are increasing, as shown in Table 5 − 9. The total expenditures by all candidates more than doubled between 1974 and 1978. The total expenditures for Senate races in 1978 was three fourths of what was spent for 435 House races in that year. These large expenditures are a consequence in part of the fact that most incumbent senators face serious and well-financed challengers.

These totals mask large variations in individual races. The range of expenditures by incumbents in 1978 was from a low of $223,874 by Mark Hatfield in Oregon to an astounding $7,460,966 by Jesse Helms in North Carolina.[12] Helms spent $12.05 per vote received! No other candidate was even close to that figure, but 12 other candidates spent $3 or

---

[12] *Congressional Quarterly Weekly Report,* September 29, 1979, pp. 2154 − 55.

TABLE 5 – 9
Senate campaign expenditures, 1974 – 1978 ($ millions)

	1974	1976	*Percent change*	1978	*Percent change*
All candidates	28.4	38.1	(+34.2)	64.7	(+69.8)
All Democrats	16.6	18.8	(+13.3)	26.7	(+29.6)
All Republicans	11.9	18.5	(+55.5)	38.0*	(+105.4)
Number spending less than $250,000	21	17	(−23.5)	14	(−21.4)
Number spending more than $1,000,000	7	10	(+42.9)	20	(+100)

* Includes the extraordinarily costly Helms race in North Carolina. Helms spent $7,460,966. If this race is excluded the total for Republican candidates is $30.5 million, an increase of 64.8 percent over 1976.
SOURCE: Calculated from Bibby, et al., 1980: 26 – 37.

more per vote received in 1978 (nine of them won). On the other hand, six candidates spent less than 50 cents per vote received (but only one of these candidates won).

The sources of contributions to Senate candidates varies somewhat from those for House candidates. Both get a higher percentage of contributions from individuals giving less than $100 but nonparty political action committees (PACs) are less important as a source of support for Senate candidates and individual contributions of over $500 are a more important source (typically about one fourth of all contributions) (Bibby et al., 1980: 24 – 25; Malbin, 1979: 26). The average amount contributed by PACs to Senate candidates was greater than that contributed to House candidates but constituted a much lower percentage of total contributions. Though PAC contributions have increased dramatically in recent elections, so did other contributions and thus "PACs . . . were responsible for about the same percentage of all Congressional-campaign contributions" (Malbin, 1979: 26).

Of greater concern in 1980 than the increase in PAC contributions was the independent campaign spending of PACs. There is no ceiling on PAC expenditures as long as the group does not contact the candidate. In essence the PAC conducts its own campaign for or against a candidate. The National Conservative Political Action Committee (NCPAC) made news in 1980 by targeting six Democratic incumbents for defeat (George McGovern, Birch Bayh, Alan Cranston, John Culver, Frank Church, and Thomas Eagleton). The NCPAC effort was largely negative—against the record of these senators rather than for the challenger. Four of the six were defeated. But it is impossible to judge the effect of NCPAC. Five other Democratic incumbents were also defeated, as were three Democratic candidates in states where the Democratic incumbent lost in the primary. The point is that 1980 was a banner year for Senate Republican candidates.

The high cost of campaigning is a relatively recent phenomenon. When he first ran for the Senate in 1938, Robert A. Taft (R—Ohio) was investigated by a Senate committee for spending more than $100,000 in a primary election (Patterson, 1972: 163). In 1956, Senator Francis Case (R—South Dakota) created a sensation by revealing that a lobbyist had contributed $2,500 to his campaign in order to influence his vote. South Dakotans in Congress were not used to receiving such large contributions. Total reported expenditures for all congressional candidates—House and Senate—in 1966 were $6,416,284, 10 percent of reported expenditures for just the Senate in 1978 and less than the expenses of Senator Jesse Helms alone in 1978! What is the explanation? It is not only inflation.

> . . . between 1964 and 1968 the consumer price index rose 12.1 percent and national income rose 36 percent whereas campaign costs increased 78 percent. Other factors, obviously are working with price increases to raise the costs of seeking office (Agranoff, 1976: 219).

One important reason for the increase is simply that expenditures are more accurately reported now. Another is the cost and use of television, but in an extensive study of political campaigns, Robert Agranoff identifies still other factors that may account for increases: increased population, more sophisticated political campaign organizations and technology, skilled fund raising (and if you have it, you spend it), more contested primaries, and greater electoral competition (1976: 223 – 26). All of these factors apply to recent Senate elections. And I would like to emphasize the matter of campaign organization and technology, only because it is seldom mentioned. Political campaigning has become a growth industry for certain public relations firms. Once the firm is given the account, it employs impressive capabilities for raising and spending money. The result is escalating cost as each new candidate judges it essential to match the fund-raising and campaign costs of the opponent. This cost spiral has brought demands for more government regulations, perhaps even public financing of congressional campaigns.

Does money win elections? In his then definitive work on election costs, Alexander Heard was appropriately circumspect (1960: 16).

> No neat correlation is found between campaign expenditures and campaign results. Even if superiority in expenditures and success at the polls always ran together, the flow of funds to a candidate might simply reflect his prior popular appeal rather than create it. Our understanding of voting behavior is not so precise that all the financial and nonfinancial factors that contribute to success can be sorted out with confidence.

In 1976 four of the five top spenders in total expenditures and three of five top spenders in cost per vote *lost.* The first four were also incumbents. So money did not buy election for these candidates. In 1978, on the other hand, the top spenders did very well—four of the five highest in total expenditures, and all five in cost per vote won. Did money improve the chances of the losers in 1976 and insure victory for the winners in 1978? Unfortunately elections are not run as control experiments, and so it is hard to say for certain. Given this doubt as to precise effect, the rule in competitive races is get as much money as you can and spend it all.

The campaign expenses for Senate races also tell us something about campaign organization. Few Senate campaigns in recent years were run out of the candidate's hat, as is still possible in many House races. Organizational charts are often deceptive. In the case of campaign organizations they are typically pure fiction. Still certain functions are performed in some manner in most large campaigns. Agranoff identifies several of these (1976: 194 – 202):

Campaign manager: "the person who puts it all together."

Public relations or media director: to direct this most important aspect of the campaign.

Legal advisor: "Every campaign is conducted within a web of state or national legal regulations."

Research director: "responsible for coordinating issue type research and voting research."

Finance director: "often . . . a multiheaded function."

Coordinator of volunteers: "Volunteers . . . must be dealt with in a systematic and professional manner."

Field organization personnel: "to organize and oversee . . . activities in the various subunits."

Special group coordinators: "Among the more common . . . are women, students, youth, labor, nationality groups, occupational or professional groups, and senior citizens."

Campaign aide: "an aide who can travel with the candidate" to handle all details of travel, schedule, etc.

It does not take much imagination to see how this basic organizational structure can expand or contract depending on the size of the state, seriousness of the challenge, availability of funds, and so on. Several thousand persons may contribute in some fashion to the campaign of a large-state senator. It should also be obvious that the incumbent has an organizational advantage since he may fill many of these posts with experienced staff from the Washington or home-state offices. Finally, one can see that the campaign experience itself may begin to socialize senators to their legislative roles in this unique institution. That is, they become aware that they cannot manage all tasks themselves and therefore must get used to others acting in their name. They also learn techniques of responding to an immense number of issues and demands. Clearly the important campaign-election period contributes to the education of a senator.

SUMMARY

The following generalizations emerge from this discussion of how senators come to Washington:

1. Representing something called states, senators experience much greater variation in representing constituents than do representatives.
2. The direct, popular election of senators presumably confirmed important changes in the intergovernmental policy process (e.g., the representation of people rather than state legislatures), though this proposition has not been systematically studied.
3. Senators experience a higher average turnover in elections than do House members, but staggered terms have, in the past, permitted somewhat greater continuity of membership than in the House. Turnover in recent elections (1976 – 80) has been so high that this continuity has been effected and the House has actually returned a higher proportion of its members than the Senate.
4. Senators are faced with well-organized and financed challengers who are successful in gaining voter recognition.
5. Members typically bring considerable political experience to service in the Senate. The institution remains attractive for experienced and ambitious politicians.
6. Senate campaigns—organization, style, substance, costs—are typically best understood in terms of the social, economic, and political characteristics of the state represented. But campaign costs are increasing in all states.

These observations bring us back to the introductory comments on the Senate as an institution. There is no legislative body quite like it anywhere in the world. It does require rather special analysis— analysis which should be revealing of the nature of the American political system. For while other, indeed most, political systems have active lower chambers, none has so powerful an upper chamber. Why we have one is informative about the special brand of American federalism that is so important in formulating, legitimizing, and implementing public policy.

6 Staff recruitment and turnover

Michael J. Malbin was on his first assignment as a journalist covering Capitol Hill. He went to interview John Kluczynski (D—Illinois), who chaired the House subcommittee that had jurisdiction for a $23 billion public works authorization bill. A committee staff aide was called in to accompany Chairman Kluczynski in case Malbin "raised any technical issues." Malbin reports (1980: 3—4):

> I began the interview with what I thought was a throwaway question. . . . What makes this issue important, I asked?
> "This is a tremendously important bill. It involves millions of dollars," Kluczynski began to answer and then paused. "No—*billions*, isn't it?" he asked, turning to the staff aide.
> The significance of that brief exchange was too clear to be missed, even by a newcomer. I was initially shocked but quickly began realizing that to understand Congress, I had better start paying attention to the role of its staff.

Malbin was quick to point out that Kluczynski's behavior on that day was exceptional. "Most members seem broadly to be in control of most

133

of what their own staffs are doing" (1980: 4). But this experience directed his attention to an important development in Congress.

> Congress as a whole has become the institutional embodiment of Kluczynski's spirit. The members cannot begin to control the workload that their staffs collectively help to generate. Yet, Congress could not function in today's world without the staff on which it has become to depend (1980: 4).

I pointed out earlier the extent to which staff growth has contributed to an expanding congressional population. In fact, it is hard for the modern visitor to House and Senate offices to imagine what it must have been like 50 years ago. Those halls must have been virtually empty. And when they returned from the floor, representatives and senators could actually say hello to the whole staff of two or three persons located in one room. Today "the member of Congress may best be understood . . . as an *enterprise*, and the analysis of phenomena like personnel turnover or elite circulation must be analyzed in terms of the dynamics within those member enterprises" (Salisbury and Shepsle, 1981: 382). The enterprise may be spread over several offices—some of which are not even located in the same building as that of the boss.

Who are these people who have contributed to the creation of an enormous network of enterprises on Capitol Hill? And where do they come from? Given the diversity of the environments within which these enterprises are located (the House and the Senate, the committees and the members' offices, the satellite locations of research units), it naturally follows that the answer may not be the same for all staffs. And before trying to answer the question for any one set, it must be emphasized that the task of generalizing is even more challenging than for the members. In the first place the individuality of the staff units (particularly the members' offices and the committees and subcommittees) presents one with a staggering array of staff positions, responsibilities, and qualifications (see Chapters 8 and 10). In fact, just counting who is and who is not staff is a demanding task since many offices and committees have part-time and temporary personnel (e.g., consultants), not to mention the legions of student interns in the summer. Further, there is considerable movement from one position to another—in an office or committee, between offices, between offices and committees, from Capitol Hill to positions outside, and vice versa. As Fox and Hammond illustrate, a number of careers are now possible on Capitol Hill, though many of the moves are lateral (1977: 63):

> In the flat organizational structure which characterizes Congress, with multiple subunits and centers of power, there are few clearly defined lines of promotion and career movement upward. Within specified subunits, a personal office or a committee, some job changes are clearly

characterized as promotions—moving from LA [legislative assistant] to chief LA, or from LA to AA [administrative assistant]. Some movement between offices is similar. . . . But other moves—from legislative assistant on a personal staff to a similar position on a committee, or from one AA or committee staff director job to another, can more readily be perceived as lateral moves. Yet the career patterns of many Hill aides are characterized by just such moves.

Following the 1978 elections and the defeat of their boss, the staff of Newton Steers (R—Maryland) advertised themselves as a unit. "Super staff seeks legislator to replace super boss hit from behind Nov. 7. Staff called 'excellent' by area newspapers."[1] While it is unusual to package a staff in this way for movement to another office, some staff of defeated members are hired by newly elected members who opt for Washington-oriented rather than local-oriented ability and experience.

We have begun an answer to the question of where staff come from. It is time to treat the matter more directly (at least within the limits of data and existing studies).

PERSONAL OFFICES

The biggest staffing problem is that faced by new representatives and senators. And the problem itself is related to the job that is to be done. It so happens that the job has grown immensely. While it can still be broadly described as involving constituency representation and lawmaking, those two tasks have become impressively more complicated, thus serving to justify increased staff. The point is that 50 years ago a newly elected representative or senator could turn to two or three trusted campaign aides and say: "Let's move to Washington." At that time, however, new members were not necessarily welcomed with open arms. As former Representative Emanuel Celler (D—New York) observed: "A freshman Congressman is a lost soul. . . . He doesn't know the rules and nobody bothers explaining them" (quoted in Tacheron and Udall, 1966: v). But the job itself was pretty well understood. And as Evron M. Kirkpatrick points out (in Tacheron and Udall, 1966: v):

> Fifty years ago it was not so important for the newcomer to become equipped for constructive legislative service early in his career. Then . . . the national legislature sat only 9 months out of 24; members spent the rest of the time at home practicing law or attending to their private affairs. The mail they received referred mostly to free seed, rural routes, Spanish War pensions, and occasionally a legislative matter. The situation is different in the modern House; most Congressmen are in daily

---
[1] Quoted in *The Christian Science Monitor*, January 10, 1979. The original ad appeared in a Capitol Hill newspaper, *Roll Call*.

contact with a host of constituent problems—and the legislative business that the individual member must help to conduct has increased enormously in volume and complexity.

It is interesting as evidence for the growing complexity of being a member of Congress that orientation sessions are now conducted for the newly elected. In fact, they are brought to Washington a month before they are sworn in.

This growth in demands and expectations, then, makes staffing a crucial exercise. Members perceive correctly that they cannot function well with political cronies in these jobs. They need bright, young professionals—in part to match those that everyone else has. Of course, campaigns also have changed, and there too more than likely, the new representative will have been aided by bright, young professionals. Therefore, recruitment by new members still includes persons from campaign staffs. New members also hire many other staff from the district or state, though there are regional differences. Fox and Hammond report that western members bring fewer staff from home because of the distances involved (and possibly because westerners simply don't want to move east) (1977: 51).

Newly elected representatives and senators are typically advised to hire persons with Hill experience. Certainly the Washington end of the job requires having staff familiar with the committee system, other staff, the Library of Congress and other research sources, the White House, lobbyists, and, perhaps above all, the bureaucracy. A recent study showed, however, that new representatives chose about one fourth of their staff from persons with Hill experience; new senators chose 19 and 30 percent from the Hill in the two years measured (Salisbury and Shepsle, 1981: 388; see also Loomis, 1979). Of the major professional positions, the legislative assistant (the LA) is less likely to come from the state or district.

The whole problem of moving people from the district or state to Washington (not to mention the subsequent problem for the members in firing them if they don't work out) is eased somewhat by the expansion of district and state operations. Table 6—1 shows a rather remarkable growth of home-based staff. Over a third of the personal staff of representatives is now based in the district, and one fourth of the Senate personal staff is in state-based offices. Naturally this growth represents a shift in workload from Washington back home (see Chapters 8 and 10). And it gives the members appointments close to the electorate.

The new senator may face an even bigger problem in recruiting staff than the representative due to the larger enterprise of the typical Senate office. Those moving over from the House have the advantage of bringing along a group of aides familiar with the Hill, if not necessarily

TABLE 6-1
Home-based personal staff for representatives and senators

	House			Senate		
Years	Number in the district	Percent of total personal staff	Mean number per representative	Number in state	Percent of total personal staff	Mean number per senator
1972	1,189	22.5	2.7	303	11.3	3
1976	1,943	28.0	4.5	n.a.	n.a.	n.a.
1977	2,058	29.6	4.7	n.a.	n.a.	n.a.
1978	2,317	33.4	5.3	816	25.0	8.2
1979	2,445	34.6	5.6	879	24.3	8.8

n.a. = not available.
SOURCE: Bibby, et al., 1980: 69-70.

with the special workings of the Senate. Salisbury and Shepsle found in 1979 that 65 percent of the staffs followed their representative when he was elected to the Senate (1981:   387). But those members fresh to Capitol Hill face a rather sizeable recruiting task since the average personal staff of a senator in 1979 was 36.2 persons.

One important source of recruits is the staff of defeated or retired senators and representatives. In 1980, 18 senators and 74 representatives did not return. We can get a rough estimate of the number of personal staffers looking for a job by multiplying those not returning by the average staff size for the Senate and House (a not altogether accurate method given that personal staffs of senators vary somewhat by state population—see Chapter 10). The results of these calculations show that approximately 650 Senate and 1,200 House personal staff were seeking employment after the 1980 election. Applying the proportions of staff that would be located in the state or district (see Table 6 —1), that leaves just under 500 Senate and 800 House staff available for hiring in Washington. Interestingly enough the large majority of these people apparently leave Capitol Hill. They do not show up either working for other members or committees. Salisbury and Shepsle found that in 1977, 78 percent of the staff of departing senators and representatives also left Congress (1981:   387). Defeat of the member apparently serves as a convenient break for moving on to other jobs.

The methods of staff development do not get very high marks from those who have studied them. *Haphazard* is a word often used to describe the procedures. "People really choose you," is the way one representative put it. "It is who the senator notices, and who we know," was the judgment of a Senate staff assistant. This same person observed that "the senator may work with a guy on an issue and then at some later time hire him." And Fox and Hammond conclude that:

"Most staff members get their jobs because they happen to be in the right place at the right time" (1977: 57; other quotes also from Fox and Hammond: 49, 57 – 58). Certainly I have never known how to advise students on an exact method for getting jobs on the Hill. Those who have been successful have either known somebody or simply moved to Washington and started knocking on doors. The growth of staff makes the task of selection more difficult for the obvious reason of greater volume but also for the less obvious reason that a larger operation is less personal, more open, with greater demands for equal treatment and representation.[2] However haphazard the methods, there is no shortage of applications. Many people with impressive qualifications want to work on Capitol Hill—or at least begin their careers there.

Those selected to work in personal offices have impressive qualifications. The professional staff are typically young and well-educated. Many are recent graduates of professional schools—primarily law but also graduate schools or journalism. A high proportion knew the member before being hired. Being in Washington itself is exciting, but a special bonus for a person in his or her first job is that the work is important, even heady. And the price is right—entering salaries are high. As noted in Chapter 3, however, with the exception of the administrative assistant, tenure is relatively brief compared to other jobs in government (Fox and Hammond, 1977: 56 – 69). The explanation in part is that it is difficult for most such people to sustain interest in a job for which they get limited public credit. Malbin explains (1980: 20 – 21):

> For most of the professionals the exhilaration does not last forever. For one thing, they quickly reach a salary level not far below the legal maximum and then stay put. Another factor may be the overcrowded and noisy offices and the unpredictable and sometimes incredibly long working hours, many of which are spent doing nothing or dreaming up new things to do while waiting for five minutes of the member's time at the end of the day. But the most basic factor, the one that ultimately starts to grate on so many staff people, is the knowledge that however powerful they may appear or however often they may have turned their own opinions into laws, they will never be anything other than surrogates for someone else. One successful young staffer who was in the middle of looking for another job captured this as a comment that could have been echoed by hundreds of his colleagues: "I just don't want to spend the rest of my life carrying someone else's water."

---

[2] Senator Patrick Leahy (D – Vermont) referred to Congress as the "last plantation"—alluding to the fact that Congress has not subjected itself to the same equal rights and equal pay laws it has enacted for the rest of the government. (*The Pittsburgh Press*, May 15, 1979).

This quotation gives real-life meaning to all the turnover statistics and lends credence to the hypothesis that many staffers view their work on Capitol Hill as a "credentialing experience" (Salisbury and Shepsle, 1981: 393). But, in addition, what Malbin reports about staff anxieties has important implications for the member of Congress. The senator or representative rapidly learns that the brightest and the best staff persons are just passing through. That realization unquestionably affects member relationships with staff and contributes to the transitory nature of most congressional offices. In essence, the personal staff of representatives and senators serves an important apprenticeship function for other governmental and satellite units. That result alone justifies greater attention to who these persons are, what they learn, and where they go. Beyond that, however, is the interesting point that one must look beyond the high return rate of House incumbents in studying the stability of that institution. As personal staffs increase and become more important in handling the many complex tasks of the modern Congress, we are well instructed to take account of the effects of the high turnover of staff as well as the high return of representatives.

To summarize, senators and representatives begin building their staffs from among those persons who have helped in the campaign. In particular, administrative assistants and press aides come to Washington with the member. With others less stress is apparently placed on district or state residence unless the person is to direct the work of the local offices. Legislative assistants are less likely to be home-grown products. Rather they are increasingly drawn from among the experts in particular areas of interest to the member (normally associated with committee work). These developments represent important changes from the small, local, state- or district-oriented staffs of some decades ago to increasingly professional, more substantively-oriented staffs of today. One of the important policy consequences is that members become more involved in more legislation than in the past, dependent in part on bright, young, ambitious people who, while loyal enough during their tenure, begin a job search soon after arriving in town.

COMMITTEES

As discussed in Chapter 3, committees had staff before it was provided to individual members. These positions were subject to the patronage system, and thus one expected turnover with a change in committee leadership. Kenneth Kofmehl observes that before the passage of the Legislative Reorganization Act of 1946, only the two Appropriations Committees and the Joint Committee on Internal Revenue Taxation "had consistently employed well-trained, technically

qualified staffs with continuity of tenure" (1977:   3). "The practice of
borrowing specialists from administrative agencies to assist the committees for rather lengthy periods—sometimes extending through
several Congresses—was quite prevalent" (Kofmehl, 1977:   3; Rogers,
1941:   13). Representatives chairing committees of lesser importance
might well use the limited staff to supplement their meager personal
staffs. Senators by law had to attach their personal staffs to the committee they chaired (Kofmehl, 1977:   4). They did not get additional
staff as chairmen.

Having a small staff did not necessarily mean that those persons
were unimportant in the development of legislation. A spectacular
example of a person with great influence was Colin F. Stam who began
his service with the Joint Committee on Internal Revenue Taxation in
1927. He "served nine different chairmen of the tax committees under
six administrations" (Kuhn, 1963:   109).

> To attorneys in the great law firms who make their living out of "the
> continuing struggle among contending interests for the privilege of pay-
> ing the least," Stam is an office word synonymous with the Internal
> Revenue Code. On Capitol Hill, in the House Ways and Means Commit-
> tee and the Senate Finance Committee, in the Treasury and its Internal
> Revenue Service, his name is one to conjure with. And among reporters
> in the House and Senate press galleries he is known as the man who
> knows all about a pending tax bill and tells nothing (Kuhn, 1963:   108).

Not all committees were so fortunate in getting directors with
Stam's qualities (Patterson, 1970:   23). The Legislative Reorganization
Act of 1946 sought to improve committee staffing—in particular to
provide greater professionalism. Gladys M. Kammerer studied the extent to which the goals were achieved in the early years following the
passage of the act and found a mixed record (1949:   27–28).

> The findings . . . show a marked superiority of Senate standing
> committees to those on the House side. . . . The more highly charged
> political atmosphere in the House of Representatives . . . may help to
> account for a more pronounced partisanship in the recruitment and
> selection of committee staffs. In addition, the House leadership took no
> positive steps to assist chairmen in locating or attracting well-trained
> professional staff members.

Since Kammerer's study in 1949, the situation has improved markedly. Committeees continue to differ in the manner and style of recruitment, but as Samuel C. Patterson concludes: "the expertise of
congressional committees and their independence from the executive
branch have been greatly enhanced by extensive and increasing reliance upon professional personnel" (1970:   22). If personal staffs are
more local, political, and generalist in their perspectives, then today
committee staffs are more national, professional, and specialist in

theirs. The overall profile of present-day committee staff shows impressive credentials. A high proportion hold advanced degrees, a very large number have law degrees (45 percent among those studied by Fox and Hammond). Not unexpectedly many staff move from personal offices to the committees. This can happen when a member moves up to a leadership position on a committee or subcommittee or possibly when a member is retiring (as a way of placing his loyal personal staff).[3] But Fox and Hammond report an even larger group come from the executive branch (34.9 percent of those studied as compared to 29.8 percent coming from other congressional offices (1977: 175). Unfortunately, there are no trend data on this important subject to determine whether the situation has changed over the years.

Saying that committee staffs are less political than personal staffs is not to say that they are nonpartisan. In his careful monitoring of committee staffs, Malbin concludes that these units are more partisan than when first authorized by the Legislative Reorganization Act of 1946. Pressures on committee and subcommittee chairmen to legislate or perish has, in turn, influenced the selection of young, aggressive, and partisan staff.

> The main reason committees have moved away from nonpartisan staffing since 1946 is the political self-interest of chairmen who want aides responsive to their political needs. Instead of civil servants with years of agency experience, chairmen began looking for young lawyers with politically compatible ambitions. . . . Instead of being asked to interpret, analyze, and react to proposals originating elsewhere, they were frequently told to seek out good publicity for their chairmen (Malbin, 1977: 25—26).[4]

When committee staff is appreciated by chairmen or ranking minority members, the access to those staff by other members is not always free and equal. Particularly in the Senate, the appointing member may use committee staff for personal office purposes. In some cases, at least in the past, committee staff were even located in the appointing senator's office. In his study of staff in 1974 —75, Stephen Isaacs found that:

> Many employees of committees do little or no work for the committees that employ them. Some are used in senators' offices, others handle

---

[3] Salisbury and Shepsle find less committee staff turnover than one might expect with a change in committee leadership, however (1981: 389). Of course, their analysis is restricted to changes in Democratic leaders not partisan shifts as occurred in 1981 in the Senate.

[4] Malbin cites the Joint Committee on Internal Revenue Taxation staff as classically nonpartisan, particularly under its directors, Colin F. Stam and Laurance N. Woodworth. This staff serves as the principal tax-policy unit for both the Senate Committee on Finance and the House Committee on Ways and Means (1977: 19—25).

"case work" and other constituent service for their senators. Yet others serve as general legislative aides to the senators.[5]

The growth of committee staff in recent years has, despite the partisan selection noted above, increased the professionalization of the staff. Even patronage has its limits under pressure of workload. Thus with the increasing programmatic demands from the executive as well as from ambitious legislators, staff has expanded to include many young professionals who are not necessarily partisan in their loyalty to a chairman. Further, the reorganization of the past few years makes it more difficult to judge who is leading a committee—thus possibly increasing the autonomy of staff.

The methods of recruitment have changed through the years—which explains the increased professionalization of committee staff. Expertise is of primary importance today as a qualification, but there are many experts in most of the subject areas treated by the committees. Therefore controlling for specialization one still finds considerable reliance on personal and political contact. Fox and Hammond explain (1977: 60):

> Recruitment depends heavily on contacts. Although hiring is based on expertise, knowledge of an opening is usually dependent on who knows whom. Most committee staff are appointed by the committee or subcommittee chairman (75.2 percent) or the ranking minority member (14 percent), although the full committee often concurs. Nearly half of the committee staff responding reported previous acquaintance with the person making the appointment.

It is useful to examine some real cases of committee staff building. In 1975 a new subcommittee was created following a reorganization of the House Committee on Interstate and Foreign Commerce. John Dingell (D—Michigan) was designated as chairman and thus was in a position to hire staff. Table 6—2 shows several of the major appointments that were made. As is evident, Dingell collected a staff of persons who were known to him. Four of those hired worked for Dingell in his other committee assignments (Merchant Marine and Fisheries; Select Small Business). Three others were known to him because they worked for another subcommittee of the Commerce Committee. Many of these persons had been active in environmental issues, "they had no background in energy. They were hired for their loyalty not for their expertise" (Malbin, 1980: 102).

---

[5] Stephen Isaacs, "Senators Found Using Committee Personnel for Own Work," *The Washington Post,* February 16, 1975. For many years the minority had a special set of committee staff problems. First they had few staff assigned to them. Second those staff assigned often belonged to the ranking member, and others were reluctant to use them. Often, in fact, minority party senators were more likely to use majority staff than minority staff (Jones, 1970: 179—80).

TABLE 6−2
Assembling two subcommittee staffs — House Committee on Interstate and Foreign Commerce

1. *Energy and Power,*	*Staff person*	*Previous position*	*Contact point*
John Dingell, chairman	Frank M. Potter, Jr. (staff director)	Subcommittee staff assistant, Merchant Marine and Fisheries Committee	Worked for Dingell in previous position
	Peter Hunt	Consulting firm on environmental issues	Met Potter when both worked on environmental issues
	Walter W. Schroeder (economist)	?	?
	Peter Stockton	Small Business Committee	Worked for Dingell in previous position
	William Demarest	Small Business Committee	Worked for Dingell in previous position
	Michael Barrett	Another subcommittee of Commerce	Dingell a member of Commerce
	James Phillips	Journalist	?
	Phineas Indritz	Another subcommittee of Commerce	Dingell a member of Commerce
	David Finnegan	Science and Technology Committee	?
	David Schooler	Harvard Law School student	?
	William Braun	Another subcommittee of Commerce	Dingell a member of Commerce
	Michael Ward	Small Business Committee	Worked for Dingell in previous position
2. *Oversight and Investigations,*			
John Moss, chairman	Michael Lemov	Another subcommittee of Commerce	Worked for Moss in previous position
	Elliot Segal	Assistant dean, Yale Medical School	?
	John Galloway	Taught at Hunter College and wrote for *Consumer Reports*	Recommended to Lemov by consumer advocates Nader and Claybrook
	Richard Falkner (succeeded by)	Another congressional staff	?
	Lovell Dodge	Director of a Nader center	?

SOURCE: Compiled from information in Malbin, 1980: 101−7; 136−37.

The second subcommittee in Table 6−2 existed before the reorganization, but a new chairman was selected in 1975, John Moss (D−California). Moss fashioned a staff to suit his goals, which were more reformist in orientation than were those of his predecessor. Like Dingell he turned to a person who had worked for him in another capacity to direct the staff. Others were drawn from public interest organizations and the universities as well as other congressional offices. Moss's predecessor relied rather heavily on the Federal Bureau of Investigation in staffing the subcommittee (Malbin, 1980: 137).

Turnover differed sharply between the two subcommittees. By 1978, Moss lost 9 of the 15 he had hired in 1975, whereas Dingell lost only two or three. The Republicans had very little staff on either subcommittee—three on the Dingell's; just one on Moss's.

Committee and subcommittee staffs differ in recruitment and operations because the units themselves differ in purpose—at any one time and certainly over time as leadership changes. This variation is maddening for those who want to develop durable generalizations about the congressional process. But it happens to be well suited to the nature and functions of an institution designed to reflect changes in the society.

In summary, there are important differences between personal and committee staffs. While often partisan, committee staffs have a slightly more professional and permanent cast to them as compared to personal staffs. Their loyalties are toward the committee and subcommittee leadership and to their particular areas of expertise. As Fox and Hammond put it: "training and expertise (tempered by political acceptability) are the essential ingredients in virtually all professional staff appointments" (1977: 66). The importance of personal and committee staff growth is that, like all expansion, it is more difficult for members to command partisan loyalty and political/electoral dedication from all staff. It is also increasingly difficult for the members to know what goes on in their name.

RESEARCH SUPPORT AGENCIES

Among the most recent staff developments is the expansion of existing research agencies—the Congressional Research Service (CRS) and the General Accounting Office (GAO)—and the creation of new units—the Office of Technology Assessment (OTA) and the Congressional Budget Office (CBO). Just as the committee staff tends to be, on the whole, more professional and specialist-oriented than personal staff, so too are the research agency staff more professional and specialist-oriented than committee staff. Though members may, on occasion, be influential in hiring staff, they are not normally as involved as they are with personal and committee staffs. Rather the task of hiring and firing typically belongs to staff directors within the agencies. Thus, with these staffs we move a further step from elections as a major source of the congressional population.

Who then are these staff persons? Where do they come from? Unfortunately Fox and Hammond do not provide comparable background data on the staff for these agencies. It is also unfortunately the case that the *Congressional Staff Directory* does not provide biographical data for all of the staffs of these important support units. What one can glean from available data and personal observation is that these staff tend to be drawn more from the universities, research institutes, and executive agencies. For example, 12 persons in the Congressional Budget Office are listed in the *Congressional Staff Directory* and nine have their biographies included. Of these nine, seven have Ph.D.s, one has an M.A., and one a law degree. Prior to joining the CBO, five of the nine had at some point worked in research institutes, five had worked in executive agencies, two in universities, two in Congress (one as an intern), and one in industry. By any test, top staff in CBO are well qualified to analyze the budget. It is notable, however, that they do not come to their jobs with congressional experience. One may expect, therefore, that constituency- or election-oriented representatives and senators will be cautious in relying entirely on their work. That is not to say that such agencies do not perform important functions and provide vital information. It is only to suggest that previous experience will be weighed by the members in judging whether and how much to rely on reports and recommendations emanating from research agencies.[6]

SUMMARY

Analyzing how staff come to Washington is a bit more complicated than analyzing the membership. Representatives and senators at least got to Washington by the same process (i.e., elections) if not always in the same way. Some staff are almost elected in the sense that their futures are tied very closely to those of the members they serve. Others in increasing numbers are a part of the permanent work force on Capitol Hill. And among these, the lawyers have long been dominant, but an increasing number of social scientists, policy analysts, planners, and technologists are now populating the staff support units.

Figure 6 – 1 summarizes how the mix of staff recruitment and selection may conceivably influence congressional action on a problem or demand. Given the member's view of the job of the office staff, these persons are likely to view problems from the perspective of the state or district being represented. Still, the increase in personal staff appears to have resulted in a more professional, public policy, lawmaking perspective as well—thus the broken line. The reverse is judged to be the case with committee staff and research agency staff have little or no state and local perspective. One might automatically believe that this trend to the professional, public policy, lawmaking perspective is an unquestioned good. It is too soon to examine that proposition but not too soon to suggest that one's answer may depend on how one views the purposes and functions of a national legislature.

---

[6] Malbin provides an interesting account of the development of the House Committee on the Budget and its staff—noting some of the relationships between the Committee and CBO (1980: 187 – 203).

FIGURE 6 – 1
A general conception of the effect of different
congressional staffs

Key: ———— Indicates primary perspective

———— Indicates secondary perspective or primary
perspective of a few staff

SOURCE: Developed by author.

HOW THEY CAME TO BE THERE: CONCLUDING REMARKS

This analysis of Congress has begun by studying the population itself: who they are in Chapter 3 and how they came to be there in Chapters 4, 5, and 6. Two conclusions are particularly prominent as one reviews what has been covered so far. *First, the number of persons legitimately involved in legislative activities at the national level has grown rather dramatically in recent decades. Second, this growth is complemented by impressive diversity in skills, training, social and political background, and employment practices.*

These developments are particularly noteworthy for what they suggest about the role of Congress in the public policy process. A growing and more diversified legislative population naturally suggests a changing concept of institutional functions. Such a dynamic set of policy actors is unlikely to be satisfied with serving as a silent or reserved partner to the executive. Indeed, much of the congressional reform which has resulted in expanded staff derived from dissatisfaction with, or impossibility of, a partnership between Congress and President

Johnson in regard to foreign and defense policy and between Congress and President Nixon in regard to domestic policy.

A more aggressive Congress will naturally be drawn into many more policy activities than one that willingly serves as a reserved partner to the executive. For example, if Congress is going to initiate proposals for resolving important issues, then the members and their staffs will become involved in defining problems, assessing alternative proposals, judging implementation requirements, and evaluating program results, in addition to the more traditional functions of authorizing a particular program and appropriating funds. Though not quite as obvious, the same can be said even if congressional assertiveness only intends to be facilitative of the policy process—that is, in providing a hearing for knowledge, opinion, and interests that are relevant to an issue or a proposal to resolve an issue. Again, much depends on what is expected or implied by this posture. Active facilitation of knowledge, opinion, and interests is likely to extend to all policy activities—from problem definition through to program evaluation and termination. The point is that if one imagines that Congress can or should play these more active roles of initiator or facilitator in the national policy process, then it follows that a highly diversified and specialized set of actors is required. Presumably this direction has been taken in recent years.[7]

Of course, productive action in pursuit of these more vigorous roles requires effective organization and leadership. Expanding the staff is not sufficient. Comment on these other matters must await our discussion of how Congress organizes to do its work. But it is not too soon to display the challenge facing the membership. Figure 6 – 2 shows how the personal and committee staff situation has changed. The membership size has stayed the same. In 1947 the ancillary personnel presented no particular management problem. In 1979, however, sheer numbers suggest an overshadowing of the membership (and the growth in research agencies alters conditions even more than is displayed in Figure 6 – 2). The chart is somewhat deceptive in that personal and committee staffs are not separate entities. Rather they are divided among the offices and committees. Even so, however, two effects of growth are important to ponder. First is the matter of whether the individual member can manage such a large increase in staff, and by implication, what the optimum staff size is for the effective operation of a congressional office or committee. Second is the likelihood that size alone may come to influence the operation and performance of staff. It would seem to follow that the larger the staff, the

---

[7] I discuss these developments in regard to energy policy in Lawrence, ed., 1979: 161–78.

FIGURE 6 – 2
Proportional growth of the congressional population, 1947 – 1979

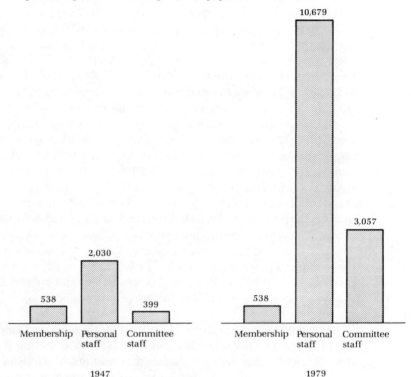

SOURCE: Compiled from data in Bibby, et al., 1980: 69 – 70.

more likely that interoffice and intercommittee staff relationships will develop that may threaten personal loyalties (e.g., to the member or to the chairman).

Neither of these matters is of great moment if Congress is to play the lesser role of partner to executive initiative in the policy process. They become more crucial if, as seems to be the case, staff growth and diversification are for the purposes of making Congress a more active participant in all phases of public policymaking and implementation.

7 Who comes to Congress, what do they want, and how do they get it?

Having provided an analysis of the congressional population, we turn now to consider that enormous set of officials, agencies, groups, and private citizens who come to Congress. A number of trends are evident—more groups active in Washington, more activity by traditional groups, more intergovernmental lobbying, more agencies advocating more programs. Philip H. Abelson, editor of *Science*, describes the trends:

> The power center that is Washington has attracted an ever-increasing number of organizations seeking to influence what goes on here. A partial enumeration of these organizations is to be seen in the Yellow Pages of the telephone book. Some 1,900 organizations are listed under the heating "Associations." Some are local or small or not particularly concerned with government. But others are large and active. Examples include the Air Line Pilots Association, the National Coal Association, and the National Education Association. In addition, many organizations, such as public interest groups, labor unions, trade organizations, and corporations, engage in efforts to influence the government.[1]

[1] Philip H. Abelson, "Power in Washington," *Science* 203 (January 12, 1979): 129.

A tourist visit to Washington typically includes the magnificent Capitol Building; the awesome, yet uninviting Supreme Court Building; and the glistening White House. Less often visited are the many large white and grey buildings housing the departments and agencies, though they are pointed out by tour guides as the bus moves from one major attraction to the next. Tourists never get to the 1600 block of K Street, Northwest, unless they are very lost. And yet visitors who are truly interested in the workings of American government should insist on this detour from the normal route. For this block contains "the equivalent of a new branch of government."[2] On either side of this broad avenue are large buildings housing a few of the associations Abelson speaks of in the statement above. Some 60 associations, corporations, and consultants—all doing business with the government—have their headquarters in buildings located between 1604 and 1666 K Street. As Jerry Breiter of the Hide, Skin, and Leather Association put it: "This is where the action is if you've got problems with the government. Any everyone's got problems with the government."[3] Of course, 1600 K Street is only one such locus of action. Many more sites are located throughout the city and the Maryland and Virginia suburbs. The point is that many people now come to Congress. The results are as described in Chapter 2—an unceasing round of demands occurring in practically every available space on Capitol Hill.[4]

WHAT DETERMINES WHO COMES?

Certainly the growth of government itself, reflecting as it does the centralization of authority in society, leads us to expect increased interest group activity. Government actions attract groups to Washington to protect their interests or to insure that they are included in the distribution of benefits. Government also creates groups that are then sustained by public programs. I have always been taken by David B. Truman's statement about the inevitable gravitation toward government. Groups are likely, according to Truman, to operate through "that institutionalized group whose powers are most inclusive." Governments are those groups with "the most inclusive power concentrations in Western society" (1951: 105—6).

> The effects of such reliance upon government are cumulative. Just as the direct and indirect efforts of an interest group may disturb the equilibriums of related groups, so its operations through and upon gov-

---

[2] *New York Times*, February 26, 1981, p. B14.

[3] Ibid.

[4] During the period in which this chapter was written, practically every major news magazine took note of the increased lobbying activity on Capitol Hill. For example, see the excellent cover story by Neil MacNeil in *Time*, August 7, 1978, pp. 14—22.

ernment are likely to force the related groups also to assert their claims upon governmental institutions in order to achieve some measure of adjustment. For example . . . the labor movement was drawn into politics in no small measure because of the use of governmental injunctive powers by employers. Both types of groups then attempted to assert their claims through the government.

Truman's example, however, suggests that some groups' gravitation to government is more inevitable than others. In a very influential little book, E. E. Schattschneider pointed out what many people knew but few acknowledged when writing about the American political system—that is, that "the flaw in the pluralist heaven is that the heavenly chorus sings with a strong upper-class accent. . . . *Pressure politics is a selective process* ill designed to serve diffuse interests. The system is skewed, loaded and unbalanced in favor of a fraction of a minority" (1960: 35, his emphasis).

Schattschneider's observations differ from those of the so-called power-elite school in that he acknowledges the existence of a pressure system. It's just that the system is limited in scope. The power elite thesis of C. Wright Mills and others postulates a relatively small coterie of decision makers drawn from the large organizations in society— including government.

> They are in command of the major hierarchies and organizations of modern society. They rule the big corporations. They run the machinery of the state and claim its prerogatives. They direct the military establishment. They occupy the strategic command posts of the social structure, in which are now centered the effective means of the power and the wealth and the celebrity which they enjoy (Mills, 1959: 4).

Mills also pointed out that, in his view, the decisions *not made* are "often of greater consequence than the decisions they do make" (1959: 4).

Fortunately, it is not necessary here to test either of these theories. Of the two, the Schattschneider view is easier to deal with because it acknowledges bias in the pressure system without necessarily attributing all decision making to a particular group. The Mills approach comes close to being a conspiracy theory, which, by definition, is difficult to prove. Our question is straightforwardly empirical—What determines who comes?

Both Schattschneider and Mills as well as Truman propose one major requirement for coming to Congress—resources. But let's begin with the *issue*. Issue awareness is a prime factor in drawing a group to Congress particularly when the issue is perceived as having a direct effect on the group in question and Congress seems likely to act. Resources are required to insure influence, however, They may take many forms: *organization, knowledge, staff, access, support by other*

groups, support by government agencies, communication capability.
Norman J. Ornstein and Shirley Elder organize these various advantages into several categories (1978:   69 — 79):

1. Physical: money and size of membership.
2. Organizational: membership skills and unity, leadership, substan-
    tive expertise.
3. Political: campaign expertise, knowledge of the process, skills in
    developing strategies, reputation.
4. Motivational: drive, ideological commitment.
5. Intangibles: overall prestige or status (often of particular lobbyists).

The Schattschneider thesis essentially states that only certain groups
will have these resources. Thus by his view, we expect the oil, steel, or
automobile industries, for example, to know what is going on, organize
a response, gain access to major decision makers in Congress, bargain
for the support of others, and communicate both their version of the
facts and their preferences as to solutions.

However fitting Schattschneider's analysis may have been when he
wrote the book in the 1950s, it does not appear to be as fully explana-
tory in the post-1960s era. The rise of citizen-based groups (or, perhaps
more accurately, groups claiming to represent citizen interests) and
the increase in the number of low-income clientele groups served by
government programs have altered the pressure system. For example,
the rise of Common Cause has to be treated as phenomenal by those
depending on either Truman, Schattschneider, or Mills for their understanding of who comes to and is received by Congress. And the
emergence of many single-issue groups and groups supportive of
specific aid or welfare programs too deserved few lines in the 1950s
literature on interest groups. Yet today these government-sponsored
groups make it difficult to reshape or terminate even those programs
which have failed—often for the very good reason that the program
has created a dependency that did not exist before. Why should any
group willingly give up an advantage provided by a federal program?
Thus, the Great Society programs of the Johnson Administration
(1964 — 69) recast the players in Schattschneider's pressure system.
None of this is to devalue the importance of the resources identified by
Ornstein and Elder. Rather it is to suggest that (1) public interest
groups like Common Cause have discovered means for gathering the
resources to compete, (2) many government programs have provided
in-house resources for low-income groups (including organization,
knowledge, staff, access, support, and communication), and (3) groups
have learned to compensate for their weaknesses by capitalizing on
those resources they have in abundance (e.g., motivation or membership unity as a substitute for lack of funds).

WHO IN FACT COMES?

On March 13, 1975, in Room 2123 of the Rayburn House Office Building, Representative Paul G. Rogers (D — Florida), gaveled to order the House Subcommittee on Health and the Environment. The group was beginning hearings on the existing federal clean air law (known as the Clean Air Amendments of 1970). Subcommittee Chairman Rogers opened the hearings with the following statement:

> When the Congress wrote the Clean Air Act nearly five years ago, I do not think it extravagant to say we established a landmark. We took steps to reverse the growing menace of air pollution which was shortening the lives of many of our citizens and lessening the quality of most others.
>
> Today, we apparently have reached a crossroads. For there are those who would put aside the progress we have made and are making.[5]

Congress had indeed enacted a landmark clean air law in 1970 — one that received broad support in both houses despite the opposition of the effected industries. As Rogers suggested, however, 1975 was a different story.

Table 7 — 1 shows the variety of groups testifying before the Rogers subcommittee. The list is specifically useful for illustrating the wide variety of interests associated with clean-air legislation and more generally useful in displaying the types of groups that make demands on Congress. As noted, five broad categories of persons made an appearance: administrators and other government actors, targets, suppliers, professionals outside government, citizen monitors. The precise proposal or program may differ (e.g., between regulation in this case, armaments, and welfare benefits), but more often than not, someone from each of these categories comes to Congress and therefore each set deserves a brief discussion.

The administrators

The title of Kenneth Crawford's book, written in 1939, conjured up the cartoonist's image of fat, moneyed, and greedy lobbyists crowding the halls of Congress. *The Pressure Boys!* No citizen could possibly condone what that title implied. Unquestionably representatives of special, private interests still roam the halls, offices, and committee rooms of Congress, but it is questionable as to whether an analysis of lobbying should begin with those persons. In fact, I prefer beginning with government agencies — federal, state, and local. If *lobbying* is defined simply as efforts to influence government decision making, then

---

[5] U.S. Congress, Committee on Interstate and Foreign Commerce, Subcommittee on Health and the Environment, *Clean Air Act Amendments —1975*, Hearings, Part 1, 94th Cong., 1st sess., p. 1.

TABLE 7–1
Organizations represented before the House Subcommittee on Health and the
Environment in regard to clean air legislation, March 13–26, 1975

Type of organization	Group represented
1. Governmental unit or association:	
a. Federal	Environmental Protection Agency
	Federal Council for Science and Technology
	Federal Energy Administration
	National Science Foundation
b. State-local	State of California (special advisor on environment)
	Department of Health, state of California
	City of Los Angeles
	National Association of Counties
	National Governors Conference
	National League of Cities
	Texas Air Control Board
	United States Conference of Mayors
2. Targets of regulation:	
a. Industries	Chrysler Corporation
	Daimler–Benz
	E. I. du Pont de Nemours
	Ford Motor Company
	General Motors Corporation
	Honda Motor Company
	Kennecott Copper Corporation
	Saab–Scania
b. Associations and institutes	American Iron & Steel Institute
	American Mining Congress
	American Petroleum Institute
	American Retail Federation
	Automotive Liaison Council
	Automotive Service Councils, Inc.
	Chamber of Commerce of the United States
	Edison Electric Institute
	Houston Chamber of Commerce
	International Council of Shopping Centers
	National Association of Industrial Parks
	National Association of Manufacturers
	National Automobile Dealers Association

surely Congress is actively and strongly lobbied by government
agencies.

Consider these facts. The bulk of the congressional agenda for any
session is made up of familiar requests—those to reauthorize programs or appropriate more money for what the government is already
doing. The familiar aphorism, the best predictor of next year's budget
is this year's budget plus a little bit more, obviously applies to programmatic requests since budgets are about programs and how to pay
for them. So—while much media attention is paid to what is new each
year, most of the decision making is directed to what is old, or at least
already on the books and familiar to legislators. Therefore, the presi-

TABLE 7–1 (*continued*)

Type of organization	Group represented
b. Associations and institutes (continued)	National Coal Association National Parking Association National Realty Committee National Retail Merchants Association National Rural Electric Cooperative Association
c. Power companies	Dairyland Power Cooperative Florida Power & Light Company Jacksonville Electric Authority Tennessee Valley Authority
3. Suppliers—pollution control equipment manufacturers	Dresser Industries Englehard Industries Gould, Inc. Industrial Gas Cleaning Institute IU Conversion Systems Matthey Bishop Universal Oil Products Company
4. Professional associations	American Medical Association American Public Health Association
5. Citizen-supported monitors	League of Women Voters National Clean Air Coalition Natural Resources Defense Council Public Interest Research Corporation Sierra Club

SOURCE: Compiled from information in U.S. Congress, Committee on Interstate and Foreign Commerce, Subcommittee on Health and the Environment, *Clean Air Act Amendments—1975*, Hearings, Part 1, 94th Cong., 1st sess., pp. xii–xiv.

dent's budgetary and State of the Union messages serve as the initial and enormously powerful lobbying effort by the executive. No other group or coalition of groups can hope to match this presentation. In fact, their efforts are essentially reactive to the details of the president's program.

Familiarity typically suggests knowledge and experience. Administering a program, justifying it before several layers of executives (e.g., agency heads, departmental secretaries, the Office of Management and Budget [OMB], possibly White House aides), and knowing where to get support for it, are all impressive advantages when it comes to influencing the members of Congress. Familiarity also extends to the workings of the legislature. Quite naturally, agencies are attentive to the comings and goings on Capitol Hill, both in terms of personnel (including the growing congressional staff) and organization. Again, no group can match the legislative liaison capabilities of the more powerful agencies.

Table 7–1 also lists a number of representatives from state and local governments. Federal domestic programs are typically administered in cooperation with state and local governments. Once the national government provides funds and organizational support for treating problems in various localities, it is not surprising that officials in those localities depend on these resources. Public officials at all levels tend to be protective of their budgets, and therefore representatives of state and local governments naturally show up as lobbyists for many programs. They may personally come to Washington or work through organizations (e.g., National League of Cities, the Conference of Mayors, National Governors' Conference, National Association of Counties, Council of State Governments). Donald H. Haider points out that "group struggle inside government is not appreciably different from that outside" (1974:   255).

> The chief distinction between public and private lobbying groups is "officiality," which means essentially legitimacy in standing. The legitimacy of governors, mayors, and county officials within the general-purpose governments over which they preside is unquestionable. But as individual or collective claimants before the federal government, they have no real formal standing as federal political actors. The legitimacy bestowed at one government level carries over to the superior level but not without a certain political devaluation in transference. Nonetheless, this legitimacy remains the essential resource which members seek to capitalize upon.

What about new programs? Most derive from the agencies, and many have the support of state and local governments. When the president wants to propose something new, he normally calls on the appropriate agency for program development. Or he may form an interagency advisory group. Or he may call a White House Conference, which is often staffed by bureaucrats from appropriate agencies. Of course, new programs also grow out of old programs and are initiated by administrators for approval by political executives, including the president. But even if a new program is formulated outside the executive, e.g., in Congress or by a citizen's group, like as not it will face comprehensive review by administrators who must bear responsibility for it if it is enacted into law. In fact, congressional committee chairmen routinely ask for a report from the appropriate agency (or OMB) on member-sponsored legislation under serious consideration before the committee. And, of course, legislation cannot be independently introduced by an interest group—it must be sponsored by a member.

These advantages of political and career executives and administrators before Congress are symbolized by the sequence of testimony in committee hearings. In the air pollution control hearings referred to earlier, Representative Rogers welcomed the first witness:

> We are very pleased to have as the first witness today to begin these hearings the Honorable Russell Train, administrator of the Environmen-

tal Protection Agency. . . . Mr. Train, we will be pleased to receive your statement.[6]

Hearings typically begin with the principal political appointee for the agency administering the current law. He or she is normally accompanied by a coterie of lesser officials, some political, some career. Administrator Train was accompanied by:

Eric Stork, deputy assistant administrator for Mobile Source Air Pollution Control.

Roger Strelow, assistant administrator for Aid and Waste Management.

Wilson Talley, assistant administrator for Research and Development.

Robert Zener, general counsel.

Of further significance is the fact that committee attendance is likely to be highest when the top officials of the agency or department are testifying. They also normally get the largest and most attentive audience among the interested and affected private groups. However important, intensive, and knowledgeable others may be, they (the private groups) must work to overcome the inherent advantages of the government representatives.

On the other hand, one should not get the impression from this description that the committee members or staff are necessarily overwhelmed by the advantages in knowledge and expertise of government administrators and professionals. This is as good a point as any to note that increased congressional staff has provided a formidable counterbalance to the agency advantages in expertise. In fact, many legislative staff come to Capitol Hill from executive agencies (see Chapter 6) and therefore possess much of the same knowledge that gives agency personnel such an advantage. Further, those Hill staffers with executive experience know something about the intelligence network by which bureaucrats keep abreast of Congress and its inner workings.

Members of Congress were not without advantages even before the recent increases in staff, however. The long tenure of the ranking committee and subcommittee members resulted in thorough acquaintance with the programs under their committee's jurisdiction. In fact, the top ranking political executives for a program seldom could come close to matching the longevity of a committee chairman. Only the career executives drawn from the ranks of the civil service were in that position. The seniority system in Congress and the merit system in the executive, therefore, have been and are two major stabilizing forces in the national policy process.

---

[6]*Clean Air Act Amendments —1975*, Hearings, pp. 2, 34.

It is also important to note that while I have initially illustrated "coming to Congress" with congressional hearings, I assume it goes without saying that most of the contact occurs outside that formal setting. Member and committee offices are often filled with representatives of one group or another seeking time with the representative, senator, committee or subcommittee chairman, legislative assistant, committee counsel or staff director, and so on. And of course, the telephone is the indispensable means of constant communication. Most staff members develop telephone neck—a physical malady associated with holding the phone to one's ear by the shoulder so as to free the hands to do other things.

The targets

By *targets*, I mean simply those persons or groups toward which the policy program is directed. Now that is easier said than listed! Given the incredible number and variety of federal programs, the task of identifying all targets is next to impossible. Fortunately, that is not at all required for present purposes. I simply want to make the point that those who stand to profit or lose from a program are likely to come to Congress.

If all of the groups affected by federal programs cannot be spotted, we surely can provide a few illustrations. In the example cited above (i.e., federal air pollution control), the program is *regulatory* in nature. Note in Table 7—1 the many industries, industrial associations, and power companies whose daily costs and operations are effected by the clean-air regulations. They come to Congress for the obvious purpose of insuring that the regulations are not so stringent as to interfere seriously with production. Theirs is a more defensive posture. They come to Congress because they want *less* done not more.

Other federal programs offer *payments* of one kind or another. In many cases these are direct payments of money, as with crop subsidies for farmers, unemployment benefits, welfare aid of various types, social security retirement benefits, etc. In other cases the payments are indirect but nonetheless result in money in the pockets of the beneficiaries, as with special postage rates for magazines, low-interest loans, tax advantages, leasing of government land, licensing of businesses, and so on. The target groups for these programs typically are there either to support what already exists or demand more.

Physical improvements represent another type of program. Presumably these projects are for the benefit of all—either for the nation as a whole, as with a highway system, or for those within a particular region, as with a flood-control project or sewage-treatment plant. Given the broad nature of the target group involved, one does not expect it to be represented as such in congressional deliberations (though, of course, the members, as well as agency personnel and, perhaps, state and local government officials will act as representatives). Suppliers, on the other hand, will certainly be there since those who build and supply materials for highways, public buildings, hospitals, sewage treatment plants, etc., benefit directly.

Another set of programs of presumed general benefit are those that fit under the general rubric of *defense*. Here too, one may expect that the organizers (i.e., the military itself) and suppliers are more likely to come to Congress than the targets or beneficiaries of a strong defense apparatus.

The government also provides many *services* —for example, education, health, transportation. These targets are more diffuse than for a direct subsidy program. One simply does not expect to find either school children or their parents very well organized to lobby in Washington for educational services. School superintendents and teachers, the suppliers of education, are very well organized, however, and very attentive to congressional developments.

This exercise in identifying a few types of government programs suggests considerable variation in the actual appearance of target groups on Capitol Hill. With the first two types, regulatory and payment programs, those directly effected are likely to come to Washington to support or oppose changes. With the next three types, physical improvements, defense, and services, the benefits are of a more general nature. In these latter cases, there is more reliance on elected representatives and government agencies to represent the interest of the program targets. On the other hand, since these latter three programs involve building, manufacturing, or providing something, it follows that the suppliers of that something will be actively involved when Congress acts on such programs.

The obvious implication of the point just made is that awareness, organization, and resources are important determinants of who comes to Congress—that is, awareness of programs and their effects, organization of those affected, and sufficient resources to get to Washington and be heard there. Those program targets without these advantages must depend on others to represent them and profit or suffer accordingly.

The suppliers

When federal outlays alone exceed $650 billion, approaching 25 percent of the gross national product, it logically follows that many persons and organizations from the private sphere are earning government dollars. The discussion above on program targets introduced several types of suppliers. They range from those who do practically nothing else but produce government material or services, as with many defense contractors, to those who are primarily in private business but do occasionally work for or sell to the government. It follows that those who do business almost exclusively with the government are going to be on Capitol Hill a lot. A major military aircraft manufacturer like Boeing is a classic example. Equally probable is the vigor of representation of these suppliers from members of Congress whose districts or states are directly profiting.

The suppliers listed in the air pollution example (see Table 7 — 1) illustrate another important point. Through regulations, government can, in effect, create an industry. In this case, establishing stringent pollution standards on what can be emitted either from the tail pipe of a motor vehicle or the tall stacks of a factory brought into being new firms or divisions of existing firms to supply pollution-control equipment. Having been created, these firms are then likely to support continued enforcement of pollution control. In this way, government programs quite naturally develop their own support.

Before leaving this category, it is well to point out that much of the activity of the suppliers may, in fact, be considerably less visible than that of other actors cited here. The American political system has never been exactly free of corruption. It is unlikely that any large system attempting to govern through public/private cooperation can ever be totally without scandal. But surely one major source of potential corruption (i.e., gaining special advantage through contributions, payoffs, kickbacks, etc.) is that associated with the private sphere supplying materials and services for public purposes as specifically defined in government programs.

The professionals

It is impossible for an active government to avoid being involved in highly technical issues in this day and age. We have witnessed, therefore, a quantum increase in the professional and technical personnel required by government, both in the bureaucracy and, more recently, in the legislature. Professionals outside government are also involved when government expands to control social and technical processes in society. Thus, for example, no public health program can be developed without drawing the medical profession toward government. The same may be said for literally hundreds of government programs and their effect on other professions—for example, airline regulation, economic controls, banking regulation, housing support, transportation plans, etc. The professionals in these circumstances are rightfully concerned about the effect of government regulations on their livelihoods. They can both provide expertise in forming the program and feedback on whether the program is effective.

Professionals outside government continue to be the major source of professionals within the government, except for the military which maintains its own training program. Many government officials retain memberships in their professional associations. Some at the higher levels of decision making move back and forth between universities or research organizations and government. Their access on the executive side may be impressive, thus forming a considerable lobbying bloc before the Congress. The full political and governmental impact of the professions has yet to be fully studied.

Citizen monitors

Along with the emergence of government-created clientele groups, perhaps no other development is as interesting and important as the rise of citizen lobbies. One hardly finds a reference to such groups in earlier works on interest groups. Today, however, Capitol Hill is virtually overrun with citizen- and consumer-group representatives. First are the broad-based groups which potentially may be involved in many different issue areas. Of the groups in Table 7 − 1, the League of Women Voters and the Public Interest Research Corporation are of this type. Premier among these groups would be Common Cause. Founded in 1970 by John Gardner, former secretary of Health, Education, and Welfare, Common Cause is supported by a general membership of over 200,000. No doubt because of Gardner's leadership, the organization has been successful in attracting a politically savvy staff. David Cohen (who recently resigned as president) and Fred Wertheimer, in particular, are respected and appreciated on Capitol Hill for their knowledge of issues and the political process. By contrast, Ralph Nader's Public Citizen organization commands less admiration on Capitol Hill. Though also effective, the Nader organization employs different tactics and is less likely to hold the confidence of the members.[7]

Second are the single-issue groups which have proliferated in recent years. The National Clean Air Coalition, Natural Resources Defense Council, and the Sierra Club are examples from Table 7 − 1. *Single-issue* is not quite an accurate description of the interest of such groups. Rather, their efforts are directed to lobbying on issues within a certain context—for example, environment, energy, taxation, civil rights, education, women's rights, and so on. These groups have the advantages of concentrated effort and intensity of commitment. In the past, political naivete prevented such groups from having much impact. The 1960s not only taught many of them the political facts of life, but it also demonstrated the effectiveness of direct action, (e.g., campaigning in a member's district, going to Washington and making demands, keeping the public informed in regard to a member's record).

---

[7] See *Congressional Quarterly Weekly Report*, May 15, 1976, p. 1197.

It is characteristic that these groups play no favorites between the political parties. Indeed, they are almost antipartisan and antipolitical in their approach. That is, they are intent on getting their way on the issue at hand and are seldom interested in accommodating the politician's problems (for example, the demands from other groups). The attitude of these groups may be, if the incumbent won't support us, we'll support someone who will. In some cases, the intensity of this political pressure has induced members into early retirement.

In summary

These five sets constitute an impressive array of demanders for members of Congress to satisfy. It is understandable that representatives and senators used to the old way of doing things simply prefer to retire. The demands of the job are much greater than ever before, calling for different types of legislators. It is quite likely that the period of the 1960s and 1970s will be looked back on as highly significant in producing a phase change in Congressional operations.

WHAT DO THEY WANT?

> Lobbying is probably as old as government; in fact . . . lobbying probably preceded government, since the establishment of a governmental system implies the accommodation of conflicting demands of participating groups. . . . Presumably, even the dictator must listen to certain key supporters (e.g., the army and the party); but compared to the elected official, he has much greater power to close off lobbying messages from many segments of the population (Milbrath, 1963:   12).

It is the case, of course, that lobbying has a constitutional base in the First Amendment. "Congress shall make no law . . . abridging . . . the right of the people . . . to petition the Government for a redress of grievances." Thus, while a great deal of newsprint is and has been devoted to attacking the special-interest and fat-cat lobbyists, it is by no means a simple matter to regulate who comes to Congress and what they do there. Even if it were not for the constitutional provision referred to above, one would want to be cautious in a democratic system in controlling citizen contact with elected decision makers. This caution is advised not only for the more obvious theoretical reasons associated with insuring the vitality of a democracy, but as well for the less obvious and highly significant reason that legislators simply need to know what people want out of government in order to make intelligent decisions.

It is not surprising, then, that congressional regulation of lobbying is slight. The Federal Regulation of Lobbying Act (Title III of the Legislative Reorganization Act of 1946) depends primarily on *disclosure* as a means of control. Lobbyists are required to register and disclose, among other things, their employers, salaries, expenses, money raised, those contributing large sums, and legislation they are seeking to influence. Abraham Holtzman summarizes the situation (1966:   106):

> In the formal legal sense, Congress has adopted rules that purport to regulate lobbying. But on the informal operational level lobbying is permitted, encouraged, and accepted as legitimate as well as useful by legislators.

Put differently, Congress is faced with meeting certain popular (mostly media) demands for controlling lobbying without at the same time interfering either with the constitutional right of citizens to make themselves heard or the legislative need for information.

It is useful to be reminded of these constitutional and practical requirements because it is easy to draw the wrong conclusions or get the wrong impressions when discussing what do they want? It is perfectly natural for people to want to improve their situation, and democratic governments have long been justified as providing a reasonable and just means for permitting that to happen. The trick is, of course, to insure that the process is reasonable and just; that, for example, access to government decision making is available to all.

I have found it useful in thinking about this important question to identify certain general interests that groups have, followed by an examination of specific issue areas. Determining what one wants from Congress is surely related to what one has now and the means by which it has been obtained, or denied. At least three general interests are involved: the *ends or goals* of congressional contact, the *beneficiaries* of these ends, and the *means* by which these ends will be achieved.

The ends

Social, economic, and *political* goals appear to dominate. Individuals or groups are attempting to raise or hold social status, improve or maintain their economic standing, increase or sustain their political access and influence. Of course, in the effort to gain more for themselves, they may also find it necessary to deny advancement to others. In fact, this process of improvement for self as denial for others is more than implicit in David B. Truman's definition of an interest group: "*Interest group* refers to any group that, on the basis of one or more shared attitudes, makes certain claims upon other groups in the society for the establishment, maintenance, or enhancement of forms of behavior that are implied by the shared attitudes" (1951:   33).

The three sets of goals identified above are not mutually exclusive. Quite the reverse, in fact. For example, economic gain achieved as a consequence of a government program may contribute to social status and result in political influence. This outcome is as likely whether the group is affluent (e.g., the oil industry benefiting from the depletion allowance) or quite poor (e.g., ghetto organizations benefiting from the poverty program). Still, individuals or groups might well be pursuing one set of goals over another, possibly assuming that other gains will follow in turn. Economic and political goals, in particular, appear to take precedence. Certain groups want economic gain above all else— again this may be the case with both those who have and those who have not. Others, for example, the civil rights organizations during the 1960s, may concentrate on political development as a first priority.

The beneficiaries

What people want when they go to Congress would normally be thought of as benefiting them directly. This is not necessarily the case, however—particularly given our inclusion of governmental groups and representatives. Some persons come to Congress to speak for others. While they may gain psychic benefits or, in the case of government agencies, stability in organization and programming, the purpose in coming to Congress is to represent or speak for others. Of course, the members of Congress themselves may legitimately purport to represent others too—after all that is why they were elected. The combinations of these representations makes for a fascinating legislative process, to be sure. Thus, for example, in a committee or subcommittee hearing there may be government administrators speaking for the program beneficiaries, the beneficiaries speaking for themselves, supporting groups speaking for the beneficiaries, citizen groups identifying a public interest—all before a membership sensitive to program effects for groups within their constituencies. Not surprisingly, committee chairmen typically ask testifying groups to identify their interests and the persons for whom they speak so that one can keep track of who presumes to represent whom.

The means

Many means are available for gaining the advantage sought. That which is sought will depend on the needs and wants of those coming to Congress. Theodore J. Lowi proposes four types of policy: distributive, constituent, regulative, and redistributive (1972: 298—310). He argues that each has special characteristics as regards the likelihood and applicability of the coercive effect of government. While an interesting and useful exercise, these categories are too abstract for our purposes. Rather, we need to consider the more specific means sought by individuals and groups for achieving their goals. We are trying to identify intentions, Lowi is trying to identify patterns of policy action (both intentions and effects).

As illustrations of the means sought by various individuals and groups coming to Congress, consider the following:

1. Get government to act less or not at all.
   Examples: Limits: tax cuts, preferential tax treatment, tax or spending limitations.
   Rescissions: reducing or terminating programs.
   Preventives: blocking action at all (possibly by controlling the agenda).
2. Get government to keep someone else from acting.
   Example: Regulation: curbing an economic practice, preventing a practice harmful to human health.
3. Get government to give you something.
   Examples: Lease: permission to use government land for extracting minerals or petroleum, agriculture purposes, other uses.
   Subsidy: supplementary payment for goods and services.
   Direct payment: payment, pensions, unemployment compensation, welfare assistance.
   Loans: low-interest or government guarantee.
   Service: education, training.
   Physical improvement: highways, schools, bridges, dams.
   Contract: agreement to produce goods or services.
   License: permission to conduct business or engage in an advantageous practice.
4. Get government to organize differently.
   Examples: Creation of a new agency.
   Upgrading an existing agency (perhaps to departmental status).
   Revamping existing procedures.

This list by no means exhausts the means for satisfying the goals of those who come to Congress from inside and outside government, but it is nonetheless impressive in this scope. It should be noted, of course, that Congress is not directly involved in granting all of these favors. Rather, Congress authorizes others to act. That authorization, and the appropriated funds to put it into effect, does begin on Capitol Hill, however, and thus the lobbying must begin there.

HOW DO THEY GET IT?

Getting what you want from Congress obviously involves access and communication. You need to make the contact with the members and then provide a message that is persuasive. The job of the lobbyist "becomes that of a communications specialist transmitting the views of his employers to decision makers in Washington and seeking to persuade, without recourse to heavy-handed pressure, those whose minds are still open to the wisdom of his organization's cause" (Rieselbach, 1973:   202). As discussed earlier the resources required for effective communication may vary greatly among groups. This variation, along with the difference in issues and receptivity on Capitol Hill, makes one cautious in generalizing about successful lobbying techniques. David B. Truman elaborates on this point (1951:   352):

> There is no single formula, no simple chronology of devices that all effective groups use in standard fashion. . . . tactics within the legislature are tremendously varied. Because the position of no two groups is precisely identical and because the resources of any single group are in part altered by the presence of other groups operating in the same area, techniques appropriate at one time may be inappropriate or unavailable at another. . . . While it would be comforting, therefore, to be able to present a sort of manual, a "how to do it," of group legislative techniques, the complexity of the legislative process will not permit it.

In support of Truman's observation, consider the following statements concerning lobbying techniques—the first two by lobbyists, the third by a member of Congress.

> I'm convinced that the grass-roots support is the important thing rather than my contacts. I know this from my experience on the Hill. . . , I can go up and explain the technical end of the thing, but it's the grass roots that lets the member of Congress know who is behind it. I would give 75 per cent to the grass roots (Milbrath, 1963:   238−39).

> * * * * *

> I'm in the business of communicating with these people, and if they don't have an open mind, I don't get to first base. I understand perfectly well that members of Congress are busy people, and I have a great deal of sympathy for that problem, but I can't be stopped by that. If a member tells me that he is too busy to see me, I find someone who is not insulated from the member, and I ask him to contact the member (Milbrath, 1963:   219).

> * * * * *

> Lobbying by other congressmen is the most difficult for me to resist. The spectacle of [another congressman] standing by the door saying

"help us out" recalls to me that he helped me out on an Indian bill (Clapp, 1963: 180).

Here are three quite different approaches. The first seeks to organize the political environment back home as a way of influencing the member. The second is the more direct approach of meeting with the member or working through an intermediary (perhaps as a means of meeting the member). And the third is a case of internal, member-to-member lobbying. At minimum, then, any inventory of lobbying techniques must include all three approaches.

Lester W. Milbrath's study of lobbying in Washington provides an evaluation of the effectiveness of various techniques by lobbyists (a sample of 99) and congressional respondents (a sample of 30 members and staff). He divided the techniques into those designed to keep communications channels open, those which employed inter-mediaries, and the direct methods of communication. I have reorganized these slightly in Table 7−2 to include the techniques used inside Washington, either direct or indirect, and those used outside

TABLE 7−2
Ratings of lobbying techniques by lobbyists and congressional respondents

	Lobbyists			Congressional respondents		
	Percent rating technique at:*			Percent rating technique at:*		
Techniques	Less than 5	5−10	Mean	Less than 5	5−10	Mean
1. Inside−direct:						
a. Personal presentation of views	9%	90%	8.4	0%	100%	8.7†
b. Presentation of research	17	82	7.4	14	85	7.3
c. Testifying at hearings	18	81	6.6	23	77	6.3
d. Bribery	98	1	0.1	96	4	0.3†
2. Inside− indirect:						
a. Contact by constituents	33	66	5.9	37	61	5.6
b. Contact by close friends	55	43	3.8	28	71	6.2†
c. Personal entertaining	87	12	1.6	100	0	0.8
d. Giving a party	89	10	1.2	96	3	0.7
3. Outside:						
a. Public relations campaigns	30	67	5.6	49	50	5.3
b. Letter and telegram campaign	44	55	4.6	70	30	3.9
c. Publicizing voting records	78	20	2.1	73	27	2.7†
d. Contributing money	83	16	1.9	67	33	3.0†
e. Campaign work	76	33	2.3	47	53	4.5†

* Percentages do not all total to 100 due to rounding.
† Indicates cases of where the congressional respondents on the average rated the technique higher than the lobbyists.
SOURCE: Milbrath, 1963: 213, 240, 257.

Washington, back in the states or district.[8] Milbrath asked his respondents to rate the technique on a scale from 0 to 10. Table 7 – 2 is useful first as an inventory of the more traditional techniques used in trying to get Congress to do what you want. But the ratings too are interesting. Both sides agree on the importance of personal, direct contact (fortunately with the exception of bribery). The congressional respondents tend to rate contact through a close friend (perhaps thinking of another member—see above) and campaign activities (contributing money or actual work for the member) higher than do the lobbyists. Overall, however, there appears to be considerable consensus on what works.

While these catalogues of lobbying techniques are useful in their own way, they fail to capture the dynamics of interaction in regard to any one bill, how contacts and communication differ among the members and between bills, or the remarkable growth in lobbying of all types during the 1970s. In part because there is no single formula, lobbyists try many techniques. But the quantum increase in participants has introduced new uncertainties. What worked well in the 1950s may no longer be so effective. Direct contact is still effective to be sure, but a lobbyist who at one time could meet with or phone a member at any time may now have to stand in line or have the call returned. Many of these new lobbyists are not the direct beneficiaries of the legislation. Rather, they are self-appointed definers of the public interest in regard to particular proposals, and they work hard to get the members of Congress to vote "right." The cozy relationship between legislator and lobbyist is more difficult to arrange than in the past. Lots of people on Capitol Hill now make it their business to monitor these relationships and demand that they be permitted to participate too (see Chapter 13 for a fuller treatment of this development). "Grumbles House Speaker Tip O'Neill: 'Everybody in America has a lobby.' "[9]

Congress itself has contributed to the increase in lobbying by playing its part in the growth of federal government programs. It should come as no surprise that a law spawning a new set of regulations brings lots of those to be regulated to Washington, or that a threatened change in the food stamp program will elicit a reaction from those depending on this form of support. But Congress has encouraged more participation and made lobbying more challenging by enacting many organizational, procedural, jurisdictional, and political reforms (see Chapter 15). Through its actions, Congress has, in essence, said: Let's bring more lobbyists to Washington and encourage them to par-

---

[8] Ornstein and Elder (1978:   82– 93) divide strategies in this way. They also point out that "influence can be particular . . . or diffuse . . ." (1978:   82).

[9] *Time,* August 7, 1978, p. 15.

ticipate in more phases of decision making, thus making life more difficult for everyone. Ornstein and Elder describe the results this way (1978: 81—82):

> All these changes altered the art of lobbying in fundamental ways. "It's not like the old days when you could see one or two people and your job was done," a corporate consultant said. "You have to work harder now, see more people." In the days when committee chairmen exercised nearly complete control of the flow of legislation, a lobbyist . . . needed only to contact a chairman and a handful of powerful senior members. But with the opening up of the system, younger legislators began to share the power—and there were many more people to be contacted and persuaded to support a lobbyist's point of view.
>
> . . . New techniques were necessary not only to persuade more skeptical and better-trained political decision makers, but also to counter the arguments of opposing groups.

In his fascinating discussion of the job of a congressman, Lewis Anthony Dexter concludes that (Bauer, et al., 1963: 405):

> A congressman must decide what to make of his job. The decisions most constantly on his mind are not how to vote, but what to do with his time, how to allocate his resources, and where to put his energy. There are far more issues before Congress than he can possibly cope with. There are very few of them which he does not have the freedom to disregard or redefine.

Many changes have occurred since Dexter wrote these words, but up until the last sentence, the only modification to make in his observation is that many more people are involved now in helping the member decide how to do the job. The last sentence is no longer appropriate, however. The increase in lobbying on all issues means that now there are very few issues which a member can unilaterally disregard or redefine. How to get it has become more complex for the lobbyist and therefore has contributed to further complicating the political and policy life of legislators in Washington. At the same time, the workload back home has also increased.

THE SPECIAL CASE OF CONSTITUENTS

Perhaps no term is more familiar on Capitol Hill than that of *casework*. Constituents come to Congress by mail and phone, sometimes in person, with requests for help in dealing with government. These cases have come to be an increasingly important part of the congressional workload.

> Casework is the basis of "constituency service." Casework is rarely self-initiated; it almost always stems from a constituent request. In offices with several caseworkers, certain subjects (for example, military,

social security, housing) are usually assigned to each caseworker, who receives and processes all letters and requests within these specific areas. In this way, they gain expertise and develop contacts with agency personnel. If the case can be handled by telephone, the agency's congressional liaison office is usually contacted. If a letter is necessary, a copy of the constituent correspondence to or request of the member is sent to the appropriate department or agency for attention.[10]

Clearly these requests are different from those characterizing classic lobbying. Those organized groups that come to Congress typically do so for the purpose of maintaining an existing program or developing a new program (occasionally to terminate an existing program). Individual constituents come to Congress in order to get services or to request that a particular program be applied fairly to their case. Janet Breslin provides the following sample of what constituents ask for (1977: 19):

> . . . assistance in obtaining delayed social security and disability benefits, denied veterans' claims and medicare reimbursements, and appeals of military decisions on such matters as hardship discharges; information on federal grant procedures, advice on developing grant proposals, and information on filing dates for special federal programs; copies of legislative bills and reports, executive branch regulations, agricultural yearbooks, infant care booklets; pictures and biographies of the senators; flags flown over the Capitol; and tourist information on Washington, D.C. and the various states; and sympathetic concern for the displaced, rejected, or frustrated citizen.

In terms of the stages of the policy process (problem definition through to program implementation and evaluation), members of Congress are, with casework, performing important program implementation and evaluation functions. They provide means by which constituents learn about programs and receive benefits—both necessary for proper implementation. And the members themselves learn something of the administration of programs and how they are accepted by their publics.

In his book, *Home Style*, Richard F. Fenno, Jr., quotes one member as saying that when he attends church festivals, "I stand at the beginning of the line and say, 'I'm the federal complaint officer'" (1978: 111). Receiving and acting on complaints is itself an important program implementation function. Casework also turns out to be an effective means for maintaining contact with those who are important in the member's policy life—that is, the departments and agencies responsible for administering programs and the local public to whom

---

[10] U.S. Congress, House of Representatives, Commission on Administrative Review, *Background Information on Administrative Units, Members' Offices, and Committees and Leadership Offices*, 95 Cong., 1 sess., 1977, p. 39.

programs are directed. Indeed, a symbiotic relationship develops out of this set of needs. Janet Breslin describes this three-cornered arrangement as it applies to senators, but her analysis is equally applicable to representatives (1977:   20).

> *The constituent* —the constituent wants help. The growth and complexity of government seems to render the individual incapable of coping. In the face of a perceived impersonal bureaucracy, it is natural for the citizen to look to the senator to intercede. . . . The constituent expects the senator to take action and to provide an adequate response from the agency.
>
> *The senator* —the senator wants to serve. He needs a competent staff to handle constituent workloads and to give attentive and timely service. He wants agencies to respond to his requests quickly and thoroughly. He wants to stay "in touch" with his constituents. He wants the constituent to know that he tried hard to be of service. He wants some public recognition of his efforts. He wants to be rewarded at the polling booth.
>
> *The agency personnel* —the agency personnel want to survive the congressional appropriations process. They want to operate with minimal congressional intervention, and so they are interested in pleasing the Senate, particularly those [members] on relevant committees. Fulfilling requests provides a convenient way to develop good agency "public relations with [Congress]."

It is not at all surprising that neither senators nor representatives are willing to have these tasks assigned elsewhere. A freshman representative explained (Clapp, 1963:   54).

> My first reaction was, "why don't they contact the executive agencies or the proper department with which these problems are associated? Why should they expect me to take care of this for them?" Gradually I came to realize that each of these problems is very important to the person writing me, and that it is important for me to treat them as significant. Many people are baffled by our bureaucracy and don't know where to turn for help. Eventually somebody says, "why don't you write your congressman?" and they do. I now realize that one of my most important functions is to help these people. If they are entitled to go through a door they cannot find, it is my job to locate that door so they can go through.

What this member has come to realize is that where there is a need for a service, so also is there a need for someone to perform that service. Apparently some members do have to learn this fact of life — they arrive in Washington with quite a different picture of the job they have been elected to do. "I thought I was going to be Daniel Webster, and I found that most of my work consisted of personal work for constituents" (Clapp, 1963:   51). Among other things, the members learn the importance of these services for reelection. It may be pronounced *ombudsman,* but it is spelled *reelection.*

The sheer volume of constituency-related work is stunning and frequently not expected by new members. Data collected by the House Commission on Administrative Review show that the average caseload per member is over 10,000 a year. Can you imagine how much mail that represents? Estimates are that the casework load has doubled in the last 10 years.[11] On the Senate side the variation is quite dramatic among the least to the most populous states. The smaller states produce 1,000 to 2,000 cases a year; those in the middle range, 2,000 to 3,000; and those with large populations range between 8,000 and 70,000. New York and California senators receive 30,000 to 50,000 cases a year, but it is Senator Kennedy (D—Massachusetts) who has the heaviest workload—more than 70,000 cases a year (Breslin, 1977: 21).

Another measure of constituency contact with members of Congress is the amount of time devoted to congressional requests by the departments and agencies. In 1962—63, the Department of Agriculture estimated that nearly 31,000 hours were spent "researching, developing, and supplying information to Congress; 13,477 letters and 43,201 telephone calls were received from congressional sources" (Clapp, 1963: 77). Equally staggering figures were reported by other departments. With the tremendous increase in casework, one may expect that these figures will have doubled in recent years. And these data well illustrate the manner and means by which federal programs result in bureaucratic growth beyond initial expectations, both in the executive and in the legislature.

At one time a constituent's contact with a member of Congress had to be on the occasion of the member's visit to the state or district, or the constituent's visit to the nation's capital. Today, however, the member hardly leaves the constituency. The sizeable increase in staff has permitted many members to establish a permanent presence at home (see Table 6—1). The decentralization of federal agencies has also contributed to this trend. That is, it is now as easy, perhaps easier, to answer constituents' requests from the state or district as from Washington.

> A number of offices, both Senate and House, are moving staff back to the state or district to handle a major proportion of the office workload. Two factors accelerating this move are the decentralization of federal agencies and the lack of office space on Capitol Hill. A number of federal agencies with which senators' and representatives' staffs deal on casework on federal project matters have well-staffed regional offices in major cities throughout the country. Casework originating within the districts is often handled by the regional agency office—hence, it makes

---

[11] U.S. Congress, House of Representatives, Commission on Administrative Review, *Administrative Reorganization and Legislative Management*, 95 Cong., 1 sess., 1977, p. 41. Casework varies, with senior members getting more than junior members.

a lot of sense for a congressman to have state or district casework staff (Fox and Hammond, 1977:   77).

Other important reasons cited for the shifting of casework to the state or district include the following (Breslin, 1977:   24):

1. Lack of space in congressional office buildings.
2. Lower staff salaries and overhead costs at home.
3. Personal contact with constituents.
4. Direct telephone lines to the agency, regional, and Washington offices.
5. Coordination between local, state, and federal programs.
6. Direct contact with local and state officials.
7. Visibility for the member in the state or district.

Fenno examined both the number of visits to the district for House members and the amount of staff resources allocated there. Representatives are paid for 26 trips home each year, yet they averaged 35 trips home in 1973. The range was considerable for the 419 members in Fenno's study: 4 to 23 trips, 129 members; 24 to 42 trips, 129 members; and 43 or more trips, 161 members. The members vary also in the amount of staff allocated to the district—from none at all to 81 percent. In seeking to explain the differences, Fenno was led to the significance of place—the region, the state, the district. But particularly telling was the dynamic relationship between the personal characteristics and perceptions of the member, and the social, political, geographical, perhaps even cultural, characteristics of the area represented. "Among the factors that appear to influence the allocation of a representative's time and money to his or her district are personal goals, family residence, distance, established local expectations, and the desire to create new local expectations" (1978:   50).

The Senate, too, takes very seriously the matter of serving constituents' wants and needs. Most senators maintain more than one office in the state—the average number is three. In some cases the staff allocated to the state nearly matches that in Washington. Perhaps as a consequence of the longer term, senators go home somewhat less frequently than House members. At least this is the finding of Eric M. Uslaner in his study of the 23 senators up for reelection in 1978. Though authorized to return home 42 to 46 times a year at government expense, 8 of the 23 (35 percent) made 23 or fewer trips in 1977, and 9 (39 percent) made the allowable 42 trips or fewer. Only six senators (26 percent) made 43 trips or more in 1977. Interestingly, five of the eight in the lowest group (23 trips or fewer) were defeated in 1978.[12]

---

[12] Eric M. Uslaner, "The Case of the Vanishing Liberal Senators: The House Did It," unpublished paper, 1979, p. 4.

State and district projects

Somewhat different from, but related to, casework is so-called project work. The sizeable number and impressive array of federal grants available for the states, counties, cities, and towns obviously stimulates the development of projects at those levels. But to apply, state and local officials and private groups must know of the existence of the grant and then often be provided with assistance as well as information and support. Congressional offices can offer such help. The application may be directed to a single agency or it may involve several agencies if a local group has developed and coordinated a series of proposals, perhaps in a large-scale urban development plan.[13]

In the case of these projects, those who come to Congress are state and local planners, department heads, special assistants, and representatives of nonprofit groups or agencies, business firms, industries, etc. Their needs vary in accordance with their knowledge and political savvy. Most states and many communities will have staff specifically devoted to getting grants. Ann Michel, director of the Office of Federal and State Aid Coordination for Syracuse, New York, states bluntly what her purpose is.

> Our first function is to manipulate the system to get as much of the money as we can into the city of Syracuse. . . . It also includes the development of a state legislative program and the follow-up lobbying effort. . . . An additional activity . . . is fairly active participation in federal legislative lobbying efforts, though that tends to be less intense than the state process (Wright, 1978: 181).

Michel cites both grant negotiation and lobbying for new legislation as important functions.

Robert Greenblatt, coordinator and chief, Federal Relations Unit of the Budget Division for the state of New York, lists a number of important functions in describing his job. Among them is lobbying in Washington.

> We try to assist both the budget examiners and the state agencies in maximizing the federal aid that comes into the state, and it's usually done by formula manipulation rather than merely applying for federal grants. The place to get in is on the ground floor when Congress is reviewing the program or initiating a program and deciding how it's going to allocate the funds (Wright, 1978: 242).

Clearly these officials are sophisticated manipulators of the system and thus are primarily coming to Congress for support—often in the early stages of program development. They may even provide information and services to members of Congress so that the members in turn will provide political backing.

---

[13] This section profits from Breslin's discussion, 1977: 21−22.

Where a state or community is not so fortunate as to have a Michel or Greenblatt available, they may require information and direct assistance in making applications, as well as support afterward. In such cases, congressional staff are more involved in manipulating rather than being themselves manipulated. On occasion the role is very active.

> Many times a senator's office will serve as the intermediary, bringing constituent groups and agency officials together to resolve disagreements. Project workers often act as salesmen for the state in negotiations with the federal government and assist in the preparation and argumentation for state groups before executive agencies (Breslin, 1977: 22).

And the payoff?

> Project workers generally will also work closely with the senator's press department to publicize the office efforts on behalf of local groups and to announce the presentation of grants for the state (Breslin, 1977: 22).

In summary, state and local officials and others eligible for federal grants come to Congress for a variety of reasons. Those who are knowledgeable about what is available (or is in the offing) may themselves shape the programs and influence their implementation with the aid of members of Congress. Those less aware require information about what is available and assistance in getting it.

THE SPECIAL CASE OF FOREIGN GROUPS

In 1938, Congress enacted the Foreign Agents Registration Act which required anyone acting for a foreign government to register with the Department of Justice. The original intent was to control the propaganda efforts of Nazi and Fascist agents before World War II. Today, however, virtually every foreign nation of significant size has a lobbying agent or agents operating in Washington (Ornstein and Elder, 1978: 51). The reason is that most national problems have international implications. Congressional decisions on what were primarily domestic issues in times past now may have critical economic, social, and political effects on foreign nations.

The examples of protective tariffs are familiar from earlier periods in American history, and they still arise from time to time (as was the concern in the 1970s about Japanese steel and automobile imports). Today two major types of foreign interests are represented. First are those nations who have come to depend on aid from the United States. Called client states, Taiwan, South Korea, and Israel fall into this category. Second are the efforts by foreign commercial interests to influence congressional decisions that are bound to affect them. The Koreans, symbolized by the activities of Tongsun Park, have cast an unfavorable image on this type of lobbying. The fact is, however, that most of this coming to Congress is like that involving domestic issues.[14]

Who actually registers as a foreign agent? Many are Washington lawyers who serve as lobbyists for domestic firms, several are former government officials, and others are public relations firms (also involved in domestic lobbying). Examples are provided in Table 7–3. Note that the fees are considerable (no doubt much higher now).

TABLE 7–3
Who comes to Congress representing foreign governments?

Registered agent	Government connections	Representing	Example of fees
Cambridge Reports	Firm of Pat Caddell, President Carter's campaign pollster	Saudia Arabia	$50,000 a year
James V. Stanton	Former representative (D – Ohio)	Republic of Korea	About $12,000 a month
Van Dyk Associates	Firm of Ted Van Dyk, former aide to Senators Humphrey and McGovern	Greece	$5,000 a month
Chester V. Clifton	Retired major general, former military aide to President Kennedy	Greece	$2,000 a month (worked for Van Dyk)
Keith Clearwaters	Former deputy assistant attorney general	Japan (Hitachi)	$100 an hour
Clark M. Clifford	Former secretary of defense, advisor to presidents	Algeria Australian Meat Board	$150,000 a year $160,000 a year
Ruder & Finn	(No direct connections – a New York public relations firm)	Iran National Airlines	Up to $507,000 a year

SOURCE: Compiled from information provided in *Congressional Quarterly Weekly Report*, April 16, 1977, p. 696.

The effort to win the right to land the Concorde at airports in the United States illustrates the impact of domestic decisions on foreign interests and the variation of involvement by members of Congress in such decisions.[15] When the United States decided against building a supersonic transport (SST), the British and French were understandably anxious to have their SSTs serve the American public. The French president and British prime minister took their case to top U.S. officials—including the secretary of state and the president. Members of Congress were responsive to environmental groups as well as to the

---

[14] This section draws heavily from Barry Hager, "Senate to Review Control of Foreign Agents," *Congressional Quarterly Weekly Report*, April 16, 1977, pp. 695–705.

[15] This brief case is a summary of material in the *Congressional Quarterly Weekly Report*, April 16, 1977, pp. 698–99.

view that permitting the Concorde to land would kill future chances of developing an American SST. Several bills were introduced to deny the Concorde landing rights. One passed the House but was defeated in the Senate and dropped in the conference. Working through public relations firms, the supporters of the Concorde sought to educate and therefore influence the public and members of Congress. "The task of the lobbyists was to impress upon the members of Congress that Franco-American relations, and international treaty negotiations generally, could be damaged by a negative Concorde decision."[16]

But the lobbyists in this case did not, indeed could not, limit their efforts to influencing Congress. They also concentrated on members of the Port Authority of New York, the Fairfax County Board of Supervisors in Virginia, and the Virginia and New Jersey state legislatures. The latter groups were all involved in making decisions about Kennedy Airport in New York and Dulles Airport in Virginia. Members of Congress from these areas, particularly New York, were also active when the Concorde lobbyists turned their attention on state and local groups. Representatives James H. Scheuer (D — New York) and John W. Wydler (R — New York) publicized the views of opponents and demanded to be included in the deliberations.

The Concorde interests engaged the services of seven prominent law firms in addition to three public relations firms. The law firms included those of former Secretary of State William P. Rogers, former Senator Charles E. Goodell (R — New York), and former Environmental Protection Agency Administrator William Ruckelshaus. Aerospatiale, the French government corporation responsible for building the Concorde, reportedly paid over $1.3 million to one public relations firm between October 1975 and October 1976. Clearly a great deal is at stake for certain foreign interests in American domestic policymaking. Because future national issues are even more likely to have international implications, lobbying by agents of foreign governments is likely to increase in the decades ahead.

CONCLUSION

This chapter has illustrated the variety of interests that come to Congress for help. They come at all because Congress has power to make important decisions affecting those interests. What this survey has demonstrated in addition is that the demands vary considerably, ranging from requests that government not act at all to proposals that the government provide money and services. Further the demands draw the members of Congress into many policy activities besides those normally associated with a legislature. Some groups want mem-

---

[16] *Congressional Quarterly Weekly Report*, April 16, 1977, p. 698.

bers to define problems as they do, others want them to formulate alternative proposals to those of the executive or competing groups, and most want their assistance in the standard legislative functions of building or opposing majorities and providing support or opposition for new and existing programs. Many constituents and some groups (e.g., public interest and consumer organizations) also want Congress to get involved in implementing and evaluating programs. Thus, while Congress does perform a primary role in approving or defeating programs, its members also play significant roles in the other policy functions of problem definition and program development, implementation, and evaluation. This participation is often at the behest of those who come to Congress and make demands.

Finally, this discussion also illuminates another important point in understanding Congress in the policy process. The pressure to be a part of program development, implementation, and evaluation—even as a secondary or appeal body—forces members into contact with the major issues and the significant others in the policy process (e.g., the administrators, targets, suppliers, professionals, citizen monitors). This extensive involvement surely does not make the job easier, but it contributes to making Congress the most powerful legislative body in the world and explains in part the need for the elaborately articulated organization which characterizes both houses. That organization is the next topic to consider.

8 How the House organizes to do its work: Offices and committees

It is useful at this point to repeat the principal orienting theme for this book, that is, picturing Congress as a population for prospective and ongoing policy networks. This reminder is helpful primarily because these next four chapters will examine formal structure and procedure. Congress is responsive and adaptive to the demands of governmental and private groups. But it does its work within an organizational framework grounded in precedent and characterized by extraordinary detail, features that are essential to the legitimizing function of Congress.

THE PROBLEM OF REPRESENTATION

What is the work to be done in Congress? Probably no legislature in the world experiences such a diverse set of demands, demands made by those from outside and from the members themselves. In part this condition is a consequence of the failure to resolve what we might call the *problem of representation.*

> *Representation* may be defined . . . as a relation between two persons, the representative and the represented or constituent, with the representative holding the authority to perform various actions that incorporate the agreement of the represented. The relation is by no means simple, since practically every type of human communication and perception can be shown to be intrinsic to representation. The relation is sociopsychological. Essentially subjective, it may, however, be affected by numerous objective conditions and events (deGrazia, 1968: 461).

The sociopsychological process of one person representing another is complicated, involving as it does an effort to serve in place of or as an equivalency for another person (who may or may not be present). But legislative representation involves more than the two-person relationship. Some of the variations are pictured in Table 8—1. Even

TABLE 8—1
Variations in representative relationships

	The represented		
The representative	*1. Individual*	*2. Group*	*3. Population (district, state, nation)*
1. Individual	A	B	C
2. Group	D	E	F
3. Institution	G	H	I

SOURCE: Compiled by the author.

though oversimplified, this display is impressive. What it suggests is considerable diversity in who is represented by whom. Among the represented is, of course, the individual constituent as suggested in the definition above. But also included are various groups, which themselves may represent individual interests in a sort of two-tiered representational system. These groups may or may not be wholly located in a legislator's state or district. There may also be occasions when the whole population of a district, a state, or even the nation constitute the represented. Clearly a legislature must develop means for facilitating these representations.

The representative may equally be the individual, acting in his or her legitimate capacity. But the representative mechanism may also be a group—for example, a legislative committee or subcommittee, a political party or its subunit. Thus, for example, Charlie Rose (D—North Carolina) acts to represent certain farm interests as an individual member of the House Committee on Agriculture, but the committee itself, or a subgroup thereof, also represents as a collectivity. It is this collective sense of representation that is referred to by Robert

Weissberg in his study of Congress. He contrasts the typical one legislator and one constituency brand of representation (B or C in Table 8 – 1) with that of institutions collectively representing a people.

> Within this tradition the central question would be whether Congress as an institution represented the American people, not whether each member of Congress represented his or her particular district (Weissberg, 1978: 535).

Not surprisingly Weissberg concludes that this collective representation does supplement individual representation (1978: 547).

> It may be impossible for one legislator to represent 400,000 people with any degree of accuracy; it may, however, be possible for 435 legislators to represent more accurately the opinions of 220 million citizens. To be sure, whether or not a particular legislator follows his or her constituency is an important question, but this question is not necessarily the most appropriate one if we ask, "Do representatives represent?"

Thus Weissberg raises prospect I in Table 8 – 1, and by implication prospects G and H as well. His discussion also implicitly introduces the classic distinction between representation as a process and representation as a consequence. This is the familiar difference between developing means by which the representative seeks to discover what the represented think and want, and the actual consequences of decision making being in line with what the represented think and want. The first does not necessarily result in the second, and the second may occur without the first.

This important distinction comes close to what Heinz Eulau has identified as the *focus* and *style* of representation. Table 8 – 1 concentrates on focus—on the targets of representation, for example, an individual constituent, a special group, or the whole population of a jurisdiction. Style refers to the means by which decisions are made by elected representatives. Eulau cites the famous speech by Edmund Burke to his constituents in Bristol in 1774. Burke argued that a representative ought to maintain "the closest correspondence" with constituents. Further, "it is his duty" to be unselfish, "to prefer their [the constituent's] interest to his own."

> But his unbiased opinion, his mature judgment, his enlightened conscience, he ought not to sacrifice to you, to any man, or to any set of men living. These he does not derive from your pleasure—no, nor from the law and the constitution. They are a trust from Providence, for the abuse of which he is deeply answerable. Your representative owes you, not his industry only, but his judgment; and he betrays, instead of serving you, if he sacrifices it to your opinion.
>
> My worthy colleague says his will ought to be subservient to yours. If that be all, the thing is innocent. If government were a matter of will upon any side, yours, without question, ought to be superior. But gov-

ernment and legislation are matters of reason and judgment, and not of
inclination; and what sort of reason is that in which the determination
precedes the discussion, in which one set of men deliberate and another
decide, and where those who form the conclusion are perhaps three
hundred miles distant from those who hear the arguments? (in Hoffman
and Levack, 1949:   115).

Burke then uttered the famous phrase summarizing his concept of the
working legislature (in Hoffman and Levack, 1949:   116):

> Parliament is not a *congress* of ambassadors from different and hos-
> tile interests, which interests each must maintain, as an agent and advo-
> cate, against other agents and advocates; but Parliament is a *deliberative*
> assembly of *one* nation, with *one* interest, that of the whole. . . . You
> choose a member, indeed; but when you have chosen him he is not a
> member of Bristol, but he is a member of *Parliament.*

Eulau quite rightly identifies in this speech a *focus* on the nation as
whole and a *style* of rational debate with each representative relying
on reason and judgment. In their study of state legislatures, Eulau and
his colleagues identified three roles—the trustee, the delegate, and the
politico. The stylistic characteristics of each were as follows (Wahlke et
al., 1962:   272—73, 277—78):

> *Trustee:* . . . sees himself as a free agent in that, as a premise of his
> decision-making behavior, he claims to follow what he considers right or
> just, his convictions and principles, the dictates of his conscience.
> *Delegate:* . . . they should not use their independent judgment or
> principled convictions as decision-making premises. But this does not
> mean that they feel equally committed to follow instructions, from
> whatever clientele. Some merely say that they try to inform themselves
> before making decisions by consulting their constituents or others;
> however, they seem to imply that such consultation has a mandatory
> effect on their behavior.
> *Politico:* Depending on circumstances, a representative may hold the
> role orientation of trustee at one time, and the role orientation of dele-
> gate at another time. Or he might even seek to reconcile both orienta-
> tions in terms of a third. In other words, the representational-role set
> compromises the extreme orientations of trustees and delegate and a
> third orientation, the politico, resulting from the overlap of these two.

That the third role, the politico, does not appear to have a separate
identity need not prevent our acknowledging the utility of the other
two. That is, most if not all legislators are likely to vary their styles
between being attentive to district demands and attentive to information or reasoning provided by other sources. For immediate purposes
we are less interested in specifying the precise number of styles of
representation than in acknowledging the variation itself.

This discussion provides context for the earlier statement that Congress has not resolved the problem of representation. Whereas politi-

cal party might play an instrumental role in determining the focus and style of representation in some legislative systems, no such tidying up goes on in Congress. The full range of relationships is permitted to exist on most issues, thus greatly complicating the organizational problems of both houses. For example, the United States Congress lacks the organizational advantage of, say, a British House of Commons. The latter solves its problem of representation with a political party solution. Individual, committee, or institutional differences in focus and style of representation are not normally permitted outside the party structure. Thus it follows that organizing the legislature is a relatively easy task.[1]

In the case of the United States Congress, failure to solve the problem of representation, or perhaps more accurately, failure to attend to the problem at all, results in at least two sets of organizations—both of which are diffuse. The first of these is directed to serving direct representational functions—most of which are perceived by members as being associated with their reelection. The second is directed to the tasks associated with lawmaking—tasks made enormously more difficult by the failure effectively to coordinate the first.

Roger H. Davidson essentially treats this matter by referring to two Congresses (and, by implication, four legislatures—two Houses, two Senates).

> One of these two entities is Congress as an institution. It is Congress the lawmaking and policy-determining body. It is Congress acting as a collegial body, performing its constitutional duties and deliberating legislative issues. . . .
>
> Yet there is a second Congress, every bit as important. . . . This is the Congress of 535 . . . individual senators and representatives. They possess diverse backgrounds and follow varied paths to win office. Their electoral fortunes depend not upon what Congress produces as an institution but upon the support and goodwill of voters hundreds or thousands of miles away—voters whom they share with none of their colleagues on Capitol Hill.[2]

Here we have the two organizational tasks referred to above. By this view Congress is both an *institution* and *collectivity*. As an institution, Congress is two representative bodies with the constitutional responsibility to pass laws. As a collectivity, Congress is two representative bodies with individual commitments and styles. Congress the institution continues, Congress the collectivity is constantly undergoing change. The trick is to organize in a fashion that connects the collectiv-

---

[1] Unless, of course, no party has a majority—a problem that plagued the Labor Party in the Callaghan Government and finally resulted in its defeat in 1979.

[2] Roger H. Davidson, "The Two Congresses and How They are Changing," paper prepared for conference on "The Role of the Legislature in Western Democracies," Selsdon Park, England, June 8–10, 1979, p. 2.

ity with the institution so that the advantages of diverse focuses and styles of representation are realized in the process of making law.

The reader may well despair at this point as to precisely where this discussion is leading. It will now lead directly into a review of how the House and Senate are organized. As we will see, both chambers have developed rather elaborate means for exercising their responsibilities as lawmaking institutions and as collectivities of elected representatives. It is to those arrangements that we turn next.

HOUSE AND SENATE—GENERAL DIFFERENCES

One hardly needs to be reminded of the important differences between the two chambers in size, length of term, nature of constituency, and basic powers. The purpose here is rather to observe that these differences are significant in explaining the organization of the two legislative bodies. Size alone is instrumental in determining how each body proceeds to do its work. The House of Representatives is considerably more formal in its proceedings, its rules more likely to be invoked as written. The Senate has fewer rules and does much of its work under agreements worked out among those involved in the debate.

The greater flexibility in the Senate also means that the distinction between committee and floor work is somewhat less clear than in the House. In his study of congressional committees, Richard F. Fenno, Jr., made the following cogent observation (1973: 190 −91):

> Since the House and Senate are different institutions, it should not be surprising that their committees are also different. Senate committees are less important as a source of chamber influence, less preoccupied with success on the chamber floor, less autonomous within the chamber, less personally expert, less strongly led, and more individualistic in decision making than are House committees.

It appears that committee work often carries over to the floor in the Senate whereas, at least in the past, the House committees enjoyed considerable floor support for legislation as reported. Thus, for example, James W. Dyson and John W. Soule found that House committees are "highly influential on roll-call voting" (in Reiselbach, 1979: 187).

Taken as a whole, I think it is fair to say that the House is more oriented toward the individualistic functions of facilitating representations from individuals and groups and discovering the basis for compromise within issues, whereas the Senate is more oriented toward the institutional functions of debating issues and discovering the basis for compromise *across* issues. It is granted that these are only very generalized distinctions, but they may prove serviceable for the student in reviewing the detail of organization in each chamber. And it is worth recalling that legislation is the result of the blending of these functions and styles since action in both houses is required.

ORGANIZING THE HOUSE OF REPRESENTATIVES

> In order to operate as a legislature capable of resolving conflict, Congress must develop an internal system of authority and action as well as establish communications with the external world. These requirements are mandatory in the sense that they must be performed if Congress is to be a legislature, but they are not fulfilled regularly with equal thoroughness and emphasis. Their fulfillment represents an equation of relationships and degrees of effectiveness, not a set of either/or alternatives (Young, 1958: 16).

In this passage, Roland Young reiterates the importance of the two activities—maintaining contact outside and developing a decision-making apparatus inside. Whatever organization emerges to meet these demands, it is assured that its elements will become involved at some point in both activities. Still, the activities themselves are distinctive enough to merit separate treatment.

Organizing to represent and serve the district

In discussing the processes and policies of Congress, David R. Mayhew, in his book, *Congress: The Electoral Connection*, asks the reader to bear in mind two prefatory points (1974a: 81—82):

> The first is that the organization of Congress meets remarkably well the electoral needs of its members. To put it another way, if a group of planners sat down and tried to design a pair of American national assemblies with the goal of serving members' electoral needs year in and year out, they would be hard pressed to improve on what exists. The second point is that satisfaction of electoral needs requires remarkably little zero-sum conflict among members. That is, one member's gain is not another member's loss; to a remarkable degree members can successfully engage in electorally useful activities without denying other members the opportunity successfully to engage in them.

As we have seen, the proof of Mayhew's assertion appears to be in the high return of House incumbents though not necessarily Senators. Clearly, where individualism or factionalism is favored over political party control, then it is eminently rational to organize so as to insure that everyone wins and no one loses. However well it seems to be working at present (and one begins to note evidence that it is not working as well as in the past), the system of allocating quite incredible resources to individual members tends to maximize the I win, you win philosophy in the House and Senate. One alternative that is familiar in other political systems, that is, political party control of the resources, has not been entertained in recent decades in the United States.

Well, how does it work out? How are House members organized to represent? Table 8—2 shows the personal resources available to all House members and how these resources have increased in recent years (exclusive of salary and retirement benefits). Calculating a total figure is difficult since certain benefits are dependent on distance from the district, office rental rates in the district, and how much certain

TABLE 8—2
Organizing to represent in the House—the perquisites

Perquisite	Amount	Comment
Official expenses:		
1. Base amount	$32,911	May be used for travel, office equipment, district office, stationery, telecommunications, mass mailings, postage, computer services.
2. Supplemental travel	Base amount of $2,250 plus additional payment based on mileage. Also one round trip for each session of Congress.	Rate set by formula.
3. Telephone	Base amount of $6,000 plus additional payment based on long-distance rates.	A member with a WATS service receives less (but not less than $3,000).
4. District office:		
a. Rental	2,500 square feet	Paid at highest rate charged to federal agencies in the district.
b. Furnishings	$27,000	A one-time payment.
Clerk hire:		
1. Staff	$288,156	For salaries of staff not to exceed 18; $15,000 may be transferred to official expenses.
2. Interns	$1,360	A two-month payment for one intern.
Other support:		
1. Franking privilege	Varies	Mail sent by frank is regulated.
2. Foreign travel	Varies	Authorized through the committees.
3. Miscellaneous (documents, file storage, gymnasium, furnishings, parking, picture framing, etc).	Varies	Chargeable to legislative branch budget.

SOURCE: U.S. House of Representatives, Committee on House Administration, *Studies Dealing with Budgetary, Staffing and Administrative Activities of the U.S. House of Representatives,* 95th Cong., 2d sess., 1978, pp. 36–59.

services are used. But the average figure for members is close to $400,000. For comparative purposes, a member of the British House of Commons gets the equivalent of less than $20,000 in support, exclusive of salary.[3] (It should be noted, however, that the British MP represents many fewer constituents—85,000 compared to 500,000 for House members).

In 1978, the House made a major change in the manner of providing support. Previously most items were paid for individually—for example, travel, telephone, postage, etc. Many of these were consolidated into an official expenses allowance which included a base amount plus certain additional allowances to compensate for district distances and differences. Many of the perquisites are not calculable from office to office but taken as a whole represent a large expense. For example, the amount of franked mail in the mid 1970s was well over 300 million pieces annually at a cost in excess of $60 million.[4] Predictably the mail increases in volume in election years (Bibby et al., 1980: 94).

These resources are organized and used differently by the members. Two important changes have occurred that have effected all members, however. First, resources have increased impressively in recent years and dramatically over a period of 50 years. Richard E. Cohen estimates that the cost of the perquisites in 1970 amounted to less than one half that in 1978 (1978: 182). Second, this increase in resources has permitted an extraordinary amount of attention to the representative function. Though I lack comparative evidence on the matter, it does seem reasonable to suggest that members are in a better position than ever before to detect how their districts are affected by pending legislation. Given the staff in the district, the mailings, the trips home, television and radio, and all of the other contacts, members are able to process their lawmaking responsibilities through a district or representative filter. Bear in mind that though we have stressed the existence of two Congresses or two major sets of functional activities (representing the lawmaking), both come together in the individual members as they do their jobs. Fenno puts it thus (1978: 215, emphasis added):

> When we speak of constituency careers, we speak primarily of the pursuit of the goal of reelection. When we speak of Washington careers, we speak primarily of the pursuit of the goals of influence in the House and the making of good public policy. Thus the intertwining of careers is, at bottom, *an intertwining of member goals.*

---

[3] The estimate of Austin Ranney in "The Working Conditions of MPs and MCs: Changing the Tools Changes the Job," paper prepared for conference on "The Role of the Legislature in Western Democracies," Selsdon Park, England, June 8–10, 1979, p. 7.

[4] Information on franked mail is provided in Congressional Quarterly, Inc., *Congress and the Nation* 4, pp. 756–59.

Not unexpectedly, Fenno discovered that junior members were more constituency attentive than senior members. In the terms in which we have been discussing this topic here, these junior members are concentrating on developing confidence in their district perspective on issues so as not to make major and costly errors in judgment, either in serving the district or in making decisions on legislation.

In Chapter 7 we discussed the increase in district-based staff for House members. The work of this local staff is more single-minded than that of the Washington staff. They are there to handle casework, be constantly attentive to events of possible importance for reelection, assist with projects, etc. Often no more than one or two persons will work in a district office and a number of volunteers or interns may be recruited.

The work in Washington is considerably more diversified and thus the staff organization is more elaborate. Space is also restricted (approximately 700 square feet for a dozen or more people). A visit to the personal office of a House member is memorable in part because of the virtual bedlam one encounters. During the summer, when student interns are everywhere, visitors hardly have a place to sit. Often one or more persons is located in the member's private office. "Offices are often noisy; decible levels oftentimes exceed 70 (the equivalent noise level of a major highway right outside the window). Keeping people working efficiently despite the closeness and clatter is no small achievement."[5] All of this pandemonium (and it is just that in certain offices) contributes to the impression that here is an operation designed for the short run—perhaps for the 18 months or so between elections (roughly the time from the general election to the next primary for many members).

Though it may not be apparent to the casual observer, there is, in fact, a distinct set of functions being performed in the members' offices. As noted earlier, the breakdown of tasks is considerably greater than that for district offices, and it has been described as follows:[6]

1. Administrative
   a. Personnel management: an increasingly important function with the growth of staff.
   b. Office management: includes managing available space; equipment leasing, purchase and use; and, of course, the critically important function of maintaining the files and other information management tasks in the age of information overload.

---

[5] U.S. House of Representatives, Commission on Administrative Review, *Background Information on Administrative Units, Members' Offices, and Committees and Leadership Offices*, 95th Cong., 1st sess., June 30, 1977, p. 38.

[6] This review is drawn from that provided in Commission on Administrative Review, *Background Information*, pp. 37 – 40.

    c. Financial management: also of increasing importance with greater resources available and the recent trend toward more restrictions on the use of funds.

2. Mail: typically the most obvious activity in the office since it physically appears stacked on every desk. The House received 17 million letters in 1970, 25 million in 1975 (an increase of nearly 50 percent in five years). ". . . the simple tasks of opening, categorizing, and routing mail can consume a number of staff working hours."[7]

3. Legislation: preparing and introducing legislation, keeping informed on pending legislation, working on committees and subcommittees to which the member is assigned.

4. Casework: discussed earlier—much is handled in the district offices but the volume of work is so great that the actual amount handled in the Washington office may not have decreased.

5. Press and public relations: one of the most important functions for insuring reelection—involves writing press releases and insuring that they are published; managing radio and television appearances and reports (members may use the House recording studio to film or record reports for home consumption); preparing newsletters, questionnaires, district town meetings.

6. Scheduling: also more complicated than ever before as the demands on a member's time increase. Staff must be aware of all hearings, markup sessions, special meetings and receptions, luncheons, appointments, while saving time for signing mail, reviewing reports, meeting with staff, and, of course, traveling to the district. Most members live their lives by the 3×5 appointment card, given to them as each day begins.

7. Federal projects: also discussed earlier (see Chapter 7)—called super casework by some, this activity is directed to insuring that the lawmaking function (where it involves largesse) contributes materially to the representative function within the member's district.

This is an impressive list of activities for a staff of 10 to 12 persons, all virtually sitting on top of one another in their Capitol Hill Office. Identifying the work to be done is one thing, accomplishing it is quite another. It must be said that members are not equally adept at either hiring or managing staff. Some members are reelected in spite of, not because of, efficient and effective staff work. And though I don't have direct evidence on the subject, I suspect that many constituents feel represented by members who are not particularly good managers of staff. It simply is the case that the standard bureaucratic criteria of good management do not always apply in measuring the effectiveness of a representative's capacity to do the job. And yet it must be further

---

[7] Commission on Administrative Review, *Background Information,* p. 38.

observed that some proposals for reform are based on these good management criteria.

Just as the work itself has expanded and is more clearly segmented than in the past, so too are the staff positions more articulated than in the past. While it is true that jobs still overlap to a considerable extent, there is more specialization than in the past. Table 8−3 shows the

TABLE 8−3
Typical staff positions in a House Washington office

Position	Responsibilities	Person in this position in office of Cecil Heftel (D − Hawaii)
Administrative assistant (AA)	Most versatile—often liaison with the district, office and staff management, some press relations, research, speech writing.	Bill Brown
Executive secretary/ office manager	Works with AA, possibly supervising the mail, filing, casework; may handle schedule and serve as member's personal secretary.	Mary Ann Nedry
Legislative assistants (LAs)	Typically a principal LA with assistants; assist in all legislative-related matters in member's committee, on House floor, with interest groups; including research and drafting of legislation.	Chris Chrisley, Valerie Lam
Press assistant	Writes press releases and speeches, maintains liaison with media, assists with radio and television reports and appearances.	Doug Carlson
Caseworkers	Handle all aspects of constituent's requests, contact agencies, respond to constituents.	Nancy Kemp, Betty Jones (located in district)
Secretary/clerks	Dictation, typing, filing—possibly some research or contact with research agencies (e.g., CRS, OTA).	Nancy Forbes, Marilyn Diego
Receptionist	Greets visitors, answers telephone, opens mail, general clerical work.	Hawley Manwarring
Equipment operator	Handles duplicating, other tasks associated with mass mailings.	

SOURCE: U.S. House of Representatives, Commission on Administrative Review, *Background Information on Administrative Visits, Members' Offices, and Committees and Leadership Offices*, 95th Cong., 1st sess., June 30, 1977, pp. 40− 42. This compilation is based on work by Susan Hammond.

typical staff positions, with the responsibilities often assumed and the persons filling these positions in one office—that of Cecil Heftel (D−Hawaii). This exercise is a bit risky given the fact that nearly 90 different titles of staff are listed with the clerk of the House. But the chances are good that these positions at least will be found in any one office.

With two or more offices to coordinate, the question arises as to how they relate to one another. John D. Macartney studied congressional district offices in Los Angeles, California, and he found variation in the organizational arrangements between the Washington and district offices. Of the 19 House members and two Senators studied, 9 had office directors in each place, 9 directed all operations from Washington, and 3 actually had principal direction from the district. He also found that in eight of the district offices of House members the top aide in the district also ranks as the top of the entire organization.[8] Surely this ranking represents considerable change from the past when serving in the district was considerably lower in prestige than serving in Washington (a problem that remains for many member organizations, it should be added).

Two important points should be made before leaving this matter of how House members are organized to represent. First, as will be seen shortly, we have less organization to describe when it comes to the members' offices even though the work that goes on is as great or greater in volume and importance as that associated with lawmaking. I believe there is a significant lesson to be learned about the roles of Congress in that fact. That lesson is simply that this district-oriented work is particularistic—directed to a great many specific problems and requests flowing from general programs, policies, and political interests (including those of the member to be reelected). It is not that problems are not repeated many times over, but rather that the outcome is typically specific in its effect on one or a few individuals. Therefore once one has said, *these* people do *this* work, little else is required for an understanding of the flow and nature of decision making.

Much lawmaking, on the other hand, is more universalistic in nature. It is designed to apply to all those who fall within the definitions included in the law. This is not to say that law does not have particular applications but rather that these applications are presumably to apply whenever a set of circumstances develop. It follows then that the organization of lawmaking will be more elaborate and, accordingly, our descriptions more detailed. I make this point to explain why many descriptions of Congress are weighted in the direction of the lawmaking function even while acknowledging the significance of constituency service.

The second point I would like you to consider is that the Washington and district office organization and activity influence how members use the organizational units of the House itself—for example,

---

[8] John D. Macartney, "Legislative Staff and District Offices," unpublished paper extracted from author's Ph.D. dissertation on "Political Staffing: A View From the District," University of California—Los Angeles, 1975, p. 40.

committees, subcommittees, research agencies, party units. In fact, a good case can be made that the members' home perspective influences how these units are established and organized. As Mayhew observes: "the organization of Congress meets remarkably well the electoral needs of its members" (1974a: 81). And I would remind the reader again that these matters of constituency service, representation, and reelection are exceedingly difficult to disentangle. All I am really saying here is that as we move now from the personal organizations of members to the institutional organization of the House, we inevitably find overlap between the representation and lawmaking functions. Committees and subcommittees are organized primarily to facilitate realization of both functions, whereas the members' offices are organized primarily to achieve the representative function (to include, of course, constituency service). Well, having gotten that out of the way, we can proceed to consider the rather elaborate manner in which the House organizes to make law.

Organizing to make law

Making law is philosophically a most intriguing process. This is not the place to get into the social function of law, but it is appropriate at least to mention it. Creating law is perhaps the principal means by which a social system attempts to identify issues, represent affected interests, and draw conclusions about what should be done. In fact, that sequence identifies a flow of activities directed toward establishing rules, specifying values, and allocating resources. The flow itself can be conceived of as moving from the issue, with all of its dimensions and related interests, to a specific course of action designed to resolve the issue (or at least change it in some way—see Chapter 13). It is interesting, however, that in the legislative process generalist participants are increasingly involved as one gets closer to final approval. Thus in order to enact a law directed to a specific condition, one must gain the support of persons who are either not associated with that condition or who have not been involved along the way.

This peculiar set of two-directional funnels—moving from the general to the specific within an issue to be resolved, while moving from the specialists to the generalists in order to get majority support— creates special organizational problems. How these problems are treated in the House of Representatives is the subject of this section. The problems themselves include primarily the matter of how best to specialize in representing interests and analyzing their views and yet insure that legislation has sufficiently broad support that its effects on other issues will have been measured. The organizational solutions in the House of Representatives are, of course, found in the committee and party systems. Using the word *solution*, however, is not meant to imply by any means that everything works smoothly at all times. It is always in order to be reminded that lawmaking in a democratic order is seldom, if ever, as tidy as the charts display, or the scholars describe.

The formal process

Having just warned the reader that reality seldom matches the formality, it is now in order to present that formal process. After all, one must first picture the object to which exceptions are made so as to understand the nature of the exceptions. Table 8 − 4 shows the major steps involved in a bill becoming a law. Senate action is included as well but will be discussed subsequently.

Though the following discussion of committees and political parties will touch on many aspects of the process, a few observations are appropriate at this point. First, the reader should not be misled into thinking that all bills are processed through these many steps. Most die in committee. In fact, perhaps the most striking feature of this display is the number of hurdles that must be overcome if a bill is to be law. The various cross marks in Table 8 − 4 are meant to indicate the points at which the legislation may die or be seriously altered. Virtually no major legislation survives intact.

Second, important differences between the House and Senate can be noted—particularly after the bills reach the floor. A book of this length could easily be written just on House floor procedures. They are incredibly complex, in large measure because the House is large and the workload is great. Bertram M. Gross employed a railroad-yard analogy in describing House procedures (1953: 338 − 39):

> One should think of many trains being run by canny engineers who will try to hold back on some occasions and to plow ahead on others. One should then visualize a tremendous number of trains lined up in the railroad yard, with their crews eager to devise means of getting a favorable signal and with gangs of switchmen roaming the yards making efforts to assure that certain trains are permanently sidetracked. Finally, one should realize that every week new trains are lined up in the yards and that every week brings closer the end of the Congress when the yards and tracks are all completely cleared and the entire process of lining-up starts over again.

Surely this word picture begins to give one the idea of what to expect when visiting the House in its bill-processing attitude.

Third, one has to be impressed with the potential for involvement by so many different persons and so many different action points. The conclusion is warranted that such an elaborate process must produce superior legislation. Yet there is another view which suggests that accountability is lost in this labyrinth. By the time a major bill is enacted into law, only the most knowledgeable observers are in a

TABLE 8– 4
From a bill to a law

Action point	House	Senate	Comments
Introduction	By a member placing it in the hopper. Receives an H.R. number.	By a member seeking recognition. Receives an S number.	Cosponsorship possible (House limits cosponsors to 25).
Committee referral	To one of 22 committees by Speaker.	To one of 15 committees by Senate president.	Assignment is not normally controversial and is actually done by parliamentarian. Action here is the first reading.
Subcommittee referral	Not mandatory—done by committee chairman.	Not mandatory—done by committee chairman.	Subcommittees more important in recent years.
Notification of appropriate agency	Comments solicited.	Comments solicited.	An important clearance point.
Hearings	Not mandatory.	Not mandatory.	Hearings may be held in subcommittee or full committee.
Reports	Subcommittee to committee/committee to floor.	Subcommittee to committee/committee to floor.	Failure to report normally kills the bill. New number may be assigned (the "Clean Bill").
Placed on appropriate calendar	5 calendars: union (money bills); House (other public bills); consent (minor bills); Private; Discharge.	2 calendars: General orders (all bills); Executive (treaties, nominations).	Major public bills in the House go on union or House calendars—others are shifted to consent calendar.
Scheduling	Major bills normally get special rule from Committee on Rules. Minor bills on call of appropriate calendar. Certain bills are privileged.	Major bills by unanimous consent agreement or majority vote. Minor bills on call of calendar.	The House Committee on Rules specifies the time and conditions for debate on major bills. Senate agreements may do the same.
Debate and amendment	May sit as a committee of the whole with lesser quorum. Debate limited. Five-minute rule on amendments.	Debate usually unlimited unless set by unanimous consent agreement.	House debate always subject to limits; Senate debate less constrained. Action here constitutes second reading.

TABLE 8– 4 (*continued*)

Action point	House	Senate	Comments
Voting	Occurs on amendments and bill itself—by voice, standing, teller, or electronic device (recorded yeas and nays).	Occurs on amendments and bill itself—by voice, standing, or roll call (recorded yeas and nays).	Motion to recommit provided in special rules in the House (for one who is opposed). Third reading follows defeat of recommital.
Motion to reconsider	Offered by member on the prevailing side, followed by motion to table.	Offered by member on the prevailing side or member who did not vote, followed by motion to table.	Purpose is to prevent reconsideration at a later date. Motion to reconsider is invariably tabled.
Dispatched to other house	House acts first on revenue measures by the Constitution, on appropriation measures by tradition.	—	Both houses may be working on legislation at the same time.

Reconciliation if different bills passed	Principal methods: 1. One house accepts the changes of the other house. 2. Request a conference.		Major bills go to conference—Speaker appoints House conferees, presiding officer appoints Senate conferees; both rely on Standing Committee recommendations. Each house votes as a bloc.
Return to each	Vote taken on conference report (no amendments).	Vote taken on conference report (no amendments).	Conference reports normally approved.
Sent to the president	Has several options: 1. Signs the bill ————————→ Becomes a law. 2. Vetoes the bill ———————→ May be overridden by ⅔ vote of both houses. 3. Does not sign the bill, ————→ Becomes law after 10 Congress in session. days. 4. Does not sign the bill, ————→ Kills the bill (pocket Congress adjourns veto). before 10-day period.		
Enumeration	Assigned either a public or private law number, in sequence of approval for each Congress (e.g., Private Law 36, 95th Congress; Public Law 202, 95th Congress).		

SOURCE: Compiled from information in Congressional Quarterly, Inc., *Congress and the Nation IV*, 1977, pp. xxxi–xxxiv; and Walter J. Oleszek, *Congressional Procedures and the Policy Process* (Washington, D.C.: Congressional Quarterly, Inc., 1978), passim.

position to identify who contributed what, when, and where. Further, the knowledge of the process itself becomes of strategic importance, not infrequently as a means for avoiding accountability on an issue — for example, supporting a measure (bill or an amendment) at one stage of the process knowing that it will be defeated at a later stage. The emphasis on a more open process in recent years (the so-called sunshine approach) is meant in part to hold members more accountable. Whether it has had that effect is debatable.

Finally, the obvious blending of executive and congressional involvement reminds us again that the legislative process is not confined to legislators. Many of the important bills are, in fact, proposed by the president and executive agencies, bills offered by representatives and senators are cleared through the agencies, hearings are conducted with major input from the executive, and, of course, the president can approve or veto a bill. These are but a few of the formal touch points. The informal are too multifarious to cite here, though mention will be made of several in subsequent discussion. These many contacts serve as important evidence for the view of Congress as a population drawn into policy networks. Clearly it is not possible in this political system to maintain political institutions as crisply segmented policy units.

The committee system.   It is commonplace to begin a consideration of congressional committees by quoting Woodrow Wilson's famous critical statement (1913:   79, emphasis added):

> The House sits, not for serious discussion, but to sanction the conclusions of its Committees as rapidly as possible. It legislates in its committee-rooms; not by the determinations of majorities, but by the resolutions of specially commissioned minorities; so that it is not far from the truth to say that Congress in session is Congress on public exhibition, whilst Congress in its committee-rooms is Congress at work.

While certainly useful, this statement does not tell us a whole lot today. For our purposes, there are more appropriate introductory statements. For example, James Bryce in *The American Commonwealth* provides an important comparative perspective for understanding the role of congressional committees (1915:   156).

> The most abiding difficulty of free government is to get large assemblies to work promptly and smoothly either for legislative or executive purposes. . . . Three methods of overcoming it have been tried. One is to leave very few and comparatively simple questions to the assembly [e.g., legislatures in totalitarian systems]. . . . Another method is to organize the assemblies into well-defined parties . . . so that on most occasions and for most purposes the rank and file . . . move like battalions at the word of command [e.g., the British House of Commons for most of its history]. . . . The third method . . . is to divide the assembly into a number of smaller bodies to which legislative and administrative

questions may be referred, either for final determination or to be reported on to the whole body [e.g., the American Congress].

We get so used to our committee system in Congress that it is easy to forget how special it is. Congress' power is directly linked with and supported by its independent committee system.

Lauros G. McConachie provides an historical and, by implication, a social context for understanding congressional committees (1898: 40):

> . . . committees are the agents, the instruments, the channels of connection between Congress and the nation.
>
> A Georgia representative recently struck out on a new line of sentiment. He confessed that he had been trying to read in the names of the House committees the history of our government. Whoever glances over their list must be impressed with the thought. Their number and their relations are largely to be accounted for by the remarkable diversity of interests in the United States, a land of many climes and of vast areas adapted to all the different pursuits of men.

The point remains valid today. The committees and subcommittees listed in Table 8—5 are a reflection not only of past and present issues, but an estimate of what the future holds as well. The committees are intentionally reflective of the social agenda—just as are the departments and agencies in the executive.

Finally it is left to that most perceptive of all students of Congress, Richard F. Fenno, Jr., to make the point that committees are vehicles for the goal achievement of their members (1973: 1).

> A member of the House is a congressman first and a committee member second. As a congressman he holds certain personal political goals. As a committee member he will work to further these same goals through committee activity. Committee membership, in other words, is not an end in itself for the individuals. Each member of each committee wants his committee service to bring him some benefit in terms of goals he holds as an individual congressman.

This is a most important statement for our purposes in this chapter since it advises one of the links between the more representative and the more policy or lawmaking type functions. Fenno identifies reelection, influence in a House, and good public policy as member goals of particular importance in the committee setting.

These fine statements by scholars through time provide an excellent introduction to the many dimensions of the congressional committee system—a system that is unique among the world's legislatures.

1. The number and types of committees. I debated whether to include all of the subcommittees in Table 8—5. The list is long, and some subcommittees have complex titles. I justified including them

TABLE 8–5
Committees and subcommittees, House of Representatives, 96th Congress

Committee	Party ratio (D – R)		Subcommittees	Party ratio (D – R)
Agriculture	27 – 15	1.	Conservation and Credit	12 – 6
	(64.3% D)	2.	Cotton	5 – 2
		3.	Dairy and Poultry	8 – 4
		4.	Department Investigations, Oversight and Research	7 – 3
		5.	Domestic Marketing, Consumer Relations, and Nutrition	6 – 3
		6.	Family Farms, Rural Development, and Special Studies	8 – 4
		7.	Forests	5 – 2
		8.	Livestock and Grains	12 – 6
		9.	Oilseeds and Rice	5 – 2
		10.	Tobacco	5 – 2
				73 – 34 (68.2% D)
Appropriations	36 – 18	1.	Agriculture, Rural Development, and Related Agencies	8 – 3
	(66.7% D)	2.	Defense	7 – 3
		3.	District of Columbia	5 – 2
		4.	Energy and Water Development	7 – 3
		5.	Foreign Operations	7 – 3
		6.	Housing and Urban Development – Independent Agencies	7 – 3
		7.	Interior	7 – 3
		8.	Labor – HEW	8 – 4
		9.	Legislative	5 – 3
		10.	Military, Construction	5 – 2
		11.	State, Justice, Commerce, Judiciary	5 – 2
		12.	Transportation	7 – 4
		13.	Treasury – Postal Service – General Government	5 – 2
				83 – 36 (69.7% D)
Armed Services	28 – 15	1.	Investigations	9 – 5
	(65.1% D)	2.	Military Compensation	9 – 5
		3.	Military Installations and Facilities	9 – 5
		4.	Military Personnel	6 – 3
		5.	Procurement and Military Nuclear Systems	8 – 5
		6.	Research and Development	7 – 4
		7.	Seapower and Strategic and Critical Materials	7 – 4
		8.	Special Subcommittee on NATO	9 – 5
				64 – 36 (64% D)
Banking, Finance, and Urban Affairs	27 – 15	1.	The City	6 – 3
	(64.3% D)	2.	Consumer Affairs	5 – 3
		3.	Domestic Monetary Policy	6 – 3
		4.	Economic Stabilization	12 – 6
		5.	Financial Institutions Supervision, Regulation, and Insurance	12 – 6
		6.	General Oversight and Renegotiation	8 – 4

TABLE 8 – 5 (*continued*)

Committee	Party ratio (D – R)	Subcommittees	Party ratio (D – R)
Banking (continued)		7. Housing and Community Development	18 – 9
		8. International Development Institutions and Finance	10 – 5
		9. International Trade, Investment, and Monetary Policy	12 – 6
			89 – 45 (66.4% D)
Budget	17 – 8 (68% D)	Task Forces:	
		1. Budget Process	9 – 2
		2. Defense and International Affairs	9 – 5
		3. Economic Policy Projections, and Productivity	5 – 4
		4. Human and Community Resources	5 – 2
		5. Inflation	7 – 2
		6. Legislative Savings	5 – 2
		7. State and Local Governments	6 – 2
		8. Regulations and Spending Limitations	6 – 2
		9. Tax Expenditures and Tax Policy	5 – 4
			57 – 25 (69.5% D)
District of Columbia	9 – 5 (64.3% D)	1. Fiscal Affairs and Health	3 – 2
		2. Government, Budget, and Urban Affairs	3 – 2
		3. Judiciary, Manpower, and Education	3 – 2
		4. Metropolitan Affairs	3 – 2
			12 – 8 (60% D)
Education and Labor	23 – 13 (63.9% D)	1. Elementary, Secondary, and Vocational Education	11 – 5
		2. Employment Opportunities	7 – 3
		3. Health and Safety	5 – 2
		4. Human Resources	5 – 2
		5. Labor – Management Relations	10 – 6
		6. Labor Standards	5 – 2
		7. Post-secondary Education	10 – 4
		8. Select Education	7 – 3
			60 – 27 (69% D)
Foreign Affairs	22 – 12 (64.7% D)	1. Africa	6 – 3
		2. Asian and Pacific Affairs	6 – 3
		3. Europe and the Middle East	6 – 3
		4. Inter-American Affairs	6 – 3
		5. International Economic Policy and Trade	5 – 3
		6. International Operations	5 – 3
		7. International Organizations	4 – 2
		8. International Security and Scientific Affairs	5 – 2
			43 – 23 (65.2% D)
Government Operations ...	25 – 14 (64.1% D)	1. Commerce, Consumer, and Monetary Affairs	6 – 3
		2. Environment, Energy, and Natural Resources	6 – 3

TABLE 8 – 5 (*continued*)

Committee	Party ratio (D – R)	Subcommittees	Party ratio (D – R)
Government Operations (continued)		3. Government Activities and Transportation	6 – 3
		4. Government Information and Individual Rights	6 – 3
		5. Intergovernmental Relations and Human Resources	6 – 3
		6. Legislation and National Security	6 – 3
		7. Manpower and Housing	6 – 3
			42 – 21 (66.7% D)
House Administration	16 – 9 (64% D)	1. Accounts	9 – 5
		2. Contracts	3 – 2
		3. Libraries and Memorials	5 – 3
		4. Office Systems	3 – 2
		5. Personnel and Police	5 – 3
		6. Printing	3 – 2
		7. Services	3 – 2
		8. Information and Computers (Policy Group)	3 – 2
			34 – 21 (61.8% D)
Interior and Insular Affairs	26 – 14 (65% D)	1. Energy and the Environment	15 – 8
		2. Mines and Mining	8 – 4
		3. National Parks and Insular Affairs	16 – 9
		4. Oversight/Special Investigations	6 – 4
		5. Pacific Affairs	6 – 3
		6. Public Lands	12 – 6
		7. Water and Power Resources	9 – 5
			72 – 39 (64.9% D)
Interstate and Foreign Commerce	27 – 15 (64.3% D)	1. Communications	9 – 4
		2. Consumer Protection and Finance	5 – 2
		3. Energy and Power	13 – 6
		4. Health and the Environment	11 – 5
		5. Oversight and Investigations	11 – 5
		6. Transportation and Commerce	5 – 2
			54 – 24 (69.2% D)
Judiciary	20 – 11 (54.5% D)	1. Administrative Law and Governmental Relations	6 – 3
		2. Civil and Constitutional Rights	6 – 3
		3. Courts, Civil Liberties, and the Administration of Justice	6 – 3
		4. Crime	6 – 3
		5. Criminal Justice	6 – 3
		6. Immigration, Refugees, and International Law	6 – 3
		7. Monopolies and Commercial Law	8 – 4
			44 – 22 (66.7% D)

TABLE 8 – 5 (*continued*)

Committee	Party ratio (D – R)	Subcommittees	Party ratio (D – R)
Merchant Marine and Fisheries	25 – 14 (64.1% D)	1. Coast Guard 2. Fisheries and Wildlife, Conservation and the Environment 3. Merchant Marine 4. Oceanography 5. Panama Canal	10 – 6 18 – 10 12 – 6 12 – 6 8 – 4
			60 – 32 (65.2% D)
Post Office and Civil Service	16 – 9 (64% D)	1. Census and Population 2. Civil Service 3. Compensation and Employee Benefits 4. Human Resources 5. Investigations 6. Postal Operations and Services 7. Postal Personnel and Modernization	5 – 3 6 – 4 4 – 2 4 – 2 4 – 2 6 – 4 4 – 2
			33 – 19 (63.5% D)
Public Works and Transportation	31 – 17 (64.6% D)	1. Aviation 2. Economic Development 3. Oversight and Review 4. Public Buildings and Grounds 5. Surface Transportation 6. Water Resources	15 – 8 14 – 7 13 – 7 11 – 7 17 – 8 17 – 8
			87 – 45 (65.9% D)
Rules	11 – 5 (68.8% D)	1. Legislative Process 2. Rules of the House	4 – 2 4 – 2
			8 – 4 (66.7% D)
Science and Technology . . .	27 – 15 (64.3% D)	1. Energy Development and Applications 2. Energy Research and Production 3. Investigations and Oversight 4. Natural Resources and Environment 5. Science, Research, and Technology 6. Space Science and Applications 7. Transportation, Aviation, and Communication	16 – 8 11 – 6 7 – 3 7 – 3 7 – 3 6 – 3 6 – 3
			60 – 29 (67.4% D)
Small Business	25 – 14 (64.1% D)	1. Access to Equity Capital and Business Opportunities 2. Antitrust and Restraint of Trade Activities 3. General Oversight and Minority Enterprise 4. Energy, Environment, Safety, and Research 5. SBA and SBIC Authority and General Small Business Problems 6. Special Small Business Problems	6 – 3 6 – 3 6 – 3 6 – 3 8 – 4 6 – 3
			38 – 19 (66.7% D)

TABLE 8 – 5 (concluded)

Committee	Party ratio (D – R)	Subcommittees	Party ratio (D – R)
Standards of Official Conduct	6 – 6 (50% D)	No Subcommittees	
Veterans' Affairs	21 – 11 (63.6% D)	1. Compensation, Pension, Insurance, and Memorial Affairs	9 – 5
		2. Education, Training, and Employment	7 – 4
		3. Housing	5 – 3
		4. Medical Facilities and Benefits	17 – 9
		5. Special Investigations	7 – 4
			45 – 25 (64.3% D)
Ways and Means	24 – 12 (66.7% D)	1. Health	6 – 3
		2. Oversight	6 – 3
		3. Public Assistance and Unemployment	6 – 3
		4. Select Revenue Measures	6 – 3
		5. Social Security	6 – 3
		6. Trade	14 – 7
			44 – 22 (66.7% D)

SOURCE: Compiled from information in *Congressional Quarterly Weekly Report,* April 14, 1979, Supplement, pp. 19 – 45.

because the substantive breakdown illustrates so many important points for this book. Here is the framework within which legislative populations are formed for participating in cross-institutional networks. One may place this breakdown along side that of the federal bureaucracy, state and local bureaucracies, major lobby groups, and Senate committees and subcommittees. Though the titles may differ, one can begin to see how the formal structure facilitates contact through coincident jurisdictions.

Consider the sheer number of work units listed in Table 8-5 — 22 standing committees with 148 subcommittees (or task forces in the Committee on the Budget). This total is up slightly since 1970 when there were 21 standing committees with 133 subcommittees. During the decade one committee was abolished (Internal Security), one was created (Budget), and one was upgraded from select to standing committee status (Small Business). These many work units result in a staggering number of work assignments. Table 8 – 6 shows the total number for all committees and subcommittees (standing and select), as well as the number of House positions on joint committees and subcommittees. The grand total is 2,561 work positions — 1,611 (63 percent) of which are with subcommittees of the standing committees. This works out to be an average of nearly six assignments per member. These totals have increased slightly since I last looked at them in 1973.

TABLE 8−6
Committee and subcommittee positions, 96th Congress

	Democrats (276)	Average per Democrat	Republicans (159)	Average per Republican	Total (435)	Average overall
Standing committees	489	1.77	267	1.67	756	1.74
Their sub-committees	1,102	3.99	509	3.20	1,611	3.70
Select committees	60	.22	31	.19	91	.21
Their sub-committees	41	.15	19	.12	60	.14
Joint committees (House members)	14	.05	9	.06	23	.05
Their sub-committees (House members)	12	.04	8	.05	20	.05
Total	1,718	6.22	843	5.29	2,561	5.89

SOURCE: Compiled from information in *Congressional Quarterly Weekly Report,* April 14, 1979, Supplement, pp. 19−45.

At that time, there were a total of 2,452 positions, an average of 5.6 per member (Jones, 1974a: 163). The large number of subcommittees means that many Democrats have an opportunity to be addressed as Mr. Chairman. Recent restrictions on the number of chairmanships to be held by any one member has spread the honor even more than in the past. A full committee chairman can chair only one subcommittee of the parent committee; no member can chair more than one legislative subcommittee (i.e., one which has the authority to report legislation); and no member can be a member of more than two committees with legislative jurisdiction.[9] As a consequence of these limits, and the opportunities they provide for junior members, nearly 55 percent of the House Democrats (151 of 276) were entitled to be addressed as Mr. or Madame Chairman in the 96th Congress. Further, since subcommittee chairmen are now elected by the party caucus of a full committee (rather than simply appointed by the committee chairman as in the past), they may be drawn from all but the lowest ranks of the full committee. In the 96th Congress, only the Committee on Ways and Means followed a straight committee seniority ranking in selecting subcommittee chairmen (i.e., the first six Democratic members below the chairman served as chairmen of the six subcommittees), a practice followed by nearly all the committees before seniority reforms were

[9] *Congress and the Nation,* 4, p. 752.

instituted. Subcommittee chairmen on the Appropriations Committee are approved by the caucus under Democratic Party rules.

Table 8–5 also includes the party ratios for the committees and subcommittees. It has been traditional to approximate the House party split in most standing committees. The exceptions are the Committees on Rules and Ways and Means, where the majority party typically has a two to one majority. The party split in the 96th Congress, 1979 –80, was 276 to 159 or 63.4 percent Democratic.[10] One can see how closely this division was followed throughout the committees and subcommittees by checking the figures under Party ratio. Table 8–7 makes this task somewhat easier, however, by displaying both

TABLE 8–7
Committees and subcommittees ranked by ratios of Democrats to Republicans

Ratio: D to R	Committees	Subcommittees (combined ratio)
Below 63.4%	Standards of Official Conduct*	District of Columbia, Administration (2)
63.4 – 64.3%	Agriculture, Banking, District of Columbia, Education and Labor, Government Operations, Administration, Commerce, Merchant Marines and Fisheries, Post Office and Civil Service, Science and Technology, Small Business, Veterans (12)	Armed Services, Post Office and Civil Service, Veterans (3)
64.4 – 65.3%	Armed Services, Foreign Affairs, Interior, Judiciary, Public Works (5)	Foreign Affairs, Interior, Merchant Marine and Fisheries (3)
65.4 – 66.3%	—	Public Works (1)
66.4– 67.3%	Appropriations, Ways and Means (2)	Banking, Government Operations, Judiciary, Rules, Small Business, Ways and Means (6)
67.4 – 68.3%	Budget (1)	Agriculture, Science and Technology (2)
68.4 – 69.3%	Rules (1)	Education and Labor, Commerce (2)
Over 69.3%	—	Appropriations, Budget (2)

Note: Subcommittee ratios less than committee ratios = 4; subcommittee ratios more than committee ratios = 12; subcommittee ratios nearly equal to committee ratios = 5.
* Set by law at 50 percent.
SOURCE: Compiled from information in the *Congressional Quarterly Weekly Report*, April 14, 1979, Supplement, pp. 19 – 45.

---

[10] The committee ratios were the subject of considerable dispute in the 97th Congress. Though their numbers had been reduced to 243 (56 percent), the House Democrats maintained favorable ratios on Ways and Means (65.7 percent), Rules (68.8 percent), Budget (60 percent), and Appropriations (60 percent). The Republicans objected, but to no avail.

groups in terms of how close they are to the party split in the House. Note that most of the committees follow the split in the House—17 of 22 are within 2 percent. Only the Committee on Standards of Official Conduct is below 63.4 percent Democratic, and the reason is that the committee is required by law to have an equal number of Democrats and Republicans. The three money committees—Appropriations, Ways and Means, and Budget are on the high side of representing Democrats, as is the Committee on Rules (a practice continued in the 97th Congress).

Subcommittee ratios tend to put the Republicans at more of a disadvantage than committee ratios. In 12 of the 21 committees with subcommittees, the subcommittee ratios were more Democratic than for the parent committee. One would normally regard a 63.4 percent advantage to be sufficient, but apparently Democrats on certain committees believe that it is not. As indicated in Table 8—6, the consequence of this disparity is nearly one full position less, on the average, for Republicans compared to Democrats (5.29 positions for the average Republican, 6.22 for the average Democrat). This matter of ratios is not inconsequential when subcommittees increasingly serve as the loci for important policy decisions.

Table 8—5 provides other information of importance for present deliberations. Observe that there are several different types of committees, for example, those that deal with:

The Budget: Ways and Means (revenues), Appropriations (expenditures), and Budget.

Foreign and Defense Policy: Armed Services, Foreign Affairs.

Governance of the District: District of Columbia.

Investigations of the executive: Government Operations.

Legislative administration: House Administration, Standards of Official Conduct, Rules.

Domestic issues: all the rest.[11]

The committees differ in prestige as well—or so it is alleged. Scholars have developed a simple means of measuring the ranking of the

---

[11] There are many useful categories of committees. The House has for years relied on a three-fold classification in making committee assignments: exclusive committees (Appropriations, Rules, Ways and Means), semiexclusive committees (e.g., Agriculture, Armed Services, etc.), and nonexclusive committees (District of Columbia, Government Operations, etc.). Ordinarily members can serve on one exclusive committee, one semiexclusive and one nonexclusive committee, or two nonexclusive committees. This rule has been violated recently. See Masters, 1961: 345–57. George Goodwin, Jr., (1970: chapter 6) proposes the useful distinction between national issue committees (e.g., Foreign Affairs, Judiciary), clientele committees (e.g., Agriculture, Interior and Insular Affairs), and housekeeping committees (e.g., District of Columbia, Government Operations). See also Bullock in Rieselbach, 1979: 62.

committees—by counting the shifts that take place when members seek reassignment. Those committees losing members are judged lower in prestige than those that are more stable. When he calculated the net shifts by a standard measure, George Goodwin, Jr. found that the Committees on Rules, Ways and Means, Appropriations, Foreign Affairs, and Armed Services were the most in demand; the Committees on Interior and Insular Affairs, Banking and Currency (now called Banking, Finance, and Urban Affairs), Merchant Marine and Fisheries, Post Office and Civil Service, and Veterans' Affairs were the least in demand. Thus, for example, Appropriations had a net gain of 59 members moving to the committee during the period of study (81st through the 90th Congresses), Veterans' Affairs had a net loss of 37 members (Goodwin, 1970:   114).[12] What this shift means for Veterans' Affairs is that it is constantly being populated with freshmen members.

Whereas this ranking is generally useful to indicate the important differences among the committees, it must be acknowledged that some members do stay on a relatively low-ranking committee for reasons associated with the district or with power in the House of Representatives. The Interior Committee is of vital interest to conservationists and members from the West, who tend to get on and stay on. Members with coastal waters or major ports in their districts naturally have an interest in what happens in the Merchant Marine and Fisheries Committee. Those are obvious cases explaining why some members stay on what by other measures are low-ranking committees. But there may be reasons associated with House politics that one might stay as well. Morris K. Udall (D—Arizona) has remained on the same committees during his nearly 20 years in the House. I never understood why, since his growing personal prestige surely would have gained him an assignment on one of the major committees. But he stayed on Interior and Insular Affairs (where he has a strong district interest) and on Post Office and Civil Service. Neither is a prestige assignment, and yet he presently chairs Interior and is the ranking Democrat on Post Office and Civil Service (foregoing the chairmanship in order to chair Interior). Here is a classic case of "you pays your money and you takes your choice." The high turnover committees have the advantage of permitting those who stay to move up quickly to positions of responsibility.

I tend to think of this committee jockeying as very much like the game of Monopoly. There are Baltic Avenue committees (Veterans' Affairs, Post Office and Civil Service); Boardwalk and Park Avenue committees (Appropriations, Ways and Means); and Atlantic Avenue committees (Interstate and Foreign Commerce, Judiciary). Whereas

---

[12] See also Bullock, (1973:   94), where he finds differences among Republicans, Northern Democrats, and Southern Democrats in how they rank committees by their transfers.

the Boardwalk group are prestigious and highly profitable in the long run, still one can build hotels sooner on Baltic Avenue. The point is that certain clever members do very well with the cheaper properties.

The cross-jurisdictional nature of many issues is also apparent in Table 8 — 5. The most obvious case is in regard to energy and environmental issues. Five committees (Government Operations, Interior, Commerce, Science and Technology, Small Business) have subcommittees which deal *directly* with energy and environmental matters; several other committees (notably Armed Services, Foreign Affairs, Public Works and Transportation, Ways and Means) deal with aspects of the energy issues. Individual departments and agencies find that they are involved with several different committees, in part because Congress normally adapts to emerging issues by making jurisdictional adjustments in its existing committee structure, rather than creating a new committee (even though it may create a new agency to treat the matter).

Note further that many committees perform investigations and oversight functions. Even though the House has an oversight committee—the Government Operations Committee—individual committees find it necessary to conduct their own investigations. No fewer than 11 committees have subcommittees that carry the label *Oversight and Investigations*, or some variation thereof. The oversight function itself will be discussed later.

2. Committee assignments. The diversity and importance of the House committee system suggest the significance of the assignment process. How does a member get on these fabled committees and their subcommittees? At one time, (before 1911) the Speaker had the authority to name the committees. Following the 1911 change, the Democrats developed a procedure whereby the Democratic members of the Committee on Ways and Means drew up the committee lists. The Ways and Means Democrats themselves were selected by the caucus. Regional representation among Ways and Means Democrats was particularly important at this time so as to give members from every area a contact on the committee.[13] In 1971 Democratic committee appointments were made subject to approval by the caucus.

At first the Republicans permitted their floor leader to appoint members to committees. In 1917, however, they too formed a committee-on-committees chaired by the floor leader. This process has continued to the present day. The committee is made up of one member from each state with Republican representation, but the members have as many votes as there are Republican representatives from their state. Thus in 1979, the member from Vermont had one vote,

---

[13] For a brief history of the process see Masters (1961: 345 — 57); Congressional Quarterly, Inc., *Guide to Congress* (Washington, D.C.: Congressional Quarterly, Inc., 1971), pp. 152 — 53; and Bullock in Rieselbach, 1979: 62 — 66.

the member from New York had 13 votes. Since the committee is rather large (47 members in 1979), a smaller executive committee does the work, which is approved by the full committee and then by the Policy Committee. The executive committee typically includes several members from the larger states.

In 1974 the Democrats changed their procedure by transferring authority to appoint committees from the Ways and Means Democrats to the Steering and Policy Committee, chaired by the Speaker. The 24-person Steering and Policy Committee includes all of the major party leaders plus a few members appointed by the Speaker and another dozen selected by regional caucuses. Thus it is broadly representative and is able to provide access for members from all parts of the country (Rieselbach, 1977:   56).

The appointing procedure itself really breaks down into two processes—one for new members and one for veterans who want to change assignments. The amount of work required obviously depends on how many members failed to return. With the number of retirements increasing in recent years, the workload is considerable. Thus, for example, in 1979 when a record number of 49 House members retired, the committee-on-committees for each party was faced with having to make decisions for more than one fourth of the total committee positions. Note in Table 8−8 that this turnover exceeds that in

TABLE 8−8
Assigning members to committees—the workload

		Democrats	Republicans	Total
1965	Freshmen assignments	86	23	109
	Transfers of veterans	35	19	54
	Totals	121	42	163
	As a percent of total committee positions	29.7%	21.5%	26.7%
1979	Freshmen assignments	85	64	150
	Transfers of veterans	39	19	58
	Totals	125	83	208
	As a percent of total committee positions	25.6%	31.1%	27.5%

SOURCE: Compiled from information in various issues of the *Congressional Quarterly Weekly Report*, 1965 and 1979.

1965 when a very large Democratic freshman class was elected in the landslide elections of 1964. Table 8−8 also shows the number of decisions made to accommodate members who wanted to change assignments. In 1979 nearly 30 percent of the total decisions by the committee on-committees were in regard to these transfers.

How does the process actually work in each case? The new members make their preferences known to the representative from their state or region who is on the committee-on-committees. In 1979 there were 42 Democratic and 35 Republican freshmen. Since the Democrats lost a few seats in the 1978 elections, the committee ratios were adjusted to reflect this shift. For example, in the 95th Congress, the Democrats had a 66.2 percent majority; in the 96th, a 63.4 percent majority. Accordingly, the number of Democrats on all but three committees was changed, in all cases reduced in percentage terms but not necessarily in absolute numbers. The new members are then aware of where vacancies exist when they apply for committee membership. Most are realistic enough to know that they are unlikely to get on the one of the top committees (Rules, Appropriations, Ways and Means). Thus their applications are normally for the next tier of committees (Armed Services; Banking, Finance, and Urban Affairs; Judiciary, Commerce, etc.).[14] This is not to say that freshmen do not get on the top-ranking committees. Increasingly, they do.[15] But the assignment is likely to come more as an appointment. That is, reacting to recent pressures for representing junior members, the leadership has sought to include freshmen but more by invitation than by accommodating preferences. At the other end are the committees on which few members want to serve and to which no one wants to transfer. Freshmen draw these assignments—in many cases, most will leave the committee in their next term. For example in 1979, only 3 of the 10 new members assigned to the Appropriations Committee were freshmen, whereas all 12 vacancies on Veterans' Affairs were filled with freshmen.

The veterans too know what positions are available and can judge their chances of making a successful move. Typically those shifting assignments are junior members (i.e., those with three terms experience or less). Having gotten an unfavorable assignment as a freshman, they seek to better their situation. In their study of committee transfers, Jewell and Chi-hung found that over 70 percent of those requesting changes were in this category (three terms experience or less) (1974: 441). In 1979 over 90 percent were in this category. As a result of this shifting a very high percentage (over 90 percent) of members get the assignments they want within five years (Gertzog, 1976: 697). Several patterns of change occur when members decide to shift commit-

---

[14] See Rohde and Shepsle (1973: 893) where they show the number of freshmen requests for committees.

[15] Bullock (1973: 89) reports that between 1947 and 1967, 18 freshmen were placed on Appropriations, 3 on Ways and Means, and none on Rules. In 1979, three freshmen were appointed to Appropriations, two on Ways and Means, and one on Rules.

tee assignments. Here are a few examples drawn from the 96th Congress:

1. Exchange assignments:
    a. Two for one. Bo Ginn (D—Georgia) drops Merchant Marine and Fisheries, Public Works and Transportation (where he is a subcommittee chairman) to go on Appropriations.
    b. Three for one. Anthony D. Beilenson (D—California) drops International Relations, Judiciary, Science and Technology to go on Rules.
    c. One for one (maintaining two assignments). Stephen J. Solarz (D—New York) drops Post Office and Civil Service, adds Budget, stays on Foreign Affairs.
    d. Two for two. Eldon Rudd (R—Arizona) drops Interior and Insular Affairs, Science and Technology, adds Appropriations, Budget.
    e. Three for two. Millicent Fenwick (R—New Jersey) drops Banking, Finance, and Urban Affairs; Small Business; Standards of Official Conduct; adds District of Columbia, Foreign Affairs.
2. Add assignments:
    a. From one to two. James R. Jones (D—Oklahoma) retains Ways and Means, adds Budget.
    b. From two to three. Bill Frenzel (R—Minnesota) retains House Administration, Ways and Means, adds Budget.

Any number of strategies are suggested by these examples. Obviously some members are willing to sacrifice breadth in committee assignments for depth. Sometimes this is necessary, given the workload of the major committees (e.g., Appropriations and Rules). Other members are willing to start fresh with new assignments (as with Representative Fenwick). Still others add work to an already busy schedule (note Representative Frenzel's assignments). The motivations are, of course, more varied than we can illustrate here. What we can do, however, is to outline the major factors influencing the process by which members and the committee-on-committees make their choices.

Like all social choice situations, committee assignments involve those who want something and those who have it within their power to give something.[16] Typically, but not exclusively, it is the rank-and-file member who wants the assignment and the committee-on-committees that has the power to grant it. The exception is when the party leadership or members of the committee-on-committees request a member to take an assignment that is not asked for—perhaps in order to block someone else or to maintain a state or regional balance

---

[16] Rohde and Shepsle (1973: 891) refer to this as a social choice process—i.e., as involving rational actors seeking to achieve goals.

on a committee. The process of getting is different from the process of giving. Let's consider each in turn.

Making preferences known to the committee-on-committees is itself a strategic decision. As noted, it involves the number and location of committee vacancies, but also to be considered is whether one's state is presently represented on the committee, the likelihood of competition from the state delegation, the suitability for one's district, the policy orientation of the committee (if it can be identified), and the number of seats likely to go to freshmen (Rohde and Shepsle, 1973: 889 – 905). All of these factors may contribute to the probability of getting a particular assignment and therefore act as signals for what and how many preferences to list. Rhode and Shepsle found that nearly two thirds of the Democratic freshmen listed three or four preferences whereas four fifths of the nonfreshmen listed just one committee (1973: 896). This result follows the expectation that the freshmen will offer a wide selection since they have no assignment. The nonfreshmen, on the other hand, typically have a specific move in mind.

Having made their preferences known, most members then lobby for the appointment.

> Many representatives seeking assignments write letters to some or all members of the Committee on Committees, setting forth arguments on their own behalf. Many also pay personal visits to the members of the committee (especially their zone representative), to the Democratic leaders, and to the chairmen of the committees they are requesting. Often letters are written to members of the Committee on Committees to support the cause of some requesters. Typically these letters came from the deans of state delegations (either from themselves alone or on behalf of the whole delegation), from party leaders or office-holders outside the House, from committee chairmen and from leaders of interest groups relevant to the work of the committees requested (Rohde and Shepsle, 1973: 890).

Note that in this survey, Rohde and Shepsle identify all of the principals involved in the second process of actually making the assignments—that is, the committee on committees, the party leaders, state delegations, and committee chairmen. A prudent requester will try to contact all such persons (see also Bullock in Rieselbach, 1979: 67 – 68).

Turning now to this second process of making the actual decisions, the committee has before it the requests and supporting documents. The task then is to match requests with assignments while at the same time maintaining harmony within each standing committee so it can get its job done and so the members are rewarded by reelection. In the several studies of the committee assignment process, the following general rules appear to be followed in making decisions.

1. Freshmen should be given at least one committee of their preference.
2. Attention will be given to state vacancies on committees where such representation is important (see below).
3. Committee chairmen (or ranking minority members) may be consulted or their communications received, but their views are not normally decisive in determining who is assigned.
4. The advice of party leaders is given special heed and may be decisive if used sparingly.
5. District interests as defined by the member will be given special attention, but a district's marginality in elections is not a prime factor in assignment (Bullock, 1972:   996 − 1007).
6. Other factors may come into play in particular cases: seniority, issue stands, interest group preferences, party loyalty, expertise, personality, race, and sex (Clapp, 1963: chapter 5; and Bullock in Rieselbach, 1979:   68 − 83).

This matter of state representation on particular committees is of special interest. As Charles S. Bullock III has shown, there has been a tendency for certain state party delegations to make a claim on a committee seat. "Retention of a committee seat for an extended period may enable a delegation to exert a proprietary claim to the seat" (1971:   527). The situation with the Democrats on the Committee on Ways and Means is best known in this connection because up until 1974 they constituted the Democratic Committee on Committees. Therefore, it made perfectly good sense to represent certain large states from the various regions in the country. In this way, the committee insured national coverage in providing access for those requesting assignments. But Bullock shows that other committees too maintained state seats over the 22-year period of his study. In particular, the following committees all had over 40 percent of the seats meeting his criteria for state control: Ways and Means (60 percent), Rules (53 percent), Armed Services (52 percent), Appropriations (49 percent), Banking and Currency (47 percent), Agriculture (43 percent), Foreign Affairs (42 percent), and Merchant Marine and Fisheries (41 percent). As expected, the committees with the highest turnover by other measures had the fewest state-controlled seats (Bullock, 1971:   533).

Charles L. Clapp concludes that: "A person's congressional career may rest largely on the kind of committee post he is given" (1963:   183). This statement must be read in the context of the importance of Congress in the national policy process. What it really says is that a member's personal influence is closely associated with committee work. Success there can mean success in other goals—for example, those identified by Fenno as crucial: reelection, influence in the House, and good public policy. It is for these reasons that we spend so much time on the assignment processes. It also explains why those processes are so complex. Clapp's statement advises us that the committee populations in particular will be drawn into policy networks. The committee is the locus of the substantive work that is of interest to other policy actors—bureaucrats, interest group representatives, state and local officials. And it is of relevance whether, as Fenno asserts, a member is on a committee primarily to get reelected, to use it as a base for influence in the larger body, or to promote particular ideas or proposals to solve public problems.

3. Committee organization, leadership, and staffs. Having gotten members on the committees, we now turn to the matter of how those committees are organized, led, staffed, and conduct their business. The primary work unit within the committee is, of course, the subcommittee. Until the 1970s the committee chairmen had awesome power in organizing the subcommittees, determining their jurisdiction, selecting the membership, designating the chairmen, and allocating staff. Not all chairmen were autocratic in exercising this authority, but many were. Dissatisfaction with these conditions led to the adoption by the House Democratic caucus of a so-called subcommittee bill of rights.[17] Each committee was required to establish a caucus that was then given many powers formerly held by the committee chairman. Of course, many committees already had caucuses. For them the directive merely formalized existing practice. Note that this move was strictly a party matter—that is, among the majority Democrats. It was designed to disperse authority and it was highly successful in doing so. The new rules also required that all committees over 20 members have at least four subcommittees. In the past, some chairmen centralized authority by not appointing permanent subcommittees (notably Ways and Means). Both subcommittee chairmen and membership are now subject to committee caucus approval, though no member can get a second subcommittee assignment until every committee member has selected a preferred subcommittee. When vacancies occur on subcommittee chairmanships, members may bid for the position in order of their seniority. If the senior member does not receive a majority vote, then the next senior member may bid for the position, etc.[18] Another change prevents committee chairmen from killing a bill

---

[17] For a summary and analysis of these changes see Norman J. Ornstein, "Causes and Consequences of Congressional Change: Subcommittee Reforms in the House of Representatives, 1970 – 73," in Ornstein, 1975:   88 – 114, and Rieselbach, 1977: chapter 3.

[18] In the 96th Congress, three junior members were successful in defeating more senior members in bids for subcommittee chairmanships. The most important of the three races was for the powerful Public Health and Environment Subcommittee (Interstate and Foreign Commerce Committee). Richardson Preyer (D—North Carolina) was the presumed heir apparent as the most senior member. But he lost in his bid, 12 to 15. Henry A. Waxman (D—California), the next ranking member, then bid and won 21 to 6. *Congressional Quarterly Weekly Report*, February 3, 1979, p. 183.

by not assigning it to a subcommittee. The rules require assignment within two weeks. These important changes appeared to allocate power in two directions—one toward more subcommittee autonomy, the other toward more party influence. But the subcommittees are continuing units and the party caucus meets only occasionally.

It is apparent in this description of the subcommittees that the power of committee chairmen has been reduced in recent years. The seniority system has been relied on in Congress for many decades to determine committee leadership.[19] It remains in place today but with modifications. The two aspects of committee leadership that are important are the means of selection and the powers to be exercised. The subcommittee bill of rights affected the chairman's power, as did certain other reforms.[20] But the means of selection, too, was altered. Prior to the 1970 reforms, the seniority system worked as follows. Once on a committee, members continued to move up as other members retired, were defeated, died, or moved to another committee. When they reached the top position in the majority party they became chairmen. It worked the same way on the minority party side, with the most senior member in committee service assuming the position of ranking minority member. In moving from one committee to another, however, a member lost seniority. Thus, for example, Dante Fascell (D—Florida) was the third-ranking Democrat on the Committee on Government Operations in the 97th Congress. If he were to move to the Committee on Appropriations in the 98th Congress, he would start over again— only being placed ahead of the freshmen assigned to the committee. One can see, therefore, why members make their move relatively early in their careers—before they accumulate seniority.

Following the 1970 reforms all nominees for chairman must be submitted to the Democratic caucus for a secret-ballot selection. The Steering and Policy Committee forwards the nominations to the caucus. In 1975, following the infusion of 75 freshmen Democrats (many elected in the wake of the Watergate scandals), three sitting committee chairmen were defeated in the caucus. This stunning action was virtually unprecedented (only two chairmen had been deposed since the 1920s) and had a sobering impact on all chairmen. Thus, while most members still rise to the top position by virtue of longevity in committee service, the present process makes it much easier to challenge a chairman and, therefore, all chairmen are con-

---

[19] There is a rich literature on seniority. See Polsby et al., 1969; Goodwin, 1959; Abram and Cooper, 1968; and Hinckley, 1971.

[20] Hinckley found much less influence of the seniority system in determining "the kind of committee chairmen selected by Congress" than was popularly advertised. For example, while southerners held more than 50 percent of the chairmanships during the 20 years of her study, they also constituted 50 percent of the Democratic membership. Hinckley, 1971:   108.

strained in their use of authority. The Republicans also vote by secret ballot in their caucus (or conference as they call it) on the nominees for ranking committee positions, but they have not ousted senior members in recent years. The Committee on Committees places the nominations before the conference.

These dramatic changes in committee organization and leadership have had a profound impact on the congressional role in the national policy process. The hardy generalizations about the locus of power no longer apply. Therefore, those who come to Congress—the agencies, interest groups, constituents—find that they must adjust to the new configurations of power. However unsatisfactory for other reasons, having strong committee chairmen left few questions about who to contact on Capitol Hill in order to get something done. Today an individual or group must plot more carefully in order to get favorable legislative action. The changes also greatly complicate the development of policy networks—those three- or four-cornered groups of officials involved in deciding policy. When power was concentrated, it was simple enough to know who to include as critical actors in an issue area. But the greater dispersion of authority, along with the increased independence of individual members, has made that task more difficult.

Among the conditions complicating analysis of contemporary legislative life is the growing impact and dispersal of committee staffs. When the committee chairman was king, the staff worked for the chairman. No one doubted who was in charge. The reforms of the 1970s were responsive to demands from junior members and the minority that staff be more widely allocated. Today it is less clear who is in charge. The growing complexity of issues, a veritable avalanche of information from the executive agencies, increased lobbying, and more democracy in House organization, all have contributed to increased staff position and influence. As Michael J. Malbin puts it: "Staff influence arises from the simple fact that members have more to do than time to do it" (1977:   17). And, of course, staff contributes to the increased workload of the members, thus justifying their own existence while at the same time creating a need for more staff. It might also be said that the decentralization in the House itself contributes to the independence and growing influence of the staff.

The work of the committee staffs includes the many administrative tasks associated with arranging the work of a committee—setting up the hearings, keeping members informed of the schedule, preparing reports, arranging for witnesses, drafting legislation, insuring that the hearings and other proceedings are printed and distributed. Samuel C. Patterson points out that staff provide intelligence, contribute to much-needed integration among the many legislative units, and often offer innovative proposals (1970:   26 — 28). As Malbin informs us, staffs can be substantively involved in every stage of lawmaking (1977: 17−18).

> For example, their ability to run committee investigations, the results of which they can skillfully leak to the media, gives them influence over the items members choose to put on the legislative agenda. Once something is on the agenda, the staff works to assemble a coalition supporting a specific piece of legislation. As it sets up committee hearings, the staff will reach as broadly as possible without sacrificing the goals the chairman, often at their urging, has adopted. Then, when a bill is "marked up" (amended and passed in committee), the staff will be expected to reconcile competing interest-group demands. When conflicts cannot be resolved, the members may then learn enough about the details to weigh the political costs of compromise. But if the major differences raised by the normally vocal interest groups can be settled otherwise, most members will be content to leave the details to the staff, as well—details that can frequently mean everything to whole industries or groups of people.

Staff operations will vary committee to committee, subcommittee to subcommittee. This variation lends further support to the view that understanding Congress today requires paying attention to the substantive breakdown within the House and Senate. That is, it is more revealing of the role of Congress in public policy to trace issues than to study institutional components (e.g., whole committees). Both Malbin and Patterson identify several types of committee staff. Malbin discusses partisan and nonpartisan staff. At first the committees hired essentially nonpartisan, professional staff. Certain committees, like Interstate and Foreign Commerce, have prided themselves on having small, highly professional staff. In recent years, however, "chairmen began looking for young lawyers with politically compatible ambitions."

> Instead of being asked to interpret, analyze, and react to proposals originating elsewhere, they were frequently told to seek out good publicity for their chairmen, either through investigations or new legislative ideas to which a chairman's name could be attached (Malbin, 1977: 26).

Patterson determined that staff adopted the dominant goals of the committees for which they worked—reinforcing the variability of staff operations. He identified a number of norms associated with their work as adapted to specific committees. These norms included limited advocacy (the classic staff posture of good public administration), loyalty to the chairman (the partisan posture noted by Malbin), deference to the members, anonymity, specialization, and limited partisanship (1970: 29−31).

As with personal staffs, the exact number and title of staff positions will differ. Still it is instructive to see what a committee staff looks like. Table 8−9 provides the breakdown for the Committee on Interstate and Foreign Commerce in the 95th Congress. Several points are worth

TABLE 8—9

Staff assignments for Committee on Interstate and Foreign Commerce and its subcommittees

	Number of assignments
Full committee—majority:	
Chief clerk and staff director	1
First assistant clerk	1
Assistant clerk	1
Professional staff member	11
Staff assistants	2
Printing editor	1
Clerical assistants	10
Documents clerk	1
Total	28
Full committee—minority:	
Minority counsel	1
Associate counsels	8
Staff assistants	3
Staff associate	1
Administrative assistant	1
Legislative assistant	1
Clerical assistants	3
Total	18
Subcommittee on Communications:	
Chief counsel	1
Economists	2
Staff engineer	1
Staff assistants	3
Office manager	1
Legislative assistants	2
Secretary	1
Total	11
Subcommittee on Consumer Protection and Finance:	
Counsel	4
Staff assistant	2
Economist	1
Legal assistant	2
Clerical assistant	2
Secretary	1
Receptionist	1
Total	13
Subcommittee on Energy and Power:	
Counsel and staff director	1
Counsel	4
Consultant	1
Research analyst	3
Research assistant	3
Administrative assistant	1
Staff assistant	5
Total	18

TABLE 8 – 9 (*continued*)

	Number of assignments
Subcommittee on Health and the Environment:	
Chief counsel	1
Assistant counsel	1
Research director	1
Senior staff associate	2
Administrative assistant	1
Research associate	1
Staff assistant	5
Total	12
Subcommittee on Oversight and Investigations:	
Chief counsel	1
Deputy chief counsel	1
Operations director	1
Chairman's counsel	1
Counsel	6
Special counsel	2
Special assistants	5
Research assistants	3
Special consultant	1
Office manager	1
Secretary	1
Staff assistants	6
Total	29
Subcommittee on Transportation and Commerce:	
Staff director	1
Counsel	1
Executive assistant	1
Legislative assistants	2
Law clerk	1
Staff assistant	1
Secretary	1
Total	8
Grand totals	
Full committee	46
Subcommittees	91
	137

SOURCE: Compiled from list in Charles B. Brownson, ed., *1977 Congressional Staff Directory* (Mt. Vernon, Virginia: Congressional Staff Directory, 1977), pp. 358 – 60.

emphasizing about this list. Note how many different titles for positions there are. Individualism does thrive on Capitol Hill! On this one committee there are 37 different staff positions. Also noteworthy is the amount of staff available to the minority. After many years, even decades, of complaining, the minority now has sizeable staff support. And, of course, the staff total is impressive—137 in all—as is the assignment of staff to subcommittees. In 1963, 14 years earlier, this committee had a total of *26 staff positions*, 17 in the full committee and 9 assigned to the oversight subcommittee. Finally, it is interesting and revealing to see the number of positions with ambiguous titles. *Professional staff member, counsel, staff assistant* are not very expressive of what a person might in fact be doing each day. *Administrative assistant, legislative assistant,* or *research assistant* are not much better. But one must not miss the lesson of the titles—that many staff are expected to perform a number of different functions. Precision in job description is not normally permitted by the multifarious demands made in the normal course of a day's work on Capitol Hill.

   4.   Committee procedures.   Certain committees have had written rules for some time, but the Legislative Reorganization Act of 1970 required that all committees provide them. This move was another effort designed to curb the arbitrary power of committee chairmen— some of whom were inclined to apply rules as they saw fit. Of course, the House rules themselves include provisions on the operation of the committee system (both Jefferson's Manual of Parliamentary Practice, which still governs the House where applicable and where not inconsistent with the House rules, and the specific Rules of the House of Representatives). House Rule XI, Clause 27 (a) provides that:

> The Rules of the House are the rules of its committees and subcommittees so far as applicable. . . . Committees shall adopt written rules not inconsistent with the Rules of the House and those rules shall be binding on each subcommittee of that committee.

Thus, to understand any one committee's procedures, it is necessary to have in hand the House rules and the committee's rules. The House rules now provide considerable detail, much of it included as a consequence of the Legislative Reorganization Act of 1970. Committee meetings, procedures, staffs, even radio and television coverage are all treated in the House rules. As you now have no doubt come to expect, the written rules of the committees vary considerably in length and topics covered. The House rules state that written rules will be adopted not that they must take particular form. The more comprehensive committee rules will cover meetings, voting, proxies, quorums, the schedule, hearings, reports, special studies, staff, minority party protections (in regard to reports, questioning, etc.), bill referral, travel, subcommittees, investigations, broadcasting, and participation in conferences. Many times the applicable House rules are repeated in the written committee rules.

   It is not possible even to begin a description and analysis of these many rules of organization and procedure. It is sufficient for present purposes to show the flow of the work. Figure 8–1 offers a picture of this movement along two tracks. On the left is the more common track for most committees—referral to a subcommittee. But the chairman, subject to a possible challenge by a majority on the committee may refer a bill to the full committee. Whichever track is followed, the

FIGURE 8–1
Normal flow of work in standing committees

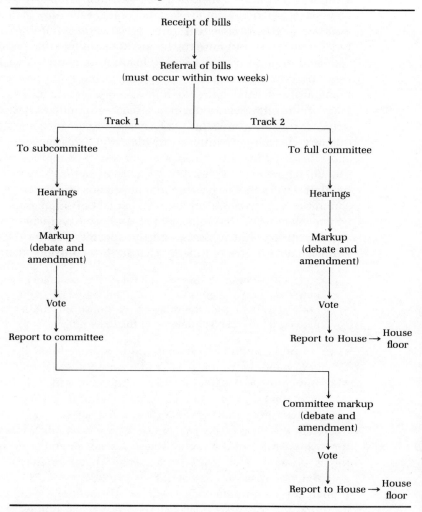

SOURCE: Compiled by author.

procedure is one of providing an opportunity for testimony through the hearings process, followed by debate and amendment in the so-called mark-up of the bill, summary and analysis in the reporting of the bill, and movement to the next stage of review (either to the full committee from the subcommittee or to the floor from the full committee).[21]

---

[21] The strategy of the markup is described by Miller (1962: 13–15) and is quoted in Oleszek (1978: 70–71). As described by Miller, the markup involves the proprietary interest of the staff, concern for the broadest support among the majority, and continual testing for weakness by the minority.

In terms of the policy process, what we have here is a sequence of the public display of an agreement. Agree and display—that is not a bad description of what goes on in the legislative arena. At each of the various levels, compromises are fashioned among those involved at that level. This work must then be delivered to another set of actors, some of whom will not have been involved at all up to this point. If the agreements themselves are not very strong, then one may predict difficulty as the number of participants expands—that is, in the full committee or on the House floor. Another way to describe this series of stages is as a process of expansion, from those most to those least knowledgeable and continuously involved. Obviously, in order to get anything enacted into law in this process, techniques and cues must be developed so that majorities can be gathered along the way.

The description of the personal offices and committee system moves one from representation to lawmaking. But the organization of Congress is still more complex, with a party system that performs a wide variety of facilitative functions and a legitimating process on the floor that is sensitive to the broader demands of legislative issues. Finally an elaborate set of unofficial groups also contribute to meeting organizational goals.

9

How the House organizes to do its work: Parties and floor action

The work of the committees is vital but not sufficient in itself to make law. We turn now to the political parties, the many unofficial groups that contribute to the work of the House, and the organization of activities on the House floor.

THE POLITICAL PARTY SYSTEM

I happened to have been in England on June 11, 1979, when the Chancellor of the Exchequer presented a bold new budget to the House of Commons. The budget included major tax reform and severe cuts in existing programs. The members of Parliament debated the document, and one week later, on June 18, the budget was in effect. There were strong reactions to the budget in the media and among the public, but the Conservative Party had a working majority in the House of Commons, and therefore it was able to put the plan into effect immediately. I mention this example primarily to illustrate what can be accomplished by a strong political party system. As will become evident in what follows, American legislative parties bear only the remotest relationship to the workings of the British party system. It is useful, then, at the start of this section to be conditioned to the fact that American political parties are mere shadows of their counterparts throughout most of the rest of the world.

Why should that be? Why aren't American parties able to deliver like, say, the Conservative Party in England? A full answer to that question would take us deeply into the constitutional order of American society. It is enough for present purposes to acknowledge that our political system lacks the mechanisms that guarantee party unity and purpose across institutions. The British prime minister comes from the legislative party; the American president does not. In fact, our president may be of one party, with the other party enjoying a majority in Congress. But even the individual members of Congress may be (and usually are) elected separately from another, whereas members of the House of Commons are linked together as representatives of their party. When I inquired of one British scholar how it was that Shirley Williams, prominent member of the Labour Government before the election, could have lost her seat in the House of Commons, he said simply: "It had nothing to do with her. She remains popular. But the tide was running to the Conservatives." In summary, our legislators do not arrive in Washington bound by national party ties, and once there they may participate in a majority party which is opposite that of the president.

It is useful to be reminded of these facts since they help shape our expectations regarding how political parties function in Congress. In saying that parties assist in the organization and management of congressional business, we are by no means implying that they direct these affairs. Rather they provide the means by which certain essential activities are accomplished—for example, assigning members to committees and subcommittees; scheduling business on the floor; informing members of pending legislation, crucial votes, and actions taken in committees; making commitments on those occasions when the legislative party is unified on an issue. These functions should not be minimized for they are essential to the movement of legislation. Nor should too much be expected from parties in performing these functions since providing the means to act is different from taking or directing those actions.

How are the parties in the House organized and led? And what role do they play in the movement of legislation? Those are the principal topics for this section.

Party organization

While their functions may differ from those of political parties in other systems, the basic organizational units are much the same—a large meeting, a number of special committees, and the party leaders. The large meeting in the case of House parties is, of course, the caucus, which the Republicans refer to as a conference. The most important meeting of the caucus occurs every two years at the beginning of each Congress when the party leadership is elected and new rules adopted. Actually this meeting now takes place in early December in the year before the new House convenes and just a month after the election of the new House. Normally one does not expect a big turnover of the leadership or major changes in the party rules, but in recent years these caucuses have been very active, particularly in the Democratic Party. After decades of inactivity, the House Democratic caucus emerged in the 1970s as a center of reform. Many of the changes in the seniority and committee systems were originated in a special caucus committee (the Committee on Organization, Study, and Review, created in 1970 and headed by Julia Butler Hansen, D—Washington— see Chapter 15) and fought over in the Democratic caucuses during the early 1970s. Meetings of the caucus were hardly covered by the press in previous congresses. Their actions became front-page news in the 92nd to the 95th Congresses. The Democratic Study Group (DSG), an organization of activist House members dissatisfied with party and committee leadership, emerged in the 1970s with a majority of House Democrats as members. They sought to revive the party caucus as a means for change precisely because they did command a majority there and were not likely to get change through other means (Ornstein, 1975: 91–92).

In addition to its role in facilitating reform, the House Democratic caucus has been the site of interesting leadership contests. In the recent past party leadership changes occurred in a pro forma fashion. When a Speaker retired, the majority floor leader became Speaker, the whip became majority floor leader, and a new whip was appointed by the majority leader. In December 1976, the majority leader, (Thomas P. "Tip" O'Neill (D—Massachusetts)), succeeded the retiring Speaker, Carl Albert (D—Oklahoma), as predicted. But a real donnybrook developed in the race to succeed O'Neill as majority leader. The House Democratic whip, John McFall (D—California), announced his intention to seek the floor leadership post, but he was challenged by Phillip Burton of California, Richard Bolling of Missouri, and James Wright of Texas. In what was perhaps the most exciting House leadership contest in a very long time, James Wright won on the third ballot. With the low man having to bow out, it took three ballots to narrow the race. Burton and Wright survived this process, and the latter won by a single vote, 148–147. Wright ran third in the first ballot, second in the second ballot, and first in the third ballot.[1]

---

[1] The definitive description and analysis of this contest is that by Bruce I. Oppenheimer and Robert L. Peabody, "The House Majority Leadership Contest, 1976," paper delivered at the 1977 meeting of The American Political Science Association, Washington, D.C., September 1–4, 1977. Peabody (1976) has studied other major leadership contests in both parties.

The role of the caucus in policy matters obviously depends on how unified the party is on the issues. For many decades, the Democrats were badly split on a number of basic issues—particularly civil rights. Further, since southern Democrats chaired many of the important committees, they saw no need to submit policy questions to the caucus for decision. The seniority system provided them with an ample base of power in the committee system. Thus the caucus met at the beginning of a Congress to reconfirm leadership and the existing rules, and hardly ever convened again until the next Congress.

It was not always so, however. During the 62d and 63d Congresses (1911−15) the Democrats met in caucus to settle party positions on pending legislation. In the 63d Congress the then majority floor leader, Oscar W. Underwood (D−Alabama), fed the president's program through the caucus for approval, and members were bound to support these agreements.

> Underwood thoroughly agreed with [president] Wilson in believing in a unified party working together to pass a definite program. For him, a binding caucus was the natural way to govern a legislative party. This device allowed debate within the party but also allowed the party to present a completely united front to the opposition party (Ripley, 1969a: 56).[2]

The Democrats have not subsequently been able to match the achievements of the binding caucus. Still, the caucus in the 1970s was more active than at any time since Underwood's leadership in dealing with both party reform and policy issues.

The Republican's use the term *conference* for a specific reason. They objected to the binding caucus of the Underwood era and thus adopted another term for the meeting of all their members (Hasbrouck, 1927: 31). Ironically though they employed the softer label, the House Republican conference has been more active than the Democratic caucus from the post-Underwood period to the 1970s. Since the 1950s, the Republicans have used their conference to initiate policy research, first through the Policy Committee, later through a Research Committee. They have also met with some frequency to discuss the policy positions recommended by the Policy Committee. John Anderson (R−Illinois), who has served as conference chairman since 1969, has stated that meetings of the conference are called:

> to consider party positions on the legislation, to plan parliamentary strategy, to publicize Republican principles, to receive reports and recommendations from the committee on policy and task forces organized and functions under the committee on research and planning, and to

---

[2] This fascinating period is also treated in Brown (1922: chapter 11); Hasbrouck (1972: chapter 1); and particularly, Fleming (1972: 234−50).

consider and take actions on matters of major importance to the entire Republican House membership.[3]

In summary, with the exception of one short period, the Democrats have until recently used their caucus primarily to confirm the incumbent leadership. Its very existence, however, permitted junior members and liberals to mount successful challenges to the organization in the 1970s. That is, once they gained a majority, these dissidents were able to use the latent powers of the caucus to oust leaders and enact reforms, even discuss substantive policy. The Republicans, on the other hand, consistently have been more united on policy and have used the conference to test the reactions of members to legislative proposals. On occasion the Republicans have even sought to initiate policy proposals by creating committees and task forces (Jones, 1970:   35 – 39).

Each party also has a number of special committees. Table 9 – 1 shows those for each party as they existed in the 97th Congress. Note that these committees perform rather basic party functions: assisting in election and reelection (the campaign committees), assigning members to committees, and performing some policy-related tasks. It is in the latter that the two parties differ the most. Just as the Democrats have not used their caucus for substantive policy purposes as much as the Republicans have used their conference, so too the Democrats have not typically used their Steering and Policy Committee for these purposes either. In fact, this group was moribund for many years, revived only in the 1970s to assume important scheduling and appointing functions. The Republicans, on the other hand, revitalized their Policy Committee in 1959, and the group has been active since that time in formulating policy statements on major issues. The weekly meetings of the Policy Committee have served as a forum for the views of the membership, quite probably contributing to party unity in the standing committees and on the floor (Jones, 1964). But the Research Committee too has developed important policy functions. Rather than depending entirely on the work of Republicans on the standing committees, the party leadership has, in recent years, sought to develop a basis for party positions on legislative issues. In the 96th Congress, the Research Committee had two task forces (one each on economic policy and energy)—in the 95th Congress it had five. While a member of the committee chaired the task forces, the membership itself was drawn from other members—mostly those from standing committees with jurisdiction for these issues. It should be pointed out that the Republicans have, no doubt, chosen to utilize these committees in this way because (1) they have traditionally been more united on policy

---

[3] Quoted in Walter J. Oleszek, "Party Caucuses in the United States House of Representatives," unpublished paper, Congressional Research Service, n.d., pp. 10 – 11.

TABLE 9– 1
Party committees, House of Representatives, 97th Congress

Committee	Functions	Composition
Democrats:		
1. Steering and Policy Committee	Schedules legislation and recommends committee assignments to caucus.	Speaker chairs, eight other party leaders also members, 29 total members in 1981.
2. Congressional Campaign Committee	Raises money for candidates provides for campaign support.	Caucus elects chairman, one member for every state or territory with Democratic representation, leadership ex officio, 52 total members in 1981.
3. Personnel Committee	Oversees the selection and operations of House administrative personnel (previously called the Patronage Committee).	Chairman appointed by Speaker, Speaker also a member, five total members in 1981.
Republicans:		
1. Committee on Committees	Recommends committee assignments to conference.	Minority leader chairs, one member for every state or territory with Republican representation, 50 total members in 1981.
2. Policy Committee	Advises conference on policy positions—legislation and party matters.	Conference elects chairman, leadership ex officio, 32 total members in 1981.
3. Research Committee	Establish task forces and conduct research on major issues.	Conference elects chairman, seven total members in 1981.
4. Congressional Committee	Raises money for candidates, provides other campaign support.	Conference elects chairman, leadership ex-officio, 57 total members in 1981.

SOURCE: Compiled primarily from *Congressional Quarterly Weekly Report*, March 28, 1981, Supplement, pp. 43 – 46.

matters, and (2) they lack the advantage of majority control of the standing committees (at least since 1952).

The caucus may be the font of all authority and thus play an important legitimating role but it is, ultimately, the leadership that shapes the role of political parties in the legislative process on a daily basis. The principal majority party leader is, of course, the Speaker. The House of Representatives differs from many of the legislatures around the world (though not those in the states) in that the parliamentary leader (that is, the person who chairs the debates) also serves as the leader of the majority party. In many legislatures this parliamentary role is nonpartisan.

The Speaker has traditionally been one of the most powerful positions in American politics. "In power and prestige," Neil MacNeil asserts, "the Speaker can be compared only with the president and the chief justice. . . . He has been the elect of the elect" (1963: 61). Such notables as Henry Clay, James K. Polk, James G. Blaine, Thomas B. Reed, Joseph G. Cannon, Nicholas Longworth, John N. Garner, and Sam Rayburn, have served as Speaker but of these, only one, Polk, was elected to the presidency. The Speaker's powers were, at one time, awesome. In addition to a large degree of control over legislation, he had impressive political powers to appoint committees, chair the Committee on Rules, and determine who would speak on the floor. Writing at the height of the Speaker's powers, Mary P. Follett quoted a House member's view of the impact of the office (1896: 301):

> When this Republic goes down . . . it will not be through the "man on horse-back" or any president, but through the man on the wool-sack in this House, under these despotic rules, who can prevent the slightest interference from individual members; who can, if he will, make and unmake laws like an emperor, hold back or give the sinews of war and the salaries of peace.

Follett concluded that "the Speaker is at the same time a moderator, a member, a party chieftain, and the most influential man in the House" (1896: 301).

By contrast, Speaker P. "Tip" O'Neill (D—Massachusetts) argues today that comparisons between him and previously strong speakers are unfair. He judges that the members are not willing to be led as in the past. As one report has it:

> . . . if leadership is a problem, so, too, is what Majority Leader Jim Wright of Texas calls "followership." The fact is that congressmen today are a young and independent breed. . . . [They don't] need the party, and . . . can ignore O'Neill with an impunity that would have stunned Sam Rayburn.[4]

What these dramatically different images tell us is simply that position with legitimate authority does not necessarily result in great power. The context within which authority is exercised makes a difference, including the interactions between leaders and followers and the independent sources of authority for the followers. And that context has changed for the Speaker of the House. I understand that I compress a great deal of history in the following statements, but they do provide a capsule history of how we have moved from an emperor Speaker to one who has difficulty exercising even legitimate authority.

1.   Joseph G. Cannon (Speaker 1903—11) exceeded the bounds of his support and therefore invited reform. His actions led to the so-called 1910 revolt.[5]

---

[4] Henry W. Hubbard, "What Ails Congress," *Newsweek*, July 2, 1979, p. 35.

[5] This dramatic confirmation between Speaker Cannon and the progressives within the Republican Party was a classic debate over the role of political party in Congress. Cannon supported a party government theory—one in which he was dominant as

2. The Speaker was removed from the Committee on Rules in 1910 and stripped of his committee appointing powers in 1911.
3. The committee chairmen emerged as powerful forces after the 1910 – 11 changes (particularly those for Appropriations, Rules, and Ways and Means).
4. Speakers in the post-1910 period were forced to depend on personal resources to be effective. Nicholas Longworth (1925 – 31) and Sam Rayburn (1940 – 47, 1949 – 53, 1955 – 61) developed strength in office; the other 10 speakers between Cannon and O'Neill were much less effective.
5. Some of the 1970 reforms were designed to reduce the power of committee chairmen by increasing the authority of the Speaker.
6. Other of the 1970 reforms increased the power of the subcommittee chairmen and the autonomy of individual members.
7. The Speaker of the 1980s, therefore, has greater authority than at any time since Cannon, but the exercise of this authority is complicated by the increased resources available to subcommittees and the rank-and-file.

What I have described is a two-directional flow of power in the House of Representatives. It seems that members were unwilling to reestablish the all-powerful Speaker, but it was inevitable that reducing the power of the committee chairmen would enhance the authority of the speakership if there were to be a coherent legislative process. At the same time, it was unlikely that the same members who nearly impeached a president would accept a role of dependency on party leadership. So now we can see the basis for O'Neill's frustration.

Among the Speaker's traditional powers are those of recognizing members, interpreting the rules and applying the precedents, assigning bills to committee (within the limits of the rules), appointing special and ad hoc committees, and providing certain other favors. To these have been added the power to nominate members for appointment to the House Committee on Rules (i.e., within his party), chair the powerful Steering and Policy Committee, and refer bills to more than one committee. Of course, the first two of these added powers apply to a Democratic Speaker.[6] Should the Republicans gain a majority in the House, they might make further changes.

The other majority party leaders include the floor leader, whip, deputy whips, and caucus chairman. The floor leader's responsibilities are revealed by the title. This person works closely with the Speaker in

Speaker. The progressives rejected this view in favor of more independence for legislators. In a sense Cannon's excesses destroyed the chance of developing a strong but responsible party organization in Congress. See Jones, 1968: 617 – 46.

[6] Robert L. Peabody discusses these powers as resources for the leaders. He adds an important exchange function by which leaders use their positions to perform favors and thus increase their resources (1976: 45 – 47).

planning the work of the House. Though the Speaker is not always in the chair (e.g., during the deliberations of the Committee of the Whole), still he has not traditionally managed the floor debates. This task has become that of the floor leader and involves scheduling, working closely with committee chairmen, paying close attention to the flow of business from the committees.

As Randall B. Ripley documents, the position of floor leader is rather recent as a separate, identifiable party office—that is, since 1899 (1967: 24). Until 1919, the majority leader was also chairman of the Committee on Ways and Means. Not surprisingly, many majority floor leaders become Speaker—8 of the 15 who have held the position since 1899 and 7 of the 9 who have held the position since 1931 (not counting Wright—the present incumbent at this writing).[7] As indicated earlier, the floor leader is elected by the caucus.

The tasks of the whip are absolutely vital for the effective operation of the party system in the House. Essentially the whip manages a communication system—maintaining contact with the rank-and-file members, the committees and subcommittees, and the other less formal groups in the House. Leaders want to know what is going on, and they also want to provide information on crucial votes. Thus the whip, who is appointed by the floor leader in the Democratic Party, has an elaborate organization. In the 97th Congress, Thomas S. Foley (D–Washington) worked with a chief deputy whip (also appointed by the floor leader) and an elaborate organization of deputy, at large, and assistant whips to collect and spread the word. The whip, too, is essentially a 20th-century phenomenon. Ripley records that the first Republican was appointed to that post by Speaker Reed in 1897. The Democrats later appointed their first whip in 1900 (Ripley, 1967: 33).

The Democratic Caucus Chairman has not been a particularly important post through time. In fact, service in the post has typically been brief—often no more than one two-year term, by tradition no more than two terms. The incumbent at this writing, Gillis W. Long (D–Louisiana), defeated two other contenders in the December 1980 Democratic Caucus. The caucus chairman is normally considered to be a member of the leadership team despite the fact that there are few powers associated with the post itself.

The minority party in Congress has become synonymous with the Republican Party since 1930. Republicans have been in the majority in the House just twice since then—in 1947–48 and 1953–54. The minority leadership arrangements differ from those of the majority party. In some respects, the minority party leader serves as a counter-

---

[7] Of the two who did not become Speaker, neither had a chance to assume the office. Charles Halleck's party lost its majority status, and Hale Boggs disappeared—presumably killed in a plane accident.

part to both the Speaker and majority floor leader. That is, he serves as the party's principal spokesman to the outside world—just as does the Speaker. On the other hand, he does not have the parliamentary duties of the Speaker, nor is he called upon by the media to speak for the House of Representatives. He also serves as his party's manager of debate on the floor—as a counterpart to the majority floor leader. The Republican floor leader also chairs the Committee on Committees but not the Policy Committee (the Democrats combine these responsibilities in their Steering and Policy Committee).

The duties of the whip in the Republican Party do not differ from those on the Democratic side, but the whip organization is different. The whip is aided by one chief deputy whip and a somewhat less elaborate set of deputy regional and subregional whips.

The Republican conference chairman does have a more significant role to play than his Democratic counterpart as a consequence of the greater role played by the conference in party affairs. In fact in the 96th Congress, John Anderson (R—Illinois) chose to remain head of the conference rather than be ranking member of the Committee on Rules when party rules forbade holding the two leadership posts.[8] The role of the conference in initiating research and discussing policy stands gives the chairman some appointive powers and results in greater public exposure than for the Democratic caucus chairman.

Table 9—2 lists the party leaders at the start of the 97th Congress, 1981—82. Note that both parties have had a large turnover in leadership in recent years. A new Democratic team was selected in 1977, though some leaders had held other posts in earlier Congresses. The House Democratic whip in the 96th Congress John Brademas (Indiana) was defeated for reelection in 1980, and Thomas S. Foley was appointed whip (Foley had been serving as the chairman of the caucus). A new position was created in the December 1980 Democratic caucus—that of chief of task forces. Speaker O'Neill has used task forces to build coalitions in support of bills—a relatively new technique born out of the conflict and divisions over difficult issues in recent years (Sinclair, 1981).

John J. Rhodes (R—Arizona) resigned as House Republican leader in 1980 (though he remained in the House). Rhodes had succeeded Gerald R. Ford in 1974 when Ford became vice president. The former whip, Robert H. Michel, defeated Guy Vander Jagt (Michigan) in the race to succeed Rhodes. Vander Jagt served as chairman of the Congressional Committee in the 96th Congress. A new team was then elected to lead the House Republicans (though several of the new leaders held other posts in the 96th Congress).

In summary, the functions of the House party organization in the

[8] Oleszek, "Party Caucuses," p. 5.

TABLE 9–2
Major party leaders, House of Representatives, 97th Congress (1981–1982)

Position	Incumbent	Previous years in position	How selected
Democrats:			
Speaker	Thomas P. O'Neill (Mass.)	4	Nominated by Caucus, elected by House
Floor leader	Jim Wright (Texas)	4	Elected in Caucus
Whip	Thomas S. Foley (Wash.)	0	Appointed by floor leader
Chief deputy whip	Bill Alexander (Ark.)	0	Appointed by floor leader
Chairman of Caucus	Gillis W. Long (La.)	0	Elected by Caucus
Secretary of Caucus	Geraldine A. Ferraro (N.Y.)	0	Elected by Caucus
Chairman of Steering and Policy Committee	Thomas P. O'Neill (Mass.)	4	By virtue of being leader of the party
Chairman of Congressional Campaign Committee	Tony Coelho (Calif.)	0	Elected by Caucus
Chairman of Personnel Committee	Joe Moakley (Mass.)	4	Appointed by Speaker
Chief of Task Forces	Richard A. Gephardt (Mo.)	0*	Appointed by floor leader
Republicans:			
Floor leader	Robert H. Michel (Ill.)	0	Elected by Conference
Whip	Trent Lott (Miss.)	0	Elected by Conference
Chief deputy whip	David F. Emery (Me.)	0	Appointed by whip
Chairman of Conference	Jack F. Kemp (N.Y.)	0	Elected by Conference
Vice chairman of Conference	Jack Edwards (Ala.)	0	Elected by Conference
Secretary of Conference	Clair W. Burgener (Calif.)	0	Elected by Conference
Chairman of Policy Committee	Richard B. Cheney (Wyo.)	0	Elected by Conference
Chairman of Committee on Committees	Robert H. Michel (Ill.)	0	By virtue of being leader of the party
Chairman of Congressional Committee	Guy Vander Jagt (Mich.)	6	Elected by Conference
Chairman of Research Committee	Edward R. Madigan (Ill.)	0	Elected by Conference
Chairman of Personnel Committee	John T. Myers (Ind.)	0	Elected by Conference

* Position created in 1980.
SOURCE: Compiled from *Congressional Quarterly Weekly Report*, March 28, 1981, Supplement, pp. 43–46.

policy process are more facilitative than managerial. The structure exists alongside the formal legislative process to tease it along. The party assists in organizing the lawmaking process in the first place, provides forums for identifying effects of law, establishes a vital communications network, encourages exchanges and compromises, and identifies the political consequences of various courses of action. Seldom does the party apparatus itself take charge of the legislative process, forcing it to produce a particular program. The exceptions would be when a particularly powerful president combines with an effective party leader in the House (as with the early years of the Woodrow Wilson and Lyndon B. Johnson administrations) or when a crisis exists (as with the economic depression of the 1930s or war). Another minor exception might be noted. Though hardly a case of taking charge of the legislative process, still one must acknowledge the efforts of the House Republicans in recent years to perform more active policy functions through the Research Committee, Policy Committee, and Conference. They are not successful very often in having their work substitute for that of the standing committees. But they definitely have had influence as a consequence of exploring alternative proposals and identifying where they agree, or cannot possibly agree (Jones, 1964).

Party at work

Though congressional parties appear weak when compared to their counterparts in other political systems, still it must be acknowledged that they continue to play a role at every stage of the legislative process. Certainly no other grouping is as pervasive in Congress as that of the political party. Committee and subcommittee members organize as Republicans and Democrats. They get their committee assignments from their respective parties, they caucus with each other, and sit together in the committee rooms. Hearings are normally conducted with due consideration of the minority party's right to question and call witnesses. Committee and subcommittee reports include minority views if there are any (though in some cases the minority may be dissenting members of the majority party). And after many years of complaining, the minority party has committee and subcommittee staff specifically assigned to it.

Once a major bill has been reported out of committee, it is normally brought before the Committee on Rules to be scheduled for floor debate. The importance of this committee for the majority party is acknowledged by the permanent two to one ratio of majority to minority members. It is generally acknowledged that the rules will be used to facilitate the workings of the majority while providing the minority with an opportunity to express itself.

On the House floor, the Democrats and Republicans sit on separate sides of the chamber, have separate conference and cloak rooms near the chamber, and normally have equal time in debating legislation (depending on whether the minority on a particular bill is, in fact, drawn primarily from the minority party). In addition, certain protections are provided for the minority party in debate—e.g., a motion to recommit a bill and the right to object to bills brought up under the Consent Calendar procedure (see below). But the work of political party outside the committees and subcommittees shows up primarily in the policy committees, the caucus or conference, and the whip system. Discussions are held on whether to take a party position on a particular bill, with the degree of party unity obviously the most important determinant of positive action. Presidential wishes too can activate party leaders in support of or opposition to legislation. The initial screening in the policy committee may favor a policy position. If so, this position is transmitted to the membership. Or on rare occasions, the policy committee may forward a particular issue to the caucus or conference for debate. Majority party leaders also must determine when to schedule particular legislation, as well as crucial votes. The point is that there is a considerable amount of party activity in regard to important legislation, but it is exceedingly difficult to lay out a specific process of party involvement. Consistent with a *facilitative* policy role, the political party in Congress is very much dependent on forces outside the party.

Table 9 – 3 provides another dimension by which people measure the party system in the Congress—the amount of party voting there. Two measures are provided: (1) the percentage of roll-call votes in which a majority of one party opposes a majority of the other party and (2) the percentage of time that the average Democrat or Republican votes with the party when they are in opposition. For the student of British politics the figures in that first column are absolutely stunning. A majority of Democrats opposed a majority of Republicans on *over* 50 percent of the roll-call votes only twice in 20 years (1964, 1965). The range of party votes is from 27 percent party votes in two years of the Nixon administrations to 55 percent during the incredibly productive first full year of the Johnson period (see discussion below).

The percentage of party votes actually is declining both in the long and short runs. Julius Turner and Edward V. Schneier, Jr., found that "the trend toward a weakening of party lines in Congress has been an unmistakable feature of 20th-century American politics" (1970: 37; see also Brady and Bullock in Dodd and Oppenheimer, 1981: 197). In 1897 – 1901 more than half the votes in the House found 90 percent of one party opposing 90 percent of the other. By 1955 – 65 – only *six percent* of the votes had this division. The relatively high average of 50 percent party votes during the Kennedy-Johnson period (1961 – 64) carried over for one year into the Johnson administration, but then it dropped to 37 percent for the last three years (1966 – 68). It was during this time that President Johnson's troubles in Vietnam and the cities began to mount. Not unexpectedly election of a Republican in 1968 meant a further reduction in the number of party votes. After all, Presidents Nixon and Ford needed Democratic votes to enact their

TABLE 9—3
Party unity scores, U.S. House of Representatives, 1961—1980

Presidential administrations	Percent of party votes	Percent voting with party	
		Democrats	Republicans
Kennedy:			
1961	50	72	74
1962	46	70	70
Kennedy—Johnson:			
1963	49	73	74
1964	55	69	71
Average	(50)	(71)	(72)
Johnson:			
1965	52	70	71
1966	41	62	68
1967	36	67	69
1968	35	59	64
Average	(41)	(64.5)	(68)
Nixon:			
1969	31	61	62
1970	27	58	60
1971	38	61	67
1972	27	58	66
1973	42	68	68
Nixon—Ford:			
1974	29	62	63
1975	48	69	72
1976	36	66	67
Average	(35)	(63)	(66)
Carter:			
1977	42	68	71
1978	33	63	69
1979	47	69	73
1980	41	69	71
Average	(41)	(67)	(71)

SOURCE: Jewel and Patterson, 1977: 390, and *Congressional Quarterly Weekly Report,* January 10, 1981, pp. 79—80.

programs. But observe that the relatively low percentage of party votes carries over to the Carter administration too.

The second and third columns of Table 9 — 3 record the percentage of time that the average Democrat and Republican voted with their respective parties when the two were in opposition. Two observations can be made about these figures. First, the Republicans consistently vote their party more than do the Democrats. At no time did they fall below the Democrats in this 20-year period; twice their average was the same as the Democrats. Second, both parties show the same pattern during this period—that is, a decline in the average partisan voting from the Kennedy—Johnson administration through the

Johnson administration and the Nixon—Ford administrations, with a recovery during the Carter administration. The explanation may be that the issues are more crosscutting in nature, less strictly partisan. Certainly the Vietnam War (with all of its domestic impacts), the civil and political rights struggles of the 1960s, and the economic and energy problems of the 1970s did not lend themselves to straight-party voting. Even the taxation and government management issues which were found to be highly partisan in earlier studies came to be less so by the end of the 1970s.[9] But party voting may also be associated with a clear and forceful program offered by the president (as with the Kennedy-Johnson administrations, 1961—65). If this latter explanation is correct, then we may witness the reappearance of more party voting during the Reagan administration—something to watch for.

It should be pointed out that another possible explanation for the decline in party votes and partisan voting may be simply the increase in the absolute number of roll calls. As will be discussed subsequently, the provision for recording teller votes and the installation of electronic voting combined with the greater autonomy of individual members, created in part by staff increases, have resulted in a phenomenal increase in roll-call votes—from 93 in 1958 to 233 in 1968 and 834 in 1978! It may be that the significant issues on which one might expect party voting are now hidden within hundreds of other votes of a more routine, nonpartisan nature. As it happens, the total number of recorded votes declined in 1979 to 672 and the percentage of party votes increased to 47 from 33, thus supporting the hypothesis. Unfortunately for the theory, the number of recorded votes declined further to 604 in 1980 and so did the percentage of party votes—to 38 percent. Clearly the effect of increased roll-call voting requires careful study before we can conclude that it explains the decline in the percentage of party votes. It is uncommonly difficult to sort out the precise influence of party in floor voting, as it should be if I am correct that political parties in Congress play a facilitative rather than managerial role in House affairs.

What is the role of party leaders in encouraging party votes? Aren't they crucial in getting out the vote? John W. Kingdon concludes that: "the leadership of neither party is particularly important. . . . Even among the groups of Republicans who turn to the party leadership the most . . . the importance of the leadership is not particularly impressive" (1973:   135). Kingdon believes that party voting is rooted in the

---

[9] There have been many studies of roll-call voting. A sample of the best includes: Truman (1959); Turner and Schneier (1970); Macrae (1958); Clausen (1973); Fiorina (1974); Matthews and Stimson (1975); Mayhew (1966); Schneider (1979). Kingdon (1973) and Kozak (1979) also studied voting but primarily through interviewing the members to judge influence on their behavior.

political life of the member—from election to the contacts members have in the House (1973:   135).

> Party voting seems to begin with constituency differences; the parties have very different demographic bases and support coalitions. Building on constituency differences are the patterns of interaction within the House. Congressmen rely heavily on informants within their own party grouping. Common campaign experiences limit the party regularity.

I am certain the reader detects that it has not been easy to reconstruct and describe the party at work. We know party exists and operates in a fashion; precisely defining that role is difficult. One should not miss the lesson in all of this, however. As I have written elsewhere:

> More commonly we have had factionalism with organizations of convenience (called political parties) designed to promote factional interests. These organizations do, indeed, perform a communication function but seldom is it more than as "upgoing transmission belts of claims and grievances."[10]

In his important study of how congressmen decide, Aage R. Clausen makes the cogent observation that "partisan bonds are treasured more in the halls of Congress than they are in the broader expanse of American politics." The importance of that statement is simply that it asks us to consider the weakness of party among the general public as the context for judging its importance in Congress. Clausen then adds (1973:   120):

> That party bonds are treasured in two large bodies such as the Senate (100 members) and the House (435) is quite understandable; it would be odd if it were otherwise. Party is a link with the past and with the constituency, and it provides a basis for establishing new friendships and working relations in the confusing whirlpools of Washington politics. Accompanying this informal intrapartisan interaction is a more formal arrangement of party officialdom in a loose party organization. The party organization's dispensation of rewards and privileges can only serve, however slightly, to augment the level of partisan cohesion that arises out of the camaraderie of the natural grouping. However, I would place a greater premium on the natural affinity between legislators of the same party as a source of party cohesion than I would on the formal party organization.

What this important statement tells us is that we may not find party at work *on* the members but rather *in* the members. The formal party organization exists to facilitate communication and expression of whatever party has come to mean. But it does not, apparently cannot,

---

[10] Charles O. Jones, "Can Our Parties Survive Our Politics," paper presented at a meeting on "The Role of the Legislature in Western Democracies," Selsdon Park, England, April 20 – 22, 1979, p. 5.

command or direct these forces. So the party system turns out to be much more subtle in influence than the committee system.

UNOFFICIAL GROUPS

A number of groups have emerged in the post-World War II House of Representatives that perform important organizational and policy functions. These groups make connections that are unlikely to develop in the ordinary course of the organizational workings of Congress. Not unexpectedly there are more groups in the House than in the Senate—another consequence of the larger size. It is likely that the weakness of party invites the proliferation of these groups. They supplement the party structure but also threaten it since they perform party-like functions.

There are several different types of unofficial groups in the House. Some form around geographical interests—the state or region. Others are more ideologically based, either within or between the parties. Some are formed to deal with particular issues, effecting either a special group (e.g., the blacks) or perhaps an industry (e.g., steel). Still other groups are quite social in purpose, though the social is never very far from the political on Capitol Hill. Each of these types deserves at least a brief discussion.

Geographical groups

The state delegation is a natural organizational unit. Thus, for example, the members of the Pennsylvania delegation are bonded to one another by a common geographical identity. More important, however, an elaborate governmental apparatus exists in the state to define problems within those borders and to measure the effects on state interests of what else goes on outside the borders. There are occasions, therefore, when state and local officials will attempt to use the congressional delegation to protect or further parochial interests.[11] Neither party nor bicameralism may act as barriers to state delegation unity, when it comes to clearly defined state interests. What is true for Pennsylvania is, of course, true for the rest of the states. Aage R. Clausen explains (1972: 79):

> The political system contained within the boundaries of the United States embraces 50 subsystems; the states of the federal union. The individual states are territorially defined units with constitutionally pre-scribed governmental systems, differentiable social, political, and eco-

---

[11] Of course, the influence of the state and its politics may be expected to vary. See Deckard (1972: 199 – 222).

nomic characteristics, and unique historical experiences. The characteristics of these subsystems have been articulated through the adaptation of their citizens to economic and social conditions under the terms of a governmental framework both imposed from without and developed from within.

Here then is a historical and geographical basis for unity on some issues.

How is this natural unity likely to express itself? First organization is necessary; second there must be an object to that organization. The most obvious organizational impetus is political party. Members are likely to have some connection with their state party and they surely have contacts with their party in Congress. Thus the state party gives a member common lenses through which to view the congressional agenda. In what is perhaps the most careful study of the influence of state party, Clausen finds that he can account for a considerable proportion of congressional voting by state party, but that its effect varies (1) among issues—showing up as most important on civil rights and welfare issues; as least important on farm and foreign policy issues for Democrats, and (2) between the parties—with the Democrats more attentive than the Republicans to state or regional party. In regard to the latter finding, Clausen speculates that (1972: 95):

> Democrats are more pragmatically oriented to assessing and carrying out the demands of their constituents, as they perceive them in the raw; Republicans, on the other hand, are a party marked by ideological principles, less pragmatic in their evaluations of policy impacts.

The impact of a state party delegation is not limited to voting. The senior member or dean of a state party delegation is often the contact for a new member in getting a committee assignment. Where a committee is thought of as having state or regional seats, the state delegation naturally is protective and seeks to retain the seat when a member resigns, retires, or is defeated (Bullock, 1971).

Where the whole state or region is effected by a particular issue, one may expect to see active lobbying by the delegations involved. Thus, for example, John H. Kessel (1964) shows how the delegation from the state of Washington cooperated in regard to economic problems in the state. In such cases one may observe cooperation between the parties and between the senators and representatives. Some state delegations—often including the senators—meet regularly just as a means of maintaining communication. Such contact is not only helpful within the Congress but in dealing with the executive too, particularly the bureaucracy. That is, members are able to exchange information about case work, dealing with the agencies, and patterns of complaints from constituents.

Issue and ideological groups

A great many groups fit into this category. I combine them simply because the task of separating is difficult and arbitrary. Most ideological groups take positions on issues. Many issue-based groups have ideological leanings. A meaningful distinction can be made between within-party and across-party groups, however. We will consider each in turn.

Certainly the premier group to consider in this section is the Democratic Study Group (DSG). No other unofficial organization can claim the same degree of structure or success. Formed in September 1959 to counter what was perceived as conservative domination in the House (an unholy alliance between Republicans and southern Democrats), the DSG grew steadily in size and influence to the point of dominant influence in all aspects of legislative decision making. During the 1950s certain northern liberals became increasingly frustrated in their efforts to achieve legislative goals. They correctly sensed that the 1958 elections provided an opportunity to increase their numbers. They contacted liberal Democratic candidates and offered them assistance in their campaigns and in Washington once they were elected. "While the actual impact of this 'help' is difficult to measure, there can be no doubt about its effect upon the new members" (Ferber, in Polsby, 1971:   25). The first chairman of the DSG made the following report to the full membership:

> We have held several meetings and have organized the Democratic Study Group on a preliminary basis. More than 70 members have attended one or more of these meetings. We have established a tentative whip organization. We have elected a temporary steering committee, responsible to the will of a majority of the board group of participating members of the House. Meetings during the past week will permit research and organizational details to go forward during the recess (Ferber, in Polsby, 1971:   257).

This description made it clear that the DSG meant business—virtually a party within a party since it had a whip system, a steering committee, and research capability. The latter function was particularly important in that it led to hiring a small staff and thus guaranteed continuance of the group. The members of the DSG contributed from their staff funds to hire a research director and the whole effort was well launched.

The DSG in recent years has constituted a majority of House Democrats—thus insuring considerable power within the House when the DSG itself was unified. The staff, too, has grown in numbers and influence.

> In practice, virtually all of DSG's activities are generated and executed by the staff, which has assumed an independent leadership role in

recent years. The DSG staff ordinarily consists of approximately 12 people, four of whom engage in legislative research. The institutionalization of the DSG has left the staff director a good deal of discretion in initiating and overseeing DSG operations (Stevens et al., 1974: 669).

Task forces have also been used for the purpose of studying particular problems, with varying degrees of success (often depending on the real interest of members, the nature of the issue, and the staff time available).

The activities of the DSG are many and varied. They include (Stevens et al., 1974:   670 − 71):

1.   Providing information to the members through fact sheets on legislative issues, weekly legislative reports with summaries of provisions of bills and background of legislative action to that point.
2.   Providing campaign services to incumbents and Democratic challengers.
3.   Increasing voting turnout among liberals on the floor through the use of a whip system.
4.   Increasing liberals' knowledge and effective use of legislative strategies (requiring, among other things, greater familiarity with the rules).
5.   Lobbying for institutional reform (e.g., changing the seniority system, reducing the power of the Committee on Ways and Means, increasing the power of the caucus, etc.)

In 1981 the DSG discontinued the practice of having members contribute funds from their clerk-hire allowance and increased the dues. DSG members paid $2,200 a year for services in 1981. William M. Brodhead (D−Michigan) served as chairman of the DSG in the 97th Congress.

No other group comes close to matching the organization, activities, and impact of the DSG. Still a Democratic Research Organization and a Republican Study Group (RSG) emerged in the 1970s as conservative counterparts to the DSG. Both have staff assistance and seek to provide legislative information for members. "We provide the basic range of services the DSG provides to its members," the Republican Study Group staff director was quoted as saying.[12]

Another group of interest is that called the Wednesday Group. Composed of liberal Republicans, this unit was organized in 1963 with an initial membership of 15.[13] Interestingly two of the founders—John V. Lindsay and Ogden Reid, both of New York—later abandoned the

---

[12] Congressional Quarterly Weekly Report, June 26, 1976, p. 1636. The RSG dues are much less than those for the DSG—$125 in 1980.

[13] On the founding see Congressional Quarterly Weekly Report, November 27, 1964, p. 2736. See also Congressional Quarterly Inc., Guide to the Congress of the United States (Washington, D.C.: Congressional Quarterly, 1971), p. 608.

Republican party. The group seeks to influence the more conservative-oriented Republican leadership and to analyze and discuss legislative issues. Appropriately they meet on Wednesday.

Another group that is issue-oriented and happens to be within the Democratic Party is the Congressional Black Caucus (CBC). As an ethnic-based group with strong issue interests, it would seem that only the circumstances of the association of blacks with the Democratic Party makes it a within-party group. Still the one black senator in recent decades, Edward Brooke of Massachusetts, was a Republican and did not belong to the CBC. The CBC was formed in response to the outrage black representatives felt in President Nixon's failure to meet with them in the early months of 1970. Meetings were held among the 13 black House members to identify issues of significance for blacks and poor people.

> During the first year (from mid-1971 to mid-1972) the CBC saw itself as "congressmen at large for 20 million black people." The functions that individual members perform for their constituents, the CBC would perform for black Americans generally. In carrying through this mandate the caucus staff attempted to provide casework services, gather and disseminate information, engage in administrative oversight, articulate the interests of specialized groups with the black community . . . and develop legislative proposals (Barnet in Mansfield, ed., 1975:   36).[14]

This bold and comprehensive approach was moderated in later years as the CBC became more selective on issues and in its activities. Still this pattern of creating a caucus for a particular group, issue, or cause has become familiar on Capitol Hill. Typically, most such organizations go through similar phases from an initial effort to represent very broad national interests to a more modest role. As expected, these individualized or tailored representational efforts are debilitating for political parties. At least in the initial stages, they tend to transcend party, traditional leadership ties, perhaps even constituency.

Other unofficial associations develop in the House that have an ideological or issue base and draw from both parties. Principal among these is the so-called conservative coalition. The coalition is essentially an alliance of convenience between conservative-minded Republicans and Democrats (the latter principally from the South). It can be traced to the 1930s insofar as cross-party voting is concerned, but no one has documented the existence of an actual organization (Brady and Bullock in Dodd and Oppenheimer, 1981:   187 – 96). Certainly no office or staff exists, as with the other groups discussed here. Yet something

---

[14] For information on other groups see Michael J. Malbin, "Where There's a Cause There's a Caucus on Capitol Hill," *National Journal*, January 8, 1977, pp. 56 – 58.

appears to go on. As Senator Paul Douglas (D—Illinois) once stated (Manley in Dodd and Oppenheimer, 1977: 79):

> Now I have to say something which all of us know although we seldom speak about it: I refer to the bipartisan, unholy alliance which exists in this body, and also in the House of Representatives, between the conservative Republicans and the conservative Democrats of the South.

Senator Everett M. Dirksen (R—Illinois), who delighted in chiding his colleague from Illinois, denied the charge: "This business of talking about unholy alliances is the sheerest 'stuff.'"

Unquestionably the two groups had policy interests in common. What they did formally to achieve their mutual goals is not clear, however. John F. Manley reached the following conclusion after careful study of the coalition (in Dodd and Oppenheimer, 1977: 81).

> Simple policy agreement may be the single most important element holding the Conservative Coalition together, but the claim that the coalition is no more than an accidental meeting of minds is excessive. There is substantial evidence of joint planning on the part of coalition leaders, and coalition observers have detected a number of cases of overt bipartisan cooperation among conservatives. . . . The coalition is, in fact, many times a consciously designed force in the legislative process, and this is true for both the committee stage and the floor stage of that process.

Of course, times and issues change. Whereas the conservatives in Congress were at one time badly outnumbered (e.g., during the first two years of the Johnson administration, 1965—66), they have in more recent years swelled their ranks and thus feel less threatened.

Another cross-party group with ideological or issue interests is the Members of Congress for Peace through Law (MCPL). The members tend to be more liberal and particularly concerned with foreign policy issues. It is bipartisan and bicameral, with over 100 members. A small staff is maintained. The principal purpose is to supply information and promote communication among those interested in major foreign policy issues. Morris K. Udall (D—Arizona) observed that "It's someplace you can go with an idea without worrying about whether you're a Republican or Democrat."[15] In this regard, the MCPL is in the tradition of bipartisan foreign policy that characterized the 1940s and 1950s. The group has several committees and often sponsors conferences.

Many other issue-based caucuses have emerged in recent years—either around a specific set of issues, as with the Steel Caucus seeking

---

[15] Quoted in Congressional Quarterly, Inc., *Guide to the Congress of the United States,* p. 610.

to improve the competitive advantage for the steel industry; or as protective of a set of interests for a particular group in society, as with the women, the elderly, the blacks, etc. Burdett A. Loomis identified 26 such groups in 1979—many of which had paid staff (in Dodd and Oppenheimer, 1981:   208 — 9). One can interpret these developments in quite different ways. On the one hand, they appear to be a healthy development in representative democracy, with the various special groups and interests receiving direct attention within the legislative process. It can be argued that this type of access is required due to the increasing complexities of legislative organization in the House. By another interpretation, however, one can interpret such developments as highly discouraging since they reflect the incapacities of the political parties to represent and organize interests, and, indeed, contribute further to the decline of party functions. Certainly it is difficult for party leadership to cope with cross-party caucuses or with intense in-party issue or ideologically based coalitions.

Social groups

The Republicans, in particular, have a number of groups that are primarily social in nature. Acknowledging that almost every form of human interaction in Congress is likely to have political effects, still the groups in this category are less self-consciously organized for those outcomes. Several of the groups—for example, the Chowder and Marching Society, SOS, Acorns—grew out of the so-called class clubs. Every incoming class of freshmen representatives organizes and elects officers. This organization serves important orientation purposes, and the Republicans even represent the five most recent classes on the Policy Committee. The social and educational functions served by the classes were judged by some members to be essential beyond their freshman year, and so the groups noted above were created. Membership is limited and is based on age, region, and committee assignment.

> These groups meet frequently, normally once a week, and a significant portion of each meeting is devoted to "going around the table," each member briefing the others on issues and political developments within his area of policy specialty. No efforts ordinarily are made to arrive at a collective judgment. (Matthews and Stimson, 1975:   74).

Other social groups include the Prayer Breakfast Group. It is "a voluntary organization open to any member who cares to participate" and "meets weekly for breakfast and an hour of prayer and fellowship" (Clapp, 1963:   39). The gym group also is acknowledged to have legislative as well as social and physical fitness purposes. "Actually a lot of work is done in the gym. . . . You can discuss informally things you don't want to call a man about" (Clapp, 1963:   40). Senator William S.

Cohen (R — Maine) tells a story about the House gymnasium that illustrates how all social relationships on the Hill can transmit important norms. During the very early days of his service in the House Cohen found the gym and went there to practice his two-handed set shot.

> Each day I put on a shooting exhibition that had older members talking about "Old Doc" finally having met his match.
>
> "Old Doc" was a not-so-old former college all-state player from South Carolina. . . .
>
> One day when everybody was in a betting mood, he said, "Okay, Cohen. Let's see what you can do."
>
> I was feeling cocky as hell and said, "Okay, but I'm not playing unless we shoot from at least 30 feet out."
>
> Doc looked at me with a sort of gun-sighting squint in one eye and said, "How long did you say you've been here?"
>
> "About three weeks," I replied naively.
>
> "Then who the hell are you to be telling me what the rules of the game are going to be?"
>
> With that, he turned and walked off the court and left me with my jaw hanging. It was my first lesson about the seniority system and the unspoken rule that freshmen should walk a little more lightly around the seasoned stalwarts (Cohen, 1981: 29 – 30).

Summary

This brief section on unofficial groups advises the reader to look beyond the formal and more visible organizational entities in the House to all of those other social and political connections that characterize the institution. Jewell and Patterson point out that (1977: 327):

> It has now become rather commonplace to observe that a legislative body, like other human groups, is a social system in the sense that it is characterized by widely shared standards of proper conduct, or norms; that each position in the legislative structure has associated with it expectations about the behavior of the people who occupy these positions; and that these expectations about positions, or rules, are interlocking in an interactional system.

The several types of groups identified here contribute to maintaining the social system in the House by transmitting the norms, developing and communicating expectations, and just plain doing the work of lawmaking.

ORGANIZING THE WORK ON THE FLOOR

It may be helpful as imagery to picture the offices, subcommittees, committees, and party apparatus as performing a filtering function in the legislative process. Clearly means must be developed to sift and winnow the incredible number of demands made upon our national legislature. A primary organizational goal then is to narrow and combine these requests and the abovementioned units perform admirably in this regard. With all this apparatus working, the volume of complex legislation that gets to the floor is still awesome. Additional means have to be employed beyond the completion of committee work to manage the flow of work. Further winnowing then is the first function to be performed by floor organization.

Other tasks to be accomplished on the floor include providing proper notice and display of the legislation; maintaining momentum in the process to prevent stoppage; insuring opportunity for debate and broad participation; making a record for administrators, the courts, and the members themselves; and, of course, reaching a final decision. Accomplishing these many feats is a considerable challenge in a body of 100 members, as with the Senate. But the House has 435 members, and therefore its means for lawmaking on the floor are suitably even more complex. Obviously, I judge it important to mention these points as background to a rather detailed discussion of House procedures. I worry about the fact that the formal structures and processes are sometimes passed over because they tend to be dry or dull subject matter. I enter a plea here to pay them heed because of the important role they have to play. More than at any other point in the policy process, the traditional institutional mechanisms are significant just for what they are—a set of procedures to insure the legitimacy of policy programs. I am not saying that informal agreements or deals are not made—only that they had better follow form when they get to the floor.

With the proper caveats having been mentioned, we can now turn to how the House is organized to move bills along once a committee has acted. Several quite logical questions are answered by the existing organization. These are:

1. What have we got to work on? Organizational requirement: an agenda. House mechanism: calendars.
2. How should the work be scheduled? (Or: what is important?) Organizational requirement: priority setting, routines. House mechanisms: House Committee on Rules, designated days, privileged matters.
3. How can important bills be displayed, debated, and changed? Organizational requirement: distribution, orderly involvement. House mechanisms: reports, limited debate, Committee of the Whole.
4. How can we reach a final decision? Organizational requirement: decision rules. House mechanisms: objectors, various types of voting (assumed and displayed majorities).

These four questions form the organizational breakdown for the rest of this section.

What have we got to work on?

A bill that is reported out of committee is accompanied by a written report prepared by committee staff and approved by a majority of the committee.[16] This report is the principal briefing document for the rest of the membership and thus typically contains the following vital information: the purposes of the bill; summary of findings from the hearings; explanation of the major provisions; how the bill will change existing law (what will be omitted, what will be added); correspondence or reports from the relevant department or agency in regard to the bill; supplemental, partial dissenting, or minority views (any of which may come from members of either party, separately or jointly filed). Committee amendments to be introduced on the floor are also included. It is appropriate here to note that the committee report is an excellent starting point for students who want to learn something of the legislative process since they can then work back to the committee and subcommittee stages or move forward to the action on the floor. But their subsequent usefulness is not limited to scholars. As Charles J. Zinn notes (1969: 14):

> Committee reports are perhaps the most valuable single element of the legislative history of a law. They are used by the courts, executive departments and agencies, and the public generally, as a source of information regarding the purpose and meaning of the law.

Reports are numbered for each Congress in the order in which they are filed with the clerk of the House and then printed by the Government Printing Office for distribution to the membership. This number is also printed on the bill below the bill number. For most members and staff, the report is the principal source of information on pending legislation, even if the policy committees or caucus subsequently discuss the bill in question.

The bill is now ready to be placed on the House agenda. Actually there are three agendas—one for money measures (revenue or tax bills and appropriation bills) called the Union Calendar, one for all other public bills called the House Calendar, and one for bills of a private nature (i.e., dealing with individuals) appropriately called the Private Calendar. As bills go on the various calendars, they are given numbers in sequence of their arrival. The two public bill calendars are best

---

[16] As Walter J. Oleszek, a leading student of floor procedures, points out (1978: 74): "Bills voted out of committee unanimously stand a good chance on the floor. A sharply divided committee vote combined with dissenting minority views usually presages an equally sharp dispute on the floor."

TABLE 9 – 4
Designated days in House legislative month

	Monday	Tuesday	Wednesday	Thursday	Friday
1st	Consent Calendar	Private Calendar	Calendar Wednesday	Open	Open
	Suspension of rules (Members)		Open		Special orders
2d	Discharge Calendar		Calendar Wednesday		Open
	District Business	Open*	Open	Open	Special orders
3d	Consent Calendar	Private Calendar	Calendar Wednesday	Open	Open
	Suspension of Rules (Committees)		Open		Special orders
4th	Discharge Calendar	Open	Calendar Wednesday		Open
	District business		Open	Open	Special orders

* Open periods may be used for special resolutions from the House Committee on Rules and privileged matters.
SOURCE: Compiled from information in Zinn (1969).

viewed merely as holding stations for bills. Seldom are bills taken up in the sequence in which they appear since they differ greatly in importance. Rather the House has an elaborate set of procedures for considering legislation. Precisely how the scheduling occurs is the next of our major questions.

How should the work be scheduled?

Table 9 – 4 shows how the House organizes its week so as to manage its workload. The designated days are designed expeditiously to handle the less important measures and can be briefly treated here.[17]

First and third Mondays:
Consent Calendar. Used for noncontroversial measures. Any member may move a bill from the House or Union Calendar to the Consent Calendar. If no objection is made, these bills are passed

---

[17] Any number of sources may be relied on for more detail on these procedures, for example, Oleszek (1978); Zinn (1969); Tacheron and Udall (1966: chapter 9); Congressional Quarterly, Inc., *Guide to the Congress of the United States* (Washington: Congressional Quarterly, 1971): chapter 2; and of course, the *Rules and Manual, United States House of Representatives*.

by unanimous consent without debate. Each party has three official objectors to study the Consent Calendar to insure that an important bill is not slipped through under this procedure. One objection carries the bill over to the next call of the Consent Calendar; three or more members objecting the second time removes the bill from the Consent Calendar, and it is returned to the House or Union Calendar. Members may also ask that a bill be "passed over without prejudice" to the next call of the calendar. *Suspension of the Rules:* Requires seconding by a majority of members present and a two thirds vote to pass. The proposition to suspend the rules is debated for 40 minutes, equally divided between supporters and opponents. No amendments to the proposition are possible, though the proposition itself may contain amendments to the bill in question. Members are given preference for motions on the first Monday, committees on the third Monday. Suspension of the rules is used to expedite noncontroversial business.

Second and fourth Mondays:
Discharge Calendar. Any member may file a discharge motion after a bill has been in a committee for 30 days or before the House Committee on Rules for seven legislative days. The motion requires the signatures of a majority of members (218) to be placed on the Discharge Calendar where it stays for seven legislative days. Any member who has signed the petition may then move that the committee be discharged on the second or fourth Monday. Debate on the motion is limited to 20 minutes, equally divided between proponents and opponents. If the motion passes, the bill is debated immediately or placed on a calendar. Given this cumbersome procedure, few such moves are successful (371 filed and 24 bills actually discharged between 1923 and 1971).[18]
District Business. The Committee on the District of Columbia may claim this time for consideration of any bills it has pending.

First and third Tuesdays:
Private Calendar. The calendar is called on these days, with bills considered in the order in which they appear. Objection by two or more members recommits the bill to committee. As with the Consent Calendar, each party has three official objectors to scan the Private Calendar for bills that do not belong.

Wednesdays:
Calendar Wednesday. One of the reforms enacted during the Cannon speakership was that of calling the committees in alphabetical order every Wednesday to permit them to call up one

---

[18] Congressional Quarterly, Inc., *Guide to the Congress,* p. 114.

of their bills from the House or Union Calendar (thus circumventing the Rules Committee). Debate is limited to two hours, equally divided, and consideration must be completed in the same legislative day. The procedure may be dispensed with, and normally is, by unanimous consent or a two-thirds majority of those voting (if a quorum is present). This procedure is seldom used—only twice successfully between 1950 and 1970.[19]

Fridays:

Special Orders. This term covers a number of actions, but here it refers to permissions granted to members to speak on a particular subject not presently before the House as legislation. These speeches are normally reserved for Friday afternoon. New members, in particular, may use this time to practice for when they will be participating in an actual debate. As one member advised (Udall and Tacheron, 1966: 196):

> Get a special order and have a few of your friends participate with you. Get the feel of being in the well of the House. . . . Practice in the somewhat stilted language of yielding to other colleagues . . . so that when you do get into the real legislative fight it isn't all new.

While all of this scheduling appears to leave little time for major legislation, the reader is reminded that some procedures are rarely used. In practice, only Mondays and the first and third Tuesdays are typically tied up with minor business, and even those days are sometimes free for other business.

What then of the major legislation? How is it scheduled? The House rules provide that certain measures are privileged and can therefore be called up at any time after a suitable waiting period (to allow members' time to read reports). These measures have to do with money or with administering House affairs. Thus, the Committees on Appropriations, Budget, and Ways and Means are permitted to bring their work before the House on a privileged basis (i.e., appropriations bills, budget resolutions, and tax bills). And so are the Committees on House Administration, Rules, and Standards of Official Conduct as regards certain personnel, rules, and administrative matters. It is the case that the Appropriations Committee, in particular, will sometimes include material in an appropriations measure that does not belong there (e.g., general policy that should be in separate legislation). In such cases, the Committee may ask the Committee on Rules for a waiver on any points of order that may be raised. If any committee with privileged legislation status wants a closed rule (see below), it must also go to the Committee on Rules to obtain it.

And finally we come to the House Committee on Rules as the most

---

[19] Congressional Quarterly, Inc., *Guide to the Congress,* p. 114.

important agency for the scheduling of major legislation. First a brief history of the committee is essential, then we can turn to its present role in setting the House agenda. The House has had a Rules Committee from the very first to recommend changes in its procedures. But between 1789 and 1849, it was a select committee, then a standing committee between 1849 and 1853, again a select committee between 1853 and 1880, and since then a standing committee. The Speaker became a member of the Committee in 1858, and in 1883 the Committee assumed the power of issuing special orders (called rules) to set the time and terms for debating major legislation on the House floor (Galloway, 1955: 340). With the Speaker chairing the committee, it assumed significant power in deciding what would or would not be debated. It was not surprising then, in 1910, that the Progressives, led by George Norris (R – Nebraska), sought to remove the Speaker from this committee. In doing so, however, the Committee was separated from party leadership and developed the potential for independence on policy issues. This potential was realized in the 1950s under the chairmanship of Howard W. Smith (D – Virginia), when southern Democrats teamed with Republicans to thwart liberal Democratic programs. At that time, the Committee had eight Democrats and four Republicans, but two southern Democrats (Smith and William Colmer, D – Mississippi) joined the Republicans on certain issues and the tie vote would defeat the measure.

When John F. Kennedy was elected president, expanding the Committee on Rules became a high priority since the prospect was that the president's program might be defeated before it ever got to the floor. The House voted 217 to 212 in 1961 to enlarge the committee from 12 to 15 members – a move made permanent in 1963.[20] Later the membership was increased again to the present 16 – 11 Democrats and 5 Republicans.

Today the Committee on Rules is much more an arm of the leadership than at any time since the Speaker chaired the committee. The Speaker nominates the Democrats to serve on the committee, and they are then approved by the caucus. The chairman is subject to approval by secret ballot in the caucus. Certain other changes were also made in the specific authority of the committee, including an important modification by which the Democratic Caucus could instruct its Rules Committee members to provide for certain amendments should a committee seek a closed rule (see below).[21]

----

[20] At the time these were major struggles. For details on the Smith chairmanship see Robinson (1963); for an analysis of the enlargement, see MacNeil (1963: chapter 15); and Cummings and Peabody in Peabody and Polsby, (1969: 253 – 80).

[21] The committee's authority to block conferences with the Senate was also curbed in 1965. Before this time the committee normally was called on for a resolution to send a bill to a conference with the Senate. A majority vote of the House was sufficient for this purpose after 1965.

Whether acting independently or as an arm of the leadership, the Committee on Rules performs significant functions in managing the flow of business on the floor. It serves the other committees by responding to requests for special orders. The sequence of its involvement and decisions is as follows:

1. A request is made by a committee for a special order to debate a bill on either the House or Union Calendars at a particular time under specified conditions. (Note: hearing this request is the initial decision made by the Rules Committee, but requests are rarely denied outright).
2. The Rules Committee holds hearings on the request at which committee members testify. Both proponents and opponents of the bill are normally present at the hearings to respond to questions by Rules Committee members. (Here then is an essentially in-house set of hearings—i.e., between members of the House).
3. A decision is then made as to whether a special order or rule should be granted and, if so, how it should be formulated.
4. The committee decides among the following options in issuing a special order (obviously influenced by the nature of the original request):
   a. An "open rule" which sets the time and length of debate and permits amendments.
   b. A "closed rule" which also sets the time and length of debate but permits only committee amendments.
   c. A "modified closed rule" which permits amendments on specified sections of the bill.
   d. Any of the above rules may provide for a substitute bill to be voted on and/or a waiver on any point of order that may be raised against the bill or any of its provisions.[22]

Each of these variations can be illustrated from the following resolution (I have taken liberties with a specific resolution introduced in the House on July 19, 1979, by excising certain material that I will introduce at the proper time).

H. Res. 305

Resolved. That upon the adoption of this resolution it shall be in order to move . [1] . that the House resolve itself into the Committee of the Whole House on the State of the Union for the consideration of the bill (H.R. 3917) to amend titles XV and XVI of the Public Health Service Act to revise and extend the authorities and requirements under those titles for health planning and health resources development, and for other purposes. [2] . [3]. After general debate, which shall be confined to the bill and shall continue not to exceed one hour to be equally divided and controlled by the chairman and ranking minority member of the Com-

---

[22] For further details on options see Matsunaga and Chen (1976: 21−23).

mittee on Interstate and Foreign Commerce, the bill shall be read for amendment under the five-minute rule. .[4]. . At the conclusion of the consideration of the bill for amendment, the committee shall rise and report the bill to the House with such amendments as may have been adopted and the previous question shall be considered as ordered on the bill and amendments thereto to final passage without intervening motion except one motion to recommit.[5][23]

Here is a classic open rule. If the House adopts this resolution (a simple majority is required for passage), it first agrees to make this bill its immediate business, regardless of what may be pending on its various calendars. The House orders itself into the Committee of the Whole (a procedure discussed subsequently) and proceeds to debate the bill (H.R. 3917 in the example given) under the terms set forth in the resolution. Note that only one hour of general debate is permitted, equally divided between the party leaders of the committee that reported the bill (Interstate and Foreign Commerce in this case). The bill is then *open* for amendment, again under the conditions of the five-minute rule that limits explanation to five minutes followed by an opposing statement, also limited to five minutes. Following amendment, the rule provides that the House will move directly to the question of final passage, permitting only a motion to recommit the bill to the committee (a final protection for the minority since only a member opposed to the bill can make the motion).

Using this same resolution, we can illustrate several variations.

Closed or modified closed rule: Simply strike the words "the bill shall be read for amendment under the five-minute rule" and insert "the bill shall be considered as having been read for amendment." The effect of this change is obvious—all opportunities to amend the bill are shut off. This language in turn may be modified by permitting amendments introduced by the sponsoring committee or in regard to specific language in the bill, or both. For example, the resolution above may read: "No amendment shall be in order to said bill *except* amendments offered by direction of the Committee on Interstate and Foreign Commerce," or "No amendment shall be in order to said bill *except* amendments with respect to the following language of the bill (specification of specific sections or words)," or some combination of these restrictions. The effect of these modifications is to control who offers amendments and what is to be amended.

Waivers of points of order: It so happens that this particular resolution did include waivers that I excised so as to present a pure open rule. Note that I entered numbers above the three dots where I removed language. At 1 the resolution read: "section 402(a) of the Congressional Budget Act of 1974 (Public Law 93—344) to the contrary

---

[23] *Congressional Record* (daily edition), July 19, 1979, p. H6212.

notwithstanding." This section of the Budget Act prohibits consideration of any new budget authority unless the bill was reported by May
15 of the preceding year. Since this bill involved budget authority, a
waiver was required. At 3 the resolution read: "and all points of order
against sections 106 and 107 of the bill for failure to comply with the
provisions of clause 5, rule XXI are hereby waived." This language is
more or less standard for a waiver. In this case, the designated sections
violated the rule against including appropriations in an authorization
bill and therefore a waiver was needed so as to prevent a legitimate
objection from a member once the bill reached the floor.

Other provisions: Any number of other provisions may be included
in a rule—depending entirely on what a committee requests or the
Committee on Rules judges is required. In the case of H. Res. 305,
provision was made at 2 that "the first reading of the bill shall be
dispensed with." Since the House rules call for three readings, this
move simply saved time with a bill that was presumably quite different
from that which had been introduced. At 4 in H. Res. 305 the original
wording included the following words: "by titles instead of by sections." Note where this occurs, i.e., in the part of the rule applying to
amending procedures. This provision permits amendments which cut
across sections and thus is preferred by members who have objections
to more than just one section. It simply is one more strategic move
that may be important in deciding the fate of the bill.

At 5 I excised the following language:

> After the passage of H.R. 3917, the House shall proceed, section 402(a) of
> the Congressional Budget Act of 1974 to the contrary notwithstanding [a
> repeat of the earlier waiver], to the consideration of the bill S. 544, and it
> shall then be in order in the House to move to strike out all after the
> enacting clause of the said Senate bill and to insert in lieu thereof the
> provisions contained in H.R. 3917 as passed by the House.

Who said that the Congress can't make "is" out of what "isn't"? What
this provision does is to change the Senate version of the bill into the
House version by a simple substitution. Only the Senate bill
number—S. 544—remains. Again, this procedural move saves a great
deal of time since the Senate bill does not need to be assigned to a
committee or debated. It is dispensed with altogether by substituting
the House bill.

H. Res. 305 offers a particularly good illustration of the work of the
Committee on Rules. One can see with this case what a crucial role the
committee plays. As I have pointed out before, the floor procedures are
vitally important as the means for legitimizing a policy action. Exceptions are made all the time, but only in accordance with accepted
practice. The exceptions represent the accommodation to political
and legal demands and thus are very carefully developed. All of this

suggests that in scheduling major bills for debate, the Committee on Rules performs a significant policy function. In essence, *it establishes the conditions under which legitimation will occur.* The requesting committee obviously has a great deal to say about these terms, representing as they do careful estimates of what is required to get a majority on the floor. But the Committee on Rules itself often gets involved and will decide which course to pursue when factions on the committee request different conditions. So, the committee serves at a crucial juncture in the policy process—that between the more substantively oriented development of a program to resolve an issue (the committee stage) and the more procedurally oriented majority approval or legitimation of the program (the floor stage). What it decides to include in the rule may determine the substance and the eventual fate of the bill.

Resolutions from the Committee on Rules are introduced by a member of the committee and are themselves subject to debate and approval or rejection by the House. If an issue is controversial, the debate over the resolution may be revealing of what is to come later. Debate is, however, limited to one hour, with half the time allotted to those who oppose the rule. One may expect the most objection to be voiced against the closed rule. Cries of gagging are heard as members charge that the majority is seeking to destroy the deliberative functions of the House. The closed rule has never been used frequently— primarily for complex tax legislation from the Committee on Ways and Means.

> . . . members of the committee are becoming increasingly reluctant to grant such requests because they are more and more persuaded that the House should be as free to work its will as the Senate, which is not bound by any such rule (Matsunaga and Chen, 1976: 22).

Following debate on the rule, a vote is taken. In the case of H. Res. 305—the example cited above—debate was very brief since, as the ranking Republican on the Committee on Rules observed: "I know of no opposition to the rule."[24] Vote was taken by an electronic device and H. Res. 305 passed 395 to 10, with 29 not voting. Not unexpectedly, few rules are defeated—only 37 in the 20 years between the 85th and 94th Congresses (Matsunaga and Chen, 1976: 151—52). In the first place, the work of the committee typically represents an agreement with the principal supporters of the legislation as it has been reported from the standing committee. Even if the requesting committee is divided, one may expect the Rules Committee members to have framed the rule by relying on a reasonably accurate estimate of the support for the bill on the floor. In the second place, members are not

---

[24] Ibid., p. H6213.

anxious to establish an anti-Rules Committee reputation. Though its power is not as great as it was in years past, still the committee performs a crucial function in the legislative process. As Walter Oleszek observes (1978:   107): "Challenging the Rules Committee is an uninviting task; members know that at some future time they will need a rule from the committee for their own bills." While it is rare for a resolution to be defeated, when it happens it typically ends the life of the bill just as surely as if it had been the subject of the vote. Technically the bill remains on the calendar, but in fact it is unlikely ever to be debated on the floor during a session if the resolution to debate it has been defeated.

The Committee on Rules is considerably more circumscribed in exercising its authority as traffic cop than it was in the 1950s. When the committee approves a rule it must file its report within three legislative days. If the member making the report does not call it up before the House in seven legislative days, then any member of the committee may do so. These rules protect against delay once the committee has acted. Further, as noted earlier, the Democratic Party Caucus can and does instruct the Rules Committee Democrats in regard to bills before them. This type of action was unthinkable in the 1950s (Matsunaga and Chen, 1976:   41).

How should important bills be displayed, debated, and changed? How should a final decision be reached?

A number of significant activities are included in these questions. Earlier I proposed that Congress, perhaps any legislature, provides means for reaching agreement on a policy issue, then displaying that agreement. "Agree and display" occurs within the subcommittee, then in the committee, again in the Committee on Rules. The display of each agreement is to a larger and larger group, thus complicating the approval or legitimation process. Knowing that final House and Senate approval is required may influence the development of the legislation in early stages. Certainly it does not profit supporters in the subcommittee to play to that audience alone. It may equally be the case, however, that those fashioning agreements at lower levels cannot predict subsequent reactions or are unwilling in any case to compromise.

What has to happen if a legislature is to perform at all well is that procedures have to be developed to move legislation while permitting interested parties to get involved along the way. Achieving these goals gets more difficult as bills move out of the committee and into the larger arena of the House floor. Thus any chamber as large as the House of Representatives must have rules of procedures and norms of behavior that will facilitate the flow of legislation.

Not unexpectedly, therefore, the House has detailed rules for its floor operations. The committee report has already been discussed. It is the most prominent display of the agreements associated with the bill in question. Therefore, certain matters must be included (see earlier discussion). Among other things, the report must show how the proposed law effects existing law. The purpose is obvious—not only must the immediate agreement be displayed, but the membership must also be informed about where this bill fits into the maze of federal policy. The committee report is distributed to all members and is "the principal means of communicating a committee decision to the entire chamber" (Oleszek, 1978:   74). It is typically the principal source of information for the members and their staffs.

The great bulk of legislation before the House is relatively minor in importance and thus the terms for debating it are very strict—that is, limited time and no amendments. I have already described these procedures when discussing the many methods for getting legislation to the floor (e.g., Consent Calendar, Suspension of the Rules, etc.). The debate on major legislation follows the agreed-upon limits established in special resolutions from the Rules Committee (see above). After approving the terms of debate the House transforms itself into a committee. This is one of the more interesting maneuvers in our legislative process, if a bit baffling to the outside observer. Reread the first several lines of H. Res. 305. Note that it makes it "in order to move . . . that the House resolve itself into the Committee of the Whole House on the State of the Union." Here specifically is how that worked in regard to H.R. 3917 on July 19, 1979:

> **Mr. Waxman:** Mr. Speaker, I move that the House resolve itself into the Committee of the Whole House on the State of the Union for the consideration of the bill (H.R. 3917).
>
> **The Speaker:** . . . The question is on the motion offered by the gentleman from California (Mr. Waxman).
>
> [The motion was agreed to.]
>
> IN THE COMMITTEE OF THE WHOLE
>
> Accordingly the House resolved itself into the Committee of the Whole House on the State of the Union for the consideration of the bill, H.R. 3917, with Mr. Moakley in the chair.[25]

Observe first that when the House sits as a committee a special chairman is appointed by the Speaker. The Speaker is then free to participate in the debate (though he seldom does). The other changes are more important, however, and justify the procedure. The quorum in the House is 50 percent plus one of the membership, or 218 members; the quorum in the Committee of the Whole is only 100 members. Amendments are debated under the five-minute rule so as to speed up

---

[25] Ibid., pp. H6213—14.

the process, and debate can be limited by majority vote of those present. All told then, the procedures of the Committee of the Whole facilitate efficient debate and amendment. Fewer members need to be present, and the legislation can be more effectively managed.

Table 9–5 provides a summary of the sequence of action on the House floor for the great bulk of major legislation. We need not review each step in detail but it is helpful to explain the rationale for certain procedures and to illustrate various steps with concrete examples. I have already discussed and provided examples of action points one through six. Let's begin then with point seven—general debate. The time for debate in the House is severely limited because of size. Two or

TABLE 9– 5
The flow of work on the House floor—major legislation

Action	Comment
1. Resolution introduced by a member of the House Committee on Rules	Resolution specifies the terms of debate.
2. Debate on the resolution	Limited to one hour, with time equally divided.
3. Vote on the resolution	Simple majority carries.
4. Motion to resolve the House into the Committee of the Whole	In order following passage of the resolution or rule.
5. Vote on the motion	Normally noncontroversial.
6. House becomes the committee	Mace is removed; Speaker steps down in favor of a chairman.
7. General debate on the bill.	Time specified in the resolution—equally divided between majority and minority floor managers.
8. Bill read for amendment.	5-minute rule applies—pro forma amendments introduced to prolong debate. Amendments must be germane to section or title being read.
9. Vote on amendments.	Done in sequence of the degrees of amendment by voice, division, teller, or recorded teller.
10. The Committee of the Whole rises:	Chairman returns the gavel to the Speaker; mace is returned.
11. Previous question is ordered.	Provided in the resolution; no more debate permitted.*
12. Vote on amendments.	Separately or en bloc by voice, division, teller, or electronic device.
13. Engrossment and third reading.	Pro forma action approved by unanimous consent.
14. Motion to recommit.	Provided for in resolution; must be introduced by a member opposed to the bill; may be with or without instructions; 10-minutes debate permitted on motions "with instructions."
15. Vote on motion to recommit.	Approval kills the bill, but it may be returned later.†
16. Vote on final passage	Normally by record vote (electronic device).
17. Motion to reconsider.	Pro forma action to prevent reconsideration of the bill later—motion typically laid on the table.‡

* If the previous question has not been ordered in the resolution, then one hour of debate is permitted after the Committee rises and amendments are in order.
† If a motion with instructions passes, the bill may be reported back to the House within seconds since the Committee Chairman merely acts for the Committee in resubmitting the bill with the required changes.
‡ The House rules provide that following a vote "it shall be in order for any member of the majority, on the same or succeeding day, to move for the reconsideration thereof" (Rule XVIII). Thus, in order to prevent later consideration, the majority moves reconsideration immediately.
SOURCE: Compiled by the author from the information in Oleszek (1978: Ch. 5); Zinn (1969); and the House Rules.

four hours is not untypical, with the time always divided between proponents and opponents. The time is literally managed by a representative on each side—appropriately referred to as the floor manager for the bill. The proponent is typically the chairman of the committee or subcommittee reporting the bill, with the ranking minority member of the same group in charge of the time in opposition. This is not to say that the proponents and opponents always divide along party lines, however.

Since general debate is often characterized by set speeches, it may strike one that it is a purposeless exercise. Such is not the case, however. Any number of purposes are served. Signals are given to undecided members. Rationales are provided which can be used by the members to justify their votes to constituents and interest groups. A record is established that may be consulted later by the implementing department or agency in the executive and by the courts if the law is challenged there. The press is informed about the strengths and weaknesses of a program. All of these purposes are directed toward the display function of the legislature—both for contemporary understanding and future interpretation. Here is an example of how the general debate proceeds:

> **The Chairman** [of the Committee of the Whole]: . . . Under the rule, the gentleman from California (Mr. Waxman) will be recognized for 30 minutes, and the gentleman from Kentucky (Mr. Carter) will be recognized for 30 minutes.
>
> The Chair recognizes the gentleman from California (Mr. Waxman).
>
> **Mr. Waxman:** Mr. Chairman, I yield myself such time as I may consume.
>
> (Mr. Waxman asked and was given permission to revise and extend his remarks).
>
> **Mr. Waxman:** Mr. Chairman, the legislation before us today.[26]

And he began to discuss the bill. Later Mr. Carter (Tim Lee Carter, R—Kentucky, speaking for the opposition) made his opening speech. Then came the shorter speeches.

> **Mr. Waxman:** Mr. Chairman, I yield three minutes to the gentlewoman from Maryland (Ms. Mikulski).[27]

Mr. Carter, too, was in a position to yield time. In this particular case the time permitted was not required, and Waxman therefore yielded back the balance of time (a not uncommon practice with less controversial bills).

Following the conclusion of general debate, the bill is read by title or section for amendment. Normally, the reading itself will be dispensed with and the bill made open to amendment—in its entirety, by

---

[26] Ibid., p. H6214.

[27] Ibid., p. H6216.

title, or by section. The amending process is often complicated when the House is debating important legislation. Again, instructions are normally included in the rule, perhaps limiting the number, type, and source of amendments. And amendments are debated under the very strict five-minute rule by which the proposer and an opponent are each limited to five minutes. In order to extend debate, members frequently introduce so-called pro forma amendments—for example, "Mr. Chairman, I move to strike the last word." No vote is taken— indeed, the member is only using the amending procedure to make a statement which he or she was unable to make in the general debate.

There are degrees of amendments. First is the amendment itself, which may in turn be amended (an amendment to the amendment). A substitute may be introduced to the amendment, and that substitute may in turn be amended. The sequence of voting is as indicated in Figure 9 −1 (the numbers in parentheses). House amendments must be germane to the section of the bill being amended.

FIGURE 9 − 1

The amending process—degrees of amendments and sequences of voting

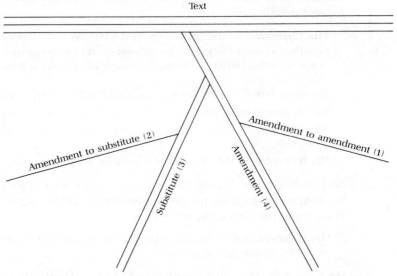

SOURCE: Congressional Quarterly, *Guide to the Congress of the United States* (Washington, D.C.: Congressional Quarterly, 1971), p. 112, as taken from *Cannon's Procedure in the House of Representatives* (1963).

It is difficult, if not impossible, to illustrate all of the variations in amending a bill. The process is used for so many different purposes—e.g., to make a public announcement, satisfy an interest, repair or refine the bill, redirect or kill a program. Actual instances are helpful, however, for understanding that what we have described here really does happen on the House floor. On September 6, 1979, the

House was in the process of amending the Foreign Assistance Appropriations for 1980. The sequence of action for a part of that day was as follows:

1. Mr. Bedell moves a pro forma amendment.
2. Mr. Miller offers an amendment to the section being read by the clerk.
3. Mr. Obey offers an amendment as a substitute for Miller's amendment.
4. Mr. Long makes a point of order noting the lack of quorum.
5. Quorum call. Proceedings resume when a hundred members respond.
6. Mr. Miller offers an amendment to Obey's substitute for his amendment.
7. Mr. McHugh offers an amendment to the original Miller amendment (an amendment to the amendment).
8. Mr. Bauman inquires as to the appropriateness of the McHugh amendment. The chair rules that it is in order.
9. The McHugh amendment to the original Miller amendment is agreed to (voice vote).
10. The Miller amendment to Obey's substitute is not agreed to, 18 to 24 on a division.
11. Mr. Miller demands a record vote and makes a point of order noting a lack of a quorum.
12. Quorum call. Proceedings resume when a hundred members respond.
13. The Miller amendment to Obey's substitute is not agreed to, 178 to 228, 28 not voting, on a recorded vote.
14. Mr. Conte offers an amendment to Obey's substitute.
15. The Conte amendment to Obey's substitute is agreed to (voice vote).
16. Mr. Obey demands a recorded vote.
17. The Conte amendment to Obey's substitute is agreed to, 395 to 12, 27 not voting, on a recorded vote.
18. Mr. Miller offers an amendment to the Obey substitute.
19. The Miller amendment to the Obey substitute is not agreed to, 44 to 62, on a division.
20. Mr. Miller demands a recorded vote.
21. The Miller amendment to the Obey substitute is agreed to, 254 to 144, 36 not voting, on a recorded vote.
22. The Obey substitute, as amended, to the original Miller amendment, as amended, is agreed to (voice vote).
23. The original Miller amendment, as amended, is agreed to (voice vote).[28]

---

[28] *Congressional Record* (daily edition), September 6, 1979, pp. H7368–78.

All four degrees of amendments are illustrated here. We can now redraw the chart with the actual examples (see Figure 9 −2). One might have thought that this complicated series of amendments, with two intervening quorum calls and three recorded votes, would have

FIGURE 9−2
Amendments offered to 1980 Foreign Assistance Appropriation, September 6, 1979

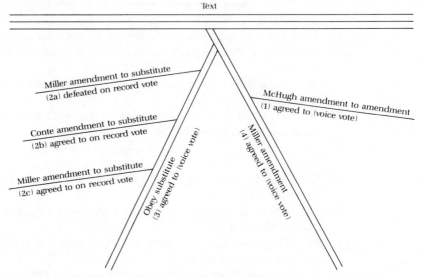

SOURCE: Compiled from *Congressional Record,* September 6, 1979, pp. H7368−78 (daily edition).

taken a very long time. In fact, due to the expeditious debating procedures and electronic voting, these several actions took place in an elapsed time of two hours and 30 minutes.

The clerk continues the reading of the bill for amendment. When no more amendments are offered, a motion is made for the Committee of the Whole to rise and report to the House. The Speaker resumes the chair. Where the rule specifies, the previous question is considered ordered, and no further debate is permitted. If no such provision is included in the rule, an additional hour of debate is permitted, and new amendments may be introduced. The Speaker then asks whether a separate vote is demanded on any amendment. If not, they are voted on as a bloc. The bill is then pro forma read a third time.

It is at this point that the minority party or other opponents to the bill have one last opportunity to change or defeat the bill. The motion to recommit the bill is always included in the rule, but it must be introduced by a member who is opposed. It goes like this:

Mr. Quillen: Mr. Speaker, I offer a motion to recommit.

The Speaker: Is the gentleman opposed to the bill?

Mr. Quillen: I am, Mr. Speaker.

The Speaker: The gentleman qualifies. The clerk will report the motion to recommit.

(The clerk read as follows.)

Mr. Quillen moves to recommit the bill, H.R. 3236 to the Committee on Ways and Means.

The Speaker: Without objection, the previous question is ordered on the motion to recommit.

(There was no objection.)

The Speaker: The question is on the motion to recommit.

(The motion to recommit was rejected.)[29]

A motion to recommit may also carry instructions for the committee to take some action. If it passes, as they rarely do, then the committee is likely to report back immediately with the change. Normally one would expect a majority to emerge in the process of debate and amendment—a majority that will then beat back the effort to recommit the bill.

Now we come to the very final stages of floor action. The Speaker announces that the question before the House is the passage of the bill. Someone may object that a quorum (218 for the full House) is not present. The bells ring throughout the offices and committee rooms—one bell for a teller vote, two for a recorded vote, three for a quorum call—and the vote is taken, by electronic device if recorded. Recorded or roll-call votes used to be very time consuming as the clerks had to read all the names of the members. Now they go very swiftly as the members simply insert a plastic card into a slot at one of the many voting stations in the chamber and press the yea, or nay, or present button. The vote is announced as it is recorded on electronic boards located on either side of the chamber. A motion to reconsider is then made and laid on the table so as to prevent later action to overturn the result. The bill is then delivered to the Senate if it has not as yet acted.

Summary

I have provided no more than a sketch of the procedures used for processing legislation on the floor. I have insisted that the formal means of debating and approving bills are important in and of themselves. They form the basic structure within which the members do their business as lawmakers. Determined majorities may take exceptional actions to be sure, but the base is normally not effected by these actions. The next bill is considered under the familiar procedures, not the recent exceptions.

---

[29] Ibid., p. H7418.

The other point of importance is that we have not directly discussed the legislative strategies that emerge in response to the formal procedures. Clearly, those supporting and opposing bills before the House will seek to gain whatever advantage they can. Knowledge of the rules is one such advantage. For many decades senior southern Democrats were masters of parliamentary procedures. Senator Richard Russell (D– Georgia) won many a day with this mastery—often in the face of a majority in the Senate who opposed him. Typically, of course, knowledge of the rules is more useful as a resource to those who seek to prevent or delay action. Those favoring a bill must know what to do on the floor, but their principal task is to muster a majority in support of the proposed legislation. The wiley student of the rules may triumph without majority support if delay or defeat is desired, however.

CONCLUSION

While I have submitted to the temptation in Chapters 8 and 9 to provide considerable organizational detail, it is significant as well to understand that volumes more could be written. I personally learned something important in the writing of this material—it simply won't do in describing Congress to understate the complexity of the formal legislative structure. The crucial legitimizing function of the legislature demands more attention to form, to rules, to precedents than might be true for institutions performing other policy functions. This survey of House organization also demonstrates the need for connecting tissue among the various units and subunits. In theory, political parties are to facilitate making connections so that the representative and analytical functions performed by committees and subcommittees will result in the House performing its legislative or lawmaking functions as well. For many reasons, parties are limited in achieving this goal. Thus it is that other groups emerge, often contributing to a fragmented lawmaking process in the House. It seems clear that the House is better organized to represent than to produce integrated legislative programs. That deficiency may be compensated for either in the Senate or with a strong and effective president. But the Senate is, itself, not too well suited organizationally to produce integrated programs, and as we know, presidents vary greatly in their understanding and knowledge of congressional strengths and weaknesses. The immediate task now is to consider the Senate and how it is organized.

10 Organizing the Senate

In his classic book on the Senate, Lindsay Rogers argued that "the role of the American Senate . . . is a paradoxical but convincing justification of the bicameral theory" (1926: 256). His was a subtle but important point—essentially that the Senate as a policy institution capitalizes on the ego centrism of its members.

> The Senate . . . plays a high and unanticipated role in the political drama. It is, however, a role that is better described than seen, and one who watches the Senate at work is disillusioned. . . . The Senate . . . is the only possible forum that the Constitution and practice under it permit. It is the only chamber where minority aspirations can find free expression and where there can be any criticism of the executive. A member of the House of Representatives is a private in the ranks. . . . Each senator, on the other hand, is a staff officer—even a prima donna. He looks upon himself not as *primus inter pares* but as *inter stellas luna minores*.
>
> Senators, perhaps, should not be taken too seriously, but the importance of the Senate must not be underestimated (Rogers, 1926: 253–55).

Surely the founding fathers intended the Senate to perform different functions than the House. One can justify bicameralism even if
both chambers are constituted in the same way—that is, as providing
double review and evaluation. But the constitution makers did not
limit themselves to this rationale. The Senate was to be populated by
those "in a more advanced age and a longer period of citizenship" (The
Federalist, 1937:   400). Senators were given longer terms, with only
one third of the chamber having to seek reappointment "every second
year." Words and phrases like *stability, security to the people,* and *due
sense of national character,* were used in *The Federalist* to justify the
Senate. Beyond these expectations, however, were those associated
with the selection of senators. By permitting state legislatures to
choose senators the constitution writers created an assembly of
ambassadors—a point they apparently well understood. As was recorded in *The Federalist*, this method had

> . . . the double advantage of favoring a select appointment, and of
> giving to the state governments such an agency in the formation of the
> federal government as must secure the authority of the former, and may
> form a convenient link between the two systems (1937:   401).

Of course, the purity of this ambassadorial role was compromised, if
not destroyed, by the ratification of the 17th Amendment.

No institution may be expected to develop precisely in accordance
with the intentions of its creators. Still the differences in composition
between the House and Senate were striking enough to insure different styles and functions for each. While both chambers have changed
through time, sometimes even exchanging functions, the differences
remain more striking than the similarities.

In general, it is fair to say that the debating function remains today
as central to Senate operations. If the House functions particularly well
as a chamber of representation, the Senate at least has the potential for
serving well as a chamber of integrated review and analysis. Open
debate is a method for discovering connections between issues. It is in
this sense that I made the point earlier that the Senate is more
oriented toward the institutional functions of debating issues and discovering the basis for compromise across issues.

The purpose of reiterating these degrees of difference between the
two chambers is simply to prepare the reader for variations in Senate
organization. Clearly, if one legislative institution sees itself as doing
different work from another, then it may be expected to vary its organization and procedures. Our discussion will follow basically the same
outline as that for the House—the offices, committees and subcommittees, political parties, and floor procedures. But the conclusions will
vary consistently with the earlier observation that the debating function is particularly important. As we will see, the state-serving tasks of
the offices are very much the same as the district-serving work in the

House, only larger in scope. But the operations of the other components differ in kind as well as degree. The committees are relied on less, the parties are even more organizations of bare convenience, and the work on the floor is more particularized to each legislative issue.

ORGANIZING TO REPRESENT AND SERVE THE STATE

The observation that the Senate functions as a forum should not lead us to believe that it lacks organization or staff. Writing at the end of the 1950s, Donald R. Matthews noted that "some of the fastest-growing 'bureaucracies' in Washington are to be found in the Senate Office Building" (1960:   82). His description of the typical office appropriately included the receptionist, guest book, pictures of the home state features, telephone ringing, busy typists' fingers, active administrative and legislative assistants.

> Beyond this, a tranquil oasis amid the noise and clutter of the "outer" and "working" rooms, is the senator's private office. Here one finds a larger, well-worn desk, several Victorian couches and leather chairs, often a huge wall map of the world, autographed pictures of politicians, framed citations and awards, and more pictures of scenic attractions (Matthews, 1960:   82).

What Matthews described 20 years ago sounds familiar for today. The effort to capture a bit of the home state is familiar, certainly the busy staff cramped into limited space is the same. The differences are (1) that the Washington staff is larger now and not all located in the senator's suite, and (2) a sizeable staff operation may be found back home as well.

Writing in the late 1970s, Elizabeth Drew described the office operations of a senator from a moderately sized state, that of John C. Culver, D—Iowa (1979:   38—39).

> Outside Culver's own office is the usual warren that makes up a Senate office suite. There are five rooms, three of them subdivided by plywood partitions. About 20 people, including staff members and summer interns, work in these rooms; 7 other handle mail in a building a half block away; and 11 work for Culver on committee matters in other offices in the two Senate office buildings.

The fast growth in staff that Matthews observed in the Capitol Hill offices in 1959 has obviously escalated. But there is much more. Drew continues (1979:   39):

> In addition, Culver maintains four offices in Iowa, where a total of 10 people work. The Iowa offices handle most of the casework for constituents. . . . One Senate aid estimates that approximately one fourth of every senator's job consists of taking care of state interests and casework.

From one busy office in 1959 to several in different locations in 1979 —
that is the measure of change in the work for senators. Increased
demands resulting from more complex events and issues explain the
need for more staff. It is worth being reminded again, however, that
increased staff too can, and normally does, result in greater workloads,
thus requiring more staff, etc.

The perquisites available to senators are listed in Table 10 − 1. Total
figures for individual senators range roughly between $700,000 and

TABLE 10 − 1
Organizing to represent in the Senate—the perquisites

Perquisite	Amount	Comment
Office expenses:		
1. Travel (round trips)	40 − 44	Total amount varies with distance.
2. Telephone/telegraph	$ 4,400 +	Additional provisions for long distance minutes adjusted for state.
3. Postage	$ 1,390 − $ 1,740	Adjusted for state.
4. Stationery	$ 3,600 − 5,000	Adjusted for state.
5. District office		
a. Rental	4,800 − 8,000 sq. ft.	Adjusted for state; paid at highest rate charged to federal agencies in state.
b. Furnishings	$ 22,500 − $ 28,500	Adjusted for state; a one-time payment.
c. Expenses	$ 7,800	Annual allowance.
Clerk—hire:		
1. Staff.....................	$ 624,431 − $1,110,237	Adjusted to state, though small states get considerably more per capita. Includes personal staff and legislative assistance for committees.
Other support:		
1. Franking privilege	Varies	Chargeable to legislative branch budget.
2. Foreign travel	Varies	Authorized through the committees.
3. Miscellaneous (documents, file storage, studios, furnishings, parking, etc.)	Varies	Chargeable to legislative branch budget.

SOURCE: Richard E. Cohen, "Congressional Allowances Are Really Perking Up," *National Journal*, February 4, 1978, p. 182.

$1,250,000 exclusive of senatorial salaries, pensions, and general sup-
port. The full Senate budget in fiscal year 1979 was just over $185
million—an average of $1.85 million per senator. Many adjustments
are made for the differences in population among the states but by no

means on a straight per capita basis. I can do no more here than to provide the reader with a general idea of the amount and kind of support that is available. The precise figures and formulas for allocation are no doubt undergoing change as this section is written. And, in any event, the methods relied on are exceedingly complex, making the legislative process seem simple by comparison. As one recent report noted:

> Much confusion surrounds Senate funding because the appropriations structure is fragmented and budgeting is nonprogrammatic. This renders an understanding of the process all but impossible to the casual observer and, one suspects, to the senators themselves.[1]

Having acknowledged the mystery surrounding the precise methods of allocation, it is possible to describe some of the effects. In regard to office allotments and expenses, practically every decision is based on the differences in state population. For example:

Number of rooms (Washington): five for less than 7 million to eight for more than 15 million.

Automatic typing equipment: four for less than 1 million to 11 for more than 13 million.

State office space: 4,800 square feet for less than 2 million to 8,000 square feet for more than 17 million.

Stationery: 15,000 letterheads and envelopes for less than 3 million to 30,000 for more than 10 million.[2]

And so it goes for many different items provided for office management. Note that the same formula is not used for all items. And, of course, the larger states tend to get cheated on a per capita basis—e.g., .0004 square feet of state office space per Californian to .014 square feet per resident of Wyoming (over 30 times greater).

The clerk hire allowance is, perhaps, the most important support available. It is provided in two categories—that for personal offices (in Washington and the state, however the senator wishes to divide it) and that for legislative assistance. The bulk of the allowance is for personal office staff, and the variation there depends upon population—again favoring small states (Wyoming with nearly $1.25 per capita; California with less than a nickel). Legislative assistance, on the other hand, is based on service on the committees where a senator does not have appointing power either as a chairman or ranking minority member (full committee or subcommittee). The special provision for legislative assistance associated with committee and subcommittee work is recognition of the need to provide special support for this work.

---

[1] U.S. Senate, Commission on the Operation of the Senate, *Budgeting in the United States Senate*, 94th Cong., 2d sess., 1977, p. 91. (Material prepared by Gayle Condon).

[2] Commission on the Operation of the Senate, p. 64 ff.

In her study of the operation of senators' offices, Susan Webb Hammond concluded that "the Senate has 100 different bureaucracies at the personal office level. Managing a small bureaucracy thus becomes an important aspect of each Senator's job."[3] The tasks to be accomplished do not vary much from those facing a House member's staff (i.e., administrative, press, legislative, constituent, and project work). But the number of staff involved will vary from that normally found in a House office to several times that number (from 13 to 71 in 1977). When Kenneth Kofmehl studied Senate office staffs in the early 1960s he found "considerable overlapping of duties among the high-level positions" (1977:   168). Though job assignments today are not as well specified as in executive agencies, still considerable departmentalization has occurred. Thus, in addition to managing offices in Washington and at home, many senators and their top aides are faced with the challenge of coordinating the work of a diverse staff in Washington itself. In her study of Senate offices, Hammond found that various techniques were used to coordinate staff work: departmental meetings, meetings of department heads with the administrative assistant, weekly breakfasts with the senator's committee and office staffs in attendance, reliance on the common experience of committee and office staffs, regular staff meetings with all in attendance, weekly reports from the state, frequent travel to the state.[4]

Senate staff positions are very much like those in the House. It's just that there are more of them. Fox and Hammond discovered similar patterns of organization to those in the House too—that is, some hierarchically organized, some highly individualistic, and others in between with central clearance but limited direction from the top, referred to as "coordinative" by Fox and Hammond (1977:   76).

Organization and use of staff in state offices also varies between the House and Senate. Though junior senators are more prone to maintain large staffs at home than are senior senators, all have shifted work in this direction.[5] Space and salary problems in Washington along with decentralization of federal agencies and the positive effect of a senatorial presence at home have combined to encourage this development.

Table 10 − 2 shows the variation in the number of staff offices and percentage of staff allocated there. In the 95th Congress a large majority of the senators had two or more offices, a surprisingly large num-

---

[3] Susan Webb Hammond, "The Operation of Senators' Offices," in U.S. Senate Commission on the Operation of the Senate, *Senators: Offices, Ethics, and Pressures*, 94th Cong., 2d sess., 1977, p. 4.

[4] Hammond, "The Operation," p. 9.

[5] As reported by Janet Breslin in "Constituent Service," in U.S. Senate, Commission on the Operation of the Senate, *Senators: Offices, Ethics, and Pressures*, 94th Cong., 2d sess., 1977, p. 23.

TABLE 10–2
State offices for senators, number and staff, 95th Congress

	Number of state offices								
	0	*1*	*2*	*3*	*4*	*5*	*6*	*7*	
Senators with	3	25	28	25	11	2	3	2	= 99*

	Percentage of staff in state				
	0–20 percent	*21–30 percent*	*31–40 percent*	*41–50 percent*	*51 per- cent +*
Senators with	37	36	14	10	2	= 99*

* One senator not reporting.
SOURCE: Compiled from Charles B. Brownson, ed., *Congressional Staff Directory* (Mt. Vernon, Va.: Congressional Staff Directory, 1977).

ber (18) had four or more. A sizeable majority also allocated more than 20 percent of their staff to state offices, with 12 senators maintaining better than 40 percent of their staff back home. Many of those with larger staffs in the state were from large western states but certainly not all.

A most interesting development is that of senators combining their state staff operations to provide more comprehensive service. In 1977 the two Democratic senators from South Dakota and the two Republican senators from Oklahoma were cooperating in this way. The latter two operated six offices in 1977 with a total staff of 24. One wonders why there could not be cooperation as well between House and Senate members, as well as some coordination with state legislative representatives. Perhaps as government programs grow in numbers and complexity, constituent service headquarters may emerge to coordinate casework at several levels of government.

Hammond quite rightly observes that office organization and operations reflect the senator's style and view of responsibilities. But the equality in state representation (two senators for each) forces accommodation of differences in the provision of resources and this too insures that staff operations will vary. So we get quite remarkable diversity in a relatively small legislative body. And these individual and state differences are accommodated, even encouraged. As we will see, they are carried along through the committee system as well so that floor activity comes to have a most serious purpose—to discover a basis for agreement among highly divergent perspectives. Pre-floor House procedures tend to reduce differences; pre-floor Senate procedures often tend to highlight them. These observations lead us into considering how the Senate organizes to make law.

ORGANIZING TO MAKE LAW

In Chapter 8 I proposed picturing the lawmaking process as two funnels—one an issue or problem defining and bill development funnel that goes from the general to the specific, the other a policy approval funnel going from specialists to generalists (or at least those less involved in preparing the bill in question). The same imagery can be used for the Senate if one simply flattens out the funnel a bit. Figure 10 — 1 shows the differences. While a somewhat imprecise exercise,

FIGURE 10 — 1
House and Senate lawmaking processes

The House

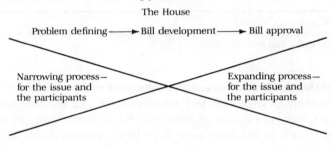

The Senate

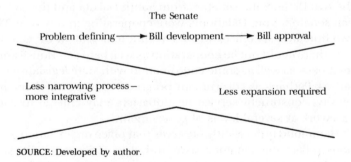

SOURCE: Developed by author.

still the chart illustrates a fundamental difference in the lawmaking processes of each House. The House's advantage in providing expertise through its committee system can create problems later in building majority support for legislation (problems that are solved by various rules—see Chapter 9). Senate committee processes are less exclusive with the result that fewer issues are resolved. What all of this says, in part, is that the committees and subcommittees play a different role in the Senate as compared to the House and that these differences influence floor activity in each chamber. Richard F. Fenno, Jr., puts it this way (1973: 190 — 91):

> . . . Senate committees, as a class, differ from House committees as a class. Whatever the differences among the committees within a given chamber or whatever the similarities between a given pair of counterpart committees, there are fundamental cross-chamber differences that render all Senate committees different from all House committees. Since the House and Senate are different institutions, it should not be surprising that their committees are also different. Senate committees are less important as a source of chamber influence, less preoccupied with success on the chamber floor, less autonomous within the chamber, less personally expert, less strongly led, and more individualistic in decision making than are House committees.

It appears that Woodrow Wilson's statement, "Congress in its committee-rooms is Congress at work" (see Chapter 8), is more applicable to the House than the Senate. It is time to examine the committees and explore these differences.

The Senate committees

To say that committees perform different functions in the Senate is not to suggest that they are unimportant in that chamber. An individual senator's day is filled with committee work. As Matthews observes, this work is of "paramount importance" to a senator since it can make "his reputation with his colleagues" (1960: 17). But often a good committee reputation prepares one for influence on the floor since many issues will carry over to that stage.

The number of committees. Table 10 − 3 provides information on all standing committees and subcommittees of the 96th Congress. The Senate has seven fewer standing committees (15 as compared to 22 in the House), thus forcing some to work with more than one House

TABLE 10−3
Committees and subcommittees, Senate, 96th Congress

Committee	Party ratio (D−R)	Subcommittee	Party ratio (D−R)
Agriculture, Nutrition, and Forestry	10−8 (56.6% D)	1. Agricultural Credit and Rural Electrification	3−2
		2. Agricultural Production, Marketing, and Stabilization of Prices	7−4
		3. Agricultural Research and General Legislation	4−4
		4. Environment, Soil Conservation, and Forestry	4−4
		5. Foreign Agricultural Policy	5−4
		6. Nutrition	3−3
		7. Rural Development	4−3
			30−24 (55.6% D)

Committee	Party ratio (D−R)	Subcommittee	Party ratio (D−R)
Appropriations	17−11 (60.7% D)	1. Agriculture and Related Agencies	8−5
		2. Defense	11−7
		3. District of Columbia	3−2
		4. Energy and Water Development	9−7
		5. Foreign Operations	6−4
		6. HUD— Independent Agencies	7−5
		7. Interior	9−6
		8. Labor, HEW	9−5
		9. Legislative Branch	3−2
		10. Military Construction	4−2
		11. State, Justice, Commerce, and the Judiciary	7−5
		12. Transportation	6−3
		13. Treasury, Postal Service, General Government	3−2
			85−55 (60.7% D)
Armed Services	10−7 (58.8% D)	1. Arms Control	4−3
		2. General Procurement	5−4
		3. Manpower and Personnel	4−3
		4. Military Construction and Stockpiles	5−4
		5. Procurement Policy and Reprogramming	4−3
		6. Research and Development	5−4
			27−21 (56.3% D)
Banking, Housing, and Urban Affairs	9−6 (60.0% D)	1. Consumer Affairs	3−2
		2. Economic Stabilization	3−2
		3. Financial Institutions	5−4
		4. Housing and Urban Affairs	6−4
		5. Insurance	2−1
		6. International Finance	4−3
		7. Rural Housing and Development	2−1
		8. Securities	2−1
			27−18 (60.0% D)
Budget	12−8 (60.0% D)	No subcommittees	
Commerce, Science, and Transportation	10−7 (58.8% D)	1. Aviation	4−3
		2. Communications	7−5
		3. Consumer	3−2
		4. Merchant Marine and Tourism	3−2
		5. Science, Technology, and Space	6−3
		6. Surface Transportation	7−4
			30−19 (61.2% D)

(Also a study group on national ocean policy, 3D)

TABLE 10-3 (*continued*)

Committee	Party ratio (D-R)	Subcommittee	Party ratio (D-R)
Energy and Natural Resources	11-7 (61.1% D)	1. Energy Conservation and Supply	6-4
		2. Energy Regulation	6-4
		3. Energy R and D	7-5
		4. Energy Resources and Materials Production	6-4
		5. Parks, Recreation, and Renewable Resources	6-4
			31-21 (59.6% D)
Environment and Public Works	8-6 (57.1% D)	1. Environmental Pollution	4-3
		2. Nuclear Regulation	4-3
		3. Regional and Community Development	5-4
		4. Resource Protection	4-3
		5. Transportation	3-2
		6. Water Resources	4-3
			24-18 (57.1% D)
Finance	12-8 (60.0% D)	1. Energy and Foundations	3-2
		2. Health	4-3
		3. International Trade	7-5
		4. Oversight of Internal Revenue Service	2-1
		5. Private Pension Plans and Employee Fringe Benefits	2-1
		6. Public Assistance	3-2
		7. Revenue Sharing, Intergovernmental Revenue Impact, and Economic Problems	4-3
		8. Social Security	3-2
		9. Taxation and Debt Management Generally	4-3
		10. Tourism and Sugar	2-1
		11. Unemployment and Related Problems	2-1
			36-24 (60.0% D)
Foreign Relations	9-6 (60.0% D)	1. African Affairs	2-1
		2. Arms Control, Oceans, International Operations, and Environment	4-3
		3. East Asian and Pacific Affairs	4-3
		4. European Affairs	3-2
		5. International Economic Policy	3-2
		6. Near Eastern and South Asian Affairs	3-2
		7. Western Hemisphere Affairs	4-3
			23-16 (59.0% D)

TABLE 10—3 (*concluded*)

Committee	Party ratio (*D—R*)	Subcommittee	Party ratio (*D—R*)
Governmental Affairs	9—8 (52.9% D)	1. Civil Service and General Services	2—1
		2. Energy, Nuclear Proliferation and Federal Services	4—3
		3. Federal Spending Practices and Open Government	4—3
		4. Governmental Efficiency and the District of Columbia	2—2
		5. Intergovernmental Relations	4—3
		6. Investigations	6—5
		7. Oversight of Government Management	2—2
			24—19 (55.8% D)
Judiciary	10—7 (58.8% D)	1. Administrative Practice and Procedure	5—4
		2. Antitrust, Monopoly, and Business Rights	6—4
		3. Constitution	4—3
		4. Criminal Justice	5—4
		5. Improvements in Judicial Machinery	3—2
		6. Jurisprudence and Governmental Relations	3—2
		7. Limitations of Contracted and Delegated Authority	2—1
			28—20 (58.3% D)
Labor and Human Resources	9—6 (60.0% D)	1. Aging	3—2
		2. Alcoholism and Drug Abuse	3—2
		3. Child and Human Development	3—2
		4. Education, Arts, and Humanities	5—3
		5. Employment, Poverty, and Migratory Labor	4—3
		6. Handicapped	3—2
		7. Health and Scientific Research	6—4
			27—18 (60.0% D)
Rules and Administration	6—4 (60.0% D)	No subcommittees	
Veterans' Affairs	6—4 (60.0% D)	No subcommittees	

SOURCE: Compiled from information in *Congressional Quarterly Weekly Report*, April 14, 1979, Supplement, pp. 4—16.

TABLE 10–4
House and Senate standing committee counterparts

House	Senate
1. Agriculture	Agriculture, Nutrition, and Forestry
2. Appropriations	Appropriations
3. Armed Services	Armed Services
4. Banking, Finance, and Urban Affairs	Banking, Housing, and Urban Affairs
5. Budget	Budget
6. District of Columbia	*None* (treated in Governmental Affairs Committee)
7. Education and Labor	Labor and Human Resources
8. Foreign Affairs	Foreign Relations
9. Government Operations	Governmental Affairs
10. House Administration	Rules and Administration
11. Interior and Insular Affairs	Energy and Natural Resources
12. Interstate and Foreign Commerce	Commerce, Science, and Transportation
13. Judiciary	Judiciary
14. Merchant Marine and Fisheries	*None* (treated in Commerce, Science, and Transportation Committee)
15. Post Office and Civil Service	*None* (treated in Governmental Affairs Committee)
16. Public Works and Transportation	Environment and Public Works; Commerce, Science, and Transportation
17. Rules	*None* (Senate rules treated in Rules and Administration Committee)
18. Science and Technology	*None* (treated in Energy and Natural Resources; Commerce, Science, and Transportation, and Labor and Human Resources Committee).
19. Small Business	*None* (treated in Select Small Business Committee)
20. Standards of Official Conduct	*None* (treated in Select Ethics Committee)
21. Veterans' Affairs	Veterans' Affairs
22. Ways and Means	Finance

SOURCE: Compiled from information in *Congressional Quarterly Weekly Report*, April 14, 1979, Supplement.

committee. Table 10 – 4 shows the general jurisdictional comparisons. Note that some Senate committees have enormously broad jurisdiction. The Senate committees on Commerce, Science, and Transportation, and Energy and Natural Resources treat matters handled in at least four House committees. Other matters treated by standing committees in the House are handled by select committees in the Senate.

The fewer number of committees and subcommittees (90 of the latter compared to 148 in the House) is to be expected given the smaller size of the Senate. As it is, senators have nearly twice as many committee and subcommittee assignments as House members—10.68 in 1979 as compared to 5.89 in the House (see Table 10 –5). Since 1970 the Senate has actually reduced the number of standing committees—abolishing three committees (Aeronautical and Space Sciences, District of Columbia, and Post Office and Civil Service), and creating two new committees (Budget and Veterans' Affairs) for a net loss of one. The number of subcommittees too has been reduced since 1970, from 109 to 90.

TABLE 10 – 5
Senate committee and subcommittee positions, 96th Congress

	Democrats (59)	Average per Democrat	Republicans (41)	Average per Republican	Total	Average overall
Standing committees	148	2.51	103	2.51	251	2.51
Their subcommittees	392	6.64	273	6.66	665	6.65
Select committees	30	.51	23	.56	53	.53
Their subcommittees	32	.54	24	.59	56	.56
Joint committees (Senate members)	14	.24	9	.22	23	.23
Their subcommittees (Senate members)	11	.19	9	.22	20	.20
Totals	627	10.63	441	10.76	1068	10.68

SOURCE: Compiled from information in *Congressional Quarterly Weekly Report*, April 14, 1979, Supplement, pp. 4–16.

The Senate has also reduced the number of committee and sub-committee positions in recent years. In 1973 there were 389 committee and 1,196 subcommittee positions compared to 327 committee and 741 subcommittee positions in 1979. As a result the average senator's committee/subcommittee positions were reduced by about five. Much of this reduction was a consequence of changes recommended by the Temporary Select Committee to Study the Senate Committee System, chaired by Senator Adlai E. Stevenson (D – Illinois). The Stevenson Committee proposed the first major change in the Senate committee system in 30 years. Its effect was to distribute power and resources more equally among the membership. The changes included the following:

1. *The committees.* Reduced in number from 31 (standing, select, joint) to 24 (15 standing committees). Formalized a distinction between major and minor committees (only two standing committees are minor—Rules and Administration and Veterans Affairs; select and joint committee assignments are also minor). Prohibited a committee from establishing subcommittees without full Senate approval. Reduced the number of subcommittees by a third. Altered jurisdictions of committees to absorb the work of abolished committees and for other purposes.

2. *Committee membership.* Limited senators to membership on two major, one minor committee (unless presently serving on three major committees). Limited subcommittee assignments on major committees to three (except for Appropriations), on minor committees to two. Required that no senator could receive a second

subcommittee assignment until all committee members had received a first assignment.

3. *Chairmanships.* Limited senators to one committee chairmanship at any one time. Limited senators to one subcommittee chairmanship on each committee. Limited major committee chairmen to one subcommittee chairmanship on major committees, one on minor committees. Limited minor committee chairmen to two subcommittee chairmanships on major committees, prohibited their chairing a minor subcommittee. (Note: the effect of all of this was to limit senators to three chairmanships in all—one full committee, two subcommittee; or three subcommittee).

4. *Staffing.* Required committee staff to reflect the majority-minority ratio, with at least one third under the control of the minority.[6]

The effect of these important changes was to provide more opportunity for junior and minority party senators to be involved in important legislative decision making and thus it attracted considerable support on the Senate floor (Davidson in Dodd and Oppenheimer, 1981: 130).

The redistribution resulting from the reforms changed the work load for individual senators from the clearly unachievable to the merely impossible. Consider the case of Senator Dennis DeConcini (D—Arizona). Serving his third year in the Senate in 1979, he hardly lacked for something to do. His assignments and rankings are as follows:

Appropriations (15th ranking of 17)
  Subcommittees: Foreign Operations (lowest ranking); Interior (7th of 9); State, Justice, Commerce, the Judiciary (6th of 7); Treasury, Postal Service, General Government (2d of 3)

Judiciary (7th ranking of 10)
  Subcommittees: Constitution (3d of 4); Criminal Justice (4th of 5); Improvements in Judicial Machinery (chairman)

Rules and Administration (6th ranking of 6)

Select Indian Affairs (3d ranking of 3)

And though limitations have been placed on the number of chairmanships which a senator can hold, senior members still wield considerable influence. Warren Magnuson (D—Washington) first came to the Senate following the 1944 election (the senior Democrat in the 96th Congress). In the 96th Congress he chaired the powerful Committee on Appropriations and served on four of its subcommittees (chairing one). He also was the senior Democrat on the Committe on Commerce, Science, and Transportation and served on three of its sub-

---

[6] For further details see *Congressional Quarterly Weekly Report*, February 12, 1977, pp. 283 — 84; and Davidson in Dodd and Oppenheimer, 1981: 120 — 28.

committees. He waived his right to the chairmanship of the Commerce Committee so as to lead the Appropriations Committee. Finally he served as the second-ranking Democrat on the Committee on the Budget. Despite all of this impressive seniority, however, Senator Magnuson was defeated for reelection in 1980.

As with the House, many Senate changes have resulted in a rather impressive distribution of chairmanships. By limiting the number of leadership positions that any one senator can hold, even the lowest-ranking senators can either chair or serve as ranking minority member on a subcommittee. All but one of the 59 Democratic senators in the 96th Congress had the privilege of being called Mr. Chairman (there were no female Democratic senators). All 53 Republican senators in the 97th Congress chaired at least one subcommittee—including two women. With so many leaders, it is not surprising that it is difficult to manage the Senate!

Like their counterparts in the House, Senate committees have considerable jurisdictional overlap. This feature has advantages and disadvantages—for example, careful review from differing perspectives as an advantage; needless duplication, perhaps even in-fighting, as a disadvantage. The whole issue of committee jurisdictions was of concern to the Stevenson Committee. In their first report, the committee recorded a quite incredible array of jurisdictional networks among committees and subcommittees for several major policy areas. The most striking case was in the energy area.

> In June 1975 the U. S. Energy Research and Development Administration, ERDA, concluded it was answerable to no fewer than 14 standing committees of the Senate, not to mention 2 select committees and 31 subcommittees or panels. Counting House and joint bodies, jurisdiction over ERDA matters was shared by a total of 99 separate committees, subcommittees, or panels. . . . Energy is probably the most striking current example of jurisdictional overlap; but the picture is not very different for environmental protection, economic policy, research and development, transportation, health, and other such topics.[7]

The committee proposed some changes in jurisdiction but such descriptors as environment, energy, economic, research, foreign or international still appear with some frequency among Senate sub-committees (see Table 10 – 3).

"Oversight" appears with less frequency among subcommittee titles in the Senate as compared to the House. In fact, only two of the 90 subcommittees have that label (one each in Finance and Governmental Affairs). Of course, if one adopts Morris Ogul's definition of legislative oversight as "behavior by legislators and their staffs, individually or

---

[7] U.S. Senate, Temporary Select Committee to Study the Senate Committee System, *The Senate Committee System*, 94th Cong., 2d sess., 1976, p. 103.

collectively, which results in an impact, intended or not, on bureaucratic behavior" (1976: 11), then much of the ordinary work of the Senate and House oversees the executive.

Table 10 −6 shows another difference between Senate and House committees. The party split in the 96th Congress was 59 Democrats (if

TABLE 10− 6
Senate committee and subcommittee ratios, Democrats to Republicans, 96th Congress

Ratio: D to R	Committees	Subcommittees (combined ratio)
Below 53.0%	Governmental Affairs	
53.0 − 53.9%		
54.0 − 54.9%		
55.0 − 55.9%	Agriculture	Agriculture, Governmental Affairs
56.0 − 56.9%		Armed Services
57.0 − 57.9%	Environment and Public Works	Environment and Public Works
58.0 − 58.9%	Armed Services, Commerce, Judiciary	Judiciary
59.0 − 59.9%		Energy and Natural Resources, Foreign Relations
60.0 − 60.9%	Appropriations, Banking, Budget,* Finance, Foreign Relations, Labor and Human Resources, Rules and Administration,* Veterans' Affairs*	Appropriations, Banking, Finance, Labor and Human Resources
61.0 − 61.9%	Energy and Natural Resources	Commerce
Subcommittee ratio less than committee ratio	= 3	
Subcommittee ratio more than committee ratio	= 2	
Subcommittee ratio nearly equal to committee ratio = 7		

* These committees do not have subcommittees.
SOURCE: Compiled from information in *Congressional Quarterly Weekly Report*, April 14, 1979, Supplement, pp. 4− 16.

one includes Harry F. Byrd, Jr., of Virginia, an Independent who gets his committee assignments from the Democrats), and 41 Republicans. Note how closely this ratio is followed in the committees. The Senate has no committees with a mandatory two to one ratio. Only one committee, Energy and Natural Resources, exceeded the ratio by more than 2 percent. The subcommittee ratios also followed closely the party split in the full Senate. Actually the Republicans have a slight advantage, if it can be called that, in the number of assignments they receive compared to the Democrats (10.76 compared to 10.63, see Table 10 −5). Being a member of the minority is considerably less frustrating in the Senate. Whereas in the House the Republicans tended to get fewer subcommittee positions than their numbers would warrant, in the Senate they actually had a slight advantage in subcommittees. In some cases there were as many Republicans as Democrats on subcommittees (see Table 10 – 3).

The various types of committees do not differ greatly from those in the House. In fact, five of the six categories used for the House apply (budget, foreign and defense, investigations of the executive, legislative administration, and domestic issues). The governance of the District of Columbia is handled in a subcommittee following the Stevenson Committee reforms. Equally, the Senate committees differ in prestige as measured by movement of senators between committees. Not surprisingly, the same type of committees as in the House, are attractive in the Senate, though with some slight differences in ranking. Most notably Goodwin found that the Committee on Foreign Relations was the most attractive (30 transfers to, just 2 from during his period of study), with Finance, Appropriations, Judiciary, and Armed Services following in that order. The Judiciary Committee ranking is also higher than that in the House. Rules and Administration, Government Operations, Post Office and Civil Service, and District of Columbia were the lowest ranking committees by this measure, in that order (Goodwin, 1970:   115). Interestingly, the latter two committees were abolished in 1979. The greater prestige of the Senate Committee on Foreign Relations as compared to the House Committee on Foreign Affairs is attributable to the greater powers of the Senate in this area—specifically the treaty-approval authority.[8]

Committee assignments.   Given the greater number of committee assignments and the effort to provide senators with at least one choice assignment, the Monopoly game played in the House is less likely to occur in the Senate. Still some senators like to move around, perhaps because they are seeking a leadership position and wish to familiarize themselves with the workings of several committees, or because they are leaders. During his long career in the Senate, Everett McKinley Dirksen (R – Illinois) appeared to employ the committee-switching strategy. He served on practically every committee at one time or other. And when he was minority floor leader he gave up his seat on the Committee on Labor and Public Welfare to a junior member. Senator John Tower (R – Texas) wanted to be assigned to that committee and so informed Dirksen.

> "You came to the right place," Dirksen told him. "I'm on the Labor Committee. I'll give you my spot." Dirksen's idea was to try to satisfy every Republican senator. "The leader," he said, "takes what's left" (MacNeil, 1970:   166).

---

[8] Matthews also ranked the committees by shifts among senators. The order of the top committees then (80th and 84th Congresses) was Foreign Relations, Appropriations, Finance, and Armed Services (Matthews, 1960:   149).

Size again explains the differences between the House and Senate committee assignment processes. Obviously the Senate process is going to be much more informal since the work load is considerably less. On the other hand, greater attention can be paid to each assignment in terms of matching the member with the committee, as well as taking into account the views of the chairman and other influentials. Historically, there have been fewer changes in the Senate committee assigning system than in the House. At first the assignments were made either on the floor itself or by the presiding officer (e.g., the president pro tempore made assignments during 1823 to 1833). As George Goodwin, Jr., observes, however (1970: 83—84):

> Election from the floor was time-consuming and contained a large element of chance. . . . In 1846 the present method . . . was adopted. Committees-on-committees, working closely with party leaders, fill vacancies; their decisions are ratified by the party caucus, usually without dissent; and the whole Senate votes on the adoption of the party lists.

The Democratic committee-on-committees is called a Steering Committee. It is chaired by the floor leader and has a large (25 in the 96th Congress) and broadly representative membership. The party whip is also a member. The size of the committee has grown in recent years so as to represent a broader spectrum of the party. The Republicans in fact call their group a Committee on Committees. The floor leader is a member ex-officio but does not chair the committee. A chairman is appointed by the chairman of the conference. The whip does not serve on the committee. Regional balance is also important for the Republicans, but the group was quite small in the 96th Congress (14 members).

As in the House, decisions are made about incoming senators and veterans who want to trade assignments. The workload for two congresses is shown in Table 10 —7. The two years represented are associated with two quite different elections—a Democratic gain in 1964, a strong Republican showing in 1978. Thus, the Democrats were somewhat busier in 1965, particularly in assigning the freshmen. Because they had many vacancies on important committees (due to losses in the 1964 election), the Republicans in 1965 had to make several decisions in moving veterans. The 1978 elections turned out several veterans in both parties, with the Republicans gaining seats. As indicated in Table 10 —7, over one third of the Republican assignments were new (28 for the freshmen, 17 for veterans). In neither year was the work load onerous, however.

The committees vary in expected ways when it comes to freshmen and veteran assignments. Table 10 —8 provides examples. Appropriations and Foreign Relations vacancies went to veterans; Commerce, Science, and Transportation vacancies went to freshmen; and both

TABLE 10—7
Assigning senators to standing committees—the workload

		Democrats	Republicans	Total
1965	Freshman assignments	14	4	18
	Transfers of veterans	9	14	23
	Totals	23	18	41
	As a percent of total standing committee positions	13.5%	22.8%	16.4%
1979	Freshman assignments	17	28	45
	Transfers of veterans	13	17	30
	Totals	30	45	75
	As a percent of total standing committee positions	20.3%	34.6%	30.0%

SOURCE: Compiled from information in various issues of the *Congressional Quarterly Weekly Report*, 1965 and 1979.

TABLE 10—8
Examples of Senate committee assignments, 1979

Committee	Change in ratio	Vacancies	Freshmen appointed		Veterans appointed	
			D	R	D	R
Appropriations	16 D—9 R to 17 D—11 R	6	0	0	2	4
Commerce, Science and Transportation	11 D—7 R to 10 D—7 R	5	2	3	0	0
Foreign Relations	10 D—6 R to 9 D—6 R	5	0	0	2	3
Judiciary	11 D—6 R to 10 D—7 R	6	2	2	1	1
Rules and Administration	6 D—3 R to 6 D—4 R	4	0	0	2	2

SOURCE: Compiled from information in *Congressional Quarterly Weekly Report*, April 14, 1979, supplement, pp. 4—16.

were appointed to Judiciary vacancies. I included the Rules and Administration Committee to show how conditions can change. Though a minor committee, Rules and Administration in recent years has had to act on reform proposals, many involving rules changes. Both majority and minority floor leaders are members of the committee.

Finally, it is useful to illustrate the switching that goes on by the veterans. All examples are from the 96th Congress and select as well as joint committees are included.

1. Exchange assignments.
    a. One for two. Howard Metzenbaum (D—Ohio) drops Select Indian Affairs, adds Budget, Labor, and Public Welfare, stays on Energy and Natural Resources, Judiciary (from two major, one minor to four major).
    b. One for one. John Durkin (D—New Hampshire) drops Commerce, Science, and Transportation, adds Appropriations, stays on Energy and Natural Resources and Veterans Affairs (continues with two major, one minor).
    c. Two for one. James McClure (R—Idaho) drops Budget, Environment and Public Works, adds Appropriations, stays on Energy and Natural Resources and Joint Economic Committee (from three major, one minor to two major, one minor).
    d. Two for two. H. J. Heinz, III (R—Pennsylvania) drops Budget and Governmental Affairs, adds Finance and Select Aging, stays on Banking, Housing, and Urban Affairs (from three major to two major, one minor).
2. Add Assignments. Donald Riegle (D—Michigan) adds Budget, stays on Banking, Housing, and Urban Affairs; Commerce Science, and Transportation; and Labor and Human Resources (from three major to four major).

One can readily determine from these examples that the overall committee assignment situation is much less restrictive in the Senate. For the most part, senators are adding to their already generous complement of committee positions. One also learns that exceptions are made to the rule of two major, one minor assignment. In particular the Committee on the Budget has come to be an allowable extra assignment. Thus if a member was serving on three major committees at the time of the Stevenson reforms, then the Budget assignment gave that person four major positions (see Riegle's case above).

Committee organization and procedures. Subcommittees are just as important to Senate committee organization as they are in the House. While the Senate has not had a specific subcommittee bill of rights certain changes have been made that have the same effect. Allocation of committee staff to subcommittees, guarantees of staffing for the minority, limitations on subcommittee assignments and chairmanships—such changes have the effect of further institutionalizing the subcommittee by insuring more stability and greater continuity. Three Senate committees, Budget, Rules and Administration, and Veterans' Affairs, do not have subcommittees. One wonders how long they will be able to resist. There are simply too many rewards associated with organizing subcommittees—for example, more leadership positions, justification for more staff, greater articulation of special interests, closer relationships with the agencies. Therefore, despite the rule now requiring full Senate approval for new subcommittees, one may expect the number of units to increase in the future.

The continuity in subcommittees from one Congress to the next is considerable. Of the 90 subcommittees in standing committees in the 96th Congress, 77 were carried over from the 95th Congress (85.6 percent). A total of 20 subcommittees were dropped, 13 were added. The greatest amount of change occurred in the Judiciary Committee (six subcommittees dropped, three added), primarily as a consequence of a dramatic change in leadership from James Eastland (D — Mississippi) to Edward M. Kennedy (D — Massachusetts).

Though a high percentage of subcommittees were retained from the 95th Congress, the high turnover of membership in the 1978 elections resulted in many changes in leadership and personnel. Four new Democratic chairmen advanced under the seniority system, as modified by the Stevenson rules (i.e., no senator may chair more than one committee). Seven new ranking Republicans advanced in the same way—sometimes with impressive results. For example, in the 95th Congress Jesse Helms (R — North Carolina) was the fifth-ranking Republican on the Committee on Agriculture, Nutrition, and Forestry. In the 96th Congress he became the ranking Republican by virtue of the fact that two higher ranking members chose to assume leadership positions on other committees, one member retired, and one member left the committee. Thus while the Senate has made changes so as to distribute committee leadership posts among the members, the seniority system is still followed in replacing chairmen and ranking members.

The situation is a bit more complicated in regard to subcommittees. A relatively high percentage of Democratic subcommittee chairmen returned—52 of the 77 subcommittees that carried over from the 95th Congress. But the sizeable changes in the Republican ranks (over 25 percent elected in 1978) resulted in major shifts in subcommittee leadership—only 30 of 77 ranking members were carried over. Again, in general the seniority system is followed, but the limitations on subcommittee chairmanships results in significant turnover following an election with many retirements and defeats of veterans. Senators naturally shop around to select those subcommittees judged to be of most value or of most interest to them. Often one finds a lower-ranking member assuming a leadership position because a more senior member (on that subcommittee) already has the requisite number of chairmanships (or ranking positions).

Table 10 — 9 shows the subcommittee change from one Congress to the next for the Committee on Agriculture, Nutrition, and Forestry. Note first that the turnover in membership is rather high—36.7 percent for the Democrats; 45.8 percent for the Republicans. The Rural Development Subcommittee membership is practically all new (six of seven

TABLE 10–9
Subcommittee membership change, 95th to 96th Congress; Senate Committee on Agriculture, Nutrition, and Forestry

					Strict	
			Leader's rank		seniority	
	New members		in 95th Congress		violated?	
Subcommittee	D	R	D	R	D	R
1. Agricultural Credit and Rural Electrification	1 of 3	1 of 2	None*	1st of 2	Yes	No
2. Agricultural Production, Marketing, and Stabilization of Prices	2 of 7	1 of 4	1st of 7	1st of 4	No	No
3. Agricultural Research and General Legislation	1 of 4	1 of 4	None*	4th of 4	Yes	Yes
4. Environment, Soil Conservation, and Forestry	2 of 4	2 of 4	4th of 6	None*	Yes	Yes
5. Foreign Agricultural Policy	2 of 5	2 of 4	2d of 4	None*	No	Yes
6. Nutrition	0 of 3	1 of 3	1st of 4	1st of 3	No	No
7. Rural Development	3 of 4	3 of 3	3d of 3	None*	No	No

* Refers to the fact that the leader was not a member of the subcommittee in the 95th Congress.
SOURCE: Compiled from information in *Congressional Quarterly Weekly Reports*, Supplements, April 30, 1977; April 14, 1979.

members). Of the 14 leadership positions for the two parties, 5 were held by the same person in both Congresses (two Democratic chairmen and three ranking Republicans). Also note the number of new members who assume leadership positions (five for the two parties) and the number who move ahead of more senior members on that committee (two—one in each party).

In summary, one finds considerable stability in the breakdown of committee work into subcommittees but somewhat less continuity in the leadership and membership of those units. Of course, it is to be expected that a large freshman class will result in more changes these days due to the distributive rules enacted in 1977. If the subcommittees stay the same but the leadership and membership changes, then we may expect growing influence for the staff. We turn to that topic next.

It is not uncommon to find only one senator in attendance at a subcommittee hearing. Yet a sizeable group of people will be behind the dais (though normally not sitting in the senators' chairs). These extras are staff aides from committee members' offices and, of course, from the committee itself (though the latter normally sit at the table below the dais). I discussed the role of office staff earlier. Suffice here to say that one of the many jobs to be performed by the senator's legislative staff is to monitor the work of those subcommittees of which he or she is a member, particularly when the senator cannot attend a meeting. Equally important is to follow subcommittee and committee action on bills of particular interest to the senator, perhaps because they effect interests in the state or because they were introduced or co-sponsored by the boss.

One expects Senate committee staffs to be larger than their counterparts in the House on a per member ratio basis. After all, Senate committees are smaller, and yet certain basic functions have to be performed by a committee regardless of size. But it is somewhat surprising to find that several Senate committees have larger staffs in absolute numbers than their opposites in the House. Fox and Hammond report that 11 Senate committees had larger staffs in the 94th Congress (1975 — 76) — in some cases (Governmental Affairs, Interstate and Foreign Commerce, Judiciary, Veterans) the Senate staff was twice as large or more (1977:   169 — 70).

As in the House, the Senate committees vary considerably in staff size — from 22 for Agriculture and Forestry to 251 for Judiciary in the 94th Congress. They also differ in the allocation of staff to the subcommittees. Thus, selecting any one committee for illustrative purposes is problematic. Still, as with the House, showing the types of staff positions for a single committee does provide the reader with useful information. Table 10 — 10 lists the positions for the Committee on Governmental Affairs, 95th Congress (as reported in the *Congressional Staff Directory*). This committee has one of the larger staffs — actually somewhat larger than is reported in Table 10 — 10.[9] As with the House, there are many different titles one might have — 27 in all for this committee. In 1963 the committee had about half or less of the staff that it reports now. Also the titles of positions are no more revealing for Senate committees than on the House side. All staff get involved in a variety of committee and subcommittee responsibilities.

A brief discussion of this matter of staff positions and allocations might be useful for directing student attention to the future. As presently organized, committee and subcommittee staff positions provide precisely the right experience in dealing with the more specialized bureaucrats. That is, work on different types of projects brings one into contact with different types of people and can, as a consequence, result in a staff more accommodating to the generalist methods of the senators. This is not to say the staff, as organized now and in the recent past, is not specialized in various ways. It is to say that their specialization is not necessarily respected every day when there is work to be done. They may be assigned to do a job which normally would fall out of their personal definition of their expertise and which would not normally be assigned to them if they were in an executive

---

[9] See *The Senate Committee System*, p. 200, where the Committee on Governmental Affairs is reported to have had a staff of 144 in 1975 (94th Congress).

TABLE 10 — 10
Staff assignments for Senate Committee on Governmental Affairs and its subcommittees

	Number of assignments
Full committee—majority:	
Chief counsel and staff director	1
Chief clerk	1
Professional staff member	2
Counsel	5
Investigator	1
Staff editor	1
Research assistant	2
Administrative secretary	1
Clerical assistant	5
Receptionist	1
Total	20
Full committee—minority:	
Chief counsel	1
Special counsel	1
Minority clerk	1
Professional staff member	2
Total	5
Subcommittee on Investigations—majority:	
Chief counsel	1
Assistant counsel	2
Chief clerk	1
Professional staff director	1
Professional staff member	3
Investigator	6
Staff editor	1
Assistant clerk	8
Total	24
Subcommittee on Investigations—minority:	
Minority chief counsel	1
General counsel	1
Executive assistant	1
Professional staff member	1
Investigator	3
Clerical assistant	3
Total	10
Subcommittee on Civil Service and General Services:	
Staff director and chief counsel	1
Professional staff member	1
Chief clerk	1
Total	3
Subcommittee on Energy, Nuclear Proliferation, and Federal Services—majority:	
Chief counsel	1
Staff director	1
Chief clerk	1
Secretary	1
Total	4

TABLE 10 – 10 (*continued*)

Number of assignments

Subcommittee on Energy, Nuclear Proliferation, and
Federal Services—minority:
Minority counsel 1

Subcommittee on Federal Spending Practices and
Open Government—majority:
Staff director 1
Chief clerk 1
Professional staff member 4
Assistant chief clerk 1
Staff assistant 1
Clerical assistant 1
    Total 9

Subcommittee on Federal Spending Practices and
Open Government—minority:
Professional staff member 2
Staff assistant 1
    Total 3

Subcommittee on Governmental Efficiency and
the District of Columbia—majority:
Staff director and general counsel 1
Professional staff member 3
Research assistant 1
Secretary 3
    Total 8

Subcommittee on Governmental Efficiency and
the District of Columbia—minority:
Minority counsel 1
Professional assistant 1
Professional staff member 1
Legislative aide 1
    Total 4

Subcommittee on Intergovernmental Relations—majority:
Staff director 1
Chief clerk 1
Counsel 5
Receptionist . .· 1
Secretary 4
Robo operator 1
    Total 13

Subcommittee on Intergovernmental Relations—minority:
Minority counsel 1
Assistant minority counsel 3
    Total 4

Subcommittee on Reports, Accounting, and
Management—majority:
Staff director 1
Chief counsel 1
Counsel 1
Chief clerk 1
Professional staff member 1
Secretary 1
Research assistant 1
    Total 7

TABLE 10 – 10 *(concluded)*

	Number of assignments
Subcommittee on Reports, Accounting, and Management—minority:	
Minority counsel	1
Minority clerk	1
Professional staff member	1
Total	3
Grand totals:	
Full committee	25
Subcommittees	93
	118

SOURCE: Compiled from list in Charles B. Brownson, ed., *1977 Congressional Staff Directory* (Mt. Vernon, Virginia: Congressional Staff Directory, 1977), pp. 171–73.

agency. Thus the ambiguity in job titles is an advantage for the senators in using the staff and for the staff in their dealings with the bureaucracy.

The development to watch in the future is that of greater insularity developing as a consequence of subcommittee stability and independence. It would be quite natural to expect specialized subcommittee staff to lose the more comprehensive approach as they become more entrenched. It may even follow that specialized subcommittee staff will begin to compete with the executive in initiating policy proposals, perhaps even becoming identified with the proposals to the exclusion of the political realities associated with the issue. If the latter happens, of course, the staff will have come to play a more active policy role, and their activities may influence the future responsibilities of the institution.

Organizing a Republican Senate

In recent years, the Republicans have not had the great deal of practice in organizing Senate committees. They have been in the majority only twice since 1932—the 80th Congress (1947 – 48) when they had a 51 – 45 margin and the 83rd Congress (1953 – 54) when they held a slim 48 – 47 margin (one senator—Morse of Oregon was an independent). In the 96th Congress, the Democrats enjoyed a 59 – 41 edge— seemingly a comfortable margin for retaining their majority in the 1980 elections despite the fact that 24 of the 34 seats up for election were held by Democrats. But the Republicans realized a net gain of 12 Senate seats, enough to give them control of the Senate by a margin of 53 – 46 (Byrd of Virginia is an Independent). The election returns surprised the Republicans and absolutely stunned the Democrats. The chairmen of the Committees on Agriculture, Nutrition, and Forestry; Appropriations; and Foreign Relations were defeated. Two select committee chairmen (Intelligence and Small Business) were also defeated, and two other chairmen (one standing, one select) retired. A total of 27 subcommittee chairmanships were made available by retirements or defeats. Thus even if the Democrats had retained a majority by defeating incumbent Republicans, considerable change would have been realized in the 97th Congress (somewhat greater than that which occurred between the 95th and 96th Congresses).

Democratic candidates did not defeat Republican incumbents in 1980, however, and thus there was a total turnover in chairmanships. When such a massive turnover (by Senate standards) takes place, one naturally expects a more youthful set of chairmen. After all, 16 of the 53 Republican senators (30 percent) in the 97th Congress were elected in 1980, and 35 (66 percent) were serving their first term! The average age of the new Republican chairmen was 56. Not one of the standing committee chairmen had served as a Republican in the Senate in 1953 — 54 when that party last had a majority (Strom Thurmond, however, served as a Democrat at that time). Three of the chairmen in the 97th Congress were serving their first term, six their second term (Jones in Sandoz and Van Crabb; 1981: chapter 4).

As expected the Republicans followed the modified seniority rule in every case for selecting committee leaders. That is, a senator serving as the ranking minority member during the 96th Congress became the new chairman unless such a move resulted in two chairmanships for that Senator. For example, Robert T. Stafford, Vermont, was the ranking Republican on the Committee on Veterans Affairs and the Committee on Environment and Public Works in the 96th Congress. He had to choose between them, and not surprisingly he selected Environment and Public Works. Actually the third-ranking Republican on Veteran Affairs became the new chairman since the second-ranking Republican too had another chairmanship. The chairmanship of the Committee on Rules and Administration in the 97th Congress was actually given to a new member of the Committee—Charles McC. Mathias, Jr., of Maryland. The reason was simply that those senators with more seniority chose other obligations which prevented them from assuming the leadership of the Committee.

The other important change that occurred as a result of the Senate elections was a large turnover in committee and subcommittee staff. It was estimated that the Republicans gained nearly 500 staff positions. That number would have been even greater except for the fact that a two to one split in staff between the majority and minority was scheduled to go into effect in 1981.[10]

---

[10] See *National Journal*, November 29, 1980, p. 1879.

The 1980 elections produced a fascinating outcome—a House and Senate organized by different political parties. This condition is not unprecedented (it has occurred twice before in this century— 1911—12 and 1931—32), but in the past it has been associated with a downswing in fortunes for the Republican Party (both houses were lost by the Republicans in 1912 and 1932). This most recent case appears to be associated with an upswing in Republican fortunes—at least as evidenced by the 1980 elections. At the committee level, one important consequence of this split control is House Democratic chairmen working with (or against) Senate Republican chairmen. A certain amount of cross-party communication is required if laws are to be passed since two sets of committees work on the same bills and committee leaders often face each other across the conference table (see Chapter 12). Therefore what is already complicated by virtue of bicameralism becomes even more intricate by virtue of split party control.[11]

---

[11] For details on these split-control Congresses see Jones, 1970 and Ripley, 1969a.

11 Beyond the committees in the Senate: Political parties and floor action

In their review of changes in Senate leadership, Norman J. Ornstein, Robert L. Peabody, and David W. Rohde remark that (in Dodd and Oppenheimer, 1977: 10):

> The evolution of Senate leadership patterns from the 1950s to the mid-1970s has both contributed to and been reflective of changes in Senate membership, committee structure, norms, and rules. That such organizational variables should be closely related is hardly surprising. But if anything, the relatively small size of the Senate, the lengthy tenure of its membership, and its pervasive collegial atmosphere have all tended to reinforce their interconnected aspects, with enhanced consequences for decentralizing and power-sharing trends in the Senate.

Due to its characteristics, the Senate, more than the House, reflects the many dilemmas and contradictions of American democracy. The size of the House itself forces some organizational resolution of these dilemmas. That is, to act at all a large body must make rules and pay them heed. As Ornstein and his colleagues observe, however, the special nature of the Senate permits delayed resolution. In fact, sometimes it seems that no effort is made in the Senate to force conclusions or to resolve conflicts. It reminds one of the faith in just plain talk that appears to support the town-meeting type of democracy. It is not always possible to pinpoint and describe how it happens—tradition, understanding, comity, even fatigue, may all play a part. What is certain, however, is that party leadership and organization cannot be expected to play consistently powerful and aggressive roles in this extraordinary second chamber.

Lowered expectations for considering the role of Senate party leaders and organization are also appropriate for treating Senate floor activity. That is, not expecting strong and efficient policy direction by the parties prepares one for the broad participation and pervasive collegial atmosphere on the floor. Who's in charge here? is a perfectly reasonable question to ask, but asking it reveals one's lack of understanding of the Senate. No one dare appear to be in charge, even if someone is.

Having set the context, we now turn to consider party leadership, party organization, and what happens when bills get to the Senate floor.

PARTY LEADERSHIP

The context described above indicates that the conditions under which party leaders operate in the Senate are limiting, to say the least. They are expected to eschew efforts to dominate the legislative process and to applaud and enhance activities bound to make it more difficult to lead—for example, facilitating involvement by substantive experts from the committees, surveying interest among other members (including those from the minority), accommodating the maximum number of requests in debate. All of this suggests that Senate leaders are less likely than their House counterparts to stand apart from the membership. There is no Senate counterpart to the Speaker of the House. The vice president, when he in the chamber, serves as the president of the Senate. Given our election system, that person may be of a different party than the majority party in the Senate.[1] The president pro tempore is by custom the senior member of the majority party and strictly speaking serves as the presiding officer when the vice president is absent. But normally this person will chair a major committee and is unlikely to spend time presiding over the Senate. For example, Strom Thurmond (R—South Carolina) held this position in the 97th Congress, but his more important post was as chairman of the Committee on the Judiciary. It is significant then that any senator (often a junior majority senator) might be in the chair when the vice

---

[1] This split party condition has occurred half the time since 1952. Richard M. Nixon (for six of eight years), Spiro T. Agnew, Gerald R. Ford, and Nelson A. Rockefeller all presided over Democratic Senates (a total of 14 of 28 years, 1952—80).

president is absent—significant because the position is hardly more than a symbol of authority toward which debate is directed and a set of ears for hearing what the Senate parliamentarian has to say in regard to a particular floor situation. Thus this lack of a Speaker produces exactly the kind of leveling which we would expect to find in the Senate. Those who sit in the chair have little or no authority, and those with leadership positions work from the floor like every one else (the floor leaders sit at the front desks to the right and left of the center aisle).

Given this situation, it is not surprising to find that few senators actually strive to lead their party. I would venture to guess that every member of the House secretly desires to be the Speaker. The same cannot be said for senators desiring to serve as floor leader. As Robert L. Peabody observes: "the great majority of Senators remain content to make their mark through legislative specialization, or so it would seem" (1976: 321). In fact, often through history the floor leader has not been the principal leader of the party. In the first decade of this century, the post changed hands practically every session. Nelson W. Aldrich (R—Rhode Island) was the generally acknowledged leader of the Senate during this period, working from his position as chairman of the Senate Committee on Finance. Since that time (i.e., after 1911), the majority leader in particular "has been consistently influential in the majority party" (Ripley, 1969b: 4). And yet he may well have to compete with other influential senators. That is guaranteed in the case of the Republicans where they divide responsibilities among several leadership positions (see below). But it is also characteristic of the Democrats who tend to center all important formal duties in the floor leader. Thus, for example, Richard B. Russell (D—Georgia) was always a central figure regardless of who served as floor leader (even Lyndon B. Johnson!). And on the Republican side, Robert A. Taft (R—Ohio) was a dominant force but served as floor leader only one year.

As one reviews the persons who have held the post of floor leader in this century relatively few names stand out as deserving special attention. Among the Democrats Lyndon B. Johnson (D—Texas), who served from 1953 to 1961, is surely the most prominent. Senator Russell summarized Johnson's qualifications as follows: "He doesn't have the best mind on the Democratic side of the Senate; he isn't the best orator; he isn't the best parliamentarian. But he's the best combination of all of these qualities" (Peabody, 1976: 323). Among the Republicans, Senator Taft was "the predominant Republican oligarch of the World War II era and its aftermath" though serving as floor leader only in 1953 (Peabody, 1976: 323). While the Johnson and Taft styles are often described as standard, they tend to be the exception not the rule.

In order to provide perspective on Senate party leaders, it is useful to consider two dimensions: (1) the extent to which they depend on the party or president for determining programmatic initiatives and proposals and (2) the extent to which they attempt to pressure legislators into supporting proposals which emerge (whatever the source). The first can be thought of as an independent/dependent dimension; the second an aggressive/permissive dimension. This then gives us four possible types of leaders:

1. *Independent, aggressive.* This type is that relatively rare party leader who independently forms his own programs and aggressively pursues support within the Senate and outside. (Robert A. Taft and Nelson W. Aldrich come the closest, though neither served for long as floor leader—probably because to do so would reduce their independence).

2. *Independent, permissive.* While independently forming his own preferences and proposals, this type of leader permits a consensus or majority to emerge on its own. (Several leaders with particular substantive policy interests—e.g., Mike Mansfield on foreign policy—would fit this style).

3. *Dependent, aggressive.* While dependent on what the system produces (i.e., either from the White House or congressional committees), this leader is aggressive in pressing it into action and insuring output. (Lyndon B. Johnson is the classic example).

4. *Dependent, permissive.* Again dependent on the system for programs, this leader is permissive as to whether, when, and how the Senate acts. (Mike Mansfield is the classic case on most issues, but most other Senate floor leaders would, on balance, fall into this category).[2]

Noting that Mike Mansfield, who served as floor leader longer than any other person in history, was independent on foreign policy does suggest an important qualification—that is, a leader's style may vary among issues. Further, these broad categories mask the degrees of difference implicit in the dimensions. Thus Robert C. Byrd (D—West Virginia) falls someplace between the aggressive and permissive extremes—not as aggressive as Johnson, surely not as permissive as Mansfield. The same might be said about Howard H. Baker, Jr. (R—Tennessee)—the majority floor leader in the 97th Congress.

The more important point that emerges from this classification exercise is that the Johnson type of leadership is exceptional. Interestingly, however, other leaders tend to get measured by the Johnson standard. There is no question that he was an extraordinarily resourceful floor leader. In a particularly revealing portrait of Johnson's technique and style, Ralph K. Huitt describes what we now know to be

---

[2] Charles O. Jones, "Senate Party Leadership in Public Policy," in U.S. Senate Commission on the Operation of the Senate, *Policymaking Role of Leadership in the Senate*, 94th Cong. 2d sess., 1976, p. 24.

a remarkable combination of intelligence, resourcefulness, and personal drive (in Huitt and Peabody, eds., 1969: 145, 148; emphasis added).

> Johnson was a legislative pragmatist. He believed it possible to do anything that was worth the effort and the price, and so considered every problem from the standpoint of what was necessary to achieve the desired objective and whether the objective was worth the cost. . . .
>
> . . . Lyndon Johnson's legislative strategy frequently reflected an acute awareness that senators must play many different and often conflicting roles and *that one task of leadership is to structure a situation so that a member can select a role which will allow him to stand with the party.*

This process sounds simple enough, and yet it is anything but simple to manage. The Senate is decreed by the constitution to be populated by equals, each representing a sovereign state. Structuring situations so that these equals can agree, while maintaining their individuality, is no small feat.

It is frequently pointed out that Johnson did not serve as majority floor leader for a Democratic president, Dwight D. Eisenhower being in the White House during the eight years that Johnson led his party in the Senate. We will, of course, never know how successful he might have been serving a Democrat, but it is hard to believe that Johnson would not have done everything possible to demonstrate to the country that he could get a presidential program enacted.

No Senate Republican floor leader has, in recent years, matched the qualities of Johnson. In another time, Nelson W. Aldrich (R—Rhode Island) matched the Johnson technique. He was called "the manager of the United States" and the "schoolmaster of the Senate" (Barry, 1924: 152 and Depew, 1922: 180). He was accused of carrying a chloroform bottle: "It is invisible. . . . He sits down beside a senator and the first thing that the senator knows he has been chloroformed, and is completely under the Aldrich influence" (Dunn, II, 1922: 64). But Aldrich was more interested in substance than Johnson and used process to his own ends.

In more recent times, Everett M. Dirksen (R—Illinois) clearly desired to be as effective among the minority Republicans as Johnson was among the majority Democrats. "In general, his style was one of remaining vague on an issue or taking an initial position from which he could negotiate: bargaining with the majority party, the president, and his own colleagues, and eventually accepting a compromise" (Jones, 1970: 168). Obviously it is more difficult to collect majorities when one is leader of the minority. By definition one must get majority party support. Thus it is not surprising that Dirksen was faulted for not doing more for the party. I interviewed a number of Senate Republican staff aides during his period of leadership and the lack of partisanship was a frequent complaint (Jones, 1970:   169).

> Dirksen is more personal, but Taft was more party oriented.
> He doesn't really push for partisan causes. He is effective but not partisanly effective.
> Dirksen is pretty much helping Dirksen—I doubt that Dirksen's leadership is helping the Republican party very much.

Table 11 — 1 provides a list of the Senate floor leaders for both parties since the emergence of the position as a significant post in 1911. Since that time the Democrats have had 12 floor leaders, the Republicans 13. Each party tends to select senators with considerable experience. Note that the average age for both sets of leaders is around 60—only two Democrats and three Republicans were less than 57 when elected floor leader, and only Democrats Kern and Johnson were elected to lead the party in their first term. Turnover of leaders is relatively high, only three Democrats and two Republicans serving 10 years or more, but remarkably enough no floor leader left office by virtue of having been defeated in the caucus. Thomas Martin withdrew in 1913 because he did not have the votes to defeat John Kern, but there are no other cases of a floor leader having been turned out by his colleagues. And finally, it is worth noting that succession from party whip to floor leader appears to emerge in recent years. Four of the last five Democratic and two of the last three Republican floor leaders served first as the party whip.

The job of being floor leader is essentially a job of managing the flow of business from the committees through the unique floor proceedings. Though the leaders vary in techniques and style (as described above), still the main task is one of management. The leader's principal advantages are those of position and location. He is a center of information and communication within his party, within the Senate, among committee chairmen, between the House and Senate, and between the White House and the Senate. The scheduling function alone insures that the floor leader will be contacted by those who want action and those who want to know what actions are being taken (e.g., the media). Thus, though the position itself has relatively few formally prescribed duties, its central location attracts attention and increases its potential for influence. As has been observed, some floor leaders are moved to take advantage of this situation to expand their functions, others are content to confine their activities, even on occasion denying invitations to do more.

Senate whips have a much less demanding job than their counterparts in the House. They essentially serve as assistant leaders in both parties, working with the floor leader in scheduling legislation and maintaining communication with the membership. Whips were ap-

TABLE 11-1
Senate floor leaders, 1911-1983

	Dates of service	Age[1]	Years in Senate[2]	Years as leader	Majority or minority	Reason for leaving post
Democrats:						
Thomas Martin, Va.	1911-13	64	18	2	Minority	Withdrew
John Kern, Ind.	1913-17	64	2	4	Majority	Not reelected to Senate
Thomas S. Martin, Va.	1917-19	70	24	2	Majority	Died
Gilbert Hitchcock, Neb.	1919-20	60	8	1	Minority	Not elected[3]
Oscar Underwood, Ala.	1920-23	58	6	3	Minority	Resigned for ill health
Joseph Robinson, Ark.	1923-37	51	10	14	Minority (4 years) Majority (10 years)	Died
Alben Barkley, Ky.	1937-49	60	10	12	Majority (10 years) Minority (2 years)	Elected vice president
Scott Lucas, Ill.[4]	1949-51	57	10	2	Majority	Not reelected to Senate
Ernest McFarland, Ariz.	1951-53	57	10	2	Majority	Not reelected to Senate
Lyndon Johnson, Tex.[4]	1953-61	45	4	8	Majority (6 years) Minority (2 years)	Elected vice president
Mike Mansfield, Mont.[4]	1961-77	58	8	16	Majority	Retired
Robert C. Byrd, W.Va.[4]	1977-	59	18	(serving)	Majority (4 years) Minority (2 years)	Serving
Average		58.6	10.7	6.5[5]		

Republicans:

		Age[1]	Service[2]			
Jacob Gallinger, N.H.	1911–18	74	20	7	Majority (2 years) Minority (5 years)	Died
Henry Cabot Lodge, Mass.	1918–24	68	25	6	Majority	Died
Charles Curtis, Kans.[4]	1924–29	64	15	5	Majority	Elected vice president
James Watson, Ind.	1929–33	64	13	4	Majority	Not reelected to Senate
Charles McNary, Oreg.	1933–44	59	16	10	Minority	Died
Wallace White, Me.	1944–49	67	13	5	Majority (2 years) Minority (3 years)	Retired
Kenneth Wherry, Neb.[4]	1949–51	57	6	2	Minority	Died
H. Styles Bridges, N.H.	1952–53	54	15	1	Minority	Withdrew
Robert A. Taft, Ohio	1953	64	13	1	Majority	Died
William Knowland, Calif.	1953–59	45	8	5+	Majority (1+ years) Minority (4 years)	Retired
Everett Dirksen, Ill.[4]	1959–69	63	8	10	Minority	Died
Hugh Scott, Pa.[4]	1969–77	68	10	8	Minority	Retired
Howard Baker, Tenn.	1977	52	10	(serving)	Minority (4 years) Majority (2 years)	Serving
Average		61.5	13.3	5.3[6]		

[1] Age at election as leader.
[2] Years of service at the time of election as leader.
[3] Hitchcock served as acting leader after Martin's death.
[4] Served as whip prior to election as floor leader.
[5] Does not include Hitchcock or Byrd.
[6] Does not include Baker.

SOURCE: Compiled from data in Ripley, *Power in the Senate* (1969b: 30); Jones (1970: 44), and *Biographical Directory of the American Congress, 1774– 1971* (Washington. D.C.: U.S. Government Printing Office, 1971).

pointed shortly after the floor leadership post itself became institutionalized—the first Democratic whip was appointed in 1913; the first Republican in 1915 (Ripley, 1969b: 33 — 35). During much of the New Deal period the Senate Republicans did not appoint a whip. After the 1936 election only 17 Republican senators were left—they hardly needed "whipping."

Both Democratic and Republican whips have assistants. In the 96th Congress, Senator Alan Cranston (D—California) was aided by eight assistant whips. Most were junior senators, and regional balance did not seem to be a consideration in their selection (three from the east, two from border-states—both from Kentucky, two from the midwest, and one from the south). Senator Ted Stevens (R—Alaska) was aided by 15 assistant whips (presumably to serve the other 25 Republican senators). Like the Democrats, the Republicans clearly use the whip apparatus as a means of socializing new senators (13 of the 15 were in their first terms in the 96th Congress).

PARTY ORGANIZATION

On paper, Senate party organization appears rationally structured for maximum policy direction and coordination. If one didn't know better from experience, one might picture a smoothly operating machine for identifying major issues and developing government programs. By this model, the policy committees would set the agenda and propose party solutions to major issues. These proposals would then be modified and endorsed by the caucus. The committee-on-committees, and perhaps even the campaign committees, would be used by the leadership to enforce support of party proposals in the standing committees. That is, recalcitrant senators would be removed from standing committees and denied campaign money. By this view, the standing committees would serve party purposes.

As noted in Table 11 — 2 the Democrats seemingly contribute further to this image of party government by having the floor leader chair all party units except the campaign committee and the legislative review committee. It would appear that Senator Byrd is in full command of the Senate Democratic Party. What you see is not necessarily what you get, however. The Policy Committee does not function as a central problem-identification and program-development agency. Still it has assumed important functions in recent years. Johnson appointed his friends and allies to the committee, and it became "a personal . . . appendage, and a center of new ideas" (Peabody, 1976: 337). When the Democrats have been in the majority the principal function of the Policy Committee has been to prepare the legislative schedule, that is, determine how and when legislation is to be debated on the floor. The

TABLE 11 – 2
Major party leaders, Senate, 97th Congress (1981 – 1982)

Position	Incumbent	Previous years in position	How selected
Democrats:			
Floor leader	Robert C. Byrd (W.Va.)	4	Elected by Conference
Whip	Alan Cranston (Calif.)	4	Elected by Conference
Chairman of Conference	Robert C. Byrd (W.Va.)	4	By virtue of being leader of party
Secretary of Conference	Daniel K. Inouye (Hawaii)	4	Elected by Conference
Chairman of Policy Committee	Robert C. Byrd (W.Va.)	4	By virtue of being leader of party
Chairman of Steering Committee	Robert C. Byrd (W.Va.)	4	By virtue of being leader of party
Chairman of Legislative Review Committee	Dale Bumpers (Ark.)	4	
Chairman of Senatorial Campaign Committee	Wendell H. Ford (Ky.)	4	Elected by Conference
Republicans:			
Floor leader	Howard H. Baker, Jr. (Tenn.)	4	Elected by Conference
Whip	Ted Stevens (Alaska)	4	Elected by Conference
Chairman of Conference	James A. McClure (Idaho)	0	Elected by Conference
Secretary of Conference	Robert Dole (Kan.)	0	Elected by Conference
Chairman of Policy Committee	John Tower (Tex.)	8	Elected by Conference
Chairman of Committee on Committees	Richard G. Lugar (Ind.)	0	Appointed by Conference chairman
Chairman of Senatorial Committee	Bob Packwood (Oreg.)	0	Elected by Conference

SOURCE: Compiled from *Congressional Quarterly Weekly Report*, March 28, 1981, Supplement, pp. 18 – 19.

staff kept track of pending legislation and prepared a tentative schedule. The committee itself advised the floor leader on priorities, and he in turn would set the final schedule for any one week in consultation with the minority floor leader. Mansfield expanded the size of the Policy Committee to include other party leaders (the secretary of the Conference, whip, and president pro tempore), the members of the Legislative Review Committee, and six other members appointed by the floor leader. Byrd has continued this practice. According to Robert L. Peabody (1976: 338): "Under Mansfield the Democratic Policy Committee . . . assumed a broader role in adopting positions on policy issues." He quotes Mansfield as saying that: "When the Democrats were in charge, we bowed to the president. Under Nixon, we function primarily as a policy determining committee."

The Democratic Conference functions primarily for organizational purposes—to select or reconfirm leadership at the beginning of the session and to approve changes in the rules. The latter has been important in recent years given the many changes in committee structure, seniority, and committee assignment procedures. Senate parties held December caucuses like their counterparts in the House for the first time in 1980.

The Democratic floor leader also chairs the Steering Committee, which makes all committee assignments. And he might be expected to have influence with the chairman of the Senatorial Campaign Committee. But neither of these is typically used as an enforcer of party policy positions. The committee assignment process is now considerably more circumscribed than in the past as a result of changes cited in Chapter 10. The Campaign Committee is broadly representative of the factions within the party. It functions primarily as a fund raising and distributing unit for all candidates.

The Republicans have, in recent years, come somewhat closer to the model described earlier despite the fact that leadership is more decentralized. The Republican Policy Committee has traditionally performed a slightly more substantive policy role than its Democratic counterpart. It is also broadly representative and includes the leadership serving ex officio (floor leader, whip, chairman and secretary of the conference). The chairmen of the Committee on Committees and Senatorial Committee (the campaign committee) are also members. The Committee meets every Tuesday for lunch, with all Republican senators invited. While they exchange views on pending legislation, the Policy Committee does not normally issue policy statements on a regular basis like their House counterpart. Staff tracks legislation and does research and reports at the request of individual senators. With majority status, the Republican Policy Committee staff will no doubt assume the same scheduling tasks previously performed by the Democratic Policy Committee staff. Meanwhile, the latter may find more time to get involved in program development.

The Republican Conference is also more likely than the Democratic Conference to meet on legislative issues—in some cases virtually under the auspices of the Policy Committee—as a result of discussion in the Tuesday luncheons. But its principal role too is organizational. And neither the Committee on Committees nor the Senatorial Committee is likely to be used to reward or punish the voting behavior of Republican senators.

Having discussed these organizational units at all leads me to caution the reader. The units do exist, the committees and conferences do occasionally meet, the staffs do have work to do. But these realities must be placed in the context of the larger reality of a small legislative body that operates quite informally. Ample opportunities exist for senators to consult with each other, on both sides of the aisle (Baker, 1980). On the other hand, it should be noted that the Senate is not the calm, relaxed, club-like institution it used to be. The pace of work

today is almost breathtaking—reducing the time available for ca-
maraderie.

PARTY AT WORK

Having said that the Senate party organization looks more impressive on paper than it does in place, let us turn now to how, or whether,
the party works in the chamber. As in the House, political party identification is one of the more obvious and prominent features of the
Senate landscape. Every Senator but one (Harry F. Byrd, Jr., Virginia) is
referred to as either a Democrat or a Republican.[3] Republicans sit with
Republicans, Democrats with Democrats, in the chamber and in the
committees and subcommittees. But there are also differences. The
minority party protections are less formal in the Senate than in the
House. That does not mean they do not exist. In fact, the casual observer may have trouble distinguishing the minority from the majority
based simply on how members are accommodated in scheduling and
debate. Permissiveness and accommodation characterize Senate behavior, and it is useful to bear that in mind in thinking about the role of
political parties. A party position may well emerge as problems and
legislative proposals are studied and debated, but it is rare for one to
have been set in advance. As in the House, party often is more within
senators when they arrive than it is a force working on them when
they do their work on Capitol Hill.

I am therefore even less able to set forth a clear and crisp description of the Senate parties at work than of the House parties. "It's
organized just like a string of sausages" (Matthews, 1960: 118). Legislation typically comes out of the committees in less finished form than
in the House. The policy committees and leadership prepare a schedule (see below), but there is less of a break between committee and
floor activity in the Senate. Often major issues are carried over to the
floor. Perhaps a strong party organization could change this feature. As
it is, however the party units (policy committees and conferences) do
not typically have a finished product to react to following committee
action. Put another way, it would be extraordinary for party to intervene with a strong endorsement or rejection when bills come out of
committees *since the process of development and compromise may
have only just started.* Many Senate features are complementary and
mutually reinforcing. Party is no stronger than it is because of how
senators get there in the first place, how they work with one another,
and how they prefer to see legislation move. In a sense, party is the
ultimate *dependent* variable.

---

[3] Byrd is elected as an Independent, but he gets his committee assignments through
the Democrats.

So—important legislation moves along in the Senate, from sub-committee, to committee, to its scheduling, and finally to the floor, without a great deal of closure, making it hard to draw firm conclusions along the way. But the end is in sight. Voting does occur. Indeed, it is increasing in frequency on the Senate floor—252 recorded votes annually on an average in the 1960s, 548 on an average in the 1970s (Bibby et al., 1980:   90). How does party fare in the voting?

First it is interesting to observe that there are fewer voting studies of the Senate than of the House. Why this should be is not altogether clear, particularly since study of Senate voting would appear to be simple by comparison. The most comprehensive analyses are now 20 years old, those by David. B. Truman and Donald R. Matthews. Truman studied just one Congress—the 81st—and he found "voting was far from haphazard," "differences between the parties on a wide range of substantive policy matters," and "the Republican bloc structure had a much more fractionated appearance than the Democratic" (1959:   90−91). He concluded that party interaction and association definitely occurred.

Though less comprehensive in his examination of voting behavior in a single Congress, Matthews provides some comparison between congresses (the 80th to 84th). He found clear differences between the parties on conservative-liberal questions and partisan support for the president. He also found the Democrats able to achieve more party unity because they were less divided on ideology. His conclusion that "party 'discipline' may be weak, but party 'identification' is strong," is consistent with what Truman found (Matthews, 1960:   123).

Table 11 − 3 presents comparable data with that presented earlier for the House (Table 9 − 3). The results are roughly similar. That is, the Senate too has relatively few party votes, where the majority of one party opposes the majority of the other. Only twice in 20 years did the number of party votes reach 50 percent or more. On the other hand, the number of party votes never fell below 32 percent; House party votes fell below 30 percent on three occasions. Other comparative observations are: House party unity scores tend to be higher than Senate scores for both parties; like the House, party unity scores tend to be less in the second session of each Congress—that is, during election years; and there is less difference between the two parties in the Senate.

Perhaps more directly indicative of partisanship in the Senate is the support of the president. Table 11 − 4 shows comparable House and Senate averages for recent presidents.[4] First note that the House pro-

---

[4] Presidential support scores are only very generally indicative of how well a president does in Congress. For example, a president may take a position in favor of a bill which has been drastically altered from the original recommendation he introduced.

TABLE 11 – 3
Party unity scores, U.S. Senate, 1961 – 1980

Presidential administrations	Percent of party votes	Percent voting with party	
		Democrats	Republicans
Kennedy:			
1961	62	69	68
1962	41	65	64
Kennedy-Johnson:			
1963	47	66	67
1964	36	61	65
Average	(46.5)	(65)	(66)
Comparable House averages	(50)	(71)	(72)
Johnson:			
1965	42	63	68
1966	50	57	63
1967	35	60	65
1968	32	51	60
Average	(40)	(58)	(64)
Comparable House averages	(41)	(64.5)	(68)
Nixon:			
1969	36	63	63
1970	35	55	56
1971	42	64	63
1972	36	57	61
1973	40	69	64
Nixon-Ford:			
1974	44	63	59
1975	48	68	64
1976	37	62	61
Average	(40)	(63)	(61)
Comparable House averages	(35)	(63)	(66)
Carter:			
1977	42	63	66
1978	45	66	59
1979	47	68	66
1980	46	64	65
Average	(45)	(65)	(64)
Comparable House averages	(41)	(67)	(71)

SOURCE: Jewell and Patterson (1977: 390) and various issues of *Congressional Quarterly Weekly Report*. Party unity votes are defined as those on which a majority of one party oppose a majority of the other.

vided impressive support to Presidents Kennedy, Johnson, and Nixon (during his first term). The House has typically been less support- ive than the Senate since 1973. Second the spread between the two parties in supporting the president is often greater in the House than in the Senate (only during the first Nixon administration was the dif- ference in the House less—16 compared to 20 in the Senate). Other observations include the consistently greater Senate over House Re- publican support for Democratic presidents and the greater House

TABLE 11—4
Average party support for president's program, 1961—1980, House and Senate

President	Senate Average percent of roll calls won by president	Senate Average percent of support D	Senate Average percent of support R	House Average percent of roll calls won by president	House Average percent of support D	House Average percent of support R
Kennedy—Johnson						
(1961—65)	86	63*	41	85	73*	37
Johnson						
(1965—69)	78	57.5*	48	86	67.5*	44
Nixon						
(1969—73)	67.5	44	64*	80	49	65*
Nixon—Ford						
(1973—77)	60	40	61*	54	38	61*
Carter						
(1977—80)	79	66.5*	46	73	62.5*	38

* Indicates administration party.
SOURCE: Jewell and Patterson (1977: 397) and various issues of *Congressional Quarterly Weekly Reports*.

over Senate Democratic support for Kennedy and Johnson but not for Carter. The overall patterns are also interesting. Democratic presidents can do respectably well if they gain sufficient support from their own party. In fact, it appears that they might win 90 percent of the roll calls if they can line up more votes from their own party (particularly in the Senate for Kennedy and Johnson, in the House for Carter). Republican presidents are not in such a good position. They are forced to rely on Democrats to do well. Republican support for Republican presidents varies little between the two houses. When Democrats provide support, as they did for Nixon in his first administration, then a Republican president scores well. The problem, of course, is that efforts to gain Democratic support may lose a Republican president support in his own party. Democrat or Republican, it is certainly the case that "presidents . . . do not control the actions of party leaders or consistently receive their support" (Edwards, 1980:   80).

Donald R. Matthews observes that: "On Capitol Hill everyone is a partisan" (1960:   145). Party is a dominant feature of the legislative landscape. But it is uncommonly hard to describe and characterize. Political party is not unlike the fog—you know it is there but you are uncertain where it came from, where it is headed, or what it's purpose is while there.

ORGANIZING THE WORK ON THE FLOOR

In his account of his involvement in lawmaking on Capitol Hill, young Eric Redman, in *The Dance of Legislation*, reported on his education regarding differences between the House and Senate (1973: 168 – 69).

> Experience . . . already taught me that the Senate was a far more intricate and subtle legislative labyrinth than the institution my college textbooks had described. Now Staggers' [chairman of a House committee with which Redman had dealings] staff taught me a parallel lesson about the House of Representatives. I had anticipated that the House might consider itself the legislative equal of the Senate, despite the condescending habit of Senators of referring to it as "the lower body." Yet I soon learned that the House really considers itself the Senate's superior. . . . Congressmen and their staffs, in fact, cherish a fine disdain for the Senate and senators, whom they regard as "hotheads" writing ill-considered, poorly drafted, and generally irresponsible legislation. . . . To House careerists—and to the career staffs of the House committees—the Senate is an unseemly, anarchic, and almost dissolute body. Congressmen of real importance and their staffs do not attach great significance to suggestions or legislation that emanate from the opposite side of Capitol Hill.

Anyone visting the two bodies at work can appreciate Redman's observations, but the differences are particularly striking on the floor of each chamber. Suppose a student studied only the House, believing that both bodies were essentially alike. Such a person might be reasonably well served with this knowledge through the committee stage in the Senate (aside from wondering where all the committee members were). But imagine the problems in relying on knowledge of House procedures once the legislation is on the Senate floor. Perhaps more than anything else, our observer would be frustrated by the lack of closure. House procedures provide many stop points, making it possible for those in the galleries to sense, if not fully understand, the method down there. Senate procedures appear anarchic by comparison.

In describing House floor procedures, I observed that several organizational requirements had to be met, an agenda, establishment of priorities, processing of routine matters, debate, opportunity to amend, and means for a final decision. While the same is true for the Senate, they do it all quite differently. I have organized the discussion into three topics: scheduling the work, organizing the day, and making decisions.

Scheduling the work

The fact that the Senate is smaller in size than the House does not mean that senators do less. Since bills cannot become law until passed by a majority in both houses, it is clear that the Senate institutional workload is as great as that of the House; thus the individual member workload is considerably greater. Add to this the incredible constituency demands for a large state like California or New York and one wonders how certain senators are able to manage the job.[5]

Since legislation spills out from the Senate committees on the floor in somewhat more raw form than in the House, it is not surprising that the Senate is in session longer hours than the House. The House is normally in session four to five hours; the Senate, six to seven hours. And the workload varies through the year. In 1975 Senate sessions averaged seven hours and 43 minutes in March, June, and November, and eight hours and 23 minutes in the busy months of July and December. The longest sessions tend to occur on Wednesday and Thursday, the shortest invariably is on Monday. Sessions typically begin at 10 A.M. or after and adjourn before 7 P.M.[6]

In the House one pictures a series of channels into which committee-reported legislation flows. In some cases, for example, as with the House calendar, the channel has tributaries—the Consent Calendar, suspensions, the Rules Committee. No such imagery is possible in the Senate. All legislation—public, private, appropriations, taxation, authorizations, significant, insignificant—goes on one calendar, the Calendar of General Orders. No filtering at all occurs as the bills tumble out of committee to be lined up in the chronological order of their reporting date. There is a second calendar—the Executive Calendar—but it is for business only the Senate has authority to conduct, that is, treaties and nominations.

Of course as in the House, the bulk of the legislation is minor and noncontroversial. Therefore, some means has to be devised to get it before the Senate in an expeditious manner, insuring that nothing major slips through. Both parties have calendar watchers (usually someone from the Policy Committee staff) to insure that the bills are truly noncontroversial, and then the majority leader simply clears the calendar of such measures by unanimous consent. As Walter J. Oleszek notes: "Once cleared [by each party], minor and noncontroversial bills generally take only several seconds or a few minutes to pass" (1978: 136). Here is an example:

> **Mr. Robert C. Byrd:** I ask unanimous consent that the Senate proceed to the consideration of the following Calendar Orders Nos. 278, 278, 280, 281, 282, 282, 284, 292, 292 and 305.

---

[5] Herb Jasper, in a study of scheduling in the Senate, noted that when asked about their concerns "more senators listed 'scheduling . . . to avoid conflicting demands' as 'very important' than any other item." Herb Jasper, "Scheduling of Senate Business," in U.S. Senate, Commission on the Operation of the Senate, *Committees and Senate Procedures*, 94th Cong., 2d sess., 1977, p. 131.

[6] Data from U.S. Senate, Commission on the Operation of the Senate, *Legislative Activity Sourcebook: United States Senate*, 94th Cong., 2d sess., 1976, p. 4. In the 94th and 95th Congresses the House had longer days on the average than at any time in the post-World War II period. Senate days for those Congresses exceeded in length those for all but two post-war Congresses (Bibby et al., 1980: 86–87).

The Presiding Officer: Is there objection to the request of the Senator from West Virginia?

Mr. Baker: Mr. President, reserving the right to object, and I shall not object, this list of Calendar order numbers has been cleared on our side. We have no objection to proceeding to their consideration and, indeed, to their disposition as the majority leader requests.

The Presiding Officer: Without objection, it is so ordered.

Mr. Robert C. Byrd: Mr. President, I ask unanimous consent that the measures be considered en bloc, that the amendments that are indicated be agreed to, and that the bills and resolutions, as amended, be agreed to en bloc.

The Presiding Officer: Without objection, it is so ordered.[7]

And so 10 bills were passed by the Senate. Other minor bills may also be passed with dispatch but with less anonymity. The sponsors may wish some recognition for the bill in the *Congressional Record*. In essence a type of consent calendar now appears to exist in the Senate whereby the majority leader lists bills to be cleared a day before they are processed on the floor (Oleszek, 1978: 136). Senators from either party then have an opportunity, primarily through watchful staff, to judge whether they object or wish to debate and amend the bills in question. Strictly speaking—by the Senate Rules—any member can move to take any bill off the calendar at any time. The new procedures encourage members to work through the floor leaders, however, so as to develop a more orderly flow of business.

One problem in employing unanimous consent procedures for passing even minor and noncontroversial legislation is that senators may not have an opportunity to study the bills. A one-day layover requirement has been provided in the Senate rules for many years. In 1970, however, a three-day layover was provided for in the rules, to apply to any bill reported from a standing committee (except declarations of war or emergency, legislative veto procedures, and executive reorganization plans). The one-day requirement can be waived by unanimous consent; the three-day requirement by agreement between the majority and minority leaders. Both are frequently waived.[8]

Unanimous consent to pass minor legislation or to permit a violation of the rules (e.g., permit a staff person floor access during debate or committees to meet when the Senate is in session) is a practice that has been used in the Senate from the beginning. In this century, however, the so-called complex unanimous consent agreement has come into use. "The purpose of such agreements was generally to set a specific date for votes on amendments to a bill and final passage of the bill itself. Also, agreements frequently limited the time allowed for

---

[7] *Congressional Record* (daily edition), August 2, 1979, p. S11342.

[8] See Jasper, "Scheduling of Senate Business," p. 132.

debate on amendments and final passage."[9] It seems then that the complex unanimous consent agreement performs very much the same function in the Senate that resolutions from the Rules Committee perform in the House. More about that later.

Robert Keith summarizes the process by which these agreements are constructed.

> The idea of fairness is central to the concept of unanimous consent. Senators are reluctant to abandon the protection of the Standing Rules in favor of unanimous consent agreements unless they are certain that their interests will be guarded. This assurance is carefully cultivated, resulting from the longstanding practice of mutual respect and consideration. The balance of the system is maintained when each senator feels that he gains as much but sacrifices no more than every other senator.[10]

In order to achieve this end, "the process . . . must be scrupulously open."[11] It is incumbent upon the party leaders to insure that they do, indeed, speak for their members in agreeing to the provisions. Their own credibility is seriously jeopardized if objection is heard once an agreement is called up on the floor.

Keith has discovered a number of important changes in complex agreements during the last quarter century. For example, they are used more frequently and are longer. But the really important change is that they are developed and applied *before floor consideration*. He notes that before 1975 agreements were developed during debate and discussion. Thus, the procedures for floor consideration were more or less pieced together along the way.

> Debate on one bill would often be conducted pursuant to three or four complex agreements. . . . An illustration . . . occurred in 1970. During consideration of two bills, the Foreign Military Sales Act and the Military Procurement Authorization Act, 22 complex agreements were entered into. Each successive agreement set terms for debate and disposition of newly proposed amendments.[12]

However casual the Senate may appear today, its procedures are considerably more orderly than in the past. Of course, agreements are still worked out on the floor during debate. Situations do arise that call for further adjustments and limitations to existing agreements.

What do these agreements look like? One may see them by paging

---

[9] Robert Keith, "The Use of Unanimous Consent in the Senate," in U.S. Senate, Commission on the Operation of the Senate, *Committees and Senate Procedures*, 94th Cong., 2d sess., 1977, p. 149.

[10] Ibid., p. 151.

[11] Ibid.

[12] Ibid., p. 159.

through the *Congressional Record,* probably running into one every third day or so, by Keith's count. Here is an example.

> *Ordered.* That when the Senate proceeds to the consideration of S. 1398 (Order No. 326), a bill to establish energy efficiency standards for industrial equipment, debate on any amendment shall be limited to 30 minutes, to be equally divided and controlled by the mover of such and the manager of the bill; and debate on any debatable motion, appeal, or point of order which is submitted or on which the Chair entertains debate shall be limited to 30 minutes, to be equally divided and controlled by the mover of such and the manager of the bill; *Provided,* that in the event the manager of the bill is in favor of any such amendment or motion, the time in opposition thereto shall be controlled by the minority leader or his designee; *Provided futher,* That no amendment that is not germane to the provisions of the said bill shall be received.
>
> *Ordered further.* That on the question of final passage of the said bill, debate shall be limited to 1 hour, to be equally divided and controlled, respectively by the Senator from Ohio (Mr. Metzenbaum) and the Senator from New Mexico (Mr. Domenici); *Provided,* That the said Senators, or either of them, may from the time under their control on the passage of the said bill, allot additional time to any Senator during the consideration of any amendment, debatable motion, appeal or point of order.[13]

Compare this agreement with the example of a House resolution in Chapter 9. Many of the same issues are covered—limiting time on amendments (done by invoking the five-minute rule in the House), dividing the time equally between proponents and opponents, limiting general debate. On the other hand, there are many differences attributable to the variation in methods for doing business in the two chambers. Among these differences are the following:[14]

1. Amendments are introduced and debated without the Senate reforming as a Committee of the Whole.
2. Since nongermane amendments are permitted by Senate rules, provision is often made to exclude them. Nongermane amendments are not permitted by House rules.
3. Debate on amendments typically comes rather soon after the motion to consider the bill. General debate comes on the question of final passage.
4. Amendments are never prohibited. There is no closed rule in the Senate.
5. The conditions for debate may be altered by agreement along the way.

---

[13] *Congressional Record* (daily edition), September 24, 1979, p. S13265.

[14] Oleszek provides a list of some of these differences, p. 142.

Referred to either as unanimous consent or time limitation agreements, they may vary considerably in form. The example above is characteristic of the more formal agreement. But they may also be very brief and not written out in advance. For example, on September 27, 1979, the majority leader asked unanimous consent "that there be a time limitation on the debt limit increase, H.R. 5269, of four hours to be equally divided . . . etc."[15] The agreements are typically approved several days before the bill is actually taken up on the floor (another difference from House procedure where the bill is normally taken up immediately upon approval of the rule). In the case of the agreement cited above, it was approved on September 24, the bill was taken up on September 28. It may be that during the interim some further restriction has become desirable. If the party leaders agree, it is entirely possible that the majority leader will request approval of such a restriction at the time that the bill is taken up or even during its consideration.

Another scheduling improvement that has been instituted in recent years is the so-called tracking system. This is no more than a method for moving several bills at once by reserving time in advance for their consideration. As Walter Oleszek observes: "The system is particularly beneficial when there are numerous important bills awaiting floor action or when there is protracted floor conflict over one bill" (1978: 140). The latter situation has been particularly troublesome for the Senate. In the event of a filibuster (see below), the Senate was, in the past, completely tied up, unable to move other legislation. However, if the Senate, by unanimous consent, agrees in advance to assign certain time periods to certain legislation, then it is in order to interrupt the filibuster so as to consider other bills. The filibuster then resumes on its own schedule.

Clearly, successful floor scheduling depends heavily on the work of the floor leaders and their staffs. They must maintain close contact with the committees so as to know what is forthcoming and be highly sensitive to the interests and priorities of their respective colleagues. They must also communicate their intentions to the membership so that there will be no misunderstandings. A periodic review of the schedule is often undertaken by the majority leader or asked for by the minority leader. Thus for example, on September 7, 1979, Senator Byrd judged it important to "say a little something about the schedule for the rest of the year." He reviewed all of the remaining legislation and warned senators that "this will involve some Saturday sessions."[16] The majority leader may also summarize accomplishments from time to time. It was on such an occasion that we learned something about this

---

[15] *Congressional Record* (daily edition), September 27, 1979, p. 13610.

[16] *Congressional Record* (daily edition), September 7, 1979, p. S12126.

matter of scheduling. Senator Byrd first praised the Senate for a very productive week, then acknowledged the cooperation of the minority leader. Minority Leader Baker responded:

> I think it has been a high point of this session that the majority leader has agreed to meet periodically with me and others to try to arrange the schedule of the Senate. We have had good success at those meetings so far, and I think it has been mutually beneficial. I know it has been helpful on this side of the aisle, in that it gives our members a chance to gain some insight into the progress of our work, and give some suggestions and hopefully insight, as it were, into the matters to come before the Senate.
>
> Since that [the scheduling] is the special province of the majority and the majority leader handles it with such cooperation and grace, I want to take this opportunity to thank him for that cooperation. . . .
>
> **Mr. Robert C. Byrd:** Mr. President, this has been my practice from the beginning. I think it is a matter that requires cooperation between the leaders on both sides of the aisle. I have found it productive, and intend to continue the practice.
>
> **Mr. Baker:** I thank the majority leader. We intend to try to continue to cooperate. I hope that soon we may have another meeting, so that we may explore further areas of cooperation.
>
> **Mr. Robert C. Byrd:** As the distinguished minority leader knows, we discussed that this morning, and we agreed to meet today.
>
> **Mr. Baker:** I know. I wanted to let our friends know we were doing that.
>
> **Mr. Robert C. Byrd:** I am not sure our friends care too much. They probably have their hands full.
>
> **Mr. Baker:** Perhaps they will care more after the time is over.
>
> **Mr. Robert C. Byrd:** Perhaps.[17]

This colloquy illustrates the comity so characteristic of the Senate, but it also is full of information. We learn that the bipartisan cooperation is not something furtive. It is proudly announced in a public setting. Both leaders established a point of reference should conflict develop later. One can almost hear future comparisons being made in regard to relationships between these same leaders on other issues or as a consequence of their having switched positions (in the 97th Congress Baker became majority leader, Byrd minority leader). Then Senator Byrd, at Senator Baker's prodding, announced that a meeting would be held today, thereby advising senators with scheduling problems or preferences to contact the leaders.

One seldom witnesses such interparty cooperation and courtesy in the House. Scheduling there is very much a partisan matter, which is the reason why a motion to recommit a bill is always included in the House resolution. No such motion is necessary in the Senate as a

---

[17] *Congressional Record* (daily edition), July 23, 1979, pp. S10275–76.

protection of the minority. The minority, whether it be partisan (that is, the minority party) or bipartisan (e.g., the conservatives on an issue), is typically consulted and accommodated along the way. They may lose the vote, but they normally have ample opportunity to state their case and to introduce their amendments.

Organizing the day

It is not easy for the person sitting in the gallery of either House or Senate to comprehend exactly what is going on at any one point. Still the greater size of the House demands more formal and orderly procedures. Therefore one can at least discern the flow of business after the fact by getting a copy of the *Congressional Record* for the day of the visit. The greater informality of the Senate makes it difficult for all but the most experienced observer to follow the action. Interruptions are frequent—not only of individual senators but of whole debates. So much of what takes place has either been agreed to in advance (as described above) or is manufactured in place to suit the needs of a particular senator. Still it is possible to describe a general order of events, with the understanding that senators can, by unanimous consent, do almost anything they choose (including having the "morning hour" occur in the afternoon—see below).

We begin by noting that the day I chose to illustrate the order of business is September 28, 1979, by the calendar and June 21, 1979, by the course of legislative business. What this means simply is that the Senate has not officially adjourned since June 21. The House typically adjourns after each day's business, and thus the legislative days and calendar days are normally the same. In the Senate, however, adjournment is less frequent. Often the Senate simply recesses from day to day and thus is out of sequence with the calendar. The legislative day of June 21, 1979, did not end until October 4, 1979.

The distinction between adjournment and recess is not trivial. By recessing the Senate can move immediately to unfinished business— that is, whatever bill is under consideration on the floor. If the Senate adjourns, then the new legislative day must begin with the regular order (see below).[18] Those wishing to delay measures obviously prefer adjournment. This is not to say, of course, that provisions will not be made for the regular order if the Senate only recesses. Rather the

---

[18] Of course, this too may be a mere formality. On October 4, when the majority leader decided to get the legislative day caught up with the calendar, at 4:15 P.M. he moved adjournment for 30 seconds. In order, he then asked unanimous consent that the reading of the journal be dispensed with, no resolutions be taken up, there be a brief period for transacting morning business, the morning business be closed, and the Senate recess. All were granted, and the Senate was then ready to take up unfinished business once it reconvened. *Congressional Record* (daily edition), October 4, 1979, pp. S14140—41.

leadership has the option of going directly to unfinished business if the legislative day does not change.

The regular order of business during a day is as follows:

1. The call to order.
2. Prayer.
3. Reading of the journal of the proceedings of the last legislative day (normally dispensed with).
4. Routine morning business.
5. Special orders.
6. Unfinished and/or new business.
7. Recess or adjournment.

A few comments or explanations are in order. The reading of the journal is required unless dispensed with by unanimous consent. One can imagine the delay involved when the last legislative day is nearly four months long (e.g., the case above, June 21 to October 4). Routine morning business is simply the period in which members introduce bills, reports and messages from the president or House are acknowledged, brief speeches given, etc. The morning hour is scheduled for two hours but may be much shorter, or longer, dispensed with altogether, or shifted to another part of the day. Special orders permit senators to deliver short speeches—up to 15 minutes. They may follow or be considered a part of morning business. One must constantly bear in mind that the Senate does not slavishly follow its own rules. Thus, for example, it is entirely possible that morning business or a special order may be interrupted, always by unanimous consent, and the Senate may go into executive session to clear a number of appointments on the Executive Calendar. It happens all the time, much to the consternation of the observer.

At some point attention will turn to legislative business. I have selected a day to illustrate what takes place. By chance I chose a long day for Senators. Table 11 — 5 shows what happened. Following the standard routine in the morning, the Senate debated and passed two bills, agreed to one conference report, and rejected a second. The several recesses were required because the House of Representatives was acting on a conference report for a resolution to continue appropriations at current rates. Unfortunately, the report got tangled up with a controversy over pay raises and the funding of abortions. Thus the Senate recessed frequently awaiting House action. At one point morning business was taken up again simply to pass time until the House acted. When the House finally did act, it insisted on its way in regard to both controversial issues and then recessed for 10 days. Senators were furious, particularly since failure to pass the report meant that federal employees would not get paid after October 1. Despite the problems

TABLE 11—5
The Senate at work—September 28, 1979

Business	Time
Call to order	10:15 A.M.
Prayer	
The Journal	
Special order (Senator Kassebaum R—Kansas)	
Routine morning business	
Conclusion of morning business	10:48 A.M.
Recess (30 minutes)	10:48—11:18 A.M.
Consideration of Industrial Equipment Energy	
Efficiency Act of 1979 (S. 1398)	11:18 A.M.
Agreement to House Concurrent Resolution 192	
(unanimous consent)	
Return to consideration of S. 1398	
Recess to meet the president of the National	
Assembly of France	12:13—12:14 P.M.
Return to consideration of S. 1398	12:14 P.M.
Passage of S. 1398 (43—39)	
Consideration of Public Debt Limit Increase	
(H.R. 5369)	
Recess (one hour)	12:36—1:36 P.M.
Return to consideration of H.R. 5369	1:36 P.M.
Senator Harry F. Byrd, Jr., recognized for 12	
minutes to make statement	
Return to consideration of H.R. 5369	
Passage of H.R. 5369 (49—29)	
Consideration of Conference Report on	
Appropriations bill (H.R. 4394)	
Passage of Conference Report on H.R. 4394	
Recess (awaiting the call of the chair)	5:57—6:47 P.M.
Routine morning business	
Recess (awaiting the call of the chair)	7:35—8:44 P.M.
Announcement by majority leader	
Recess (awaiting the call of the chair)	8:46—9:38 P.M.
Consideration of Conference Report on	
continuing resolution on appropriations	9:38 P.M.
Rejection of Conference Report (9—55)	
Final recess till 12:00 A.M., September 29, 1979	11:22 P.M.

SOURCE: Compiled from *Congressional Record* (daily edition), September 28, 1979, pp. S13617—S13744.

caused by rejecting the report, a large majority of senators voted against it. Senator Warren Magnuson (D—Washington and chairman of the Senate Committee on Appropriations) observed that "we can just call time-out here in the football game and bide our time and see what the House does." Senator Byrd was highly upset.

Mr. Robert C. Byrd: Mr. President, there will be no more roll-call votes today. But the Senate will be in session tomorrow.

In the event the president wishes to exercise his constitutional right to call the other body into session tomorrow, he will not have to call this body into session. The Senate will meet, ready to do business with the other body, if the other body were to be called back by the president.

Several Senators: Hear! Hear![19]

I reiterate that no day is typical. Legislatures in authoritarian regimes have routine orders and typical days. The United States Senate is involved in too many major issues to be so predictable.

Making decisions on the floor

The flow of work on the Senate floor is both less complicated than in the House and more difficult to follow. Table 11 — 6 summarizes the

TABLE 11 — 6

The flow of work on the Senate floor—major legislation under unanimous consent agreements

Action	Comment
1. Unanimous consent agreement introduced.	Generally establishes time limit on amendments and debate on final passage. May restrict nongermane amendments and specify time for final vote.
2. Presiding officer calls up the bill.	May come at any time after morning business but normally not on the same day as the agreement.
3. Floor managers speak to the bill (summarize its purpose).	Majority and minority senators from the committee sponsoring the bill will be managers.
4. Introductory speeches.	Other members may speak in general about the bill.
5. Committee amendments taken up.	Often introduced and approved en bloc and incorporated into the bill as original text for further amendment.
6. Vote on committee amendments.	May be acted on by unanimous consent.
7. Individual amendments introduced.	May be introduced to any section of the bill. Debate limited by agreement.
8. Vote on individual amendments.	May be by voice, division, or roll call.
9. Engrossment and third reading.	Incorporates all of the amendments. Reading is normally by title only.
10. Question put on final passage.	Put by the presiding officer.
11. Final vote on the bill.	May be voice, division, or roll call. Roll call is typical for important bills.
12. Motion to reconsider.	Normally tabled, preventing reconsideration at a future time.

SOURCES: Compiled by the author from information in Congressional Quarterly, *Congress of the United States* (Washington: Congressional Quarterly, Inc., 1971), pp. 115 – 16; Oleszek, 1978: 155 – 64; and Zinn, 1969: 25 – 27.

various steps, with comments. Again we see major differences from the way in which the House does its business on the floor. The Senate moves rather directly to amendments, without reforming itself as a

---

[19] *Congressional Record* (daily edition), September 28, 1979, p. S13743.

committee. The whole amending process is much less restrictive. Senators roam about freely in amending the bill and normally have ample time for debate. There are degrees of amendments, just as in the House, and they are voted on in the same logical order (see Chapter 9). General debate may proceed on final passage, in part because amending is so characteristic of Senate floor action that debate upon first consideration may be irrelevant to the bill in its final form. Again, we have an indication of the difference in the relationship of committees to the floor in the two chambers. The House procedures are based on the assumption that what comes out of committee will survive more or less intact on the floor; Senate procedures are based on just the opposite assumption.

To illustrate the process consider the bill for which a unanimous consent agreement was obtained on September 24, 1979 (see p. 313). On September 28, the presiding officer (Senator Howell Heflin, a first-term Democrat from Alabama) announced that: "Under previous order, the Senate will now proceed to the consideration of S. 1398."[20] The clerk read the title, and it was then announced by the presiding officer that a committee amendment striking all after the enacting clause and substituting other language would be before the Senate. The new language was printed in the *Congressional Record* and the presiding officer then repeated the terms of the unanimous consent agreement. The majority leader asked unanimous consent that the time originally allotted to Senator Pete Domenici (R—New Mexico) be allotted to Senator Lowell Weicker (R—Connecticut). Senator Howard Metzenbaum (D—Ohio) shared the time equally with Weicker. Senators Weicker and Metzenbaum delivered opening remarks and answered initial questions regarding the bill. Senator Domenici offered an amendment that was accepted by both Weicker and Metzenbaum and approved by voice vote. No further amendments were introduced, and the presiding officer announced:

> The bill is open to further amendment. If there be no further amendments to be proposed, the question is on agreeing to the committee amendment in the nature of a substitute, as amended.
>
> The committee amendment in the nature of a substitute, as amended, was agreed to.[21]

The presiding officer ordered the amendments to be engrossed (i.e., a final copy of the amended bill be produced), and the bill was read a third time. Senators Weicker and Metzenbaum delivered final speeches and yielded back their remaining time. The presiding officer asked, "Shall the bill pass?" The yeas and nays were ordered (requiring support of one fifth of those present). "The clerk will call the roll." The

---

[20] Ibid., p. S13620.

[21] Ibid., p. S13626.

bill passed 43 to 39, with 18 not voting. Senators Alan Cranston (D—California) and Ted Stevens (R—Alaska), the party whips, announced that several senators were "necessarily absent," noting how two senators from each party would vote if present. Senator Metzenbaum moved to reconsider the vote. Senator Weicker moved to lay the reconsideration motion on the table, which was agreed to. S. 1398 was then ordered to be printed.

While S. 1398 was handled with considerably more dispatch than most major legislation, still it provides a rather complete illustration of all the stages in Table 11 — 6. The bill itself sought to improve the efficiency of industrial pumps and motors—possibly saving up to 700,000 barrels of oil a year.

Can important legislation reach the floor without a unanimous consent agreement? On any day but Monday, any senator may move to take up a bill out of its order on the calendar. Consideration may proceed until the president of the Senate calls up the unfinished business of the Senate, at which point further action on the bill under consideration is postponed (in essence, it becomes unfinished business). Legislation is, of course, enacted in this way. There are, however, several problems in attempting to manage major legislation without unanimous consent agreements. First and foremost is the threat of a filibuster. The word itself has virtually become synonymous with the Senate. It is derived from the Dutch, French, and Spanish words meaning freebooter or buccaneer. George B. Galloway identifies it first with the House of Representatives in 1853 (1955: 559—60):

> In the course of a long speech on the Military Academy bill Congressman Abraham W. Venable of South Carolina had denounced the actions of American filibusterers (freebooters) in Cuba. His speech provoked Congressman Arnold G. Brown of Mississippi who said: "When I saw my friend standing on the other side of the House filibustering, as I thought, against the United States, surrounded as he was by admiring Whigs, I did not know what to think. It seemed to me he had taken formal leave of his old state rights friends and gone over to the Whigs."

It is a fact that delaying tactics were frequently tried in the House during the 19th century, and with considerable success. Repeated teller votes, disappearing quorums, frequent amendments—these and other techniques were used until Speaker Thomas B. Reed made a number of rulings in the 51st Congress to curb such practices. But the tradition of debate in the Senate has preserved the filibuster in robust form throughout the decades.

Rule XIX of the Standing Rules of the Senate states that:

> When a Senator desires to speak, he shall rise and address the Presiding Officer, and shall not proceed until he is recognized, and the Presiding Officer shall recognize the Senator who shall first address him. No

Senator shall interrupt another Senator in debate without consent, and to obtain such consent he shall first address the Presiding Officer, and no Senator shall speak more than twice upon any one question in debate on the same day without leave of the Senate, which shall be determined without debate.

Note the control that is conferred to the senator who has the floor. Once recognition is gained, and in the absence of a unanimous consent agreement, the member cannot be interrupted without consent and does not lose the floor unless he or she speaks twice on the same question (a difficult matter to judge). Nowhere does it suggest that the senator's remarks must be relevant to the issue at hand. In 1947, Senator Glen H. Taylor (D—Idaho) "spoke for 8½ hours on fishing, baptism, Wall Street, and his children."[22]

The Senate is not totally helpless in the face of endless talking, however. In the first place, fatigue can take its toll where just a few senators are involved. Once a senator sits down, the command of the floor is ended. Still some senators have demonstrated incredible stamina. The record is held by Senator Strom Thurmond (then a Democrat from South Carolina—he later switched parties) who held the floor for 24 hours and 18 minutes in 1957.[23] More troublesome, of course, are the team filibusters where several senators take turns. These exercises can go on for a very long time unless the bill is withdrawn or cloture is invoked. The first action is, of course, a victory for the filibusterers. The second closes down debate by an orderly procedure.

The Senate adopted its cloture rule in 1917. Its original provisions required a vote of two thirds of the senators present and voting to close debate (e.g., if 66 senators are present and voting, then a vote of 44 senators is required to stop debate). The rule was changed in 1949 to require two thirds of the entire Senate membership, not just those present and voting. And in 1959 the rule was changed again. The new provisions stated that:

1. A motion to close debate must be signed by 16 senators.
2. Following a quorum call, a roll-call vote is taken on closing debate.
3. Two thirds of the senators present and voting must agree.
4. If the requisite number of senators agree, then debating time for any senator is limited to one hour.
5. No new amendments are in order except by unanimous consent.
6. No dilatory motions or amendments or nongermane amendments are in order.

---

[22] *Congressional Quarterly Weekly Report,* October 1, 1977, p. 2065.

[23] Other impressive performances: Wayne L. Morse, also a party switcher from Republican to Independent to Democrat (Oregon), 22 hours, 26 minutes in 1953; Robert M. LaFollette (R—Wisconsin), 18 hours, 23 minutes in 1908.

While slightly less restrictive, the 1959 version of Rule 22 was not likely to forestall a determined band of filibusterers. Thus, Senate liberals regularly sought to modify the rules. In 1975 they were successful in changing the number required to close debate for all business except changes in the Standing Rules from two thirds of those present and voting to three fifths of the entire membership (60 senators if there are no vacancies). Rules changes would still require a two-thirds vote.[24]

Table 11−7 shows the increased use of Rule 22 over the years since its adoption in 1917. During the first period approximately one at-

TABLE 11−7
Senate cloture votes, 1917−1977

Time period	Successful	Unsuccessful	Total
1917−59	4	18	22
(42 years)	(18%)	(82%)	
1960 −69	4	19	23
(10 years)	(17%)	(83%)	
1970 −74	13	42	55
(5 years)	(24%)	(75%)	
1975 −77*	18	14	32
(3 years)	(56%)	(44%)	
Totals	39	93	132
	(30%)	(70%)	

* Totals to October 1, 1977.
SOURCE: Compiled from information supplied in *Congressional Quarterly Weekly Report,* October 1, 1977, pp. 2064, 2066.

tempt was made every two years, on the average. In fact twice during the early period no cloture efforts were made for five years running (1928−32, 1955−59). This lack of cloture motions did not mean there were no filibusters, only that no one tried to halt them. Business began to pick up in the 1960s when there was an average of 2.3 cloture efforts each year and at least one every year. By the 1970s cloture votes were quite regular—an average of just over 11 per year, with 21 occurring in 1974! The success ratio improved somewhat in the 1970s, though not impressively. Had the three-fifths rule been in force, however, another 19 cloture efforts would have passed, raising the success ratio to nearly 60 percent. Thus, there was a strong incentive among the antifilibuster group to adopt the three-fifths rule in 1975.

During the debate on the Rule 22 changes in 1975, one Senator James B. Allen (D−Alabama) displayed a new wrinkle in minority obstructionist techniques—the postcloture filibuster-by-amendment. Senator Allen had perfected this method in previous years and he relied on it heavily to prevent a change in Rule 22. The technique

---

[24] See *Congressional Quarterly Weekly Report,* March 1, 1975, pp. 450 −51.

reminds one of the obstructionist tactics in the House during the reign of Speaker Reed. In order to prevent action, the postcloture filibusterer introduces a string of amendments and objections to any unanimous consent motions designed to speed debate (e.g., to dispense with the reading of the journal). Allen was successful in delaying but not defeating the rules change, which finally passed on March 7, 1975.

Senator Allen's worries about the possible effects of a change in Rule 22 were well founded. As shown in Table 11 − 7, the success ratio of cloture motions improved dramatically after the change to a 60 percent majority. In fact, 9 of 10 cloture motions were successful between September 24, 1975, and September 23, 1976.

The postcloture technique was used with considerable success in 1977 by two liberal Democrats determined to kill legislation designed to end price controls on natural gas. Senators James Abourezk (South Dakota) and Howard M. Metzenbaum (Ohio) launched a standard filibuster, but cloture was invoked by a wide margin (77 − 17). Abourezk and Metzenbaum then tried to amend the bill to death. Once cloture is invoked further debate is limited to 100 hours. However, quorum calls and votes on amendments submitted before the cloture vote are not counted against the 100 hours. The senators had filed 508 amendments before cloture. They began to call them up for consideration, repeatedly demanding roll-call votes. They also insisted that the clerk read the amendments, and they frequently asked for quorum calls. Senator Russell Long (D − Louisiana − son of a champion filibusterer) observed in reference to Senator Metzenbaum: "I never saw a man come in here and become an ace filibusterer so fast."[25]

The Abourezk-Metzenbaum postcloture filibuster was ended in dramatic fashion. Majority Leader Byrd called up the amendments himself so as to have them declared dilatory and thus not in order. Vice President Walter Mondale made one of his rare appearances in the chair and cooperated with the majority leader. Mondale recognized Byrd over and over again, ignoring the requests of other senators to be heard. Abourezk believed he had assurance that these rulings could be appealed. When no appeals were permitted, Abourezk shouted: "Mr. President, I make the point of order that this is a steamroller."[26] Other senators also sought to get the floor to protest the methods being used. Byrd finally responded in an emotional outburst − reminding the Senate of the many efforts he had made to break the impasse and charging that the delay tactics constituted "abuse of the Senate." Many senators were frustrated by the delaying tactics, but the tradition of free debate and minority rights is strong in the institution. Thus several members rose to object to the steamroller

---

[25] *Congressional Quarterly Weekly Report*, October 8, 1977, p. 2064.
[26] Ibid., p. 2136.

tactics. Abourezk and Metzenbaum then ended their filibuster, citing the obvious lack of support from the Carter administration (given that the vice president cooperated with Byrd).

Thus the filibuster by amendment was at an end, but it was uncertain whether future efforts could be stopped in the same manner. That is, appeals to the rulings of the chair, if permitted, would also take a great deal of time, thus accomplishing the same end as a vote on the amendment itself. In 1979, therefore, a further change was made in Rule 22. After cloture has been invoked, a final vote must occur after 100 hours of debate. All quorum calls and votes are counted in the 100 hours, but provision is made to extend the time for debate if approved by a three-fifths vote. Further, every senator would be guaranteed at least 10 minutes to speak even if to do so extended the time beyond 100 hours.[27] It is worth pointing out that 10 minutes in the House is considered a luxurious amount of time—most members are restricted to five minutes.

Typically, the exceptional circumstances require the most explanation. This greater attention should not distract the reader from understanding that most legislation is not subject to such complications. The major lesson from studying the various forms of filibuster is to illustrate the importance of the unanimous consent procedure. When it breaks down, the Senate has difficulty as a legislative body. Put another way, the norms of courtesy and comity are effective in insuring an extraordinarily civil legislative process. When they are absent, however, the system breaks down since the norms themselves do not permit alternative or fail-safe methods for enacting legislation. A further lesson from recent reforms is simply that these norms have declined in importance, and thus means have been developed to insure movement of legislation.

SUMMARY

It is said that when the House rapidly passed the bulk of his energy program in 1977, President Carter believed that the same would happen over in the Senate. He was, of course, very wrong. The Senate proceeded to emasculate his proposals, employing a very different legislative process than the House. It is not that one cannot predict success or failure in the two legislative bodies on Capitol Hill. It is rather that to do so on the basis of what happens in one chamber is likely to be either disappointing or disastrous. As we have seen, the Senate is a very special legislative body—both in comparison with others around the world and certainly in comparison with the House of Representatives.

---

[27] See *Congressional Quarterly Weekly Report*, February 24, 1979, p. 320.

12 Getting together in the legislative process

Making law requires a great many formal get-togethers. I have already introduced and described many of these conclaves—the committee and subcommittee hearings and markup sessions, party caucuses, House and Senate floor proceedings. This chapter will concentrate primarily on the formal connecting points between the two chambers and between Congress and the president.

GETTING THE HOUSE AND SENATE TOGETHER

The two legislatures that make up the United States Congress very seldom come together as one. There is no provision in the Constitution for them to act as one sitting body. Typically the only time during the year that the members actually all join one another is to hear the president deliver the State of the Union Message. They work separately on similar issues and yet are compelled to present a single bill to the president for his signature. Thus means must be devised for accommodating differences.

Approving the work of the other chamber

The least complicated method for passing the same bill in both houses is simply for one house to await the action of the other, then pass the same bill. When a bill comes over from the other chamber it normally is referred to the appropriate standing committee. This referral invariably occurs in the House, but Senate Rule XIV states that "every bill and joint resolution of the House of Representatives which shall have received a first and second reading without being referred to a committee, shall, if objection be made to further proceeding thereon, be placed on the Calendar."[1] What this rule means, in essence, is that bills passed by the House can go directly on the Senate Calendar without going first to a committee. This procedure is no guarantee that the bill will be passed by the Senate without amendment or in the same form as in the House, but it does remove one important stage (the committee) where changes might be made.

The two chambers are not likely to be so acquiescent in regard to most major legislation as to pass whatever comes to them from the other house. Typically different versions of a bill are developed and approved by the two houses. These differences may be ironed out informally and the compromise introduced and passed by both houses. Walter J. Oleszek notes an example of this happening when a southern senator threatened to filibuster "both the required motion to appoint conferees and the conference report itself" (Oleszek, 1978: 183). In that case the threat of obstruction encouraged the members to work out their differences. But there may be reasons associated with timing or the probable membership of a conference or, possibly, a change in the circumstances leading to the demand for legislation that may stimulate an informal accommodation.

Similarly there may be strategic reasons for one house acceding to the amendments passed by the other house. Perhaps the amendments are minor in nature, or possibly the leadership judges that a conference may deadlock or otherwise jeopardize the passage of needed legislation.

The conference

For the student of the legislative process, however, the really interesting procedure is when the two houses come together formally in conference to work out the differences in legislation. This procedure has its precedent in English parliamentary practice, dating from the 14th century. It was adopted in the very first Congress (Horn,

---

[1] United States Senate, *Senate Manual* (Washington, D.C.: U.S. Government Printing Office, 1963), Rule XIV, p. 16.

1970:   166).[2] Until 1974 all conference proceedings were closed to the public. Congressional reformers were always critical of the secret conference as constituting, in the words of Senator George W. Norris, a "third house" which is often "the most important branch of our legislature" (Galloway, 1955: 321). George B. Galloway noted that (1955; 320):

> It is alleged that Congress surrenders its legislative function to these committees; that under this secret system lobbyists are able to kill legislation they dislike; and that "jokers" designed to defeat the will of Congress can be inserted without detection. Critics say that the system delegates too much power into the hands of a few men who are not really held to answer for what they do.

It follows logically that having a secret conclave between senior senators and representatives at the conclusion of legislative action in each house is bound to lead to a conspiracy theory. But junior members and reformers had more than logic to support their claims about the power of these meetings. There was ample evidence in earlier times of the power of conferences, despite the restrictions on the jurisdiction and procedures of these meetings. Being held in secret and with no written record, it was not unusual for conferences to undo much of what had been passed in the two houses. Further, the fact that the meetings were out of public view led to various strategies of accommodation within each house. As one senior House member told me many years ago: "We let them have what they want within reason, knowing that we can get what we want in conference." Senator Albert Gore (D—Tennessee) described the conference as follows:

> It is here, in secret meetings often not even announced until the last minute, that a few men can sit down and undo in one hour the most painstaking work of months of effort by several standing committees and the full membership of both houses (Peabody, et al., 1972:   158).

In 1974 a total of 12 conferences were held in public, approximately 10 percent of the total. In 1975 conferences were automatically open unless members voted at the beginning of each meeting to close them. In that year 44 percent of the meetings were open. The overall effect of this change has been to insure that conferences are an extension of legislative action within the two houses. Or, put another way, the provision for open meetings makes it less likely that the conferees can start afresh, ignoring the agreements worked out in the House and Senate.

---

[2] For the historical development of the conference see Ada C. McGown, *The Congressional Conference Committee* (New York: Columbia University Press, 1927) and Lauros G. McConachie, *Congressional Committees* (New York: Thomas Y. Crowell, 1898).

Conference appointments and procedures

How do conferences come into being? And what are the procedures under which they do their work? The house with the "papers" (the bill as originally passed by one house plus any amendments attached by the other) requests a conference. The request is a direct consequence of disagreement with the amendments attached by the other house. This request normally passes by unanimous consent in the Senate. In the House, the request may be approved by unanimous consent, or by acceptance of a rule from the House Committee on Rules, or by simple majority vote without a rule if the originating committee agrees.[3]

Once the two houses agree on meeting in conference, the presiding officer for each chamber appoints the conferees or managers — normally assigning those designated by the committee chairmen responsible for the bill. The number selected will vary with the complexity of the issues involved, but typically those from both parties who have played important roles will be included. Often the House and Senate will send different sized delegations since seniority and participation in the legislative action on the bill determine who is appointed. *Each house votes as a unit* so the difference in size does not give either an advantage. A majority on each side must vote for the report for it to be forwarded to the two chambers.

I have selected a simple case to illustrate approval of a conference. The Senate passed a bill to restructure the Federal Law Enforcement Assistance Administration. The House amended the bill and returned it to the Senate. Senator Edward M. Kennedy (D—Massachusetts), then chairman of the Senate Committee on the Judiciary, requested Senate approval of a conference.

> **Mr. Kennedy:** Mr. President, I move that the Senate disagree to the amendment of the House, and that the Senate request a conference on the disagreeing votes of the two houses thereon, and that the chair be authorized to appoint conferees on the part of the Senate.
>
> The motion was agreed to, and the presiding officer appointed Mr. Kennedy, Mr. Biden, Mr. DeConcini, Mr. Baucus, Mr. Heflin, Mr. Thurmond, Mr. Laxalt, Mr. Dole, and Mr. Cochran conferees on the part of the Senate.[4]

The next day, the House responded positively to the request for a conference.

> **Mr. Gudger:** Mr. Speaker, on behalf of Mr. Rodino, the chairman of the Committee on the Judiciary, I ask unanimous consent to take from the Speaker's table the Senate bill (S. 241) to restructure the Federal Law

---

[3] Congressional Quarterly, *Guide to the Congress of the United States* (Washington, D.C.: Congressional Quarterly, 1971), p. 118. On the details of conference makeup and procedures see also Oleszek, 1978: chapter 8; Zinn, 1979: chapter 8; and the House and Senate rules.

[4] *Congressional Record* (daily edition), October 18, 1979, p. S14802.

> Enforcement Assistance Administration . . . with the House amendment
> thereto, insist on the House amendment, and agree to the conference
> asked by the Senate.
>
> **The Speaker:** Is there objection to the request of the gentleman from
> Washington? The chair hears none and, without objection, appoints the
> following conferees: Messrs. Rodino, Kastenmeier, Danielson, Gudger,
> Mazzoli, Hall of Texas, McClory, Ashbrook, and Hyde.
>
> (There was no objection.)[5]

Note that on this bill there were nine conferees from each house.
The Senate delegation included five Democrats and four Republicans;
the House delegation was made up of six Democrats and three Republicans. In both cases all were members of the Judiciary Committees of
the respective bodies. The difference in ratios of Democrats to Republicans in the respective chambers explains the difference in the
makeup of the two delegations.

The composition of conference committees is not always so simple.
As noted in Chapter 10 the two houses do not have absolutely parallel
jurisdiction between their committee systems. What is treated in one
Senate committee may be considered in more than one House committee. Often a particular issue falls within the jurisdiction of different
committees in each house. And there are spectacular instances in
which several committees are involved. Perhaps the most remarkable
case in recent years was that of the conference on the Carter energy
package in 1977.[6] The House and Senate passed different legislation in
form and substance. The House approved one bill. The Senate divided
the major sections into separate bills. The House worked through five
committees and then coordinated the results by the use of an Ad Hoc
Committee on Energy (composed of many of the members from the
five committees with jurisdiction). The Senate worked through two
committees and did not coordinate the results. Five separate bills were
passed and sent on to conference. Thus a huge conference (28
senators, 25 representatives) had to cope with a highly controversial
and incredibly differentiated set of legislative actions. Further complicating the process was the fact that different senators worked on
different portions of the energy package. For example, 18 senators
from the Committee on Energy and Natural Resources served as conferees for the natural gas bill. It took nearly a year before all parts of the
program finally cleared the conference. Many sections were noncontroversial, but Speaker O'Neill insisted that all sections be voted on at
the same time in the House. Thus even though the Senate method of

---

[5] *Congressional Record* (daily edition), October 19, 1979, p. H9444.

[6] This account is based on material in various *Congressional Quarterly Weekly Reports*, 1977, 1978; Charles O. Jones, "Congress and the Making of Energy Policy," in
Lawrence, ed., 1979: chapter 14, and Light, "The National Energy Plan and the Congress," also in Lawrence, ed., 1979: chapter 15.

dividing the sections into separate bills prevailed, the House held the noncontroversial bills until the Senate passed the highly conflictual tax provisions.

What the example of the energy conference suggests is that these meetings are likely today to be a microcosm of the preferences and struggles displayed in each house. In fact, a conscious effort is made to reflect the views of the principal participants, often directly through appointments of conferees. This was not always so in the past when only the most senior committee or subcommittee members from each house were appointed.

Conferences typically met on the Senate side of the Capitol before 1962. In that year a truly titanic struggle developed between the two committees which meet the most frequently in conference—the House and Senate Committees on Appropriations.[7] Location of the meetings was the superficial problem. The more fundamental issues were the tendency of the Senate committee to increase House-approved appropriations bills, the origination of appropriations bills in the House (assumed from their constitutional right to originate revenue measures), and some deep-seated institutional jealousy (mostly on the part of representatives toward the Senate).

The battle began near the close of the 1961 session of Congress when a House appropriations subcommittee chairman requested an evening conference be held on the House side of the Capitol. The Senate Appropriations Committee chairman, Carl Hayden (D—Arizona), refused. Later the House approved a conference report that was objectionable to the Senate and then adjourned sine die at 4:21 A.M. The Senate either had to approve the report or there would be no appropriation at all.

> Senators were outraged. Democratic leader Mansfield denounced the House's lack of courtesy and complained that the Senate had taken a "shellacking." Republican leader Dirksen threatened a roll-call show-down: "Are we a coordinate branch of the legislative establishment, or are we not?" (Horn, 1970: 168).

Though definitely miffed that the House would put them in this position, the Senate passed the conference report, but "many vowed it would never happen again" (Horn, 1970: 169).

When the second session began, House Appropriations Committee Chairman Clarence A. Cannon (D—Missouri) informed his counterpart in the Senate, Carl Hayden, that henceforth he wanted to alternate the site of conferences between the House and Senate sides of the Capitol Building. The House committee also passed a resolution favoring the alteration of chairmen between representatives and senators

---

[7] For the details of this struggle see Fenno, 1966: 635—41; Horn, 1970: 165—72; Pressman, 1966: chapter 1.

(senators had normally served as conference chairmen). The Senate countered with its own demand.

> . . . Senate Appropriations would like to have half of the appropriations bills originate in the Senate and half in the House. Once that was done, the Senate committee would be delighted to confer on the House side in connection with Senate-originated bills and on the Senate side . . . concerning bills initiated in the House (Horn, 1970: 169).

This tradeoff was not acceptable to the House, and an impasse resulted. As the end of the fiscal year approached, executive agencies began to get very nervous. Clearly something had to happen to get the two committees working with each other or the federal government would cease to function.

To make a long story short, "two five-man negotiating teams, one from each committee, finally met on 'neutral ground' in the Old Supreme Court chamber midway between the Senate and the House" (Fenno, 1966: 641). All conferences were to be held in the neutral zone for the rest of the session, and a joint committee was to make recommendations for a more permanent settlement at the beginning of the next Congress. The joint committee was never appointed, but a special conference room was created when the east front of the Capitol Building was extended in 1963. This room, EF — 100, straddles the line between the House and Senate sides of the Capitol.

Understandably this dispute was followed carefully in the press and was depicted as a contest for power and prestige between two old men — both Hayden and Cannon were in their 80s. No doubt this characterization was partially correct. For present purposes, however, the conflict is revealing of the importance of conferences and of the bargaining situation which exists. A complex set of political connections is represented by the conference. One may witness negotiations between and within committees (or subcommittees), parties, and institutions. Thus, for example, House conferees will negotiate among themselves as members of the same or different committees (where more than one is represented) and political parties. They also may have to negotiate with House leaders since they, after all, represent the full House. And, of course, they will deal with the Senate conferees, who in turn have their own set of connections to manage.[8]

These special bargaining circumstances, where the negotiators represent several different constituencies, obviously limit options and restrict behavior. In some cases, however, a chamber will be even more explicit by instructing its conferees not to compromise in regard to certain provisions. Often these instructions strengthen the hand of the

---

[8] For further details on these negotiations see Vogler, 1971: chapter 5.

conferees who may use them primarily to get their way, either directly or by threatening to break off the conference to get further instructions if the managers from the other house do not capitulate. Typically the House is more prone to using these tactics.

The bargaining is also restricted by the rules and precedents. Both houses restrict conferences to consideration of the differences between the two houses and to the material in the legislation (new material not considered by either house cannot be inserted). These rules are not always as limiting as might be supposed. Sometimes the differences between the two versions are so great that the conference in fact has great latitude. Perhaps one house has substituted a totally different bill for the one passed in the other house. Or special arrangements might be agreed to between the two houses, as with the 1977 energy legislation, which provide considerable discretion for the conference. It also happens that the rules are waived by unanimous consent in both houses, thus permitting extraordinary changes to be made by a conference.

What a conference looks like

The physical arrangements for the conference are quite different than for other committee meetings. The members sit at a long table, representatives on one side, senators on the other. Typically attendance is lower among senators than House members. "Some senate conferees never do attend" (Horn, 1970: 155). Three or four rows of chairs are placed behind each set of conferees for staff. Provision is made also for the press and other spectators. For an important bill, those with an official purpose (members and staff) may easily number 50 to 70 persons. Another 100 to 150 press, staff from other committees or member offices, agency personnel, and general public may also crowd into the room. So—we have a picture of a room with a long table stacked with files and documents, a staff hovering over the members (more evident on the Senate than House side), and a large number of persons observing the proceedings, some attentive, others not. The noise level is typically quite high, the ventilation poor, and klieg lights may be switched on and off. Working under these conditions requires incredible concentration.

It was precisely in this setting that an important conference between the House and Senate Budget Committees took place in May, 1980. Each house had passed a budget resolution, and a conference was called to work out the differences. The first meeting was held in the hearing room of the House Committee on the Budget (Room 210 in the Cannon House Office Building). It was 90 degrees outside, and with the air conditioning reduced to save energy it was evident that the room would soon be hot and stuffy. Every seat was filled, and people stood in the doorways. Photographers and television camera crews moved around the table. One had to strain to hear the members. A House member shouted: "Let's get a mike that works." Conferees from both sides frequently asked for order in the room. At one point a rumbling was heard in the hallway making it impossible to hear anyone. A large hand cart filled with glasses finally worked its way down the cavernous hallway. It was difficult to determine when the conference began since no announcement was made on who was to chair the meeting or what was to be discussed first. I was told later that this was unusual and was due to the fact that the former Senate Budget Committee chairman, Edmund S. Muskie (D—Maine), had just become secretary of state, and the present House chairman, Robert Giaimo (D—Connecticut), was in the hospital. Presumably they would have brought more order to the proceedings.

Once a conference is underway it often meets frequently and at some length to complete its work. In the case I am reporting on here, the two committees were under some pressure to meet a deadline of May 15 for passing the first budget resolution (a deadline they missed). Thus, the conferees were prepared to meet into the evening for several days. I returned to Room 210 in the late afternoon of the first day's meeting to see what progress had been made. The room was still packed, and the members were trying to negotiate despite the noise and movement all around them. By this time all members were in shirt sleeves. It was sweltering inside, and the place smelled like a locker room. All the windows were open, surely making the air conditioning work as hard as if it had been turned up.

I was assured by a staff member that committee leaders from the two houses do get together privately to estimate what can be realized by way of compromise within these public sessions. The two committee staffs also communicate continuously (though it should be noted that there were several instances in the conference described above when it was apparent they had not communicated). Thus, the openness of the proceedings forces extra communication between the House and Senate. Still the agreements reached outside the committee room must be discussed and ratified within that room as well. And when meeting in an open conference the members can be assured of pressure from lobbyists (those from the government as well as from private and public interest groups) and the press. The former learn quickly in open meetings when things are not going well for them and can seek to influence members along the way. The latter report selected details of conference proceedings, thus informing the public, providing the basis for editorials and other interpretive commentary, and encouraging greater participation in conference decisions.

The conference report

Once agreement has been reached, a report is prepared by committee staff (those from the committees represented) that summarizes the recommendations and explains the specific changes. No minority report is permitted, though conferees may register their disapproval by refusing to sign the report. If agreement cannot be reached on certain amendments, this fact is reported to each chamber, and the amendments in disagreement must then be considered separately and eventually reconciled by each chamber.

A conference report is privileged business in both the House and Senate, which means simply that it can be called up at any time. The report cannot be amended for the obvious reason that it represents accommodations reached between the two houses. Thus, the report is accepted or rejected as a whole, though a conference may be requested by either house to consider further adjustments.

The differences in structure and rules often cause problems in House-Senate relationships. A difference that has particularly troubled House members participating in conferences is that of nongermane Senate amendments. In effect, the Senate was able to include material in a bill that had never been considered by the relevant House committees. In 1972 the House changed its rules to permit separate debate (up to 40 minutes) on any Senate amendment that would be ruled nongermane if introduced into the House. A majority vote was required to approve the amendment, and if rejected the conference report would be returned to the Senate minus the rejected amendment. This change had the desired effect for House members of reducing the number of nongermane amendments in the Senate.[9]

What happens on the floor with regard to a conference report? Here is an actual case. On November 2, 1979, Senator Magnuson (D—Washington) interrupted debate on the Migration and Refugee Assistance Act to ask consideration of a conference report on legislation to restructure the Milwaukee Railroad. It apparently was urgent that the report be approved so as to forestall possible bankruptcy for the railroad. After the report was read the presiding officer said: "Without objection, the Senate will proceed to the consideration of the conference report."[10] Senators Magnuson and Packwood (R—Oregon) explained the urgency of the report, two other senators commented on the need for the legislation, and the presiding officer stated: "the question is on agreeing to the conference report. The conference report was agreed to."[11] The Senate then returned to its debate on refugee assistance. The whole action took only minutes.

---

[9] *Congressional Quarterly Weekly Report,* November 4, 1972, p. 2931.

[10] *Congressional Record* (daily edition), November 2, 1979, p. 15754.

[11] Ibid., p. 15755.

On that same day (November 2) the House was debating the Education Amendments of 1980. Mr. Staggers (D—West Virginia) first interrupted the debate to ask for House approval of a conference with the Senate on the Milwaukee Railroad Restructuring Act. As he explained:

> . . . we have reached informally an agreement with the Senate. We would confirm that agreement by signatures and bring it back to the House and file it and try to get it completed today because there is an emergency in the western states.[12]

Here is a case where agreement had already been reached, and a conference was requested to confirm it. The conferees were appointed principally to sign the report. Approximately two hours after requesting the conference Mr. Staggers again interrupted debate on the education amendments to present the conference report and request its immediate consideration. Several members spoke in favor of the report and it was approved as follows:

> **Mr. Staggers:** Mr. Speaker, I move the previous question on the conference report.
>
> (The previous question was ordered.)
>
> **The Speaker pro tempore:** The question is on the conference report.
>
> (The conference report was agreed to.)
>
> (A motion to reconsider was laid on the table.)[13]

No two congressional actions are ever exactly alike. Approval of this report came more quickly than for most major bills. And the appointment of conferees two hours before formal approval of the report is unusual, though not without precedent. There is very little that either house cannot do by unanimous consent. Note that in both houses it was in order to interrupt the proceedings because conference reports are privileged matter. In the House, however, the action required the cooperation of the members in not objecting since reports normally must be available to members for three days in advance of floor action.

Appropriations conferences

Conferences between the appropriations committees (actually the subcommittees) are typically annual events. Seldom may one expect the two groups to arrive at the same figures, and seldom is one house willing to accept the figures of the other without face-to-face bargaining. Stephen Horn describes the appropriation conference as "a continuing institution" (1970: 155).

---

[12] Ibid., p. H10187.
[13] Ibid., p. H10215.

> The conferees are usually old colleagues. The subcommittee chairmen have been bargaining and trying to persuade one another sometimes for a decade or more. While a conference is ad hoc, it is also in a very real sense a continuing institution. In the short run the issues may change; the participants seldom do. If a group of conferees is unsuccessful this year, there is always next year.

Since their subject matter is more stable than that for other committees, the appropriations conferences are more likely than other conferences to develop routines. As Richard F. Fenno, Jr., notes: "The House and Senate are normally in agreement as to how appropriations conferences should be convened, how they should be conducted, and how their results should be disposed of" (1966: 620). Of course, this agreement on routines results from shared perceptions and expectations regarding the purpose and function of a conference. Fenno again (1966: 624−25):

> The Appropriations conference committee is a viable institution in part because House and Senate members . . . share some basic expectations about what the conference should accomplish and what rules of the game should be observed. . . . House and Senate participants report the same basic perceptions. Both see the conference as a struggle which inevitably culminates in a negotiated settlement of some sort.

Agreeing on what to expect by way of procedure does not guarantee agreement on the specifics. In fact, the expectation of conflict may contribute to it. Fenno quotes a senator and a representative on their expectations (1966: 625):

> **Senator:** Its a knockdown drag out affair until you get agreement. It's a lot of fun if you like that sort of thing.
> **Representative:** It's psychology, being stubborn, being boisterous—even walking out if something is important.

Also contributing to conflict are the images that members of each house have of themselves and each other. In fact, these perceptions led to the 1962 stalemate over the location and leadership of conferences.

Floor approval of appropriation conference reports is often more complicated than that for other reports, in part because conferences may not always agree on all amendments. Amendments in disagreement are considered by the full chamber after approval of the report. Table 12−1 shows the sequence of action in each house for a conference report on a supplemental appropriations bill in 1979 (i.e., a bill providing additional appropriations beyond those originally allocated). Note that approval is sought first for the conference report as signed by a majority of managers for each house. Attention is then directed to those Senate amendments which were in disagreement. Of the 50 such amendments, only two were in actual disagreement. The other 48 were in so-called technical disagreement. This is simply the means by which any unauthorized appropriations or legislation (which is prohibited in appropriations measures) in a Senate amendment is voted on by the House, as provided for in House Rule XX. The House amended some of the Senate amendments in disagreement, thus requiring further affirmative action by the Senate so that the bill would pass both houses in the same form.

Senate action was swift, though senators were not pleased that the House refused to support one Senate housekeeping item. The report was subjected to almost no debate. As indicated in Table 12−1, Senator Magnuson moved its adoption, followed by requests that the Senate agree to the House amendments to the Senate amendments.

TABLE 12−1
Sequence of House and Senate floor action on Conference Report on 1979 Supplemental Appropriations

House action (July 17, 1979)

1. Jamie Whitten (D−Mississippi), chairman of House Committee on Appropriations, calls up report.
2. Whitten and Silvio Conte (R−Massachusetts), ranking Republican on Appropriations, recognized for 30 minutes each.
3. Whitten explains the report and presents a table comparing House, Senate, and conference actions (table takes up 20 pages of *Congressional Record*).
4. Whitten yields to other members for supportive speeches.
5. Conte explains the report, including the amendments in disagreement.
6. Conte and Whitten handle questions from the floor, sometimes yielding to other members for responses.
7. Whitten moves the previous question, which is ordered.
8. Speaker states the question and announces that "the ayes appeared to have it."
9. Robert Bauman (R−Maryland) objected to the vote "on the ground that a quorum is not present."
10. Absent members were notified and a vote was taken by electronic means. Result: yeas 284, nays 132, not voting 18. "So the conference report was agreed to."
11. The Speaker called on the clerk to designate the first amendment in disagreement.
12. Amendments in disagreement were considered in turn (a total of 50 amendments were in disagreement, of which 2 were in true disagreement, 48 in technical disagreement).
13. The House receded from its disagreement and concurred with 38 Senate amendments, receded from its disagreement and concurred with amended Senate amendments in 11 instances, and insisted on its disagreement to one Senate amendment.

TABLE 12 – 1 (*continued*)

Senate action (July 20, 1979)

1. Warren Magnuson (D—Washington), chairman of Senate Committee on Appropriations, requested immediate consideration of report.

2. The presiding officer, hearing no objections, announced the report as present business.

3. Magnuson briefly explained the report.

4. Milton Young (R—North Dakota), ranking Republican on Appropriations, announced support for the report.

5. Two other Senators made brief statements on the report.

6. Magnuson moved adoption.

7. The presiding officer announced that the motion was agreed to.

8. Magnuson asked unanimous consent that the Senate concur with House amendments to 10 Senate amendments. No objection.

9. Magnuson asked unanimous consent that the Senate concur with the House amendment to an additional Senate amendment. No objection.

10. Magnuson moved that the Senate recede from the one amendment to which the House disagreed. Agreed to.

SOURCE: Compiled by author from *Congressional Record* (daily edition), July 17, 1979, pp. H6014 – 54; July 20, 1979, pp. S10050 – 52.

Winning a conference

The final topic to consider in regard to House-Senate conferences is the matter of which body predominates. In his study of selected conferences for the period 1928 – 48, Gilbert Steiner found that the House delegations were more influential than those from the Senate (1950: 170 – 72). Fenno found just the opposite in studying appropriations conferences. While warning that winning in conferences does not suggest "dominance of the appropriations process as a whole," Fenno concluded that "the simplest answer to the question of who wins in conference appears to be: *the Senate*" (1966: 663, his emphasis). He found that of 331 conference decisions over a 15-year period, the Senate position was favored 56.5 percent of the time, the House position was favored 30.5 percent of the time, and the difference was split 13 percent of the time. The Senate position was particularly favored on appropriations for the Departments of Agriculture; Health, Education, and Welfare; Justice; and Interior. Stephen Horn found very much the same pattern in his study of appropriations conferences in 1965 (1970: 160 – 61).[14]

David J. Vogler has produced the most recent and comprehensive study of which house wins in conference. He coded 297 conferences

---

[14] John F. Manley's findings on revenue measures in conference were similar (1970: 272 – 79).

for five congresses (79th—89th) and confirmed the dominance of the Senate (winning 59 percent of the time compared to 32 percent for the House and 9 percent split). Vogler did find important differences among policy areas (ranging from 78 percent Senate victories for appropriations, 48 percent Senate victories for taxes and economic policy) among the committees, and between congresses. But the overall conclusion was clear—the Senate wins more than the House (Vogler, 1971: 55—64).

Why should this be so? The results are particularly puzzling given the conventional wisdom that House members are typically better prepared on specifics than senators. One would think, therefore, that House members could outmaneuver senators in conference. As Fenno points out: "By general agreement, the House conferees are better prepared, better organized, better informed, more single-minded in their interest, and employ a more belligerent bargaining style" (1966: 668). How is Senate dominance to be explained? Fenno believes that (1966: 669):

> It flows from the close structural identity of the Senate and the Senate Appropriations Committee. When the Senate conferees go to the conference room, they not only represent the Senate—they are the Senate. The position they defend will have been worked out with a maximum of participation by Senate members and will enjoy a maximum of support in that body.

Gerald S. Strom and Barry S. Rundquist are not persuaded by this argument. They doubt that judging which side wins in conferences is a good measure of dominance in the legislative process (a point Fenno also makes in regard to the whole appropriations process). Strom and Rundquist believe that the chamber which acts first on a bill probably has the most influence (1977: 450).

> We would expect that conferees from this chamber [the one that acts first] would have the most incentive to induce the other conferees to leave their prior gains intact by conceding to their conference requests. Thus for the victor [those acting first], conferences are a means toward ensuring what has been won elsewhere not an arena for new victories.

Since appropriations begin in the House, it is not surprising that the Senate wins—but they win on a turf already established by the House. Strom and Rundquist demonstrate that when the Senate acts first, the House wins in conference (the Senate won 72 percent of the time when the bill first passed the House; the House won 71 percent of the time when the bill first passed the Senate). Their conclusion is that the Senate wins not because of the identity between conferees and the chamber but "because it acts second" (1977: 452).

These findings are supported by a study by John Ferejohn in which he found the House to be quite successful in maintaining its projects in conferences and also realizing some success in preventing Senate projects. Often it was the Senate's effort to increase the budget that was at issue. Thus it is not exactly correct to state that the Senate wins a battle that may already be 90 percent over. Ferejohn states that (1975: 1042, 1045):

> House approval of a new project generally implies Senate approval but the converse is not the case . . . If one were to accept Fenno's and Vogler's results at face value, groups desiring federal expenditures would be well-advised to concentrate their efforts on the Senate Appropriations subcommittees. My findings indicate a different strategy may be preferable. If an interest group wants to add a project to a bill, it should concentrate on the House subcommittee since a project there will almost certainly survive the whole process.

These interesting studies put the conference in proper perspective. Important as these meetings are, they represent the culmination of a great deal of work by both houses. Conferences are ad hoc committees seeking to identify where agreement is possible. That they occur at the close of the process for major legislation tends to exaggerate their importance on occasion. Their work is vital, but one must be reminded that it is applied to legislation already well developed in the two houses. It is even likely that stories in the past about the all-powerful conference were somewhat embellished—no doubt for good practical political reasons. Power is often realized through misperceptions.

Joint committees

Conferences are joint House-Senate ad hoc committees created for the specific purpose of working out agreements on different versions of a bill on the same subject. Joint committees, on the other hand, are created by statutes or joint House-Senate resolutions and may carry over from one Congress to the next. Typically they do not have the authority to report bills—the Joint Committee on Atomic Energy was an exception. They have been created for several purposes: to manage a facility common to both houses (e.g., the Joint Committees on Printing and the Library), to investigate legislative organization and make recommendations for change (e.g., the Joint Committees on Budget Control and Congressional Operations), and to investigate major policy issues and make recommendations (e.g., the Joint Economic Committee and the Joint Committees on Defense Production, Internal Revenue Taxation, and Reduction of Federal Expenditures).

Several joint committees are no more than means by which the standing committees in each house can communicate on problems faced by each side. The Printing and Library Committees are made up of selected members from the House and Senate committees concerned with internal administration. The Internal Revenue Taxation Committee (now called the Taxation Committee) is the oldest joint committee, created in 1926. It offers important staff work for the two taxing committees (Senate Finance, House Ways and Means) and also provides a way for the leadership of those important standing committees to discuss common problems. The staff has been an extraordinary asset, according to John F. Manley, a principal student of congressional tax policy (1970: 310).

> In performing its tasks for the Ways and Means Committee and the Senate Finance Committee the staff is expected to follow certain norms, including objectivity, bipartisanship, and neutrality. . . . "Our job," according to Chief of Staff Laurence N. Woodworth, "is to see that members of Congress get the facts on both sides so they can make their own decisions."

Other important joint committees in recent years have been the Joint Committee on Atomic Energy (JCAE) and the Joint Economic Committee (JEC). Both were created in 1946—by the Atomic Energy Act and the Employment Act. The JCAE had authority to supervise the Atomic Energy Commission and could draft and report bills. It developed very impressive power but was abolished in 1977.[15] The JEC was created primarily to receive and study the annual economic report from the Council of Economic Advisers.[16]

Joint committees have not enjoyed great popularity on Capitol Hill. As George Goodwin, Jr., notes, problems associated with institutional rivalries and standing committee prerogatives prevent this type of cooperation (1970: 45).

> How large will the new committee be? If there is to be one vote per member . . . will the committee be even-numbered and therefore susceptible to tie votes? Should the committee meet on the Senate or on the House side of the Capitol? Shall the chairman be a representative or a senator? Would a single bicameral hearing tend to deprive certain groups of their prized access to Congress?

The matter of chairing joint committees has been resolved by simply rotating leadership between the houses with each session or each Congress. But the other problems, plus the simple pull of gravity toward each chamber, have resulted in limited effective use of this means of getting together. The JCAE is an interesting recent case study in this connection. As nuclear energy came to be more controversial and as the broader issue of energy came to dominate the congressional agenda, the JCAE was abolished in 1977 and its jurisdiction assumed by the regular standing committees of each house.

---

[15] Harold P. Green and Alan Rosenthal (1963) studied the JCAE at the height of its influence.

[16] The creation of the JEC is discussed in Bailey (1950).

TABLE 12–2
Joint committees, 89th – 96th Congresses

Congress	Number of joint committees and (subcommittees)		Committees added	Committees dropped
89th	8	(14)	—	—
90th	8	(15)	—	—
91st	7	(15)	—	Organization of Congress
92d	8	(15)	Congressional Operations	—
93d	9	(16)	Budget Control	—
94th	7	(14)	—	Budget Control, Reduction of Federal Expenditures
95th	4	(5)	—	Atomic Energy, Defense Production, Congressional Operations
96th	4	(5)	—	—

SOURCE: Compiled from various issues of the *Congressional Quarterly Weekly Report*.

Table 12 – 2 indicates that joint committees are actually declining in use. Only four remain: Economic, Library, Printing, and Taxation. The high point for joint committees was in the 93d Congress with nine committees and 16 subcommittees.

GETTING TOGETHER WITH THE PRESIDENT

The founding fathers definitely had a legislative role in mind for the president. As Stephen J. Wayne observes, however, the president's legislative "duties were designed to prod and check the Congress but not to usurp its powers" (1978: 3). The presidential-congressional policy connections as outlined in Article II include the power to make treaties and appointments "by and with the Advice and Consent of the Senate," fill vacancies when the Senate is in recess, give Congress "Information of the State of the Union," recommend "Measures as he shall judge necessary and expedient," convene one or both of the houses "on extraordinary Occasions," and adjourn them if they cannot agree on adjournment. These are rather variable contacts—some designed as congressional checks on the executive (as with the treaties and appointments), others to provide congressional input (the State of the Union and recommendation of legislation), and still others to guarantee that Congress will convene in emergencies and that it will leave town when its work is done.

The continuous contact between the two institutions is actually provided for in Article I, Section 7, Clause 2, which reads:

> Every Bill which shall have passed the House of Representatives and
> the Senate, shall, before it becomes a Law, be presented to the President
> of the United States; If he approves he shall sign it, but if not he shall
> return it, with his Objections to that House in which it shall have origi-
> nated, who shall enter the Objections at large on their Journal, and
> proceed to reconsider it.

It is this constitutional requirement that the president sign a bill into
law that makes him an active participant in the legislative process.
Louis Fisher reports that "one critic of the Constitution called [the
veto] 'a political error of the greatest magnitude, to allow the executive
power a negative, or in fact any kind of control over the proceedings of
the legislature'" (1972: 22). Had this power not been included it
seems unlikely that the president would have capitalized to the same
extent on his prerogatives to give "Information of the State of the
Union" and recommend legislation. In other words, it is fair to conclude that the president's influence on the front side of legislation is
enhanced by his authority to say yes or no at the final stage. Of course,
Congress may still have the last word, but it can do so only if two
thirds of the members of both houses are determined to do so. When
the president says he wants something, he must garner a majority of
those voting in both houses. When he doesn't want something, however, he only needs the support of one third plus one in only one
house.

The veto process

How does this process of bill signature actually work? Like all important stages in the lawmaking process it reflects the political context
within which an issue emerges and is acted on. Figure 12−1 displays
the steps that are followed after both houses have approved the same
bill. Enrollment occurs first. It is one of those crucial and exacting procedures which gets no public attention. The final bill must incorporate
every amendment as approved by the two houses. Scores, even hundreds, of changes may be involved. Even punctuation is critically important at this stage since misplaced commas, semicolons, or decimal
points may result in important changes in meaning. The enrolled bill
is then hand delivered to the White House and a signed receipt
obtained.

Presidential decisions on whether or not to sign a bill into law
depend on substantive and strategic considerations. The departments
or agencies effected by the bill, the Office of Management and Budget,
and the president's immediate advisers provide counsel to the president on such matters. Included among substantive or programmatic
concerns are the extent to which a bill satisfies the original presidential request, the feasibility or suitability of a program not requested, the

FIGURE 12–1
From a bill to a law after House and Senate approval

Congressional action

1. Papers to enrolling clerk of originating house.
2. Enrolled bill printed on parchment paper.
3. Enrolled bill certified by officer of originating house (secretary of the Senate or clerk of the House).
4. Bill examined by Committee on House Administration for accuracy.
5. Bill signed first by the Speaker in every case, then by the president of the Senate while each house is sitting.
6. Bill sent to the White House.

Presidential action

10 days remaining* (except Sundays)

Action	Result
1. President signs.	Law.
2. President does not sign.	Law after 10 days.
3. President returns with objections (vetoes).	Returned to originating house.

Fewer than 10 days remaining*

Action	Result
1. President signs.	Law.
2. President does not sign.	No law.

Returned to originating house →
- Congress does not act. → No law.
- Fails to get ⅔ vote in one house. → No law.
- Approved by ⅔ vote in both houses. → Law.

* Refers to the number of days before congressional adjournment, beginning with the day of delivery of the enrolled bill to the White House.
SOURCE: Compiled from material in Zinn (1979), and the U.S. Constitution.

relationship of the legislative action to existing law on the same or a related subject, and the constitutionality of the legislation.

The strategic considerations may be many and varied. First is the simple matter of timing. A bill passed early in the session may be vetoed because there is ample time within which to get it passed again in the form the president prefers. On the other hand, when a bill is absolutely essential for continuing a vital program, a veto late in the session may force congressional concessions. And a president in some cases may prefer having a bill to which he objects strongly on his desk with fewer than 10 days left in the session. The Constitution provides for the so-called pocket veto in these circumstances. Since Congress is not in session to receive his objections, he does not have to register them (though presidents often send a message anyway). The bill is killed without his having to do anything.

Other strategic considerations include an estimate by presidential advisers as to whether members of Congress are open to compromise or whether they are adamant and prepared to override the president's veto. Normally a president does not prefer to have his vetoes overridden, particularly if the action is taken by a Congress in which his party has a majority. Thus, careful evaluations are necessary to determine congressional mood (and most vetoes are sustained—see Table 12—3). Associated judgments are made about public attitudes—those of special publics or interest groups and those of the general public as reflected in polls and the media. If a president thinks a veto is popular outside the halls of Congress, it may be worth it to risk being overridden. More likely, however, is that the veto will be sustained under such circumstances. Throughout these considerations presidential advisers analyze the gains and losses attendant to the veto. While it is a powerful weapon, it is rather blunt—much more so than the scapel-like tool available to those governors who can item veto, that is, negate certain sections of a bill. The president must say either yes or no.

The potential for saying no is itself an impressive resource relied on more or less skillfully by all presidents. It is a particularly important source of influence for a president whose party is not in the majority in Congress. Such presidents, for example, Ford, Nixon, Eisenhower for three Congresses, Truman for one Congress, lack the potential for realizing majority support within their own party and thus find the threat of veto a useful weapon in their congressional relations. Stephen J. Wayne explains in describing the Nixon and Ford administrations (1978: 159):

> A potential veto constituted an important part of both administrations' legislative strategy. Liaison aides used the threat of a presidential veto to influence the Democratic majority to tailor its legislative proposals so that they would be acceptable to the president. Timmons [legisla-

tive aide for Nixon and Ford] estimated that there were 20 to 30 measures that were "cleaned up sufficiently" due to the threat of a veto. Since it made little sense to push for legislation that the president might veto, the congressional staff tried to get veto signals as early as possible. In the domestic area, OMB [the Office of Management and Budget], in conjunction with the Domestic Council, gave the signs.

The threat of veto is by no means limited to presidents without congressional majorities, however. Franklin D. Roosevelt was a master of this technique. He used it to provide Congress with continuous signals as to his legislative interests.

> Of great importance to Roosevelt, perhaps greater than the veto itself, was his threat to use it unless Congress sent him the bills he could approve. He constantly gave party leaders his views on certain pending legislation, letting them know unequivocally whether he would approve or veto (Jackson, 1967: 205).

The point is that some presidents use every available tactic to get what they want from Congress. Minority party presidents are forced into that position by virtue of limited party support in Congress. But majority party presidents too may be aggressive in pursuing a particular program.

Table 12−3 provides an historical survey of presidential vetoes since 1865. The 16 presidents before 1865 used the veto 58 times. Over half of these were exercised by three presidents—Jackson, Tyler, and Pierce. Seven presidents before 1865 vetoed no bills at all. According to Carlton Jackson, John Tyler was the most effective president in using the veto during this early period. He "carried the veto to its fullest extent in the period before the Civil War" (Jackson, 1967: 85).

Andrew Johnson's problems with Congress are well known and reflected in his veto record. Congress regularly overrode the vetoes (the highest percentage of overrides in history). Beginning with the Grant administration some presidents began to veto private pension and relief bills. Cleveland in particular gained a reputation for turning back such legislation as unnecessary or fraudulent, and he holds the all-time record for the average annual number of vetoes.

The modern era of presidential-congressional relations begins with the second Roosevelt (though it should be noted that Woodrow Wilson also evaluated the work of Congress against a standard of his own programmatic interests). Roosevelt holds the record for the most vetoes, though his annual average is below that of Cleveland. Approximately half of Roosevelt's vetoes were of private bills, but that still leaves over 300 vetoes of public bills. It is fair to say that with Roosevelt the veto became an important means by which the president sought to influence the legislative process. Since Roosevelt the most active use

TABLE 12−3
Presidential vetoes, 1965−1977

President	Years in office	Bills vetoed	Average per year	Direct vetoes	Pocket vetoes	Vetoes over-ridden	Percent over-ridden*
A. Johnson	3.88	28	7.2	21	7	15	71.4
Grant	8.0	92	11.5	44	48	4	9.1
Hayes	4.0	13	3.3	12	1	1	8.3
Garfield	.54	0	0	0	0	0	—
Arthur	3.46	12	3.5	4	8	1	25.0
Cleveland	4.0	414	103.5	304	110	2	.7
Harrison	4.0	44	11.0	19	25	1	5.3
Cleveland	4.0	170	42.5	42	128	5	11.9
(Cleveland							
totals)	8.0	584	73.0	346	238	7	2.0
McKinley	4.54	42	9.3	6	36	0	—
T. Roosevelt	7.46	82	11.0	42	40	1	2.4
Taft	4.0	39	9.8	30	9	1	3.3
Wilson	8.0	44	5.5	33	11	6	18.2
Harding	2.42	6	2.5	5	1	0	—
Coolidge	5.58	50	9.0	20	30	4	20.0
Hoover	4.0	37	9.3	21	16	3	14.3
F. Roosevelt	12.08	631	52.2	371	260	9	2.4
Truman†	7.77	250	32.2	180	70	12	6.7
Eisenhower	8.0	201	25.1	83	118	3	3.6
Kennedy	2.83	25	8.8	14	11	0	—
L. Johnson	5.17	30	5.8	16	14	0	—
Nixon	5.58	43	7.7	24	16‡	5	20.8
Ford	2.42	66	27.3	45	16	12	26.7
Carter ('77 − '78)	2.0	19	9.5	6	13	0	—

* Percent of direct vetoes only since pocket vetoes cannot be overridden.
† The combined Roosevelt−Truman years do not add up to a multiple of four years due to the change in the inauguration date in Roosevelt's first term (see 20th Amendment to the Constitution). Roosevelt's first term was 46½ months long (March 4, 1933 to January 20, 1937).
‡ Includes one pocket veto later declared to be invalid in the federal courts since it was rendered during a congressional recess, not an adjournment.
SOURCE: Compiled from data in Congressional Quarterly, *Guide to the Congress of the United States* (Washington, D.C.: Congressional Quarterly, Inc., 1971), p. 583, and *Congressional Quarterly Weekly Report*, November 18, 1978, p. 3326.

has come in split-party administrations—Truman, Eisenhower, Nixon, and Ford.

Veto messages may be very short and direct or they may be lengthy and elaborately argued. For example, on November 2, 1978, President Carter pocket vetoed a bill authorizing the establishment of the Legionville National Historic Site in Pennsylvania. In a brief message, the president pointed out that the site does not meet the standards set by the Department of the Interior. "Further, the site has been altered by such modern intrusions as a railroad and an interstate highway."[17]

---

[17] *Congressional Quarterly Weekly Report*, November 18, 1978, p. 3327.

However, when he vetoed the Energy and Water Development Appropriations bill on October 5, 1978, President Carter offered a detailed justification. After all, in refusing to sign the bill he was eliminating many so-called pork-barrel projects for the ensuing fiscal year. He was particularly critical of the water projects.

> I respect the hard work and good intentions of the members of Congress who have prepared this legislation. . . . But this bill . . . contains provisions for excessive, wasteful water projects and ill-advised limitations on efficient program management; these require that I disapprove HR 12928 in its present form.[18]

The president noted that several sections of the bill were satisfactory but that "the American people have the right to expect that their government will pursue . . . goals effectively, efficiently and with the budgetary discipline and careful planning essential to reduce inflation and continue economic growth."[19] He urged Congress to revise the bill.

No two veto messages are exactly alike but this one on water projects is typical of what a president tries to accomplish on an important piece of legislation. In this case President Carter amplified the issues by stressing inflation and government waste. Yet sensitive to the possibility of being overridden on such an important bill for individual members, he invited Congress to try again. Not surprisingly, supporters of the measure in the House (as the originating chamber) acted quickly to override the veto. The issue was brought before the House on the same day that the veto message was issued. The House leadership on both sides of the aisle favored overriding. But the White House, including the president, engaged in extensive lobbying among the members with good results. The final vote to override the veto was 223 to 190, far short of the required two-thirds majority. Since two-thirds approval of both houses is required to override, the Senate did not act.[20]

The signature

The veto often has important political implications, as has been demonstrated above. The approval of a bill may also involve high politics. In the first place the president has the option of permitting a bill to become law without his signature (see Figure 12 − 1). He may do this when he disapproves of a part of the bill but estimates that Congress will override his veto or when he judges that the bill is essential for the

---

[18] *Congressional Quarterly Weekly Report*, October 14, 1978, p. 2973.

[19] Ibid., p. 2974.

[20] Summarized from a description in *Congressional Quarterly Weekly Report*, October 7, 1978, p. 2721.

continuance of a vital government program. By permitting the bill to become law after 10 days he registers his disapproval (he may even issue a statement to that effect), and he sets up a situation in which he can blame Congress later if his analysis of weaknesses proves to be correct.

Finally there is the signature itself. The act may be perfunctory in the case of many lesser bills. Or the president may capitalize on it as a photo opportunity. Members of Congress who have been active in the development of the bill are invited to the Oval Office, along with interested and involved others, for the signing ceremony. The president may then sign the bill with several pens and present them to many of those assembled around his desk.

When a bill becomes a law in any one of the methods noted here — presidential signature, override of a veto, or without a presidential signature after 10 days—it receives a Public Law number (or Private Law number) in the order in which it was finally approved by each Congress. In the future the law will be referred to by this number, and the Congress in which it passed (e.g., PL 96 − 70 — the 70th law approved in the 96th Congress). The law in its original form (i.e., the enrolled bill) is then forwarded to the General Services Administration for permanent deposit as a document in the National Archives.

The laws are available to the public in three forms (Zinn, 1979: chapter 16):

1. *Slip Laws.* Each law is published separately for immediate availability in the documents room of both houses, or by subscription or purchase from the superintendent of documents. The Office of the Federal Register, General Services Administration, prepares the slip laws, provides marginal citations to laws mentioned in the text, and includes historical information on the passage of the bill.
2. *Statutes at Large.* A bound volume of laws is prepared by the General Services Administration for each session of Congress — called the Statutes at Large. The laws are included in chronological order, along with helpful reference material regarding the effect of the new statutes on earlier laws and the legislative history of each statute.
3. *United States Code.* This document "contains a consolidation and codification of the general and permanent laws . . . arranged according to subject matter (Zinn, 1979:   37). The current status of laws is outlined (with amendments). Not all the language from the amendments is repeated since it is available in the Statutes at Large. The code is prepared by the House Committee on the Judiciary. New editions are prepared every six years, with cumulative supplements published after each session of Congress.

SUMMARY

Nelson W. Polsby observes that (1976: 190 — 91):

> In the light of our constitutional history . . . conflict between the two branches [Congress and the presidency] should come as no surprise. Indeed, the system was designed so that different branches would be captured by different interests and so that they would have to come to terms with one another peaceably in order to operate the system at all. . . . if the Constitution can be said to grant legitimacy to anything, surely it legitimizes conflict between Congress and the president.

Polsby's observations can be applied as well to the differences between the two branches of Congress. The House and Senate were also designed to be captured by different interests. What the Constitution has divided, it also demands be united. Formal and informal associations exist to connect the chambers with each other and with the president. I have discussed only the most formal relationships in this chapter— the conference, joint committees, the legislative powers of the president (principally the veto). I turn next to a fuller treatment of the congressional role in the on-going cross-institutional policy process.

13 Congress and the policy process: Program development

The congressman is involved in a complex web of relationships due to his part in the ongoing drama of policymaking. He is involved in each of the three acts of this play: policy formulation, policy enactment, and policy implementation. . . .

Instead of viewing the function of Congress as that which is suggested by the title lawmaker, it might be more useful to think of Congress as one of the major intersections of a policy communications network that extends across most policy domains (Clausen, 1973: 1, 2).

To this point, Congress has been described as a political institution with an identifiable and growing population, an elaborate organization in each house, and a complex set of lawmaking processes. The remaining chapters will examine Congress in the context of the larger national policy process. As Aage R. Clausen observes in the quotation above, Congress is a crucial switchboard through which most policy message must flow. As the system's principal legitimizer, Congress is a stage on which one may witness all the principal actors participating in issue-related dramas. Thus one is fully justified in concentrating on the structure and management of the approval processes on Capitol Hill.

It is also useful to view the Congress through a wide-angle lens, however. As Clausen suggests, Congress is "one of the major intersections of a policy communications network." What if we were to look at Congress from the perspective of a network of persons active in developing and implementing a government program? That is precisely the approach taken in these final chapters. Having described the institutional structure and characteristics of Congress, I now ask you to examine it from a different angle. I suggest that you adopt an issue- or policy-oriented perspective by which *Congress is seen as a population for prospective and ongoing policy networks.* What happens by this approach is that one simply pulls back from the absorbing details of the legislative process and concentrates on the role of the legislature in the larger policy process. The focus is on legislator participation in issue analysis, and program development, approval, implementation, and evaluation. There is no reason to believe that legislators restrict themselves to one of these activities or that they act the same way for every issue. What David C. Kozak demonstrates for voting is applicable to other forms of congressional behavior too.

> . . . Congressmen do not make up their minds in a set way or in the same fashion on each and every floor vote. Their decision behavior is highly variable. Who congressmen hear from, where they get their information, and how and when they make a decision vary from vote to vote and according to issue characteristics. These variations are patterned in that differences in legislative behavior are associated with different kinds of votes. How members behave and reach decisions clearly depends on the type of vote at hand (Kozak, 1979: 363).

The institution of Congress—that elaborate set of House and Senate organizations and processes described in earlier chapters—has awesome powers of approval when compared with the rest of the world's legislatures. This ultimate authority to say yes or no to proposed legislation naturally encourages other participants in the policy process, including presidents, to include members of Congress in their activities. It is just as logical for Congress, in turn, to accommodate these requests in its organization—in staffing, in its committees and subcommittees, in creating research agencies (CBO, OTA, CRS), in allocating resources. In periods of reduced presidential authority (e.g., when the president's party does not have a majority in Congress or during the post-Watergate era) congressional participation in the full range of policy activities may even be greater than normal. One may also expect expansion of congressional policy participation with the expansion in the number and size of government programs. The post-World War II period has witnessed both developments. Between 1946 and 1980 there was split-party control between Congress and the White House nearly 50 percent of the time (16 of 34 years) compared to just 13 percent of the time between 1900 and 1946 (6 of 46 years). And during the 1960s, in particular, the nation experienced virtually an exponential growth in federal programs.

This chapter will concentrate on the nature of the policy process, the idea of policy networks, and variable House and Senate involvement in program development. In Chapter 13 attention will be directed to House and Senate involvement in program execution, the expansion and greater articulation of the congressional population in recent decades, and the tendency for Congress to want to dominate the policy process.

THE POLICY PROCESS

For the time being, I suggest that you ignore national political institutions—Congress, the presidency, the bureaucracy—and concentrate on those activities normally or logically associated with solving a problem. At the most simplified level these activities involve identifying and defining the problem, analyzing the options for solving it, selecting the best option, and applying the solution. That process may occur within a matter of seconds when the problem is immediate, the number of persons affected is small, and the resources are available. For example, suppose you are the only person to observe a young child struggling to stay afloat in a swimming pool. If you can swim (resource is available), you no doubt will jump into the pool and lend assistance. The situation gets more complicated if you can't swim and more complicated yet if more than one child is struggling to stay afloat.

Public policy issues typically affect many persons over an extended period of time and require vast resources for their resolution. The activities associated with governmental action on such issues are many and varied, but they can be generally classified into two broad categories: those directed to program development and those directed to program execution. The program development activities involve getting the problem to government and acting on it there. The program execution activities involve government application of resources to the problem and analysis of effects. Table 13−1 summarizes the many activities from the initial perception that a problem exists to its resolution or change. This list more or less represents an inventory of possible activities. It is not a model of required sequential movement— either in the sense that one activity flows directly to the next as a sort of relay race or that there is a preconceived degree of fulfillment demanded for each activity. Rather the various steps are proposed as logically following one from the other. They suggest what to look for in studying what happens in government in regard to such public prob-

TABLE 13 – 1
The policy process

Phase		Activities		Initial product
	Problem	Perception	⟶	Problem
		Definition		
	to	Aggregation/		
		Organization	⟶	Demand
	government	Representation		
		Agenda setting	⟶	Priorities
		Formulation		
		Research		
		Analysis	⟶	Proposal
		Selection		
	Action	Legitimation		
		Identification		
	in	of interests		
		Communication	⟶	Program
	government	Bargaining		
		Compromise		
		Appropriation		
		Formulation	⟶	Budget
		Legitimation		
	Government	Implementation		Structure
		Organization		Rules
	to	Interpretation	⟶	Service, payment,
	problem	Application		controls, etc.
	Program	Evaluation		Support, adjustment,
		Specification		cancellation, etc.
	to	Measurement	⟶	
		Analysis		
	government	Recommendation		
	Problem	Resolution		Relative solution,
	Resolution or change	Termination	⟶	social change

Program development activities (bracketing the upper phases)
Program execution activities (bracketing the lower phases)

SOURCE: Adapted from similar table in Jones (1977: 230 – 31).

lems as unemployment, poor housing for low-income groups, labor management relations, steel imports, etc.

Notice that I have identified a product from each of the various activities. Again these products follow logically—from a problem to a demand to do something, from the demand to a set of priorities among demands, from priorities to a proposal, etc. But I am not suggesting the fulfillment of special criteria nor a systematic method for each product. For example, in some cases the problem may be very well specified, perhaps because of scientific research and analysis. In other instances it may be poorly specified, possibly because there is no time or resources for systematic investigation. As with the policy activities the list of products is offered primarily as a guide.

At this point I ask you to consider political institutions once again—specifically those provided for in the Constitution. It seems apparent that the founding fathers did associate certain policy activities with the three branches. Table 13—2 identifies several constitutional provisions as explicitly or implicitly assigning policy functions

TABLE 13—2
The distribution of policy activities in the U.S. Constitution

Policy activity	Constitutional provision	Distributed to	Comment
Definition	Art. II, Sec. 2, 3 (require opinions, state of the union)	President	Implicit
Representation	Art. I., Sec. 2, 3 (election of House, Senate)	Congress	Direct
	Art. II, Sec. 1 (election of president)	President	Indirect
Agenda setting	Art. II, Sec. 3 (state of the union, recommend measures)	President	Explicit
Formulation	Art. I, Sec. 8 (congressional powers)	Congress	Implicit
Legitimation	Art. I, Sec. 7, 8 (bill to law process, congressional powers)	Congress, President	Explicit
	Art. II, Sec. 2 (treaties, appointments)	Congress, President	Explicit
Appropriation	Art. I, Sec. 8, 9 (congressional powers)	Congress	Explicit
Implementation	Art. II, Sec. 1, 3 (presidential power)	President	Explicit
	Art. III, Sec. 2; Art. VI (judicial power)	Courts	Implicit
Evaluation	Art. I, Sec. 9 (accounting of public money)	Congress	Explicit
	Art. II, Sec. 3 (state of the union)	President	Implicit
	Art. VI (supreme law of the land)	Courts	Implicit

SOURCE: Compiled by author.

to one or more of the branches. The president's powers to "require the Opinion, in writing, of the principal Officer in each of the executive Departments" and to "give to the Congress Information of the State of the Union, and recommend to their Consideration such Measures as he shall judge necessary and expedient" are what we might call the front-end activities. They explicitly or implicitly assign to the president the tasks of defining problems, setting priorities, and formulating proposals to cope with public problems. Congress, the House of Representatives in particular, is directly assigned the representative function. However, since the Constitution more explicitly directed the president to set priorities and formulate measures, one can assume that congressional representation was intended to be reactive to presidential initiative. That certainly is the way it has developed.

Congress is very explicitly given the final say in regard to legislation, including appropriations. The president has a role to play, but Congress can still have its way (unless it adjourns within 10 days of having presented a bill to the president—Sundays excepted). And the Constitution is equally explicit in directing the president to "take Care that the Laws be faithfully executed." The role of the courts in implementation is less explicit, following from their jurisdiction in certain cases in law.

Finally the Constitution directs Congress to publish "a regular Statement and Account of the Receipts and Expenditures of all public Money", a rather explicit command to evaluate how the government spends money. Presidential and judicial evaluation activities follow from the president's power to provide information on the State of the Union and the command that "Judges in every State shall be bound" by "the supreme Law of the Land."

Thus the Constitution does offer a policy process model, as indicated in Figure 13—1. It is interesting that while one can legitimately

FIGURE 13—1

Policy process model suggested by the Constitution

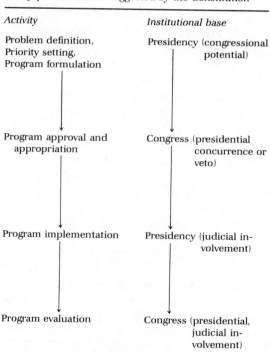

Activity	Institutional base
Problem definition, Priority setting, Program formulation	Presidency (congressional potential)
Program approval and appropriation	Congress (presidential concurrence or veto)
Program implementation	Presidency (judicial involvement)
Program evaluation	Congress (presidential, judicial involvement)

SOURCE: Compiled by author.

infer an institutional base for the various activities, still the Constitution explicitly or implicitly provided for involvement by other branches. There is, in short, good constitutional basis for the kind of cross-institutional policy process that has emerged through time. Separation of powers, with checks and balances, is best interpreted as *separated institutions sharing power.*

It is this cross-institutional participation in various policy activities that is of particular interest to us here. Members of Congress are not now, nor have they ever have been, willing to accept exclusive presidential involvement in policy initiation. In their analysis of congressional-bureaucratic relationships, Ripley and Franklin cite the following major issues in which Congress was responsible for initiation: medicare, social security disability insurance, pension reform, the 18-year-old vote, political campaign reform, air pollution, reduced role in the Vietnam War, control of chemical additives in foods, creation of a consumer protection agency, automobile safety standards, food programs for the poor, increases in the minimum wage (Ripley and Franklin, 1980:   218).

But it is not whole institutions doing the unexpected in the policy process that we are searching for here. Nor is it even likely that Congress as such was responsible for initiation of the legislation cited above by Ripley and Franklin. Much more probable is that *selected* members and staff were moved to define problems and design proposals to solve those problems. For whatever reason, they were drawn into a network of decision makers on these issues. They may even have formed the core of the policy actors in program development. More about that later. It is enough at this point to suggest that legislators may get involved in various policy activities, often depending on the issue at hand. This fact encourages one to trace issue and program development, alert to those points at which legislators are active participants. It is this more issue- or policy-oriented perspective on Congress that is adopted in this section of the book.

POLICY NETWORKS

Roger H. Davidson remarks that (in Welch and Peters, 1977:   30):

> Nothing is more natural than for interested individuals or groups to cluster about those government agencies whose decisions affect them directly. With the rise of the welfare state and its attendant philosophy of positive government, these relationships were formalized and invested with theoretical underpinnings of "interest group liberalism."

When a government program is put into effect, those groups effected, either positively or negatively, can be expected to pay close attention to further government action. Many times these clienteles will have been associated with the origination of the program. Thus one expects to find organizations associated with and supportive of the following programs: labor with the minimum wage, farmers with commodity support programs, hospital administrators with hospital construction support, oil producers with depletion allowances, etc. It also follows that these private organizations and the government agencies will be associated with members of Congress and their staff, again because of the power of that institution to approve program expansion, contraction, or abolition.

Various labels have been attached to what Davidson refers to as "these ingrown arrangements in various policy fields" (Welch and Peters, eds., 1977: 30). J. Leiper Freeman referred to policy subsystems (1955), Douglass Cater spoke of subgovernments (1964), Dorothy B. James observed cozy little triangles (1974), and Ernest S. Griffith noted that: "one cannot live in Washington for long without being conscious that it has *whirlpools* or centers of activity focusing on particular problems" (1939: 182). The precise label is not important except as a convenience of expression. What is important is the frequent observation that the politics of making policy is characterized by cross-institutional communication within specific policy or issue areas.

Given the incredible variety and complexity of issues, it is quite natural to wonder if these interactions among groups, bureaus, and committees might not be considerably more varied than is implied by any one of the labels above. In introducing still another label, Hugh Heclo finds that "the *iron triangle* is not so much wrong as it is disastrously incomplete." He summarizes the concept as follows (in King, 1978: 102):

> The notion of iron triangles and subgovernments presumes small circles of participants who have succeeded in becoming largely autonomous. . . . Iron triangles and subgovernments suggest a stable set of participants coalesced to control fairly narrow public programs which are in the direct economic interest of each party to the alliance.

Heclo proposes that other types of networks also exist—those comprising a larger number of participants that are much more porous than the iron triangles. He refers to issue networks that are the reverse image of the autonomous and well-bounded iron triangles (in King, 1978: 102).

> Issue networks . . . comprise a large number of participants with quite variable degrees of mutual commitment or of dependence on others in their environment. . . . Participants move in and out of the networks constantly. Rather than groups united in dominance over a program, no one, as far as one can tell, is in control of the policies and issues.

Thus the search for patterns of communication and contact in regard to policy issues may turn up a small and tightly organized coterie of persons drawn from decision makers and implementors, as well as from the groups for whom the program has been developed—the *cozy little triangle.* Or it may produce a more open community of actors, sometimes larger, sometimes smaller, with less direct commitment to the program being considered. I refer to these networks as *sloppy large hexagons*. There are innumerable examples of the triangle. Examples of the issue network include many social welfare programs or foreign policy issues where participation may expand merely because the program has become a public issue. Legislators, political executives, a wide variety of interest groups, policy analysts, and many other individuals and public officials feel quite free to participate in the development and implementation of welfare programs. These same persons, on the other hand, may be very reluctant to involve themselves in the development and implementation of a farm subsidy or labor-management relations program.

Emmette S. Redford has brought some order to this whole matter of policy relationships by identifying micropolitics, subsystem or intermediary politics, and macropolitics. In essence he distinguishes among issues and the means available for treating those issues. First are the relatively narrow, one-on-one requests that are made of government officials. More often than not these requests do not "engage the response of effective countervailing interests" (Redford, 1969: 84). The request may come from an individual, a company, or a community (perhaps through a member of Congress) to a government agent who has the authority to grant it. Redford points out that rules, standards, or administrative procedures, impartially and impersonally applied, may be the best method or system for handling these minor issues (1969: 85–88). He also observes that any such effort to establish routines to handle such matters may be threatened by political connections—including those with members of Congress (1969: 91). Perhaps we might label these *cozy little connections*. Earlier we discussed case work in congressional offices (to include work on district projects). Much of this work is micropolitical and frequently is a consequence either of perceived inequities in existing rules or administrative processes, or of a determination to gain a favor not likely to be granted by those rules and processes. Members and their staffs are actively drawn into *implementation* in these cases.

Redford's discussion of subsystem or intermediary politics does not differ significantly from that of others mentioned above. This is the politics of the cozy little triangles, often with administrative, congressional, and industrial corners. He does, however, offer several interesting propositions in regard to this type of issue politics (Redford, 1969: 102–5):

> First, subsystems provide stability for existing equilibriums among interests.
>
> Second, subsystems provide continuous access and superior opportunities for influence to high-quantity, aggregated interests.

Third, subsystems provide some access and representation to interests that are not dominant.

Fourth, substantial changes in the balances among interests served by subsystems can be expected to occur only through macropolitical intervention that modifies the rules and roles operating in the systems.

These propositions suggest that the policy triangles do perform important functions within the political system. An implicit advantage from those cited by Redford is that they prevent an overloading of the macropolitical system.

"The distinguishing factor," for macropolitics "is the breadth of involvement" (Redford, 1969: 107). The issues of very broad significance are treated at this level. They may burst forth as new issues, or more commonly, they "are forced upward out of subsystems." David C. Kozak refers to these as "hot issues" (1979: chapter 6). These issues typically involve the president and congressional party leaders at the national level. They are the bases of the sloppy large hexagons referred to earlier. Most if not all members of Congress are expected to have opinions on such issues. Many if not most members will participate in program development and approval activities. A large number of members are also attentive to how programs designed to treat these issues are implemented.

The three types of policy networks identified here are summarized in Table 13−3 along with examples of congressional involvement in each. The cozy little connection is restricted to contacts between those who want a favor and those with authority to grant it. Sometimes these contacts are made to correct, or gain an exception to, existing programs. Many times they are no more than an effort to gain an advantage. The cozy little triangle also is characterized by limited participation and access, but entry is possible if one can demonstrate definite interest or expertise (e.g., a member of Congress with a constituency or with professional background in the issue at hand). The principal function of the triangle is to stabilize policy—to establish predictable outcomes, to reduce surprise. Finally, the sloppy large hexagon describes those interactions on highly visible, public issues for which there is considerable demand that large numbers of public figures be involved. Access is virtually unrestricted because of the scope of the issue. In fact, most members of Congress cannot afford to ignore the issue. I cite gas rationing as an example. Widespread constituency interest in such a program insures that all members will pay attention to this issue and prepare a response to any proposal.

In addition to the many variations in the patterns of communication among participants in the development and implementation of programs, it is reasonable to expect changes in these patterns over time. Thus circumstances may develop to expand participation and to

TABLE 13–3
Characteristics of policy networks

Type of network	Characteristics			Example of congressional involvement
	Number of participants	Access	Functions	
1. Cozy little connection (micropolitics)	Very few (one-on-one)	Restricted (on demand)	Provide favors	Casework, projects
2. Cozy little triangle (intermediary politics)	Few (legislators, administrators, clientele)	Less restricted (interest/expertise)	Stabilize policy	House Subcommittee on Tobacco on price stabilization
3. Sloppy large hexagon (macropolitics)	Many (legislators, administrators, leaders, clientele, publics)	Unrestricted (demand involvement)	Acknowledge issue, initiate action	Floor consideration of gas rationing plan

SOURCE: Compiled by author.

change the configuration of interaction. A good example can be found in the rather dramatic expansion of several energy issues as a consequence of the Arab oil embargo in 1973 and various nuclear power plant accidents in the 1970s (most notably at Three Mile Island in Pennsylvania).

> The *cozy little triangles* which had come to characterize the development of energy policies had become *sloppy large hexagons.* Demands by environmentalist and public interest groups to participate in decision making, involvement by leadership at the highest levels in response to crisis, and the international aspects of recent energy problems have all dramatically expanded the energy policy population. . . . the expansion is up, out, and over—*up* in public and private institutional hierarchies (e.g., the involvement of presidents of companies and countries, rather than just low-level bureaucrats, and of congressional party leaders rather than just subcommittees); *out* to groups that declared an interest in energy policies . . . , and *over* to decision-making processes in other nations or groups of nations (Jones in Hollander, 1979:   105).

The change in participation from the triangle to the hexagon is not the only possible shift. In his classic work, *The Governmental Process,* David B. Truman talks about "converting the controversial into the routine" (1951:   444).

> What the administrator is forced to seek is a means of converting the controversial into the routine. This conversion may be largely achieved . . . by the legislative declaration. The administrator then inherits an adjustment among conflicting interests, a mandate, within the terms of which he must operate as long as the respective forces retain the relationships arrived at in the legislative stage. No question arises concerning what groups shall enjoy what measures of access to the administrative agency.

In our terms, Truman has identified movement from macropolitics characterized by the sloppy large hexagon to intermediary politics characterized by the cozy little triangle. Surely it is the wish of many interests to convert the controversial into the routine, particularly if the routine favors them. The point is that highly visible, controversial, or hot issues eventually may be submerged into the routine operations of government or may be supplanted by other, more controversial issues. And it is also possible that what begins as a macro or intermediary political issue remains so. Here are some examples for each case:

1. From intermediary politics to macropolitics (triangle to hexagon): many policy issues associated with petroleum following the Arab oil embargo, nuclear power following Three Mile Island.

2. From macropolitics to intermediary politics (hexagon to triangle): medicare for the aged, cigarette labeling, regulating automobile safety, federal aid to education.
3. Begins as intermediary politics and stays there: countless examples—research, training, highway construction, agriculture price supports.
4. Begins as macropolitics and stays there: the war on poverty as a classic example, but many other welfare-related programs also classify as do many foreign policy issues.

The micropolitical issues may also experience change over time. Favoritism itself may become an intermediary or macropolitical issue. President Carter regarded the many water projects in the west as a result of cozy little connections. His effort to reduce these projects created a significantly larger issue among members of Congress—even affecting support for other programs. These one-on-one contacts between individuals, groups, or industries also may be to correct inequities of macro or intermediary political decisions. Or they may be the means by which such decisions are made effective. That is, the broader policy may be one of so-called distributive politics whereby favors of various kinds (public works, contracts, subsidies) are distributed among those who seek them.

To summarize, those who study policy issues rather than institutional units (like a congressional committee or bureaucratic agency) have found it convenient to rely on a concept of communication among a cluster of persons associated with different formal groups. But the pattern of communication and the number of participants may vary across issues and over time. Three ideas are particularly useful to us, then, in studying Congress as a population drawn into policy networks:

1. That the members and their staffs (personal and committee) may be involved, over time, in a wide range of policy activities on an issue, in association with bureaucrats, interest group representatives, and consultants.
2. That these associations may be quite stable in regard to certain narrow issues and quite volatile in regard to other broad issues.
3. That these associations may change gradually or abruptly over time.

Finally, the particular patterns cited here (the connections, triangles, and hexagons) are prototypes only. They do give us something to look for in studying congressional participation in the policy process. But they by no means exhaust the possibilities for cross-institutional and public-private interaction on policy issues. Thus for example, we may expect to find considerable variation in goals and personnel among the connections, triangles, and hexagons, with the policy issue itself often explaining much of the difference.

CONGRESS AND PROGRAM DEVELOPMENT ACTIVITIES

We turn now to consider congressional involvement in program development activities—those associated with getting problems to government (perception, definition, aggregation, representation, and agenda setting) and with acting on them once there (formulation, legitimation, and appropriation)—see Table 13 — 1. Bear in mind that the focus in this section is on the *activities* not on the *institution*. That is, we are not solely trying to explain how, for example, Congress establishes means for defining problems or setting an agenda but rather how the actions of members and staff contribute to achieving these functions for a particular issue. It may well be, of course, that Congress will be the center of such activity for certain issues (see below), but we may not discover that fact unless attention is directed more broadly to the activity rather than to the institution.

Ripley and Franklin observe different relationships among public and private groups for different types of policy. They identify five groups of participants (the president and centralized bureaucracy, the bureaus, Congress, the subcommittees, and the private sector) and postulate that persons from these groups may be drawn into program development for different issues. They then propose six types of issues or policies, three each in the domestic and foreign/defense areas (Ripley and Franklin, 1980: 20 — 28, 212 — 18).[1]

1. Domestic
    a. Distributive policy: provides subsidies, grants, or benefits— low visibility, classic pork barrel politics.
    b. Regulatory policy: seeks to maintain competition (antitrust, licensing) or protect the public (environmental standards, consumer protection)—visible at first, may accommodate the regulated industry.
    c. Redistributive policy: transfers wealth from one sector or class to another, as with many welfare programs—high visibility, often ideological.
2. Foreign and Defense
    a. Structural policy: associated with military personnel and material—low visibility, often distributes benefits among congressional districts (e.g., military bases).

---

[1] Ripley and Franklin rely on categories borrowed from Theodore J. Lowi and Samuel P. Huntington.

    b. Strategic policy: implements "the basic military and foreign policy stance of the United States toward other nations"— visibility varies, normally involvement at high levels.

    c. Crisis policy: deals with immediate, large-scale, unforeseen issue—normally high visibility, typically presidency-centered.

Ripley and Franklin identify patterns of relationships for each of these types of policy. They assert that subsystem politics (the cozy little triangles) characterizes distributive and structural policies (1*a* and 2*a* above). The important relationships are between bureaus, subcommittees, and those affected in the private sector. Redistributive and strategic policies (1*b* and 2*b* above) are normally more visible and thus tend to involve many more persons at high levels in both institutions (Congress and the presidency). These are the macropolitical issues that may be characterized by sloppy large hexagons. Regulatory policies may also involve a great many actors, particularly in the early stages of program development. The refinements and details of policy may be worked out at the subsystem level, however. And finally, crisis policy typically is responded to within the presidency.

This effort by Ripley and Franklin to identify patterns of relationships as characteristic of different types of policy is an important first step. It advises us to look for variations in participation by those associated with public and private institutions. At several points in their analysis, Ripley and Franklin also encourage us to look for changes in patterns within particular policies over time. But their effort is not intended to discriminate among the many real issues that fit into each of their six categories or among the several activities associated with program development for any one issue. Thus, for example, one may expect differences in precise relationships among participants for many of the programs that Ripley and Franklin identify as distributive policies—grants for scientific research, airport construction, mass transit facilities, income tax deductions for interest on home mortgages. We may expect variation among these programs in terms of who is involved, where they come from, how they communicate, and what they decide.

However, even more important for present purposes is to imagine that participation, communication, and decision-making methods may vary *within* an issue from one set of policy activities to the next (see Table 13—1). It is in conceiving of the policy process in this way that one breaks out of the dominant institutional mode and is encouraged to analyze congressional participation, with others, in various policy networks. The proposal, then, is to analyze congressional participation in all of the activities associated with program development for a particular issue. The expectation is that this participation will vary in quantity and quality from one activity to the next, one issue to the next, and one time period to the next.

How can members of Congress and their staffs justify getting involved in other than the legitimation activities that are traditionally associated with a legislature? What kinds of information and experience can they bring to these other activities? A brief review of program development activities is in order.

Problem to government

1. Perception/definition of problem. Members of Congress are highly sensitive to public problems. The demands of the office itself insure that the successful representative and senator will organize his or her political life to search for and receive public problems (principally those in the state or district). Most notable in this regard is the campaign. For representatives these events come so frequently that they are virtually in a perpetual search for district problems. The campaign experience is instructive but so are the frequent visits to the district, the mail, phone calls, and the work of the district office.

Much of this intelligence about state or district problems is gained by the members through an unsystematic but normally reliable process of personal absorption. Representatives in particular often know more about the geographical area that constitutes their district than anyone else. This knowledge is typically honed by the threat posed by a primary or general election opponent. An exception to the more personally developed information is that gained by polls, a device increasingly used by members of both houses.

Members also can claim expertise in problem definition by virtue of their work in Washington. Personal staffs may be directed to study particular problems—often those affecting the state or district. And of course, the committees and subcommittees are constantly engaged in problem identifying and defining activities in the hearings and staff reports. Similarly, the various congressional research agencies may also be requested to prepare analyses of the causes and effects of public problems.

These Washington-based definitional activities tend to be more systematic than those associated with the state or district-based activities mentioned above but less systematic than those of the bureaucracy. It is also the case that whereas representatives typically have an advantage over senators in knowing their constituency, senators have a staff advantage over representatives that sometimes prepares them to comprehend better the relationships among various problems.

2. Aggregation and representation. Senators and representatives are likewise very active and experienced in facilitating the aggregation of those whom they perceive to be effected by a problem. This talent follows from their need for electoral support at home and their experience in enacting legislation in Washington. In some cases, members insist that those affected get together so as to present a stronger, more united front in Washington. And, conversely, they may discourage presentation of demands if groups are divided and in conflict. Again I must stress that we are merely noting how and why *members of Congress* get involved in other than the familiar policy approval activities. Policy actors from elsewhere in the government and from the private sphere are also involved in these early stage activities of definition and aggregation.

It should also require no more than a brief mention that the members of Congress and their staffs are experts in representing. Just as they are well trained and organized to campaign and get reelected, so too are they well prepared to represent. In fact, the one activity follows from the other. This is not to say that they are always good at representing, or that others are not also involved in that activity, but only to stress that the members are predictably and legitimately active here.

3. Agenda setting.   Members of Congress, in particular the party and committee leaders, are often actively involved in the process of setting priorities among public problems to be treated. The leaders can provide important information about the mood and interests of the membership. They can supply predictions about how members will react to certain priorities. But not even party leaders are normally in a position to establish priorities on their own. As Richard E. Neustadt observes: "Congressmen need an agenda from outside, something with high status to respond to or react against. What provides it better than the program of the President?" (1960:   6– 7). The president and his aides often consult with members of Congress and their staff, but priority setting has typically been an executive-centered activity.

What about those instances when the president is of a different party from that of the majority in Congress? As Neustadt mentions, the presidential program may also be something for Congress to react to. But what if the president doesn't want much of anything from Congress—or intends to let present programs expire, programs that a majority in Congress support? In such cases, members of Congress have been much more active in establishing priorities. For example, in his study of the Eisenhower administration, James L. Sundquist concludes that congressional Democrats definitely established priorities to counter those of the Republican president, and in spite of a lack of cooperation by their own party leadership. Speaker Sam Rayburn and Senate Majority Leader Lyndon B. Johnson worked rather closely with the popular president.

> The [Democratic] activists were constrained to proceed independently to organize their own bloc in each house of the Congress, rally support for specific measures inside and outside the legislature, and press for action on them. They could also work with the Democratic National Committee . . . and particularly with the Democratic Advisory Council established by [Paul] Butler late in 1956.

> The Senate activist bloc, the corresponding House bloc (organized as the Democratic Study Group), and the national committee and advisory council came to comprise a triangle of communication and mutual reinforcement that by-passed the party's leadership in Congress. By 1960 it had come close to isolating the leadership (Sundquist, 1968: 395−96).

The Nixon administration also encouraged congressional Democrats to be more active in setting priorities. Ralph K. Huitt describes the situation as follows (in Mansfield, ed., 1975: 76).

> Nixon did not seem to want anything from Congress. To be sure, he initiated domestic programs and proclaimed priorities, but he seemed to lose interest in them quickly. In fact, Congress found itself upbraiding him for not really trying to get what he said he wanted, which many members wanted more than he did.

Nixon's style and lack of programmatic drive may have encouraged many congressional Democrats to establish their own priorities, but they were not successful in creating a process for doing so. Weak party leadership and rather continuous reform were but two of many factors preventing the development of a coherent counterprogram.

In summary, neither house of Congress is well structured to set priorities. Bicameralism, the decentralized committee system, and a highly dependent party leadership are obstacles to this end. At the same time, members can provide information about what their constituents think is important. They can provide equally useful information on the many special interests likely to be touched by government programs. It is for these reasons, as well as the realization that Congress must approve government programs, that the members are drawn into agenda-setting activities.[2]

Action in government

1. Formulation. As indicated in Table 13−1, program formulation may involve doing research on the various options for treating a problem, analyzing the advantages and disadvantages of these options (to include review of the effects from each), and eventual selection of one option or a combination of options. Members of Congress can bring a great deal of wisdom to these activities, again working in concert with others. Congressional hearings are often designed to explore policy options—typically including that of continuing an existing program. Committees and subcommittees are structured by membership and staff operations to provide political analysis of political options. Over time these units become impressive banks of information on the feasibility of proposals.

---

[2] For additional discussions of agenda setting, see Cobb and Elder (1972), Bachrach and Baratz (1970), and Schattschneider (1960).

Political feasibility is a crucial consideration for program formulation. But Ralph K. Huitt questions whether it makes sense to speak of a
total legislative system to include Congress, the interest groups, executive agencies, and the press, in making strategic choices on what is
feasible (in Ranney, 1968:   272).

> It is more accurate, I think, to begin with the committees and speak of
> the *policy system*, which is focused about each pair of committees,
> House and Senate, that shares similar, if not identical jurisdiction.

Huitt observes that there are large national interest groups and high
level executive departments "ranging across a broad sweep of the legislative spectrum."

> More common than the giants by far are the groups with a single interest
> (albeit a broad one, like higher education), and the executive agency with
> one or a handful of bills, all of whose business is done with a single
> committee in each house (in Ranney, 1968:   272).

According to Huitt, "this organization . . . around specialized concerns shapes the entire system that makes legislation" (in Ranney,
1968:   274). For present purposes we can interpret these comments as
reinforcing the view that it is the member's knowledge of specialized
interests that contributes to program formulation—from the research
into options to the selection of one proposal over another.

It should be pointed out that the participation of members of Congress in formulation activities is often highly subjective. The evidence
they offer is biased in favor of the interests they represent. One is
expected to have preferences on Capitol Hill. Selective presentation of
data is a common and accepted practice. Staff reports are typically
prepared for someone or some group and for a clearly specified purpose. The objectivity or fairness is presumed to be a result over time of
subjective arguments forcefully presented.

The reforms during the 1970s increased Congress' capacity to formulate programs independent of the executive. The creation of the
Congressional Budget Office and the Office of Technology Assessment,
the provision for a stronger research agency in the Library of Congress
(the Congressional Research Service), and the large increases in personal and committee staffs contributed to greater research and analytical skills on Capitol Hill. Program formulation has been centered in
Congress for certain issues in the past. We may expect it to occur there
in the future, both as a consequence of inaction elsewhere and in
response to, or as a counterforce to, proposals developed elsewhere. A
further result of this increased analytical capacity may well be more
active participation by members in executive-centered program
formulation—partly due to demands by the members themselves,
perhaps due as well as to a recognition of their growing competence.

2. Legitimation. It is within this set of legitimation activities that legislators typically excel. Given the nature of our constitutional system most national government programs must be traceable to majority support in Congress. Others besides legislators participate in building legislative majorities however, and there are all kinds of approval processes which take place outside Congress—in letting contracts, setting standards, issuing licenses, etc. (Jones and Matthes in *Encyclopedia of Policy Studies,* 1982).

The activities associated with majority building in a legislature include the identification of the principal interests to be satisfied, communication among these interests, bargaining, and determination of a compromise. Virtually the entire legislative process as described in the previous chapters is designed to accomplish these goals—the organization and appointment of committees and subcommittees, assigning bills, the hearings and markup sessions, the scheduling of bills for floor debate, and amending process, and voting. The Congress is composed of two majority-building machines, which then must meld their products before legitimation is complete.

One must not be misled, of course, into believing that each proposal for government action on a public problem represents a significant challenge to the majority building talents of legislators. There are such cases, to be sure. It took several decades before majorities were fashioned for federal aid to education, medical care for the aged, federal civil and voting rights laws. If all legislative proposals were so conflictual, congressional turnover would no doubt be high—the result of fatigue. As it is, however, most proposals are to do a bit more of what is already being done, extend what is being done for some to others, or do something similar in another area. As Huitt notes (in Ranney, 1968: 274):

> What is most feasible is what is purely incremental, or can be made to appear so. Paradoxically, it is politically attractive to tout a proposal as "new" so long as it is generally recognized that it is not new at all but a variation on a familiar theme.

The advice contained in this wisdom is: Try to go where the majority already is. Even if you want to do something truly new, you are advised to begin with what is feasible. Huitt speaks of "finding halfway houses . . . which supply at least part of what is needed under the guise of doing something else" (Ranney, 1968: 274). A classic case is the means by which we finally got a federal aid to education program. Having just enacted a popular War on Poverty program, the education aid proposal was based on the number of persons in a school district below the poverty line rather than the number of students, the economic base, the condition of the schools, etc.

R. Douglas Arnold notes a distinction between "separate coalitions for each new expenditure program" and "a single umbrella coalition for a whole collection of diverse programs" (1979: 210). In the first the necessary support is garnered by extending the program to each state and congressional district regardless of need. The second umbrella-type coalition relies on what Arnold calls multiple-program logrolls. The exchange of support between urban and rural Democrats for programs affecting each is an example of the umbrella coalition. Of course, building and maintaining such a group typically depends on strong party leadership and structure. As Arnold notes, however (1979: 212):

> The days of Lyndon Johnson and Sam Rayburn passed, and their successors, Mike Mansfield and Carl Albert, were much less inclined to function as coalition leaders. Yet party leaders are the only ones who *could* arrange and enforce the complex series of trades necessary to assemble an umbrella coalition for diverse programs.

We may also expect to find members of Congress getting involved in other legitimation processes. Certainly they will be attentive to federal contracts to be awarded in their states and districts. They may show up at public hearings for setting pollution standards or licensing a nuclear power plant (or be instrumental in organizing others to testify). And they may challenge the expertise of a government technician who has been given the authority to develop a procedure, build a dam, set a standard, design a weapon. The rationale for involvement by a member may again be constituency interest, but it may also be the result of the member's understanding of the law which provides for the bureaucratic approval process.

3. Appropriation. The budgetary process runs parallel to the substantive lawmaking process. Few laws can be enforced, few program goals can be realized without money. Until the passage of the Budget and Impoundment Control Act of 1974, the formulation of a budget was centered primarily in the executive. Though sensitive to the views of members, the Office of Management and Budget (and its predecessor, the Bureau of the Budget) had the responsibility of preparing the document for submission to Congress.

In essence, the 1974 Act created a budgetary formulation process in Congress. Budget Committees were established in each house, a Congressional Budget Office with a professional staff was authorized, and a procedure was developed for setting money limits for the authorizing and appropriations committees. Congress now takes a comprehensive view of taxing and spending and seeks to control both. As Dennis S. Ippolito sees it, the new congressional participation in budget formulation offers several advantages (1978: 119):

> First, the new budget process provides Congress with the mechanism to act on fiscal policy and to challenge executive dominance in eco-

nomic management. Second, Congress can use the budgetary process to make priority choices by considering spending decisions in relation to each other. The budget resolutions therefore also make it possible for Congress to specify how its priorities differ from those of the president. Third, Congress has developed budgetary staff and information resources that reduce considerably its reliance on the executive for budget data and analysis.

Approval of the taxing proposals is centered in the House Committee on Ways and Means and the Senate Committee on Finance. Authorization of expenditures must precede appropriations, and this action is taken in the several authorizing committees. And appropriations are handled in the two appropriations committees. All of these actions are legitimation processes like those described above—that is, actions requiring majority support in both houses. We needn't repeat the earlier discussion. But two points are worth mentioning.

1. Approval of appropriations is a separate action from approval of a program. Therefore they may not come out the same. That is, the money appropriated for a program may be less (it can't be more) than the amount authorized. Thus different forces may be at work in the two legitimation processes.

2. The new budget system has affected the approval processes for taxation, program authorization, and appropriation. When Congress approves budget resolutions it is in essence establishing limits for the standing committees—limits which did not exist in the past. The potential for conflict is considerable (LeLoup, 1980; Schick, 1980). Thus for example, in 1980 the House passed a budget resolution directing its committees to reduce spending by $6.4 billion. Appropriations Committee chairman Jamie L. Whitten (D—Mississippi) defied the resolution in regard to appropriations for Saturday mail delivery. Much to the chagrin of the Budget Committee chairman, Robert N. Giaimo (D—Connecticut), Speaker O'Neill appeared to support Chairman Whitten: "If the Budget Committee was to say to the Appropriations Committee, 'you can't do this,' they would be transgressing on the rights of the Appropriations Committee." Chairman Giaimo responded by charging that the Speaker was undermining the budget process. "It undermines what the leadership told us to do. The Budget Committee didn't dream this up by itself."[3]

To summarize, one may expect to find members of Congress and their staff actively involved in all functional activities associated with program development. They can justify involvement because of their knowledge and understanding of constituencies, and the many private and public interests affected by government programs, as well as expertise on the special topics of their committees and subcommittees

---

[3] Both quotes from the *New York Times*, June 17, 1980.

and ultimately their authority to approve laws. This general survey of activities suggests quite varied participation. We may expect:

1. Active participation by many members and staff in legitimation activities (including appropriations).
2. Variable participation by members and staff in problem definition, interest aggregation, program formulation, and formulation of the congressional budget.
3. Limited participation by members and staff in agenda setting.

COMPARING ACTION ON SPECIFIC BILLS

The tremendous variation in legislator involvement in program development is illustrated by comparing what happens on specific bills at any one time or what happens over time in regard to a particular program. Consider a few of the many available studies of a bill becoming a law—campaign finance reform by Robert L. Peabody and colleagues (1972), the federal aid to education program by Eugene Eidenberg and Roy Morey (1969), civil rights legislation by Daniel M. Berman (1966), a national health service corps by Eric Redman (1973), and the classic study of the Employment Act of 1946 by Stephen K. Bailey (1950). Each of these studies provides quite different answers to the following questions.

1. Who participated in what program development activities?
2. Did this participation vary between the House and Senate? If so, how did it vary?
3. Which activities were centered in Congress? Which in the executive?
4. How and when did legislators and staff communicate with each other? With other participants?
5. How aware of program development were the less active legislators and staff?

These are but a few of the more obvious questions one might ask, with quite variable results.

David E. Price has conducted one of the few systematic analyses of legislators' participation in program development activities. Based on a study of 14 major bills Price, like Huitt, first warns against generalizing about participation in policy activities, "particularly if the unit of analysis remains the entire executive or legislative establishment."

> Legislative initiatives are diverse and scattered phenomena, while various policymakers hardly find themselves possessed of equal incentives and resources, the system does display considerable "slack." Differences between individuals, committees, and agencies sometimes display fixed patterns attributable to "external" determinants. But the free-

dom of individuals and decision-making units to determine their own legislative roles is often considerable (Price, 1972: 292).

In what was a most useful exercise for our purposes, Price identified who was involved in six program development activities for fourteen bills. The activities closely parallel those relied on in Table 13−1.

Those listed in Table 13−1	Price's counterparts
Perception/definition	Information gathering
Aggregation/organization	Interest aggregation
Representation/agenda setting	Instigation/publicizing
Formulation	Formulation
Legitimation	Mobilization, Modification

Table 13−4 summarizes Price's observations about the relative involvement of executive, legislative, and interest group participants—

TABLE 13−4
Variation in participation in program development activities (14 bills, 89th Congress)

Program development activity	Source of participants (number of bills)						
	a Primarily executive	*b* Primarily legislative	*c* Primarily interest groups	Mixed a,b	b,c	a,c	a,b,c
Information gathering (perception, definition)*	6†	—	1	4	1	2	—
Interest aggregation (aggregation/organization)	—	7	—	7	—	—	—
Instigation/publicizing (representation/agenda setting)	1	2	—	3	2	5	1
Formulation (same)	2	3	—	2	—	—	7
Mobilization (legitimation)	—	2	—	8	1	—	3
Modification (legitimation)	—	13	—	1	—	—	—

*The labels in parenthesis represent the policy activities used here—see Table 13−1.
† Figure represents the number of bills on which participants drawn from the executive were primarily involved (N = 14).
SOURCE: Developed from the work of David Price, *Who Makes the Laws?* (Cambridge, Mass.: Schenkman, 1972), Table 7, pp. 290−91.

whether actors from these sources were primarily involved or whether they worked together with others, hence the several mixed categories. Several conclusions emerge from this table.

1. Information gathering tended to be centered more in the executive—six bills where executive actors were primarily involved, six others where they worked with others (*a, b* and *a, c*).
2. Interest aggregation and modification tended to be centered more in the legislature—the latter heavily so.

3. Instigation/publicizing, formulation, and mobilization were characterized by considerable mixing of participants.
4. Legislators were primarily involved in more activities than either executive or interest group actors—information gathering being the only activity in which they were not the principal actors for at least one bill.

The three groups of participants also varied in their involvement across policy activities for the different bills studied by Price. I assigned scores to each group depending on whether they were primarily involved in an activity (3 points), shared involvement with another group (1½ points each), or shared with the other two groups (1 point each). By this simple scoring system the following variations were identified:

1. Congressional dominance (members of Congress active in all activities, little sharing with others).
    Fair packaging.
    Campaign finance.
    Cold war GI benefits.
2. Congressional sharing with interest groups (members of Congress active in most activities, some sharing with lobbyists).
    Traffic safety.
3. Congressional sharing with executive (members of Congress active in most activities, some sharing with members of executive).
    Cigarette labelling.
    Oceanography.
    Poverty amendments.
4. Executive sharing with Congress (members of executive active in most activities, some sharing with members of Congress).
    Foreign investors' tax.
    Medical complexes (heart disease, cancer and stroke research).
5. Sharing among all groups (significant involvement of groups in several activities).
    Medicare.
    Sugar Act amendments.
    Unemployment insurance.
    Elementary and secondary education.
    Fair labor standards.

James L. Sundquist also found important differences in policy responsibility and participation among several major bills during the Eisenhower, Kennedy, and Johnson administrations. Though Sundquist's analysis of program development activities is less systematic than Price's, his rich descriptive material provides further support for the impressive variation in congressional policy participation

(Sundquist, 1968: 390 —91 and passim). Ripley and Franklin likewise identify variations among important bills—executive dominance, joint program development, congressional dominance, and stalemate—but as noted earlier they do not discriminate among the several program development activities (1980: 219).

The point to be emphasized from these variations is that they reinforce the utility of viewing Congress as a population variably drawn into the policy process as associated with different issues. It is clear that the members and their staffs participate broadly in policy activities, and this participation varies greatly among various types of issues. Price contributes even more evidence to support this conclusion when he examines differences among congressional committees. As with individual members, he found that certain committees and subcommittees were active in different types of activities. He cautiously concluded that some committees specialize in "the formulation and publicizing of legislation" and others specialize in "the 'maturing' and compromising of proposals with an eye to eventual mobilization" (Price, 1972: 311 —12).

CONCLUSION

The Congress is the most critical government institution for maintaining a constitutional democracy. Its legitimacy as the lawmaker stems from the electoral connections with the people. This authority to pass on all government programs justifies congressional involvement in other program development activities (problem definition, aggregation, agenda-setting, formulation) and guarantees that those responsible for and benefitting from these programs (political executives and bureaucrats at all levels of government, as well as public and private interest groups) will often draw members and their staffs into fuller participation in the early stages of program development. For the student of legislatures the policy process perspective offers a different view of the role those institutions play in the political system. The formal structure and procedures of the lawmaking process are undeniably important for maintaining the legitimacy of government programs, thus justifying the scholar's attention. But focusing on issues, how they get to government, and who acts on them there, provides quite a different window for studying legislative behavior. We have done no more in this chapter than provide clues as to where to look and what to look for. In summary, these clues are:

1. Look for congressional involvement (members and staff) in all activities logically associated with developing a government program.

2. Look for congressional participation in policy-associated networks (cozy little connections, cozy little triangles, sloppy large hexagons).

3. Above all, look for variation—in who participates in what, in how this participation changes over time, in how the participation differs between issues, bills, committees, the two chambers, the political parties.

14 Congress and the policy process: Program execution

Traditional concepts of the separation of powers typically assign program execution to the executive. By this view Congress authorizes a program and appropriates the money to administer it; the president supervises the implementation of the program and judges whether it is suitable. Therefore Congress is not expected to play a significant role as government moves toward the problem or as the program is returned to government for evaluation (see Table 13–1).

Most students of the national political system do not accept this separation of functions doctrine either as a theory or a description of reality. If Congress had less constitutional discretion in shaping its role in the policy process, one could imagine a more compartmentalized government. But Article I of the Constitution gives Congress very broad powers, and thus it has roamed about quite freely in performing administrative and evaluative tasks. Not only that, but Congress has as well forced administrators to perform the more political tasks associated with program development. As Morton Grodzins argued (in Goldwin, ed., 1964: 127).

> [The] activities of the administrator do not sound significantly differ-
> ent from the activities of many congressmen. And they are not. The
> higher administrator . . . performs an intrinsically political role. The
> reason such a role is possible for the administrator is the same reason
> that accounts for the interference in administration on the part of the
> legislator. The administrator can play politician, just as the politician
> can play administrator, because the parties are without program and
> without discipline.

This interlacement of administrative and legislative roles has become more complex in recent years with the growth of government at
all levels. We have witnessed the expansion of the presidency, and
many observers have viewed that development with alarm. Watergate
and its aftermath, culminating in the resignation of President Nixon,
reduced the power of the presidency and, in so doing, drew attention
to the reality of bureaucratic preeminence. It is not that the agencies
gained that much authority as a consequence of Watergate. Rather we
have come to realize the full extent of their critical role in decision
making. Lawrence C. Dodd and Richard L. Schott warn us not to
concentrate so much on individual presidents when studying institutional relationships (1979:   7—8).

> Such a perspective . . . tends to ignore the fact that the "executive" is
> much more than the presidency; the executive is essentially two related
> but often conflicting institutions: the presidency and the bureaucracy.
> The increased power of the executive, in short, results from not only the
> emergence of an imperial presidency but also the emergence of the
> modern administrative state.

This advice is very wise indeed, but it complicates even further our
task of trying to understand the policy relationships between Congress and those who presumably are organized to do Congress'
bidding.

In this chapter we will first examine the more traditional incursions
of the members of Congress into program execution—approving appointments, enacting legislation, and particularly oversight in its many
forms.[1] We will then consider more recent involvements by Congress
in program implementation and evaluation—developments such as
the new budget procedures, sunshine and sunset laws, and the expanded legislative veto. These new developments raise a significant set
of issues—those associated with the expansion of the congressional
population and what it means for legislative participation in the policy
process. These trends will be discussed, as will their implications for

---

[1] I have already discussed casework and campaigning—both of which may involve
members in program implementation and evaluation. Case work in particular, is a form
of administrative behavior, and it can lead to program evaluation by the members and
their staff.

the various forms of network and subsystem politics referred to in Chapter 13.

TRADITIONAL INVOLVEMENTS

Opinions differ rather dramatically on whether members of Congress should be actively involved in the administrative process.[2] Those who believe in legislative supremacy typically support congressional follow through. Those who believe in presidential supremacy typically refer to such activity as congressional interference. The legislative supremacists are convinced that no authorized government action can possibly be defined as being out of bounds for the Congress. To do so is to compromise the representative and democratic character of the political system. As Charles S. Hyneman observes: "If Congress is to have the supreme authority to say what the government is to do, then it must be in a position to describe what it wants done in as much detail as it thinks necessary" (1950: 81). On the contrary, those stressing executive dominance often emphasize a strict separation of powers doctrine. By this view legislatures have a legitimate role to play, but they should not be authorized to roam freely among the activities assigned to other institutions.

It is difficult to deny the legislative supremacy rationale since it is based on standard democratic theory. If members of Congress wish to pursue an investigation or limit the discretion of an agency head or specify an administrative procedure, it is hard to maintain that they cannot or should not act in that way. On the other hand, however academic the separation doctrine may be, it has become very real with the growth of technical issues and a specialized bureaucracy trained and organized to treat such issues. Dodd and Schott point out that (1979: 2):

> The administrative state is . . . in many respects a prodigal child. Although born of congressional intent, it has taken on a life of its own and has matured to a point where its muscle and brawn can be turned against its creator . . . . Protected by civil service tenure, armed with the power to issue orders and rules that have the force of law, supported by strong clientele and interest groups, and possessing a wealth of information, knowledge, and technical expertise, it goes forth to battle its institutional rivals on equal, and sometimes superior, terms.

I am reminded of the familiar grade school teacher's trick for distinguishing *may* and *can.* "Can I open the window?" "You can but you *may* not." For the present context we alter the question: "May we (the

---

[2] See, for example, the discussion by Roger Davidson and his coauthors of the three dominant views of Congress—the literary theory of balanced institutions, the executive force theory, and the party government theory (Davidson, et al., 1966: chapter 1).

members of Congress) get involved in this technical aspect of program execution?" And the answer sometimes is: "You may but you *cannot*." Congress does have the authority to intervene under most circumstances, but it often lacks the capability to do so.[3]

Congress, nevertheless, does intervene in administration—often frustrating the bureaucratic experts. As Grodzins sees it (in Goldwin, ed., 1964: 114):

> The congressional interference is constant, effective, and institutionalized. It may be pegged on the broadest issues of national policy or on purely personal considerations, but it is most frequently exercised on behalf of local interests—individual, group, and governmental.

Much of this so-called interference is formal and institutional in nature. That is, the involvement is a direct consequence of congressional authority, and the methods are associated with lawmaking and other legislative prerogatives—approving appointments; program authorization, appropriation, and auditing; and legislative oversight. With some of these techniques Congress uses its ordinary powers to influence administrative decision making, with others it defines a specific role for itself on a case-by-case basis (requiring reports and consultation or giving itself a second chance with a veto). Each of these methods requires discussion.

Appointments

The Constitution directly involves the Senate in the appointing process by stating that the president "shall nominate, and by and with the Advice and Consent of the Senate, shall appoint Ambassadors, other public Ministers and Consuls, Judges of the Supreme Court, and all other Officers of the United States, whose Appointments are not herein otherwise, provided for, and which shall be established by Law" (Article II, Sec. 2). For much of the 19th century the appointing process was used in a highly partisan way to reward political supporters. No one doubted that the spoils system, as it was popularly known, was an important method for the Senate to influence who decided what in the executive. The custom of senatorial courtesy logically emerged. By this custom, the president cleared appointees within a particular state with a senator or senators of the president's party from that state. In essence this system permitted senators to make appointments. The custom has not held for national appointments though any president

---

[3] Of course, the courts may also limit congressional involvement, but they are often hesitant about doing so. The reader should also be reminded that Congress in recent years has sought to increase its capacity to cope with technical issues—see Chapter 15.

is well advised to inform senators and House members when appointing persons from their state or district so that they can make an announcement locally. As David R. Mayhew and others have demonstrated, "credit claiming" is a time-honored congressional practice (Mayhew, 1974a: 52ff., Fiorina, 1977: Ch. 5).

The spoils or patronage system was substantially reformed with the passage of the Pendleton Act of 1883, establishing a permanent civil service. Expansion of the merit system and further provisions for job security now leave very few positions available for presidential appointment and thus for direct influence by senators. Thus congressional involvement in program execution through the appointing process is much more limited than in the last century. Still, Senate hearings are held on major appointments, and while very few are actually rejected (even when the president is of a different party from the majority party in Congress), senators seek to put the nominee on record in regard to controversial issues.[4] No one has ever tried to measure the precise influence that these hearings have on the nominee, but there does seem to be little doubt that the senators think it is worth trying to impress the candidate with their views.

Program development

I have already described in some detail the extent to which Congress is involved in program authorization and appropriation. But the emphasis before was on these actions as influential in determining the shape and direction of a program (i.e., as program development activities). Here we want to consider briefly the extent to which Congress reaches into program implementation through its power to authorize and appropriate. In a sense what we are considering here is the amount of detail included in the law and the extent of the resources provided for implementing the law. In his most interesting and provocative book, *The End of Liberalism*, Theodore J. Lowi speaks of "restoring rule of law." Lowi is worried about the growth in administrative discretion. It is his view that no delegation of power ought to be granted "to an administrative agency that is not accompanied by clear standards of implementation" (Lowi, 1969: 297– 98). His position illustrates how program development can dominate program implementation and evaluation. If it were possible for those writing the laws to create uniformly applicable rules for every program, then the bureaucrat would simply apply those rules to each case. There would

---

[4] Between 1941 and 1971 only 28 appointments were actually rejected, though many hundreds were withdrawn and several thousand were not acted on. The highest rate of approval in this period (99.5 percent) was for Richard M. Nixon in 1969 – 71; the lowest (82.2 percent) for Harry S Truman in 1947 – 49. Congressional Quarterly, *Guide to the U.S. Congress* (Washington, D.C.: Congressional Quarterly, 1971), p. 228.

be no interpretation, only application (see Table 13−1). And evaluation would simply measure whether the rule was in fact applied.[5]

Unfortunately, the condition that concerns Lowi does in fact exist. Laws are often vague and programs are often approved with many of the details still to be resolved. It is under these conditions that administrators often play the role of the politician. They are left to develop crucial aspects of the program, which forces them to seek support for their decisions. The corrective for this condition is typically a rather unsystematic process by which adjustments are made in subsequent authorizations and appropriations. These adjustments may be the consequence of new demands, but they may also result from the members' evaluation of program effects and a determination to shape or even dictate future implementation. I am reminded of frustrations expressed by members of Congress concerning the implementation of the Air Quality Act of 1967, particularly in regard to the establishment of air quality regions. In the Clean Air Amendments of 1970, Congress simply declared that every state would be an air quality region—what was to be implemented in the 1967 Act was implemented by decree in the 1970 Act (Jones, 1975:   ch. 7).

Suffice it to say at this point that the process of program development involves a complex set of dynamics between Congress and the executive. The precise product is typically a result of a complex series of associations that each has with the other and with those to whom the program is directed. Often the degree of explicitness in the law is explained by these dynamics. In other words, the congressional reach into program administration may well be the consequence of the politics characterizing a particular issue.

Legislative oversight

In 1973, the Select Committee on Committees in the House of Representatives (popularly known as the Bolling Committee after its chairman, Richard Bolling, D−Missouri) held hearings on committee reorganization. One major topic was legislative oversight of program implementation. John C. Culver (D−Iowa) was particularly distressed about congressional capacities to oversee the executive.

> I am a member of the Government Operations Committee. I am also a
> member of the House Foreign Affairs Committee. I can assure you that to
> my knowledge and satisfaction, we are completely devoid of any plans in
> the Government Operations Committee for a systematic, organized, ra-
> tional review of the operations of the federal government on anything

[5] In a most interesting exercise, Richard F. Bensel finds that a rule of law standard may be incompatible with a strong party organization (1980:   734 − 44).

approximating a regularized basis. . . . there is no comprehensive plan for systematic review of operations of the federal government.[6]

A number of scholars testifying before the Committee expressed the belief that the central problem was that of incentive. John Bibby testified: "The regularization of oversight will not take place until the Members think it is worth their while to invest time, staff, and other resources in it."[7] Richard F. Fenno, Jr., agreed.

> It is easy for us to say more staff, more information, more computers. But I think there is the problem that lies with you [the members], and I have to turn that question back to you. Why don't you [engage in oversight]?[8]

Representative Culver was not prepared to accept that response.

> It may be easy for you to come here and say that, but it is easier for you to come here and say nothing. I think that it would be very useful for you to come here and say . . . that we need a greater degree of coordination in congressional oversight, that we need to elevate the whole subject and aspect of congressional activity to a far more serious level of consideration and recognition in congressional context, and then to give us some specific recommendations.[9]

Nelson W. Polsby then restated the Bibby-Fenno position in somewhat more practical terms.

> I would answer Mr. Fenno's question of why doesn't oversight take place. I think it is probably because the relevant committee and subcommittee chairmen don't want to, and the reason they don't want to is because they have made some political judgments of their own about what their priorities ought to be.
> . . . it seems to me that at the core of your [Culver's] complaint is essentially a political disagreement with a large number of the committee chairmen who have appeared before you.[10]

Later in a set of hearings specifically devoted to the oversight issue, Morris S. Ogul also agreed with his academic colleagues but raised the broader issue of the lack of a centralized and coordinated congressional agenda.

---

[6] U.S. Congress, House of Representatives, Select Committee on Committees, *Committee Organization in the House,* panel discussions, 93d Cong., 1st Sess., June 13, 1973, p. 19.

[7] Ibid., p. 15.

[8] Ibid., p. 22.

[9] Ibid., p. 22.

[10] Ibid., p. 23.

Mr. Ogul: . . . The third point is the most difficult for me, and that is the idea of a comprehensive scheme for oversight. The reasons for that is I think it would be desirable but I don't see oversight as a technical process.

I see it as involving, just as legislation does, very substantial priority choices, policy choices, really decisions on what is important and not important. Were there a central mechanism in Congress for setting that kind of an agenda, then I would be delighted to see the implementation.

Mr. Culver: Isn't that what I was actually talking about, so you have the totality of perspective essential to make these kinds of tradeoffs and to be able systematically to determine whether in actual fact, for example, you ever looked into the Justice Department and not have to rely on the memory of an individual chairman to be able to tell you?[11]

These exchanges illustrate the complexities associated with congressional oversight. The fact is that members of Congress have lots to do in performing their duties associated with constituency service and passage of legislation. Organizing themselves to oversee the implementation of government programs is an enormous undertaking. Yet many members are sensitive to the need for follow-through to determine whether congressional intentions are in fact realized.

A reasonable argument can be made that legislators are not temperamentally suited to perform the oversight function. After all, most see themselves as lawmakers. Typically it is the development of proposals, the fashioning of compromises, and the building of majorities that get public attention, nationally and locally. Certain people are attracted to legislative work because of these lawmaking activities. Following through to the execution of the law may be equally demanding, but it tends to get less media coverage. Furthermore the findings may be ambiguous or embarrassing. Sometimes it is better politically *not* to know how it all came out (Campbell, 1969: 410; Weiss, 1970: 58). Then there is also the problem associated with programs primarily symbolic in nature, (i.e., where the act of passing a law itself is viewed as being responsive to a demand). How does one judge the success of such programs beyond the impact of their having been enacted at all? Under such circumstances, evaluation criteria are difficult to establish.

Several factors guarantee that congressional oversight will be discussed and promoted, but they also insure that it will be more and more difficult to achieve. First is the obvious expansion in the number of government programs. In particular, the great domestic breakthrough during the 1960s produced a virtual quantum jump in the federal government's agenda for social action. Second is the sizeable amount of executive discretion permitted in administering many complicated government programs. Political executives and in turn career bureaucrats have been directed by Congress to establish procedures, set standards, allocate resources. In some cases one can spot a

---

[11] *Committee Organization in the House*, June 22, 1973, p. 264.

total policy process occurring within the executive—including all the activities associated with program development, that is, problem definition through to the allocation of funds. The point is that under these conditions oversight is not limited simply to the matter of program administration but must include as well the judgments made about program formation.

Related to this expansion of administrative discretion is a third factor—the growth of large-scale, multipurpose programs. The War on Poverty, federal aid to education, medical care for the aged, public housing, various energy and environmental programs, all were responsive to demands for nationally coordinated efforts to solve public problems. But multipurpose programs typically have multiple goals, both stated and unstated, a development that justifies greater congressional oversight but insures only limited success. In addition, as a fourth factor, programs are often intended to have indirect effects, effects that are sometimes the principal goals. Using a tax program to affect social behavior is an example. The direct effect is that of raising revenue; the indirect effect may be to equalize resources or conserve energy.

Fifth, not only have we witnessed horizontal expansion of government programs in the sense that they tend to have a broad effect (e.g., environmental regulations and their influence on the economy and energy production), but we have witnessed vertical expansion as well. That is, many national domestic programs are administered at the state and local levels of government. In some cases the cooperation of citizen or other private groups is required for implementation. Deil S. Wright identifies a complex picket-fence federalism in which national, state, and local officials are involved in developing and administering highway, welfare, education, health, transportation, urban renewal, public housing, and agriculture programs. "Financially the entire system has become increasingly interdependent, and the states and local units depend more than ever before on external, intergovernmental sources of revenue" (Wright, 1978: 65– 66).

Taken together these developments further strain Congress's limited capacity to engage in effective oversight. Ironically the various types of expansion referred to above—in goals, number of programs, number of officials involved, executive authority—guarantee an increase in the demands for effective oversight while at the same time creating conditions under which comprehensive congressional monitoring is exceedingly difficult. In summary, a body of reluctant legislators is faced with demands that they accomplish what everyone concedes is impossible.

How does Congress cope with this difficult chore? I will treat this question in two parts. First I will review those techniques that have traditionally been employed to oversee the executive. Later I will discuss developments that are responsive to recent demands for more evaluation.

In his book, *Congress Oversees the Bureaucracy*, Morris S. Ogul distinguishes between manifest and latent oversight activities. This distinction is useful in separating the views that people have of oversight. There are those who see it as a definable activity in and of itself—"We will now do legislative oversight." Others take a broader view, identifying oversight as a latent function of many legislative activities. Ogul fits in this second group. He defines *legislative oversight* as "behavior by legislators and their staffs, individually or collectively, which results in an impact, intended or not, on bureaucratic behavior" (Ogul, 1976: 11).

This dichotomy between the more narrow, manifest activities and the broader, latent activities also provides a suitable basis for categorizing traditional oversight efforts. Those fitting the first type include:

1. Investigations of the executive by special and standing committees.
2. Requiring periodic reports from executive agencies regarding their performance—in general or in regard to specific programs.
3. Auditing the expenditures by the executive.

The first two activities produce great quantities of written record which may in turn serve as the basis for changes in legislation. They represent the most faithful implementation of Section 136 of the Legislative Reorganization Act of 1946 which states that:

> To assist the Congress in appraising the administration of the laws and in developing such amendments or related legislation as it may deem necessary, each standing committee of the Senate and the House of Representatives shall exercise continuous watchfulness of the execution by the administrative agencies concerned of any laws, the subject matter of which is within the jurisdiction of such committee; and, for that purpose, shall study all pertinent reports and data submitted to the Congress by the agencies in the executive branch of the Government.[12]

Investigations are generally a well-recognized activity among the public since certain of them have received a great deal of media attention. Reportedly, the first investigation of administration occurred in 1792—an inquiry by the House into the defeat of General St. Clair's expedition against the Indians. Joseph P. Harris reports that 185 investigations were officially reported as having taken place between 1789 and 1919. Today that many and more can take place in one Congress—236 in the 82d Congress; 215 in the 83d (Harris, 1964: 264).

Reports from executive agencies can, of course, be one major source

---

[12] U.S. Congress, Senate Committee on Government Operations, *A Compilation of the Legislative Reorganization Act of 1946*, 83d Cong., 1st Sess., 1953, p. 26.

of investigations. But the volume of reports is staggering. Ogul counted 460 reports in 1969, just from the cabinet-level departments (not counting those from lesser agencies). It is no doubt correct that the total number of reports is well into the thousands. Ogul quotes one member as saying: "We have to keep the wastebaskets full to survive" (1976: 177).

However, the more spectacular congressional investigations have been launched as a consequence of well-publicized events, not executive reports. And they have varied as to topic and source within Congress (though most of the major investigations in recent decades have been launched in the Senate). They include:

The Truman Committee: created as a special Senate Committee in 1941 to investigate national defense contracting. The seven-member committee was the result of a resolution introduced by Senator Harry S Truman (D — Missouri) who acted on complaints from home about waste in the construction of Fort Leonard Wood. As Donald H. Riddle concludes: "Through its example the Committee enhanced the influence and prestige of Congress and set a high standard against which subsequent committees may be judged" (1964: 165).

The Kefauver Crime Investigation: conducted by a special Senate committee in 1950 to investigate crime across state borders. Senator Estes Kefauver (D — Tennessee) first proposed the investigation and became the chairman of a special committee set up when a jurisdictional dispute arose between the committees on the Judiciary and Interstate and Foreign Commerce. Many of the Kefauver hearings were televised.

The McCarthy Hearings: conducted by the Permanent Investigations Subcommittee of the Senate Committee on Government Operations. When the Republicans became the majority party in 1953, Senator Joseph R. McCarthy (R —Wisconsin) chaired the full committee and the investigations subcommittee. He launched investigations of the armed forces—notably the Army—charging that the communists had infiltrated the services. The famous Army — McCarthy hearings were eventually chaired by Senator Karl E. Mundt (R —South Dakota). These hearings commanded large television audiences. Senator McCarthy was later censured by the Senate for his activities. The House Committee on Un-American Activities also gained a reputation for its investigations of subversion.

The TFX Contract Investigation: also conducted by the Permanent Investigations Subcommittee of the Senate Committee on Government Operations. The controversy was over the awarding of a defense contract to build a fighter plane to General Dynamics

Corporation rather than the Boeing Corporation. Senator Henry Jackson (D—Washington) requested the investigation (Boeing is located in the state of Washington).

The Watergate Investigations: conducted initially in 1973 by a Select Committee on Presidential Campaign Activities. The seven-member committee was chaired by Senator Sam Ervin (D—North Carolina). The Committee's hearings escalated beyond campaign activities with revelations from the trial of those who broke into the Watergate Office Building. The House Committee on the Judiciary then launched its own investigation preparatory to judging whether impeachment of the president was warranted.

As suggested by this small sample of investigations, the results of congressional inquiry can vary from criminal indictments, to changes in the law, censure (or other disciplinary action) of members of Congress, changes in administrative practices, even removal of a president. In some cases there is no direct action taken by Congress, and yet the publicity associated with the investigation can have an important impact. Joseph P. Harris notes that (1964: 270):

> The possibility of a congressional investigation acts as a constant deterrent against improper and unauthorized executive acts . . . . Administrative incompetence, faulty administration, and occasionally corruption of executive officers have not infrequently been exposed by investigation.

At the same time, however, this technique tends to be blunt, episodic, unsystematic. Harris again (1964: 270):

> Spurred on by the prospect of publicity and party advantage, committees have often conducted such inquiries with more zeal than discretion and have been guilty of unfortunate excesses and failure to act in a judicial manner. Undoubtedly, capturing headlines has been at times of more interest to members of committees than ascertaining facts.

The third manifest oversight activity is that of monitoring the expenditures of the executive. Congress is required by the Constitution to publish "a regular Statement and Account of the Receipts and Expenditures of all public Money . . . from time to time" (Article I, Section 9). The Congress has always been sensitive to the need for performing this task. The House created a Committee on Expenditures in Executive Departments in 1816; the Senate created a counterpart in 1842. (Galloway, 1955: 274).[13] Neither committee was notably successful, though both survived even the 1946 committee reorganization (the name was changed to Government Operations in 1952).

---

[13] Joseph P. Harris points out that Congress actually established a set of committees in each house to examine individual departments (1964: 129).

The really important change in auditing procedures occurred in 1921 with the passage of the Budget and Accounting Act. Prior to that time the audits were conducted by the Treasury Department. The General Accounting Office (GAO) was created as an agency independent of the executive with the responsibility for overseeing and auditing government expenditures and filing reports with Congress. GAO has auditing responsibilities which have in recent years taken it beyond what is normally regarded to be the standard audit. It was quite a natural development associated with the expansion and growing complexity of government programs that Congress would direct the GAO to assume broader evaluative functions. After all, the audit itself takes one deeply into programmatic details. As Joseph Pois points out:

> The self-initiated reviews of economy, efficiency and program effectiveness, which are central in the functioning of the GAO, are indispensable in underpinning GAO's capability to be of service to the Congress. These reviews, for which the GAO also used the rubric "auditing," go far beyond what had, at least in the past, been understood by the term "audit." As the Comptroller General points out, GAO auditing "includes not only examining accounting records and financial transactions and reports but also checking for compliance with applicable laws and regulations; examining the efficiency and economy of operations; and reviewing the results of operations to evaluate whether the desired results, including legislatively prescribed objectives, have been effectively achieved."[14]

The auditing functions of GAO, as broadly conceived in the statement above, may have several impacts on program execution. First there is the anticipatory reaction by administrators trying to estimate the methods, extent, and impact of the review or audit. Second is the effect of the expanded use of the GAO by members of Congress to provide information and analysis on program execution. The comptroller general pointed out that in 1966 special requests from committees and members constituted 8 percent of the workload of a professional staff of about 2,400; in 1977 requests were estimated at 34 percent of workload of a professional staff of 3,800.[15] That increase alone forces administrators to be more attentive to congressional wishes. In addition, it has the effect of further institutionalizing congressional involvement in implementation and evaluation. Finally

---

[14] Joseph Pois, "The General Accounting Office as a Congressional Resource," in U.S. Congress, Senate, Commission on the Operation of the Senate, *Congressional Support Agencies,* 94th Cong., 2d Sess., 1976, p. 32.

[15] Cited in Pois, p. 34.

there is the impact of the information itself on the future implementation of a program.[16]

GAO reports are received by the two Government Operations Committees (the Senate committee is now Governmental Affairs). The two committees may then conduct investigations, but they have only limited legislative authority. That is, they must depend on other committees to develop and report legislation based on their investigations. It is not surprising that these committees have never been highly prestigious assignments, ranking 14th of 19 House committees and 13th of 15 Senate committees in Goodwin's preference ranking (1970: 114−15). As Dodd and Schott point out, effectiveness in investigation depends in part on authority to write legislation—to carry through with the changes required. But the committees are dependent on others to complete their work. Dodd and Schott also observe that investigations launched as a consequence of auditing reports may take the Government Operations committees deeply into the jurisdictions of other committees (1979: 165−68). All standing committees and subcommittees tend to be very protective of their turf. Any group with cross-cutting jurisdiction, the committees on Government Operations or the Budget, may find that it is interfering with any number of cozy little triangles when pursuing an investigation.

In summary, the auditing function is self-expanding with the growth of government. It "can uncover administrative problems of which Congress was simply unaware" (Dodd and Schott, 1979: 252), and it is surely "one of the potentially strongest means of legislative control of administrative performance" (Harris, 1964: 128). But comprehensive evaluation of government programs is an unlikely result of the auditing function as presently organized. Given the volume of material now available from GAO alone, it is likely that the members will pick and choose information to suit their personal predispositions. When there is too much to do one does what is most interesting or rewarding.

These more traditional, manifest oversight activities—investigations, reports, and auditing—do not add up to a very impressive, systematic review of policy implementation by the executive. Typically, it seems, the effect of oversight has been more a matter of the executive agencies trying to stay ahead of Congress. That is, knowing that investigations and reports are always possible, or concerned as to what the GAO may uncover, the agencies in effect oversee themselves. This effect may be as positive as if Congress were conducting comprehensive and systematic oversight—at least until and unless the agencies discover that they needn't be so attentive.

---

[16] One should not leave the impression that the GAO is all seeing and all knowing. The workload is enormous, and as Allen Schick observes: " . . . GAO . . . cannot inspect every administrative action affecting the availability of funds" (1980: 497).

Perhaps the best way to stay ahead of Congress and avoid the investigative reporting/auditing type of oversight is to maintain close and cordial relationships in regard to the recurring legislative associations. For it is often in the ordinary, everyday connections between Congress and the executive that the former learn what is going on in policy execution and that the latter are able to judge the values and special interests of the legislators. We turn then to the activities which have more latent oversight potential. They include:

1. The authorization and appropriation processes.
2. Approval of government organizational changes and personnel procedures.
3. The legislative veto.

I have already alluded to the obvious impact Congress has in policy execution by virtue of the detail provided in authorization and appropriation measures. Reference at this point is to the periodic review of programs for purposes of extending and financing them. Normally this process occurs annually for appropriations, and thus a continuity exists within the appropriations subcommittees that lays the basis for effective oversight.

Here is the situation. A program is proposed or an extension (or expansion) is requested. The agency first comes before the relevant authorizing committees (or subcommittees) for approval. Specific funding for the next fiscal year must then be requested from the relevant appropriation subcommittees. Under these circumstances, conditions are right for a review of what is happening within the agency. Committee members, if they are able and willing, can capitalize on this opportunity. As Ogul points out: "The legislative hearing provides a potentially useful forum for oversight activity. If that potential is not regularly and systematically developed . . . it still remains there to be seized" (1976: 162). What better time to determine program effectiveness than when the agency wants more?

As it happens, however, this potential is not fully realized for several reasons. Agency representatives do not simply appear before the committee emptyheaded and emptyhanded. They come fully prepared to justify their programs, and typically they bring large quantities of supporting material, much of it designed to demonstrate favorable constituency effects.[17] They are followed by interest group representatives who also support the program in question. And by no means least important are the advocates among the members themselves. Bear in mind that many of these programs, for which the hearings may serve as an oversight opportunity, were initially supported by

---

[17] For evidence on bureaucratic strategies in regard to building congressional support, see Arnold, 1979.

the committee. Put differently, often the cozy little triangle that created the program sits in judgment over the program at this stage of reauthorization and appropriation.

> The appropriations process and the authorization of programs are subject to strong pressures from within and without Congress in behalf of spending programs. The counter pressures that exist are usually much less potent, for congressional organization in effect invites and facilitates the spending pressures by its dispersal of decision making among many largely autonomous committees and subcommittees (Harris, 1964: 101 — 2).

Another standard legislative function with oversight potential is that associated with creating an executive in the first place and reorganizing it afterward. What is the connection between organization and oversight? If a lawmaking body is acting in a comprehensive and rational manner, it may be expected to establish unambiguous program goals, guidelines for reaching those goals, and a facilitative organization. Presumably the legislators would then monitor organizational performance and make adjustments where structure itself appeared to be at fault (e.g., relocating the administrative unit, reallocating responsibilities, changing personnel procedures, etc.). By this conception, program substance and organization are presumed to be closely connected, at least to the extent that all program evaluations will review structure and personnel as contributing to program results.

By now it should come as no surprise that the Congress does not engage in anything approaching this particular brand of rational behavior. Congress is remarkably inconsistent among the departments and agencies in the extent to which it gets involved in orgranizational matters. Joseph P. Harris found that of the 124 major administrative units within the cabinet-level departments, 68 had been created by statute, 56 by executive action (1964: 22). Most of the subunits of the other agencies were created by executive action. Congress may get very involved in questions of organizational location—as with the issue of whether the War on Poverty program should be placed in the Executive Office of the president or given to a department—but it seldom if ever carries through from legislative goals to detailed organizational arrangements for accomplishing those goals. Those matters are left to administrative discretion, as is preferred by most public administrators.

Does Congress ever terminate an agency? In his study of this question, Herbert Kaufman found the answer to be: very seldom. Even where an agency was killed, he found that the activities were not terminated. The reasons are very much those associated with the program support normally realized in the authorization and appropriations process.

> Once a service or program gets started, it seems to continue thereafter, just as conventional wisdom holds. Why this happens is no mystery; services and programs are instituted because they fill a need not otherwise met, whereupon people begin to count on them and to plan in the light of them. Terminating them would therefore cause hardship and even suffering, the effects of which radiate outward through the society. . . . these social costs tip the balance against termination. Government officers dare not ignore them the way private interests can. Governmental activities therefore tend to go on indefinitely (Kaufman, 1976: 64).

Even temporary agencies can have long life, successfully resisting efforts to evaluate their purpose and accomplishments. Thus, for example, certain House members sought to abolish the Federal Energy Administration (FEA) in 1976. The FEA was created as a temporary agency in 1974. It had just a two-year life. Representative Floyd J. Fithian (D—Indiana) made the following observations in the unsuccessful effort to disband the agency.

> Mr. Speaker, the House will soon have the opportunity to determine the future of the Federal Energy Administration, one of the fastest growing bureaucracies in Washington.
>
> The easiest course of action . . . would be to simply extend the Agency's temporary mandate. . . . Indeed, rubber stamping the proposal to continue the FEA would be something of a traditional response to a bureaucracy's desire to perpetuate itself.
>
> The House of Representatives has many fine traditions, traditions which should be cherished and perpetuated. Assisting in the entrenchment of temporary agencies is, however, not among them.[18]

The FEA was later abolished, but its functions were absorbed by a new cabinet-level Department of Energy.

Congress also may get involved periodically in the personnel policies of the executive. The landmark legislation is well known—the Pendleton Civil Service Act of 1883 that marked the beginning of greater professionalism and less patronage, the Ramspeck Act of 1940 extending coverage of the civil service, the Veterans' Preference Act of 1944 giving returning veterans a preference in hiring, and the Civil Service Reform Act of 1978 which provided the most extensive set of changes since the 1883 act. Congress also has enacted legislation regarding pay and retirement, right to organize, loyalty, staff size, and political activities. In some cases, this legislation is a result of the members' evaluation of government programs or is a means by which

---

[18] *Congressional Record,* May 17, 1976, p. E2598 (daily edition).

judgments are made about the effectiveness of government administration. But as with the organizational changes noted above, it is seldom if ever that Congress coordinates its actions on personnel with those on either the organization or substance of public policy.[19]

In his book, *Political Organizations*, James Q. Wilson establishes the following theme: "The behavior of persons who lead or speak for an organization can best be understood in terms of their efforts to maintain and enhance the organization and their position in it" (1973: 9). While perhaps an unorthodox perspective, Wilson's views certainly do provide one with a basis for understanding what otherwise appears to be inconsistent, sporadic, and obdurate congressional-executive relations. If we simply expect both legislative committees and executive agencies to act protectively, then their activities typically make sense. Such expectations tell us to look for congressional involvement in organizational and personnel matters when the members judge it in their best interests to do so. This view is at odds with the comprehensive, rational approach introduced earlier, but it appears to be more useful in explaining what happens.

The final technique in this list of broader functions which may have latent oversight effects is that of the legislative veto. As with the other activities in this section, oversight may be a by-product of an action primarily designed to achieve other purposes. The legislative veto is defined

> as a statutory mechanism which renders the implementation of executive proposals, advanced in pursuance of statute, subject to some further form of legislative consideration and control. To illustrate, the Reorganization Act of 1949, as renewed by Congress in 1961, authorizes the president to propose plans reorganizing the structure and functions of government agencies. However, a plan proposed by the President cannot go into effect until it has lain before Congress for 60 days during which time either house can disallow it by a simple majority (Cooper and Cooper, 1962: 467—68).

The point is that Congress reserves for itself *a second say* in regard to authorization for the executive to act. A rather recent development, the technique "remained uncrystallized in form until 1939" (Cooper, 1956: 129).[20] It has been used primarily as a check on performance, according to Joseph Cooper, where the executive has "obligations which cannot subsequently be effectively checked through the appropriations process" (1956: 130). In the case of reorganization plans,

---

[19] Harris (1974) treats the issue of Congressional control of the civil service in chapter 7. Hugh Heclo notes that bureaucrats need support from all sides but they are in a position to "play presidents and congressional committees against each other" (1977: 22).

[20] Harris notes that Congress first experimented with the legislative veto as early as 1932 (1964: 204).

disapproval by one house was sufficient to kill the plan. In addition to reorganization proposals, the legislative veto has been used with more specifically substantive policy decisions—deportation of aliens, disposal of surplus property, and agreements with other countries regarding nuclear energy materials.

Veto by congressional committee is also possible in some cases. As already discussed, congressional committees influence the work of executive agencies through the normal workings of the authorization and appropriations processes. But formal provisions are sometimes included in legislation that require a department or agency to consult with a committee before making a decision—a veto-like power. Joseph P. Harris identifies the following types of committee veto (1964: 217—38):

1. Come into agreement legislation—provisions requiring the agency to submit proposals to the committee for approval (done mostly for real estate transactions by the military).
2. Termination of business enterprises—provisions requiring the Department of Defense to submit to the appropriations committees any plans for terminating commercial activities by the military (e.g., manufacture of cable, cement mixing, coffee roasting) and transferring the work to private firms.
3. Committee approval before appropriations—provisions requiring that the authorization committee approve an action before funds are appropriated (used for certain public works projects).
4. Advance reports—provisions requiring reports 30 to 90 days before an action is to be taken; no mention made of committee veto (used most for nuclear energy policy). "The effect of the requirement is the same as though a formal veto power were granted, since the advance report puts a committee on notice and enables it to inquire into proposed actions or plans" (Harris, 1964: 233).

Needless to say presidents have been wary of such actions by Congress to involve itself in program administration, and they have occasionally vetoed measures with these provisions. Note that most of the programs subjected to committee approval are those of great interest to the members because of their constituencies—military installations and contracts, public works. Thus the committee veto is in some respects like casework as a form of congressional involvement in administration. Whether or not Congress includes provisions for advance notice of administrative actions, one can expect (1) attentiveness on the part of the members to any programs with direct effect on the district and (2) sensitivity among agency heads to these congressional interests.

The list of traditional involvements by Congress in program implementation and evaluation is rather imposing—casework, appointments, program authorization and appropriation, program auditing, and the many techniques of legislative oversight (investigations, reports, approval of organizational changes, and the legislative veto). Our review of each of these techniques suggests, however, that *involvement does not derive from a coordinated and comprehensive outlook by Congress of an administration.* Rather we have seen that Congress seldom if ever acts as a whole institution. The techniques of congressional participation in program execution have tended to facilitate the involvement of individual members and the committees when special interests are affected by administrative action. The item-by-item discussion suggests the lack of any systematic approach by Congress to program administration. Yet when taken as a whole, congressional intrusions are more or less predictable in the way Grodzins suggested (i.e., "exercised on behalf of local interests—individual, group, and governmental"). Unfortunately this rule is not acceptable to those like former Representative Culver, who prefer a comprehensive, coordinated, and continuing congressional review. And in the 1970s many members were elected who favored the Culver point of view. A new perspective was introduced which resulted in important changes in the congressional approach to program execution.

THE NEW INVOLVEMENTS—CONGRESS REACHES OUT

In their study of the use of concurrent resolutions as a means for administrative accountability, Cornelius P. Cotter and J. Malcolm Smith speculate about certain insufficiencies of the United States Congress (1956: 966):

> Perhaps the moral of the study is that we must free congressmen from constituency loyalties and subject them to strict party discipline if we wish to insure that available techniques for the legislative control of administration are effectively employed to serve an interest which is broad and public.

This view of the Congress as too parochial is rather widely shared among critical observers of that institution. The party discipline solution has been frequently proposed in the past; it is less popular today. Thus, for example, in a much heralded report by the American Political Science Association's Committee on Political Parties, issued in 1950, it was stated that (1950: 2):

> Compromise among interests is compatible with the aims of a free society only when the terms of reference reflect an openly acknowledged concept of the public interest. . . . Parties have the right and the duty to announce the terms to govern participation in the common enterprise. The emphasis in all consideration of party discipline must be

on positive measures to create a strong and general agreement on policies.

The party solution to the perceived problems of Congress is attractive since it provides a means for uniting what the Constitution divided—the executive and the legislature. Unfortunately certain basic problems develop to prevent this marriage. First, the president may be of a different party than the majority in Congress (in fact, that condition has occurred more than half the time, 1953—85). Second, the national party has very limited influence in congressional nominations and elections. Third, the Congress is composed of two very different chambers, with party and leadership playing different roles in each. Different majority parties may even control the two chambers (as in the 97th Congress). And fourth, cabinet officials seldom have political party experience, nor is such experience normally judged to be important for the exercise of their responsibilities.

Given these political and institutional realities, it is not surprising that the party solution was not implemented when conditions favored congressional assertiveness over the executive in the 1970s. What were these conditions? From the White House came the disastrous Vietnam policies, the escalating costs of Johnson's Great Society programs, Nixon's arrogant declarations of presidential authority, and, of course, the constitutional crisis caused by Watergate. From Capitol Hill came the perceived abuses of power by committee chairmen, ethical lapses by important congressional figures, failures of leadership to cope with presidential excesses, and inattentiveness to the long run-effects of many domestic programs (for a more complete discussion, see Chapter 15).

Following the reelection of Richard M. Nixon in 1972 these many factors contributed to extraordinary media and public attention to Capitol Hill activities. It was almost as if the decline in the presidency—powers and office—forced Washington watchers to turn their eyes to Congress. During the final days of the Nixon presidency, it seemed that the nation came to depend on Congress for leadership and that the members themselves doubted their capacity to lead. A veritable avalanche of reform was forthcoming—more practically than had been enacted to that time. Many of the changes were directed to the internal workings of Congress. But virtually all of the proposals had important implications for the role of Congress in program execution. In fact taken as a whole, the reforms add up to a highly pretentious effort on the part of Congress to involve itself as never before in all of the associated activities of the policy process.

The reforms themselves are discussed in greater detail in Chapter 15. Suffice here to say that most of them were intended to expand the role of Congress in the policy process. Of particular interest are those changes that had the effect of expanding congressional activities in program execution: sunshine and sunset laws, expanded use of the legislative veto, the growth of staff, and the creation of a new budget process.

Sunshine laws. Beginning in 1973 both houses began to hold more open committee meetings. Before that time approximately 30 to 40 percent of the meetings (hearings and markup sessions) were closed. In 1975 only 7 percent were closed (15 percent in the Senate, less than 3 percent in the House).[21] This openness naturally encouraged greater participation by the members and interest groups in all aspects of legislative work. Lobbyists could follow developments first hand, even "passing notes to members in conferences."[22] The openness is said to have many effects on legislative deliberations—greater partisanship, less compromising, better preparation for meetings by members and staff, fewer errors in reports. In addition, it appears to encourage greater involvement by members in all phases of the policy process. The argument is that the increased access for special interests leads to efforts to insure that victories gained in Congress are guaranteed later in program implementation. The tendency therefore is to include more details in legislation than might otherwise occur and to develop means for program evaluation to guarantee that the legislative goals are realized.

Sunset laws. Though not as yet enacted by Congress, the so-called sunset laws provide a regularized process for congressional review of program execution. As passed by the Senate in 1978, most programs would be subject to comprehensive review every 10 years. If not then reauthorized, the programs automatically would be terminated (the sun would set on that program). The House did not act on the bill. The importance of this effort is in illustrating once again the frustrations members feel concerning the growth of government programs and the congressional incapacities for conducting oversight. By requiring a comprehensive review, some members believe that they will be able to do what they otherwise have not done. Such a law, if enacted and enforced, would force Congress to be involved more in policy implementation and evaluation. One result surely would be even greater growth in congressional bureaucracy since comprehensive reviews of large government programs can only be conducted by professional analysts. Further, additional staff would be required to process the agency reports justifying continuation of programs.

---

[21] *Congressional Quarterly Weekly Report,* January 24, 1976, pp. 152–54.

[22] Quote from former Representative Wayne Hays (D—Ohio), in *Congressional Quarterly Weekly Report,* January 24, 1976, p. 152.

Expanded use of legislative veto.   "Legislative vetoes are putting rabbits to shame on Capitol Hill."[23] This controversial technique (see earlier discussion of its development) has proliferated in recent years, primarily as a reflection of conflicts between Congress and the executive, as well as the growing concern among members of Congress about their capacity to control actions by the agencies. By 1980, some 167 laws contained legislative veto provisions. Nearly one fourth of these (42) were enacted during the Carter administration. This development represents one of the most dramatic examples of congressional intrusions into program implementation. It reflects a lack of trust between the institutions as Congress is, in essence, unwilling to permit the executive freely to administer programs. In a sense the legislative veto extends the program development process. Those interests which have been successful in the lawmaking process are given a chance to guarantee a favorable interpretation in the administrative rule-making process. And those interests losing out earlier in the process are given a second chance.

> Lobbyists who have not prevailed for their employer in regular legislation or in the rule-making process in the agencies now will have another chance to block federal actions they don't like—in effect, a second or even a third bite of the apple.[24]

As with the sunset laws, effective use of the legislative veto also will result inevitably in more congressional staff. Monitoring and analyzing administrative actions requires time, resources, and expertise. Most members of Congress are already overburdened. Thus, more and more staff will have to be hired.

Congressional staff increases.   Growth of staff has already been mentioned as a logical consequence of other developments associated with the expanded role of Congress in the policy process (sunset laws, legislative veto). But increasing personal and committee staffs for the purpose of promoting more effective program development can easily result in greater congressional involvement in program execution. What happens simply is that staff work on all of the early policy activities (problem definition, interest aggregation, formulation of proposals, etc.—see Table 13–1), and it inevitably takes these professionals into the full cycle of policy-related decision making. They are analysts, after all, and they understand that everything in government is ultimately connected to everything else. A member of Congress is elected from a state or district to represent his or her constituency and participate in making law. These are weighty responsibilities—

---

[23] *Congressional Quarterly Weekly Report,* March 8, 1980, p. 661.
[24] Ibid.

constituting more than enough work to keep a person fully occupied. Without a staff, therefore, a senator or representative is more likely *to restrict participation* to those activities directly associated with the expectations of relevant publics. With a staff, the members can expand their horizons considerably—doing more of what they have done in the past and extending themselves to activities previously assigned to others. Further, they will be urged by their staffs to grow in these ways.

The new budget process. The Budget and Impoundment Control Act of 1974 represents the most ambitious effort of Congress to integrate its many legislative activities through a more orderly budgetary process. Prior to 1974 an administration budget was sent to Capitol Hill, there to be distributed among the many authorization committees and appropriations subcommittees in each house and never again to be treated as a whole document. Appropriations for the departments and agencies were approved in no particular order—often it was well into the new fiscal year before Congress completed action on an agency's budget. It took a challenge by a Republican president (Richard M. Nixon) to a Democratic Congress for large-scale reform to occur. In essence, President Nixon suggested that Congress was incapable of acting intelligently on the budget. He "blamed the Democratic Congress for just about all of the economic and fiscal woes of the republic," according to John McEvoy, staff director for the Senate Committee on the Budget. McEvoy believed, however, that (in Shepsle, ed., 1980:   2):

> It was not as if Congress had not earned its vulnerability as the target for President Nixon's onslaught. Things really were out of control. Five times between 1965 and 1974, Congress had attempted to discipline itself by imposing arbitrary percentage reductions midstream in the appropriation process. Each empowered the president to reduce spending which had already been enacted. Those spending ceilings failed for a number of reasons. They were not thought through, and as soon as people began to feel the pinch of the programs that were being reduced, supplemental appropriations had to be made to make up the difference.

The combination of the president's criticism (plus his own bold actions in impounding funds) and congressional awareness of the limitations of the present system led to major changes in the budget process (LeLoup, 1980:   chapter 2; Schick, 1980:   chapters 2, 3). The 1974 Act made significant organizational and procedural changes. Budget committees were created in each house, a Congressional Budget Office (CBO) was established to provide independent budget analysis, the fiscal year was changed from July 1—June 30 to October 1—September 30, and procedures were set forth for Congress to conduct a comprehensive review of all authorizations and appropriations. The sequence of action under the new procedure is as follows (Havemann, 1978:   34—35; Ippolito, 1978:   104):

1.	President submits current services budget to Congress (in essence an estimate of the cost of maintaining current programs).		November 10
2.	President submits annual budget to Congress.		Fifteen days after Congress meets
3.	Congressional Committees make budget recommendations to the two budget committees.		March 15
4.	Congressional Budget Office (CBO) reports to the budget committees on alternative budget strategies.		April 1
5.	Budget committees report first budget resolution.		April 15
6.	Congress adopts first budget resolution.		May 15
7.	Congressional committees report all authorizing legislation.		May 15
8.	Congress passes all spending and revenue bills.		Labor Day plus seven
9.	Congress adopts second budget resolution.		September 15
10.	Congress passes budget reconciliation bill.		September 25
11.	New fiscal year begins.		October 1

This drastic revision of the congressional budgetary process includes several opportunities for comprehensive analysis of fiscal policy. The current services budget gives the budget committees an early overview of the costs of maintaining programs at current levels, the preparation of the first budget resolution forces Congress to consider the costs of new and existing programs, and the preparation of the second budget resolution demands a full-scale review of actions by the standing committees, with reconciliation required if the committees have exceeded the limits in the resolution.

While most critics give the new process mixed evaluations, none is prepared to argue that the old system was better. Certainly problems have arisen as the political context has changed. When first developed, the procedure permitted Congress to protect its prerogatives against a hostile administration. Presidents Nixon and Ford were threatening to reduce programs that were popular on Capitol Hill. An important shift occurred during the Carter administration, and Congress was itself faced with having to reduce programs. As Robert N. Giaimo (D–Connecticut), Chairman of the House Committee on the Budget, observed:

> I think we're being tested now in economic affairs because of the very real crisis that's out there. And the jury is really out on whether Congress has the necessary fortitude to bite the bullet and make the hard choices.[25]

Our present concern is less with the future effectiveness of the new procedures than with their potential for encouraging greater involvement by members of Congress in program execution. The temptations are great to duplicate, or substitute for, the work of the executive.

---

[25] Quoted in Timothy B. Clark and Richard E. Cohen, "Balancing the Budget a Test for Congress—Can it Resist the Pressures to Spend?" *National Journal*, April 12, 1980, p. 592.

Given the fundamental importance of the budget to all government activity, it is not at all surprising that budget committee members and their staffs (including the CBO) are drawn toward evaluating existing programs. It is equally unsurprising that mutual suspicion grows between the two branches. The president may be expected to be even more protective of his budget than in the past. And in part as a consequence of this behavior, congressional budgeteers are likely to be even more active in producing separate analyses. Thus what began in part as a partisan reaction by a Democratic Congress to a Republican President's budget behavior now makes cooperation difficult even when the two institutions are presumably controlled by the same party.

Further tensions have been created within the institution itself, particularly in an era of budget-cutting politics. In the most comprehensive review of the new congressional budget procedures, Allen Schick concludes that "the new process enlarges the potential for conflict within Congress because it expands the scope of participation and compels Congress to make more explicit budget choices than before" (1980: 80). He also notes that the new budget committees are placed in an adversarial position in regard to the other congressional committees. Therefore, one consequence of this major reform may well be to encourage members and committees to get more involved in each other's affairs, as well as in the affairs of the executive.

CONGRESS AS A TOTAL POLICY PROCESS

In his essay on parliamentary government, Ernest Barker made a fundamental point applicable to all governments through time (1951: 70).

> Every human institution tends naturally to institutionalism. It exaggerates itself. Not content with discharging its specific function, it readily seeks to encroach. This is a tendency shown by each and all of the four institutions of representation—by the electorate; by the system of party; by the parliament; by the cabinet. All are necessary: all are equally necessary; but each is apt to think that it is specially necessary, and each is apt to claim predominance over the others.

Barker viewed this tendency toward encroachment as unfortunate, yet inevitable (1951: 71).

> Instead of seeing itself as a part, which must play its function as such and claim no more than that, each institution is prone to see itself as a whole, to regard itself as a rounded O, and to claim a total sovereignty. That is an aberration. There is no sovereignty of the electorate. There is no sovereignty of party. There is not even a sovereignty of parliament. . . . There is no sovereignty of cabinet. . . . The only thing sovereign is the whole system of representation—the whole system of reasoning debate, which runs through all the parts; which needs each party and

every part; which needs, above all, the inter-adjustment and balance of all the parts.

Substitute our own institutions for those of Britain, in particular Congress for parliament and the president for the cabinet, and one has in this statement the classic justification for the separation of powers and checks and balances. James Madison never said it any better. The natural tendency to encroach requires that each institution be checked. By this view, which was certainly dominant at the Constitutional Convention, a balance among the institutions must be achieved. Each must have the authority to do its job and yet sufficient checks must be available to prevent serious encroachments. For Barker this balance produces the partnership that is essential for good government. "Any society, to be worthy of the name, must consist of *partners* who enjoy a say in the affairs of the society. When a society ceases to be that, it ceases to be a society" (Barker, 1951: 68).

The pertinence of this analysis for the present discussion is simply this. The work of Congress has traditionally had an impact on program execution. But often the effect was indirect, a by-product of activities primarily associated with program development (e.g., casework, authorization and appropriation, oversight). Recent reforms (growth in staff, expanded use of the legislative veto, a more comprehensive and coordinated budgetary procedure) encourage even more direct and systematic congressional participation in program execution. Interestingly these changes appear to have been made to a substantial degree as a consequence of perceived excesses by the president—particularly during the Johnson and Nixon administrations. That is, Congress was moved to expand its capabilities to deal with all aspects of foreign and domestic issues because many members came to believe that Presidents Johnson and Nixon had exceeded their authority (Jones in Mann and Ornstein, 1981: chapter 8). In this context, the importance of the Watergate crisis was that the lack of trust between the two branches encouraged Congress to encroach on the executive—in Ernest Barker's words: "to see itself as a whole, to regard itself as a rounded O, and to claim a total sovereignty."

The demands are enormous on any institution with pretentions of total sovereignty. A branch of government that intends to establish a total policy process within itself has set a formidable challenge. But meeting such a challenge is conceivable within the executive due to its hierarchical structure. A president who decides to do it all himself will encounter many problems, but at least he has some advantages in that the bureaucracy is organized, on paper at least, to be attentive to his priorities.[26] Congress is quite another story. Strictly speaking no one is

---

[26] He is, however, limited in other ways—the four-year term, requirement for congressional approval of his program, potential for challenge in the federal courts, limits in capacity to command a sizeable bureaucracy.

in charge. The collective decision to expand the policy activities—for example, into program execution—is unlikely to result in anything approaching coordinated and systematic direction of the bureaucracy. Therefore it is not surprising that one has difficulty analyzing the precise effect of what I have called the new involvements. Congress has definitely made an effort to improve its capacities for monitoring program implementation and engaging in program evaluation. But the full effects of the changes are as yet unknown.

PROGRAM EXECUTION ACTIVITIES AND POLICY NETWORKS

The program execution activities appear to move the action away from the legislature. As displayed in Table 13−1 they are:

Program implementation:
  Organization.
  Interpretation.
  Application.

Program evaluation:
  Specification.
  Measurement.
  Analysis.
  Recommendation.

This work traditionally has been associated with the bureaucracy. It appears to require consistent participation by specialists—those persons with the time and expertise to provide predictable policy application across issues. Legislators can seldom be expected to offer these advantages, though the recent explosion in congressional staff permits them to entertain (and justify) greater involvement.

Under normal circumstances then one would expect that the policy networks, particularly if they tend to be cozy little triangles, will vary in population through the set of policy activities (problem definition through to program evaluation). For example, primary and secondary participation in triangles or subsystems may vary as indicated in Table 14−1 (the White House is not included in this exercise). Note that the bureaucrats are expected to be the primary actors in program implementation and evaluation, with group representatives seeking to influence their decisions (possibly through their access with legislators).

What if Congress makes a conscious decision to participate more actively in program execution? Greater secondary participation by the members in the kinds of traditional functions cited early in this chapter (appointments, program development, oversight) is unlikely to have much of an effect in the bureaucratic-centered triangle. When Congress acts more directly, however, either (1) to alter the shape of the

TABLE 14–1
Expected participation in traditional cozy little triangles: Problem definition to program evaluation

Policy activities	Primary participants	Secondary participants
Problem definition	Group representatives, bureaucrats	Legislators
Agenda setting	Legislators, bureaucrats	Group representatives
Formulation of proposals	Group representatives, legislators, bureaucrats	—
Approval of proposals (including appropriation)	Legislators	Group representatives, bureaucrats
Program implementation	Bureaucrats	Group representatives, legislators
Program evaluation	Bureaucrats	Group representatives, legislators

SOURCE: Compiled by author.

policy network or (2) to substitute its decisions for those of the bureaucrats, then we have the potential for some fundamental changes in the workings of the policy process. Sunshine laws, sunset laws, and the new budgetary process are examples of the first type of change; the expanded use of the legislative veto and the growth of staff are examples of the second. Let's consider the effects of each type of change.

The first set of reforms is designed to increase participation directly (as with the sunshine laws) or indirectly by demanding greater coordination and comprehensive review (as with sunset laws and budget reform). An important effect of these changes, therefore, may well be to encourage shifts from intermediary or triangle politics to macro or hexagon politics (see Table 13–3). It may well be that in making these changes Congress is only reflecting public demands. Whatever the ultimate cause, the point is that these moves effect program execution in part by *increasing participation and altering the configuration of the network.* Other groups and legislators are invited to be more attentive to program execution. The budgetary reforms have the additional potential effect of establishing a new locus for decision making—one which is less susceptible to traditional intermediary or triangle politics whether in program development or program execution. The new budget committees are charged with the responsibility of formulating budget resolutions and monitoring the work of the other committees. When the economy is growing and revenues are high, the budget committees simply offer an orderly method for doing business. When revenues fall off and there are demands to balance the budget, the two committees must decide priorities. The process itself seeks to coordinate the intermediary politics so characteristic of the other standing committees. That it is sometimes unsuccessful is beside the point. The process now exists and some members take it seriously.

The second set of reforms (legislative veto and staff growth), may have the effect of drawing legislators and their staffs into primary participation in program execution. This may occur as a consequence of the fact that more legislative actors are monitoring and evaluating program implementation and thus bureaucrats and group representatives must acknowledge their presence. But more fundamentally legislative actors are thrust directly into program implementation since the legislative veto in essence adds another decision point to that stage of policy action. Thus the legislative veto and the impressive growth of staff resources have the potential of changing the expectations associated with who does what in program execution.

CONCLUSION

Generalizing about congressional participation in the policy process is somewhat easier for program development than for program execution. Whereas congressional prerogatives permit considerable monitoring of program execution, actual behavior by members has been episodic and unsystematic. Many legislators are frustrated by this reality and have pressed for change. As Representative Culver lamented: "There is no comprehensive plan for systematic review of operations of the federal government." Therefore changes have been instituted that affect the role of Congress in program execution. It is too soon to tell for certain what the effects of these changes will be. It is not too soon to speculate, however. Two developments in particular are identified which deserve further exploration.

1. Many reforms have been enacted which represent significant encroachments by Congress into what are normally considered executive functions. Serious questions are raised as to whether Congress can be effective if it tries to create a total policy process within itself.

2. The encroachments have the potential of significantly effecting the structure and operations of the policy process—possibly by producing a shift from intermediary or triangle politics to macro or hexagon politics.

These observations take us beyond the immediate topic for this chapter, but provide an effective introduction to the next topic—congressional reform.

15 Reforming the Congress: When and how

Any institution with the principal functions of facilitating political representation and bargaining will always be subject to considerable criticism. When Congress is doing its job well on a divisive issue, it may not be enacting any legislation at all. Or when a law is passed it is normally the result of bargaining and compromise, and the very essence of compromise is that nobody wins or loses *everything*. Therefore it is unlikely that congressional performance will get a positive rating from those judging the institution from their own self-interest. Senator Alben W. Barkley's famous story of Farmer Jones illustrates another dimension of the public evaluation of Congress. Barkley learned that Jones planned to vote for his opponent in a primary race. This news stunned Barkley since he had been doing favors for Jones for over 30 years (cited in Matthews, 1960: 218).

> He hurried to see Jones and reminded him of his many labors on his behalf.
>
> "Surely" Barkley said, "you remember all these things I have done for you?"
>
> "Yeah," said Farmer Jones sullenly, "But what in hell have you done for me lately?"

The public approval ratings of Congress are typically quite low (Vogler, 1980: 6). Seldom do they exceed those of the president. In recent years they were the highest for Congress when it was enacting a high proportion of Johnson's Great Society program. When the public displayed great dissatisfaction with President Nixon during the height of the Watergate crisis, they held similarly low opinions of Congress—27 percent approval for the president in January, 1974; 21 percent approval for Congress (Jones in Dodd and Oppenheimer, 1977: 252).

> At least superficially, it would appear that the public ratings of Congress are associated with those of the president, though always a bit lower. This finding lends little support . . . to the theory that the public turns to Congress as an alternative when the president fails. Rather, the public would appear to group the two [institutions]—disillusionment with one leads to disillusionment with the other (Jones in Dodd and Oppenheimer, 1977: 252).

Congress the institution is unlikely very often to satisfy a majority of people. "They're not doing anything." "I didn't get all of what I wanted." "What have they done for me lately?" "They're no better than the crook in the White House—probably worse." Attitudes like these sum up to a highly critical view.[1] Still, until recently both representatives and senators had a relatively high rate of return. This puzzle led Richard F. Fenno, Jr., to ask: "If our congressmen are so good, how can our Congress be so bad?" (in Ornstein, ed., 1975: 278). His response, in part, was simply that the members work hard at winning approval for themselves but not very hard at gaining public support for the institution. In fact, they often campaign against their own institution. Public disapproval and the failure of the members to support and defend the institution make Congress vulnerable to media criticism and ridicule. The total effect of these forces is devastating to congressional self esteem. A reform pathology appears to have functioned almost constantly in recent years. It goes something like this:

> **Observation:** "I didn't get all of what I wanted" or "What have they done for me lately?"
>
> **Generalization:** Congress is sick.
>
> **Diagnosis:** The _____ are at fault. (*Instructions:* Fill in the blank with one, more than one, or all of the following: committees, parties, leaders, staff, budget processes, elections).
>
> **Cure:** Reorganize, change rules, increase staff, etc.

Notice that one moves from a complaint about substance, about not getting what one wants or expects to get, to an organizational or pro-

---

[1] For an analysis of various factors that effect congressional popularity and how these factors differ between the two institutions, see Parker, 1977: 93–109.

cedural change. People often conclude that institutional structure or special interests are at fault, and so they propose to reform decision making. Sometimes they are right, and a new method of doing things results in different policy products. More often, however, the diagnosis is wrong, and structural changes result in more of the same or a new set of dissatisfactions (either for the reformer or for someone else).

Congressional reform is a fitting last major topic for this book since it acts like a mirror to reflect many of the themes emphasized in these pages. It follows that those justifying change have been moved to make judgments about people, organization, processes, and product. Their words and actions tend to reveal images they have of what Congress is and what it should be. But special attention to this topic is suitable for another reason. The decade of the 1970s witnessed more reform practically than had been approved in the rest of congressional history. Many of these changes have been discussed throughout the book. It remains, however, to discuss the dynamics of political reform and identify the major reform eras in congressional history, with special attention to the remarkable 1970s.

THE REFORM PSYCHOLOGY

One should not generalize about congressional reform from the last decade. The 1970s are interesting to us primarily because they are different from other decades. Congress can be changed, but it reforms itself and it is not moved very often to enact large-scale reforms. It takes more than criticism to stir Congress—in fact, the members become inured to constant censure. Speaking more generally about political reform, William J. Crotty points out that (1980: xxv):

> Reform movements have their own momentum. Times of robust activity are followed by long periods of seeming passivity. A single incident, volatile, dramatic, and well publicized, can set off a chain reaction of events that lead to a pressure for change. The modifications introduced in response to the public outcry may be merely cosmetic in effort to pacify the public and head off meaningful change. Or they can lead to fundamental and innovative efforts to restructure approaches to a problem.

In the case of Congress a reform movement must be strong enough to influence the members to make changes. For whereas Congress has the authority to reform other national institutions, those institutions do not in turn have the authority to reform Congress. Under what conditions is Congress likely to be moved to reform itself? Clearly the members themselves must perceive the need for change—and this perception must be widespread in order to create the reform psychology. For a short time Congress had a Joint Committee on Congressional Operations (1971 — 77) to conduct studies of Congress on a continuing basis—a sort of what to reform next mission. The committee was not notably successful, however, for the very good reason that reforms require considerably more collective support than a joint committee can possibly muster.[2]

The more likely stimulus for reform is an action or series of actions perceived by members to be a direct threat to the institution. This threat may be from *outside Congress but inside the government,* as with an aggressive president who seeks to minimize the role of Congress or a Supreme Court that reduces congressional authority. If enough members conclude that Congress is too weak to respond adequately to such threats, then the reform condition is set. Or the threat may come from *inside* Congress, as with the arbitrary exercise of power by party or committee leaders, or cumbersome procedures that are perceived to be interfering with effective lawmaking. In recent years another threat has developed—that from *outside the government.* Public evaluations of congressional performance in the polls or by public interest groups may also be perceived as threatening the integrity of the institution and therefore lead to reform.

Naturally the threat will be interpreted differently by the members, often depending on partisan considerations or how it is each member analyzes the personal effect of change. Therefore, it is not surprising that perception among members of the need for change is not automatically followed by agreed-upon reforms. Proposals are introduced, disagreements emerge, debate and analysis take place, compromises are fashioned, support is developed, and sometimes reforms are enacted. It may also be the case that the threat itself passes and the mood for reform may dissipate. The central point about reform is that it follows from, and must be sustained by, worry among the members that Congress cannot do its job well. Therefore, the threat as a stimulus to reform must persist.

Reforms may have many different purposes. Some are designed simply to reduce pressure and are therefore quite symbolic in nature. Whatever the long-term effect may be, the short-term purpose is to satisfy those demanding change. Or as Samuel C. Patterson observes: "The brute fact is that legislative reforms very often are not changes at all and should not be considered to be changes. There are mere amenities, which make legislators more comfortable" (in Welch and Peters, eds., 1977:   217). So the purpose may be no more than providing higher salaries or better working conditions (including staff support). Other purposes include streamlining procedures for better coordination, permitting the majority to act on controversial policy

---

[2] A document was published to advertise the purpose and potential for the Joint Committee. U.S. House of Representatives, *The Joint Committee on Congressional Operations,* 92d Cong., 1st Sess., 1971 (Document No. 92 — 187).

issues, and reallocating power. Or the reform may be strictly ad hominum—that is, designed to get rid of certain people, typically because they have obstructed the legislative process.

It is the very nature of a response to a threat that primary consideration is given to the short-run goal of reducing the threat rather than the long-run effects of making change. In fact reforms are seldom analyzed for all possible effects. Often a blind faith in change for its own sake is demonstrated by many reformers. Making the change is immediately gratifying, and beyond that, it buys time since the members can justifiably argue that the institution should not be tested again until the reform has had a chance to work.

ANALYZING CONGRESSIONAL REFORM

This short-run orientation of the reform psychology suggests the need to create a framework for analyzing congressional change. In particular we need to identify the different objects of reform, the immediate changes that may be realized, the contribution of these changes to accomplishing the various functions of Congress, and, finally how the reform effects the status of the institution in national politics.[3]

The objects of reform

The targets or objects of congressional reform differ greatly, consistent with the variation in what is perceived to be at fault. The following goals can be identified:

1. *Jurisdictional:* where the object is the basic authority of the institution to participate in national policymaking (e.g., in budget making or approving military actions).
2. *Electoral:* where the object is congressional campaign and election procedures.
3. *Procedural/organization:* where the object is the rules and formal organization of Congress.
4. *Political:* where the object is the redistribution of power among party and committee leaders, and how that power is exercised.
5. *Analytical:* where the object is congressional capacity for doing independent policy analysis.
6. *Ethical:* where the object is the personal conduct of the members and staff.

---

[3] I have relied heavily in this section on a paper I wrote for a conference on legislative reform called "How Reform Changes Congress," published in Welch and Peters, ed., 1977: 11—29.

Changes realized

What happens as an immediate result of enacting a reform? These short-run changes are important and may be quite varied. They may or may not affect the announced object of the reform. Changes of the following sort may be realized:

1. *Criticism:* whatever the precise reform, one immediate result may be a lessening of criticism, if not necessarily a rise in institutional esteem among the public.
2. *Personnel:* new people may assume positions of responsibility— quite simply, the faces may change on Capitol Hill.
3. *Authority:* Congress may allocate itself more power, or the location of decision making may shift from one group or person to another.
4. *Process:* decisions may be made differently from in the past—in terms of the information relied on, the flow of work, the number of people involved.
5. *Output:* the laws may change or Congress may be more active in its other work—oversight, communicating with constituents, identifying issues.

Clearly the reforms can result in some of these changes and not others. You may see reduced criticism, even higher ratings for Congress in the opinion polls, and little else. Or one can imagine removing some persons from positions of authority, replacing them, and giving the new people more authority, all with little change in output. Analyzing reform *as change* is not as simple as it might appear.

Functions served

Roger H. Davidson and Walter J. Oleszek discuss the House of Representatives in organic terms. They point out that as an organization the House must adjust both to its external environment and to its internal needs. Innovation or reform designed to facilitate the organization's interface with its external environment is called adaptation. And that designed to relieve the internal stresses and tension is called consolidation (Davidson and Oleszek, 1976: 39 — 41). Elsewhere I refer to the fact that legislatures are two-faced. They

> must face the people—searching out and receiving public problems. They must also face the law—developing public policy and seeing to its implementation. Put another way, legislatures are really two objects: a collectivity and an institution. As a collectivity, individual representatives act as receptors, reflecting the needs and wants of constituents. As an institution, the legislature has to make laws, arriving at some conclusions about what ought to be done about public problems (Jones, 1974b: 138).

Davidson, too, speaks of two Congresses. The first "Congress as an institution . . . performing its constitutional duties and deliberating on legislative issues." The second is "Congress-as-career-entrepreneurs."

> This is the Congress of 535 individual senators and representatives. They come from diverse backgrounds and have followed various paths to win office. Their electoral fortunes depend not on what Congress produces as an institution but on the support and good will of voters . . . who are not shared by any of their colleagues on the Hill (Davidson in Crotty, ed., 1980: 284 – 85).

These several observations are really related to the functions performed by Congress. Broadly speaking, Congress represents (implied in the discussion of the external environment, adaptation, the face to the people, Congress-as-career-entrepreneurs) and it makes law (variously described as meeting its internal needs, consolidation, the face to the law, Congress-as-institution). And though these tasks are by no means easy to reconcile, still the legislature was designed as the principal democratic institution for joining the two functions.

There are functional equivalents for representation and lawmaking in the activities that constitute the policy process (see Table 13 – 1). Some activities are oriented more toward the people and their problems (representation), some toward developing a proposal and getting it approved (lawmaking). For example:

Representative or adaptive functions:

1. *Problem definition and representation, and agenda-setting:* identifying problems and judging which should be acted on in government.
2. *Program implementation:* interpreting and applying the law.
3. *Program evaluation:* measuring the effects of policy programs.

Lawmaking or consolidative functions:

1. *Program formulation:* developing proposals to solve public problems.
2. *Program approval:* building majorities for proposed programs.
3. *Program budgeting:* building support for appropriations.

The point is that reforms may have effects beyond the immediate change realized. They may also facilitate or impede the functioning of Congress in the policy process by affecting its capacities to perform the various kinds of work cited above.

Institutional effect

Another matter to consider in congressional reform is its overall effect on the relative place of the institution in the Washington power structure. In Chapter 1, I proposed three interpretations of the division of power among the institutions—legislative primacy, presidential primacy, and mixed government (cooperative or adversarial). We need do no more here than refer to those categories and suggest to the reader that reform can contribute in the long run to realization of one set of relationships over another. It should also be noted that reformers may have intentions to affect the relationship among the institutions in a particular way but be unsuccessful. Or it may never have occurred to them to have such an effect, and yet their reforms may in fact have profound impact on the way the institutions share power.

Summary

The principal lesson from this review of reform intentions and effects is that, like all organisms, Congress is integrated into its environment through a complex set of internal and external interlacements. It is therefore not in the least surprising that when one set of connections is disturbed, others are affected as well. For it is a fact that people and institutions (which are, after all, collections of people) get used to doing things in a particular way over time. Disruptions are never easily confined.

It is also characteristic of reform movements, however, that their supporters seldom will set about analyzing the possible effects of change in advance or evaluating the impacts once the change has been made. As noted earlier, the reform psychology does not normally accommodate thoughtful analysis of effects. It is responsive to short-term threats and seeks immediate relief. There is also a serious question as to whether we have available either the methods or the knowledge to conduct intelligent analysis of the manifold changes and effects that may occur as a result of enacting reforms. Put differently, the science of reform is quite crude, if it exists at all.

This same lack of desire and knowledge helps to explain the limited amount of evaluation once a reform has been set in place. Donald T. Campbell argues that "most ameliorative programs [i.e., reforms] end up with no interpretable evaluation" (1969:   409 – 10, his emphasis).

> . . .*specific reforms are advocated as though they were certain to be successful.* For this reason, knowing outcomes has immediate political implications. Given the inherent difficulty of making significant improvements by the means usually provided and given the discrepancy between promise and possibility, most administrators [or reformers] wisely prefer to limit the evaluations to those the outcomes of which they can control. . . . Ambiguity, lack of truly comparable comparison bases, and lack of concrete evidence all work to increase the administrator's [or reformer's] control over what gets said, or at least to reduce the bite of criticism in the case of actual failure. There is safety under the cloak of ignorance.

Campbell supports our earlier conclusion (Chapter 14) that the knowledge to conduct proper evaluation of reforms is often lacking. In addition, he points out that this very ignorance may sustain reform despite its failure. Campbell also believes that the desire for evaluation is normally lacking (1969: 410, his emphasis).

> If the political and administrative system has committed itself in advance to the correctness and efficacy of its reforms, *it cannot tolerate learning of failure.* To be truly scientific we must be able to experiment. We must be able to advocate without that excess of commitment that blinds us to reality testing.
>
> This predicament, abetted by public apathy and by deliberate corruption, may prove in the long run to permanently preclude a truly experimental approach to social amelioration.

One can readily see from this discussion how much reform can reveal about the institution to which it is directed. It is an activity intimately associated with the creation, maturation, and survival of institutions. Proposals for change naturally raise questions about the what, where, when, who, and how of the work and functions of the existing apparatus.

REFORM ERAS

I identify three major reform eras for the modern Congress. First is the period in which power was consolidated in the speakership and subsequently dispersed—from the 51st Congress and the establishment of the Reed Rules to the 61st Congress and the removal of Speaker Cannon from the Committee on Rules. Second is the post-World War II reform era in which Congress sought to reorganize itself so as to cope with the increasing complexity of public issues and match the growing power of the president. Third is the extraordinary period of the 1970s which witnessed an outpouring of reforms designed to curb the power of committee chairmen and increase the capacity of Congress to participate actively in all phases of the policy process.

As will soon become apparent, most of the reform takes place in the House of Representatives not the Senate. The reasons for this concentration of effort tell us something about the differences in function and style of the two chambers. Being more the place of representation, the House has immense organizational problems. The members are naturally pulled toward the special interests of their individual districts. Designing means by which compromises will be fashioned so that laws may be passed is a constant challenge in that body.

The Senate is a more deliberative body, by design and therefore by inclination of the membership. One does not expect the elaborate organization and detailed procedures required in the House. Strict adherence to written rules is not necessary—in fact, it may even be harmful. Likewise, one would not expect frequent reform. Rather, changes are likely to occur over time and may not be formally presented or ratified. The fact that rules are made to be broken in the Senate suggests that it can adapt to changing circumstances more readily than is true in the House. Still reforms have been enacted in that august body too—as will be discussed subsequently.

From Reed to Cannon—The rise and fall of the Speakership

In their article analyzing House leadership, Joseph Cooper and David W. Brady observe that (1981:   411):

> The legacy the House of the 19th century left to that of the 20th was a set of rules which placed the majority firmly in control of the House and centralized power in the hands of the Speaker as the agent of this majority. It was this legacy the House rejected when it revolted against the Speaker in 1910. In so doing it not only stripped the Speaker of many of his important powers, but also paved the way for a metamorphosis in the nature of the House as a political institution.

Rather dramatic reforms began this period of strengthened party and leadership, and equally dramatic reforms ended it.

Partisanship was extremely bitter in the 1880s and 1890s, so much so that it virtually brought legislative action to a standstill. Whichever party was in the minority engaged in delaying tactics to prevent the House from acting on legislation. Either members would introduce dilatory motions of various kinds and demand the call of the roll, or they would ask for a determination of whether a quorum was present and then absent themselves. The latter tactic was effective during the 50th and 51st Congresses due to the small margins of control by the majority party (the Democrats held 52 percent of the seats in the 50th Congress; the Republicans held 52 percent of the seats in the 51st Congress). Thomas B. Reed (R—Maine) sought to get a change in the rules when he was in the minority but failed, apparently because the Democrats, knowing they would be in the minority in the next Congress, intended to use the same tactics. According to one journalist, the Democrats were determined (Robinson, 1930:   188):

> . . . to filibuster in the next House against revenue legislation, territorial bills, contested election cases, and every other measure when by so doing the minority can hope to reap a party advantage. It is clear that the Democrats in the next Congress will filibuster against any and every proposition to amend the rules so as to give the majority that control of the business of the House to which it is justly entitled.

Thus, the Democrats, who were more often than not in the minority during these years, were not about to approve a change which might prevent future obstructionism on their part. As Charles F. Crisp (D—Georgia) declared: "We live in this country under written constitutions. These constitutions are made not to protect the rights of majorities but to protect the rights of minorities" (Robinson, 1930: 188). Crisp later served as Speaker himself.

The Democrats were true to their intentions in the 51st Congress. On January 21, 1890, however, Speaker Reed made the first of his important rulings to curb dilatory actions by the minority. Richard P. Bland (D—Missouri) demanded a teller vote on a motion to adjourn, and Reed refused on the grounds that Bland simply wanted to obstruct the proceedings. In an appeal the Speaker's decision was upheld and the first skirmish was over.

Having lost this first encounter, the Democrats prepared to do battle on the next. They were determined to withdraw from the chamber on quorum calls, thus forcing the Republicans to be in the House chamber at all times.

> The disappearing quorum was in most cases only temporarily effective; but in the 51st Congress, the narrow majority and the expressed determination of the Speaker to secure reforms establishing effective majority rule and the equally evident determination on the part of the minority to fight such reforms to the last ditch, made it absolutely vital. Without a quorum it was evident that little could be accomplished (Robinson, 1930: 205).

Matters came to a head on January 29, 1890, when an election case was brought before the House. A Democrat demanded a roll-call vote. A quorum was 165, and only 161 Republicans were in the chamber. Several were sick and not able to attend. The call of the roll produced 162 yeas, 3 nays, and 163 not voting. "On Recapitulation, two Democrats amid the laughter of their colleagues withdrew their votes, making the result yeas 161, nays 2, not voting 165" (Robinson, 1930: 297). After announcing the vote and hearing Mr. Crisp shout "no quorum," Speaker Reed directed the clerk to "record the following names of members present and refusing to vote." Reed then read off names of members whom he observed as present in the chamber.

> At once the House was in an uproar. There was an explosion as violent as was ever witnessed in a legislative body. The Speaker's recital of the names was interrupted by passionate remonstrance. His course was denounced as revolutionary. . . . Reed remained unruffled (McCall, 1914: 167).

The battle between the Speaker and the Democrats continued for three days. With each new motion the Democrats refused to vote, and Reed called enough names to produce a quorum. At one point the Speaker summarized his position in what turned out to be one of the classic statements of the strong party leadership model.

> The object of a parliamentary body is action and not stoppage of action.
>
> Primarily the organ of the House is the man elected to the Speakership. It is his duty in a clear case, recognizing the situation, to endeavor to carry out the wishes and desires of the majority. . . .
>
> Whenever it becomes apparent that the ordinary and proper parliamentary motions are being used solely for purposes of delay and obstruction . . . it then becomes apparent to the House and to the community what the purpose is. It is then the duty of the occupant of the Speaker's chair to take under parliamentary law, the proper course with regard to such matters (Robinson, 1930: 182).

As Neil MacNeil concluded, "it took an extraordinary man" to make these decisions—one fully prepared to suffer humiliation if his strategy failed (1963: 51). But the strategy succeeded, and the speakership was immensely strengthened. For his part, Reed was characteristically modest.

> Great events do not turn upon one man. The House of Representatives was ready and ripe for change, and the people stood ready to approve. What all the world wanted was easy to do (Robinson, 1930: 182).

In addition to his rulings on the floor (which were subsequently incorporated into the House rules), Reed turned the Committee on Rules into an important center of power. He made it "the steering committee of the majority party, responsible for determining the House's legislative program" (MacNeil, 1963: 53). The legislative management problems were obviously quite severe by the end of the century, and Reed was determined to solve them. He developed the concept of the special rule for determining the when and how of floor debate. The Committee had only five members—the Speaker as chairman, plus two other Republicans (the chairmen of the Committees on Appropriations and Ways and Means) and two Democrats. Once Reed and his Republican colleagues agreed on a special rule, the Speaker's custom was to present it to the Democrats "with grim sarcasm" and say, "Gentlemen, we have decided to perpetrate the following outrage" (Brown, 1922: 88).

The House Republicans suffered disastrous losses in the mid-term elections in 1890—capturing the fewest House seats since their creation as a national party. Reed was once more minority floor leader. He assumed the chair again in the 54th Congress when the House Republicans gained the most seats in their history, and he remained Speaker in the 55th Congress. David Henderson (R — Iowa) served as Speaker for two congresses after Reed's retirement, and then Joseph B. Cannon (R —Illinois) assumed the office.

Cannon lacked Reed's sense of humor and elegant manner. But he

inherited all of the power that Reed had contributed to the speakership, and Cannon used it all, even adding "his own embellishments."

> Cannon controlled the House in its entirety, and he made the House
> subservient to his will by the ruthless way he used his arbitrary powers.
> No bill could be passed without his advance permission; the appoint-
> ment of every member of every House committee was Cannon's sole
> responsibility. Cannon controlled all avenues for promotion in the
> House, and the members of the House shrank deeper into obscurity
> under his domination than ever before (MacNeil, 1963: 53).

Thus the reform condition was set. If the dilatory tactics of the 1880s
made the House ripe for Reed's rulings, the arbitrary exercise of
power by Speaker Cannon encouraged more reform.

The new changes were directed at the Speaker's control of the
agenda through his domination of the Committee on Rules and his
control of the standing committees through his power of appointment. The struggle began on March 17, 1910. Speaker Cannon was
overruled by the House on a scheduling question. In the ensuing
parliamentary maneuvering, George W. Norris (R — Nebraska) thought
he had found a way to introduce a change in the House rules (for
details see Jones, 1968: 617 — 46). Norris describes it in his autobiog-
raphy as follows (1961: 126):

> It was the hour for which I had been waiting patiently. I had in my
> pocket a resolution to change the rules of the House. Unknown to any-
> one . . . I had carried it for a long time, certain that in the flush of its
> power the Cannon machine would overreach itself. The paper upon
> which I had written my resolution had become so tattered it scarcely
> hung together.

The point was that Norris had to find a way to get his resolution
directly to the floor without going through the powerful Rules
Committee—chaired by Speaker Cannon. The Norris resolution increased the size of the Rules Committee, removed the Speaker from
the committee, and took away his power to appoint members to the
committee. After a lengthy debate which carried over to March 19,
Cannon ruled that the resolution was not in order. Norris appealed
Cannon's ruling to the House, and the Speaker was again
overruled—many progressive Republicans voting with the Democrats
against Cannon. The resolution was then passed, and the first dramatic change had occurred in reducing the authority of the Speaker.

The second major change occurred when the Democrats won control of the House in the 1910 mid-term elections. The incoming Democratic leadership was pledged to legislative reform. The new Speaker,
James Beauchamp Clark (D — Missouri), " had publicly taken a position
on the subject" and therefore, in essence, was a party to the reduction
of his own authority (Brown, 1922: 172). Meeting in caucus in 1911,

the Democrats selected the members to serve on the Committee on Ways and Means and then authorized that group to assign members to other committees.

> It was the first time in the history of the House of Representatives that the power to appoint the standing committees of the House had been taken from the Speaker and marked, therefore, the most radical reform that had yet been attempted in that body (Brown, 1922: 175).

Summary

In a relatively short period of time between Reed and Cannon the House witnessed the rise and fall of the all-powerful Speaker. The reviews of the 1910 — 11 changes were mixed. Many viewed them as absolutely essential to protect the representative system. As John Nelson (R — Wisconsin) argued in the debate: "We are free representatives of the people, and we want freedom here for every member of every party."[4] Others were highly critical. George Rothwell Brown viewed the changes as threatening the balance of power (1922: 12 — 13):

> No more paradoxical action has ever been committed by the American people than in the destruction of the power of the speakership in the name of popular liberty. It is the paradox which has obscured the basic principle of government involved — that with responsibility there must be power.

Brown's analysis would undoubtedly draw the support of Reed and Cannon. But by applying the framework outlined earlier we can be a bit more precise. Table 15 — 1 summarizes the many changes and

TABLE 15 — 1
The Reed and Cannon Reforms analyzed

Framework for analysis	Reed (51st Congress)	Cannon (61st Congress)
1. Objects of reform	Procedural/organizational, political	Procedural/organizational, political
2. Changes realized	Authority	Criticism, personnel, authority, process, output (possibly)
3. Functions served	Lawmaking/consolidative	Representative/adaptive
4. Institutional effect	Legislative primacy	Mixed government (cooperative at first)

SOURCE: Compiled by author.

effects of the two sets of reforms. Note that though the objects were the same, the immediate changes realized were much more extensive in 1910 — 11. Speaker Cannon's leadership had come under a great deal

---

[4] *Congressional Record*, March 17, 1910, p. 3304.

of criticism. He was rightly charged with having thwarted the members of his own party in their effort to participate in legislative decision making. They judged that his removal was not sufficient. The system itself had to be changed. Reed, on the other hand, was viewed as somewhat of a hero for having unplugged the legislative process. The results in terms of functions served and institutional effect realized were different in each case. The Reed rules contributed to *a more coherent lawmaking process*, thus encouraging a greater role for Congress in the national government. The Cannon reforms were specifically designed to decentralize power—to encourage greater *adaptation to the various interests* to be served by Congress. Cooperation with the Wilson Administration was realized at first, but a more adversarial mixed government emerged later with the rise of virtually autonomous standing committees.

The post-World War II reforms

The Reed and Cannon reforms resulted from internal threats to the House—that is, from cumbersome procedures and autocratic use of power by the Speaker. The reforms enacted in the immediate post-World War II period resulted from a realization by members that congressional organization had to be modernized. The stimulus to this realization was the growing power of the president. Thus there was more of an *outside* threat than was the case for earlier reforms.

In his study of *Congressional Politics in the Second World War*, Roland Young observes that: "The organization and procedures of Congress were designed for periods of relative domestic tranquility, with full opportunity for public deliberation" (1956: 228–29). During the war a great deal of power had to be delegated to or assumed by the president and the bureaucracy. And while the committee system in Congress continued to perform important policy functions, it was also the subject of much criticism. Standing committees continued to proliferate, jurisdictional disputes were inevitable, and coordination among the committees was difficult, sometimes impossible, to achieve. "At the end of the war strong voices demanded that 'Congress regain its powers,' as the phrase went" (Young, 1956: 234).

There were two principal methods by which Congress might reestablish itself as a coequal branch—by reducing the power of the executive and bureaucracy or by increasing its own capacities to deal with complex domestic and foreign issues. A report issued in 1945 by the Committee on Congress of the American Political Science Association left no doubt about how it felt (1945: 3).

> Congress must modernize its machinery and methods to fit modern conditions if it is to keep pace with a greatly enlarged and active executive branch. This is a better approach than that which seeks to meet the problem by reducing and hamstringing the executive.

This attitude seemed to be shared by other critics and by the members themselves. Consequently a Joint Committee on the Organization of Congress was created in 1945 to study proposals for change and make recommendations to the House and Senate. The Committee was chaired by Senator Robert M. LaFollette, Jr. (Progressive—Wisconsin) with Representative A. S. Mike Monroney (D—Oklahoma) serving as vice chairman. There were six members from each house with equal representation from each party.

Notice the sharp contrast in reform conditions and means for taking action between the Reed-Cannon and post-war periods. Reforms were effected in the heat of intense floor battles during the earlier periods. But in 1945 an effort was made to produce rational change to accomplish agreed-upon goals. The hot reforms of the Reed and Cannon speakerships were the result of direct, intense threats to the policy preferences of the reformers. The cool reforms of 1946 resulted from a more diffuse threat associated with the perceived decline in congressional influence. Perhaps this difference explains why "few of the objectives of the 1946 Act were achieved" (Davidson and Oleszek, 1977: 52).

The Joint Committee's recommendations were passed by both houses with little debate and few changes. The principal targets for reform were the committee system, budgeting procedures, oversight, staffing, and lobbying. The committee and budgeting changes were presumably designed to effect the most change. At the time, the House had 48 standing committees, the Senate had 33. These were pared to 19 and 15 respectively. As noted in Table 15–2, the Committees on Interior and Insular Affairs in each house consolidated many committees, as did the Administration Committees. Together these four committees (two in each house) accounted for 27 committees that existed before 1946.

The budget changes in 1946 foretold the Budget and Impoundment Control Act of 1974. The taxing and appropriations committees in each house were directed to prepare a legislative budget, including estimates of receipts and expenditures. Congress was then prohibited from appropriating money beyond receipts available without authorizing an increase in the federal debt. Unfortunately the Congress was not prepared to implement this procedure. After rather abortive efforts to enact and enforce legislative budgets in 1947 and 1948, the system broke down completely in 1949 and was not tried again (though Congress tinkered with other procedures in later years).

There were no other major reform actions until 1961. In that year mounting frustration with the dominance of Southern Democratic committee chairmen led to important changes in the policy role of the Committee on Rules. The power of the committee as an independent force was considerable since it played a crucial role in scheduling

TABLE 15 – 2

Consolidation of standing committees, Legislative Reorganization Act of 1946

	Number of committees consolidated
House (10 committees carried over intact):	10
Armed Services	2
Banking and Currency	2
Education and Labor	2
House Administration	10
Interior and Insular Affairs	6
Judiciary	4
Post Office and Civil Service	3
Public Works	4
Veterans' Affairs	3
	46
Two committees abolished	2
	48
Senate (8 committees carried over intact):*	8
Armed Services	2
Finance	2
Interior and Insular Affairs	5
Interstate and Foreign Commerce	4
Judiciary	3
Post Office and Civil Service	2
Rules and Administration	6
	32
One committee abolished	1
	33

* Two committees did undergo name changes, however—Education and Labor to Labor and Public Welfare, and Public Buildings and Grounds to Public Works.
SOURCE: Compiled from list in Galloway, 1955: 276 – 78.

legislation for floor debate. In 1949 the House curbed the power of the committee to delay legislation by enacting the 21-day rule. Legislative committee chairmen were permitted to bring a bill directly to the floor for consideration if the Rules Committee failed to act on the request for a rule within 21 calendar days. This rule was repealed in 1951.

Democratic liberals continued to press for change but were unsuccessful. The last two years of the Eisenhower administration (1959– 60) convinced them that action was necessary. Democrats had gained 49 seats in the 1958 election, and many northern Democrats were determined to enact liberal legislation. Their efforts were frequently thwarted by the Rules Committee. Though the Democrats had an eight to four margin on the committee, two southern Democrats, chairman Howard W. Smith (Virginia) and William Colmer (Mississippi), often voted with the four Republicans. When this happened a tie was the result and the request for a rule therefore defeated.

With the election of John F. Kennedy to the White House, liberal

Democrats decided to try again to break the grip of the Rules Committee. They were justifiably concerned that Kennedy's domestic program might well be bottled up by the so-called unholy alliance of southern Democrats and Republicans. With the backing of Speaker Rayburn, a proposal to enlarge the committee from 12 to 15 was passed by the House by a very narrow margin, 217−212. The change was temporary—for the 87th Congress only. The enlargement was made permanent in 1963. In 1965 the 21−day rule was reinstituted (only to be dropped again in 1967), and the power of the Rules Committee in regard to sending bills to conference was removed. The first volleys had been fired in the battle to reduce the power of committee chairmen.

Summary

Table 15−3 analyzes the post-war reforms and shows some similarities between the two sets. Of course, the first set was much more

TABLE 15−3
The major post-World War II reforms analyzed

Framework for analysis	1946 Act	1961−1965 reforms
1. Objectives of reform . . .	Jurisdictional, procedural/ organizational, analytical	Procedural/organizational, political
2. Changes realized	Personnel, authority, process	Personnel, authority, process, output
3. Functions served	Lawmaking/consolidative	Lawmaking/consolidative
4. Institutional effect	Mixed government	Mixed government (cooperative)

SOURCE: Compiled by author.

comprehensive in scope and intention but interestingly less political. The breadth of the changes realized therefore is somewhat deceptive. There were changes in personnel, authority, and process, but one questions how significant they were. Reorganization was the thing to do and was overdue. Not to have reorganized would undoubtedly have had more significant long-term effects on congressional power.

The Rules Committee reforms were in many ways more important since they derived from major political considerations. The raw power to determine policy product was seen to be involved. While by no means solving all the problems created by the seniority system and its facilitation of southern Democratic power, the changes did represent the growing strength of junior members for rearranging House politics. By the 1970s a full-scale assault was launched to reshape Congress.

A decade of reform—the 1970s

In 1970 Charles A. Reich, a professor of law at Yale University, published a book about the 1960s called *The Greening of America*. The title had such a fresh quality to it, denoting an era of purity and new growth—almost like the coming of spring. But the book is filled with bitterness and censure. For Reich, the promise of youth was stifled by the product of corporate America. Something had to give in order for the new flowers to grow (Reich, 1970: 14).

> . . . a true definition of the American crisis would say this: we no longer understand the system under which we live, hence the structure has become obsolete and we have become powerless; in turn, the system has been permitted to assume unchallenged power to dominate our lives, and now rumbles along, unguided and therefore indifferent to human ends.

Whether or not one agrees with Reich's descriptions and prescriptions, it is unquestionably true that he reflected growing discontent with public decisions and the way in which they were being made. Still the political system showed itself to be resistant to making large changes in the short run. Separation of powers, bicameralism, staggered terms, federalism—all those features the founding fathers built into the system to resist the passions of the masses—did play a part in the resistance. Thus for example in 1968, at the very high point of the 1960s rebellion, the Democrats nominated Hubert H. Humphrey for president and the Republicans nominated Richard M. Nixon. It would have been difficult to select two candidates more representative of traditional views within each party. Further, the percentage of House members returning to office in 1968 was the highest in recent years (see Table 4−2). Senators were not so fortunate—possibly portending problems ahead (see Table 5−4).

The 1968 election also showed many signs of change for the future. The Democratic convention was tumultuous, and many changes were made in the ensuing years. The critics of the 1960s became actively involved in electoral politics in the 1970s. Retirements in the House began to increase in 1970 and escalated throughout the decade. The greening of America may have occurred in the 1960s, but it had its effect in Congress during the 1970s.

Earlier I noted that members of Congress may perceive their status and authority to be threatened from the inside (e.g., due to excessive leadership), from outside Congress but inside government (e.g., in response to an aggressive president), and from outside government (e.g., in response to the media and citizen groups). The Reed-Cannon and post-World War II reforms were more or less stimulated by a singular source. Not so with the reforms of the 1970s. Liberal Democrats—most of whom belonged to the Democratic Study Group (DSG)—were motivated to make changes because of the power of committee chairmen. They were determined to modify the seniority system and reallocate power within the House of Representatives. But there were threats from outside the institution too. The election of Richard Nixon to the White House was viewed by many Democrats as cause for alarm; his overwhelming reelection in 1972 brought the two institutions into direct conflict over the budget, domestic programs, executive privilege, impoundment of appropriated funds, use of intelligence services, and the president's war powers. And throughout the 1970s the media and citizen groups (notably Common Cause and the Ralph Nader organization) steadily criticized Congress and called for reform.

Clearly the dissatisfaction with congressional organization and performance was growing rather dramatically inside the institution itself during the 1960s. Membership in the Democratic Study Group grew steadily until the organization had a majority of House Democrats. The DSG then began to work through the previously moribund House Democratic Caucus to restore its authority to approve committee assignments so as to discipline members and eventually curb the authority of the powerful committee chairmen. There were some successes in the 1960s in the reorganization of certain committees (Education and Labor, Post Office and Civil Service) and disciplining of a few members (Davidson and Oleszek, 1977: 43–45). More important, however, was the experience gained by the reformers. They learned a great deal about the strategy of reform and the need to be persistent.

One excellent strategy was that of appointing a caucus committee to study the seniority system and make recommendations to insure that committee chairmen would be responsive to the caucus. Julia Butler Hansen (D—Washington) was appointed to lead the 11-member committee, and the group came to be known as the Hansen Committee. Though the DSG resolution was modified as it passed the caucus, the group left little question that they intended the Hansen Committee to devise means by which committee chairmen could be held accountable to the caucus. It should be noted that the Republicans were working on the same problem at this same time. The Republican group was headed by Barber B. Conable (R—New York).

But these actions within the two parties take us ahead of the story. Table 15–4 shows the many reforms of the 1970s. Note that a major reform act was passed in 1970 before the seniority system modifications. This particular set of changes was the result of the work of the Joint Committee on the Organization of the Congress.[5] First organized

---

[5] The work of the Committee and the Act itself are described in detail in Congressional Quarterly, *Congress and the Nation,* vol. III (Washington, D.C.: Congressional Quarterly, 1973), pp. 382–96.

TABLE 15 – 4
The decade of congressional reform, 1970 – 1979

Year	Reform approved
1970	Legislative Reorganization Act (organizational and procedural changes). Provision for nonvoting delegate in the House of Representatives, District of Columbia.
1971	Seniority system modifications (House Democrats and Republicans). Authorization of computer services for the House.
1972	Federal Election Campaign Act. Office of Technology Assessment (OTA) established. House electronic voting system approved.
1973	War Powers Act. Seniority system modifications (House Democrats, Senate Republicans). Steering and Policy Committee activated (House Democrats). House Select Committee on Committees established (Bolling Committee). House subcommittee bill of rights. Open House committee meetings (mark-up sessions). Closed rule modified (House). House staff increases.
1974	Federal Election Campaign Act. Congressional Budget and Impoundment Control Act. Congressional Budget Office (CBO) created. Steering and Policy Committee to assign committees (House Democrats). Hansen Plan adopted in House (organizational, leadership, party, committee changes). Speaker nominates Democrats to House Committee on Rules.
1975	Senate filibuster reform ($^3/_5$ of the Senate). Conference proceedings open to the public. Seniority system modifications (House and Senate Democrats). Open Senate committee meetings (mark-up sessions). House Committee on Internal Security abolished. House staff increases. Open House party caucuses. Commission on the Operation of the Senate established. Junior senators staff assistance.
1976	House Commission on Administrative Review created (Obey Commission). Senate Temporary Select Committee to Study the Senate Committee System created (Stevenson Committee). House perquisites revised.
1977	Senate Committee system revised (names, membership, appointments, limits on chairmanships, staffing). Ethics Codes adopted (House and Senate).
1978	Congressional approval of constitutional amendment giving the District of Columbia full representation in Congress (sent to states for ratification).
1979	Senate filibuster reform (post-cloture). Reduction of dilatory floor votes (House).

SOURCE: Compiled from Congressional Quarterly, *Congress and the Nation,* Vols. III and IV, and various issues of the *Congressional Quarterly Weekly Report,* 1977 – 79.

in 1965, the Committee held hearings in that year and filed a report with recommendations in 1966. The Senate acted in 1967, the House did not. In 1970, a special subcommittee of the House Committee on Rules framed a reform bill, drawing in part on the work of the Joint Committee. Many of the changes proposed in the bill were of a house-keeping variety—encouraging greater openness in the lawmaking process, expediting floor proceedings, providing the minority with certain prerogatives, insuring that members have ample time for reading committee reports, and increasing the research and analysis capabilities of Congress. The bill passed both houses by wide margin.

If the more senior members thought that support of the 1970 Act might stave off more fundamental reform, they were soon disabused of any such notion. Actually the 1970 Act hardly touched the fundamental concerns of the DSG and its supporters among Senate liberals. The Hansen and Conable committees were already at work developing proposals to change the seniority system when the House agreed to the minor Senate changes in the 1970 Act. And once their work was done, it seemed inevitable that committee chairmen would no longer wield the power of feudal barons—as had been charged so frequently in the past. Once the door of reform was cracked open in 1971, it was very difficult to close it again. Change upon change was made, with the Senate consistently lagging behind but eventually enacting many reforms similar in kind to those in the House.

A review of Table 15—4 suggests several types of reforms. First are the many changes designed to reduce the power of committee chairmen. The seniority system modifications that made the appointment of chairmen subject to caucus approval, the so-called subcommittee bill of rights that dispersed authority and staff to the subcommittees, the limitation on the number of committee and subcommittee assignments and chairmanships, the reduction in political authority of the House Committee on Ways and Means, all fit into this category. Most of these changes were made within the party caucuses as rules to be followed in each party. One consequence was a strengthening of the party apparatus, which suited the reformers since party provided a means for reducing the independence of committee leaders. On the other hand, the increased independence of the subcommittees made it difficult for party leaders to monitor and coordinate the lawmaking process.

The second set of reforms enacted during this period were those directed toward increasing congressional power in relationship to the executive. Included in this second category would be the creation of the Office of Technology Assessment (OTA) in 1972—designed as it was to give Congress greater capacity for independent policy analysis; the War Powers Act of 1973, which limited the president's authority to commit troops abroad without congressional approval; and the

Budget and Impoundment Control Act of 1974, which developed a more independent role for Congress in the budgetary process while limiting the president's authority in regard to controlling funds once they were appropriated.

The third type of reform evident in Table 15−4 is that directed to making the Congress look good, or at least better, to outside forces. In particular, the election campaign acts designed to limit expenditures, the ethics codes for each house, and further actions to open the process to public view would fit into this category. But Common Cause also fought hard to change the seniority system and was, presumably, pleased with the results.

In summary, one can see how the many reforms listed in Table 15−4 were specifically directed to remedy the perceived excesses and insufficiencies of internal organization and leadership, to reduce the perceived inequities between congressional and presidential authority and presence, and to quiet the strong criticism from the press and vocal citizen groups.

Whole books have been written on the complex political machinations involved in enacting this full menu of reforms—one sizeable volume just on the House Select Committee on Committees—the Bolling Committee (Davidson and Oleszek, 1977).[6] We can't possibly begin to describe all of these developments. It is important, however, to record that several committees in each house conducted research and produced reports and recommendations for approval by the party caucuses or full assemblies. Many of these reports were issued as public documents and thus provide extraordinarily rich sources for students to analyze the motivation and rationale for reform. Included among these groups are the following:

1. The Joint Committee on the Organization of the Congress (1965). The Committee held public hearings in 1965 and issued its report in 1966. Senator A. S. (Mike) Monroney (D−Oklahoma) and Representative Ray J. Madden (D−Indiana) cochaired the 12-member committee (six from each house).

2. The Democratic Caucus Committee on Organization, Study, and Review—the Hansen Committee (1970). A House Democratic Party Committee was established to develop reform proposals for the seniority system and committee organization. The committee was used on three important occasions—in 1971 to propose seniority modifications, in 1973 for strengthening the party subcommittees, and in 1974 for developing a set of counter proposals to those recommended by the Bolling Committee (see below). Since the Hansen group was a party committee, no public documents were produced.

---

[6] Other works on congressional reform during this period include: Welch and Peters, eds., (1977); Ornstein, ed., (1975); Rieselbach (1977); Reiselbach, ed. (1978); and Dodd and Oppenheimer, eds. (1977, 1981).

3. The Republican Conference Task Force on Seniority (1970). Headed by Barber B. Conable, this group recommended changes in the seniority system which were adopted by the Conference in 1971. No public documents were produced.

4. The Joint Committee on Congressional Operations (1970). This committee was created by the Legislative Reorganization Act of 1970 for the purpose of conducting continuous study of congressional organization and procedure. The committee conducted occasional hearings and issued reports. It was a 10-member committee with the chairmanship alternating between the House and Senate. The committee was abolished in 1976.

5. The House Select Committee on Committees—the Bolling Committee (1973). Chaired by Richard Bolling (D—Missouri), this bipartisan, 10-member committee (five Democrats and five Republicans) held extensive hearings and issued a report with a full range of recommendations for changes in the committee system. David Martin (R—Nebraska) served as vice chairman. The proposals did not survive the Democratic caucus. Rather the Hansen Committee (see above) was charged with modifying the recommendations.

6. The Senate Commission on the Operation of the Senate (1975). This nine-member group was composed of persons outside the Senate and was charged with producing a study of the organization and operations of the Senate. Former Senator Harold E. Hughes (D—Iowa) served as chairman. Many detailed studies were produced by the staff and associated scholars. No hearings were conducted, but a final report was issued identifying numerous problems in Senate operations and making recommendations for change.

7. The Senate Temporary Select Committee to Study the Senate—the Stevenson Committee (1976). Like the Bolling Committee in the House, this was a bipartisan group with an equal number of Democratic and Republican members (six of each). Adlai E. Stevenson III (D—Illinois) served as the chairman and Bill Brock (R—Tennessee) was cochairman. The Committee held hearings and produced extensive research into the committee system. Its recommendations were largely accepted by the Senate.

8. The House Commission on Administrative Review—the Obey Commission (1976). This group was created after the scandal associated with Wayne L. Hays (D—Ohio), chairman of the House Committee on Administration. Among other things, Hays was charged with paying a mistress, Elizabeth Ray, with House funds. The 15-member commission was composed of eight House members and seven private citizens. David R. Obey (D—Wisconsin) served as chairman. Primarily a study commission, the group relied on detailed studies by a professional staff in making recommendations about the administrative and management practices in the House. The recommendations were not

adopted, primarily because the House appeared tired of enacting reforms.

This collection of committees, commissions, and task groups is really quite astounding. One or two reform groups in a decade made news in the past. To have eight in such a short period of time almost detracts from the significance of any one. For a time in the 1970s reform groups overlapped. One really needed a program to keep track of who was doing what. Interestingly, reform, which normally is designed to upset routines, had itself become routine.

Summary

It is premature to judge the manifold effects of the reforms enacted during the 1970s. The scope of reform complicated the task of the analyst. In addition, so little time has passed that any very firm conclusions are just not possible. Still one can speculate, and Table 15—5

TABLE 15—5
The reforms of the 1970s analyzed

Framework of analysis	Types of reform			
	I Inside		II Congress and the presidency	III Responsive to outside pressures
	A. Housekeeping	B. Power		
1. Objects of reform	Procedural/ organizational, analytical	Procedural/ organizational, political	Jurisdictional, procedural/ organizational, political, analytical	Electoral, procedural/ organizational, political, ethical
2. Changes realized	Process	Personnel, process, output (?)	Personnel, authority, process, output (?)	Criticism, process
3. Functions served	Lawmaking/ consolidative	Representative/ adaptive	Lawmaking; consolidative	?
4. Institutional effect	Mixed government (cooperative or adversarial)	Mixed government (cooperative or adversarial)	Mixed government (adversarial)	?

SOURCE: Compiled by author.

represents an effort to do just that. I have categorized the many reforms into three broad types:

I. Those changes designed to be attentive to perceived insufficiencies with the way Congress is organized and led. Included here are the housekeeping type reforms of the Legislative Reorganization Act of 1970 and the strongly political moves associated with reducing the power of committee chairmen. These actions were responsive to threats from the *inside*. Many of these reforms were designed to democratize the House by providing more access to more people.

II. Those changes designed to restore the balance of power between Congress and the presidency. The War Powers Act and Budget and Impoundment Control Act are the principal efforts in this category— efforts responsive to threats from *outside Congress but inside government*.

III. Those changes designed to improve the image of Congress with the public. The campaign finance, ethics, and sunshine laws were responsive to threats from *outside* the government and represented further democratizing actions in Congress.

The effort in Table 15—5 to determine the objects of reform, the changes realized, the functions served, and the institutional effect was partially successful. Easiest to judge are the objects of reform since they are imputed from the intentions and justifications as evident in hearings, committee reports, and debates. Note that taken together the actions covered the full range of objects—much broader coverage than the reforms of the Reed—Cannon or post-war periods (see Tables 15—1 and 15—3). One is less confident about identifying all of the changes which might have occurred from these reforms. The most obvious changes are those affecting process, actual authority, and personnel. It is much more difficult to judge whether criticism has been reduced and tougher yet to determine the effect on output—what Congress produces by way of public policy. One assumes that the important committee, subcommittee, and budgetary reforms have had an impact on legislative results—on the substance of the laws themselves—but the precise effects require careful study.

Also highly speculative is the assessment of the functions served by, and the broader institutional effects of, the recent reforms. Particularly difficult to judge is which policy functions are facilitated by these changes. For the fact is that both the more representative or adaptive and the more consolidative functions appear to be served. Many analysts of congressional reform speak of a two-directional effect of what has been done. Leroy N. Rieselbach puts it this way (1977:   87):

> Those who put a high premium on prompt, efficient solutions to policy problems seek to move toward a more centralized legislature. They are prepared to sacrifice openness and multiple channels of communication—that is, responsiveness—in favor of effective resolution of policy issues—that is, responsibility . . . . On the other side are those, equally committed to reform, who place the ultimate value on a free, open deliberative process. As the price for responsiveness they are prepared to endure a decentralized scheme of things, seemingly irrespon-

sible, that reaches decisions slowly and only after considerable negotiation and compromise.

Our representative/adaptive functions are similar to Rieselbach's responsiveness; the lawmaking/consolidative functions similar to his definition of responsibility. Saying that the reforms are two-directional does not necessarily mean that they are equally weighty in both directions. In fact, it seems apparent that the inside reforms affecting the power of committee chairmen were more pervasive in their impact than the housekeeping or the more broadly institutional reforms. The result? On balance, the representative or responsiveness functions appear to be better served than the lawmaking or consolidative functions. Put differently, the changes seem to have created a more decentralized and democratized legislative body in which individual members and subcommittees have more authority and resources to participate in the policy process. Party leaders lack the resources to consolidate this diverse participation. In Rieselbach's words, responsiveness won out over responsibility.

Finally, in regard to the effect of these reforms on the institution itself, the whole purpose of change has surely been to increase the role of Congress in national policymaking. This goal was particularly appropriate during the Nixon—Ford administrations when congressional Democrats sought to challenge the Republican presidents. But intentions and subsequent effects are often not the same. Perhaps the most that can be said at this point is that mixed government has resulted from the last decade of reform. The members of Congress have improved their capacities to participate in the policy process as individuals and small groups. Much of this capability has been adversarial in nature. Congress has been more active in its opposition to the policy initiatives of recent administrations and in producing its own alternative proposals. Cooperation is, of course, possible should a president decide to acknowledge the changes in Congress and be moved to work with, instead of against, that institution (see Chapter 16).

CONCLUSION

Congress changes whether or not specific reforms are enacted. It is also the case that congressional reforms are seldom fully successful in achieving the intended effects. There is often a reform psychology in the short run that simply cannot be fully attentive to longer term effects of change. However, reform eras always provide a range of perspectives on the role of Congress in the national policy process and are therefore particularly useful periods of study for students of Congress.

I have identified three major reform eras—the fascinating Reed —Cannon period in which congressional leadership was the principal focus of attention; the post-World War II period in which important questions were raised about the capacity of congressional organization and leadership to meet the challenges of modern America; and the remarkable 1970s in which a whole range of institutional and political issues were raised. When one steps back to consider all three periods, it is interesting how much more complicated the reform issues have become—a development befitting the growing complexity of public policy problems themselves. In the Reed—Cannon period, attention was rather easily focused on the simple question of how much authority should be allocated to the Speaker of the House. Matters were more complex after World War II and downright intricate by the 1960s and 1970s.

Two other observations are of particular value in this analysis. First, observe that the question of which functions are to be emphasized is never resolved. Roger Davidson's two congresses can never quite become one. Efforts to reform in the direction of representation or responsiveness are inevitably followed by efforts to consolidate or centralize. Congress appeared to go in both directions in the 1970's, probably with the result that it increased its capability for participating in all policy functions without at the same time resolving the two congresses dilemma.

Second, one is struck by the extent to which Congress is engaged in a continuous effort to maintain an important and active role in the national political system (with mixed results). War, technology, complex social and economic issues, a growing bureaucracy, all act as pressures to limit the involvement of Congress in public policy. But the institution fights back. And when a president is particularly assertive in competing with or ignoring Congress, the reform condition is set. We may not be able to judge the precise effects of the changes that are made, but one thing is very clear from this brief review: Congress remains a strong and viable political institution fully capable still of playing and protecting its constitutional role.

16 People, place, and policy

April 27, 1981: I am just beginning to compose the last words for this book on the United States Congress. Ordinarily I would not mark the date on which I write. The relevance in this case springs from my feeling of deja vu. It was exactly four years ago that I went to Washington to collect the material for Chapter 2. Today as I write, Congress has just returned from the Easter work period. Tomorrow evening, President Ronald Reagan, recovering from an assassination attempt, is scheduled to address Congress in regard to his economic package. Four years ago, President Jimmy Carter presented his energy proposals on Capitol Hill. Many of the actors have changed and different policy imperatives command their attention, but somehow I feel as though I have been there before. "This ceaseless agitation" continues.[1]

---

[1] I couldn't resist counting the committee and subcommittee meetings for this second week—four years later. The totals were 142 House and 83 Senate meetings—a total of 225 meetings compared with 250 for the week in 1977. It might also be noted that important changes occurred in the lives of four of the seven persons whose schedules I collected. John J. Rhodes resigned as minority leader in 1980, William S. Cohen ran for the Senate in 1978 and won, Edmund S. Muskie resigned his Senate seat in 1980 to become secretary of state, and George McGovern was defeated for reelection in 1980.

This book has been about the people on Capitol Hill, the place called Congress, and the policy functions served by those people in that place. The order of topics itself is important. I thought it necessary first to identify the players and their manifold connections to the outside—to the public and its problems, if you will. Second I had to describe the organizations and procedures that have developed through the years to receive and process the requests and demands directed to Congress. My sense of logic then dictated that I ask you to draw back from the machinery and the people who make it work to consider how congressionally centered activities fit into the national policy process. Throughout I have sought to note trends and provide historical context, but I also found it necessary to include a separate chapter on congressional reform movements.

As a final exercise I plan to offer a reprise of a few of the major themes associated with the principal topics of people, place, and policy. Comprehending the developments associated with each topic should provide insights into the political role of the modern Congress and how it has adapted to social change.

PEOPLE

Chapters 3 through 7 focus on three main topics—who constitutes the congressional population, how they came to be there, and how their work attracts those who want something from the national government. As regards the population, one has to be impressed with its tremendous growth in recent years, entirely due to the increase in congressional staffing. Whereas executive branch employment actually declined, 1970−79, the number of employees working for the House and Senate (not including other employees included in the legislative branch budget—e.g., the General Accounting Office) increased by 54 percent during that same period.[2] Of course, total legislative branch employment is still miniscule compared to that in the executive branch, but the growth is significant and has had an important effect on Capitol Hill and elsewhere in the government.

Who are all of these people? For the most part they are bright, well-educated, ambitious, and energetic. And they like being involved in politics. They enjoy the rewards of directly participating in important ways in resolving the crucial issues of our times. In his interesting and thought-provoking article "The Crisis of Competence in Government," James L. Sundquist states that: "Deep-seated trends have been, and are, at work that will make effective government even more difficult to attain in the 1980s than it has been in the decade just ended

---

[2] Calculated from data in U.S. Department of Commerce, Bureau of the Census, *Statistical Abstract of the United States* (Washington: U.S. Government Printing Office: 1979), p. 277.

and those that have gone before" (in Pechman, ed., 1980: 531). Failure to attract competent persons does *not* appear to be one of these deep-seated trends causing a crisis in government. By almost any measure one wishes to employ, it must be said that able people go to work each day on Capitol Hill.

Turning to how they get there, it is noteworthy first that congressional elections have held a poor second place to presidential elections as objects for research among scholars. In recent years, however, the gap in analysis has been narrowed. Researchers have been particularly fascinated with high return rates of incumbents—a phenomenon that turns out to be characteristic in recent years of the House but not the Senate. Thus another important "people" topic is the comparative turnover (over time and between chambers) of the members themselves. A high return rate of House incumbents is featured along with an increase in retirements to produce a relatively stable turnover in that chamber in recent years. Senate incumbents have not enjoyed the same advantage as their House colleagues. In fact, the turnover in recent elections has been nothing short of phenomenal. It is by no means clear what the increases in staff and the variability in membership between the two houses have to do with policy decisions, but we are well advised as students of Congress to begin measuring their impact.

Another significant matter associated with the people of Capitol Hill is the lack of systematic, centrally directed means for recruitment and selection. As a consequence, recruitment and selection are costly—in money, time, and effort. As students of politics we have to be impressed that such a variegated system can continue to function over time—producing people who display a relatively high degree of consensus on the functions of Congress.

Finally the theme of Chapter 7 stresses the scope and intensity of interests that are drawn to Capitol Hill in order to get something there. Many of the developments associated with the congressional population encourage more participation by a wider variety of special interests. The growth in staff is an obvious case in point—more people make more contacts. Less obvious is that the individualized nature of the recruitment and selection or election of members and staff increases the extent of participation. Often one has to tailor demands and strategies to a particular constituency in order to have impact. It is not sufficient to go to one place, one leader, or one group to get your way in the legislative process.

PLACE

I selected the term *place* for a very specific reason. As with the courts, but in contrast with the executive, so much of what Congress does happens in an identifiable place. It is there, up on Capitol Hill, that Congress acts. This is not to detract from the role of members back in the district. It is rather to emphasize the importance of the location to which one can go and watch the legislature at work.

I have emphasized *the ceremony of lawmaking* in Chapters 8 through 12. Congress has the power to pass laws. In our system of separated institutions, this power is very real since it can be exercised independently of the executive. Thus the trappings and formalities of lawmaking have a special significance in that they guarantee others will come to the Hill. Congress will remain a major policy institution so long as it maintains and protects this legitimating authority.

The design and organization of this congressional place just has to intrigue any serious student of politics. The sheer elaboration of complex mechanisms for representing on the one hand and forcing compromise and conclusions on the other is awesome yet admirable. The differences between the House and Senate have been stressed throughout because they add yet another dimension to the intricacies. The greater size of the House alone dictates a need for enforcing a highly articulated set of procedures in order to get closure on issues. The Senate can operate less restrictively, permitting issues to remain open throughout much of the process and allowing wide participation among the members.

Since so much of their structure is designed to facilitate representation of interests, it is particularly fascinating to watch how two such different bodies try to consolidate or compromise views so that a law can be passed. In many political systems, political parties perform this consolidative function. Then try to do so in Congress as well but are impaired by lack of a coordinating mechanism from realizing notable success. Still party persists as an organizing principle in both houses and even appears to have been strengthened in recent reforms.

Finally, one of the most fascinating and least studied marvels of this congressional place is the coming together of two such diverse bodies to produce a single piece of legislation. Often responsive to different interests, relying on different procedures, and inducing different behavior, the House and Senate must develop means for joining their work. It is no wonder that interest groups in America are strong and resourceful. The founding fathers placed so many hurdles in their way as to contribute to the survival of the fittest.

The more general point to be made in these several chapters (8 through 12) is that the fittest, and those still in training, continue to come to Capitol Hill because crucial decisions are made there that affect their interests. Lowi (1969) is unquestionably correct in observing the growth of administrative discretion. Still Congress is involved in more policy issues than in the past so that its overall role in the policy process remains important. Further, administrative "discretion" is more accurately "delegation." Those who want something from government (see Chapter 7) are well advised not to forget the distinction. After all, that which is delegated may be reclaimed. Therefore congressional support can never be taken for granted.

POLICY

I hope I have not strained the reader's patience in my organization of this book. First I simply told a story about some of what happens on Capitol Hill during a week. Then in turn I asked you to think about Congress as a growing population of actors (Chapters 3—7) and as an organized place for representing and lawmaking (Chapters 8—12). Clearly both of these perspectives contribute to one's understanding of the American policy process. Not satisfied, however, I introduced another section (Chapters 13 and 14) that proposed yet another accounting—that of Congress fitted within the national decision-making apparatus. I found the notion of policy networks useful in promoting this third approach because it encourages one to connect the people and groups within Congress to various policy issues and activities (see Table 13—1). This perspective followed the chapters on Congress as a formal legitimating institution—an appropriate placement since it reminds the reader that the members and their staffs play important roles in policy activities other than majority building.

It does not take long for one to be persuaded that legislators and their staffs are involved in program development activities. Typically all one has to do is identify the associated activities (problem definition, aggregation, formulation, etc.), and many examples come to mind (constituency contact, congressional hearings, staff research). The separation of powers model, however, does not prepare us to expect very extensive congressional participation in program execution beyond the traditional impacts associated with approval of appointments, explicitness in the statutes, and legislative oversight. Thus it is particularly interesting to observe the expansion of legislative involvement in program execution and its effect on policy networks. In the short run, at least, this expansion has contributed to a new politics in Washington.

Chapter 15 treats the matter of Congress's policy toward itself. In it we learn that Congress is not often moved to reform itself, in part because it is, and always has been, designed to be accommodative, adaptive, and flexible. Excesses occur, however, and when they are perceived as threats to the integrity of the institution, reforms are enacted. More often than not the members perceive threats to the representational function as being the most serious. Thus moves toward greater centralization of decision making (by their own leaders or the president) are typically checked. Congress tries to protect its right to reflect national diversity, thus frustrating those who prefer a more unified and systematic national policy process.

WHERE DOES CONGRESS STAND TODAY?

In Chapter 1, I identified four interpretations of or perspectives on presidential-congressional interaction—congressional primacy, presidential primacy, mixed government—cooperative, mixed government—adversarial. I concluded that the Carter administration had an adversarial relationship with Congress. This was partially, perhaps primarily, due to the president's attitude toward a Congress controlled by his party (Jones in Mann and Ornstein, 1981: chapter 8). The relationship appeared to suit many Democrats in Congress, however, since they had grown accustomed during the Nixon—Ford administrations to an expanded policy role. Many of the reforms of the 1970s were specifically designed to be confrontational—reducing presidential authority and increasing congressional capacities to participate actively in a full range of policy work.

How do we describe the present situation? All one can do is speculate since major political shifts occurred in 1980. Among these changes is the landslide election of a conservative Republican, Ronald Reagan, despite a tremendous Democratic advantage in party registration; the election of a Republican majority in the Senate; a sizeable increase in the number of House Republicans; and an apparent national mood to stabilize, perhaps reverse, the long-standing trend toward a larger federal government. Reflecting on these changes and incorporating them with the developments of the 1970s, one is led to speculate as follows in regard to the four types of relationships:

Congressional primacy: An unlikely future outcome given the complexity of issues and increasing demand for coordinated policy development. A strengthened Congress is one able to compete with, not dominate, the executive.

Presidential primacy: Somewhat more likely than the above but still remote during the Reagan administration given the strength of the Democrats nationally and in the House of Representatives. Continued economic crisis or war may lead to a greatly strengthened executive, however.

Mixed government—cooperative: The most likely result as evidenced by the early months of the Reagan administration. Despite split party control (Republican president and Senate, Democratic House), the importance of economic issues and the apparent public support for a lesser government role combine to encourage greater cooperation than in the recent past.

Mixed government—adversarial: A predictable outcome following the midpoint of the Reagan administration unless the Republicans also capture control of the House in the 1982 elections. Split-party control offers a prime condition for adversarial presidential-congressional relations unless a crisis intervenes.

I see two purposes being served by this brief exercise. First it reveals that Congress is likely to continue performing a stronger role in the policy process than in the recent past (i.e., before 1972). The imperial presidency is unlikely to re-emerge in the near future. In fact, we may be as close to what the framers intended in separating the institutions as we have ever been. Second the exercise may encourage the reader similarly to make estimates of the status of presidential-congressional sharing of power. These estimates can then serve as a useful starting point for analyzing the how, when, and why of political change.

Having come full circle, I now conclude this analysis of the United States Congress. This remarkable body never ceases to interest and amaze me. It commands our attention as citizens because it has been designed to reflect our national will. In this spirit, I close with the practical wisdom of one of the greatest congressional leaders, Thomas Brackett Reed, Speaker of the House of Representatives, 1889—91, 1895—99 (McCall, 1914: 256):

> Freedom never meant the best government in the abstract, it only meant the government best fitted to the people governed. We have not the best laws in the United States that wise men could dream of. What we have is the best laws our people are fit for; and as they grow in knowledge and sense the laws follow in laggard procession. But they follow.

Appendix: Writing a term paper on Congress

The United States Congress is unquestionably the most documented political institution in the world. That is both good news and bad news for the student. The good news is that rich and fascinating material is available on every facet of the legislative process. The bad news is that the volume of documentation itself can be overwhelming. The purposes here are to encourage the reader to do research on Congress and to make the task easier by providing a brief guide to the documents.

RESEARCH ON LAWMAKING

Suppose I wanted to trace the history and politics of a particular bill.[1] Table A—1 shows the major documents that are available for such a project. I will shortly discuss each of these in turn. First I should tell you, however, that I find it extremely difficult to use those documents until I have an overview of the legislation—what happened when and where. The best place to begin is with the Rand McNally of

---

[1] I have relied heavily in preparing this appendix on Goehlert (1979), Schmeckebier and Eastin (1961), and Congressional Quarterly, *Guide to the Congress of the United States* (1971).

444

TABLE A–1
Studying how a bill becomes a law

The process	The documents	Where indexed
1. Bill introduced and referred to committee	Bills, resolutions	CIS/Index, Congressional Index, Digest of Public General Bills and Resolutions
2. Committee hearings, staff work	Hearings, prints	CIS/Index, Monthly Catalog of U.S. Government Publications, Public Affairs Information Service Bulletin, Cumulative Index of Congressional Committee Hearings
3. Committee report	House and Senate reports	CIS/Index, Congressional Index, Monthly Catalog of U.S. Government Publications
4. Floor action	Calendars, Congressional Record, House and Senate journals	CIS/Index, Indexes to Congressional Record and Journals
5. Conference action	Conference reports	CIS/Index, Congressional Index, Monthly Catalog of U.S. Government Publications
6. Presidential statements	Weekly compilation of presidential documents	Index to Weekly Compilation
7. Veto	Veto message (Congressional Record)	CIS/Index, Index to Congressional Record, Monthly Catalog of U.S. Government Publications
8. Veto override	Congressional Record, House and Senate journals	Indexes to Congressional Record and Journals, Congressional Index
9. Law	Slip law, Statutes at Large, U.S. Code	CIS/Index, Congressional Index, Indexes to Statutes at Large, U.S. Code

SOURCE: Compiled with modifications and additions from Goehlert (1979: 4).

the legislative terrain—that is, the publications of the Congressional Quarterly, Inc.[2] This private organization has been providing detailed

---

[2] The Congressional Information Service (CIS) announced in May, 1981, that it would begin a legislative history service in the Summer, 1981. Microfiche and paper copies of all official publications associated with the history of significant public laws will be available within 30 to 90 days of the enactment of the law.

descriptions and analyses of major congressional activities since 1945. Their coverage includes presidential involvements and more recently the work of the Supreme Court. There are three major sources of information—*Congress and the Nation*, Volumes I through IV; *Congressional Quarterly Almanac* (issued annually); and the *Congressional Quarterly Weekly Report*. The source used depends on how much one wants to know and when it was that Congress acted on the bill in question.

> *Congress and the Nation:* This remarkable set of volumes provides an overview of major congressional actions by topic (foreign policy; economic policy; health, education, and welfare, etc.). Key votes, biographical data, vetoes, election statistics, nominations, etc., are also provided. The material is compiled from the *Almanacs* (see below). Volume I covers the period 1945—64. Subsequent volumes cover presidential administrations—II, 1965—68; III, 1969—72; IV, 1973—76.

> *Congressional Quarterly Almanac:* Somewhat greater detail on legislation is provided in this annual compilation of major congressional actions. Again organized by issues, the summaries compile material scattered through the *Weekly Reports.* Voting scores, roll-call votes, election statistics, lobbying information, etc., are included. The *Almanac* is the logical place to begin, therefore, unless your bill is in the current year for which the *Almanac* has not yet been issued.

> *Congressional Quarterly Weekly Report:* The bedrock of material for subsequent volumes is the detailed reporting done each week in this extraordinary publication. The format for the *Weekly Report* has changed through the years, but a major effort has always been made to include coverage of committee and floor action on major legislation. Also offered are special reports, superb election coverage, roll-call votes, major presidential activities, lobbying registrations, and details on internal congressional politics. A cumulative index is provided each quarter—an essential service for those wishing to trace legislative action on a bill.

The Congressional Quarterly publishes many other books, monographs, and reports of use for studying issues, laws, and the members. Some of the books are included in the references (e.g., Oleszek, 1978; Ornstein and Elder, 1978; Dodd and Oppenheimer, eds., 1981). Other reference materials include:

> *Guide to the Congress of the United States* (1971, 1976)—essentially a text on the history, organization, procedures, and powers of Congress.

Guide to U.S. Elections (1975, with supplements)—descriptions and data on national and gubernatorial elections (including primaries).

America Votes (biennial)—state-by-state compilation of data on national and gubernatorial elections (including primaries). The data are collected by the Elections Research Center, Richard M. Scammon, director.

Contemporary Affairs Reports —special analyses of political topics (e.g., lobbying, elections) and policy issues (e.g., energy, health care).

Washington Information Directory (annual)—essentially a directory to cozy little triangles, this reference book lists all the major congressional committees and subcommittees, executive agencies, and interest groups associated with various policy issues.

Congressional Insight —a weekly publication since 1976 that concentrates on the congressional agenda—what is likely to happen, when, and where.

Editorial Research Reports —detailed analyses of specific issues, presenting historical analysis and the pros and cons.

Another private publication that includes material of interest to congressional scholars is the *National Journal*. Less exclusively directed to Congress than the *Congressional Quarterly Weekly Report*, the *National Journal* is essentially a weekly magazine with in-depth articles on selected topics. These articles can provide the student with background information on issues, legislation, and political dynamics.

When one has produced a sequence of action on a bill and gained insights into the political maneuverings, then the documents become comprehensible and of great use in providing vital details on congressional actions. Table A−1 provides a simple listing of the major points in the legislative process, the documents which one can use to find out what happened at that point, and the indexes for identifying the proper document. Notice that the CIS/Index is listed for practically all entries. This index is published by the Congressional Information Service (CIS) and it provides abstracts of many congressional documents. It is the logical place to begin a documents search after one has mapped the territory. (For details on other indexes see Goehlert, 1979: 31 − 47).

The documents differ substantially in what they have to offer the student.

1. Bill and resolutions: These documents simply include the proposed law as offered at any one point—introduction, committee report, passage by one house. Students may save themselves a search by

going directly to hearings, reports, or the *Congressional Record,* since bills and resolutions are printed in those documents along the way. In fact bills introduced in previous congresses may be very difficult to find.

2. Hearings: The hearings are perhaps the most important documents of all for understanding the politics of an issue. Often they contain the transcript of testimony and questioning before a congressional committee or subcommittee along with accompanying articles and reports relevant to the issue at hand. One gets a good picture of who wants what, as well as the major points at issue between the members, the agencies, and the various interest groups. Hearings are a little intimidating at first, but with a little practice, students will find that they can skim them rather quickly and learn a great deal. (See Schmeckebier and Eastin, 1961:   151 – 52, on the problems of finding hearings).

3. Prints: These documents contain research that the committee has requested in regard to an issue. It may be a staff report or work done by outside consultants. (P.S.: Hearings and staff reports can be very useful sources for papers in other courses. Practically no subject of importance in American society escapes attention on Capitol Hill).

4. Reports: Once a committee has acted favorably on a bill, it sends the bill to the floor with an accompanying report. This document permits one to take stock of legislative action to this point. It explains the purpose of the bill, shows where it fits into existing law, summarizes what has happened, contains executive reactions, and may contain minority or additional views.

5. Calendars: Published every day that the House is in session, the calendars provide information on bills reported out of committee and on which action has been taken. A final edition is published at the end of a session and includes all bills which failed to become law.

6. *Congressional Record:* Produced for every day that Congress is in session, the *Record* contains the full proceedings (including votes) in both the House and Senate. Members are, however, given a chance to edit their statements. The daily edition is bound every two weeks and at the end of a session (the permanent bound *Record*). It was first made available in 1873. Before that time proceedings were available in the *Annals of Congress* (1789 – 1824); *Register of Debates* (1824 – 37); and *Congressional Globe,* (1833 – 1973).

7. Journals: Published at the end of each session, the House and Senate journals contain the essentials of chamber action on legislation including votes. A separate *Executive Journal* is printed for the Senate's executive actions (treaties, nominations).

8. Conference reports: These reports simply record the agreements reached between the Senate and House conferees.

9. Slip laws, Statutes at Large, U.S. Code: These documents are discussed in Chapter 12.

10. *Weekly Compilation of Presidential Documents:* Just as the title suggests, this document contains the public statements of the president. Those of importance to legislation typically also show up in hearings, reports, and the *Congressional Record.*

In addition to these many documents, students of lawmaking will want to become familiar with the House and Senate rules and precedents. The simplest method for doing so is to study Oleszek (1976) or Zinn (1978). But each house publishes its revised rules every two years. Precedents are also updated periodically.

RESEARCH ON THE MEMBERS

It is equally interesting to focus on individual members of Congress in preparing term papers. Perhaps one wants to analyze the annual activity of a member, study the relationships between the member's state or district and legislative record, compare committee chairmen or party leaders. Many of the documents discussed above are relevant to the study of members since they include such information as the questions members ask in committee hearings, participation in floor debates, etc. But many other government documents and private sources are also available.

Table A–2 directs the student to various topics and where information may be obtained in doing research on those topics. Most of these sources provide the primary data for the particular subject, and therefore one must do whatever calculations are required to answer the question at hand. Most imposing are the extensive data archives available through the Inter-University Consortium for Political and Social Research (ICPSR) at the University of Michigan. For example, this consortium has available on computer tape all election statistics and roll-call votes from the very first Congress. Thus one can conduct very sophisticated historical or contemporary analyses using these data. Many colleges and universities are members of ICPSR, and therefore students have access to the data. The least complete and reliable data are those on such topics as congressional staff (not even the current directories are totally reliable), biographical background of the members, and campaign finance (historical data are almost worthless). One must be cautious, therefore, in using these data or very clever in identifying research questions for which poor data are useful.

Students should also be encouraged to examine the papers of members. Many members have donated papers to the Library of Congress. Others have contributed them to libraries within their states or districts. This scattering is a disadvantage to the scholar who wishes to

TABLE A–2
Studying the members of Congress

Topic	Source
1. State or district characteristics	*Statistical Abstract of the United States* (annual) (G),* *Congressional District Data Book* (G), *County and City Data Book* (G)
2. Biographical information on members	*Congressional Directory* (G), *Biographical Directory of the American Congress, 1774 – 1971* (G), *The Almanac of American Politics* (P), *C.Q. Congress and the Nation* (P)
3. Congressional staff	*Congressional Directory* (G), *Congressional Staff Directory* (P)
4. Election statistics	*Statistical Abstract of the United States* (G), *America Votes* (P), *C.Q. Guide to U.S. Elections* (P), ICPSR† *Historical Election Returns* (U), ICPSR *Candidate Name and Constituency Totals* (U)
5. Voter attitudes and behavior	ICPSR *National Election Studies, 1948 – 1980* (U)
6. Campaign finance	Reports of Federal Election Commission (G), Citizen Research Foundation Studies in Campaign Finance (U)
7. Committees and subcommittee membership	*Congressional Directory* (G), *C.Q. Almanac* (P)
8. Introduction of bills	*Congressional Record* (G), CIS/Index (P)
9. Roll call voting	*Congressional Record* (G), *House and Senate journals* (G), *C.Q. Almanac* (P), ICPSR *United States Congressional Roll Call Voting Records* (U)

* The letter following each entry indicates whether the source is the government (G), a private firm (P), or a University-based organization (U).
† ICPSR stands for Inter-University Consortium for Political and Social Research, located at the University of Michigan.
SOURCE: Compiled from information in Goehlert (1979), and Schmeckebier and Eastin (1961).

study several selected members. It turns out to be an advantage for present purposes, however, since it is very likely that a library near your college or university has such a collection. Those students at Bradley University, University of Oklahoma, University of Michigan, Harvard University, and University of Texas are particularly blessed since the papers of Everett McKinley Dirksen, (former Senate Republican leader), Carl Albert (former Speaker), Gerald R. Ford (former House Republican leader), Thomas P. (Tip) O'Neill (present Speaker), and Lyndon B. Johnson (former Senate Democratic leader), respectively are (or will be) located near by. The Dirksen Center in Pekin, Illinois, is a particularly active research library for students of Congress.

OTHER RESEARCH

I have used the topics of lawmaking (tracing legislation) and the characteristics of individual members simply as a way of introducing you to the large number of government and private sources for studying Congress. These same sources can be relied on for studying committees, political parties, leadership, relationships between the two houses and with the president, lobbying, the congressional agenda and how it changes over time, and on and on. I understand that writing term papers can be an unhappy experience. That does not have to be the case in doing research on Congress. I grant that the material available is voluminous and therefore intimidating at first glance. I think you will find that a little patience in mapping the territory first, then sampling the rich record of congressional conversation and decision making will be rewarding. It is to these ends that I have included this brief guide.

References

Abram, Michael, and Joseph Cooper. 1978. "The Rise of Seniority in the House of Representatives." *Polity* 1 (Fall): 52–85.

Abramowitz, Alan. 1980. "A Comparison of Voting for U.S. Senator and Representative in 1978." *American Political Science Review* 74 (September): 633–40.

Agranoff, Robert. 1976. *The Management of Election Campaigns*. Boston: Holbrook.

American Political Science Association, Committee on Congress. 1945. *The Reorganization of Congress*. Washington, D.C.: Public Affairs Press.

American Political Science Association, Committee on Political Parties. 1950. "Toward a More Responsible Two-Party System." *American Political Science Review* 44: 1–99.

Arnold, R. Douglas. 1979. *Congress and the Bureaucracy*. New Haven, Conn.: Yale University Press.

Bailey, Stephen K. 1950. *Congress Makes a Law*. New York: Columbia University Press.

Baker, Gordon E. 1966. *The Reapportionment Revolution*. New York: Random House.

Baker, Ross K. 1980. *Friend and Foe in the U.S. Senate*. New York: Free Press.

Barber, James David. 1965. *The Lawmakers*. New Haven, Conn.: Yale University Press.

Barker, Ernest. 1951. *Essays in Government*. 2d ed. New York: Oxford University Press.

Barone, Michael, et al. 1975. *The Almanac of American Politics*. New York: E. P. Dutton.

Barry, David. 1924. *Forty Years in Washington*. Boston: Little, Brown.

Bauer, Raymond, et al. 1963. *American Business and Public Policy*. New York: Atherton.

Bensel, Richard F. 1980. "Creating the Statutory State: The Implications of a Rule of Law Standard in American Politics." *American Political Science Review* 74 (September): 734 – 44.

Berman, Daniel M. 1966. *A Bill Becomes a Law*. New York: Macmillan.

Berry, Jeffrey M. 1977. *Lobbying for the People*. Princeton, N.J.: Princeton University Press.

Bibby, John, et al. 1980. *Vital Statistics on Congress*. Washington, D.C.: American Enterprise Institute.

Breslin, Janet. 1977. "Constituent Service," in U.S. Congress, Senate Commission on the Operation of the Senate. *Senators: Offices, Ethics, and Pressures*, 94th Cong., 2d. sess.: 19 – 36.

Brown, George R. 1922. *The Leadership of Congress*. Indianapolis: Bobbs-Merrill.

Bryce, James. 1915. *The American Commonwealth*. New York: Macmillan.

Bullitt, Stimson. 1961. *To Be a Politician*. Garden City, N.Y.: Anchor Books.

Bullock, Charles S., III. 1971. "The Influence of State Party Delegations on House Committee Assignments." *Midwest Journal of Political Science* 15 (August): 527 – 46.

———. 1973. "Committee Transfers in the United States House of Representatives." *Journal of Politics* 35 (February): 85 – 120.

———. 1975. "Redistricting and Congressional Stability, 1962 – 1972." *Journal of Politics* 37 (May): 569 – 75.

Burnett, Edmund Cody. 1964. *The Continental Congress*. New York: W. W. Norton.

Burnham, Walter Dean. 1975. "Insulation and Responsiveness in Congressional Elections." *Political Science Quarterly* 90 (Fall): 411 – 35.

Campbell, Donald T. 1969. "Reforms as Experiments." *American Psychologist* 24 (April): 409 – 29.

Cater, Douglass. 1964. *Power in Washington*. New York: Random House.

Clapp, Charles L. 1963. *The Congressman: His Work As He Sees It*. Washington, D.C.: Brookings Institution.

Clausen, Aage R. 1972. "State Party Influence on Congressional Policy Decision." *Midwest Journal of Political Science* 16 (February): 77 – 101.

———. 1973. *How Congressmen Decide: A Policy Focus*. New York: St. Martin's Press.

Clem, Alan L., ed., 1976. *The Making of Congressmen: Seven Campaigns in 1974.* North Scituate, Mass.: Duxbury Press.

Cohen, Richard E. 1978. "Congressional Allowances Are Really Perking Up." *National Journal* 10 (February 4): 180 –83.

Cohen, William S. 1981. *Roll Call.* New York: Simon & Schuster.

Cooper, Joseph. 1956. "The Legislative Veto: Its Promise and Its Perils." *Public Policy* 7: 128 –74.

Cooper, Joseph, and Ann Cooper. 1962. "The Legislative Veto and the Constitution." *George Washington Law Review* 30 (March): 467 –68.

Cooper, Joseph, and David W. Brady. 1981. "Institutional Context and Leadership Style: The House from Cannon to Rayburn." *American Political Science Review* 75 (June): 411 –25.

Cotter, Cornelius P., and Malcolm J. Smith. 1956. "Administrative Accountability to Congress: The Concurrent Resolution." *Western Political Quarterly* 9 (December): 955 –66.

Crotty, William J., ed. 1980. *Paths to Political Reform.* Lexington, Mass.: Lexington Books.

Dahl, Robert A. and Charles E. Lindblom. 1953. *Politics, Economics, and Welfare.* New York: Harper Torchbooks.

Davidson, Roger, et al. 1966. *Congress in Crisis: Politics and Congressional Reform.* Belmont, Calif.: Wadsworth.

Davidson, Roger, and Walter J. Oleszek. 1977. *Congress Against Itself.* Bloomington: Indiana University Press.

Deckard, Barbara. 1972. "State Party Delegations in the U.S. House of Representatives: A Comparative Study of Group Cohesion." *Journal of Politics* 34 (February): 199 –222.

de Grazia, Alfred. 1968. "Representation—Theory." *International Encyclopedia of the Social Sciences* 13: 461 –65.

Depew, Chauncey M. 1922. *My Memories of 80 Years.* New York: Charles Scribner's Sons.

Dodd, Lawrence C., and Bruce I. Oppenheimer., eds. 1977. *Congress Reconsidered.* 1st ed. New York: Praeger Publishers.

————., eds. 1981. *Congress Reconsidered.* 2d ed. Washington, D.C.: Congressional Quarterly Inc.

Dodd, Lawrence C., and Richard L. Schott. 1979. *Congress and the Administrative State.* New York: John Wiley & Sons.

Drew, Elizabeth. 1979. *Senator.* New York: Simon & Schuster.

Dunn, Arthur W., II. 1922. *From Harrison to Harding.* New York: G. P. Putnam's Sons.

Edwards, George C., III. 1980. *Presidential Influence in Congress.* San Francisco: W. H. Freeman.

Eidenberg, Eugene, and Roy Morey. 1969. *An Act of Congress.* New York: W. W. Norton.

Erikson, Robert S. 1971. "The Advantage of Incumbency in Congressional Elections." *Polity* 3 (Spring): 395 – 405.

————. 1972. "Malapportionment, Gerrymandering, and Party Fortunes in Congressional Elections." *American Political Science Review* 66 (December): 1234 – 45.

Fenno, Richard F., Jr. 1966. *The Power of the Purse.* Boston: Little, Brown.

————. 1973. *Congressmen in Committees.* Boston: Little, Brown.

————. 1978. *Home Style.* Boston: Little, Brown.

Ferejohn, John. 1975. "Who Wins in Conference Committees?" *Journal of Politics* 37 (November): 1033 – 46.

Fiorina, Morris P. 1974. *Representatives, Roll Calls and Constituencies.* Lexington, Mass.: Lexington Books.

————. 1977. *Congress: Keystone of the Washington Establishment.* New Haven, Conn.: Yale University Press.

Fishel, Jeff. 1973. *Party and Opposition.* New York: David McKay.

Fisher, Louis. 1972. *President and Congress: Power and Policy.* New York: Free Press.

Fleming, James S. 1972. "Reestablishing Leadership in the House of Representatives: The Case of Oscar W. Underwood." *Mid-America* 54: 234– 50.

Foley, Michael. 1980. *The New Senate.* New Haven, Conn.: Yale University Press.

Follett, Mary P. 1896. *The Speaker of the House of Representatives.* New York: Longmans, Green.

Fox, Harrison W., Jr., and Susan W. Hammond. 1977. *Congressional Staffs.* New York: Free Press.

Freeman, J. Leiper. 1955. *The Political Process.* New York: Random House.

Galloway, George B. 1955. *The Legislative Process in Congress.* New York: Thomas Y. Crowell.

Gertzog, Irwin N. 1976. "The Routinization of Committee Assignments in the U.S. House of Representatives." *American Journal of Political Science* 29 (November): 693 – 712.

Goehlert, Robert. 1979. *Congress and Law-Making: Researching the Legislative Process.* Santa Barbara, Calif.: Clio Books.

Goldwin, Robert A., ed. 1964. *Political Parties, USA.* Chicago: Rand McNally.

Goodwin, George Jr. 1959. "The Seniority System in Congress." *American Political Science Review* 53 (June): 412 – 36.

————. 1970. *The Little Legislatures: Committees of Congress.* Amherst: University of Massachusetts Press.

Gore, William, and Robert Peabody. 1958. "The Functions of a Political Campaign: A Case Study." *Western Political Quarterly* 11 (March): 55 – 70.

Green, Harold P., and Alan Rosenthal. 1963. *Government of the Atom.* New York: Atherton Press.

Griffith, Ernest S. 1939. *The Impasse of Democracy.* New York: Harrison-Hilton Books.

Gross, Bertram M. 1953. *The Legislative Struggle.* New York: McGraw-Hill.

Haider, Donald H. 1974. *When Governments Come to Washington.* New York: Free Press.

Hamilton, Alexander; John Jay; and James Madison. 1937. *The Federalist.* New York: Modern Library edition.

Harris, Joseph P. 1964. *Congressional Control of Administration.* Washington, D.C.: Brookings Institution.

Hasbrouck, Paul D. 1927. *Party Government in the House of Representatives.* New York: Macmillan.

Havemann, Joel. 1978. *Congress and the Budget.* Bloomington: Indiana University Press.

Hazelton, George C., Jr. 1897. *The National Capitol.* New York: J. F. Taylor.

Heard, Alexander. 1960. *The Costs of Democracy.* Chapel Hill: University of North Carolina Press.

Heclo, Hugh. 1977. *A Government of Strangers.* Washington, D.C.: Brookings Institution.

Hinckley, Barbara. 1971. *The Seniority System in Congress.* Bloomington: Indiana University Press.

————. 1980. "House Re-Elections and Senate Defeats: The Role of the Challenger." *British Journal of Political Science* 20: 441–60.

Hoffman, Ross J. S., and Paul Levack. 1949. *Burke's Politics.* New York: Alfred A. Knopf.

Holtzman, Abraham. 1966. *Interest Groups and Lobbying.* New York: Macmillan.

Horn, Stephen. 1970. *Unused Power: The Work of the Senate Committee on Appropriations.* Washington, D.C.: Brookings Institution.

Huckshorn, Robert J., and Robert C. Spencer. 1971. *The Politics of Defeat.* Amherst: University of Massachusetts Press.

Huitt, Ralph K., and Robert L. Peabody. eds. 1969. *Congress: Two Decades of Analysis.* New York: Harper & Row.

Hyneman, Charles. 1950. *Bureaucracy in a Democracy.* New York: Harper & Row.

Hyneman, Charles S., and George W. Carey., eds. 1967. *A Second Federalist.* New York: Appleton-Century-Crofts.

Ippolito, Dennis S. 1978. *The Budget and National Politics.* San Francisco: W. H. Freeman.

Jackson, Carlton. 1967. *Presidential Vetoes: 1792–1945.* Athens: University of Georgia Press.

Jacobson, Gary C. 1980. *Money in Congressional Elections.* New Haven, Conn.: Yale University Press.

James, Dorothy B. 1974. *The Contemporary President.* Indianapolis: Bobbs-Merrill.

Jennings, M. Kent, and L. Harmon Zeigler., eds. 1966. *The Electoral Process.* Englewood Cliffs, N.J. Prentice-Hall.

Jewell, Malcolm E., and Chu Chi-Lung. 1974. "Membership Movement and Committee Attractiveness in the U.S. House of Representatives." *American Journal of Political Science* 18 (May): 433–41.

Jewell, Malcolm E., and Samuel C. Patterson. 1977. *The Legislative Process in the United States.* 3d ed. New York: Random House.

Jones, Charles O. 1964. *Party and Policy-Making: The House Republican Policy Committee.* New Brunswick, N.J. Rutgers University Press.

—————. 1968. "Joseph G. Cannon and Howard K. Smith: An Essay on the Limits of Leadership in the House of Representatives." *Journal of Politics* 39 (August): 617 – 46.

—————. 1970. *The Minority Party in Congress.* Boston: Little, Brown.

—————. 1974a. "Between Party Battalions and Committee Suzerainty." *The Annals* 411 (January): 156 –68.

—————. 1974b. "From the Suffrage of the People: An Essay of Support and Worry for Legislatures." *State Government* 47 (Summer): 137 – 41.

—————. 1975. *Clean Air: The Policies and Politics of Pollution Control.* Pittsburgh: University of Pittsburgh Press.

—————. 1979. "American Politics and the Organization of Energy Decision Making." *Annual Review of Energy* 4: 99 –121.

Jones, Charles O., and Dieter Matthes. 1982. "Policy Formation." *Encyclopedia of Policy Studies.* New York: Marcel Dekker.

Kammerer, Gladys M. 1949. *The Staffing of the Committee of Congress.* Lexington, Ky.: Bureau of Government Research.

Kaufman, Herbert. 1976. *Are Government Organizations Immortal?* Washington, D.C.: Brookings Institution.

Kazee, Thomas A. 1980. "The Decision to Run for Congress: Challenger Attitudes in the 1970s." *Legislative Studies Quarterly* 5 (February): 79 –100.

Keefe, William J. 1980. *Congress and the American People.* Englewood Cliffs, N.J.: Prentice-Hall.

Kelly, Alfred H., and Winfred A. Harbison. 1948. *The American Constitution: Its Origins and Development.* New York: W. W. Norton.

Kessel, John H. 1964. "The Washington Congressional Delegation." *Midwest Journal of Political Science* 8 (February): 1 –21.

King, Anthony, ed. 1978. *The New American Political System.* Washington, D.C.: American Enterprise Institute.

Kingdon, John W. 1973. *Congressmen's Voting Decisions.* New York: Harper & Row.

Kofmehl, Kenneth. 1977. *Professional Staffs of Congress.* 3d ed. West Lafayette, Ind.: Purdue University Press.

Kostroski, Warren L. 1973. "Party and Incumbency in Postwar Senate Elections: Trends, Patterns, and Models." *American Political Science Review* 68 (December): 1213 –34.

Kozak, David. 1979. "Contexts of Congressional Decision Behavior." Unpublished Ph.D. Dissertation, University of Pittsburgh.

Kuhn, Delia, and Ferdinand Kuhn, eds. 1963. *Adventures in Public Service.* New York: Vanguard Press.

LaFollette, Belle C., and Fola LaFollette. 1953. *Robert M. LaFollette.* New York: Macmillan.

Lawrence, Robert, ed. 1979. *New Dimensions to Energy Policy.* Lexington, Mass.: Lexington Books.

LeLoup, Lance T. 1980. *The Fiscal Congress: Legislative Control of the Budget*. Westport, Conn.: Greenwood Press.

Loomis, Burdette. 1979. "The Congressional Office as a Small (?) Business, New Members Set Up Shop." *Publius* 9 (Winter):   35—55.

Lowi, Theodore J. 1969. *The End of Liberalism*. New York: W. W. Norton.

———. 1972. "Four Systems of Policy, Politics, and Choice." *Public Administration Review* 33 (July/August):   298—310.

MacNeil, Neil. 1963. *Forge of Democracy*. New York: David McKay.

———. 1970. *Dirksen*. New York: World.

Macrae, Duncan, Jr. 1958. *Dimensions of Congressional Voting*. Berkeley: University of California Press.

Malbin, Michael J. 1977. "Congressional Committee Staffs: Who's in Charge Here?" *The Public Interest* 47 (Spring):   16—40.

———. 1979. "Campaign Financing and the 'Special Interests.'" *The Public Interest* 56 (Summer):   21—42.

———. 1980. *Unelected Representatives: Congressional Staff and the Future of Representative Government*. New York: Basic Books.

Manley, John F. 1970. *The Politics of Finance: The House Committee on Ways and Means*. Boston: Little, Brown.

Mann, Thomas E. 1978. *Unsafe at Any Margin*. Washington, D.C.: American Enterprise Institute.

Mann, Thomas E., and Norman Ornstein, eds. 1981. *The New Congress*. Washington, D.C.: American Enterprise Institute.

Mann, Thomas E., and Raymond E. Wolfinger. 1980. "Candidates and Parties in Congressional Elections." *American Political Science Review* 74 (September):   617—32.

Mansfield, Harvey C., Sr., ed. 1975. *Congress Against the President*. New York: Praeger Publishers.

Masters, Nicholas A. 1961. "Committee Assignments in the House of Representatives." *American Political Science Review* 55 (June):   345—57.

Matsunaga, Spark M., and Ping Chen. 1976. *Rulemakers of the House*. Urbana: University of Illinois Press.

Matthews, Donald R. 1960. *U.S. Senators and Their World*. Chapel Hill: University of North Carolina Press.

Matthews, Donald R., and James A. Stimson. 1975. *Yeas and Nays*. New York: John Wiley & Sons.

Mayhew, David R. 1966. *Party Loyalty Among Congressmen*. Cambridge, Mass.: Harvard University Press.

———. 1974a. *Congress: The Electoral Connection*. New Haven, Conn.: Yale University Press.

———. 1974b. "Congressional Elections: The Case of the Vanishing Marginals." *Polity* 6:   295—317.

McCall, Samuel W. 1914. *Thomas B. Reed*. Boston: Houghton Mifflin.

McConachie, Lauros G. 1898. *Congressional Committees*. New York: Thomas Y. Crowell.

McGown, Ada C. 1927. *The Congressional Conference Committee.* New York: Columbia University Press.

McKay, Robert B. 1965. *Reapportionment.* New York: Twentieth Century Fund.

Milbrath, Lester W. 1963. *The Washington Lobbyists.* Chicago: Rand McNally.

Miller, Clem. 1962. *Member of the House.* Edited by John W. Baker. New York: Charles Scribner's Sons.

Mills, C. Wright. 1959. *The Power Elite.* New York: Oxford University Press.

Neustadt, Richard E. 1960. *Presidential Power.* New York: John Wiley & Sons.

Norris, George W. 1961. *Fighting Liberal.* New York: Collier Books.

Ogul, Morris. 1976. *Congress Oversees the Bureaucracy.* Pittsburgh: University of Pittsburgh Press.

Oleszek, Walter J. 1978. *Congressional Procedures and the Policy Process.* Washington, D.C.: Congressional Quarterly Press.

Olson, David M. 1978. "U.S. Congressmen and Their Diverse Congressional District Parties." *Legislative Studies Quarterly* 3 (May): 239 –64.

Ornstein, Norman J., ed. 1975. *Congress in Change.* New York: Praeger Publishers.

Ornstein, Norman and Shirley Elder. 1978. *Interest Groups, Lobbying and Policymaking.* Washington, D.C.: Congressional Quarterly Press.

Patterson, James T. 1972. *Mr. Republican: A Biography of Robert A. Taft.* Boston: Houghton Mifflin.

Patterson, Samuel C. 1970. "The Professional Staffs of Congressional Committees." *Administrative Science Quarterly* 15 (March): 22 –37.

Peabody, Robert L. 1976. *Leadership in Congress.* Boston: Little, Brown.

Peabody, Robert L., and Nelson W. Polsby, eds. 1977. *New Perspectives on the House of Representatives.* 3d ed. Chicago: Rand McNally.

Peabody, Robert L., et al. 1972. *To Enact a Law: Congress and Campaign Financing.* New York: Praeger Publishers.

Pechman, Joseph, ed. 1980. *Setting National Priorities: Agenda for the 1980s.* Washington, D.C.: Brookings Institution.

Polsby, Nelson W. 1968. "The Institutionalization of the U.S. House of Representatives." *American Political Science Review* 62 (March): 144 –68.

Polsby, Nelson W., et al. 1969. "The Growth of the Seniority System in the U.S. House of Representatives." *American Political Science Review* 63: (September): 787 –807.

Polsby, Nelson W. 1970. "Strengthening Congress in National Policy-Making." *The Yale Review* 59 (June): 481 –97.

————, ed. 1971. *Congressional Behavior.* New York: Random House.

———— . 1976. *Congress and the Presidency.* 3d ed. Englewood Cliffs: N.J.: Prentice-Hall.

Polsby, Nelson W., and Fred I. Greenstein, eds. 1975. *Handbook of Political Science 5.* Reading, Mass.: Addison-Wesley Publishing.

Pressman, Jeffrey L. 1966. *House vs. Senate: Conflict in the Appropriations Process.* New Haven, Conn.: Yale University Press.

Price, David E. 1972. *Who Makes the Laws?* Cambridge, Mass.: Schenckman.

Ranney, Austin, ed. 1968. *Political Science and Public Policy.* Chicago: Markham.

Redford, Emmette S. 1969. *Democracy in the Administrative State.* New York: Oxford.

Redman, Eric. 1973. *The Dance of Legislation.* New York: Simon & Schuster.

Reich, Charles A. 1970. *The Greening of America.* New York: Random House.

Riddle, Donald H. 1964. *The Truman Committee: A Study in Congressional Responsibility.* New Brunswick, N.J.: Rutgers University Press.

Rieselbach, Leroy N. 1973. *Congressional Politics.* New York: McGraw-Hill.

————. 1977. *Congressional Reform in the Seventies.* Morristown, N.J.: General Learning Press.

————, ed. 1979. *The Congressional System.* 2d ed. North Scituate, Mass.: Duxbury Press.

Riker, William H. 1955. "The Senate and American Federalism." *American Political Science Review* 49 (June):   452 – 69.

Ripley, Randall B. 1967. *Party Leaders in the House of Representatives.* Washington, D.C.: Brookings Institution.

————. 1969a. *Majority Party Leadership in Congress.* Boston: Little, Brown.

————. 1969b. *Power in the Senate.* New York: St. Martin's Press.

Ripley, Randall B., and Grace A. Franklin. 1980. *Congress, the Bureaucracy, and Public Policy.* Homewood, Ill.: Dorsey Press.

Robinson, James A. 1963. *The House Rules Committee.* Indianapolis: Bobbs-Merrill.

Robinson, William B. 1930. *Thomas B. Reed: Parliamentarian.* New York: Dodd, Mead.

Rogers, Lindsay. 1926. *The American Senate.* New York: Alfred A. Knopf.

————. 1941. "The Staffing of Congress." *Political Science Quarterly* 54 (March): 1 – 22.

Rohde, David W., and Kenneth A. Shepsle. 1973. "Democratic Committee Assignments in the House of Representatives: Strategic Aspects of a Social Choice Process." *American Political Science Review* 67 (September):   889 – 905.

Salisbury, Robert H., and Kenneth A. Shepsle. 1981. "Congressional Staff Turnover and the Ties-That-Bind: Congressman as Enterprise," *American Political Science Review* 75 (June):   381 – 96.

Sandoz, Ellis, and Cecil Van Crabb, eds. 1981. *A Tide of Discontent.* Washington, D.C.: Congressional Quarterly Press.

Schattschneider, E. E. 1960. *The Semi-Sovereign People.* New York: Holt, Rinehart & Winston.

Schick, Allen. 1980. *Congress and Money.* Washington, D.C.: The Urban Institute.

Schlesinger, Arthur Jr. 1973. *The Imperial Presidency.* Boston: Houghton Mifflin.

Schmeckebier, Lawrence F., and Roy B. Eastin. 1961. *Government Publications and Their Use*. Washington, D.C.: Brookings Institution.

Schwarz, John E., and L. Earl Shaw. 1976. *The United States Congress in Comparative Perspective*. Hinsdale, Ill.: Dryden Press.

Shepsle, Kenneth. 1978. *The Giant Jigsaw Puzzle: Democratic Committee Assignments in the Modern House*. Chicago: University of Chicago Press.

——————., ed. 1980. *The Congressional Budget Process*. St. Louis, Mo.: Center for Study of American Business, Washington University.

Sinclair, Barbara Deckard. 1981. "The Speaker's Task Force in the Post-Reform House of Representatives." *American Political Science Review* 75 (June): 397 – 410.

Snowiss, Leo M. 1966. "Congressional Recruitment and Representation." *American Political Science Review* 60 (September): 627 – 39.

Stealey, O. O. 1906. *Twenty Years in the Press Gallery*. New York: Publishers Printing.

Steiner, Gilbert Y. 1950. *The Congressional Conference Committee*. Urbana: University of Illinois Press.

Stevens, Arthur G., Jr. et al. 1974. "Mobilization of Liberal Strength in the House 1955 – 1970: The Democratic Study Group." *American Political Science Review* 68 (June): 667 – 81.

Strom, Gerald S., and Barry S. Rundquist. 1977. "A Revised Theory of Winning in House-Senate Conferences." *American Political Science Review* 71 (June): 448 – 53.

Sundquist, James L. 1968. *Politics and Policy: The Eisenhower, Kennedy, and Johnson Years*. Washington, D.C.: Brookings Institution.

Tacheron, Donald G., and Morris K. Udall. 1966. *The Job of the Congressman*. Indianapolis: Bobbs-Merrill.

Tansill, Charles C., ed. 1927. *Formation of the Union of the American States*. Washington, D.C.: U.S. Government Printing Office.

de Toqueville, Alexis. 1945. *Democracy in America*. New York: Alfred A. Knopf.

Truman, David B. 1951. *The Governmental Process*. New York: Alfred A. Knopf.

——————. 1959. *The Congressional Party*. New York: John Wiley & Sons.

Turner, Julius, and Edward V. Schneier, Jr. 1970. *Party and Constituency: Pressures on Congress*. Baltimore: Johns Hopkins Press.

Volger, David J. 1971. *The Third House: Conference Committees in the United States Congress*. Evanston, Ill.: Northwestern University Press.

——————. 1980. *The Politics of Congress*. 3d ed. Boston: Allyn & Bacon.

Wahlke, John C., et al. 1962. *The Legislative System*. New York: John Wiley & Sons.

Wayne, Stephen J. 1978. *The Legislative Presidency*. New York: Harper & Row.

Weiss, Carol H. 1970. "The Politicization of Evaluation Research." *Journal of Social Issues* 26 (Autumn): 57 – 68.

Weissberg, Robert. 1978. "Collective vs. Dyadic Representation in Congress." *American Political Science Review* 72 (June): 535 – 47.

Welch, Susan, and John G. Peters, eds. 1977. *Legislative Reform and Public Policy*. New York: Praeger Publishers.

Wilson, James Q. 1973. *Political Organizations*. New York: Basic Books.

Wilson, Woodrow. 1913. *Congressional Government*. Boston: Houghton Mifflin.

Wright, Deil S. 1978. *Understanding Intergovernmental Relations*. North Scituate, Mass.: Duxbury Press.

Young, Roland. 1943. *This is Congress*. New York: Alfred A. Knopf.

————. 1956. *Congressional Politics in the Second World War*. New York: Columbia University Press.

————. 1958. *The American Congress*. New York: Harper & Row.

Young, James Sterling. 1966. *The Washington Community, 1800 – 1828*. New York: Columbia University Press.

Zinn, Charles J. 1969. *How Our Laws are Made*. Washington: U.S. Government Printing Office.

Additional sources

There are many other major works on Congress in addition to those cited in the references. Some of the more important books are listed below.

Alexander, De Alva Stanwood. 1916. *History and Procedure of the House of Representatives.* Boston: Houghton Mifflin.

Bailey, Stephen K. 1966. *The New Congress.* New York: St. Martin's Press.

Bailey, Stephen K., and Howard D. Samuel. 1952. *Congress at Work.* New York: Henry Holt.

Beard, Edmund, and Stephen Horn. 1978. *Congressional Ethics: The View From the House.* Washington, D.C.: Brookings Institution.

Berman, Daniel M. 1964. *In Congress Assembled.* New York: Macmillan.

Bibby, John F., and Roger Davidson. 1972. *On Capitol Hill.* Hinsdale, Ill.: Dryden Press.

Blair, George. 1967. *American Legislatures.* New York: Harper & Row.

Bolling, Richard. 1965. *House Out of Order.* New York: Dutton.

————. 1968. *Power in the House.* New York: Capricorn.

Bradshaw, Kenneth, and David Pring. 1972. *Parliament and Congress.* Austin: University of Texas Press.

Burnham, James. 1959. *Congress and the American Tradition.* Chicago: Henry Regnery.

Burns, James MacGregor. 1949. *Congress on Trial.* New York: Harper & Row.

Carr, Robert K. 1952. *The House Committee on Un-American Activities.* Ithaca, N.Y.: Cornell University Press.

Carroll, Holbert. 1966. *The House of Representatives and Foreign Affairs.* Boston: Little, Brown.

Chamberlain, Lawrence H. 1946. *The President, Congress and Legislation.* New York: Columbia University Press.

Chartrand, Robert L., et al., eds. 1968. *Information Support, Program Budgeting, and the Congress.* New York: Spartan Books.

Cherryholmes, Cleo H., and Michael J. Shapiro. 1969. *Representatives and Roll Calls.* Indianapolis: Bobbs-Merrill.

Chiu, Chang-wei. 1928. *The Speaker of the House of Representatives Since 1896.* New York: Columbia University Press.

Clark, Joseph S. 1964. *Congress: The Sapless Branch.* New York: Harper & Row.

Cleaveland, Frederick N., ed. 1969. *Congress and Urban Problems.* Washington, D.C.: Brookings Institution.

Congressional Quarterly, Inc. 1976. *Powers of Congress.* Washington, D.C.: Congressional Quarterly, Inc.

Cummings, Milton C., Jr. 1966. *Congressmen and the Electorate.* New York: Free Press.

Dahl, Robert A. 1950. *Congress and Foreign Policy.* New York: W. W. Norton.

Davidson, Roger H. 1969. *The Role of the Congressman.* New York: Pegasus.

deGrazia, Alfred, ed. 1966. *Congress: The First Branch of Government.* Washington, D.C.: American Enterprise Institute.

Dexter, Lewis A. 1969. *How Organizations Are Represented in Washington.* Indianapolis: Bobbs-Merrill.

————. 1969. *The Sociology and Politics of Congress.* Chicago: Rand McNally.

Dodd, Lawrence C. 1975. *Congress and Public Policy.* Morristown, N.J.: General Learning Press.

Ewing, Cortez, A. M. 1947. *Congressional Elections, 1896–1944.* Norman: University of Oklahoma Press.

Farnsworth, David N. 1961. *The Senate Committee on Foreign Relations.* Urbana: University of Illinois Press.

Ferejohn, John. 1974. *Pork Barrel Politics: Rivers and Harbors Legislation, 1947–1968.* Stanford, Calif.: Stanford University Press.

Froman, Lewis A. 1963. *Congressmen and Their Constituencies.* Chicago: Rand McNally.

Froman, Lewis A., Jr. 1967. *The Congressional Process: Strategies, Rules, and Procedures.* Boston: Little, Brown.

Fuller, Hubert Bruce. 1909. *The Speakers of the House.* Boston: Little, Brown.

Galloway, George B. 1961. *History of the House of Representatives.* New York: Thomas Y. Crowell.

Getz, Robert S. 1966. *Congressional Ethics.* Princeton, N.J.: Van Nostrand.

Green, Mark J., et al. 1972. *Who Runs Congress?* New York: Grossman.

Griffith, Ernest S. 1961. *Congress: Its Contemporary Role.* 3d ed. New York: New York University Press.

Groennings, Sven, and J. P. Hawley. 1973. *To Be a Congressman: The Promise and the Power.* Washington, D.C.: Acropolis Books.

Hacker, Andrew. 1963. *Congressional Districting: The Issue of Equal Representation.* Washington, D.C.: Brookings Institution.

Hamilton, James. 1976. *The Power to Probe: A Study of Congressional Investigation.* New York: Random House.

Harris, Joseph P. 1953. *The Advice and Consent of the Senate.* Berkeley: University of California Press.

Haynes, George H. 1938. *The Senate of the United States.* 2 vols. Boston: Houghton Mifflin.

Henderson, Thomas A. 1970. *Congressional Oversight of Executive Agencies: A Study of the House Committee on Government Operations.* Gainesville: University of Florida Press.

Hinckley, Barbara. 1978. *Stability and Change in Congress.* New York: Harper & Row.

Holtzman, Abraham. 1970. *Legislative Liaison: Executive Leadership in Congress.* Chicago: Rand McNally.

Jacobson, John E. 1974. *Constituencies and Leaders in Congress.* Cambridge: Harvard University Press.

Jewell, Malcolm E., ed. 1962. *The Politics of Reapportionment.* New York: Atherton.

———. 1962. *Senatorial Politics and Foreign Policy.* Lexington: University of Kentucky Press.

Jones, Rochelle and Peter Woll. 1979. *The Private World of Congress.* New York: Free Press.

Josephy, Alvin M., Jr. 1975. *On the Hill: A History of the American Congress.* New York: Simon & Schuster.

Keefe, William J., and Morris Ogul. 1981. *The American Legislative Process: Congress and the States.* 5th ed. Englewood Cliffs, N.J.: Prentice-Hall.

Kingdon, John W. 1966. *Candidates for Office: Beliefs and Strategies.* New York: Random House.

Kirby, James C., Jr., ed. 1970. *Congress and the Public Trust.* New York: Atheneum.

Kirst, Michael W. 1969. *Government Without Passing Laws: Congress' Non-Statutory Techniques for Appropriations Control.* Chapel Hill: University of North Carolina Press.

Koenig, Louis W. 1965. *Congress and the President.* Chicago: Scott, Foresman.

Kolodziej, Edward A. 1966. *The Uncommon Defense and Congress, 1945–1963.* Columbus: Ohio State University Press.

Leuthold, David A. 1968. *Electioneering in a Democracy.* New York: John Wiley & Sons.

Loewenberg, Gerhard, and Samuel C. Patterson. 1979. *Comparing Legislatures.* Boston: Little, Brown.

McInnis, Mary., ed. 1966. *We Propose: A Modern Congress.* New York: McGraw-Hill.

McPhee, William N., and William A. Glaser, eds. 1962. *Public Opinion and Congressional Elections.* New York: Free Press.

Morgan, Donald G. 1966. *Congress and the Constitution.* Cambridge: Harvard University Press.

Morrow, William L. 1969. *Congressional Committees.* New York: Charles Scribner's Sons.

Munger, Frank, and Richard F. Fenno, Jr. 1962. *National Politics and Federal Aid to Education.* Syracuse, N.Y.: Syracuse University Press.

Murphy, Thomas P. 1974. *The New Politics Congress.* Lexington, Mass.: Lexington Books.

Murphy, Walter F. 1962. *Congress and the Court.* Chicago: University of Chicago Press.

Olson, David M. 1980. *The Legislative Process: A Comparative Approach.* New York: Harper & Row.

Oppenheimer, Bruce I. 1974. *Oil and the Congressional Process.* Lexington, Mass.: Lexington Books.

Orfield, Gary. 1975. *Congressional Power: Congress and Social Change.* New York: Harcourt Brace Jovanovich.

Patterson, James T. 1968. *Congressional Conservation and the New Deal.* Lexington: University of Kentucky Press.

Pitkin, Hanna Fenichel. 1967. *The Concept of Representation.* Berkeley: University of California Press.

Polsby, Nelson W., ed. 1971. *Reapportionment in the 1970s.* Berkeley: University of California Press.

Reid, T. R. 1980. *Congressional Odyssey: The Saga of a Senate Bill.* San Francisco: W. H. Freeman.

Riddick, Floyd M. 1949. *The United States Congress: Organization and Procedure.* Manassas, Va.: National Capitol Publishers.

Ripley, Randall B. 1972. *Kennedy and Congress.* Morristown, N.J.: General Learning Press.

————. 1978. *Congress: Process and Policy.* 2d ed. New York: W. W. Norton.

Robinson, James A. 1962. *Congress and Foreign Policy-Making.* Homewood, Ill.: Dorsey Press.

Rothman, David J. 1966. *Politics and Power: The United States Senate, 1869–1901.* Cambridge: Harvard University Press.

Saloma, John S., III. 1969. *Congress and the New Politics.* Boston: Little, Brown.

Schmidhauser, John R., and L. L. Berg. 1972. *The Supreme Court and Congress.* New York: Free Press.

Schneider, Jerrold E. 1979. *Ideological Coalitions in Congress.* Westport, Conn.: Greenwood Press.

Schuck, Peter H., ed. 1975. *The Judiciary Committees.* New York: Grossman.

Schwab, Larry M. 1980. *Changing Patterns of Congressional Politics.* New York: D. Van Nostrand.

Scott, Andrew M., and Margaret A. Hunt. 1966. *Congress and Lobbies.* Chapel Hill: University of North Carolina Press.

Shaffer, William R. 1980. *Party and Ideology in the United States Congress.* Lanham, Md.: University Press of America.

Shannon, W. Wayne. 1968. *Party, Constituency and Congressional Voting.* Baton Rouge: Louisiana State University Press.

Siff, Ted, and Alan Weil, eds. 1975. *Ruling Congress.* New York: Penguin Books.

Truman, David B., ed. 1965. *The Congress and America's Future.* Englewood Cliffs, N.J.: Prentice-Hall.

Uslaner, Eric M. 1974. *Congressional Committee Assignments: Alternative Models for Behavior.* Beverly Hills, Calif.: Sage Publications.

Vinyard, Dale. 1968. *Congress.* New York: Charles Scribner's Sons.

Wallace, Robert Ash. 1960. *Congressional Control of Federal Spending.* Detroit: Wayne State University Press.

White, William S. 1956. *Citadel: The Story of the U.S. Senate.* New York: Harper & Row.

————. 1965. *Home Place: The Story of the U.S. House of Representatives.* Boston: Houghton Mifflin.

Index

A

Abourezk, James, 324–25
Acorns, 244
Administrative assistant (AA), 135, 138–39, 190
Administrative Review, House Commission on, 432
Aeronautical and Space Sciences Committee (Senate), 277
Agriculture, Nutrition, and Forestry Committee (Senate), 273, 286–87
Agriculture Committee (House), 23, 198, 212
Air Quality Act (1967), 384
Albert, Carl, 224
Aldrich, Nelson W., 296–99
Allen, James B., 323–24
Ambassador, confirmation hearings of, 26
Amending process
  in House of Representatives, 247, 260–63
  in Senate, 313
America Votes, 447
Anderson, John, 225, 231
Annals of Congress, 448
Annapolis Convention, 2

Appointments, Senate involvement in, 26, 382–83
Appropriations Committee
  House, 139–44, 198, 209, 212
  Senate, 25, 274
Appropriations conferences, 336–39
Armed Services Committee
  House, 198, 209, 212
  Senate, 274
Arms Control and Disarmament Agency, 25
Articles of Confederation, 1–2, 107
Assistant whip (Senate), 302
Atomic Energy, Joint Committee on, 341–42
Atomic Energy Act, 342
Atomic Energy Commission, 342

B

Baker, Howard H., Jr., 24, 297, 311, 315
Baker v. *Carr*, 75
Banking, Finance, and Urban Affairs Committee
  House, 198–99, 209
  Senate, 274
Banking and Currency Committee (House), 212

Barkley, Allen W., 409
Baumann, Robert, 38
Bayh, Birch, 123, 129
Beilenson, Anthony D., 210
Bellmon, Henry, 25
Bibby, John, 385
Bicameralism, 5, 369, 427
Bills
  in House of Representatives
    amendments to, 247, 260–63
    debate on, 257–60
    display of, 256–57
    passage of, 263
    reporting of, out of committee, 247
    scheduling of, 247–56
  in Senate
    amendments to, 313
    floor action on, 319–25
    scheduling of, 309–16
  signature of, by president, 349–50
  veto process of, 344–49
Blacks, in Congress, 67
Blaine, James G., 228
Bland, Richard P., 419
Boeing Corporation, 390
Boggs, Hale, 230
Boland, Edward P., 22
Bolling, Richard, 224, 384, 432
Bolling Committee, 384, 431–32
Brademas, John, 231
Braithwaite, Karl, 40, 42
Brock, Bill, 432
Brodhead, William M., 241
Brooke, Edward W., 25, 67, 242
Brown, Arnold G., 321
Buckley v. *Valeo*, 102
Budget, congressional, 14–16, 372–74, 402–4
Budget and Accounting Act (1921), 391
Budget Committee
  House, 199
  Senate, 277, 285
Budget Control and Congressional Operations, Joint Committee on, 341
Budget and Impoundment Control Act (1974), 25, 372, 402, 424, 431
Bumpers, Dale, 39
Burke, Edmund, 181–82
Burton, Phillip, 224
Byrd, Harry F., Jr., 281, 291, 305
Byrd, Robert C., 297, 302, 310–11, 314–15, 318–19

C

Calendar of General Orders (Senate), 310
Calendar Wednesday (House), 249–50
Calhoun, John C., 5
Campaigning
  for House of Representatives, 94–101
  for the Senate, 127–32

Cannon, Clarence A., 331–32
Cannon, Joseph G., 9, 228–29, 417, 420–23
Capitol Building, original structure of, 54
Carter, Jimmy
  energy program of, 14, 16–18, 437
  relationship with Congress, 9, 124, 234–35, 348–49, 364, 401
Carter, Tim Lee, 259
Case, Francis, 130
Casework, 169–75
Caseworker, role of, 190
Caucus, in House of Representatives, 223–27
Caucus chairman, position of, 229–30
Celler, Emanuel, 135
Census, effect of, on congressional districts, 75–76
Chandler, Albert B., 120
Checks and balances, 5
Chowder and Marching Society, 244
Church, Frank, 123, 129
Citizen lobbies, development of, 161–62
Civil Service, 383
Civil Service Reform Act (1978), 395
Clark, James Beauchamp, 421
Clay, Henry, 228
Clean Air Act (1977), 21–22
Clean Air Amendments (1970), 153–55, 384
Cleveland, Grover, 347
Closed rule (House), 252–53
Cloture rule (Senate), 322–25
Cockburn, Sir George, 54
Cohen, David, 35, 161
Cohen, William S., 22–23, 119, 244–45
  schedule of, 28, 30, 32
Collins, James M., 22
Colmer, William, 251, 425
Commerce, Science, and Transportation Committee (Senate), 274, 277
Commerce Committee (House), 22
Committee hearings, 51
Committee reports (House), 247, 448
Committees
  counterparts of, in Senate and House, 277
  House, 196–97
    assignments to, 207–13
    number and types of, 197–207
    organization, leadership, and staffs, 213–19
    and party ratios, 204–5
    procedures in, 219–21
  Senate, 273
    number of, 273–85
    organization of, 285–91
    procedures in, 285–91
    staff, 288–91
  and staff recruitment and turnover, 139–44
  typical week in, 18–27
  workings of, 27–35
Common Cause, 35, 101, 152, 161, 428
Conable, Barber B., 428, 432

Concurrent resolutions, use of, 398
Conference (Senate and House), 327–29
    appointments to, 329–33
    appropriations, 336–39
    description of, 333–35
    procedures for, 329–33
    report, 335–36, 448
    winning of, 339–41
Conference of Mayors, 156
Congress, U.S., *see also* House of Representatives *and* Senate
    and appointments, 26, 382–83
    as billion dollar Congress, 14–16
    budgetary process in, 14–16, 372–74, 402–4
    busyness of, 13–14
    characteristics of members of, 62–67
    comparing action in, on specific bills, 374–77
    current status of, 442–43
    documents of, 447–49
    growth of, 54–62
    historical perspective on, 3–9
    housing of, 60–61, 439–41
    and legislative oversight, 280, 384–98
    members' sensitivity to public problems, 367
    people in, 438–39
    policy networks in, 358–65, 406–8
    and the policy process, 352–58, 404–6, 441–42
    press coverage of, 43–49
    and program development, 365–74, 383–84
    program execution activities, 406–8
    public approval ratings of, 410
    ratio of staff to members, 59
    reforms, 409–11
        analysis of, 413–17
        eras of, 417–35
        functions served by, 414–15
        institutional effect of, 415–16
        in the 1970s, 427–33
        objects of, 413–14
        post-World War II, 423–26
        psychology behind, 411–13
        and the Speaker of the House, 418–23
    study of modern, 9–12
    and sunset laws, 400, 407
    and sunshine laws, 400, 407
    and use of legislative veto, 396–97, 401
    writing a term paper on, 444–51
Congress and the Nations, 446
Congressional Black Caucus (CBC), 242
Congressional Budget Act (1974), 253–54
Congressional Budget Office (CBO), 144, 370, 402
Congressional districts
    creation of, 74–76
    organization of House to represent, 185–92
Congressional Globe, 448
Congressional Information Services (CIS), 447
Congressional Insight, 447

Congressional Operations, Joint Committee on, 411–12, 432
Congressional primacy, 4–6, 9, 442
Congressional Quarterly Almanac, 446
Congressional Quarterly Weekly Report, 446–47
Congressional Record, 448
Congressional Research Service (CRS), 144, 370
Congressional staff
    characteristics of members of, 67–69
    growth of, 56–59, 134
    House, 216–19
    increases in size of, 401–2
    recruitment and turnover of, 133–45
    Senate, 267–71, 288–91
    typical week for, 40–43
Congressional Staff Directory, 144–45
Consent Calendar (House), 234, 248–49
Conservative coalition (House), 242
Constituents, special case of, 169–75
Constitution, U.S.
    Article 1, 3
    on composition of Congress, 72
    policy process model suggested by, 356–57
Contemporary Affairs Reports, 447
Continental Congress, 1
Coolidge, Calvin, 9
Cooper, Joseph, 42
Coordinator of Information, 57
Corruption, and lobbying, 160
Council of Economic Advisors, 342
Council of State Governments, 156
Cranston, Alan, 108, 129, 302, 321
Credit claiming, 383
Crisis policy, 366
Crisp, Charles F., 419
Culver, John C., 129, 267, 384–86, 398
Cunningham, George V., 41

                    D

de Tocqueville, Alexis, 13–14
DeConcini, Dennis, 279
Defense Production, Joint Committee on, 341
Democratic Caucus (House), 251, 256, 428
Democratic Caucus Committee on Organization, Study, and Review, 431
Democratic Committee on Committees (Senate), 283
Democratic party
    dominance of Congress by, 67
    House organization of, 224, 226–31, 233–38, 251, 256, 428
    Senate organization of, 302–4
Democratic Research Organization, 241
Democratic Study Group (DSG), 224, 240, 428, 430
Deputy whips, position of, 229–30
Dingell, John, 142
Dirksen, Everett M., 243, 282

Discharge Calendar (House), 249
Distributive policy, 365
District Business Calendar (House), 249
District of Columbia Committee
    House, 199
    Senate, 277, 282
Dole, Robert, 123
Domenici, Pete, 320
Domestic policy, 365
Dornan, Robert K., 99
Douglas, Paul, 243
Drummy, Maureen, 41
Durkin, John, 285

E

Eagleton, Thomas, 123, 129
Eastland, James, 286
Economics, Joint Committee on, 341–43
Editorial Research Reports, 447
Education of the Handicapped Act, 25
Education and Labor Committee (House), 199, 428
Eisenhower, Dwight D.
    administration of, 368, 376, 425
    relationship with Congress, 9, 346, 348
El Paso Alaska Company, 25
Election
    for House of Representatives, 76–78
    for Senators, 109–14
Emery, David, 23
Employment Act (1946), 342, 374
Energy, Department of, 395
Energy and Natural Resources Committee (Senate), 275, 277, 281
Energy Research and Development Administration (ERDA), 22
Environment and Public Works Committee (Senate), 275
Ervin, Sam, 92, 390
Executive Journal, 448
Executive secretary to representative, role of, 190
Expense allowance, of legislators, 187, 268–69
Export Administration Amendments, 35

F

Familian, Gary, 99
Fascell, Dante, 214
Favoritism, 364
Federal Corrupt Practices Act (1975), 101
Federal Elections Campaign Amendments (1974), 101
Federal Elections Commission, 102
Federal Energy Administration (FEA), 395
Federal Law Assistance Administration, 329
Federal Regulation of Lobbying Act (1946), 162–63

Federalist, 4–5, 10, 107, 266
Fenwick, Millicent, 210
Filibuster, 314, 321–25
Finance Committee
    House, 209, 373
    Senate, 275
First Amendment, 162–63
    and campaign finance, 102, 104
Fithian, Floyd J., 395
Floor leader
    House, 229–30
    Senate, 296–301
Flowers, Walter, 22
Foley, Thomas S., 23, 230–31
Food Day Conference on World Hunger, 26
Ford, Gerald R.
    on congressional budget, 14–15
    as House Republican leader, 231
    relations with Congress, 9, 124, 234–36, 346, 348, 403
Foreign Affairs Committee (House), 199, 212, 282
Foreign Agents Registration Act (1938), 175
Foreign and defense policy, 365–66
Foreign groups, special case of, 175–77
Foreign Relations Committee (Senate), 26, 275, 282
Fowler, Wyche, 17
Franking of mail, 187
Frenzel, Bill, 210
Frey, Louis, 22
Fuqua, Don, 22

G

Gabusi, John, 42
Gardner, John, 101, 161
Garin, Geoffrey, 40
Garner, John N., 228
General Accounting Office (GAO), 58, 144, 391–92
General Dynamics Corporation, 389–90
General Services Administration, 350
Geographical groups, in House of Representatives, 238–39
Gerrymandering, 73
Giaimo, Robert N., 334, 373, 403
Gibson, Kenneth, 24
Ginn, Bo, 210
Goldwater, Barry, 123
Goodell, Charles E., 177
Gore, Albert, 328
Government Operations Committee (House), 199–200, 214, 392
Governmental Affairs Committee (Senate), 276, 282, 392
Guide to the Congress of the United States, 446
Guide to U.S. Elections, 447

H

Hamilton, Alexander, 4, 107, 114
Hansen, Julia Butler, 224, 428
Hansen Committee, 428, 431
Harding, Warren G., 9
Hatfield, Mark, 26, 128
Hawkins, Paula, 67
Hayakawa, S. I., 108, 124
Hayden, Carl, 331–32
Hays, Wayne L., 432
Heflin, Howell, 320
Heftel, Cecil, 190
Heinz, H. J., III, 32, 40, 110, 116, 285
    schedule of, 34
Helleck, Charles, 230
Helms, Jesse, 128, 130, 286
Henderson, David, 420
Hollings, Ernest F., 25
Hoover, Herbert, 9
House Administration Committee (House), 200
House calendar, 247–49, 252
House Commission on Administrative Review, 21
House of Representatives, *See also* Representatives
    approval of work of Senate, 327
    changes in size of, 73–74
    committee system in, 197–221
    conferences between Senate and, 327–41
    general differences between Senate and, 184–85
    joint committees with Senate, 341–43
    organization of, 185–221
    work on floor, 245–64
    political party system in, 222–38
    and the problem of representation, 179–84
    reasons for deciding to run for, 88–94
    relations of, with president, 343–50
    support in, for president, 307–8
    typical week in, 35–36, 38–39
    unofficial groups in, 238
        geographical groups in, 238–39
        issue and ideological groups in, 240–44
        social groups in, 244–45
Hughes, Harold E., 432
Human Resources Committee, 25
Humphrey, Hubert, 123, 427
Humphrey, Muriel, 120

I

Ideological groups, in the House of Representatives, 240–44
Imperial presidency, 7
Incumbency
    and campaign finance, 100
    in House of Representatives, 78–83
    in Senate, 114–17

Inter-University Consortium for Political Research (ICPSR) at University of Michigan, 449
Interest group(s)
    beneficiaries of, 164
    definition of, 163
    development of, 150–52
    goals of, 163–64
    means of, 164–65
    techniques of, 166–69
Interior and Insular Affairs Committee
    House, 200, 424
    Senate, 424
Internal Revenue Taxation, Joint Committee on, 139–40, 341–42
International Relations Committee (House), 35, 38
Interstate and Foreign Commerce Committee (House), 21, 142, 200, 216–18
Issue groups, in the House of Representatives, 240–44

J

Jackson, Andrew, 347
Jackson, Henry, 123, 390
Jay, John, 4
Jefferson, Thomas, 6
Johnson, Andrew, 347
Johnson, Lyndon B.
    administration of, 376, 405
    relations with Congress, 9, 234–36
    as senator, 296–98, 302, 368
Joint committees, 341–43
Jones, James R., 210
Judiciary Committee
    House, 200
    Senate, 276, 282, 286

K

Kassebaum, Nancy L., 67
Katz, Allan, 42
Kefauver, Estes, 389
Kefauver Crime Investigation, 389
Kennedy, Edward M. (Ted), 39, 123, 172, 286, 329
Kennedy, John F.
    administration of, 376
    relations with Congress, 9, 234–35, 251, 425–26
Kern, John, 299
Kluczynski, John, 133–34

L

Labor and Human Resources Committee (Senate), 276
LaFollette, Robert M., 127, 424

Lamphere, Phylis, 24
Law(s); *see* Bills
Leahy, Patrick J., 25, 138
Lee, Blair, 114
Legionville National Historic Site, 348
Legislative assistant (LA), 134–36, 139, 190
Legislative expansion, 4
Legislative oversight, 280, 384–98
Legislative primacy, 4, 5–6, 9, 442
Legislative Reorganization Act (1946), 56–57, 139–41, 163, 388
Legislative Reorganization Act (1970), 219
Legislative veto, 396–97, 401
Library, Joint Committee on, 341–42
Library of Congress, 58
    Congressional Research Service, 58
    Legislative Reference Service, 56–57
Lindsay, John V., 241
Lobbying, 156; *See also* Lobbyists
    by constituents, 169–75
    definition of, 153–54
    determination of who, 150–52
    by foreign groups, 175–77
    goals of, 163–64
    reasons for, 162–65
Lobbyists; *see also* Lobbying
    administrators as, 153–58
    citizen monitors as, 161–62
    professionals as, 160–61
    suppliers as, 159–60
    targets of, 158–59
    techniques of, 166–69
Long, Gillis W., 230
Long, Russell, 39, 324
Longworth, Nicholas, 228–29

M

McC. Mathias, Charles, Jr., 292
McCarthy, Joseph R., 389
McCarthy Hearings, 389
McClure, James, 285
McEvoy, John, 402
McFall, John, 224
McGovern, George, 33, 41, 123, 129
    schedule of, 33
Maclay, William, 110
Macropolitical issues in Congress, 361, 363
Madden, Ray J., 431
Madison, James, 4–6, 10, 107, 114, 405
Magnuson, Warren, 279–80, 318, 335, 338
Majority leader
    role of, 23
    typical schedule of, 27, 29
Mansfield, Mike, 26, 40, 297, 303
Manual of Parliamentary Practice (Jefferson), 219
Marginal districts, recruitment of candidates in 85

Markup sessions, 19
Martin, David, 432
Martin, Thomas, 299
Members of Congress for Peace through Law (MCPL), 243
Merchant Marine and Fisheries Committee (House), 201, 212
Merit system, 383
Metzenbaum, Howard M., 285, 320–21, 324–25
Michel, Robert H., 231
Micropolitical issues in Congress, 364
Middleton, John, 40–41
Midterm election, 76
Migration and Refugee Assistance Act, 335
Miller, Clem, 97
Milwaukee Railroad Restructuring Act, 335–36
Minority leader
    role of, 24
    schedule of, 29
Modified closed rule (House), 252–53
Mondale, Walter, 324
Monroney, A. S. (Mike), 424, 431
Moss, John, 143
Moynihan, Daniel P., 26
Mundt, Karl E., 389
Muskie, Edmund S., 32–33, 40, 123, 334
    schedule of, 32

N

Nader, Ralph, 161, 428
National Association of Counties, 156
National Clean Air Coalition, 161
National Conservative Political Action Committee (NCPAC), 129
National Governors' Conference, 156
National Journal, 447
National League of Cities, 24, 156
National Resources Defense Council, 161
Nelson, Gaylord, 24
Nelson, John, 422
New Jersey plan, 2–3
Nixon, Richard M.
    appointments of, 383
    and presidential primacy, 7
    relations with Congress, 9, 234–36, 346, 348, 369, 402–3, 405, 427–28
    and Watergate, 380, 390, 399
Norris, George W., 113, 251, 328, 421

O

Obey, David R., 21, 432
Obey Commission, 21, 432
Office of Legislative Counsel, 56
Office of Management and Budget, 344, 372
Office of Technology Assessment (OTA), 144, 370, 430
Ogul, Morris S., 385–86

One-person, one-vote principle, 75
O'Neill, Thomas P. "Tip," 168, 224, 228–29, 231, 330, 373
  typical schedule of, 16–17, 27–29
Open districts, recruitment of candidates in, 85
Open rule (House), 252–53
Organization, Study and Review Committee (House), 224
Organization of Congress, Joint Committee of, 424, 428, 430–31
Ornstein, Norman J., 41

P

Packwood, Robert W., 335
Park, Tongsun, 175
Patronage system, 383
Patterson, William, 2–3
Pendleton Civil Service Act (1883), 383, 395
Pepper, Claude, 119
Personal offices, turnover and recruitment of staff for, 135–39
Pierce, Franklin, 347
Pocket veto, 346
Policy networks in Congress, 358–65, 406–8
Policy process in Congress, 352–58, 404–6, 441–42
Political action committees (PACs)
  campaign contributions of, 129
  and campaign finance, 103–4
  contributions of, to campaigns, 100
Political parties
  in House of Representatives, 222–38
  potential role of, in Congress, 8
  in Senate, 295–308
  solution of, to problems of Congress, 399
Polk, James K., 228
Pork barrel legislation, 349
Post Office and Civil Service Committee
  House, 201, 428
  Senate, 277, 282
Postcloture filibuster-by-amendment, 323–24
Prayer Breakfast Group, 244
President, legislative role of, 343–50
Presidential-congressional relationships, 380
  adversarial mode, 8–9, 443
  congressional primacy, 4–6, 9, 442
  cooperative mode, 7–9, 442
  presidential primacy, 6–7, 9, 442
Presidential primacy, 6–7, 9, 442
Press aide, 139
Press assistant, 190
Press coverage, of congressional activity, 43–49
Pressure politics, 151
Preyer, Richardson, 213 n
Primary election, 76, 109
Printing, Joint Committee on, 341–42
Prints, 448
Private Calendar (House), 247, 249

Private law number, 350
Program development activities in Congress, 365–67, 383–84
  agenda setting, 368–69
  aggregation and representation, 367–68
  appropriation, 372–74
  formation, 369–70
  legitimation, 371–72
  perception/definition of problem, 367
Progressive party, 127
Protective tariffs, 175
Public law number, 350
Public Works and Transportation Committee (House), 201

Q–R

Quay, Matthew S., 112
Railsback, Thomas, 119
Ramspeck Act (1940), 395
Randolph, Edmund, 2
Ray, Elizabeth, 432
Rayburn, Sam, 228–29, 368
Reagan, Ronald, 437
  relations with Congress, 125, 236
Recommit, motion to, 263
.Recruitment
  of representatives, 84–94
  of senators, 119–27
Redistributive policy, 365
Reduction of Federal Expenditures, Joint Committee on, 341
Reed, Thomas B., 106, 228, 230, 321, 324, 418–23, 443
Register of Debates, 448
Regulatory policy, 365
Reid, Ogden, 241
Representatives, *see also* House of Representatives
  characteristics of, 62–67
  choice of
    and campaign finance, 94–105
    creation of district, 71–76
    as incumbents, 78–83
    and recruitment, 84–94
    types of elections, 76–78
  functions performed in offices of, 188–89
  perquisites of, 186–87
  personal staff of, 135–39
  staffing problem of new, 135–36
Republican Committee on Committees (Senate), 283
Republican Conference Task Force on Seniority, 432
Republican party
  House organization of, 224–27, 230–38
  Senate, control of 81st by, 291–93
  Senate organization of, 291–93, 295, 298–99, 304

Republican Study Group (RSG), 241
Republicanism, 4
Research support agencies, 353
  and staff recruitment and turnover, 144–45
Reynolds v. *Sims,* 108
Rhodes, John J., 24, 29, 231
Riegle, Donald, 285
Rogers, Paul G., 22, 156
Rogers, William P., 177
Roosevelt, Franklin D., 6–7, 9, 347
Rose, Charlie, 180
Ruckelshaus, William, 177
Rudd, Eldon, 210
Rule 22, 322–25
Rules and Administration Committee (Senate),
  276, 282, 284–85, 292
Rules Committee (House), 201, 209, 212, 228–29,
  233, 250–56, 417
Runoff elections, 76, 109
Russell, Richard B., 264, 296

S

St. Clair, congressional inquiry into defeat of,
  388
Scheuer, James H., 177
Science and Technology Committee (House),
  22, 201
Select Committee on Committees (House), 384,
  431–32
Senate; *see also* Senators
  appointive powers of, 382–83
  approving work of House of Representatives,
    327
  committees in, 273
    chairmanships of, 280
    number of, 273–85
    organization and procedures of, 285–91
  conferences with House of Representatives,
    327–41
  distinction between adjournment and recess,
    316
  early history of, 110–14
  general differences between House and, 184–
    85
  joint committees with House of Representa-
    tives, 341–43
  lawmaking in, 272–91
  organization of, 265–67
  organization of Republican, 291–93
  organization of work on floor, 308–25
    of day, 316–19
    making decisions on floor, 319–25
    scheduling, 309–16
  political parties in, 295–308
  relations of, with president, 343–50
  serving and representation of states, 267–72
  staffing of, 267–71

Senate; *see also Senators—Cont.*
  support in, for president, 306–8
  typical week in, 37, 39–40
Senate Commission on the Operation of the
  Senate, 432
Senate Republican Policy Committee, 20, 24
Senate Temporary Committee to Study the Senate, 432
Senatorial courtesy, 382
Senators; *see also* Senate
  campaigning of, 127–32
  and change of tenure, 114–17
  characteristics of, 62–67
  perquisites of, 268–69
  personal staff of, 135–39
  reasons for loss of election, 117–19
  recruitment of, 119–27
  representation of, 107–9
  staffing problem of new, 135–36
  types of elections, 109–14
Seniority system in Congress, 157, 214
Separation of powers, 4, 5, 427
Seventeenth Amendment, 113–14, 120, 127, 266
Sierra Club, 161
Slip laws, 350, 449
Small Business Committee (House), 201
Smith, Howard W., 251, 425
Social groups, in House of Representatives, 244
Solarz, Stephen, 210
SOS, 244
Speaker of the House, 251
  position of, 227–29
  reforms of position, 418–23
  schedule of, 21, 28–29
Special Orders (House), 250, 252
Spoils system, 383
SST (supersonic transport), 176
Staff; *see* Congressional staff
Stafford, Robert T., 292
Staggers, Harley O., 22, 336
Stam, Colin F., 140
Standards of Official Conduct Committee
  (House), 202
State delegations, impact of, in House of Repre-
  sentatives, 238–39
State of the Union message, 155, 326
Statutes at Large, 350, 449
Steel Caucus, 243–44
Steering and Policy Committee (House), 208,
  214
Steers, Newton, 135
Steiger, William A., 41–42
Stevens, Ted, 25, 302, 321
Stevenson, Adlai E., III, 278, 432
Stevenson Committee (Senate), 278–80, 282, 286
Stork, Eric, 157
Strategic policy, 366
Strelow, Roger, 157
Structural policy, 365

Student interns, 188
Sturgeon, Daniel, 112
Sunset laws, 400, 407
Sunshine laws, 400, 407
Supreme Court, U.S., on congressional districts, 75
Suspension of the Rules (House), 249–50

T

Taft, Robert A., 130, 296–97
Talley, Wilson, 157
Tax Reduction and Simplication Act (1977), 39
Taxation, Joint Committee on, 342–43
Taylor, Glen H., 322
Team filibuster, 322–25
Temporary Select Committee to Study the Senate Committee System (Senate), 278
Tenure, of senators, 114–17
TFX Contract Investigation, 389–90
Thurmond, Strom, 123, 292, 295, 322
Ticket fillers, 84
Time limitation agreements (Senate), 314
Tourism, 150
Tower, John, 24, 282
Tracking system (Senate), 314
Train, Russell, 156–57
Trans-Alaska Gas Project, 25
Truman, Harry S,
  appointments of, 383
  relationship with Congress, 9, 346, 348
  as senator, 389
Truman Committee, 389
Tunney, John, 124
Tyler, John, 347

U

Udall, Morris K., 28, 31, 206, 243
  schedule of, 28, 30–31
Unanimous consent (Senate), 310–11, 314
Underwood, Oscar W., 225
Union Calendar (House), 247–49, 252
United States Code, 350, 449
Urban Affairs Committee (House), 209

V

Vander Jagt, Guy, 231
Venable, Abraham W., 321
Veterans' Affairs Committee
  House, 202, 209
  Senate, 276–77, 285
Veterans' Preference Act (1944), 395
Veto, process of, 344–49
Vietnam War, 236
Virginia plan, 2–3

W

Waivers of points of order (House), 253–54
War Powers Act (1973), 430
Warncke, Paul, 25
Washington Information Directory, 447
Watergate, 380
Watergate Investigations, 390
Waxman, Henry A., 213, 257, 259
Ways and Means Committee (House), 202, 207–9, 212–13, 255, 373, 422
Wednesday Group, 241–42
Weekly Compilation of Presidential Documents, 449
Weicker, Lowell, 320–21
Wertheimer, Fred, 161
Wesberry v. *Sanders*, 75
Whip
  House, 229–31
  Senate, 299, 302
Whitten, Jamie L., 373
Williams, Harrison, 24
Wilson, Woodrow, 120–21, 196, 273
  and presidential primacy, 6–7
  relationship with Congress, 9, 347
Women, in Congress, 67
Wright, James C., 38, 224
Wright, James C., Jr., 23, 27
Wydler, John W., 177

Y–Z

Young, Andrew, 17
Young, Milton, 66
Youth Employment Act, 24
Zablocki, Clement J., 38
Zener, Robert, 157

This book has been set VIP, in 10 and 9 point Zapf Book Light, leaded 2 points. Chapter numbers are 48 point Beton extra bold and chapter titles are 16 point Zapf Book Demi-bold. The size of the type page is 30 by 47 picas.